CONTEMPORARY COLLECTIVE BARGAINING

CONTEMPORARY COLLECTIVE BARGAINING

FOURTH EDITION

Harold W. Davey

Iowa State University

Mario F. Bognanno

University of Minnesota

David L. Estenson

University of California—Berkeley

Prentice-Hall, Inc.
Englewood Cliffs, New Jersey 07632

Library of Congress Cataloging in Publication Data

DAVEY, HAROLD W.
  CONTEMPORARY COLLECTIVE BARGAINING.

  Includes bibliographies and index.
    1. Collective bargaining–United States.
I. Bognanno, Mario Frank.   II. Estenson, David.
III. Title.
HD6508.D28 1982   331.89'0973   81–19965
ISBN   0-13-169771-4   AACR2

Editorial/production supervision and interior design by Natalie Krivanek
Cover design by Miriam Recio
Manufacturing buyer: Ed O'Dougherty

Printed in the United States of America
10 9 8 7 6 5 4 3 2 1

ISBN 0-13-169771-4

Prentice-Hall International, Inc., *London*
Prentice-Hall of Australia Pty. Limited, *Sydney*
Prentice-Hall of Canada, Ltd., *Toronto*
Prentice-Hall of India Private Limited, *New Delhi*
Prentice-Hall of Japan, Inc., *Tokyo*
Prentice-Hall of Southeast Asia Pte. Ltd., *Singapore*
Whitehall Books Limited, *Wellington, New Zealand*

CONTENTS

5   CONTRACT NEGOTIATION: PRINCIPLES, PROBLEMS, AND PROCEDURES   108

6   BALANCING THE RIGHTS OF LABOR AND MANAGEMENT   149

9   RESOLUTION OF FUTURE TERMS DISPUTES 209

10   NEGOTIATED WAGE ISSUES 226

11   NEGOTIATED ECONOMIC SECURITY PACKAGES AND OTHER "FRINGES"   246

12   JOB SECURITY AND INDUSTRIAL JURISPRUDENCE   278

13   *LABOR MARKETS AND BARGAINING—*
THEORY, STRATEGY, AND EVIDENCE   **304**

14   THE ECONOMIC IMPACT OF COLLECTIVE BARGAINING 332

15   PUBLIC SECTOR COLLECTIVE BARGAINING 369

16 *EMERGING COLLECTIVE BARGAINING RELATIONSHIPS IN HEALTH CARE, PROFESSIONAL SPORTS, AND HIGHER EDUCATION* 408

17 *COLLECTIVE BARGAINING: THE CHALLENGES AHEAD* 439

PREFACE

Contemporary Collective Bargaining discusses the practice of collective bargaining in the United States today. The practical focus of Harold W. Davey's previous editions is carefully preserved and reinforced: *what* collective bargaining is really all about, *why* collective bargaining is this way, and *how* collective bargaining works.

However, in many ways this book is significantly different from the third edition: it has grown from thirteen to seventeen chapters, the order in which specific subjects are presented has been changed, and new topics have been substituted for the old, improving all the original chapters. This edition contains more data and statistical tabulations, and references have been updated; questions for discussion, thought, and research have been added to each chapter.

In other respects, this book is *not* different from the third edition. Important examples are Chapter 5, "Contract Negotiation: Principles, Problems, and Procedures," Chapter 7, "Contract Administration," and Chapter 8, "Grievance Arbitration"; they retain their original practical focus and continue to reflect Harold W. Davey's unique touch and insight. However, these chapters were updated to fill in the gaps created by new legal developments in areas like minority and women's rights, fair representation, and finality of arbitration. An appendix to Chapter 5 is devoted to the subject of *calculating settlement costs*.

This book's third edition contained normative judgments about "good" or "bad" practices and assertions about what "ought to be." While we have modified this practice, it remains one of the book's identifying characteristics. We share professional judgments with the reader, drawing on our combined academic and practical experiences in collective bargaining; however, the difference between facts and judgments remains clear.

Chapter 1 gives readers a definition of collective bargaining and our plan for the book. Following the advice of reviewers, Chapter 2 is now a brief review of significant historical developments in U.S. labor policy. The next six chapters examine public policy, unit structure, negotiations, contract administration, and the grievance arbitration process. Among these practical, micro-oriented chapters regarding the operation of contemporary labor relations, Chapter 6 contains a fresh treatment of how the U.S. collective bargaining institution functions through reliance on processes which permit a balancing of management rights against union rights. Chapter 9, "Resolution of Future Terms Disputes," concludes the book's treatment of collective bargaining *process* topics. This chapter's new richness is found primarily in discussions about interest arbitration.

The substantive issues discussed at the bargaining table and the resulting content of the labor agreement are presented in Chapters 10, 11, and 12. These chapters contain in-depth examinations and analyses of negotiated wage, fringe benefit, and job security issues, respectively. Chapter 10 has been considerably reorganized and the subjects of job evaluation and incentive systems are given greater emphasis. Chapter 11 was almost completely rewritten. Critical subjects such as ERISA, HMO legislation, coordination of public and private benefits, and fringe benefit cost as a rising share of payroll costs are now highlighted. The impact of these subjects on pension, health, and related fringe benefit negotiations is fully discussed. Chapter 12 remains basically unaltered; however, new topics such as affirmative action programs, discipline and discrimination and minority rights are now included.

Chapters 13, 14, 15, and 16 are new. The subjects in these chapters have been placed later in the book because we did not want to interrupt the flow of discussion relevant to "hands-on" institutional processes and other subject matters of collective bargaining proper. Moreover, we felt that with the practical side of collective bargaining well understood, readers would be in a better position to appreciate the more abstract content of Chapter 13 on labor market economics and bargaining behavior. Similar considerations hold true for Chapter 14, which delves into the economic impact of collective bargaining. A synthesis of numerous empirical studies, this chapter bridges the gap between microdecisions and macroconsequences. Relative union wage gains, COLA and price inflation, and productivity are among the subjects discussed. The triangular relationship of labor to management and of both to government is examined, leading to a discussion of the nation's experiments with incomes policies.

Finally, Chapters 15 and 16, on collective bargaining in the public sector and on the emergence of collective bargaining in the fields of health care, professional sports, and higher education build on the concepts, procedures, and laws discussed in the first part of the book. These chapters present a final and very important lesson, namely that collective bargaining is a dynamic and adaptive institution which has applications beyond the manufacturing, construction, and mining industries, i.e., the traditional union sectors in the United States.

A book is never the product of authors alone. Although Mario F. Bognanno and David L. Estenson are primarily responsible for this edition, Harold W. Davey's excellent third edition was its basis. Conscientious reviewers gave our manuscript a careful and critical reading. We followed many of their suggestions for revision and rewrite. We are particularly thankful to Herbert G. Heneman, Jr., Professor Emeritus, University of Minnesota; Anthony V. Sinicropi, University of Iowa; R.J. Shuster, Youngstown State University; and Marcus H. Sandver, Ohio State University.

Several colleagues were helpful in discussions over content, clarity, strengths, and weaknesses of the book. We wish to acknowledge assistance received from Ross E. Azevedo, University of Minnesota; Frederic C. Champlin, University of Oklahoma; James B. Dworkin, Purdue University; Daniel G. Gallagher, University of Iowa; Gregory S. Hundley, University of Oregon; and Hoyt N. Wheeler, University of South Carolina.

We are grateful to the University of California and the University of Minnesota for institutional support and we owe a special debt of appreciation to Ms. Donna D'Andrea and Mrs. Marjorie Whitehill, Industrial Relations Center, University of Minnesota for clerical coordination and service.

On a personal note, Mario's wife Peggy deserves special thanks for her unfailing assistance and encouragement throughout this project.

Harold W. Davey, Ames, Iowa
Mario F. Bognanno, Minneapolis, Minnesota
David L. Estenson, Berkeley, California

CONTEMPORARY COLLECTIVE BARGAINING

COLLECTIVE BARGAINING TODAY

1

INTRODUCTION

Sometime before the year 2000 we will reach that moment when collective bargaining in America ends its second hundred years. Collective bargaining began when several employees chose to join together and bargain with their employer rather than to quit and seek better wages, hours, and working conditions elsewhere. In the almost two hundred years of evolving public policies, of union growth and decline through several cycles, of increasingly large and complex workplaces, one element remains central to collective bargaining: employees at a common workplace joining together to change through bargaining their wages, hours, and conditions of employment.

Today collective bargaining is a vital element of modern life, affecting the distribution of billions of dollars, and directly or indirectly influencing the pay and working conditions of a majority of employed Americans. Collective bargaining is an activity of intense interest to those directly involved; it is at once rational, emotional, and amusing in its games and histrionics. It can be violent. No year passes without injury or death erupting out of the confrontations of extreme labor dispute. It is a serious activity to employers, to employees, to their unions, to the economy, to the public, and to government.

This book is about the practice of collective bargaining today. In this book we report the current public policy applicable to collective bargaining; we describe the state of collective bargaining practice; we analyze some of the behaviors in collective bargaining; and we analyze and report those behaviors that seem to work better than others.

WHAT IS COLLECTIVE BARGAINING?

For our discussion in the rest of the book, *collective bargaining* is defined as a continuing institutional relationship between an employer entity (government or private) and a labor organization (union or association) representing exclusively a defined group of employees (appropriate bargaining unit) concerned with the negotiation, administration, interpretation, and enforcement of written agreements covering joint understandings as to wages or salaries, rates of pay, hours of work, and other conditions of employment. Of major importance is the fact that the collective bargaining relationship between employer and union is *a continuous one*, involving contract administration as well as contract negotiation.

Descriptions of collective bargaining that stress strategy and bluffing unfortunately convey the idea that negotiation of contracts is all there is to the process. Laymen envisage shirt-sleeved men in a smoke-filled room at midnight with a strike deadline staring them in the face. Such a melodramatic picture is, of course, a true one in particular cases at particular points in time. Yet it is never accurate as a portrayal of the *totality of the bargaining relationship*. Contract negotiation is vitally important but it is never the whole story.

When employer and union negotiate a contract, they are reaching a joint understanding on a written statement of policies and procedures under which they must live together for one to three years (perhaps longer in some cases). It is the process of *living together under the agreement* that gives meaning and significance to the written instrument. Experience in contract administration is the crucial factor in determining whether the collective bargaining relationship will be a constructive one. As Neil Chamberlain and the late Harry Shulman stressed in 1949, the negotiation of a contract is to labor relations what the wedding ceremony is to domestic relations. In their view, "the heart of the collective agreement—indeed, of collective bargaining—is the process for continuous joint consideration and adjustment of plant problems."[1]

The term "collective bargaining" was reputedly coined by Sidney and Beatrice Webb, the famed historians of the British labor movement.[2] It was first given wide currency in the United States by Samuel Gompers and has long been an accepted phrase in our labor relations vocabulary. It has proved to be a useful shorthand term for describing a continuous, dynamic, institutional process for solving problems arising directly out of the employer–employee relationship.

Our definition of collective bargaining is deliberately elastic to cover the complete range of organized or institutional relationships between unions and employers. Collective bargaining is a system made up of a set of *continuous* processes; it is customary and helpful to distinguish *negotiation* of contracts (the "legislative" phase of the union–employer relationship), *administration* of contracts (the "executive" phase), and *interpretation* or *application* of contracts (the "judicial" phase).

THE PARTIES IN COLLECTIVE BARGAINING

The chief participants in collective bargaining do not act for themselves. They are representatives of their respective. institutions, the workers organized into a trade union and the collective entity of the corporation, business firm, or public agency. Collective bargaining is always representative on the employees' side. The interests of nonsupervisory employees are represented to employers by an institutional hierarchy ranging from shop stewards, committee members, and local union officers to the top officers and staff personnel of the national union. The bargaining is thus clearly "collective" on the union side. Union X is the *exclusive bargaining representative* of *all* employees in a defined unit for purposes of negotiating with their employer with respect to wages, hours, and other terms or conditions of employment. The representative standing of Union X is frequently based on certification by the National Labor Relations Board (NLRB) after having won a secret-ballot election conducted by an NLRB field examiner.

In most cases, bargaining is also collective on the employer's side. Those who negotiate and administer contracts for the corporate or agency employer are acting in a representative capacity. Although there are still owner-managers who speak for themselves in collective bargaining, the corporation and public agency are the dominant form of organization in

1. Harry W. Shulman and Neil W. Chamberlain, *Cases on Labor Relations* (Brooklyn: Foundation Press, 1949), p. 3.

2. See Vernon H. Jenson, "Notes on the Beginnings of Collective Bargaining," *Industrial and Labor Relations Review*, 9 (January 1956), 225–34.

the American economy. In any corporate enterprise, professional managers handle the employer's interests in labor relations. The managers of the enterprise speak in the name of the directors or elected officials. The latter in turn represent the legal owners, the stockholders, or the electorate. The representative nature of the process on both sides of the bargaining table is most apparent in what is usually called multiemployer bargaining. In such a bargaining structure it is customary for an employers' labor relations association to speak for the member employers in negotiating with one or more unions representing the combined employees of the associated employers.

For these reasons, collective bargaining typically involves organized group relationships rather than individual dealings between principals. It is an institutionalized representative process. The contract or agreement sets forth the procedures whereby the continuing relationship between management and union is carried forward.

Certain differences between the union as an institution and the corporation as an institution play an important role in shaping the nature and direction of the bargaining process and the respective goals of the parties.[3] Arthur M. Ross observed in 1948 that the trade union is a political agency operating in an economic environment. This deceptively simple characterization emphasizes a fact of life about unions that many employers and students of labor relations still fail to comprehend. *Union leadership is elected at all levels.* Pressure is thus always operating on union leaders to prove that they are *doing something* for the represented employees. The union is in this sense a highly political agency, as is any other service organization whose leadership is elected. The ears of union leaders are constantly subjected to the haunting political refrain of their rank-and-file constituents, "What have you done for us *lately?*"

This basic characteristic of unionism is helpful in explaining why union bargaining demands sometimes appear to be of a blue-sky nature to the detached observer or the cost-conscious employer. There should, however, be comfort in the knowledge that informed union leaders do realize they are operating in an economic environment. They know that the surging aspirations of the rank and file must, in the final analysis, be tempered by economic reality.

In short, the union is a body politic in which authority flows from the bottom up. This causes the dynamics of union policy determination to differ sharply from those of the corporation, where authority flows from the top down. On economic issues, for example, it is comparatively easy for management to formulate its policy in cost terms. The union approach on economic issues is necessarily conditioned by such "political" consider-

---

3. Arthur M. Ross, *Trade Union Wage Policy* (Berkeley: University of California Press, 1948), *passim.*

ations as rank-and-file aspirations, gains made by other unions, and the growth and survival requirements of the union as an institution.[4]

Reconciliation of the economic calculus of the employer with the union's "political" approach is often a difficult task. It serves to make collective bargaining as a process the despair of those "rational" observers who yearn for order and precision in determining the price of labor.

STRUCTURAL VARIATIONS IN BARGAINING RELATIONSHIPS

Variety in U.S. labor relations patterns is shown by the many diverse structures for bargaining purposes. The most familiar bargaining structure involves a single employer negotiating with one or more unions. However, many important bargaining relationships involve an employer association and one or more unions negotiating a so-called multiemployer agreement.

Another structural arrangement is generally referred to as "coalition bargaining" or "coordinated bargaining." The structure applies to situations where several unions dealing with a large employer, such as General Electric or Westinghouse, combine forces for bargaining purposes and negotiate with the employer on a united-front basis.

An older version of coalition bargaining has been practiced for many years in some labor market areas by the principal craft unions in the building trades who negotiate on a joint basis with a contractors' association. In a limited number of industries, we can observe what amounts to national bargaining between an employer association and one or more unions.

Generally speaking, however, the structure of bargaining in the United States can be described as decentralized or even "fractionalized" in character. The significance of fractionalization is diminished in some industries by the force of pattern bargaining. Without wishing to exaggerate the force of key settlements on other contracts, many negotiations today are clearly conducted in terms of both constraints and compulsions imposed by policies originally established in other negotiations.

Public sector bargaining takes place in a variety of forms. At its simplest, it may be a professional negotiating team representing the public agency bargaining with representatives of the union. More often than not, however, other avenues for bargaining complicate the proceedings. Unions may choose to do their bargaining directly with elected officials by involving themselves in electoral politics and by lobbying. Elected officials may choose to intervene with the professional employer negotiating team, or fail to implement or fail to pass legislation implementing the terms of

---

4. *Ibid., passim.*

agreement negotiated by the employer representative. The latter action forces the union to bargain directly with elected officials, and forces union involvement in the political process.

The structure of the bargaining relationship is basic to collective bargaining; it determines who negotiates with whom. We discuss the possible arrangements in Chapter 4.

THE SUBJECT MATTER OF COLLECTIVE BARGAINING

In simple terms, collective bargaining covers two basic subject matter categories: (1) *the price of labor*, broadly defined to include not only wages as such but any other working conditions or term of employment involving direct monetary outlays, such as pension plans, group life insurance plans, paid vacations, and so forth; (2) *a system of industrial jurisprudence*, that is, policies and procedures governing on-the-job relationships that apply to all workers covered by the contract in like fashion in like circumstances. It embraces the vitally important function of collective bargaining in substituting a rule of law in shop relationships for the former arbitrary discretion of supervision.[5]

We can also define the subject matter of collective bargaining by utilizing statutory expressions of coverage as contained in sections 9(a) and 8(d) of the National Labor Relations Act.

Section 9(a) covers the subject matter of collective bargaining by the now-familiar phrase "rates of pay, wages, hours of employment, or other conditions of employment." Section 8(d), the first legislative attempt to define the obligation to bargain in good faith, describes the area covered by the duty to bargain as including "wages, hours, and other terms and conditions of employment."[6]

The differences between 9(a) and 8(d) are not important for our present purpose. Both make clear that from a public policy standpoint the subject matter of collective bargaining remains essentially what it has always been—the price of labor, the hours of work, and policies and procedures

---

5. Sumner H. Slichter, *Union Policies and Industrial Management* (Washington, D.C.: Brookings Institution, 1941).

6. Section 8(d) made its appearance as new language in the Taft-Hartley Act of 1947. When to provide footnote citations for statutory provisions can be troublesome. When using the term "National Labor Relations Act," we are generally referring to the federal law as it stands, unless otherwise stated. The full statutory citation which embraces the original National Labor Relations Act of 1935 (Wagner Act), the Labor Management Relations Act of 1947 (Taft-Hartley Act), and the Labor Management Reporting and Disclosure Act of 1959 (Landrum-Griffin) is as follows: 49 Stat. 449 (1935), as amended by Pub. L. No. 101, 805th Cong., 1st Sess. (1947), and Pub. L. No. 257, 86th Cong., 1st Sess. (1959); 29 U.S.C. 151–68, 29 F.C.A. 151–68.

relating to any phase of the employment relationship. Current contracts that run over one hundred printed pages in length are *in essence* similar to the one-page documents negotiated by craft unions with employers in the 1890s. Whether the contract is one or two hundred pages in length it is still dealing with wages, hours, and other terms and conditions of employment. The range, diversity, and complexity of issues treated in collective bargaining have expanded, but collective bargaining as a process and the essential nature of its coverage remain generically the same. Nearly all management and union representatives hold firmly to the view that collective bargaining should be limited to negotiating and administering contracts that cover, in the late J. M. Clark's happily succinct phrase, "wages and human relations on the job."[7]

ALTERNATIVE APPROACHES
TO THE CONTENTS OF COLLECTIVE BARGAINING

What collective bargaining looks like depends a great deal on what trade, industry, service, or profession one is examining. *All* genuine collective bargaining deals in one fashion or another with the price of labor and human relations on the job. Beyond this it is hazardous to generalize. There is truly a protean diversity both in bargaining structures and in the treatment of substantive and procedural problems.

One natural contrast is between *craft* and *industrial* bargaining. Historically, skilled workers organized on a craft basis were the first to form stable, durable national unions. Their basic objectives have remained essentially the same over long periods of time. For example, building trades craft unions have sought to control employment opportunities exclusively for members in good standing, to increase steadily the monetary compensation for journeymen, and to protest their carefully defined work jurisdictions against encroachment by other unions and against dilution of skills by the employer.

Such craft unions do not seek detailed contractual restriction of employer discretion in on-the-job situations. The business agent servicing a craft union in the construction field limits his attention to making sure that union wage scales are being observed and that no nonunion workers or itinerant journeymen without permits are employed on any project. Such a concentration on enforcing union scale and closed shop conditions makes for comparatively short written agreements between contractors and building trades unions. In bulky contrast are the contracts negotiated

---

7. John Maurice Clark, *Guideposts in Time of Change* (New York: Harper & Row, 1949), p. 148.

between manufacturing firms and industrial unions. The latter typically represent *all* nonsupervisory production and maintenance employees (skilled, semiskilled, and unskilled) in inclusive bargaining units.

Industrial union negotiators necessarily emphasize inclusion in *their* contracts of detailed statements of policy and procedure governing on-the-job rights and relationships because realistically they cannot control employer hiring or otherwise limit the supply of labor in a particular labor market. Membership in an industrial union is based on the industry in which the worker is employed rather than on the nature of the work performed. Industrial union leaders are, in their fashion, just as interested in job security for their membership as are leaders of the highly skilled journeyman craft groups.

The industrial union leader must concentrate on *job security on the job.* He seeks to negotiate detailed rules and procedures governing layoffs, recalls to employment, promotions, transfers, and the like, with seniority as the primary (if not sole) criterion whenever possible. Also, nearly all industrial contracts confine the employer's right to discipline to cases where he can prove "good and just cause." Finally, in an uncertain climate created by technological change, plant relocation, and industrial structural change, union representatives in manufacturing are particularly concerned with negotiating provisions to reduce the adverse impact of any such changes on incumbent employees.

The contract between an employer and an industrial union is thus often a lengthy document that may run more than a hundred closely printed pages. Contract administration in a large factory tends to be formalized, structured, and institutionalized. Sheer numbers prevent the informal approach to grievance adjustment that is still possible in craft bargaining situations or in small manufacturing establishments.

Contract administration in a large public bureaucracy (where industrial unionism is growing rapidly) is perhaps the most formalized of all; this can be attributed in part to complex contracts and in part to the sometimes complementary, sometimes competing—but always formalized—civil service procedures.

This aspect of industrial union contracts helps to explain why the bulk of grievance arbitration in the United States appears to be generated from medium and large industrial units rather than from small firms or craft units. Using an impartial arbitrator to make a final and binding decision as the last step in the contract's grievance machinery is regarded as standard operating procedure by most large firms and the unions with which they bargain. Yet arbitration is seldom needed by employers and craft unions in building and construction or in small manufacturing establishments.

Diversity is also well illustrated by noting which bargaining issues are of central importance to the parties. The price of labor is a key issue in nearly every negotiation. Beyond this, it is difficult to generalize. Unions in manufacturing stress seniority (length of service) as a primary criterion governing layoffs, recalls, and promotions. Building trades unions do not concern themselves in the same fashion with seniority from a collective bargaining contract standpoint. They attempt to achieve security for members by controlling entrance to the trade. They function as an employment agency for the various contractors with whom they negotiate. The craft union's seniority system is internal to the union.

Unions in the hotel and restaurant field have a special interest in provisions governing split-shift employment. This is not even a problem for most other unions. Craft unions with closed shop contracts do not stress contractual control of the employer's right to discipline. Industrial unions, however, invariably regard as a must a contract clause limiting the employer's exercise of the disciplinary prerogative to cases of "good and just cause."

Professional associations or unions representing teachers have a special concern over establishing through negotiation their voice in such matters as classroom size, curriculum, nonclass functions required of the teacher, credit for class preparation time, and so forth. These are serious problems for *teachers as such*, but are not a concern for other unions. In any industry geared to assembly-line operations, a critical problem area is likely to be the length and spacing of relief periods and coffee breaks. In other lines of work, periodic rest may be less essential and thus of minor importance as a bargaining problem.

For those industries on continuous-shift operations (three shifts of eight hours each in a twenty-four-hour period), the paid lunch period while on the job is sometimes a critical issue. This problem can be even tougher when those on continuous shift with a paid lunch period are working side by side with other workers who are in the plant for eight and a half hours with a thirty-minute *unpaid* lunch break.

Piece rates or incentive standards are serious bargaining problems in industries where labor cost is a substantial percentage of total cost (such as the garment and shoe industries). Employers who pay by the hour, however, are faced with difficulties in developing and maintaining performance standards for "measured day work."

Perhaps enough has been indicated on the variety-diversity theme to point up the fact that there is no such thing as a typical collective bargaining contract. The more contracts one studies, the more one is impressed with the fascinating variety of policies and procedures developed by the parties in reaching a mutually satisfactory accommodation, contract after contract, on the deceptively simple problems of wages, hours, and other conditions of employment.

In the remaining chapters, we discuss in some detail the variety of policies and procedures that may be negotiated in a contract. We discuss the division of rights under the agreement, grievance and arbitration procedures, discipline, job security and seniority provisions, and the pay package, especially the many ways in which the pay package may be designed.

PUBLIC POLICY AND COLLECTIVE BARGAINING

Collective bargaining is a means for setting private, mutually agreed, terms governing the employer–employee relationship. At some point it is inevitable that the collective, privately determined terms interfere with what might be considered public interests. Allowing private decision making has the considerable advantage of letting people with the most knowledge and most at stake choose a suitable "portfolio" of terms. Public interference has the undesirable feature of requiring an outsider's decision.

On the other hand, private collective bargaining imposes costs on others; for instance, a strike or lockout of steel workers or fire fighters can be very serious to others in the community. Collective bargaining best represents the interests of a majority of employees; occasionally, interests of a minority are overlooked or harmed. Both of these cases invite public intervention. Government jurisdiction usurps the private jurisdiction in order to protect individual rights (such as rights of equal opportunity or free speech) and the interests of customers of and suppliers to the firm or agency (such as the disruption of commerce from strike or collusion by a union and employer to restrict trade).

Public policy in the United States restricts many activities and tactics of employers and unions. Legal restrictions on collective bargaining in the private sector primarily have been on tactics and procedures. These restrictions are intended to limit somewhat the harm to innocent third parties by encouraging settlement and limiting conflict. For example, employers and unions must both bargain in good faith, though they are not required to settle and may, under most circumstances, strike or lock out. An exception to the freedom to strike includes prohibition during times of national emergency. And unions cannot strike against one employer in order to put economic pressure on another employer. The union and employer are free with a few exceptions to write their own terms and conditions of agreement; the contract terms are not mandated by outside agents and the contract is recognized as legal.

Regulation of the collective bargaining process extends beyond the negotiation phase. The bargaining unit—that is, who may be represented by the union in a particular work setting is determined by the National Labor Relations Board. The NLRB supervises secret-ballot employee elections on whether or not they desire union representation. Thus, unions represent workers who choose a particular union as their representative.

Employees may choose not to have a union; that too is their right under contemporary public policy.

Unions themselves are regulated. To insure that unions are honest and responsive agents of their members, the political process within the union must meet certain standards of democracy. Union officials must comply with disclosure and other obligations in handling members' money. Although these regulations are neither perfect nor always enforced, most unions are responsible representatives of the interests of the rank and file.

In the public sector, regulation of collective bargaining is widely disparate and to some extent experimental. At one extreme, public sector collective bargaining is unrecognized in any statute, and regulation is left to judicial interpretation of common law. At the other extreme, there exists detailed legislation on what is a bargainable subject and what is not, on what tactics employers or unions may use and what tactics they may not use, and on the method for resolving unsettled disputes; perhaps including compulsory contract arbitration.

Because public policy sets the rules of conduct under which collective bargaining operates, it is vital to understand what our public policies are in order to understand collective bargaining. In Chapter 3 we discuss in detail the regulation of most of our private sector collective bargaining. Throughout the rest of the book we discuss public policy regulations and issues where appropriate.

Public policy concerns include more than those issues directly involved in union operation and collective negotiation. Does collective bargaining lead to inflation? This is one question of public concern today. Because of our slowing growth in productivity, we might ask what impact unions have on the efficiency of our economy? These questions are some of the macro-aspects of the collective bargaining process. These issues are discussed in Chapter 14 on the economic impact of collective bargaining.

COLLECTIVE BARGAINING OUTSIDE THE UNITED STATES

An industrial relations system viable in one country may, for many reasons, not be suitable to the legal, economic, social, and institutional requirements of another country. Readers unfamiliar with collective bargaining in places other than North America are warned that customs and practices differ tremendously. Usually unions outside North America direct their primary effort toward political activity rather than negotiation with the employer on wages, hours, and conditions of employment. In parts of northern Europe, for example, employee representatives serve on the board of directors of private corporations; the employee's representative has a mandate to participate in all aspects of corporate decision making. As another example, in Australia private sector bargaining impasses go to mandatory arbitration; strikes are prohibited (but, as with the public sector in the U.S., not unusual). One book cannot possibly do justice to all the labor relations practices around the world.

The present volume has a parochial and modest objective. We shall be concerned primarily with analysis of collective bargaining policies and procedures that fit the legal, economic, political, and social milieu of the United States. Our discussion is geared to U.S. experience and U.S. conditions.

PLAN OF DISCUSSION

We have two goals for our presentation in the following chapters. First, and foremost, we discuss specifically the practice of contemporary collective bargaining. We hope the attentive reader, by the end of the book, will understand the main currents of contemporary practice and will have an appreciation for the variation and invention among those who practice collective bargaining. Second, we attempt to present a broader picture of the collective bargaining process, including the changing currents of labor relations from its outset in the eighteenth century to the happenings in the emerging sectors today, and including the implications of collective bargaining for our society and our economy.

To understand collective bargaining today, one must understand the rules of the game as determined by public policy. In the next chapter we discuss the development of current policy and the development of unions. Then, in the following chapter, we summarize the important features of current regulation of the collective bargaining process.

Before collective bargaining begins, the bargaining unit must be fixed. This is discussed in Chapter 4 where the topics covered include the selection of the union by employees, the determination of which employees the union represents, and the association by unions and employers into larger bargaining structures.

Chapters 5 through 9 describe various aspects of the collective bargaining process. Included in these chapters is discussion of negotiation and settlement of disputes over the terms of agreement. We also discuss the collective agreement, the nature of this contract, and the means by which the contract is applied day to day. Most important is the means by which disputes over the interpretation of the contract are settled during the life of the agreement.

The negotiation and administration of an agreement is one part of collective bargaining; the other part is what are the actual terms and conditions of employment specified in the contract. In Chapters 10, 11, and

12 we consider contract contents and issues, including such topics as wage levels and wage differentials, the increasing importance of indirect forms of pay and work rules, discipline, and dismissal.

In Chapter 13 we depart from our emphasis on practice and consider bargaining theory and the relationship of collective bargaining to labor markets in a more analytical format. This emphasis carries over to Chapter 14, where we discuss and analyze some of the economic effects of collective bargaining.

Chapters 15 and 16 deal with what we consider to be emerging sectors of collective bargaining—the public, health care, sports and educational sectors. It is not that these are necessarily the most important sectors for collective bargaining: a strong case can be made, for example, that collective bargaining in the steel, coal, or railway industries is more important. But the emerging sectors, as the name implies, are the areas of greatest change, and these are the areas generating the most current attention and interest. In keeping with the theme of a book on contemporary collective bargaining, we reflect that interest. We conclude with a chapter outlining the challenges, performance, and future of collective bargaining in the United States.

In the next chapter we begin with a brief history of collective bargaining.

Questions for Discussion, Thought, and Research

1. A union leader noted, "We incorporate as many of the rank-and-file demands as possible. Our job is to narrow down their proposals from the ridiculous to the unreasonable. Although some of our initial proposals may appear to be of a blue-sky nature, it is the management negotiator's job to say no." What are some of the political reasons behind this strategy?

2. What issues are typically covered in a labor agreement? Examine a labor agreement. What proportion of the contract is devoted to the discussion of the price of labor, compared to items which relate to a system of industrial jurisprudence?

3. Is it possible for a union to become too democratic? Are maximum democracy in a union and maximum effectiveness in representing the interests of union members mutually exclusive goals? Discuss.

4. One observer noted, "In collective bargaining negotiations, the element of trust is indispensable." He went on, "The system can best be characterized as 'negotiators lying with honor.'" Are these two statements inconsistent?

5. Why do unions place so much emphasis on seniority? Is this emphasis likely to continue in the next decade?

6. In what sense does collective bargaining create a system of jurisprudence?

7. What factors are most important in causing people to join labor organizations? What factors are most influential in keeping people from joining? Explain.

8. What is your definition of the phrase "collective bargaining"? How does your definition differ from that presented in Chapter 1?

9. In general terms, how would you characterize U.S. policy toward collective bargaining? Do you agree with this policy thrust? Discuss.

10. To what extent are union and employer bargaining goals variously influenced by economic and political factors? From a practical viewpoint, does it really matter whether economic or political factors dominate the goal formation process? Discuss.

Selected Bibliography

At the end of each of the remaining chapters we list a brief bibliography. Primarily, the readings are books rather than articles; they are intended to serve as a starting place for further inquiry. Many of the best studies and certainly the most current information appear in articles. Listed below are some places to look to find current information and articles.

Indices: The most comprehensive index is *Work Related Abstracts*. Other useful indices include *Business Periodicals Index* and the *Public Affairs Information Service* (PAIS).

Some journals that carry collective bargaining topics include *Industrial Relations, Journal of Labor Research, Labor Law Journal, Collective Bargaining in the Public Sector,* and *Industrial and Labor Relations Review.*

Very relevant and topical papers and discussions appear in the annual proceedings of the Industrial Relations Research Association and the National Academy of Arbitrators.

Prentice-Hall, the Bureau of National Affairs, and Commerce Clearing House publish labor relations reporting services.

A rich variety of articles, monographs, and statistical reports emerges from the U.S. Department of Labor. The department's *Monthly Labor Review* reports many of tbe latest events and statistics.

For an introduction to American labor relations see Dunlop, John T., and Derek L. Bok, *Labor and the American Community.* New York: Simon and Schuster, 1970.

DEVELOPMENT OF
COLLECTIVE BARGAINING

2

This book is about contemporary collective bargaining. It is doubtful, however, that we can understand collective bargaining today without understanding something of the major events that led to current practices and institutions. In this chapter we pay particular attention to two areas, the development of unions and the development of laws regulating collective bargaining.

The American emphasis on collective bargaining owes a great deal to the type of unions which have survived in the United States, and to how the surviving unions have evolved through the years. Other countries have unions, but they are primarily political agents, or they emphasize bargaining of a quite different character compared to American unions. Unions, even in the United States, are not uniform. For example, craft and industrial unionism have been conflicting concepts of what unions should be. To some extent, these differences remain today, and continue to influence the process of collective bargaining.

Today collective bargaining is heavily regulated. (These regulations are summarized and discussed in the next chapter.) Current regulation is relatively recent in origin; other approaches have been tried. The type of legal or regulatory approach affects the relative success of unions versus employers, the type of workers who successfully unionize, and the extent of and intensity of conflict in collective disputes. As public policy regulating collective bargaining has changed, so has the collective bargaining process.

In the following pages, in rough chronology, we trace some of the important changes in collective bargaining.

THE FIRST UNIONS

The first union in the United States was formed in 1792 by shoemakers (called Cordwainers at the time) in Philadelphia. The union of shoemakers was soon followed by unions of printers, cabinet makers, masons, coopers, and tailors. These early unions included workers sharing a single craft who sought goals we recognize today in modern craft unions: a minimum wage for craft work and job security, especially through control of apprentice entry.

What change brought about the desire of craft workers to form unions? The most important change appears to have been improved transportation and expanded credit, which permitted much larger productive units. The larger organizations sold their products over a wider geographic area and competed for labor over a wider geographic area. Capital requirements for larger businesses made it unlikely that a journeyman would become a master tradesman. Thus, for most craft workers their livelihood depended upon their lifelong wage earnings rather than earnings from business ownership. As trade expanded, wage earnings were under constant competitive pressure from producers in other geographic areas (undercutting the price of the firm they worked for) and from wage earners moving in from other geographic areas. Unions arose for a conservative purpose, to maintain the status of the craft worker and to preserve the wage of lifelong craft workers against the expanding competitive pressures which threatened to undermine their current positions and earnings.

The early unions were not formed by factory workers; it would take more than a century before factory work would be organized in substantial volume. The early unions were not formed by the least advantaged wage earners. Early unions formed within the relatively skilled and privileged occupations, in large part to preserve their relatively skilled and privileged status.

NINETEENTH-CENTURY JUDGES

In 1792, when the first union appeared, there was no legislation applicable to unions or collective bargaining. It was up to judges to decide legal policy based on their interpretation of the principles of common law. Common law represents the precedent of court decisions made without the guidance of legislation. Only with the twentieth century did legislation (statutes) replace common law regulation of collective bargaining. Thus, public policy in this area was ruled by judges for the entire century.

Philadelphia Cordwainers

In 1806 the first court case relevant to labor unions was decided. The judge applied the common law doctrine of criminal conspiracy to the Cordwainers' union. This doctrine says that what one man may do (threaten to quit unless a higher wage is paid) many combined may not do (threaten to strike unless a higher wage is paid). Workers participating in concerted action were convicted of crimes.

Though the law was clear, it was not always successful at stopping union activity. Juries were reluctant to convict union members. And the courts intervened only after the union had organized and, perhaps, already achieved its initial objective. As we found recently with unions in the public sector, outlawing unions or collective bargaining does not always put an end to successful union activity.

Commonwealth v. Hunt

In 1842 the Massachusetts Supreme Court issued a famous decision that served as a precedent that limited, but did not eliminate, the doctrine of criminal conspiracy. Chief Justice Shaw argued for the Court that unions were not necessarily seeking illegal ends, such as high wages through "conspiracy." He argued that unions may serve legal purposes as well, such as cultural or social advancement of members. This ruling discouraged the application of the criminal conspiracy doctrine to unions, since the prosecution had to demonstrate that the union was seeking an unlawful end. With the decline of the conspiracy doctrine, other judicial approaches toward unions and collective bargaining were tried.

Equity Courts

Beginning about 1880, reaching a peak in the 1890s, and lasting until 1932, another judicial device was used against unions. Equity courts are designed to prevent harm from happening. They issue temporary restraining orders or injunctions without a trial. Rulings are made by judges without a jury. Failure to abide by the injunction is contempt of court, which can be immediately punished by imprisonment.

Equity courts offered several advantages to employers not found in other types of proceedings. First, equity courts issue judgment without a jury. Juries have historically been much more sympathetic to unions that have judges. Second, the initial, temporary injunction was usually made without any chance for a union representative to argue against the employer version. Thus, the judge heard only the employer interpretation of events. Third, the decision and remedy came before, or in the early stages of, a strike, boycott, or picket. Equity courts were often able to stop unions before they could act. From the employers' perspective, this was far superior to a protracted court battle long after the union had ended a successful strike. Fourth, judges, who favored employers against unions, often issued injunctions without any clear indication that what the union sought was illegal or harmful.

Despite the antagonism held by judges toward unions, unions survived, grew, and sometimes prospered during the nineteenth century. This growth is discussed in the next three sections. Injunction against union strikes, boycotts, or pickets was ended for the most part in the private sector with the passage of the Norris-LaGuardia Act in 1932. Any remnants of the conspiracy doctrine were ended at this time as well. Active intervention by Congress and state legislatures ended most common law policies toward collective bargaining. Today common law prevails only over some very small employers and their employees, and over some state and local government employees.

EMERGENCE OF THE NATIONAL UNION

As transportation improved, local unions in one geographic area found themselves competing against labor or goods produced by labor from other geographic areas. It became apparent that local unions could not negotiate wages and working conditions without regard for wages and working conditions of comparable workers in other locales. National unions arose to equalize to some extent wages and working conditions among local bargaining groups, and to prevent employers from playing one local against another during bargaining.

The first national union was formed in 1852 by printers (called the National Typographic Union). Like other national unions of this era, this was a union of local bargaining groups that performed the same type of work. Toward the end of the century national unions formed rapidly, reaching 171 by 1909.[1]

1. Lloyd Ulman, *The Development of Trades and Labor Unions* (Berkeley: Institute of Industrial Relations, University of California, 1961), p. 383.

Today the national union (usually called an international because some locals are in Canada) is the dominant level of labor organization. The national union charters and disciplines local unions, sanctions local strikes and supports local unions with funding in their sanctioned strikes, and sends representatives to assist locals with their bargaining. The national union works to organize new locals. And the national represents local unions with multiemployer or multiplant employer negotiations. In general, the national is most active in coordinating local negotiations when the product market is national in scope. Where the product market is local, such as in the construction industry, the national is less involved in local negotiations.

Knights of Labor

The Knights of Labor was a short-lived labor organization different in many ways from conventional trade unions. The Knights had a national membership of working people organized into local assemblies. Local assemblies, unlike trade unions, did not include only workers from a common trade. Assemblies organized around communities, industries, nationalities, and workplaces, as well as conventional trades. Assemblies often included the skilled and relatively unskilled.

National leaders of the Knights of Labor sought goals and favored means different from those of the trade unions. The Knights' leaders sought the cooperation of labor and capital. Several producer cooperatives were formed under the sponsorship of the Knights, though all were to fail. Though several important strikes were supported by the Knights, the leadership was in principle antistrike, preferring arbitration of disputes instead. Though some political lobbying was undertaken (including support for legisled eight-hour days, weekly pay laws, equal pay for equal work, and health and safety laws), the leadership was diffident toward building a political party for labor.

Though not supportive of strikes and bargaining, much of the Knights' growth followed successful strikes by assemblies within the organization. After the Railway Strike of 1877, the Knights grew from its Philadelphia base into a national movement. Following a successful strike against Jay Gould's railroads in 1885, the Knights jumped in membership from 100,000 to 700,000 by the following year. Working people, especially the less skilled who were not represented by trade unions, joined in the hope they could resolve their grievances against employers.

Given the general goal of "cooperation," but the lack of any clear means—whether politics, strikes, or some other weapon—of forcing "capital" to cooperate, there was little the Knights could offer working people in helping them resolve grievances. The Knights of Labor declined as fast as it grew following a series of unsuccessful strikes, including an attempted general strike for an eight-hour day. It disappeared in the 1890s. Perhaps if the Knights had been clearer in purpose—whether the purpose was formation of a political party of labor or solid support for selected strikes—the character of the labor movement in the United States today would be broader in scope and put much less emphasis on local bargaining and contract administration.

The American Federation of Labor

The Knights of Labor and the national trade unions were able to coexist for a time. Many of the trade unionists in fact held dual memberships in their trade and the Knights. The two types of labor unions, however, were not especially compatible. Anti-trade union groups within the Knights criticized trade unions for their concentration on the interests of their own trade and not the interests of the broader labor movement. Trade unionists, on the other hand, criticized the Knights for accepting scab laborers as members. Both types of organizations competed for the allegiance of craft labor. But the interests of skilled craft labor were not advanced effectively when lumped in with less skilled labor. Other union members were not always supportive of the wage premiums paid craft labor, and skilled workers lost some bargaining leverage when lumped in with easily replaced unskilled workers. Finally, the trade unions eschewed the utopian ideas of the Knights of Labor, favoring instead pragmatic, short-term goals.

In 1886, at the height of the Knights of Labor success, another national labor organization, called the American Federation of Labor (AFL), was formed. This was an organization that essentially accepted the existing economic system and sought to advance member interests through collective bargaining. It was an organization that believed that the greatest labor solidarity was achieved when each craft had its own union. It was an organization of limited authority, made up of autonomous national trade unions. And it was an organization where member unions were granted exclusive jurisdiction to organize workers performing a particular type of work. There would be no dual unionism in the AFL. Workers would not have split allegiance between unions, and employers would not be able to set one union against another.

The federation of trade unions had several purposes. It negotiated and then defined the boundaries of the member international unions. It encouraged and assisted locals and internationals. For example, the AFL aided in efforts at national boycotts and sought strike assistance from other affiliates for particularly difficult strikes. It provided information to its members, the public, and the press about the trade union movement. It sought to influence public opinion in a way favorable to trade union views. In later years the federation also attempted (sometimes successfully) to secure favorable national legislation.

The AFL was financially starved in its early years. But it survived and sometimes prospered. Its successor, the AFL–CIO, exists to this day.

Wobblies

In 1905 another national labor union, the Industrial Workers of the World, sometimes called the IWW or Wobblies, was formed. Like the Knights of Labor, this was to be a short-lived movement seeking ends very different from the AFL unions. The IWW, however, was never able to achieve the membership size of the Knights, though the legacy of this union was larger. Part of this legacy is a number of folk heroes including Joe Hill, Big Bill Haywood, and Mother Jones.

The IWW was founded upon radical, syndicalist principles, although as the union grew a mixture of ideologies developed. The syndicalist goal was eventual control of business by workers. As an intermediate step, they attempted to organize workers in common industries. Industry unions were intended to be the "shadow" management of the industry until the time workers controlled the industry. The IWW was the first union concentrating on organizing all workers within an industry, rather than, say, only workers performing a particular craft.

The IWW leadership initially came out of the Western Mine Federation. The Wobblies' greatest strength was in the mines and logging camps of the West. The union's constituents were the large mass of unskilled and semiskilled workers ignored for the most part by the AFL unions.

The most notable IWW success, however, occurred on the east coast with the Lawrence, Massachusetts, textile strike of 1912.[2] An AFL union represented a small minority of textile workers. Unrepresented by any union were the vast majority of less skilled workers, at least until the IWW came along. Many of the IWW supporters in Lawrence were recent immigrants, a group that trade unionists argued could not be successfully unionized. This prediction proved false: the strike ended with a victory for the IWW. Among other achievements, the work week for women and children was cut to fifty-four hours.

When successful, such as in the Lawrence strike, the IWW objectives and means were not radically different from those of a typical labor union. In Lawrence the objectives were better wages and working conditions. These strikes proved that the less skilled workers in mass production work could organize, that the many nationalities could work together, and, despite tremendous opposition, that they could successfully obtain concessions from employers. This demonstration foreshadowed the next, great union development.

The IWW, however, was to have no part in this development. During

---

2. This strike provides the setting for part of E. L. Doctorow's novel *Ragtime*.

World War I virtually all the leaders of IWW were imprisoned as subversive. With the leadership imprisoned, the union declined rapidly, dissolving during the early 1920s.

VIOLENCE IN LABOR DISPUTES

In the period from the 1870s until the 1930s many major strikes occurred throughout the country. More often than not, these were violent affairs that sometimes brought the commerce of economic sectors or whole communities to a halt. A typical sequence might go like this: (1) declaration of a decrease in wages or working conditions by the employer, or demand for improved wages and working conditions by the union, (2) employees picket, strike, or threaten to strike, (3) issuance of an injunction against striking or picketing and troops, police, or private militia brought in to enforce the injunction, (4) an attack by troops, police, or private militia against strikers or picketers, or destruction of private property by workers or those sympathetic to their cause, (5) reaction, spread of disorder beyond the bounds of original dispute, more violence, and (6) a period of widespread, protracted conflict. Sometimes these disputes ended with an agreement favorable to labor, other times the union failed entirely. Either way, the disputes were usually long and bitter, with little room for compromise in the positions of both sides.

Railway Strike of 1877

The Railway Strike of 1877 was perhaps the major strike of the nineteenth century. It was a series of strikes against several railroads in several states. Strikes in all states were a reaction to substantial cuts in pay by the railroads and the use of larger trains requiring fewer employees to operate. The most violent confrontation occurred in the state of Pennsylvania.

The governor called troops out to stop railway strikers in Pittsburgh, even before any property was damaged. The first militia activated, however, joined the strikers. The next militia brought in removed the picketers by opening fire with a Gatling gun. Many were killed or wounded. A crowd, composed of railway workers and other citizens, then turned on the militia, eventually routing them from the city. Several troops were shot as they retreated. What followed was rioting, looting, and burning of railway cars and stores in Pittsburgh and, to a lesser extent, in other cities in Pennsylvania. The strike spread to all parts of Pennsylvania, bringing railway transport to a halt.

A similar, less violent scenario was followed in other states. This series of strikes proved the potential for substantial damage in labor-capital disputes.

In the 1890s and early 1900s a number of violent strikes took place. Labor was to lose them all. Brief summaries of four strikes follow.

Homestead Mills

In 1890 Carnegie Steel raised the price for steel and in 1892 lowered the wage to steel workers—represented by the Amalgamated Association of Iron, Steel, and Tin Workers—at their Homestead Mill. Because the Amalgamated refused to agree to the decrease, and in an effort to force agreement, the company locked the workers out of the mill. Pinkerton guards were hired to protect the mill. As they arrived at the plant they were met by mill workers. A battle ensued, and scores of guarders and workers were killed or wounded before the Pinkertons withdrew. The company kept the plant shut until the workers, financially strained, agreed to return to their jobs and to dissolve their union. The company, however, did not gain an unadulterated victory; raising prices while lowering wages was to harm its public image for years to come.

Pullman

In 1894 the Pullman company, a manufacturer of railway cars, cut wages to its employees by 22 percent. The employees struck in protest. They were aided by railway workers throughout the country who refused to move Pullman cars. The sympathy boycott against Pullman rail stock substantially reduced rail traffic throughout the country.

A familiar strike pattern resulted. Injunctions against the unions for their strike and boycott were sought. In this case, not only was a state court involved, but a federal court was involved because of disruption in the flow of mail. Both federal and state troops were called to end the strike, boycott, picketing, and demonstrations. In Chicago at least a score of strikers were killed by troops. Riots of protest followed; railway stock was burned. The end result, however, was not favorable to the Pullman workers. And the union of railway workers that assisted them with the boycott was fatally damaged.

Coeur d'Alene, Idaho, and Cripple Creek, Colorado

These two mining areas were the place of a decade of labor strife during the 1890s and early 1900s. Both periods of strikes and protests began with a reduction in wages and working conditions by the mine owners. In Coeur d'Alene the daily wage was reduced, in Cripple Creek the work day was increased. The mine rebellion was quelled, but only after heavy troop involvement, mass arrests, and the dynamiting of many of the mines.

General Strikes

The four strikes just summarized are a sample of labor protest that occurred during this period. It had a countrywide effect—the examples here are from Pennsylvania, Illinois, Idaho, and Colorado—but strikes occurred in all parts of the country. The examples above are from manufacturing, mining, and transportation, but no mass operation industry was immune. Despite the serious union losses—achieved at great cost to employers and the public—union efforts were not stopped and more serious strikes were to come.

In 1934 three general strikes took place in different parts of the country involving, at least initially, different industries. A general strike covers all workplaces within a geographic area; it is a strike of all employees against all employers.

In San Francisco the Pacific Coast Longshore Union was striking against and picketing the shipping industry. In order to clear the way for ships to load and unload at the docks, the National Guard was called in. Several picketers were killed during the guard attempts to clear the docks. In reaction to these deaths, a strike in support of the longshore workers was undertaken by other workers in the city. Similar general strikes nearly occurred in Portland and Seattle at this time. The longshore workers prevailed in this dispute; it was the beginning of collective bargaining for longshore workers.

In Minneapolis the dispute began with a strike by coal truckers, followed by a strike by other truck drivers. Because the delivery of goods was stopped, other businesses in the city were slowed. Efforts were made by police and specially appointed deputies, made up of managers, lawyers, doctors, and other people from wealthier occupations, to keep trucks moving, thereby breaking the strike. Working people supporting the striking truckers met the police and "special deputies" in a downtown battle known as "The Battle of Deputies Run." In the melee one of the special deputies was killed. Later, some of the picketers would be killed. What began as a truck strike gradually drew more and more of the community into joining one side or the other. At the peak of the strike, all commerce in the city came to a halt.

In Toledo the strike began against some manufacturers supplying parts to the auto industry. Reacting to assaults on nonstriking workers, the National Guard was sent to assure peace. A confrontation between the guard and strikers left several dead or seriously wounded. Further clashes were to follow with hundreds more injured, although none fatally. A settlement favorable to the striking workers ended the confrontation.

These very brief descriptions of a small handful of strikes that occurred from 1870 to 1935 illustrate several lessons about strikes and managing strikes:

1. In an interdependent economy, a strike of one trade or industry group—especially in key transportation, mining, and manufacturing sectors—can severely diminish the production of other economic sectors.

2. Strikes against one employer or group of employers often spilled over to strikes and boycotts against other employers. The most extreme form of this type of strike is the general strike stopping all commerce within a community. These broad-based strikes were often violent and extreme in character.

3. Despite police, employer-hired security agents, state and federal militia, and clear judicial disapproval, strikes were not stopped.

4. The more flagrant the abuse against strikers, the more sympathy they gained for their cause from the wider public. The very efforts intended to stop unions carried the seeds for union renewal and victory.

A new policy was needed to deal with unions and labor disputes. Attempts to quash unions had proven unproductive. What was needed was a policy to contain disputes and promote industrial peace. Such a policy was crafted in a succession of legislative acts. These are discussed later in this chapter.

ANTITRUST LEGISLATION AND COLLECTIVE BARGAINING

Growth of very large business enterprises led to legislation by the federal government regulating their business activities. One of the first pieces of such legislation was the Sherman Antitrust Act of 1890. The act was intended to stop "combinations" that restrain "trade and commerce." Injunctions, criminal prosecution, and triple damage civil awards were permitted as sanctions under provisions of the act.

It remains a controversy to this day whether or not Congress ever intended the Sherman Act to apply to labor unions or any action—strike, picket, or boycott—taken by a union. The act neither explicitly includes nor explicitly excludes labor unions. Whether Congress intended application to labor unions, the federal courts were to apply the statute to labor unions.

The first Supreme Court decision was in 1908 in a famous case known as

Danbury Hatters.[3] A national union of hat makers attempted to organize workers of all the large manufacturers of hats. Most were unionized, but some manufacturers—including Loewe's in Danbury, Connecticut —proved difficult. To make matters worse from the union's perspective, Loewe paid less than union employers and enjoyed some competitive advantage against union manufacturers that had higher labor costs. The union undertook a nationwide boycott against Loewe in order to force the company to bargain collectively. AFL union members refused to buy Loewe hats or to do business with merchants selling Loewe hats. This reduced orders for Loewe hats from all over the country. Loewe sued the union for triple damages under Sherman Act provisions and, in the *Danbury Hatters* decision, won an award of half a million dollars from the hatters' union. The Supreme Court ruled that the boycott was an unlawful restraint of interstate "trade and commerce."

In 1914 Congress amended the Sherman Act when it passed the Clayton Act. The AFL thought that the clarifying language in section 6 of the Clayton Act exempted labor unions from coverage by the antitrust regulation. Section 6 declared that labor is not a "commodity or article of commerce." In *Duplex,*[4] however, the Supreme Court disappointed hopeful members of the AFL. The Court ruled that labor unions were not by their existence illegal, but actions by labor unions that restricted the flow of interstate trade and commerce were still violations of the act. *Duplex* reaffirmed the Court's decision in *Danbury Hatters.*

To complete the story of antitrust applications to collective bargaining, we must add something about other legislation that we discuss in greater detail later in the chapter. In 1932 Congress passed the Norris-LaGuardia Act and in 1935 the Wagner Act. Both pieces of legislation were favorable to unions; both are among the first efforts by Congress to explicitly regulate the collective bargaining process. This legislation was used by the courts to reinterpret Congress' intent in passing the Clayton Act.

In 1941, in *Hutcheson,*[5] the Supreme Court removed strikes and boycotts by labor unions for the most part from antitrust prosecution. As long as the intent of the union was to secure better conditions for labor, and as long as strikes and boycotts were used only as a temporary means to effect change in the *labor market*, then unions were exempt. If, however, the union attempted to control the *product market*, then this was (and is today) a potential violation of antitrust legislation.

In a series of decisions over the next forty years, the Supreme Court has refined this distinction. The most general test is whether the union *and* employer act in concert to restrict other firms (and employers) from the

---

3. *Loewe* v. *Lawlor*, 208 U.S. 274 (1908).
4. 254 U.S. 443 (1921).
5. 312 U.S. 219 (1941).

product market. If the union *and* employer act together for this purpose, it may be an antitrust violation.

EBB AND FLOW

Union membership growth has not been a relentless upward march. Instead, growth has come in brief, rapid spurts, sometimes followed by loss of membership. The largest burst came in the late 1930s and early 1940s, but the pattern was established long before this. The following listing indicates the extent of fluctuation between 1887 and 1934.

DATE	MEMBERSHIP	DATE	MEMBERSHIP
1887	703*	1915	2583
1897	447	1920	5048
1900	869	1925	3519
1905	2022	1930	3393
1910	2141	1934	3609

*510 members in Knights of Labor.

Membership in thousands of people.

Source: Leo Wolman, *The Growth of American Trade Unions (New York:* National Bureau of Economic Research, 1924); and Leo Wolman, *Ebb and Flow in Trade Unionism* (New York: National Bureau of Economic Research, 1936).

Union membership shrank with the collapse of the Knights of Labor in the 1890s. AFL internationals grew rapidly in the late 1890s and early 1900s, remained static for a decade, then spurted ahead during World War I. A good part of this gain was subsequently lost during the 1920s.

What caused the uneven growth of union membership? Trade unions grew rapidly during periods of rapid employment growth, especially following an economic depression. Trade unions grew rapidly during the tight labor markets of both world wars. Periods of rapid growth are not characterized by more of the same, but by a new characteristic to the labor movement. The Knights of Labor attracted (and lost) a new type of union member. Vigorous expansion of craft unionism corresponded to the push for strong national unions. The early part of this century saw some of the first signs of successful industrial unionism as well. For example, the United Mine Workers, an industrial union affiliated with the AFL, won important victories in the coal fields of Pennsylvania at this time.

Successful unionism provokes employer reaction. Employer association, political and legal offensives, changes making management more responsive to worker desires, and strike-breaking efforts are used to slow and perhaps recapture gains made by unions. Employers may be caught unaware for brief periods, but the momentum has not been an exclusive province of unions.

The 1920s, for example, was a period marked by intense employer efforts to rid their work force of union representation. These efforts were not entirely negative; many firms adopted more progressive employment practices. And employer arguments met some receptive listeners; wages were growing rapidly in this prosperous period even without union representation. The 1920s was also a period of change for which the craft orientation of the AFL was ill suited. New employment was not in craft work, but in machine work. It was this group that would provide the next major impetus for union growth. Gains were to come, however, only with the initial resistance of the AFL.

EMERGENCE OF INDUSTRIAL UNIONISM: FROM CIO TO AFL–CIO

As organized labor entered the depression years of the 1930s, the union membership represented a rather limited selection among the working class. Union members were the most skilled and best paid. They were not the unskilled or semiskilled workers found in mass production industries. AFL unions in general showed little interest in organizing this group, and what little interest was shown was primarily negative.

Within the AFL there was, however, a small group of industrial unions—the United Mine Workers (UMW) and unions in the apparel industry. These unions organized skilled and unskilled workers within their industry.

Craft unions lived uncomfortably with the notion of industrial unions. They feared, sometimes correctly, that the industrial union would capture groups of craft workers lodged within a variety of industries. For example, a carpenter working at a coal mine might be a member of the carpenters union, or a member of the UMW, or both. The carving of jurisdiction was perhaps the main reason for the antipathy which the AFL internationals felt for industrial unions, and the problem that was to prove so difficult in reconciling the two groups in the years to come.

In the early 1930s, the industrial unions within the AFL urged that new efforts be made to unionize the large majority of working people who were not union members. The Depression had spawned anger at business, worker concern over jobs, and favorable legislation that promised success. To further their intent, the group in 1935 formed the Committee for Industrial Organization within the AFL. It immediately clashed with the craft-dominated leadership of the AFL. The two groups separated and, in

1938, the Committee of Industrial Organization became an independent federation of national unions called the Congress of Industrial Organizations (CIO).

If unsuccessful in converting their AFL fellows, the CIO was extremely successful in converting workers to the cause of industrial unionism. It was to organize industrial unions in the steel and aluminum, auto, rubber, oil and refining, and glass and meat packing industries, among others. In 1937 it led successful drives to organize workers at United States Steel and General Motors. In the latter effort a novel new technique, the sit-down strike, was employed. This technique was to prove successful in other organizing devices.

Stunned and threatened by the success of the CIO, the old AFL internationals launched major organizing drives of their own. Since pure craft unions had limited membership potential, they also organized some of the noncraft workers as well. The AFL and CIO were rivals. The AFL even established rival industrial unions to compete with the CIO counterpart. The AFL, with its geographically diverse organizational base, financial muscle, and experience in organization and negotiation, was able, once started, to surpass the efforts of the CIO and gain a membership lead. The CIO, however, proved once and for all that mass production workers could unionize and bargain collectively. Most of our largest unions today were formed at this time.

Because the CIO emerged from the AFL, it had many similar characteristics. It was not politically radical; it was to evict several unions for refusal to sign noncommunist pledges. Its goals were similar to those of the AFL, focusing on collective bargaining, willing to find an accommodation with business, and continuing to rest primary strength with the national unions, not with the new federation, and not with locals.

Many leaders within both organizations continued to meet, and maintained friendships from the old AFL days. From 1937 onward there were continued attempts at reconciliation between the AFL and CIO. The issue of rivalry became increasingly critical in the post-World War II period. Competing unions began raiding the opponent membership. Despite considerable exertion on both sides, the net gain to either side was minuscule. Efforts were made in the 1950s to limit raiding by signing pledges. Further cooperative efforts were to come.

In 1955 Walter Reuther, heading the CIO, and George Meany, heading the AFL, agreed to merge the two federations. The result was the American Federation of Labor-Congress of Industrial Organizations (AFL–CIO). George Meany, representing the larger AFL, became president of the new federation.

REGULATING COLLECTIVE BARGAINING:
THE BEGINNING

Congress for the most part left public policy toward collective bargaining in the hands of the judiciary until the 1930s. Exceptions to this tendency include the perhaps inadvertent application of antitrust statutes to union boycotts, and legislation regulating collective bargaining in the railroad industry. In the 1930s, however, Congress passed two major pieces of legislation that fundamentally changed public policy toward collective bargaining, and that today form the foundation for the regulation of collective bargaining. The era of regulation marked the end to over a century of fluctuating efforts to suppress collective bargaining, and the beginning of efforts to make collective bargaining work better.

The first major legislation, known as the Norris-LaGuardia Act, freed unions from the threat of injunction. The Supreme Court, as discussed earlier, was also to use Norris-LaGuardia to reinterpret and then free unions from most antitrust prosecution under the Sherman Act. Thus Norris-LaGuardia demolished the main legal weapons used against unions, leaving unions free to use economic sanctions against employers (except where people or property are injured or destroyed).

Norris-LaGuardia did nothing to restrict employer efforts to stop union organization of the workplace. Unions could strike without fear of injunction, but nothing in this law requires the employer to bargain with the union or to do anything in any way that recognizes the union.

Norris-LaGuardia has two main features. The first restricts judges from issuing injunctions against strikes, or activities such as picketing that publicize a strike or other labor dispute. Second, it made "yellow-dog contracts" not enforceable in court. A *yellow-dog contract* was a signed promise by an employee not to join or support a union. Signing this contract was required as a condition of employment by some antiunion employers. The contract was enforceable in the courts—that is, the courts could order unions not to interfere with the contractual obligations of the employee not to join a union, until Norris-LaGuardia.

Norris-LaGuardia was preceded by another statute with a more activist approach toward collective bargaining. In the earlier section on violence in labor disputes it was apparent that the railroad industry was particularly troubled by strikes. These strikes were not subdued strikes over contract terms, but lengthy, intense struggles over the existence of an employee organization. These strikes had an extremely disruptive consequence on the nation's economy, since products did not easily flow from plant to consumer without an operating rail system.

To minimize this railroad disruption, Congress had at various times passed legislation attempting to promote compromise. For example, the Erdman Act of 1898 protected the right of railroad employees to organize and bargain collectively, and, in order to facilitate collective bargaining, it provided for mediation and arbitration. This act was declared unconstitutional by the Supreme Court. But similar legislation was to reappear in 1926, and this time to withstand the test of constitutionality.

The Railway Labor Act provides for freely selected collective bargaining representatives, for mediation, and for voluntary arbitration. Company dominated unions were outlawed. The premise for this act, and for those to come—including the Wagner Act—was that the process of collective bargaining is a means to end labor disputes. Since unions practically could not be eliminated (over a century of experience supported this), then the alternative was a reconciliation of employer and employee interests. By promoting compromise and resolution, labor disputes could be minimized and, therefore, the disruption of interstate commerce could be minimized.

Protection of interstate commerce was an important aspect of selling the constitutionality of this public policy approach toward collective bargaining. The federal government jurisdiction is confined to interstate matters. Even today, those limited number of private employers not engaged, directly or indirectly, in interstate commerce, are outside the jurisdiction of federal statutes.

The Railway Labor Act was amended in 1934, and several times since then. Today this act regulates collective bargaining in the railway and airline industries.

It should be noted that, in the time since the passage of the Railway Labor Act and the Wagner Act, excepting a brief transition period, we have not had labor disputes even close to the destructive force of those in earlier times.

The Wagner Act

The second major legislative act of the 1930s was passed in 1935. The National Labor Relations Act, generally known as the Wagner Act, was based on principles already established in the Railway Labor Act. By getting employers to negotiate with *representative* organizations chosen by employees, industrial peace would be promoted, and interstate commerce protected.

The Wagner Act favored employees and unions over employers. Whereas Norris-LaGuardia removed weapons used against unions, but left employers free to oppose union organizing, the Wagner Act *required* employers to bargain collectively with a union of the employees' choosing. Public policy had clearly moved to the employees' side with passage of the Wagner Act.

The act created the legal right for employees to form and to join labor organizations, to bargain collectively, and to engage in concerted activity. In order to protect this right, certain employer actions, called unfair practices, are proscribed, including the support of company unions and discrimination in employment against union members or supporters. The act *requires* employers to bargain with elected representatives of the employees. (Provisions of this act are discussed in greater detail in the next chapters.) The intent of these restrictions and requirements is to resolve differences—to compromise—rather than to engage in protracted combat until one side or the other capitulates.

To enforce these employer restrictions, the Wagner Act provides an agency to administer and to enforce provisions of the act. The agency was (and is today) called the National Labor Relations Board. The board was to supply specific interpretation to the general standards of employer conduct created in the Wagner Act. And the board was to oversee employee elections concerning union representation, including determination of who was eligible to vote, supervision of the election, and certification of the results.

This second duty of the National Labor Relations Board deserves emphasis. Under the Wagner Act, employers must bargain with representatives of the employees' choosing. Union pressure on an employer cannot force union recognition unless the affected employees, through a secret ballot, choose that union as their representative. If employees do not want a union, then the employer cannot be coerced by others into bargaining with a union. And if employees want a different union, then the employer must bargain with that union.

The Wagner Act was a significant departure from past policy. We had moved from a policy of antagonism to collective bargaining to a point of active encouragement.

Taft-Hartley

The industrial disputes record of 1946 can be better understood if we remember that collective bargaining was in its infancy in most key industries when World War II came upon us. At the time of Pearl Harbor (December 7, 1941), management and unions in many newly organized industries were still in the fighting stage. The war forced them into a shotgun marriage. Frictions, resentments, and misunderstandings were concealed by the pressures for uninterrupted production. After V-J Day in August 1945, the lid blew off.

The year 1946 did not prove that collective bargaining was a failure. It did reveal that bargaining in good faith had yet to be tried, in many cases, and in others was a long way from perfection. This was especially true in the newly unionized, critical mass production industries like steel, automobile, and electrical appliance manufacturing. The year 1946 was abnormal in several respects. The severe wave of major strikes was, in part at least, the explosive result of too rapid change in fundamental relationships and attitudes.[6] Too much readjustment was needed in too short a time. The wartime necessity for self-restraint helped to conceal the fact that these adjustments had not been made.

When revising national labor policy in 1947, the Congress chose to ignore the exceptional aspects of 1946, looking only at the staggering total of man-hours lost due to strikes in 1946. Employer and public pressure to "do something" about the situation proved to be overwhelming. The end result was the Labor Management Relations Act, generally called the Taft-Hartley Act, a law that contained nearly all the restrictions on unions then urged upon the Congress by the National Association of Manufacturers and the U.S. Chamber of Commerce.

Technically, the 1947 law was "an act to amend the National Labor Relations Act and for other purposes." The "amendment" was roughly five times as long as the 1935 statute and contained many new provisions and concepts. Although properly rated as one of the most controversial laws in our history, experience under the 1947 law did not bear out either the extravagant hopes of its supporters or the worst fears of its opponents.

The Taft-Hartley Act left intact most of the Wagner Act, including employer unfair labor practices and the interpretation and election supervision duties of the National Labor Relations Board. Added to these provisions were six union unfair labor practices. The Taft-Hartley amendment in effect balances the interests of employers against the interests of unions represented in the Wagner Act. Two examples: unions must bargain in good faith under Taft-Hartley just as employers must under Wagner; and *unions* must not *force* employers to discriminate against employees in order to encourage or discourage union membership under Taft-Hartley, just as employers must not discriminate against union employees under Wagner. Union unfair labor practices are summarized in the next chapter.

Taft-Hartley created new obligations for unions, such as the duty to represent employees, and new restrictions on union security, such as outlawing the closed shop (with limited exceptions) and permitting states to pass more restrictive union security laws. The act also provided a procedure to deal with national emergency strikes. Specifics of this act are summarized in the next chapter.

Landrum-Griffin Act

The final major labor legislation was the Labor-Management Reporting and Disclosure Act of 1959. This act is better known as the Landrum-Griffin Act. The Landrum-Griffin Act is dwarfed in comparison to the importance of the Wagner and Taft-Hartley acts. Nevertheless, besides tightening some

6. Table 3–2 shows the dramatic increase in the number of days idle during strikes in 1946.

of the language in Taft-Hartley, Landrum-Griffin made significant changes in the regulation of union governance.

Landrum-Griffin passage followed a series of hearings in the Senate on racketeering in the operation of several large unions. The McClellan committee found a number of abuses by union officials against members. Criminal action in the misuse of union funds was also found by the committee.

This act placed controls on the authority of union officers in both administration of the union and of funds collected by the union. As part of this provision, unions are required to send regular reports to the Department of Labor on their administrative and financial status.

The act required union constitutions and regular elections of union officers. It protected union member rights to express their views about candidates for union election and about the conduct of union affairs. Failure to conduct a fair election allows the secretary of labor to ask the courts for a new election to be supervised by the Department of Labor.

UNION MEMBERSHIP GROWTH
AFTER 1935[7]

Two related events during the middle 1930s brought on a surge of union growth unlike any other in U.S. history. First, the Norris-LaGuardia Act ended the primary antiunion legal weapon, the injunction, and the Wagner Act encouraged and aided union organizing by placing a variety of restrictions on employers. Second, the CIO began organizing a huge potential constituency in the mass production industries. Answering the CIO challenge, the AFL also began organizing this same constituency, the one that it had so long ignored. From less than 4 million members in 1935, unions grew to over 14 million members a decade later.

The post-World War II period was a period of slow growth. The craft and industrial workers were already organized. Although union membership was to grow, the rate of increase was slower than the rate of increase in employment. Employment was growing fastest in the less unionized service sector, and not as fast in the heavily unionized mass production, distribution, or handicraft sectors.

Future growth requires a new style of unionism, one that appeals to, and one that can effectively represent, the service worker. Just as craft unionism, at least in part, gave way to industrial unionism, future growth depends upon service unionism.

The only successful area of service unionism is the only area of

7. Table 3–4 shows figures on union membership from 1958 to 1978 and on union and association membership from 1968 to 1978.

substantial new union growth during the post-World War II era. Public sector union growth, beginning about 1960, has kept the decline (in percent unionized) from falling even more.

Public Sector Unionism

Although public sector unions have been around for decades, substantial membership growth came only after the year 1960. Growth occurred at the federal, state, and local levels, and in all regions of the country.

Public sector collective bargaining is in some ways different from collective bargaining practiced with private sector craft and industrial unions. For example, while, for the most part, craft and industrial union collective bargaining is regulated by the National Labor Relations Act, public sector collective bargaining is regulated by a variety of legislation at the federal, state, and local level, and by common law.

Because of the contemporary development of public sector collective bargaining, and because it is distinctive enough on some dimensions from private sector collective bargaining, we have devoted an entire chapter to this topic.

SUMMARY OF UNION GROWTH

Beginning around the year 1800, a number of small craft unions were organized. Despite a hostile legal environment, they survived and grew. First, the number and size of the individual local craft unions grew. Then, the many local unions grew into one national union for each type of craft work. Important decisions and control were increasingly found at the national union level. Growth of national unions paralleled the growth of national product and labor markets. In 1886, a federation of national craft unions, called the American Federation of Labor (AFL), was created.

In the late nineteenth and early twentieth centuries two new types of labor unions erupted, only to disappear shortly thereafter. The Knights of Labor tried to organize all working people. Except for some vague notions of cooperation, neither the goals nor the means to achieve these goals was ever established by the Knights; while it lasted, the Knights were an ineffectual labor representative. The Industrial Workers of the World represented the mass production worker, not the elite craft worker represented by the AFL unions. A radical but occasionally effective union, the Wobblies faded during World War I. Organization of mass production workers awaited another union.

This union was the Congress of Industrial Organizations (CIO), an offshoot of the AFL. The CIO, aided greatly by the antibusiness climate of the 1930s, and by the very favorable provisions of the Wagner Act, began to organize national unions in the auto, steel, rubber, electrical appliance, and other mass production industries. Many of our largest unions today came out of the early CIO period. The AFL, confronted with the CIO challenge, responded with the vigorous drive to organize industrial workers as well. During World War II, the AFL was to surpass the membership size of the CIO. Between 1935 and the end of World War II, union membership grew from almost 4 million to almost 15 million.

After World War II, with the major production industries already unionized, union membership growth slowed drastically. The AFL and CIO rivalry resulted more in stealing members from each other rather than reaching a new membership. A reconciliation between the two federations of national unions began in the 1950s, culminating in a merger in 1955 that formed the American Federation of Labor-Congress of Industrial Organizations (AFL–CIO).

The postmerger period has seen a gradual increase in the number of union members, but a gradual decrease in the proportion of employees who belong to labor unions. The only remarkable development has been in the public sector, which has been transformed from an area of limited union activity to an area that surpassed the private sector in percent union membership during the 1970s.

SUMMARY OF PUBLIC POLICY

In general terms, public policy toward collective bargaining can be one of suppression, toleration, encouragement, or regulation. All four government postures toward unionism and collective bargaining can be illustrated in U.S. experience.

Broadly speaking, public policy from the revolutionary war period until 1842 was one of suppression. Union activity was stymied by the courts under English common law concepts of criminal conspiracy in restraint of trade. Following the famed 1842 decision, *Commonwealth of Massachusetts* v. *Hunt*, unions were able to achieve some operational effectiveness, although they were still subject to severe judicial scrutiny as to whether their activities were for (what courts regarded as) lawful purposes sought by lawful means.

From 1842 to World War I, public policy toward unions, as reflected in court decisions, followed an uncertain line between toleration and continued suppression. Whenever unions resorted to economic pressure, from roughly 1900 on, they were likely to be blocked by court action through injunctions or antitrust prosecutions.

Passage of the Norris-LaGuardia Act began a lengthy period of "encouragement" of unionism and collective bargaining. Prior to 1932 the public policy deck was stacked against unionism, with the exception of a brief period of emergency legitimacy during World War I and the Railway Labor Act of 1926. At the bottom of the Great Depression, however, the pendulum swung toward a policy of "encouragement." The Wagner Act of 1935 was clearly the high point of unblushing *encouragement* of unionism and collective bargaining. It also marked the beginning of the *regulation* phase. Five employer practices were prohibited as unfair. The National Labor Relations Board was charged with implementing the national labor policy of encouraging the practice and procedure of collective bargaining.

The Wagner Act period, 1935–47, was basically one of government encouragement of collective bargaining. At the same time, the specific prohibition of unfair practices for employers initiated the era of regulation in an inclusive and permanent sense. Also, the National Labor Relations Board representation case duties, notably its determination of appropriate units for bargaining in particular cases, demonstrated that performance of a service function can have an important regulatory impact. The board's unit decisions have vitally influenced the structure of unionism and the structure of bargaining relationships.

During wartime both employers and unions were operating under the constraints of National War Labor Board policy and the voluntary no-strike–no-lockout pledge taken by top management and union leaders shortly after Pearl Harbor. Joint concern for the effective prosecution of the war obscured the fact that tensions were building just below the surface. Long restrained by wartime regulations, some unions were anxious to capitalize on their increased economic power. At the same time, there were some "unreconstructed" employers who looked upon a return to private bargaining as an opportunity to crush the unions with which they had been obliged to deal. Such confrontations made 1946 the most serious strike year in our history.

The Taft-Hartley Act of 1947, in part a reaction to the intense strike activity of 1946, ended the one-sided preference for unions found in the Wagner Act. Taft-Hartley placed restrictions on union practices similar in some ways to Wagner Act restrictions on employers. Some union sanctions, such as the secondary strike or boycott, were also limited. The result of Wagner plus Taft-Hartley was an act favorable to the process of collective bargaining, at least within limits, but not strongly favoring either the employer or employee side.

The positive side to this evolution should not be overlooked. The values of regulated collective bargaining came to be appreciated by many employers and labor leaders as well as by government representatives. When both employer and union find that the true locus of power lies outside their relationship, such as in the courts, it is difficult for them to develop constructive private arrangements. Both parties are under pressure to shape their policies and strategies to persuade the government third force. Neither is required to face up to the necessity for establishing a satisfactory, enduring relationship with the other party.

Growth of public sector unions during the period after 1960 was aided greatly by public policies by the federal government and by many state governments which encouraged collective bargaining. Because public sector collective bargaining is left to the many states, rather than governed by one federal statute, a great variety of public policies, ranging from suppression to encouragement to regulation exist in the public sector today.

Questions for Discussion, Thought, and Research

1. Has U.S. public policy toward collective bargaining been one of suppression, tolerance, encouragement, or regulation?

2. How is it possible that two philosophically divergent organizations like the AFL and CIO managed to merge in 1955 into the AFL–CIO? What similarities did the two organizations share?

3. Compare and contrast the policies and goals of the Knights of Labor, "Wobblies," and AFL. Why did only the AFL survive?

4. Historically speaking, what economic changes brought about the desire of craft workers to form unions?

5. Explain the role of the courts during the early years of union development in America. Go beyond the text and explain the reason for their antagonism toward unions.

6. What role did the strike play in motivating the U.S. Congress to pass legislation favorable to collective bargaining?

7. What are the arguments, pro and con, for extending the antitrust provisions of the Sherman Act to unions?

8. What caused the uneven growth in union membership prior to passage of the Wagner Act in 1935?

9. Today it is common to hear individuals defame collective bargaining on the grounds that it is too closely tied to industrial "conflict" rather than to "cooperation." Do you agree with this assertion? Explain your answer. Taking a historical view, did Congress legalize collective bargaining to advance the notion of conflict or cooperation?

10. What is an injunction? How did the injunction differ from the yellow-dog contract as a means to thwart union efforts?

Selected Bibliography

Gregory, Charles O., and Harold A. Katz, *Labor and the Law* (3rd ed.). New York: W.W. Norton & Co., Inc., 1979.

Rayback, Joseph G., *A History of American Labor*. New York: Free Press, 1966.

Taft, Philip, *Organized Labor in American History*. New York: Harper & Row, Pub., 1964.

Taylor, Benjamin J., and Fred Witney, *Labor Relations Law* (3rd ed.). Englewood Cliffs, N.J.: Prentice-Hall, 1979.

Ulman, Lloyd, *The Rise of the National Trade Union*. Cambridge, Mass.: Harvard University Press, 1955.

THE PUBLIC POLICY
FRAMEWORK FOR
COLLECTIVE BARGAINING

3

During this century, for better or worse, employer practices have been increasingly restricted by public regulation. We regulate, among other things, decisions about pay, employment, retirement, and safety, all topics that are important to collective bargaining. Usually the intent is to protect employees. Employer restrictions are of two sorts: (1) standards, usually minimums or maximums, that apply to a large set of employers and workplaces, or (2) requirements that encourage an employee voice in setting pay, hours, and working conditions through collective representation and the process of bargaining. Collective bargaining allows an employer and employee group to tailor rules to conditions perhaps unique to their workplace. This chapter is about restrictions on collective bargaining practices.

Increasingly, however, public policy is directed toward the first alternative of setting standards. New sequences of the alphabet, such as OSHA, EEO, and ERISA, have become prominent. This trend has an important implication for collective bargaining; discretionary areas for joint union-management agreement are compressed. Often, traditional collective agreements conflict with other public regulations. In later chapters we discuss the implication of other public policies for the practice of collective bargaining.

Besides encouraging, and sometimes discouraging, collective bargaining by unions, public policy serves another purpose: to protect the general public from the effects of labor disputes. Long before we had any public policy in this area, we had strikes. Often the early strikes were long and violent, severely disrupting the economy. Regulation of employers and unions realistically cannot stop strikes, but by making the process toward compromise more efficient, by restricting practices most disruptive to the public, and by requiring employers and unions to work toward agreeing, public policy can reduce public inconvenience and the interruption of commerce from strikes.

Public policy limits, conditions, and controls relationships between unions and management in the United States in a more pervasive fashion than in any other country in the free world. Thus, no realistic understanding of contemporary collective bargaining policies and procedures is possible without first considering the legal framework within which the practitioners of bargaining must operate, both as to contract negotiation and administration.

The cornerstone of federal policy in the field of labor relations law is the National Labor Relations Act of 1935 (Wagner Act), as amended substantially in 1947 by the Labor Management Relations Act of that year (Taft-Hartley Act) and again in 1959 by the Labor Management Reporting and Disclosure Act (Landrum-Griffin Act).[1] More recently, the National Labor Relations Act was granted extended coverage through the 1974 Health Care Amendments, which brought health care institutions under its jurisdiction. Another major federal labor relations policy is the Railway Labor Act. Passed originally in 1926 and amended several times since then, this act covers labor relations in the railroad and airline industries.

The national labor policy since 1935 has been to encourage the practice and procedure of collective bargaining and the freedom of employees to form and join unions of their own choosing. Since 1947, federal law has also sought to protect employees in their right to refrain from self-organization and collective bargaining if they so desire.

To effectuate such broad policy objectives, federal law prohibits as "unfair" certain specified employer and union practices that when committed interfere with or nullify the employee rights just mentioned. Federal

1. We are generally referring to the current federal law on labor relations as one statute—the National Labor Relations Act or the act—except where otherwise indicated.

law also establishes machinery for peaceful determination of questions in a variety of cases concerning employee choice as to representation or nonrepresentation.

ROLE OF THE NATIONAL LABOR RELATIONS BOARD

The federal administrative agency principally charged with administration of our national labor relations policy is the National Labor Relations Board.[2] Throughout its lifetime since 1935 the NLRB has had two primary functions: (1) investigation and, where necessary, prosecution and adjudication of cases involving charges that unfair labor practices have been committed; and (2) determination in particular cases, customarily by the technique of secret-ballot elections, as to whether workers desire to be represented by labor organizations for purposes of collective bargaining with their employers as to wages, hours of work, and other conditions of employment.

The NLRB thus performs both *regulatory* functions (unfair labor practice cases) and *service* functions (representation cases) in the field of union-management relations. The board has been a storm center of controversy over the years.[3] Controversy and problems continue today.[4] Such criticism can be better understood if not justified when one remembers that the NLRB has always had the unenviable task of deciding cases in substantive problem areas where partisan convictions are strongly held and conflict of interests is both natural and unavoidable. At one time or another, both employers and the unions have been extremely critical of particular board decisions, policies, and procedures. Furthermore, both management and organized labor in their political roles have sought to influence presidential appointments to the board. They have tried to mold the agency to fit their conceptions of what should be by a variety of pressures. Both sides have appeared to prefer an NLRB that would be "impartially" in their own favor.

2. For a detailed two-volume account of the origin of the National Labor Relations Board, see James A. Gross, *The Making of the National Labor Relations Board* (Albany: State University of New York Press, 1974).

3. In the late 1930s the NLRB was assailed as being, among other things, "a drumhead court-martial," "a Spanish inquisitory tribunal," and a "modern Judge Fury." This last characterization was applied to the board by the famed *New York Times* correspondent, Arthur Krock. The torrent of criticism was so severe that *Fortune* magazine entitled a 1938 article on the board and its operations, "The G——— D——— Labor Board." This was not, by the way, *Fortune's* appraisal of the board but a reflection of the tone of criticism that *Fortune* was investigating. See *Fortune*, 8 (October 1938). See also Harold W. Davey, "Separation of Functions and the National Labor Relations Board," *University of Chicago Law Review*, 7 (February 1940), 328–46.

4. J.H. Fanning, "We Are Forty—Where Do We Go?", *Labor Law Journal*, 23 (January 1976), 3–10. In this article, Fanning, the NLRB's senior member, outlines problems and possible remedies with which the board is concerned.

Attacks on the NLRB have marred its image and, in some cases, its performance. It is sometimes a far cry from the impartial, quasi-judicial administrative tribunal which Congress intended it to be. In retrospect, it is also clear that many criticisms leveled at the board should have been directed at the law the board was administering.

The Wagner Act was *intentionally* one-sided in favor of unions, in the sense that it prohibited employer practices and gave maximum encouragement to employees to unionize and to bargain collectively. Such a statutory bias was designed to redress a lack of balance heavily weighted in the employer's favor. The Taft-Hartley Act of 1947 was described by its supporters as an "equalizing" law because of its many specific restrictions and prohibitions of union conduct. The unions dubbed it a "slave labor law" at the time but have somehow managed to live with it. It is scarcely to be wondered that the NLRB has been under a steady drumfire of criticism through the years. It is charged with the unenviable task of administering a statute that is in a real sense schizophrenic. A few words about the organization and administration of the NLRB are in order as a prelude to the more substantive analysis which follows.

THE NLRB'S ORGANIZATIONAL STRUCTURE AND ADMINISTRATION

The NLRB does not initiate unfair labor practice complaints or election petitions on its own motion. Rather, the board's functions are triggered when an employee, group of employees, union, or employer files a complaint or petition. The later filings are made at one of the board's 49 regional and local offices, which are staffed with professionals trained in labor law and industrial relations. As a general matter, when regional office staff members are assigned cases, they work with parties in an attempt to voluntarily settle the dispute or to remedy the alleged unfair labor practice violation. Partially as a result of these efforts, only a small fraction of the 50,000 or more cases of all types filed these days at the regional and local offices of the NLRB actually find their way on appeal to either the five-member board or to the office of the general counsel in Washington, D.C.

When election petitions are filed, the regional directors have authority to investigate the petitions, make unit rulings, schedule and conduct secret-ballot elections, and certify the election results. Appeals from the regional directors' decisions and election procedures can be made to the NLRB.

In instances when unfair labor practice complaints are filed, the regional directors have authority to investigate the complaints and then to issue *formal* complaints if labor law violations are uncovered. After a complaint is formally issued, the regional office prosecutes the matter of violation before one of the board's administrative law judges (ALJs). Any of the parties to the ALJ's hearing may appeal his decision to the NLRB. When the regional directors decide on behalf of the general counsel that a formal complaint ought not to be issued, the complaining party may appeal for a reversal of this decision to the general counsel in Washington, D.C.

The nationwide network of regional and local offices of the NLRB is supervised by the office of the general counsel. Appointed by the President with consent of the Senate to a four-year term, the general counsel is also (mainly) responsible for the investigation and prosecution of alleged violations of the labor law. This function was once the responsibility of the NLRB itself.

Between 1935 and 1947 the general counsel's office was the prosecuting agency for the board. It was the board's counsel that would make findings of unfair labor practices and issue formal complaints. Since the union could not commit an unfair practice until 1947, all of these actions were taken against employers. They complained about this organizational arrangement because the complaints would then go to the counsel's parent body—namely, the board—for trial. The appearance of having the board serve as both prosecutor and judge violated their sense of judicial fairness. The Taft-Hartley amendments of 1947 remedied this organizational problem, along with other provisions in the Wagner Act.

The membership of the board was also expanded from three to five persons, appointed by the President with the consent of the Senate for staggered five-year terms. More pointedly, the general counsel's office was made separate from and independent of the board. Since 1947 the board has functioned primarily as a quasi-judicial organization which decides cases generally brought to it upon review of regional directors' and ALJ's decisions. The parties to the board's cases can seek judicial review of its decisions in the federal courts.

The NLRB does not have enforcement authority in its administration of the labor laws. Thus, to have its orders and decisions enforced, the board must use the U.S. courts of appeals. We will return to a review of some of the NLRB's administrative problems later in this chapter.

SCOPE OF THE PRESENT ANALYSIS

No attempt is made here to evaluate all the criticisms that have at times nearly engulfed the board and the legislation under which it operates. The focus is on selected statutory provisions and board decisions whose impact has been on the private discretion of employers and unions engaged in collective bargaining.

PUBLIC POLICY PROBLEM AREAS
TO BE COVERED

Since it is not possible to cover the law relating to all important policy areas, the selection process, although painful, had to be undertaken. In this chapter, we consider federal regulation of the process and substance of collective bargaining and federal regulation of representation.

The principal topics selected for analysis include the following:

1. A capsule summary of selected Taft-Hartley provisions.
2. NLRB policy on the scope of bargaining and the statutory duty to bargain.
3. Public policy on union security provisions, state right-to-work legislation, and Section 14(b).
4. Statutory restrictions on collective bargaining procedures, including limitations on the right to strike.
5. Public policy on union representation procedures.
6. Enforcement of board decisions and enforcement and administration problems provoking proposals for labor law revision.

State labor relations legislation is of vital importance to collective bargaining, but the analysis here is limited mainly to federal law. No detailed consideration can be given to such important matters as the state of the law relating to the weapons of economic conflict (for example, strikes, lockouts, and boycotts); proposed legislation to bring union activity under the antitrust laws; the impact of those sections of Landrum-Griffin that deal primarily with control of internal union affairs; or the Railway Labor Act.

In the past, several writers have been optimistic enough to hope that the incidence of employer and union unfair labor practices would decline as practitioners on the two sides became more professional in their relations with one another. However, regardless of whether or not the parties have become more professional, the fact is that the NLRB's unfair practice caseload has been running at record high levels with no prospect of diminishing appreciably.[5]

By the same token, some have thought that the 1955 merger of the AFL and the CIO would remove some of the NLRB's problems in representation cases. This has also not proved to be the case. The board still must wrestle with some thorny bargaining unit questions. In fact, under the 1974 health care amendments, the board was charged with the responsibility of determining appropriate units in the health care industry in such a way as

5. See Table 3–3.

to prevent excessive unit proliferation and fragmentation, which, we shall see in Chapter 4, has been a nagging problem in the public sector.[6]

Under President Eisenhower, the board was charged by the unions with being promanagement in key decisional areas. Under presidents Kennedy and Johnson, the board was attacked by management for being prounion. The Nixon and Ford labor boards were labeled as conservatives; Carter's and President Reagan's will surely be considered prolabor and promanagement, respectively.

The criticism will doubtless never end. Some of it has been unfair, even vicious. Some has been healthy, constructive, and probably deserved.

CAPSULE SUMMARY OF SELECTED TAFT-HARTLEY PROVISIONS

Most readers of this book are generally familiar with the contents of Taft-Hartley. Nevertheless, a brief review of some of the more important provisions of the act may be helpful at this stage. Such a summary will permit more economical discussion of the specific problem areas selected for analysis.

Employers are prohibited by the act from engaging in the following actions:

1.   Interfering with, restraining, or coercing employees in the exercise of their rights of self-organization and collective bargaining through representatives of the workers' own choosing.
2.   Establishing and maintaining company-dominated labor organizations by financial assistance or in other ways.
3.   Discharging or otherwise discriminating against their employees for joining a union or for being active in support of a labor organization.
4.   Discharging or otherwise discriminating against their employees for testifying in an NLRB case.
5.   Refusing to bargain collectively with a union elected by a majority of employees in a unit appropriate for collective bargaining purposes.

The foregoing is a summary, in the authors' words, of section 8(a) of the act. With some changes in wording, these are the same five unfair practices originally prohibited by the Wagner Act. Under Taft-Hartley, certain other aspects of employer conduct are prohibited in conjunction with certain of the prohibited unfair union practices.

---

6. Allan L. Bioff, Lawrence J. Cohen, and Kurt L. Hanslowe, eds., *The Developing Labor Law, Cumulative Supplement 1971–75*, 1976, p. 128.

Unfair union practices are not as easily summarized or counted. Therefore, a narrative form is used for describing prohibitions and controls of union activity under the act.

Taft-Hartley imposes severe restrictions on the means that unions can use to induce workers to join. It prohibits labor organizations from restraining or coercing employees in the exercise of their rights under section 7, one of which (as noted earlier) is the *right to refrain from* forming and joining unions and engaging in concerted activity. This limitation has had considerable impact on the means of conducting both organizing compaigns and strikes.

Unions are prohibited from coercing an employer in the selection of *his* representatives for purposes of collective bargaining or the adjustment of grievances. This provision is intended to leave the employer free to bargain through a multiemployer association for labor relations purposes *or* to stay out of such an association if he prefers to bargain on a single-employer basis.

The act prohibits unions from pressuring an employer to discriminate against one of his employees and thus commit an unfair practice himself. Unions cannot force an employer to discharge an employee who is in bad standing with the union in question, unless the reason for his bad standing is failure to tender periodic dues (or, originally, the initiation fee) required as a condition of employment under a legally valid union security provision of the contract.

Just as employers are prohibited from refusing to bargain in good faith with a labor organization lawfully entitled to exclusive representation rights under the act, so also unions have been prohibited since 1947 from refusing to bargain collectively in good faith with employers.

Unions are prohibited from charging initiation fees to prospective members that the NLRB may find to be "excessive or discriminatory under all the circumstances." Also, unions may not pressure employers into making money payments for services not performed or not to be performed where the payment is held to be "in the nature of an exaction."

The Secondary Boycott Ban

The most controversial, complex, and publicized area of union unfair practices is found in section 8(b)(4), which prohibits or restricts union use of economic pressure in a variety of ways.

Under section 8(b)(4), unions are prohibited from:

1. Engaging in secondary boycotts.
2. Forcing an employer to bargain unless the union in question is the certified bargaining agent.
3. Forcing an employer to cease bargaining with a duly certified union.

4.   Forcing an employer to assign particular work to employees of one union rather than another unless the employer is failing to comply with an NLRB order or certification.

The fourth prohibition declares the jurisdictional strike to be an unfair labor practice. In any such case the NLRB, by section 10(k), is instructed to transform itself into what amounts to a compulsory arbitration board to make a final and binding determination of the work assignment issue if the matter is not resolved by the conflicting unions within ten days.

The ban on secondary boycotts is, clearly, the most important of the prohibitions. The term *secondary boycott* appears nowhere in the statute. This is a useful shorthand term for characterizing the type of indirect economic pressures prohibited by the act. The most common form of secondary boycott involves the application of economic pressure against an employer with whom the union has no dispute in order to force him to cease doing business with an employer with whom the union *does* have a dispute or whose employees the union is seeking to organize.

Certain loopholes in the Taft-Hartley ban on secondary pressures were plugged by 1959 Landrum-Griffin amendments. For example, negotiation of "hot cargo" clauses is specifically banned as an unfair practice under Landrum-Griffin. A *hot cargo clause* is labor relations slang for a contract provision wherein the employer agrees not to discipline employees for refusing to handle "struck work." Some were more broadly worded to extend to products made under unfair conditions. "Unfair" in such usage is usually equated with "nonunion" in the union's eyes.

Discussion of the law of secondary boycotts is specifically avoided here primarily because it lies outside the mainstream of our concentration on public policy as it affects ongoing bargaining relationships between company X and union Y.

Organized labor holds that federal law is too sweeping in its condemnation of secondary pressures. Union leaders distinguish between what they regard as legitimate uses of secondary pressures and those that they might tacitly concede to be out of bounds. The law, however, basically reflects the view of the late Senator Robert A. Taft that one cannot draw a meaningful legislative line between "good" and "bad" secondary boycotts.

Historically, the secondary boycott was often used to unionize the employees of company X who could not be induced to join union Y by direct approaches. Pressure was applied to other firms to cause them to cease doing business with nonunion company X. The latter, upon feeling the economic pinch, would then urge its employees to sign up with union Y.

Such indirect unionizing through the employer may have been defensible tactics when workers had no legislative or judicial protection of their rights, particularly when the target firm posed a genuine threat to wage and working standards that the union had established elsewhere in the industry or labor market area. Under modern conditions, however, it does not seem unreasonable to require that unions conduct their organizing campaigns in "front door" fashion.

Since 1935 the right of workers to form and join unions and to engage in concerted activities has been protected by law against employer interference, coercion, and restraint. Since 1947 the workers' right to refrain from unionizing or concerted activity has been similarly protected. In the absence of unlawful employer coercion, if the employees of company X have made clear that they do not wish to be represented by a labor organization their right to remain nonunion should be respected and protected.

Demarcation of "secondary" from "primary" remains a current issue, particularly among unions in the construction industry. Courts have interpreted Taft-Hartley to mean that subcontractors working on the same construction site are each separate employers. Efforts by unions to close down all subcontractors on a construction site because of a dispute with one subcontractor is an illegal secondary activity under this interpretation. Unions have argued that subcontractors are an extension of the general contractor; therefore, a labor dispute with any subcontractor is also a dispute with the general contractor. In 1976 Congress amended Taft-Hartley to support the union interpretation, but under very heavy employer pressure President Ford effectively vetoed the legislation. This likely will continue as a controversy in collective bargaining.

SCOPE OF COLLECTIVE BARGAINING

Statutory Duty to Bargain
and Bargainable Issues

Perhaps most fundamental to national labor relations policy has been the requirement that employers bargain collectively in good faith with the certified representatives of their employees.[7] How to determine presence or absence of good faith continues to be a controversial policy issue.[8] Particularly controversial as well as important to persons engaged in collective bargaining is the board's now famous *Borg-Warner* doctrine.[9]

7. For a study of the effect of this provision in action see Philip Ross, *The Government as a Source of Union Power: The Role of Public Policy in Collective Bargaining* (Providence, R.I.: Brown University Press, 1965).

8. For a penetrating review of NLRB policy see James A. Gross, Donald E. Cullen, and Kurt L. Hanslowe, *Good Faith in Labor Negotiations: Tests and Remedies,* Cornell Law Review, 53 (September 1968), 1009–35.

9. Affirmed by the U.S. Supreme Court in *NLRB* v. *Wooster Division of Borg-Warner Corporation*, 356 U.S. 342 (1958).

The NLRB recognized three categories of bargaining proposals, each with a distinct set of rules. Mandatory subjects are those that fall under the category of "wages, hours, and other terms and conditions of employment," as stated in section 8(d) of the NLRB. Both the employer and the union are required to bargain in good faith over all mandatory subjects. Negotiation over wages, hours, and other terms and conditions of employment is considered crucial to the establishment of a comprehensive labor-management agreement. Sections 8(a)(5) and 8(b)(3) of the NLRB therefore require that both parties engage in bargaining over mandatory subjects. However, bargaining in "good faith" does not require making a concession. Other factors such as willingness to meet and discuss the merits of an issue determine whether good faith requirements have been met. Mandatory subjects (unlike permissive subjects) may be legally pressed to the point of impasse.

Permissive subjects are those topics which fall outside of the "wages, hours, and other terms and conditions of employment" category. Bargaining over these subjects is totally voluntary. Since neither party is compelled to bargain over permissive subjects, it follows that insistence to the point of impasse on their inclusion in the contract as a condition to the execution of the contract is a violation of the bargaining duty. In fact, it is an unfair labor practice for either party to press for a concession over a permissive issue to the point of impasse. Unions, therefore, typically urge that collective bargaining remain fluid and dynamic in order to blur the distinctions between categories and make more subjects open to bargaining.

Prohibited subjects are those proposals that are illegal and forbidden under the NLRB. Bargaining over these subjects is, of course, not required and their inclusion in the contract is not allowed even if the other party agrees to the proposal. The "closed shop" proposal is an example of an illegal subject.

Examples of subjects that have at one time been deemed mandatory are vacations, nondiscriminatory union hiring halls, group life insurance plans, pension and retirement benefits, union security, checkoff clauses, plant rules covering rest or lunch period, safety rules, no-strike clauses, Christmas bonuses, merit raises, and discharge of employees.

Examples of permissive issues are as follows: benefits to present retirees; price of meals in a cafeteria operated by an independent caterer; a clause establishing terms and conditions of employment for strikebreakers; a clause fixing the size and membership of bargaining teams; strike insurance; and a requirement that contract ratification be by secret ballot.

Subjects which had not been considered matters for mandatory bargaining may over a period of time move from the permissive to the mandatory category. This tendency to expand the area of mandatory issues stems from an increasingly liberal interpretation of the phrase "wages, hours, and other terms and conditions of employment." For example, the NLRB had previously held that the employer was not required to bargain over a purely economic decision to make technological improvements, to relocate operations, to subcontract, and related managerial decisions. More recently, however, the NLRB has held that, even though motivated by legitimate business interests, such decisions must be negotiated to the extent that job security or working conditions are affected.[10]

The difficulty in creating two classes of bargaining issues can be highlighted through stating two propositions, each of which commands support, and then seeing where the logic of each proposition leads. The first proposition is that an employer and a union should retain full private discretion on what matters to bargain about so long as neither seeks to compel the other to agree to something unlawful. This statement is consistent with the presumed consensus as to the virtues of "free" collective bargaining.

The second proposition holds that no party to collective bargaining should be permitted to frustrate the process by insisting to the point of impasse on a demand *outside the normal scope of collective bargaining*, even though such demand is not unlawful *per se*.

The sticking point in each case relates to the good faith concept. One can feel strongly about the desirability of the NLRB's staying out of the arena of collective bargaining and yet it is hard to object when the board's help is sought in cases where stubborn adherence to a nonmandatory proposal appears to be in fact "bad faith bargaining." If the board were suddenly to announce that it would no longer listen to unfair practice charges where the basis of the charge was insistence on a lawful but nonmandatory proposal as a condition precedent to agreement on all other phases of the contract, the probability is that such self-limitation of its discretion might open a Pandora's box of frivolous or malicious proposals as a guise for concealing refusal to bargain.

The NLRB guideline must be related to the same basic question in each case at all times: Does the demand or proposal fall within the statutory concept of wages, rates of pay, hours of work, and other conditions of employment? The guideline should be applied by the NLRB in a manner that will permit a maximum of discretion to the parties in determining the subject matter and procedures of collective bargaining.

The NLRB's "Totality of Conduct" Doctrine

Distinguishing between mandatory and nonmandatory bargaining proposals (demands) and relating this to the presence or absence of good faith is admittedly a sticky proposition. The task becomes stickier when the

10. See *Dixie Ohio Express*, 167 NLRB 72, 66 LRRM 1092 (1967).

board goes to the point of deciding that good faith is absent (or bad faith is present), even though no single act was illegal and where a contract resulted but where the course of bargaining conduct viewed in its entirety is held to constitute bad faith bargaining. This, in summary, was the board's finding in the *General Electric* case.[11]

It is difficult to write in a detached way about the board's "totality of conduct" approach as applied in the *General Electric* case. The danger is real that one's views about "boulwarism" as a negotiating strategy will affect critical judgment as to the wisdom of the board's decision.[12] To be specific, we do not believe boulwarism is an approach calculated to yield durable and constructive employer-union relations. At the same time we might question the board's finding that GE's use of this strategy of bargaining can properly be held to be a violation of the act.

Good faith is a subjective thing. Overt behavior is not always a reliable index of its presence or absence. A good offer by management is not necessarily proof of good faith, nor is a skimpy one necessarily proof of bad faith.

As Gross, Cullen, and Hanslowe have pointed out, it is interesting to speculate how the NLRB might have ruled on a case of what they term "union boulwarism," that is, one where the union goes through the forms of bargaining, does not insist on any illegal or nonmandatory proposals, and wants to sign an agreement, *but only one matching the terms of an existing area or industry pattern.*[13]

The futility of the board's approach in the GE situation is underlined by considering the operational significance of the standard remedy of a directive to cease and desist in such a case. How can the board through such a directive induce GE to change its frame of mind without necessarily changing any of its actions? Again, as Gross, Cullen, and Hanslowe have suggested, the board is in the anomalous position of finding GE guilty of everything in general and nothing in particular.[14]

If one is to be this critical of the board, the obligation to offer constructive alternatives is a "mandatory" one. This is easier said than done. It seems clear that the board should be more precise than it has been

---

11. 150 NLRB 192 (1964).

12. "Boulwarism" refers to a practice invented by Lemuel Boulware, a vice president for General Electric. Briefly, the plan calls for careful company analysis of employee preferences, the state of the marketplace, and information presented by the union, followed by a company-formulated wage and working conditions offer. This offer will not be altered by the company unless the union presents new information. Unwillingness to engage in the normal "give-and-take" of bargaining is the most distinguished aspect of this approach (though the resulting settlement may in fact be no different than one arrived at by "give-and-take").

13. Gross, Cullen, and Hanslowe, *Good Faith in Labor Negotiations*, p. 1030, footnote 19.

14. *Ibid.*, p. 1031.

on what types of bargaining conduct it regards as illegal. Also, the board could be clearer than in the past on evaluating the reasonableness or unreasonableness of particular bargaining proposals and perhaps more cautious on the matter of inferring bad faith. Perhaps the board should be required to set out the criteria it will use in determining whether or not a particular party is bargaining in good faith.

UNION SECURITY

Section 14(b), Taft-Hartley and State Right-to-Work Laws

To a professional trade unionist, perhaps the most irritating provision in the Taft-Hartley Act is one small innocent-appearing sentence, section 14(b), which reads as follows:

> Nothing in this act shall be construed as authorizing the execution or application of agreements requiring membership in a labor organization as a condition of employment in any State or Territory in which such execution or application is prohibited by State or Territorial law.

In layman's terms, Congress is saying: "On the subject of union security clauses in collective bargaining agreements, a state law that is more restrictive than ours will prevail over the federal statute." Thus, 14(b) reverses the usual constitutional presumption by making state law superior to federal. It does so in an area of extreme sensitivity.

Repeal of 14(b) has been a major AFL–CIO goal. The federation has made all-out lobbying efforts against 14(b) in 1965, 1966, and 1969. Recently, in 1977, the issue was brought up again, and similarly defeated. More specifically, it was decided not to include the repeal of 14(b) in the package of revisions constituting the Labor Reform Law of 1977, in hopes of increasing its chances of passage.[15]

Union members have always shown resentment at being required to work alongside employees who refuse to join the labor organization doing the bargaining with the employer. Ever since *Commonwealth* v. *Hunt* (1842),[16] feelings have run strong against these "free riders." At the same time, powerful sentiment has always existed against compelling workers to join unions against their will. Thus, the union security issue is by no means a new one. It has always had an explosive character. Requiring by contract that a worker join a union before or at some point after his hiring has often been a source of bitter conflict and misunderstanding.

15. *Congressional Quarterly Weekly Report*, 35, No. 31 (July 30, 1977), 1604.
16. The dispute in the *Hunt* case, 45 Mass. 4 Met. III (1942), involved concerted refusal to work for any employer using a nonunion workman.

Membership requirement clauses have been constantly in the public eye through court decisions and legislative enactments. Federal and state legislation on this subject constitutes an important restriction on the discretion of employers and labor organizations in contract negotiation. The nature of these restrictions has not changed much in recent years, nor have the arguments for and against such public policy controls.

The struggle goes on at the legislative level, with no end in sight. Unionists generally regard a state right-to-work law (one which bans any form of union security clause) as a prime target for elimination. Employer forces in right-to-work states generally strive to keep such laws on the books. The battle seems to be more over symbol than substance. Recent statistical analyses indicate, at most, that a right-to-work law modestly affects the fortunes of the union movement.[17] Many union leaders assert that part of the cause of their relative and, recently, absolute decline in membership is the fact that corporations have been relocating plant operations to the South, where the preponderance of right-to-work states are located. Unions historically have failed to organize the South and their drive to eliminate right-to-work laws there, as well as to strike down section 14(b) of the Taft-Hartley Act, has netted little success. The data in Table 3–1 make the point. States with right-to-work laws and states located in the South are also the states which rank the lowest in terms of union membership as a percentage of nonagricultural employment.

Many other factors besides the presence or absence of right-to-work laws determine relative state unionization. Foremost among these factors is the industry-occupation mix of the state. Some types of work and some types of workers are more amenable to union organizing efforts than other types of work or workers. Other factors include work and community values that characterize the state, other local political policies (especially the relative likelihood of law enforcement agency involvement in alleged crimes by strikers or union organizers versus alleged crimes against strikers and union organizers), the extent of urbanization (unions are more likely to prosper in large urban areas), and the resolve that employers in the area have to oppose the union movement. Allowing for these other factors virtually eliminates the apparent correlation between right-to-work laws and low levels of state unionization.

Yet the blunt fact is that proponents of right-to-work legislation hope that such a law will make it more difficult for unions to solidify their financial and organizational positions in particular bargaining relationships. Unions view right-to-work laws as a threat to their "right to exist." Even if the practical impact is not large, the motives of the participants

17. See Keith Lumsden and Craig Peterson, "The Effect of Right-to-Work Laws on Unionization in the U.S.," *Journal of Political Economy*, 83 (December 1975), 1237–48; and William Moore and Robert Newman, "On the Prospects for American Trade Union Growth: A Cross-Section Analysis," *Review of Economics and Statistics*, 57 (November 1975), 435–45.

Table 3–1

Distribution of Membership of National Unions by State and as a Proportion
of Employees in Nonagricultural Establishments, 1978

State	MEMBERSHIP (THOUSANDS) 1978[a]	1978 Ranking	MEMBERSHIP AS A PERCENT OF EMPLOYEES IN NONAGRICULTURAL ESTABLISHMENTS 1978	1978 Ranking
All States	20,459	—	23.6	—
Alabama[b]	257	22	19.2	25
Alaska	43	46	26.2	13
Arizona[b]	122	30	13.8	37
Arkansas[b]	109	33	15.0	33
California	2,184	2	23.7	17
Colorado	172	27	15.2	32
Connecticut	296	18	21.9	22
Delaware	52	43	21.0	23
Florida[b]	367	16	11.7	46
Georgia[b]	271	20	13.6	38
Hawaii	120	31	32.1	6
Idaho	47	45	14.3	36
Illinois	1,497	4	31.5	7
Indiana	643	8	29.3	10
Iowa[b]	212	26	19.2	26
Kansas	117	32	12.8	42
Kentucky	274	19	22.4	21
Louisiana[b]	227	24	16.0	30
Maine	74	39	18.3	27
Maryland–District of Columbia	458	14	21.0	24
Massachusetts	611	9	24.5	14
Michigan	1,223	6	34.6	3
Minnesota	411	15	24.4	15
Mississippi[b]	103	35	12.7	44
Missouri	578	10	30.0	8
Montana	67	41	24.1	16
Nebraska[b]	92	36	15.3	31
Nevada[b]	80	37	22.9	20
New Hampshire	48	44	13.2	40
New Jersey	683	7	23.0	19
New Mexico	54	42	12.1	45
New York	2,753	1	39.2	1
North Carolina	147	28	6.5	50
North Dakota	34	47	14.6	35
Ohio	1,294	5	29.5	9
Oklahoma	138	29	13.4	39
Oregon	232	23	23.1	18
Pennsylvania	1,595	3	34.2	4
Rhode Island	108	34	27.1	12
South Carolina[b]	76	38	6.7	49
South Dakota[b]	24	50	10.3	48

Table 3-1 — *Continued*

	MEMBERSHIP (THOUSANDS)		MEMBERSHIP AS A PERCENT OF EMPLOYEES IN NONAGRICULTURAL ESTABLISHMENTS	
State	1978[a]	1978 Ranking	1978	1978 Ranking
Tennessee[b]	303	17	17.7	28
Texas[b]	575	11	11.0	47
Utah[b]	68	40	12.9	41
Vermont	33	48	17.4	29
Virginia[b]	258	21	12.7	43
Washington	496	13	33.1	5
West Virginia	226	25	36.8	2
Wisconsin	522	12	27.8	11
Wyoming[b]	28	49	14.9	34
Membership not classifiable[c]	60	—	—	—

[a]Based on reports from 125 national unions and estimated for 49. Also included are local unions directly affiliated with the AFL-CIO and members in single-firm and local unaffiliated unions.
[b]Has the right-to-work law.
[c]Includes local unions directly affiliated with the AFL-CIO.
Note: Because of rounding, sums of individual items may not equal totals.
Dashes indicate no data in category.

Source: *Directory of National Unions and Employee Associations, 1979*, Bureau of Labor Statistics, U.S. Department of Labor, 1980, p. 71.

insure continued controversy and the continued symbolic importance of this issue.

Few knowledgeable people are neutral on right-to-work legislation. One's viewpoint is conditioned principally by value judgments as to unionism and as to the proper role of public policy in relation to collective bargaining as a process. There can be no scientific position for or against right-to-work legislation.

A Note on the Agency Shop

State right-to-work laws typically ban any contractual provision requiring union membership as a condition of employment at any time before or after hiring. Such legislation thus invalidates not only closed shop contracts but also union shop provisions and maintenance of union membership clauses. One strategem designed to circumvent these prohibitions is the agency shop provision. Under an agency shop arrangement, the union certified as the bargaining agent receives dues money from the new employee as though he were a member, but he is not obligated to join the union. The agency shop has appealed to some unions as a practical solution to the "free rider" problem.

At least fifteen states permit the negotiation of "fair share" or agency shop clauses in the public sector.[18] These laws provide that, while a public employee may not be required to join a union, the latter may require the nonunion employee to pay a portion of regular dues and other assessments. In theory, the payment represents the nonunion employees' fair share of the costs to the union for representing them.

Closed Shops and Closed Unions: Are They Special Cases?

The original closed shop rationale was directly related to a formal four- or five-year apprenticeship program leading to acquisition of journeyman status.[19] For labor quality control, it used to make sense to relate this training regimen to closed shop provisions with the unions functioning as employment agencies. These arrangements have lost much of their validity under current labor market conditions. In any event, it is unlikely that closed shop contracts will again become a valid form of union security under federal law. One important exception to this, contained in section 8(f) of the act, applies to the construction industry, and allows an employer and a union to enter into a prehire agreement that contains a union security clause requiring membership within seven, instead of the normal limit of thirty, days. This provision closely approximates the old closed shop agreements.[20]

The true problem still relates to *closed unions*, historically associated with craft unions in the building and construction field and in the railroad industry. Firm government action is recommended to eliminate cases of *de facto* closed shop arrangements being maintained by "closed" unions. The usual case was one where the local union members stubbornly refused to admit blacks into apprenticeship programs. No defense is possible for a labor organization which discriminates against applicants on the basis of race, creed, color, or sex. Unions in a democracy cannot be regarded as *bona fide* labor organizations if they are not in fact genuinely "open." The only legitimate restriction on union entry should be one relating to a person's ability to learn the craft or trade in question.

Fortunately, the cancer of closed unions has been vigorously attacked by both government agencies and the AFL–CIO. All unions affiliated with the AFL–CIO and most of the major unaffiliated organizations have constitu-

18. See Table 15–8.

19. Closed shops require union membership as a condition for employment.

20. Allan L. Bioff, Laurence J. Cohen, and Kurt L. Hanslowe, eds., *The Developing Labor Law, Cumulative Supplement, 1971–75* (Washington, D.C.: Bureau of National Affairs, 1976), p. 374.

tional provisions on membership that are above reproach.[21] Serious pockets of discrimination remain, however, in some local unions in some areas, where the membership clings to a policy that should be labeled for what it is—*white racism*.

The Taft-Hartley approach to the closed union problem was oblique and generally unsatisfactory. Seemingly, unions were obligated to accept into membership anyone offering to pay the customary initiation fee and dues. Workers could be expelled from the union under the union's own rules, but employers could not be required to discharge employees for being in bad standing unless the reason for lack of good standing was nonpayment of dues.

The act thus operated only to protect workers from the *employment consequences* of arbitrary restrictions on admission or undemocratic expulsions. It overlooked or disregarded the fact that arbitrary denial of admission to union membership can operate to the serious detriment of employees even if it does not actually cost them their jobs. Also, arbitrary expulsion from a union, even if it does not result in discharge from employment of the expelled member, can undermine the democratic structure of the union.

Taft-Hartley thus did not meet head-on the problem of discriminatory or undemocratic union admission and exclusion policies. However, in 1964 the board made a powerful contribution to the antidiscrimination drive in its *Hughes Tool* decision.[22] In this case, the NLRB held that "the duty to equal representation . . . is inherent in the exclusive representation status accorded [to labor organizations] by the statute." Thus, it found that to refuse to process the grievance of a (black) nonunion member of the bargaining unit was an unfair labor practice which, if continued, could result in the union's loss of certification. Going further, in 1974 the board held that a union which has won majority status may be denied certification for discrimination on the basis of race, national origin, or alienage.[23] However, this stand was overruled by the board in 1977.[24] Current board law is that it will not consider issues relating to alleged union discrimination (of any kind) as a bar to certification provided that the unit's members encounter no interference in exercising their right to select a bargaining agent. The appropriate vehicle for resolving discrimination violations under sections 8(b)(1)(A), 8(b)(2), and 8(b)(3) is *via* unfair labor practices

21. The Brotherhood of Locomotive Firemen removed its race bar in 1963. Since that date the AFL–CIO has been able to say that no affiliated union has racial restrictions in its constitution. Informal exclusion through local union departure from or defiance of national union policy is something else again. See Ray Marshall, *The Negro and Organized Labor* (New York: Wiley, 1965), particularly chapters 5 and 6.

22. *Hughes Tool Co.*, 147 NLRB 1573 (1964).

23. *Bekin's Moving and Storage, Inc.*, 211 NLRB 138 (1974).

24. *Handy-Andy, Inc.*, 288 NLRB 59 (1977).

proceedings and the revocation of certification may be the resulting remedy.

The Landrum-Griffin Act of 1959, with its much-publicized "bill of rights" for individual union members, developed still another avenue of insuring internalized fair treatment for individual unionists. Landrum-Griffin protection of union members against undemocratic union policies, however, has no particular value as an instrument for eliminating discriminatory admission or hiring hall policies.

Title 7 of the 1964 Civil Rights Act (amended) is the statute which explicitly outlaws discrimination in the admission to, and expulsion from, a union based upon race, color, sex, religion, or national origin. These limits apply to virtually every aspect of employment and/or union membership. There are some exceptions. For example, it is not an "unfair employment practice" for an employer, union, or employment agency to judge an individual based on sex, religion, or national origin in those certain instances where such factor(s) is a bona fide occupational qualification (BFOQ) or is reasonably necessary to the normal operation of that particular enterprise.

Although the Equal Employment Opportunity Commission (EEOC) which administers the civil rights statutes originally did not have the power to enforce Title 7 of the act, it was granted, through the 1972 amendments, the power to initiate court action against civil rights violators.

Before bringing court action, however, the commission must try to obtain statutory compliance through mediation and conciliation. The EEOC has the same broad investigating powers as the NLRB under the Taft-Hartley Act, and thus has access to documentary evidence and the right to summon witnesses and take testimony.

Another program that battles closed unions is affirmative action. Through the Affirmative Action Program, employers, particularly contractors, who wish to do business with the federal government are required to actively strive to eliminate employment barriers erected against minorities and women in their companies. The program is administered by the Labor Department's Office of Federal Contract Compliance Programs (OFCCP). The contracting agency of the OFCCP, if necessary, will impose affirmative action plans on particular contractors that set out minority employment goals and timetables which differ according to the available labor supply. Unions, if they are to supply such labor, must admit women and minorities to membership since, with the seven-day union shop clause allowed in the construction industry, union membership is almost a necessary condition for employment.

It is not enough for an organization to stop discriminatory practices. Oftentimes, it must take affirmative action to remedy the effects of past discrimination. Thus, the discriminatory effects of old seniority systems must be remedied. In these instances, employers and unions must tackle the vexing problem of building a new system which affirms the rights of minorities previously discriminated against while not penalizing the rights, of, say, innocent white male employees. As a practical matter this remains a challenging, perhaps impossible, task. We know for certain that the use of quota programs as a means to offset the effects of past discrimination is extremely controversial[25] and that the use of "tests" to guide the decision to hire, assign work, or even to build a seniority roster is permitted, provided the test is "job related."[26] The latter is hard to prove.

The extent to which Affirmative Action Programs and the EEOC have succeeded in making inroads into discrimination is hotly debated. One can conclude, however, that there is considerable room for improvement.[27]

Legislation and court decisions alone are not enough to wipe out the remaining bastions of union discriminatory conduct. More than a legal remedy is called for to eliminate the racist attitudes of white trade unionists at the local union level. Employers can be of direct help by refusing to tolerate or condone existing discrimination by members of labor organizations with which they have contractual relationships. There is some evidence that concerned unions will crack down harder on local unions that persist in flouting the clear mandate of the national union's constitution. The trusteeship device is one mechanism to achieve this purpose. Strong worker education programs of an "outreach" type are urgently needed in many cases.

This discussion of closed shop-closed union can be concluded on the encouraging note that the incidence of union member discrimination against nonwhites is declining. Public pressure, legislation, the courts, increased activity of the AFL–CIO itself—all are contributing to progress toward genuine internal equality. But much more remains to be done.

25. This was the issue in the famous case of *United Steelworkers of America (AFL)* v. *Weber*, 47 U.S.L.W. 4857 (U.S., June 27, 1979). A five-to-two majority of the U.S. Supreme Court ruled that a training program voluntarily negotiated by the Steelworkers and Kaiser Aluminum and Chemical was legal. The training program admitted half black, half white, even black entrants with less seniority than nonadmitted whites, until the black proportion of skilled workers (about 1 percent) mirrored the population (about 39 percent).

26. *Griggs* v. *Duke Power Co.*, 401 U.S. 424 (1971).

27. A study conducted by Morris Goldstein and Robert Smith concluded that the effect of a compliance review program on contractors was generally favorable for black males, while black females received little benefit. Morris Goldstein and Robert Smith, "The Estimated Impact of the Anti-Discrimination Program Aimed at Federal Contractors" *Industrial and Labor Relations Review*, 29, No. 4, (July 1976), 542.

STATUTORY RESTRICTIONS
ON COLLECTIVE BARGAINING PROCEDURES

Restrictions on Renegotiation
and Termination

The framers of the Taft-Hartley Act paid considerable attention to procedures for renegotiation or termination of existing collective agreements. The act specifies directly certain procedural requirements that must be adhered to by management and the union.

In non-health care sectors, the party wishing to terminate or to make changes in an existing contract must serve notice of such intention on the other party not less than sixty days prior to the expiration date of the current contract. Negotiations therefore presumably begin at least sixty days before the "old" contract is due to expire. If agreement has not been reached within thirty days prior to the expiration date, the act imposes a further obligation to notify the Federal Mediation and Conciliation Service of the existence of the unresolved dispute. Resort to economic force during the sixty days prior to the expiration of an agreement is for all practical purposes an unfair labor practice prohibited by a stringent provision that makes strikers subject to discharge without recourse.

The 1974 amendments to the act provided even more stringent notice requirements for labor disputes in the health care industry. According to these amendments, any party wishing to modify or terminate a contract in the health care sector must serve notice on the other party at least ninety days prior to the expiration of the current contract and give notice to the Federal Mediation and Conciliation Service at least sixty days prior to the expiration date.[28] In addition, because of the critical nature of the services provided by health organizations, a union is required to serve notice of its intent to strike a health care institution ten days in advance of such action.

The legislative intent is clear. Congress wished to insure sufficient time for full bargaining over any proposed contract changes. It is hard to quarrel with such an objective. The point may be urged, however, that the parties are in the best position to work out suitable renegotiation procedures. The law nevertheless casts all contract renegotiations into an inflexible procedural mold.

Although there is nothing intrinsically unreasonable in the procedural regulations of the Taft-Hartley Act described above, these objections should be noted:

28. Allan L. Bioff, Laurence J. Cohen, and Kurt L. Hanslowe, eds., *The Developing Labor Law, Cumulative Supplement, 1971–1975* (Washington, D.C.: Bureau of National Affairs, 1976), p. 297.

1. The law allows no room for negotiation of alternative procedures to suit special situations.
2. The penalties for violation of the sixty- or ninety-day "freeze" are exceptionally severe upon employees.
3. The law in practice may encourage evasion of fundamental responsibilities on a legal technicality. If one party fails to live up to the precise letter of the law, the other party may contend that he is thereby relieved from further bargaining obligations. This tactic could increase rather than reduce industrial strife.

These arguments may be tempered somewhat in the case of the health care sector. Here, reliance on the ten-day strike notice should offer a facility's administrator ample time to prepare for the continuity of patient care in the event of a strike. However, we need not dwell longer on the law's procedural restrictions. In many relationships the negotiation machinery is set in motion well in advance of the sixty- or ninety-day statutory requirement.[29] Considerable experimentation is going on with approaches for handling problems of a continuing nature that carry over from one contract to the next, such as shifting manpower requirements in a technologically dynamic situation. There is also renewed interest in the utility of prenegotiation exchanges of viewpoints on probable "tough" issues well in advance of either statutory or contractual deadlines. There is increasing joint concern over how to minimize the incidence of crisis bargaining. The use of FMCS's highly publicized "resolution by objectives" services bears witness to this fact. Joint study committees operating between contracts in many relationships are still another indication of increasing private concern and responsibility.[30]

Restrictions on the Right to Strike

The right of the union to strike and the right of the employer to lock out employees are essential concomitants of the free collective bargaining process. The will to agree in collective bargaining is conditioned by the presence of the ultimate sanction of resort to economic force.

The Wagner Act placed no statutory restrictions on the right to strike. The Taft-Hartley Act specifically outlaws several types of strikes, including the following:

29. Some employers and unions have developed the practice of "exploratory" bargaining conferences as much as one year ahead of the date for initiating formal negotiations.

30. For a knowledgeable but not particularly sanguine view of such committees, written from a historical perspective, see William Gomberg, "Special Study Committees" in *Frontiers of Collective Bargaining*, eds., John T. Dunlop and Neil W. Chamberlain (New York: Harper & Row, 1967), pp. 235–51.

1. Any strike by federal government employees.
2. Any strike to achieve an objective that is unlawful under the act (such as a strike to secure a closed shop contract).
3. Any strike to force an employer to violate the act (for example, one to compel him to cease bargaining with a duly certified union).
4. Any general or sympathetic strike (outlawed by clear implication by the complete legislative ban on secondary boycotts).
5. Any jurisdictional strike.

These are the principal outright prohibitions of strike action. Severe limitations on the right to strike are also provided in sections dealing with contract renewal procedures, as just noted, and in connection with any labor dispute that may be designated by the President as of a "national emergency" character. Such designation calls into play a special chain of procedures under Title II of the act. These restrictions are discussed in Chapter 9. The restrictions or prohibitions would appear to be of sufficient scope to make the phrase "except as provided herein nothing shall be construed as abridging the right to strike" sound a bit hollow.

Many state legislatures have been active in placing their own prohibitions and limitations on the right to strike. The variety in state patterns is so great that no summary analysis can do it justice. Some states require a majority vote by affected employees before any strike can be called. Mandatory cooling-off periods are called for in other state statutes. Strikes in violation of collective agreements, strikes by government employees or public utility workers, strikes in the nature of a secondary boycott or a jurisdictional strike—these and many others are often outlawed at the state level.[31]

Most students of union-management relations agree that the number and duration of work stoppages has been encouragingly low in most years since 1946. To some extent, this is attributable to the impact of federal or state legislation. However, the comparatively low number of man-hours lost as a result of strikes is also due in some measure to the growing maturity of the parties in labor relations (see Table 3–2).

The reduced incidence of economic force in labor disputes can be attributed to the combination or "mix" of the following elements:

1. The increasing maturity, self-restraint, and economic sophistication of the parties in bargaining.

---

31. In the third edition (1972) of this text, we noted that only two states, Hawaii and Pennsylvania, had legalized the right to strike by government employees. We also noted that this flat prohibition would break down. Today, the states of Alaska, Minnesota, Montana, Oregon, Vermont, and Wisconsin must be added to the list of states permitting public sector strikes under limited circumstances. The list will continue to grow.

2. The declining practical value of economic force as a means of inducing agreement in highly mechanized operations that can be run for lengthy periods of time by supervisory employees.

3. The increasing impatience of the *general public* and also of *particular publics* adversely affected by the operational impact of strikes, such as airline and subway passengers or newspaper readers and advertisers.

4. Recent growth of collective bargaining in the public sector where the right to strike is not generally recognized and where alternative procedures must therefore be used in most instances.

5. Recognition by many employers and unions in key bargaining relationships that their decision making, including the decision to use economic force, is no longer (if it ever was) a purely private affair, and an appreciation of the necessity of considering the public interest.

Table 3–2

Work Stoppages in the United States,
Selected Years 1940–78

YEAR	NUMBER OF STRIKES	NUMBER OF WORKERS INVOLVED (THOUSANDS)	DAYS IDLE (THOUSANDS)	PERCENT OF PRIVATE NONFARM MAN-HOURS IDLE
1940	2,508	577	6,700	0.10
1945	4,750	3,470	38,000	.47
1946	4,985	4,600	116,000	1.43
1947	3,693	2,170	34,600	.30
1950	4,843	2,410	38,800	.33
1955	4,320	2,650	28,200	.22
1960	3,333	1,320	19,100	.14
1965	3,963	1,550	23,300	.15
1970	5,716	3,305	66,414	.37
1975	5,031	1,746	31,237	.16
1978	4,230	1,623	36,922	.17

Source: *Handbook of Labor Statistics,* Bureau of Labor Statistics, U.S. Department of Labor (annual); and *Current Wage Developments,* Bureau of Labor Statistics, U.S. Department of Labor, November 1980, p. 25.

The complex of statutory and practical limitations on economic force and the decline in its use should not obscure the continuing validity of the proposition that the *right* of employees to strike and the *right* of employers to lock out employees or to "take" a strike are *essential elements of free collective bargaining* as we have always understood it in the United States. The knowledge that economic force *may* and *can* be used as a last resort is a powerful factor in keeping the parties at the negotiating table. We join those who question the viability of collective bargaining as a method for setting wages, hours, and other conditions of employment in those public sector jurisdictions where the strike is prohibited.

Under contemporary conditions of economic interdependence, the strike is rarely used. It has become literally a last-resort device where negotiation, mediation, and other efforts to reach a peaceful solution have failed. The meaningfulness of bargaining, however, is still directly related to preserving the right to use economic force. If this most powerful of incentives to reach agreement should be eliminated by law, collective bargaining would cease to be either free or productive. Viable alternative procedures are constantly being sought, as we shall note in Chapter 9, but no magic formula to insure meaningful negotiation has yet been developed.

Wildcat Strikes

Section 301's provision for damage suits by employers and unions against each other for breach of contract and its designation of the federal courts to enforce both agreements to arbitrate and arbitration awards have contributed without doubt in some degree to improving both the quality and stability of contract administration. Also, the law's stricter conception of agency since 1947 has caused many national unions to exercise tighter control over their locals to curb wildcat strikes.

When wildcats do occur, there is a visible need either for instant arbitration or injunctive relief if the significance of the contractual no-strike pledge is not to be rendered a nullity. The matter of timing makes the damage suit approach under section 301 an unsatisfactory one from the employer's viewpoint. It is likely therefore that we shall see increased usage of expedited arbitration for wildcat situations, with the arbitrator being granted the power to assess damages as the situation may dictate.

The causes of greater stability in administration of collective bargaining agreements received a substantial boost in June 1970 when the U.S. Supreme Court took the bit in its teeth and specifically overruled the much-criticized *Sinclair* case (370 U.S. 195 [1962]), which had held that a wildcat strike in defiance of a contractual no-strike pledge was unenjoinable as a "labor dispute" under Norris-LaGuardia. The now famous *Boys Markets* (398 U.S. 235 [1970]) decision establishes several prerequisites for the issuance of an injunction to enforce contractual no-strike agreements. They are as follows:

1. The strike must be over an issue the parties are obligated to arbitrate.
2. The injunction must be conditioned on arbitration of the underlying dispute.
3. The strike must be occurring or imminent.

4. The strike has or will cause lasting injury to the employer.
5. The canons of fair treatment must support the issuance of an injunction.

In general, the Supreme Court's stance is to enjoin a wildcat strike if it is over an issue which is subject to the parties' final and binding grievance arbitration agreement. An exception to this generalization, however, was recently affirmed by the high court in *Buffalo Forge Co.* v. *Steelworkers* (428 U.S. 397 [1976]). In a five-to-four decision, the Supreme Court ruled that injunctive relief under *Boys Markets* is not permissible against "sympathy strikes"—that is, a strike in which the employees in one bargaining unit observe the picket line of employees in another unit. The Court reasoned that the work stoppage was not "over" an issue which was remotely subject to arbitration.

The various limitations and prohibitions on the right to strike can probably be credited with the declining union use of economic force in recent years, although this is difficult to pinpoint, as noted earlier in this analysis.

Individual Rights

The law's emphasis on individual rights in grievance presentation (section 9) and in internal union affairs (Landrum-Griffin) has contributed to greater union leadership awareness of the need to do a complete representation job.[32] The NLRB's stress on the duty of fair representation is an important manifestation of the intensified concern for individual rights in today's highly institutionalized framework of union-employer relations. This emphasis has to be counted as a plus factor, although it must be said that overzealous concern for the individual can result in an unstabilizing, even chaotic, environment which militates against effective collective bargaining. For a detailed discussion of individual rights, see the section entitled "The Duty of Fair Representation" in Chapter 7.

REPRESENTATION ELECTIONS

Recognition cases occur whenever the NLRB determines that "a question of representation exists." Such a case may arise in a variety of ways. The most common involves a labor organization petitioning for NLRB certifica-

---

32. For a comprehensive discussion of the individual employee in relation to the collective structure, see Clyde Summers, "The Individual Employee's Right Under the Collective Agreement: What Constitutes Fair Representation," in National Academy of Arbitrators, *Arbitration—1974*, *Proceedings, 27th Annual Meeting* 1975).

tion on the basis that a majority of employees in a unit appropriate for collective bargaining desire it to represent them, and the employer in question doubts the majority status of the petitioning labor organization. Other common situations involve two or more labor organizations seeking to represent the same body of workers (no dispute on the appropriate unit) or different bargaining units being claimed as appropriate by the unions in question. A precise definition of a bargaining unit and a listing of the criteria for determining the appropriateness of a bargaining unit will be made in Chapter 4.

Another type of representation case concerns the reverse side of the coin wherein the board receives a petition for *decertification* on the grounds that the incumbent union no longer represents a majority in the appropriate bargaining unit. Recognition cases may also arise out of such technical issues as eligibility to vote, the appropriate payroll date for making up voter eligibility lists, alleged improper interference with elections, and so forth.

A representation case involves an investigation to determine whether a question of representation exists within the meaning of the act. The most common factual matter is whether a particular petitioning union is entitled to be certified by the board as exclusive bargaining representative. Such questions are typically resolved by conducting a *secret-ballot election*.

Each year since 1935, the NLRB has conducted several thousand elections in representation cases. Every election held represents a civilized alternative to economic force. The board's services in this area therefore make an incontestable contribution to the cause of peace and stability in labor relations. Union recognition was *the* major cause of strikes prior to 1935. Extensive use of the NLRB's election procedures has virtually eliminated recognition as a cause of strikes.

Representation Rules and Procedures

Minimal conditions for the NLRB to conduct an election require that 30 percent of members within a bargaining unit sign authorization cards requesting representation. Sometimes more than one union files for representation. As long as one union meets the 30 percent criterion, other unions may join the election with 10 percent authorization. Demonstrated interest below 50 percent authorization is probably insufficient for the union to win an election. Unions seldom file until they have exceeded 50 percent.

To win the election, 50 percent plus one of *those persons actually voting* must favor one of the election alternatives. If the choice is between union X and no union, one alternative must win. If the choice is among union X, union Y, and no union, and if no alternative receives a majority of votes, a runoff election is held between the top two vote choices, such as union X versus union Y or union Y versus no union.

Decertification elections follow the same pattern as certification elections. To call an election, 30 percent must request decertification. Elections require a majority of those voting.

Additional restrictions have been placed on when certification or decertification elections may be held. Some of the following are among the more important:

1. A valid contract bars, under most circumstances, a rival union from attempting to gain certification. The contract serves as a bar for up to three years. A rival union must file a petition for a new election not more than ninety days and not less than sixty days before either the termination of the collective agreement or three years of a longer contract has expired, whichever comes first.[33]

2. Another election cannot be conducted for a period of one year after a valid election. If no union wins the election, the employer is allowed a one-year respite from union organizing pressure. If a union wins, the election restriction is designed to limit bad faith delays by employers attempting to encourage decertification.

3. Employers can never actively participate in the process of collecting decertification authorizations. Employer interference such as financial support or supervisor solicitation are grounds for an election to be set aside.

Once employees demonstrate sufficient interest for a representation election, an election date is set by the NLRB and a brief campaign begins. Over the course of many years, the NLRB defined rather strict rules governing election conduct in order to achieve "laboratory conditions." Such rules restricted "promises of benefits, threats of economic reprisals, deliberate misrepresentations of material facts by an employer or a union, deceptive campaign tactics by a union, or a general atmosphere of fear and confusion."[34] The primary intent of national labor law and of the NLRB in regulating elections is to let employees *without coercion* determine whether or not they want a union and, if so, which union. The NLRB campaign rules had the intended purpose of protecting free employee choice.

As we have learned with other forms of regulation, the best intentions can lead to unintended results. The NLRB has been extensively criticized for its extreme restrictions on campaign behavior. One angle of criticism contends that the volume and complexity of rules makes violation likely, thereby encouraging delay and appeal. As we discuss in the next section of

33. *Deluxe Metal Furniture Co.*, 121 NLRB 995 (1958).
34. *Sewell Manufacturing Co.*, 138 NLRB 66 (1962).

this chapter, delays and extensive litigation are probably the most serious problems in public labor policy today. Another angle of criticism questions the behavioral assumptions underlying board rulings. Some challenge the proposition that the campaign actually changes voting behavior to a significant degree. For example, behavioral research by Julius Getman, Stephen Goldberg, and Jeanne Herman[35] challenging some behavioral assumptions of the board, may have contributed to a temporary relaxation of board campaign restrictions.[36]

Employer Policy Toward Unionization

In the private sector, while unions are generally recognized as the legitimate, as well as legal, representatives of the worker, their organizing efforts are generally resisted by management. Many companies, if not most, succeed in convincing their employees that union representation "is not right for them." This general antiunion attitude has taken many forms in recent years. In December 1977, the Council on Union-Free Environment was established as an offshoot of the National Association of Manufacturers. Its purpose is to help employers resist unionization. Few managers in personnel or labor relations in recent years have not received heavy solicitation for books and seminars on how to beat unions in certification and decertification elections. The number of books and programs suggests a large employer clientele. Indeed, Jerome M. Rosow, president of the Work in America Institute, observed at the 1979 annual meetings of the Industrial Relations Research Association that during recent years a major segment of private management in the United States has taken the most aggressive stance in a generation toward unions.

Perhaps this more aggressive employer stance as much as anything else has caused an approximate 10 percentage point decline in elections won by unions over the last decade (unions now win less than half of certification elections), and a fourfold increase in the number of decertification elections won by employers.[37] The number of decertifications, however, is still small in number (less than 1,000 per year during the 1970s) and most decertifications are for small bargaining units.

A similarly generalized policy for resisting union organizing action is

35. Julius G. Getman et al., *Union Representation Elections: Law and Reality* (New York: Russell Sage Foundation, 1976).

36. *Shopping Kart Food Market*, 228 NLRB 190 (1977) set aside the restrictive board policy of invalidating the results of an election when one party's misrepresentation of the truth during the campaign may reasonably be expected to have affected the election. Within a year however, the board reversed this ruling (*General Knit of California*, 239 NLRB 101 [1978]) by again agreeing to set aside any election where a substantial misrepresentation of truth is made. These closely timed reversals are examples of the ping-pong the board plays with the collective bargaining process.

37. *Annual Report of the National Labor Relations Board*, various years.

hard to identify in most public jurisdictions under bargaining statutes or executive orders. We have discovered few such policies in our experiences in federal and state labor relations. Numerous factors explain this variance between public and private labor relations. Perhaps the two most often referenced are:

1. Public employees, as white-collar, professional, and technical workers, are in a better position than blue-collar, private employees to self-evaluate the costs/benefits of unionization.
2. Public employers, unlike their private sector counterparts, often times perceive the union as a valuable political ally that ought not to be alienated.

Clearly, labor relations practitioners in the public and private sectors differ with respect to policy toward unionization. An interesting twist, however, was recently recorded. In 1976, the United Auto Workers achieved a major bargaining goal when General Motors agreed to assume a "neutral posture" in regard to UAW organizing efforts among production workers in unorganized parts of the giant corporation. In 1979 the United Rubber Workers achieved a similar agreement from some of the "Big Five" tire companies. Employer election conduct may be a more important bargaining issue in future contract negotiations.

ADMINISTRATION, ENFORCEMENT, AND REFORM

Each congress during the second half of the 1970s seriously considered, with at least some administration support, labor law reform. In each congress a reform law was close to enactment. Pressure for reform erupted less from the substance of the law—the part we have just discussed—than from administration and enforcement of the law. At the heart of the dissatisfactions and controversies is enforcement of unfair labor practice provisions. Other problems center on union organization.

Before outlining enforcement provisions and problems, we turn to a problem that is less a topic of legislative reform, but still a serious concern to people who engage in collective bargaining. NLRB regulations interpreting and applying national labor law are unstable, sometimes inconsistent, and often unpredictable. Most union-management relations can work reasonably well under many different regulations, provided the parties know what the standards are. Continued vacillation by the board, unfortunately, even leaves labor lawyers perplexed on just what to advise their clients. Uncertainty as to how the board majority may view a particular bargaining demand or proposal intrudes upon and disrupts the process of bargaining and serves as a constant invitation to litigate instead of to bargain the disputed matter. Litigation, in turn, exacerbates the problem of enforcement.

Inconsistency by the board has two sources. First, in order to expedite affairs, the five-member board often sits in three-member panels. How the board rules on a given case depends to some extent upon which random combination of three hears and decides the case. Second, appointments to the NLRB for many years through several presidents have been "political" in nature. Each new political combination sparks another direction, in some way contrary to the recent past standards. Some of this may be inevitable, but much of it could be avoided if employers and unions who seek to politicize the NLRB could be made to appreciate the long-run wisdom of emphasizing the board's quasi-judicial role. The best way to accomplish this objective is to make board member and key staff appointments solely on the basis of labor relations expertise and demonstrated capacity to function in a judicially detached manner.

Unfair Labor Practices

As we have already observed, the National Labor Relations Board initiates no action; nor does the board enforce its findings. It responds to complaints and asks a U.S. appeals court to enforce its findings. Complaints are filed at one of thirty-three regional offices plus sixteen smaller field offices operating under the direction of the general counsel. Investigators at each office determine the merits of each complaint and decide whether or not to pursue any further action. Ninety to 95 percent of all unfair labor practice cases are settled in the field through withdrawal, dismissal, or settlement in a median time of about forty to fifty days. In 1978, 68 percent of the unfair labor practice complaints were filed against the employer, 31 percent against the union, and 1 percent against both the employer and the union.[38]

Remedies for unfair labor practices can take the form of cease-and-desist orders, reinstatement of workers, and orders for back pay. If the court of appeals agrees with the board, and in the large majority of cases it does agree, awards and orders are enforced through contempt-of-court procedures. In 1978 the board ordered 5,533 workers reinstated (72 percent accepted reinstatement) and back pay for 8,623 workers (amounting to $13.4 million).[39]

For the huge majority of cases—of employers and unions—the board and the administrative operation of the board determine a settlement that

38. *Annual Report of the National Labor Relations Board, 1977*, p. 15.
39. *Ibid.*

is final and this is rendered reasonably quickly. Considering the resources of the board, its duties, and the enormous and alarming recent increase in workload (see Table 3–3), it performs its duties well. Problems occur not in the majority of cases, but in the small minority of cases where one party or the other wishes to violate the intent of national labor law.

A union or an employer determined to avoid the requirements of the act can do so, although its effort will involve some cost. The tactics, used especially by a small percentage of employers, is to stall, delay, and appeal any order for years, then pay the relatively nominal amount of the settlement. The worst monetary cost (other than lawyers' fees) is back pay to any workers fired for a reason that is an unfair labor practice. Not all the salary that would have been earned must be paid, only the difference between what would have been earned had the employee not been fired and the earnings of the employee on a new job. Since most employees cannot afford to wait years for the case to be settled, they find new jobs at a pay rate that is seldom drastically less than their old pay rate.

Table 3–3

National Labor Relations Board Caseload,
Selected Years 1967–77

YEAR	COMPLAINTS FILED	UNFAIR LABOR PRACTICE COMPLAINTS FILED	PERCENT ALL COMPLAINTS UNFAIR LABOR PRACTICE
1967	30,425	17,040	56
1969	31,303	18,651	60
1971	37,212	23,770	64
1973	41,077	26,487	64
1975	44,923	31,253	70
1977	52,943	37,828	71
1978	53,261	39,652	74

Source: *Handbook of Labor Statistics, 1977*, Bureau of Labor Statistics, U.S. Department of Labor, 1977, p. 317; *Forty-Second Annual Report of the National Labor Relations Board*, 1977, p. 266; and *Forty-Third Annual Report of the National Labor Relations Board*, 1978, p. 2.

The median time for a case pursued to the full board is twelve months from complaint to decision.[40] A determined union or employer can delay the procedures for much longer. Once the board decides, the order goes to an appeals court for deliberation and enforcement, a process that can take years. Court decisions for back pay go to the board for assessment. Disputes as to the amount can last for a few additional years. One reported case took almost twenty years from the time of complaint without any remedy effected, although an unfair labor practice was found and rein-

40. John H. Fanning, chairman of the National Labor Relations Board, Address before the Section of Labor Relations Law, American Bar Association, August 9, 1977.

statement and back pay were ordered.[41] Recently, a small number of employers have been repeatedly found guilty of unfair labor practices. Once one case is finally settled, they commit the same offense again. They continue because the cost of an unfair labor practice is less than the cost of collective bargaining.

Proposals for labor law reform, not surprisingly, frequently establish much higher penalties for an unfair labor practice. Some examples of proposed changes include double back pay for workers "unfairly" dismissed (an example of an unfair firing is for reasons of union membership), assessment of damages to employees by the board for failure to bargain in good faith, time limits for appeal of board orders, and loss of federal contracts for repeated violations. Current public policies are likely to be an area of either reform or continued efforts to reform during the next decade.

Representation Elections

Since the mid-1950s, union membership has been declining as a percentage of the total labor force (see Table 3–4). More serious, however, from the perspective of organized labor, is that in 1971 and 1975 the absolute number of union members declined relative to the preceding year for the first time since 1960. This decline can be attributed to job creation that is largely confined to traditionally nonunion occupations, in nonunion industries, and in nonunion geographic areas; whereas job contraction has been in those occupations, industries, and areas where unionism has been well established. Unions have had difficulty in the past few years in organizing new members in the job-creating areas, particularly in the South which has been traditionally antiunion.

Part of the organizing problem that unions confront is by now a highly refined employer strategy of using every NLRB and court procedure to delay. Delay can be particularly devastating during an organizing campaign. If delays are long enough, all election momentum is lost and the union must essentially start over. A small proportion of employers use tactics of intimidation such as discharging union sympathizers. Although this is an unfair labor practice, the sanctions are so small and the delays so long, as just discussed, that an employer willing to break the law faces few constraints.

Employers can delay by challenging every procedural ruling at the administrative level, thereby forcing the full board to hold a hearing. In 1977 it took 286 days for a fully contested representation case to be decided by the board.[42] Employers (and, in fact, sometimes unions) challenge

---

41. Sherman F. Dallas and Beverly K. Schaffer, "Whatever Happened to the *Darlington* Case?" *Labor Law Journal,* 24 (January 1973), 3–11.
42. Fanning, Address.

Table 3–4

Union Membership as a Percent of Total Labor Force
and of Employees in Nonagricultural
Establishments, 1958–78*

(numbers in thousands)

Year	Membership excluding Canada	TOTAL LABOR FORCE Number	Percent members	EMPLOYEES IN NONAGRICULTURAL ESTABLISHMENTS Number	Percent members
Unions and associations:					
1968 ...	20,721	82,272	25.2	67,897	30.5
1969 ...	20,776	84,240	24.7	70,384	29.5
1970 ...	21,248	85,903	24.7	70,880	30.0
1971 ...	21,327	86,929	24.5	71,214	29.9
1972 ...	21,657	88,991	24.3	73,675	29.4
1973 ...	22,276	91,040	24.5	76,790	29.0
1974 ...	22,809	93,240	24.5	78,265	29.1
1975 ...	22,361	94,793	23.6	77,364	28.9
1976 ...	22,662	96,917	23.4	80,048	28.3
1977 ...	22,456	99,534	22.6	82,423	27.2
1978 ...	22,880	102,537	22.3	84,446	27.1
Unions:					
1958 ...	17,029	70,275	24.2	51,324	33.2
1959 ...	17,117	70,921	24.1	53,268	32.1
1960 ...	17,049	72,142	23.6	54,189	31.5
1961 ...	16,303	73,031	22.3	53,999	30.2
1962 ...	16,586	73,442	22.6	55,549	29.9
1963 ...	16,524	74,571	22.2	56,653	29.2
1964 ...	16,841	75,830	22.2	58,283	28.9
1965 ...	17,299	77,178	22.4	60,765	28.5
1966 ...	17,940	78,893	22.7	63,901	28.1
1967 ...	18,367	80,793	22.7	65,803	27.9
1968 ...	18,916	82,272	23.0	67,897	27.9
1969 ...	19,036	84,240	22.6	70,384	27.0
1970 ...	19,381	85,903	22.6	70,880	27.3
1971 ...	19,211	86,929	22.1	71,214	27.0
1972 ...	19,435	88,991	21.8	73,675	26.4
1973 ...	19,851	91,040	21.8	76,790	25.9
1974 ...	20,199	93,240	21.7	78,265	25.8
1975 ...	19,553	94,793	20.6	77,364	25.3
1976 ...	19,634	96,917	20.3	80,048	24.5
1977 ...	19,902	99,534	20.0	82,423	24.1
1978 ...	20,246	102,537	19.7	84,446	24.0

*Totals include reported membership and directly affiliated local union members. Total reported Canadian membership and members of single firm unions are excluded.

Source: *Directory of National Unions and Employee Associations: 1979,* Bureau of Labor Statistics, U.S. Department of Labor, 1980, p. 59.

several types of decisions: the scope of the bargaining unit (which determines who votes and, for that reason, sometimes who wins), the validity of authorization cards (for example, were they coerced?), and often alleged violations of NLRB election rules.

Not too surprisingly, recent attempts at labor law reform propose to limit procedural abuses. Although some of the violation of at least the spirit of the law is obvious, reform carries certain risks. Foremost is the chance of trampling legitimate and important questions and objections under the march to a quick procedural conclusion. The list of proposed reforms matches the list of complaints: (1) proposals that elections be held within a fixed amount of time, (2) rules by the board setting criteria for bargaining unit determination (thus avoiding delays while the board settles the unit question on a case-by-case basis), and (3) requirements that the board use injunction powers granted under section 10(L) of the act to get workers discharged for union support back to work quickly.

SUMMARY

Most employers and *most* unions engage in good faith bargaining year after year with minimal contact with the NLRB. The good faith employer seldom needs to worry about unfair practice charges. Neither does the good faith labor organization. Such parties need only the service aspects of the board's functions, such as resolving questions of representation under section 9. There is seldom any compelling need to concern themselves with the NLRB because the requirements of our national labor policy *for the most part* do not interfere seriously with the even tenor of normal bargaining relationships.

At the margin, however, current federal law and the board's rulings, practices, and procedures can and do permit abuses, create uncertainties, and, perhaps, negatively affect collective bargaining relationships. J. P. Stevens and Company is cited as a case in point. This southern-based textile firm repeatedly was found guilty of unfair labor practices, yet it chose to pay fines rather than to bargain with the Amalgamated Clothing and Textiles Workers Union. The company was able to delay negotiating for seventeen years, not reaching agreement with the union until October 1980. Thus the winds of reform will and should continue to blow until steps are taken, even at the margin, to improve our national labor policy.

In order to implement national labor policy, organized labor and management must establish an interorganizational structure designed to make feasible such a relationship. Chapter 4 will spell out in detail the structural problems associated with the creation of a collective bargaining relationship.

Questions for Discussion, Thought, and Research

1. How does the function of the general counsel differ from the function of the five-member board? What is the purpose of separating the general counsel from the five-member NLRB?

2. Union X has a legal strike against A. In an effort to exert more pressure on employer A, union X organizes a picket line at company B in order to force B to stop buying products produced by A. Is the union guilty of a secondary boycott? What are the legal terms assigned to employer A and employer B?

3. Describe the process the board uses to determine which bargaining agent to certify. What is the procedure for decertification?

4. In representation or unfair labor practice cases, does the NLRB go searching for cases to process? Why?

5. What is section 14(b) of the Taft-Hartley amendments, and why is the right-to-work section opposed by organized labor? What are the arguments for and against right-to-work laws?

6. Explain the significance of the following cases:
   Sinclair
   Boys Market
   Buffalo Forge v. *Steelworkers*

7. How are NLRB orders enforced? Can an NLRB decision be appealed?

8. Which federal labor law imposes the duty of fair representation on a union? What are some of the requirements for meeting this duty?

9. The *Borg-Warner* case recognized three categories of bargaining proposals: (a) mandatory, (b) voluntary or permissive, (c) illegal. The difficulty is often in determining which items fall within the first two categories. Should an employer and union have full discretion on deciding which items they may bargain? Explain.

10. The chapter presents evidence that unions are losing more NLRB elections than in the past. Is the process to blame? Are the unions to blame? What areas of labor law reforms would you suggest, if any?

Selected Bibliography

Aaron, Benjamin, and Paul Seth Meyer, "Public Policy and Labor-Management Relations," *A Review of Industrial Relations Research*, 2. Madison, Wis.: Industrial Relations Research Association, 1971, pp. 1–60.

Bioff, Allen L. *et al.*, ed., *The Developing Labor Law,* Cumulative Supplements 1971–75 and 1976. Washington, D.C.: Bureau of National Affairs, 1976, 1977.

Bok, Derek C., "Reflections on the Distinctive Character of American Labor Law," *Harvard Law Review,* 84 (April 1971).

Brown, Douglass V., "The Role of the NLRB," *The Next Twenty-Five Years of Industrial Relations.* Madison, Wis.: Industrial Relations Research Association, 1973, pp. 111–17.

Estey, Marten S., Philip Taft, and Martin Wagner, eds., *Regulating Union Government.* New York: Harper & Row, Pub., 1964.

Getman, Julius G., Stephen B. Goldberg, and Jeanne B. Herman, *Union Representation Elections: Law and Reality.* New York: Russell Sage, 1976.

McCulloch, Frank W., and Tim Bornstein, *The National Labor Relations Board.* New York: Praeger, 1974.

Millis, Harry A., and Emily Clark Brown, *From the Wagner Act to Taft-Hartley.* Chicago: University of Chicago Press, 1950.

National Labor Relations Board, *Annual Report* (periodic). Washington, D.C.: Government Printing Office.

Ross, Philip, *The Government as a Source of Union Power: The Role of Public Policy in Collective Bargaining.* Providence, R.I.: Brown University Press, 1965.

Taft, Philip, *Rights of Union Members and the Government.* Westport, Conn.: Greenwood Press, 1975.

Wellington, Harry H., *Labor and the Legal Process.* New Haven, Conn.: Yale University Press, 1968.

BARGAINING UNITS

4

Understanding the structure of collective bargaining relationships is essential to meaningful analysis of the problems faced by employers and unions in contemporary bargaining. This chapter is concentrated on recent developments in the structure of collective bargaining.

THE EXCLUSIVE BARGAINING RIGHTS CONCEPT

A collective agreement negotiated by an employer and labor organization contains statements about employment terms concerning a certain group of workers. The workers covered by each agreement are said to constitute a *bargaining unit*. Thus, for purposes of collective bargaining, unions represent bargaining unit members.

As a matter of law, if a majority of the workers in an (appropriate) bargaining unit can show that they wish to have a bona fide labor organization to represent them in collective dealings with their employer, then the labor organization is entitled to *exclusive* bargaining rights. In other words, the union or association shown to have been designated by a majority of employees in an appropriate unit serves as and must be recognized as the exclusive bargaining agent for all employees in the unit, whether or not the employees are members of the union or association.

This concept of exclusive bargaining rights is a distinctive and important aspect of U.S. labor relations.[1] The *quid pro quo* for enjoying such rights is the employee organization's legal obligation to negotiate and administer agreements applying to all employees in the unit. Increasing emphasis has been given recently to the problem of giving meaning to the right of employees to be represented by "unions of their own choosing." This theme will be developed later in the chapter.

VARIETY IN BARGAINING UNIT STRUCTURES

The employee composition of the bargaining unit is frequently an issue of vital importance. How the unit is defined may be the determining factor in whether union X is, in fact, entitled to representation rights. When an employer is first approached by a union with a demand that he bargain collectively, his initial response is often, "Which workers do you claim to represent?"

In most private sector cases there is no dispute over the bargaining unit. A craft union will normally seek a unit consisting of employees performing the work covered by its jurisdiction, as spelled out in its charter from the AFL–CIO and its own constitution. An industrial union typically will request that the bargaining unit consist of all nonsupervisory production and maintenance employees of company X. In labor relations jargon, this is called a "P & M" unit.

Bargaining unit disputes are more commonplace among emerging public sector bargaining relationships. A civil service union may seek a unit consisting of employees in a single department of state, county, or municipal government, whereas the state, county, or city administrator may wish to bargain with a unit consisting of civil service employees across all departments or agencies. At issue is the "scope" or "breadth" of the unit.

Sharp conflicts do develop in some cases over the appropriate structure

1. In many other countries worker representation is on a pluralistic basis. This is in part a function of unionism having a strong ideological orientation (such as democratic socialist, communist, or Christian in both France and Italy).

of the unit for bargaining. Even where the general scope of the unit is agreed upon, differences may arise as to whether particular "gray zone" employees should be included or excluded (should time study clerks in a factory or officers in a fire department be in or out?).[2]

A more fundamental conflict can develop when an industrial union seeks exclusive bargaining rights for a P & M unit and one or more craft unions are at the same time petitioning for separate bargaining units. The craft–industrial unit issue has been a headache for the National Labor Relations Board (NLRB) ever since the split between the original American Federation of Labor and the rival Committee for Industrial Organization in November 1935.[3] Although the two federations merged in December 1955, after some twenty years of internecine warfare, the unit controversy still flares up periodically, as we shall see presently.

Among the newer types of unit controversies we should list problems arising from coalitions of unions seeking to bargain on a coordinated basis with an employer "conglomerate" (that is, a company with production operations in a variety of different fields). Coalition bargaining with conglomerate employers is discussed later in this chapter.[4]

Contemporary collective agreements reveal an astonishing variety of structural patterns. The usual bargaining structure throughout manufacturing and mining industries continues to be the P & M unit. Craft bargaining units prevail in such industries as printing, building and construction, railroads, and airlines.

In some industries (such as coal mining) one union dominates the representational front and negotiates master contracts with employers. In others the pattern of bargaining units may be diverse and complex. Not infrequently, one will find an industrial union such as the United Auto Workers (UAW) or the International Association of Machinists representing most of the nonsupervisory employees in a P & M unit, but the manufacturer in question may also be negotiating separately with one or more unions representing specific craft employee groups who have chosen to remain outside the P & M structure.

Modern metropolitan newspapers have traditionally bargained with a dozen or more labor organizations, including the International Typographical Union, the American Newspaper Guild, the Photoengravers, and the

---

2. Hoyt N. Wheeler, "Officers in Municipal Fire Departments: Are They Supervisors?", *Labor Law Journal*, 28, No. 11 (November 1977).

3. For an absorbing and exhaustive account of the twenty years of rivalry between AFL and CIO unions, see Walter Galenson, *The CIO Challenge to the AFL* (Cambridge, Mass.: Harvard University Press, 1960). The Committee for Industrial Organization became the Congress for Industrial Organizations in 1938.

4. See, for example, William L. Chernish, *Coalition Bargaining: A Study of Union Tactics and Public Policy* (Philadelphia: University of Pennsylvania Press, 1969).

Pressmen.[5] The newspaper unit structure is usually a complex of craft and industrial groupings. A prime contractor in the construction field typically negotiates with seven basic craft unions, plus a number of "specialty" unions. In urban construction, bargaining increasingly is on a multiemployer basis. The contractors negotiate through a labor relations association with a joint council made up of many, but not always all, of the craft unions concerned. When all building and construction units are not parties to a master multiemployer agreement, problems can easily arise from differing contract expiration dates or from the unwillingness of a particular union to settle after all other labor organizations have agreed on future terms.

The concept of multiemployer bargaining has taken a unique twist in the public sector in Hawaii. Through their Public Employment Relations Act, they established statewide bargaining units that include both state and local workers. Thus, all state and local employees doing similar work are in the same bargaining unit, and the several public "employers" involved are bargaining on a united front basis. This has greatly simplified the bargaining process and has done much to avoid the overfragmentation of bargaining units that afflicts other state and local governments.[6] We will return to the problem of fragmentation later in this chapter.

Bargaining units can be enormous in their coverage (for example, in the private sector, the General Motors–UAW master agreement covers about 400,000 employees and, in the public sector, the state of Minnesota–AFSCME, Council 6, contract covers more than 15,000 state employees) or they can embrace a mere handful of employees.[7]

The bargaining unit universe is thus remarkably diverse and varied in its composition. The most common structure involves a particular grouping of employees represented by a labor organization negotiating with a single employer on a craft or industrial basis. Nevertheless, multiemployer bargaining, company-wide contracts, and coalition or coordinated bargaining with conglomerate employers appear.

Scholars can expound readily on the superiority of one form of bargaining structure over another. It is not an easy matter to win adherents to such preferences in the real world of collective bargaining. History is hard to reverse. Short-run factors in particular labor markets are often decisive in

5. During the decade of the 1970s, several mergers occurred or were in the negotiation stage. Changes in technology broke many of the traditional skill boundaries; diversity of organizations became as obsolete as the old equipment.

6. Jack E. Klauser, "Multi-employer Bargaining in the Public Sector of Hawaii," *Journal of Collective Negotiations*, 6, No. 1 (1977), 73–79.

7. In fact, under certain circumstances a bargaining unit of one employee can be held appropriate. The City of New York has bargained collectively with a union representing an appropriate unit of two shoemakers. In 1968, Harold W. Davey served as arbitrator in a dispute involving General Electric and the Teamsters, which were representing two employees. The latter constituted the entire appropriate unit in a GE warehouse in Indianapolis.

determining whether a given group of employees is, for example, to be unionized by the Teamsters or by the UAW, by the American Federation of Teachers or by a local unit of the National Education Association. Logic often plays a minor role.

There are no purely objective criteria to determine the greater appropriateness of one bargaining structure over another. Most employees of any given employer share some common goals and interests. Considerations of efficiency—on the part of the union representing employees and the employer coping with employee unions—suggest larger units to bargain over common interests. Most small employee groups, on the other hand, have interests and goals different from those of other employees; they may, for instance, have different skills or different working conditions. In larger units, the nonshared interests of employee groups are sometimes ignored, primarily because they are relatively unimportant to other members of the bargaining unit. The structure of the bargaining unit to some extent always involves a tradeoff between considerations of the common interest along with efficiency and perhaps effectiveness in bargaining and considerations of the important specific interests of the many skill groups and work groups.

CRITERIA FOR DETERMINING THE APPROPRIATENESS OF PROPOSED BARGAINING UNITS

In the private sector, the National Labor Relations Board has always been on the hot seat in any case where the key issue was what constituted an appropriate unit for purposes of collective bargaining, because the board has the statutory duty to *decide* in each case what shall be the appropriate unit or units. In most cases, all parties concerned agree on the delineation of the appropriate bargaining unit. When a unit dispute exists, however, either between company X and union Y or between two or more unions seeking certification for different units of representation, the board has the unenviable task of deciding which unit (or units) is "appropriate" for assuring to employees "the fullest freedom" in exercising their guaranteed rights under the act.

The national labor policy makes clear that it is the employees who should decide whether they wish to be represented by a union for purposes of collective bargaining or whether they wish to refrain from the exercise of their statutory right to self-organization.[8] In this context,

8. It is desirable to quote Section 7 in its entirety at this point. The italicized words were added to the original Section 7 (Wagner Act) by the Taft–Hartley Act (1947). Section 7 reads as follows:

therefore, it is logical that the *desires of the employees concerned* should be of paramount significance in determining which employees are to be in the bargaining unit.

The NLRB normally accords great weight to the desires of employees in unit cases. Where the unit question is in dispute, however, the board's decision necessarily cannot honor the claims of all competing organizations. The NLRB generally gives short shrift to the employer's unit preference, no matter how logical it may be, if the pattern of unionization among his employees has taken a different course. When the employer and union agree on the structure of the bargaining unit, the board will usually accept the joint determination of the parties.

The desires of the employees in particular cases will always be a factor of great importance, but many other factors or criteria are relevant to a decision of unit issues. These include the following:

1. The bargaining history in the plant or industry.
2. The membership eligibility requirements of the union or unions involved.
3. The presence of a "community of interest" among the employees in the unit sought as appropriate.
4. The similarity of wage scales, hours, and working conditions among employees in the unit sought as appropriate.
5. The form or extent of present self-organization among employees.
6. The presence of a "functional coherence and interdependence" among the work operations covered in the unit sought as appropriate.
7. The organization of the employer's business and its relationship to the proposed bargaining unit, including geographic considerations if more than one plant is involved.

In cases of partial unionization, the NLRB is again considering the extent and manner of self-organization among employees. Formerly, the board had dismissed union petitions to organize a bargaining unit in only one department of a multidepartment enterprise on the grounds that structural

---

Employees shall have the right to self-organization, to form, join, or assist labor organizations, to bargain collectively through representatives of their own choosing, and to engage in *other* concerted activities for the purpose of collective bargaining or other mutual aid or protection, *and shall also have the right to refrain from any or all of such activities except to the extent that such right may be affected by an agreement requiring membership in a labor organization as a condition of employment as authorized in section 8(a) (3).*

The last part of section 7, quoted above, refers to a valid union shop agreement.

logic called for a bargaining unit embracing all nonsupervisory employees. For instance, in cases involving department stores, supermarkets, and the like, the NLRB will recognize partial organization and establish, as appropriate, units that constitute only a part of the larger unit that might ultimately be deemed more logical. Thus, in two cases involving J. C. Penney Company, the board determined that units restricted to employees in the service department of an auto center were appropriate bargaining units.[9]

OLD AND NEW
STRUCTURAL PROBLEMS

Continuing structural problem areas for the NLRB and practitioners of bargaining include:

1. The craft versus industrial unit issue, with its companion problem of craft severance from an industrial unit.
2. Multiemployer bargaining structures and other forms of centralized bargaining arrangements, with the variety of problems posed by increased policy-making authority in the hands of the international union.

Among the newer structural problems we may list:

1. Coalition bargaining and interunion and international coordination in bargaining with employers.
2. Unit problems and related structural difficulties posed by the new laissez-faire, "first come, first served" organizational approach of unions attempting to reach the unorganized.
3. Union organization of hospital units.
4. Fragmentation problems in state, county, and municipal units.
5. Bargaining units in the federal sector—effects of the Civil Service Reform Act of 1978 and various executive orders.

We shall first review the old or perennial structural problems and then take up some of the newer structural challenges.

---

9. *J. C. Penney Company*, 196 NLRB 446, 80 LRRM 1027 (1972) and 196 NLRB 708, 80 LRRM 1071 (1972).

The Craft–Industrial Unit Controversy

The craft–industrial structural controversy is almost as old as the labor movement. Following the 1935 split between the AFL and the CIO, the NLRB was frequently put on the spot in rival union disputes over representation rights. Section 9(b) imposed on the board the duty to decide in each such case on the appropriate unit. There was no way to "duck" this responsibility. In 1937 the board developed what can be regarded as a sound pragmatic solution consistent with its statutory duty.

The board's 1937 answer, known as the *Globe doctrine*, was also an ingenious approach to coping with the vexing political problems of the majority and minority rights. The board applied it in cases where one or more AFL unions were petitioning for separate craft unit(s) as appropriate and an industrial union (CIO) was urging the appropriateness of a single plant-wide P & M unit. In such cases, the NLRB held that, *when the considerations were evenly balanced*, it would allow the desires of employees in the minority craft group(s) to determine its decision.[10]

The ballots of employees in the disputed group(s) were segregated and counted separately. If a majority in a craft group voted for the petitioning AFL affiliate, the NLRB concluded that the employees desired a separate unit for purposes of collective bargaining. If a majority voted for the CIO union, this was interpreted by the NLRB as signifying a desire to be included in the broader industrial or P & M unit.

During the Wagner Act era, the board did not follow the *Globe* formula unless it found that the considerations were "evenly balanced" as between a separate craft unit(s) and an inclusive P & M unit. In 1947 Congress amended section 9(b) in a way that was presumptively favorable to self-determination by minority craft groups.

The amended 9(b) served to encourage craft separatism in a number of industries where industrial or P & M bargaining units had been operating for some time.

The *Mallinckrodt* Doctrine

In 1967 the board chose *Mallinckrodt Chemical Works* as a vehicle for reexamination of the issue as to the circumstances justifying craft severance.[11] Under *Mallinckrodt*, the board considers *all* the following factors as relevant to a proper decision in any severance case:

1. Status of the employees as craftsmen working at their craft or of employees in a traditionally distinct department.

---

10. *Globe Machine & Stamping Co.*, 3 NLRB 294 (1937), involved three AFL craft unions and the UAW. The board held that in cases such as this, "where the considerations are so evenly balanced, the determining factor is the desire of the men themselves."
11. *Mallinckrodt Chemical Works, Uranium Division*, 162 NLRB 387 (December 30, 1966).

2. Existing patterns of bargaining relationships, their stabilizing effect, and the possible effect of altering them.
3. Separate identity of the employees within the broader unit.
4. History and pattern of bargaining in the industry.
5. Degree of integration and interdependence of the production system.
6. Qualification and experience of the union seeking to represent the employees.

This sounds commendably thorough on the board's part. Board member Fanning predicted, however, that consideration of *all* these factors "will inevitably make bargaining history the controlling consideration, and inasmuch as the issue cannot arise except where there is a bargaining history, the application of *Mallinckrodt* factors will effectively rule out craft severance."

It seems clear that craft groups finding themselves unhappily locked into a P & M unit are not going to find the road out easy under *Mallinckrodt*. Perhaps the road should not be made easy for them. On the other hand, it goes against the grain to say that any group of employees should be constrained for any length of time to be represented in collective bargaining by a union or unions not of their own choosing.

There appears to be no completely effective or satisfying answer to the problem of craft severance. One can easily find fault with Congress for seeking to "move in" on the board's discretion in determining units. One can also be critical of a sweeping policy that would sanction either automatic exit upon demand or the freezing of craft groups within P & M units against their manifest will.

The only effective approach seems to be a carefully eclectic one, weighing the special circumstances in each case as it arises. The long-run results of so doing may be inconsistent and will doubtless be unsatisfactory to any who seek a simplistic formula.

Will Craft–Industrial Unit Disputes Decline?

Clashes between proponents of craft unionism and industrial unionism will probably never cease entirely, although the cost and futility of interunion raiding was demonstrated conclusively long ago.[12] In fact, the wastefulness of raiding was a key consideration leading to the merging of

---

12. The basic futility of raiding was conclusively demonstrated in the thorough statistical analysis made by Joseph Krislov, which showed that, although particular affiliated unions might have gained by raiding, the net overall percentage change as between AFL and CIO unions was negligible. See Joseph Krislov, "Raiding Among the 'Legitimate' Unions," *Industrial and Labor Relations Review*, 8 (October 1954), 19–29.

AFL and CIO in 1955.[13] Since the merger, craft–industrial unit conflicts have diminished considerably, although craft groups within P & M units frequently allege that their bargaining interests are being neglected. As an example, the UAW faced a delicate problem in satisfying the wage demands of its skilled trade components in both the 1973 and 1976 negotiations in the automobile industry.

A related source of tension, stemming not from craft–industry unit differences, but from differences in work performed by separate groups belonging to the same union, has become evident in the rubber and steel industries. The rubber industry basically has two components; the tire-producing sector and the nontire, rubber producing sector. Members of the Big Five rubber companies vary considerably in the proportion of tire products to other rubber products produced, but workers in the tire sectors have traditionally been paid a higher wage. This differential has been the source of considerable animosity between the groups, and negotiators for the union have the task of satisfying both groups at once. Similarly, a few years ago in the steel industry the Steelworkers Union was unsuccessful in its attempt to negotiate a wage and incentive package agreeable for both the steel mill workers and the miners. The latter element of the Steelworkers Union closed down mines in Minnesota's Iron Range and in upper Michigan for more than four months over a demand for parity with the "inside" locals, who were seen as having an unnecessary advantage on the incentive issue.

The declining incidence of interunion warfare should probably be regarded on balance as a constructive development. We should acknowledge, however, that when rival union conflicts come to an end (through merger or otherwise) the cherished concept of "unions of their own choosing" loses much of its meaning. Employees currently seeking to unionize for the first time are often realistically limited to one union and to one form of bargaining unit structure.[14] They do not have the opportunity to shop around for the labor organizations competing for their allegiance.

The NLRB's Preference for Multiplant Units

Concerned about this lack of choice, George Brooks and Mark Thompson have been highly critical of the NLRB's strong predilection for multiplant units with its consequent adverse effect on free choice of

13. See Mark L. Kahn, "Recent Jurisdictional Developments in Organized Labor," in Harold W. Davey, Howard S. Kaltenborn, and Stanley H. Ruttenberg, eds., *New Dimensions in Collective Bargaining* (New York: Harper & Row, Pub., 1959), pp. 3–28. Also Arthur J. Goldberg, *AFL–CIO: Labor United* (New York: McGraw-Hill, 1956).
14. See George W. Brooks and Mark Thompson, "Multiplant Units: The NLRB's Withdrawal of Free Choice," *Industrial and Labor Relations Review*, 2 (April 1967), 363–80.

representation in particular plants.[15] The certified union on a multiplant basis may not be serving the needs of employees in a particular plant, but the remedy of selecting another labor organization is difficult to achieve.

Brooks and Thompson contend that the NLRB has already made clear to the parties in multiplant units how to continue living in their "carefully protected world," through avoiding such hazards as decertification, craft severance petitions, independent unionism, or the nuisance of elections. They can do so, say Brooks and Thompson, by merely inserting in their contract a clear statement of intent to bargain on a multiplant basis, carefully listing the plants covered thereby and always taking pains to use the words "agreement" and "unit" in the singular. In this way, it is asserted, the multiplant unit becomes invulnerable to separatism by the dissatisfied at any one plant. The board's formal policy on this is that the single unit is appropriate unless it has been effectively merged by bargaining history, or the plant is so integrated with another plant that it has lost its separate identity. Also, when a plant is acquired by a multiplant company in which previous bargaining has been on a multiplant basis, the NLRB allows a self-determination election in which those employees can determine whether they want to be represented as a single unit or to be included in the existing multiplant unit structure.[16]

The trend toward more inclusive bargaining units appears likely to continue, however. The requirements of bargaining will take priority over self-determination goals, particularly where the former accommodate the institutional security needs of the union involved and also make sense in terms of the structural development of the employer. The Brooks–Thompson critique is relevant, however, to the following discussion of multiemployer bargaining, centralized bargaining, and multiunion, coalition, or coordinated bargaining. Their indictment should not be casually dismissed.

The Logic of Centralized Bargaining Structures and Multiemployer Bargaining

Structural forms of bargaining developed by both management and organized labor have been influenced by the apparent need for increasing centralization of authority over policy determination. There is a constant pressure to match organizational strength with coextensive organizational strength wherever possible.

Centralization of bargaining structures has been in evidence for some

---

15. Brooks and Thompson would permit elections on a plant basis without regard to whether the plant in question is already a part of a multiplant unit. *Ibid.*, p. 378.

16. Bureau of National Affairs, "Labor Relations Expediter," *Labor Relations Reporter* (current), LRX 56–57.

time. It is a corollary of the increasing size of many business and labor organizations.[17] As a corporation or a labor organization expands, the possibility of effective local determination of basic policies (let alone conduct of actual negotiation in collective bargaining) diminishes accordingly.[18]

This basic shift in the locus of power in bargaining relationships scarcely needs illustration. In many unions, particularly in manufacturing, there has been a steady acceleration of power in the hands of the international union at the expense of its member locals. On the management side, the pattern of centralization is most clearly visible in the rapid development of employer associations for labor relations, chiefly when the key labor organization in the field is more powerful than individual employers in the industry affected.

Highly centralized bargaining characterizes such industries as automobiles, steel, and rubber. Although contracts are still signed on a company-by-company basis, the negotiations themselves are hard to distinguish from formal multiemployer bargaining.

The UAW and the major auto companies still preserve the appearance of separate negotiations, but employers engage in constant communication and information sharing as the nearly simultaneous negotiation sessions go forward. In steel, eleven major companies bargain on a united front basis with the Steelworkers Union, although each company signs its own agreement.[19] For some time, the major rubber companies have conducted virtually simultaneous negotiations with the United Rubber, Cork, Linoleum and Plastic Workers of America, AFL–CIO. Once again we can note a high degree of coordination on the management side, even though the bargaining remains technically on an individual company basis.[20]

In the industries mentioned, it is most unlikely that the *de facto* centralization on the employer side will be transformed into *de jure*

17. According to BLS, reporting on membership for some 174 national unions, in 1978 the 14 largest unions, each having a total membership of over 500,000, represented 57 percent of the total membership in unions. For comparison, this service noted that the 84 smallest unions, having membership totals of less than 25,000 members, accounted for a mere 2.4 percent of all union members. See Bureau of Labor Statistics, U.S. Department of Labor, *Directory of National Unions of Labor Statistics,* 1979, Bulletin 2079 (Washington, D.C.: Government Printing Office, 1980), p. 61. These figures dramatize the extent to which there has developed a concentration within the labor movement not unlike the concentration of a more familiar nature in the big business category.

18. Not that local bargaining is no longer prevalent or effective. See, for example, John J. Collins, *Bargaining at the Local Level* (New York: Fordham University Press, 1974).

19. During the 1977 iron mine strike in Minnesota and Michigan over "local" issues, the companies stuck fairly close together, although United States Steel, the largest of the group, had to do some policing to keep potentially wayward members in line.

20. Perhaps more accurately, these industries can be characterized by two distinct bargaining levels. At the centralized company–industry level, wages, fringes, and some working condition terms are negotiated. At the local level, working condition terms applicable only to the local bargaining unit are negotiated. Union members are governed by two contracts: a central (master) agreement and a local agreement.

multiemployer structures and contracts. Information sharing, coordination in strategy, and constant communication are already well developed, but the technical bargaining structure in all probability will remain on a single-company basis. An important consideration is the justifiable fear of running afoul of federal antitrust legislation. Furthermore, steel, automobile, and rubber have been noted for the fierce individualistic autonomy displayed by the corporate giants involved.

Formal multiemployer bargaining has long been a popular bargaining structure when many small employers are confronted by a union that is far more powerful economically than any of them individually. When small employers must negotiate with a union representing all or nearly all of the workers in the particular industry or labor market area, the pooling of management strength and knowhow in a multiemployer organization for labor relations purposes makes complete sense from the employers' standpoint.

Employer labor relations associations developed first in highly competitive, small-firm industries such as men's and women's clothing, trucking, and baking, rather than in oligopolistic industries such as automobiles, steel, and meatpacking. The large and powerful firms in the latter case are reluctant to surrender any portion of their existing sovereignty to a central labor relations policy committee. They still consider their individual economic strength sufficient to warrant effective separate negotiations with the chief labor organization involved, although "cooperation" among the corporate giants is visibly increasing.

The continued growth of multiemployer bargaining arrangements is favored by both management and union needs for greater institutional security. Whether the industry be oligopolistic or competitive, the unions involved never feel entirely secure when employers are only partially organized. The economic power of an industrial union rests not on control of the labor supply but on control of the employer through negotiated job security provisions and union shop clauses. With some exceptions, such as longshoring, industrial unions do not concern themselves with the employer's hiring policies. Nor are they in a position to restrict entrance to the trade, as are many craft unions. The institutional security of an industrial union depends on consolidating its position in the industry by unionizing all employers if possible, and certainly all the major ones. When an industry is only partially unionized, the unorganized segment represents a constant threat to (or restraint upon) standards negotiated with the union firms. Textiles and chemicals are two examples of partially unionized industries where the unions involved are always "insecure."

Such considerations are basic to union drives for full unionization of an industry in order to take wages out of competition and to insure effective similarity in basic employment conditions. Once these objectives have been achieved, the institutional security of the union (or unions) in question is assured. The union leadership can then become more "states-manlike," particularly when industry coverage takes the structural form of a multiemployer bargaining unit. Associational bargaining sharply reduces the possibility of successful rival unionism and effectively narrows the options of the employees involved.

Where formal multiemployer bargaining arrangements are not feasible, as in the case of oligopolistic industries dominated by a few large firms, union emphasis will often be on pattern bargaining as the most effective instrumentality for achieving an approximation of uniformity on basic economic provisions, major fringes, and key contract clauses governing on-the-job relationships. Again, the underlying motivation is union institutional security flowing from the achievement and protection of desired standards.

A comparable logic often lies behind management support for multiemployer bargaining arrangements. Under an associational union agreement, an employer may actually be paying higher wages and benefits than would have been the case under single-company bargaining. However, if the employer knows that principal competitors are operating under approximately the same conditions, the employer is freed from the fear of being "whipsawed" by the union or of being undersold in the market by other employers paying "substandard" wages.

The multiemployer agreement, by taking wages out of competition, removes important unknown factors in the employer's advance calculations. It reduces risk and uncertainty and promotes stability. In spite of the continued homage paid to the competitive ideal in our economy, most employers prudently seek to avoid the risks of competition when they can. Multiemployer bargaining arrangements are frequently a product of management desire to avoid the hazards of competition.

The necessity for equalizing bargaining strength has also been a powerful stimulus to multiemployer bargaining. A union organizing an industry with strong central employer control has to unionize the entire industry before it can achieve a power position equal to the employers' united front. Employers in an industry controlled by a single union have a similar incentive to combination. Such employers are individually incapable of negotiating effectively with a labor organization whose power is coextensive with the industry as a whole. It is in the self-interest of such employers to combine into a labor relations association under such circumstances.

Multiemployer Bargaining Structures: Boon or Curse?

The arguments for and against multiemployer bargaining retain a lively interest for most observers of the collective bargaining process. The controversy illustrates a major finding in this analysis, as stressed in the preceding chapter, namely, the fascinating variety in bargaining arrangements.

There is no model structure in collective bargaining that can be scientifically approved as best for all concerned in all situations. How one views multiemployer bargaining as a structural form depends greatly on his expectations and assumptions. For example, multiemployer bargaining clearly promotes stability at the expense of some loss of discretion and flexibility in local union–management relationships. Whether this is viewed as a plus or a minus depends on the relative importance one attaches to stability, on the one hand, and local autonomy, on the other.

To take one more illustration, multiemployer bargaining promotes wage uniformity for particular categories of labor. It insures similarity in the timing and amount of changes in wage levels and basic fringes in the entire unit covered by the master contract. Most parties to multiemployer arrangements, whether they be union or management, favor taking wages out of competition. Such a development will not be regarded favorably by those who prefer single-employer bargaining as a matter of principle or who fear that consumer costs will be higher when wages are not determined "competitively" through the market mechanism.

The arguments for and against multiemployer bargaining do not change appreciably over the years. We shall outline them at this point.

The Case for Multiemployer Bargaining

The principal arguments in favor of multiemployer bargaining include the following:

1. Determination of wage policy on a multiemployer basis (particularly when the bargaining is genuinely industry-wide or area-wide) will effectively remove wages as a competitive element in cost. Such a stabilization through application of uniform standards enables employers to know where they stand on the vital element of labor cost in comparison with their competitors in the industry or in the area.
2. Removal of labor cost as a competitive item will intensify product and market competition in other areas such as managerial efficiency, worker productivity, quality of product, and distributive efficiency. The consumer should actually benefit from this intensified nonwage competition.
3. Multiemployer bargaining is generally more mature and responsible than individual plant negotiations. The employers and the union may be expected to have an informed and farsighted understanding of the future impact of their wage bargain.
4. Multiemployer bargaining permits effective joint efforts to withstand

the ruinous competition from nonunion sectors of the same industry or from low-paying producers of substitutable products in other industries. As multiemployer bargaining approaches genuine industry-wide arrangements, the submarginal firm is either brought into line or frozen out.

5. The individual employer actually has more of a voice under multiemployer bargaining than he is likely to have under pattern bargaining. Also, multiemployer bargaining can be sufficiently flexible to permit special departures from the industry norm when this is necessary. Under pattern bargaining, on the other hand, the individual firm faced by a very powerful union may have to swallow the whole pattern on a take-it-or-else basis.

6. Multiemployer bargaining should have greater beneficial effects in relation to general economic stability than bargaining on an individual employer basis for the following reasons:
   a. In multiemployer bargaining serious consideration can be given to the relationship between increases or decreases in wage rates and the volume of employment opportunities. This is an unlikely possibility under a fractionalized bargaining structure.
   b. General wage movements may be slower and less extreme under multiemployer bargaining arrangements than is frequently the case under individual plant bargaining. To the extent that this is the case, multiemployer bargaining may operate as a restraining influence in inflationary periods and as a cushioning or stabilizing force during deflationary periods.

7. Multiemployer bargaining arrangements permit workable accommodations between the simultaneous needs for uniformity and diversity. The interdependent structure of our economy increasingly requires central determination of major policy issues in the interests of uniformity. This can best be done through multiemployer bargaining. At the same time, the genuine values of democratic labor relations can be preserved by providing for a maximum of decentralization in administration and implementation of centrally negotiated collective agreements.

The Case Against Multiemployer Bargaining

The arguments generally raised against multiemployer bargaining include the following:

1. Multiemployer bargaining on wages and other economic demands will produce an undesirable uniformity rather than equitable stabilization

of labor costs. Wages cease being a measure of employee productivity and the result will be joint collusion against consumer interests.

2. Instead of raising the intensity of nonwage competition, multiemployer bargaining will produce a cost structure so high that new firms will be unable to enter the industry. Multiemployer bargaining subsidizes labor inefficiency and results in undesirable economic concentration at the consumer's expense.

3. Wage rigidities in a declining market will increase unemployment, reduce purchasing power, and simultaneously keep upward pressure on aggregate prices.

4. Individual firms will be unable to achieve policies suited to their own needs. They will be bound by the terms of a master agreement in those negotiations where they had little chance to secure recognition for their particular problems and requirements.

5. Multiemployer bargaining destroys decision-making authority by local unions. Such a result completely negates the concept of the union as an instrument for democratization of industrial relations. The subordination of the local union to the international union is not limited to negotiation of major policy issues but takes place in contract administration as well.

6. Centralized bargaining structures, particularly when industry-wide in scope, are antagonistic to the principles of the competitive free enterprise system. Monopoly power is strengthened on both sides of the bargaining table. It is unrealistic to assert that management and union "giants" will under organized bilateral monopoly be "responsible" and sensitive to consumer interests. As consumer frustration and anger increase, the demand for increased public intervention will lead eventually to wage–price–investment controls and to the end of the private enterprise economy as we know it.

Detached analysis of multiemployer bargaining as a structural form requires the conclusion that a purely favorable or unfavorable verdict is not appropriate. The source and direction of the arguments listed must be carefully noted. In any event, academic controversy over the merits of multiemployer bargaining has not visibly affected the practitioners. Multiemployer bargaining structures have proven to be remarkably durable and seem to have been generally satisfactory to the parties.

Perhaps the most publicized examples of multiemployer bargaining structures are those in trucking and construction. These are also industries where the tacit employer–union collusion against the best interests of the consumer is always a possibility. James R. Hoffa's amoral end-justifies-the-means approach in labor relations caused him to be regarded as chief villain of the labor movement. His stormy career could form the basis for an interesting digression.[21] However, we shall simply note the dedication Hoffa had to enlarging the coverage of multiemployer trucking contracts to approximate true national bargaining in this industry. Most trucking firms, understandably concerned about the economic strength of the Teamsters, appear to support multiemployer contracts just as vigorously as Hoffa himself did. Only through such a structural form can trucking management hope to negotiate with the Teamsters on approximately equal terms. For economic power reasons, the Teamsters *and* the truckers *jointly favor joint bargaining*.

In the building and construction field, particularly in urban areas, the bargaining is often on a multiemployer basis between the basic craft unions and various employer construction associations. In construction, labor cost represents a substantial portion of total cost. The wage bill is perhaps a bit stiffer than it might be if there were more complete multiemployer bargaining. Current practice generally involves separate negotiations at different times with several contractors' associations. This suggests that management in the construction industry might improve its bargaining leverage through greater unity among contractors of all types.

SOME STRUCTURAL PROBLEMS
WITH NEW DIMENSIONS

Another important aspect of the centralized bargaining structure trend relates to what is termed "coalition bargaining" or "coordinated bargaining."[22] The structural phenomenon that has given prominence to coalition bargaining is the growth of "conglomerate" enterprises. Union efforts at coalition bargaining are not new.[23] However, the drive to achieve company-wide contracts with conglomerates is a new twist.

21. Much has been written about the Teamsters and James R. Hoffa. One of the most thorough and absorbing works is that of Ralph and Estelle James, *Hoffa and the Teamsters* (Princeton, N.J.: D. Van Nostrand, 1965).

22. The terms "coalition bargaining" and "coordinated bargaining" are used interchangeably by some writers. Others seek to draw neat distinctions between the two. Management practitioners generally speak of coalition bargaining whereas union spokesmen prefer the term coordinated bargaining. Both are talking about what Lynn Wagner has termed "multi-union bargaining" in his analysis of the legal aspects of this structural phenomenon. See Lynn E. Wagner, "Multi-Union Bargaining: A Legal Analysis," *Labor Law Journal*, 19 (December 1968), 731–42. Wagner uses the term coalition bargaining to apply to situations where two or more unions bargain jointly for a common "master agreement" covering all the employees which they purport to represent. He applies the term coordinated bargaining to circumstances where two or more unions representing separate bargaining units are negotiating jointly for individual unit contracts containing common terms.

23. Multiunion bargaining in a more conventional sense is a familiar thing in building and construction and in the metal trades. In many cases, the multiple craft unions involved maintain their craft identity while at the same time negotiating as a joint union council with either a common single employer or with a multiemployer association.

The best-known example of union coalition bargaining with conglomerates involves the IUE (International Union of Electrical, Radio and Machine Workers, AFL–CIO), together with some eleven other AFL–CIO unions negotiating with General Electric and Westinghouse.[24] It is by no means the only one. The Industrial Union Department (IUD) of the AFL–CIO has established more than fifty interunion "coordinating committees." Most of these committees are set up on an employer basis and have been initiated with the hope that the interunion cooperation will be a continuing thing rather than just a contract-time association.

It is important to consider the possible impact on bargaining structures from such an intensified union emphasis on coalition or coordinated bargaining. The heart of the coalition bargaining matter is comparative economic strength. The unions' concern relates to the felt compulsion to match institutional management power. Which structural arrangement is the most logical and which bargaining unit is most appropriate are of secondary importance. The unions participating in coordinated bargaining efforts remain conscious of their traditional autonomy and organizational lines. However, they have a paramount interest in developing a united front in negotiating with conglomerate employers. The conglomerate illustrates an important structural change on the management side of the bargaining table. Whether it will be paralleled by organic structural changes on the union side is an intriguing question.

Another continuing structural trend on the management side is corporate expansion of production and distribution beyond the bounds of one country. This change toward multinational corporations presents unions in one country with a difficult bargaining problem: employers may threaten to move production to another country if they find union demands sufficiently unattractive. Thus, national unions around the world face "whipsawing" by the multinational employer. If a union in nation A settles for employment terms X, the multinational can effectively demand terms Y better than or equal to terms X from the union in country B by threatening to move jobs to country A. Natural responses to the growth of multinational corporations are multinational unionism or multinational bargaining coalitions.[25]

Obstacles to extensive international cooperation by unions, however, appear formidable. In fact, little true transnational bargaining has yet occurred, although some information has been exchanged among the

24. For an optimistic union analysis of the 1966 bargaining with GE and Westinghouse, see David Lasser, "A Victory for Coordinated Bargaining," *AFL–CIO American Federationist*, April 1967. For a less sympathetic analysis, see a monograph by William L. Chernish, *Coalition Bargaining: A Study of Union Tactics and Public Policy* (Philadelphia: University of Pennsylvania Press, 1969).

25. Although many North American unions carry "International" in their name, few have members beyond the bounds of the U.S. and Canada.

national unions. Obstacles to international union cooperation include the following:

1. Nation by nation, as mentioned in Chapter 1, practices of collective bargaining vary tremendously; it is exceedingly difficult to reconcile several modes of practice into one common bargaining framework.
2. Labor regulations differ by nation. Often, the regulation of one nation contradicts the regulation of another. Finding a common settlement area that does not violate at least one nation's regulation may be an impossible task.
3. Union structures vary nation by nation. Unions have organized around industries, around skill groups, around religion or ideology, or around political parties. Cooperation between a broad-based political union in one nation and a union representing a narrow skill group in another nation, for example, is difficult because they share few of the same objectives.
4. Economic conditions differ among nations at any given time. In one nation, where unemployment is high, jobs may be most important. In another nation, where unemployment is low, better pay or working conditions may be most important to union supporters. Reaching agreement on transnational union bargaining will be difficult if higher wage rates must be traded for fewer jobs, or more jobs traded for lower wage rates.[26]

The Laissez-Faire Approach to Organizing the Unorganized—Its Impact on Bargaining Structures

In the days of Samuel Gompers, great stress was laid on the importance of unique or exclusive jurisdiction. Each affiliated union had an assigned territory to which its organizational ambitions were to be confined. In a craft-dominated federation, this principle of one union to a trade or craft made sense as a means of avoiding what Gompers regarded as a cardinal sin, that is, dual unionism.[27]

One reason why the CIO was anathema to old-line AFL craft unionists

---

26. For a discussion on this general topic, see Howard D. Samuel, "Transnational Collective Bargaining: An Idea Whose Time Has Not Come," *Labor Law Journal*, 29 (October 1978), 619–24.

27. For a perceptive analysis of the erosion of the Gompers unique jurisdiction concept, see Benjamin S. Stephansky, "The Structure of the American Labor Movement," in *Interpreting the Labor Movement* George W. Brooks et al., eds., (Madison, Wis.: Industrial Relations Research Association, 1952), pp. 39–69.

was that John L. Lewis took over the exclusive jurisdiction idea on behalf of industrial unions, thus seeking to foreclose any craft organizing within steel, automobiles, and other basic manufacturing industries. Once the AFL recovered from the shock of the early CIO successes, many of its affiliated unions went into direct competition with the CIO by organizing on an industrial basis as well as seeking to maintain or create craft units within P & M domains. Twenty years of union organizational warfare had a shattering effect on the old concept of unique or exclusive jurisdiction. When the two rival federations were at last ready to merge there was a tacit recognition in both camps that merger was possible only through accepting the representational holdings of each AFL and CIO affiliate at the time as being appropriate, whatever they may have been, and then continuing to enforce the 1953 no-raiding agreement.[28]

In the years since the merger of AFL and CIO in 1955 there has not been any appreciable amount of tidying up of organizational status, either through organic merger of rival unions or through surrender by any union of membership territory already acquired. The voices of the structural purists have been muted. Furthermore, drives to organize the unorganized have been led mainly by unions such as the Teamsters that have displayed a thorough lack of concern over whether the employees they were signing up might not more logically have been unionized by another organization.

The enterprise shown by the Teamsters in recent years has made it our closest approximation to the British concept of a "general" union. The Teamsters have readily adapted their structural bargaining forms in custom-made fashion to the requirements and preferences of employee groups choosing them for representational purposes. In one case, it may be a conventional P & M unit; in another, a strict craft unit or a multiple-craft structure. Among the more unusual categories currently represented by Teamsters locals we can list the following: registered nurses, retail department store employees, soya bean processing mill employees, public school teachers, policemen, and flight attendants.

If one starts from the premise that employees are better off being bargained for by *some* union rather than *no* union, there is no cause to be concerned about the new approach to organizing the unorganized. If, however, one assumes that there should be *some* correlation between union specialization in employment categories and ability to provide effective representation, there is room to doubt whether the laissez-faire approach is likely to prove optimal from the standpoint of either the employees concerned or the labor movement as such. Whatever one's view may be, it is a fact that much organizing initiative has been successfully undertaken in recent years by the "wrong" unions.

28. See David L. Cole, "Jurisdictional Issues and the Promise of Merger," *Industrial and Labor Relations Review*, 9 (April 1956), 391–405.

Some intriguing examples of the new organizing approach can be found in the public sector. Although unions with traditional jurisdictional rights in government employment have shown substantial growth since January 1962, considerable organizing initiative has also been displayed by some unions that are generally private sector oriented. In Austin, Minnesota, for example, the city's police officers are represented by the Amalgamated Meatcutters and Butcher Workman's International. This illustration is by no means unusual or atypical.

Union Organization of Hospital Units

Prior to 1974, the NLRB claimed jurisdiction only over proprietary hospitals and nursing homes and was excluded by statute from asserting jurisdiction over nonprofit hospitals. Until that time, nonprofit hospitals had been excluded from the definition of "an employer" in Section 2(2) of the National Labor Relations Act.[29]

In 1974, however, the act was amended to include a new category of employer, namely, the "health care institutions."[30] In Section 2(14) a health care institution is broadly defined to include previously exempted nonprofit hospitals, health maintenance organizations, and clinics. It also brings proprietary hospitals and nursing homes under the special provisions now applicable to health care institutions. For example, there are more stringent notice requirements in anticipation of terminating or modifying contracts in health care institutions than apply to other organizations.[31] There are also special notice requirements to be met before a union may strike or picket at a health care institution.[32]

During the congressional hearings leading to the passage of the aforementioned amendments to the act, concern was expressed that unit fragmentation might become a problem in the health care industry and inpatient care. Congress, in response to this concern, directed that the board give due consideration to preventing proliferation of bargaining units in the health care industry.[33]

The board, in 1975, established a five-unit structure for use in the determination of appropriate bargaining units in hospitals. This structure established the following as separate bargaining units: (1) registered nurses (RN); (2) all other professionals; (3) technicals, including licensed practical nurses (LPN); (4) business office clericals; and (5) service and maintenance

29. 61 Stat. 137, 29 USC 152(2) (1947).
30. 88 Stat. 395, 29 USC 152(2) (14) (1974).
31. 88 Stat. 395, 396, 29 USC 158(d) (1974).
32. 88 Stat. 395, 396, 29 USC 158(g) (1974).
33. Allan L. Bioff, Lawrence J. Cohen, and Kurt L. Hanslowe, eds., *The Developing Labor Law: The Board, the Courts, and the National Labor Relations Act Cumulative Supplement 1971–75* (Washington, D.C.: Bureau of National Affairs, 1976), p. 128.

employees.[34] The board has allowed other units, established prior to 1975, to remain as they are but encourages them to reorganize following the new guidelines whenever a change is considered.[35]

There are numerous unions and employee associations involved in the organization of health care workers. The largest ones have been the Service Employees International Union (SEIU), Local 1199 of the Retail, Wholesale and Department Store Union, and the American Nurses Association, while, as mentioned earlier, the Teamsters have also been active.[36]

A final structural consideration in the health care industry includes the positioning of physicians in unit questions. In a controversial board decision, it was decided by a four-to-one vote that "residents" and "interns" are primarily "students," not "employees," and therefore are without rights under the act.[37] This determination was controversial. Member Fanning, while dissenting, noted that apprentices, trainees, and students in other occupational walks of life have never been exempt from the definition of an "employee" because of such status. Thus, consistency and past practice weighed against the NLRB's decision, and it was reversed by a U.S. appeals court in 1979.[38]

In general, physicians and dentists have shown increasing interest in collective bargaining. Practically nonexistent before 1972, some twenty-six organizations had become established and claimed a total membership of over 16,000 doctors and dentists by 1973. Both the American Medical Association and the American Dental Association have opposed unionization in these professions on the grounds that unionization is the very antithesis of individualism and would necessarily downgrade the profession.[39]

Fragmentation Problems in State, County, and Municipal Sectors

Congress showed concern about fragmentation of hospital units, in part, because the problem of fragmentation or proliferation of bargaining units has been a problem in state, county, and municipal units for some time.

---

34. *Ibid.*

35. *Ibid.*, p. 133.

36. A. Elliot Berkeley, ed., *Labor Relations in Hospitals and Health Care Facilities*, Proceedings of a Conference Presented by the American Arbitration Association and the Federal Mediation and Conciliation Service, June 10–11, 1975, (Washington, D.C.: Bureau of National Affairs, 1976), p. 47.

37. *Cedar–Sinai Medical Center*, 233 NLRB 57 (1976), 91 LRRM 1398 (1976).

38. *Physicians National House Staff Assn.* v. *Murphy*, 85 LC 11,205 (1979).

39. Mario F. Bognanno, James B. Dworkin, and Omotayo Fashoyin, "Physicians' and Dentists' Bargaining Organizations: A Preliminary Look," *Monthly Labor Review*, Bureau of Labor Statistics, U.S. Department of Labor, June 1975, p. 33.

Although most administrative and legislative bodies would rather deal with a single union, that goal seems a long way off. To make matters worse, there are a few government officials who think that the "divide and conquer" technique is still effective. Thus, largely as a result of this kind of thinking, there is a multiplicity of bargaining units in most large cities and municipalities.

The City of New York provides the clearest example of the problems of fragmentation. When negotiations in that city began, the scope of bargaining was very limited, and so there was little concern about the long-range consequences of a large number of small bargaining units. Later, when bargaining was mandated by law, the unions became involved in intense rivalry over wages, hours, and conditions of employment. Unions representing essentially the same types of workers in different departments tried to outdo each other, which resulted in chain reactions, whipsawing, and unnecessarily delayed bargaining.

Once excessive fragmentation has developed, it is not easily overcome. One possible solution is to encourage multiemployer bargaining by employees in similar occupational groups. For example, the amalgamated units of the International Union of Operating Engineers, Local 49, and twenty-one suburban municipalities in the Minneapolis–St. Paul area, represented by the Metropolitan Area Management Association (MAMA), have negotiated on a multiemployer basis for nearly a decade. Consequently, a common wage scale exists for road maintenance and equipment operators employed by these cities. Both groups are represented by labor relations experts and significant bargaining economies have resulted. Since 1973, the various communities comprising MAMA and the Teamsters' Local 320, representing police officers, have adopted a similar bargaining structure. However, it was not until 1977 that the twenty-three police departments represented by MAMA negotiated their first master agreement with Local 320. This attempt at multiemployer bargaining was short-lived. As a result of unit decertifications, Local 320 and MAMA abandoned this structure by 1980.

In both of these instances, while the certified bargaining unit in question is local in scope, the municipalities and unions involved have entered voluntarily into multiemployer bargaining in an effort to regularize wages and benefits, and to control the use of "leapfrogging" and "whipsawing" as bargaining tactics.

Multilevel bargaining was initiated in New York City in an attempt to minimize the problem of "me-too-ism." In the early 1970s, the city began to bargain on wages, pensions, and other matters of uniform concern across bargaining units. Thus, for example, a union representative and the city's Office of Labor Relations may bargain on, say, salaries for given occupational titles on a city-wide basis. A different bargaining pair may handle negotiations for another set of job titles.[40] The multilevel bargaining effort predated the move to consolidate bargaining units in New York City, which numbered 323 in December 1970. Robert D. Helsby, initial chairman of the state's Public Employment Relations Board (PERB), and Arvid Anderson, initial chairman of New York City's Office of Collective Bargaining (OCB), as well as many of the city's administrative and union leadership had identified fragmentation as a serious labor relations problem demanding treatment. Thus, in 1967 following the adoption of the Taylor Act and the creation of the state's PERB and city's OCB, a quasi-formal program based on neutrality and cooperation from all sides was begun to remedy the ills of fragmentation which had been set in place years earlier.

Multilevel bargaining as a method to resolve city-wide issues also helped to open the door to consolidation. By December 1977 the number of bargaining units in New York City stood at 92. The principal means used to bring about this consolidation were as follows:

1. Through an informal educational process, it became widely understood that fragmentation was weakening collective bargaining in New York City.
2. Departments of city government or employee organizations would petition the OCB for unit consolidation and the OCB would review the matter.
3. The OCB often took the initiative and would review the appropriateness of a given unit structure.
4. Some units were simply dissolved by the OCB because the job titles contained therein had become obsolete or vacant.
5. Under a reorganization of the state's judicial system, action is anticipated which will transfer a small number of court-related bargaining units from the OCB's jurisdiction to the state's PERB jurisdiction.

The state of Hawaii has drawn on statutory powers to prevent fragmentation among public sector units which combine similar occupation across political subdivisions into a single bargaining unit. The following were established as bargaining units on a statewide basis:

1. Nonsupervisory employees in blue-collar positions.
2. Supervisory employees in blue-collar positions.
3. Nonsupervisory employees in white-collar positions.

---

40. Public Personnel Administration, *Labor Management Relations*, 1 (current), 5226. Also, the New York story is based on lengthy discussions with Robert D. Helsby and agents of the city's OCB.

4. Supervisory employees in white-collar positions.
5. Teachers and other personnel of the department of education under the same salary schedule.
6. Educational officers and other personnel of the department of education under the same salary schedule.
7. Faculty of the University of Hawaii and the community college system.
8. Personnel of the University of Hawaii and the community college system, other than faculty.
9. Registered professional nurses.
10. Nonprofessional hospital and institutional workers.
11. Firemen.
12. Policemen.
13. Professional and scientific employees, other than professional nurses.

Also, the several employers, defined in the state's Public Employment Relations Law as including the governor, the several mayors of the four counties of Hawaii, the Board of Education, and the Board of Regents, bargain on a multiemployer basis when each has employees in a particular bargaining unit.[41] For the unique government structure of Hawaii this procedure seems to be working well, but other, more generally applicable solutions, are needed to solve the problems of the majority of cities and states.

In the next section we will discuss, among other things, the problem of fragmentation in the federal sector and the provisions in Executive Order 11491 that focus on this problem.

Bargaining Units in the Federal Sector

The early experience of federal employees with collective bargaining was similar to that of other employees in the United States.[42] Blue-collar skilled craftsmen were the first to be organized, starting in the 1830s when employees in government naval yards struck to obtain the ten-hour day. Over the following three decades federal employees pushed for, and largely received, such demands as "prevailing wage" statutes, and an eight-hour day for most employees. In 1883, Congress passed the Pendleton or Civil Service Act, which established the Civil Service Commission to implement the merit principle for selection, placement, and

41. Jack E. Klauser, "Multi-employer Bargaining in the Public Sector of Hawaii," *Journal of Collective Negotiations*, 6, No. 1 (1977), 73–79.
42. Murray B. Nesbitt, *Labor Relations in the Federal Government Service*, (Washington, D.C.: Bureau of National Affairs, 1976), p. 97.

promotion of employees, and provided that Congress would regulate wages, hours, and working conditions for federal employees. With the role of Congress identified, federal unions, now national in scope, lobbied to improve their members' employment status. This, in turn, led to the infamous "gag rules," issued as executive orders by Presidents Theodore Roosevelt and William Howard Taft. These orders attempted to stop these political activities by prohibiting federal employees from complaining to Congress regarding working conditions. The Lloyd–LaFollette Act of 1912, however, struck down these orders and guaranteed federal employees the right to petition Congress, and also recognized the right of federal employees to join unions. During the following years, the pendulum seemed to swing away from federal unionism. In 1947, the Taft–Hartley Act explicitly prohibited federal employees from striking. Violation of the law is a felony.

Relations seemed to "normalize" during the following years, and in 1962 President John F. Kennedy issued Executive Order 10988. Having the force of law, this order formally authorized limited collective bargaining rights for employees of the executive. There were a succession of executive orders after 1962 and in 1978 Congress passed and President Jimmy Carter signed the Civil Service Reform Act. An in-depth analysis of executive orders and the Civil Service Reform Act is reserved for a later chapter. We will outline in the next few paragraphs the structure of bargaining in the federal sector.

The basic purpose behind the succession of federal regulations has been to bring federal labor relations into line with practices and procedures in the private sector. Parallel to the NLRB, the Federal Labor Relations Authority (FLRA) hears petitions and then determines bargaining units within federal civilian agencies. The FLRA, like the NLRB, is mandated by law to consider both a community of interest among employees and the efficiency of operation of the agency in making its unit determinations.[43]

By 1975, there were in excess of 3,600 separate bargaining units of federal employees.[44] The developing inter- and intra-agency variations in employment relations, as well as the huge direct and indirect outlays for bargaining prompted the Federal Labor Relations Council (a predecessor of sorts to the Authority) to recommend key changes to the President that would have the effect of consolidating units. The FLRA now has the authority to consolidate bargaining units upon request of an agency or union without an election. Thus, efforts to contain unit proliferation in the federal sector are under way.

---

43. 92 Stat. 1201, 5 USC 7112(a) (1978).
44. U.S. Civil Service Commission, Bulletin 711–34, April 30, 1976, p. 14.

SUMMARY

In final summary on other structural problems treated in this chapter we can note as follows:

1. Single-plant P & M units should continue to be the most prevalent in manufacturing. Multiple-craft arrangements will remain dominant in building and construction and in many service industries such as airlines, railroads, and perhaps newspapers.
2. The long-term trend toward centralized bargaining structures should continue, notwithstanding some resurgence of local union initiative. Structural logic and bargaining efforts to obtain company-wide contracts both will serve to promote greater centralization.
3. The craft-industrial controversy will remain with us, but its intensity should be reduced by the impact of technology (prefabricated construction, for example) and by the observed looser patterns of organizing the unorganized.
4. Craft severance from P & M units will be rare under the *Mallinckrodt* approach. The NLRB will continue to receive both deserved and unjust criticism for its decisional policies in this and in other representational case matters.
5. The problem of fragmentation of bargaining units, particularly with respect to state, county, and municipal units, will in all probability be an increasing one. The voluntary multiemployer bargaining arrangement mentioned previously in the Minneapolis–St. Paul area case is the only one of its kind known to the authors, but it is expected that arrangements similar to this will become more common in the future. Fragmentation in the federal sector is being reduced, and will pose a smaller problem in future years.

In Chapter 5 we shall examine the negotiation phase of collective bargaining. The subsequent three chapters will focus on the administration and interpretation phases of the collective bargaining relationship.

Questions for Discussion, Thought, and Research

1. From a union's perspective, the appropriate unit often is the unit which the union feels is most likely to win an NLRB decision. From an employer's perspective, the appropriate unit often is the group of employees most likely to lose an NLRB election. What are the strengths and weaknesses of this approach?

2. Recently, the state of Minnesota consolidated its more than 115 bargaining units into 16 statewide bargaining units. From a union perspective, what are the strengths and possible weaknesses of statewide bargaining units?

3. In some states, fire department officers are included in the same bargaining unit as rank-and-file fire fighters. What rationale could there be for putting supervisors in a bargaining unit with nonsupervisors?

4. Why is multiemployer bargaining prevalent in some industries and virtually unheard of in other industries? What factors give rise to multiemployer bargaining units?

5. What is the NLRB policy toward P & M units?

6. What are the causes of the trend toward centralization of bargaining structures?

7. Does the centralization of bargaining units undermine the union's ability to be democratic? Are the wishes of the rank and file better reflected in centralized bargaining structures?

8. Briefly, summarize the arguments for and against multiemployer bargaining. Which set of arguments do you find more compelling? Why?

9. What are the advantages and disadvantages of fragmented bargaining structures? Do fragmented structures tend to favor unions or employers?

10. Distinguish between multiplant and multiemployer bargaining.

Selected Bibliography

Abodeely, John E., *The NLRB and the Appropriate Bargaining Unit.* Philadelphia: Industrial Research Unit, Wharton School of Finance and Commerce, University of Pennsylvania, 1971.

Berkeley, A. Elliot, ed., *Health Care Facilities, Labor Relations in Hospitals and Proceedings of a Conference Presented by the American Arbitration Association and the Federal Mediation and Conciliation Service.* June 10–11, 1975, Washington, D.C., Bureau of National Affairs, 1976, p. 102.

Chandler, Margaret K., "Craft Bargaining," in John T. Dunlop and Neil W. Chamberlain, eds., *Frontiers of Collective Bargaining.* New York: Harper & Row, Pub., 1967, pp. 50–74.

Galenson, Walter, *The CIO Challenge to the AFL.* Cambridge, Mass.: Harvard University Press, 1960.

Hayford, Stephen L., William A. Durkee, and Charles W. Hickman, "Bargaining Unit Determination Procedures in the Public Sector: A

Comparative Evaluation," *Employee Relations Law Journal*, 5 (Summer 1975), 84–103.

Nesbitt, Murray B., *Labor Relations in the Federal Government Service*. Washington, D.C.: Bureau of National Affairs, 1976, p. 545.

Seidman, Joel, "Bargaining Structure: Some Problems of Complexity and Dislocation," *Labor Law Journal*, 24 (June 1973), 340–50.

Stieber, Jack, *Public Employee Unionism: Structure, Growth, Policy*. Washington, D.C.: Brookings Institute, 1973.

Taft, Philip, *The Structure and Government of Labor Unions*. Cambridge, Mass.: Harvard University Press, 1954.

U.S. Bureau of Labor Statistics, *Directory of National and International Unions* (current). Washington, D.C.: Government Printing Office.

Wagner, Lynn E., "Multi-Union Bargaining: A Legal Analysis," *Labor Law Journal*, 19 (December 1968), 731–42.

Weber, Arnold R., "Stability and Change in the Structure of Collective Bargaining," in Lloyd Ulman, ed., *Challenges to Collective Bargaining*. Englewood Cliffs, N.J.: Prentice-Hall, 1967, pp. 13–36.

Weber, Arnold, ed., *The Structure of Collective Bargaining*. New York: Free Press, 1961.

CONTRACT NEGOTIATION: PRINCIPLES, PROBLEMS, AND PROCEDURES

5

The importance of the negotiation phase of the collective bargaining process is underlined by the blunt fact that if negotiation fails, for whatever reason, there is no contract and thus no viable bargaining relationship. In the drama of collective bargaining as a continuous process, therefore, nearly all actions over time by management and union representatives are geared, consciously or unconsciously, to the period of actual contract negotiation. This usually takes place in contemporary bargaining every two or three years, although many contracts are still negotiated annually, and some for longer than three years.

PROCEDURAL CHALLENGES IN CONTRACT NEGOTIATION

Among the procedural challenges, we may list the following:

1. How to "sell" a new policy or approach developed by management or union leadership to the constituents of both.

2. How to prevent collective bargaining contracts from expanding into "Roman codes" that are too detailed and technical for the average working mortal to comprehend.

3. How to negotiate out of a contract policies and procedures that are no longer pertinent or essential but that may be regarded as sacrosanct by one party or the other (such as outmoded working rules negotiated originally to cover a condition that no longer exists, but whose continuance may benefit some incumbent employees).

4. How to develop effective procedures for joint consideration of such long-range continuing problems as the impact of technological change and industrial relocation, outside the crisis atmosphere of contract negotiation periods.

5. How to improve grievance adjustment machinery to insure prompt handling on the merits at the lower levels by line foremen and union stewards.

6. How to insure the procedural rights of the individual worker, thereby complying with the statutory requirement of fair representation, without sacrificing institutional objectives of stability in contract administration.

The last two problems are reserved for the subsequent discussion of contract administration. The others are considered briefly in the present chapter.

PREPARATION, THE FIRST STEP

Most experienced union and management negotiators agree that the time to begin preparing for the next contract negotiation is immediately after the current agreement has been signed and put into effect. In a constructive relationship, both parties are constantly looking ahead. They do not take pride in recent accomplishments, or lick their wounds after a real or fancied defeat in negotiations just concluded.

The nature of advance preparation for negotiations will vary considerably in terms of the size and importance of the bargaining relationship. If the company and local union in question are part of a multiemployer bargaining setup, their roles may be limited. If it is customary in a particular relationship to use a pattern set by an industry leader as a policy guide in negotiations, a great deal of advance preparation may not be necessary. Many bargaining relationships do not differ greatly from what they were fifteen or twenty years ago and involve comparatively uncomplicated bargaining issues.

As a general proposition, however, most employers and unions do a great deal of factual spadework and opinion-seeking in preparation for negotiations. The larger industrial unions have a rather elaborate apparatus for obtaining accurate information on rank-and-file demands and pressures. They are also adept in the use of modern public relations techniques for "creating" membership enthusiasm for future contract demands regarded as critical by the leadership.

No prudent management, whether the enterprise be small, medium, or large, can afford not to anticipate and prepare for negotiations. It is now standard practice to schedule conferences between line supervision and industrial relations personnel to discuss contractual changes desirable from management's standpoint at the next negotiation. The ink is scarcely dry on a new contract before it is carefully examined by both the employer and the union for flaws, policy "booby traps," or troublesome ambiguities requiring clarification. This assumes that errors are not so serious as to require an immediate mutual consent adjustment.

In medium to large enterprises, it is also customary for both parties to analyze the nature and sources of grievances as a guide to contract trouble spots. When contract language proves to be either ambiguous or unworkable, the grievance procedure usually reveals the fact in short order. Daily contract administration thus provides much of the raw material for future demands and counterproposals at the bargaining table.

Technical Preparation for Bargaining

The increasingly technical nature of certain problem areas in contemporary collective bargaining makes it mandatory that the parties prepare thoroughly in advance of actual negotiation time. The truly professional touch is essential when it is clear that a complicated new proposal will be a crucial negotiation item.

For example, the employer may expect to be required to bargain on a union demand to scrap the current incentive system and convert all bargaining unit personnel to payment on the basis of weekly or monthly salaries. A great deal of study and data preparation are needed for intelligent discussion of such a demand. To take another example, bargaining on health and welfare plans has become so technical and specialized in recent years that both management and union often need to bring in "hired mercenaries" to work out the substantive and procedural content of the package of benefits.

Other "technical" issues requiring considerable advance preparation include the following:

1. Revision of the existing pension plan to provide for increased benefits, the option of early retirement, and an "escalator" clause.
2. Proposal by management for elimination of written (or customary) work rules rendered obsolete by changed technology and work methods.
3. Proposal to write a clause into a previously silent contract on management's right to subcontract work under certain conditions.
4. Revision of contract seniority language to provide for interplant transfers of employees displaced by the closing of a plant.
5. Incorporation into the contract of a profit-sharing plan or a productivity-gains-sharing plan.
6. Establishment of a special joint committee for consideration of basic problems of a continuing nature to avoid crisis bargaining.
7. Changing the basic work week from, for example, forty hours down to thirty-five or less, involving some difficult scheduling problems.
8. Bringing the collective agreement into compliance with equal opportunity and affirmative action laws.
9. Tying wages and benefits to a price index, and adapting contract language when price indices are revised (as the CPI was in 1978).

Nearly all issues in bargaining demand more thorough preparation than was formerly the case. Fortunately, the number and quality of data sources continue to improve, particularly on wage problems. The parties are inclined to rely increasingly on such data to support their respective positions on the basic wage issue. Many major unions and large companies have their own economic research units to supply factual ammunition on wages and other collective bargaining issues. Exhibits tailored for particular negotiations may contain data prepared by staff economists. The substantial improvement in "official" data has reduced the need for self-help in this area. The bargaining can be more objective when both parties are agreeable to arguing their cases in terms of data published by the Bureau of Labor Statistics, the Federal Reserve Board, or a state agency whose information is jointly regarded as reliable.

Management Preparation for Bargaining

It is easy to stress the importance of careful preparation for bargaining but somehow more difficult to lay down a meaningful prescription as to how to do it. The scale of preparation will depend both on the bargaining requirements of the parties and their economic resources. There will be a difference between the preparations by General Motors and the UAW, on the one hand, and those of a small machine shop and a local lodge of the IAM.

Some preparation techniques or procedures used by major companies are summarized below. The small firm may utilize some of these, but will not have the resources or the need to use others. The listing includes:

1. Thorough study of the current contract with a view to discovering any sections or language which may call for modification at the upcoming negotiations.

2. Systematic analysis of prior grievances for clues to defective or unworkable contract language or as an indicator of probable union demands.

3. Frequent conferences with line supervision for the dual purpose of better training of supervision in contract administration and receipt of intelligence as to how the contract is working out in practice.

4. Conferences with other employers in the same industry or area who deal with the same union to exchange viewpoints and anticipate the union's demands.

5. Use of attitude surveys to test the reactions of employees to various sections of the contract that management may feel require change or modification.

6. Informal conferences with local union leaders (stewards, shop committeemen, or business agents, as the case may be) to discuss the operational effectiveness of the contract and to send up trial balloons on management ideas for change at the next negotiations.

7. Systematic use of a commercial reporting service on labor relations for the purpose of keeping abreast of developments that may affect forthcoming contract negotiations.

8. Collection and analysis of economic data on matters of importance in the next negotiations.

9. Review of any arbitration decisions under the current contract as an aid in proposing changed contract language during negotiations.

10. Participation with the union(s) in prenegotiation conferences to agree on ground rules and sources of data for upcoming negotiations.

11. Participation with the union(s) in informal but scheduled talks, starting perhaps as much as one year prior to actual negotiation time to consider probable problem areas.

12. Development of programs to cost out contract proposals.

13. Development of a contingency plan for a strike.

14. Review of corporate objectives and forecasts as groundwork for a negotiation strategy.

A study by Meyer S. Ryder, Charles M. Rehmus, and Sanford Cohen reported that most companies in their sample made effective use of "bargaining books."[1] The nature and shape of such books can be basic or elaborate, depending on the requirements and choice of the user. The utility of such a book lies in its breaking down of the contract on a clause-by-clause basis, with notations on past management and union proposals and their fate in prior negotiations. In ongoing negotiations, this organized reference makes it easier "to cope with the disorder of bargaining." Such bargaining books would also be of value to union negotiators.

Calculations, Computers, and Negotiations

Contracts are becoming more complex. As bargaining units expand (see Chapter 4), issues and therefore contracts cover many more diverse circumstances. Evolution of the form of pay from direct pay to other types of indirect or "fringe" pay add to the contract. Each fringe requires a contract clause. Longer duration contracts require adjustment in pay through time. Especially in an inflationary period, year-to-year adjustments in pay, including cost-of-living allowances, can become complicated. Add to this the contractual debris of past negotiations and you have a serious administrative problem for both unions and employers: how to track and analyze everything in the contract.

Anything less than systematic efforts to compute contract costs can result in serious errors and long-term problems. Management errors may include overestimation leading to a costly strike or underestimation putting the firm at a competitive disadvantage. For management, simple contract costing methods such as multiplying the current number of employees by the average increase in direct pay may omit many other important costs. Besides direct pay increases, the following considerations may apply:[2]

1. The effect of direct pay on other wage costs such as:
    a. employer social security payments;
    b. pension payments if pensions are tied to past earnings;
    c. time not worked (paid vacations, for example, are now more costly) and;
    d. overtime.
2. Nonpayroll costs such as insurance.
3. Costs for time off from work.

1. Meyer S. Ryder, Charles M. Rehmus, and Sanford Cohen, *Management Preparation for Collective Bargaining* (Homewood, Ill.: Dow Jones–Irwin, 1966).
2. For a thorough treatment, see Michael H. Granof, *How to Cost Your Labor Contract* (Washington, D.C.: Bureau of National Affairs, 1973).

4. Anticipated cost-of-living adjustments, including their effects on other wage costs such as social security.

5. Effects of anticipated changes in staffing. What matters is not the size of the work force today but the size for the duration of the contract. New labor-saving methods, for example, reduce the cost of the agreement.

6. Spillover to workers within the company but outside the bargaining unit.

7. Timing of pay increases. Raises in pay toward the end of the contract are obviously less costly than equal raises at the beginning of the contract.

8. Shift differentials and incentive wages (the latter may also be changed by raising the direct pay base).

The appendix to this chapter was added to expedite discussion about contract cost calculations. It presents a hypothetical bargaining unit. The cost of this unit's wages and fringe benefits (i.e., "compensation") package is computed. Then we demonstrate how to cost out the unit's new agreement. Any in-depth review of the appendix, however, should be preceded by a reading of chapters 10 and 11, dealing with negotiated wages and fringe benefits, respectively.

Computers may be useful in costing out complicated contracts. The primary advantage lies in the ability to quickly evaluate each negotiating proposal. The primary disadvantage is cost.

Computers serve other useful purposes in negotiation. Complicated contracts covering multiple unions or multiple employers may require computers just to keep everyone informed about the current state of negotiations on each clause within the contract. Computers can be used for analysis in preparation for negotiation as well. An example would be classifying grievances, complaints, and arbitration awards against contract clauses for quick retrieval. Employers and unions may find much larger data bases useful in preparation, especially data on competitor contracts and wage settlements elsewhere in the industry or locale.[3]

UNION PREPARATION FOR BARGAINING

Unions vary considerably in the manner and extent of their advance preparation for negotiations. A building trades craft union business agent will discuss future demands with his executive board. He may sound out

---

3. Several readings on this topic may be found in Abraham J. Siegel, ed., *The Impact of Computers on Bargaining* (Cambridge, Mass.: MIT Press, 1970).

craftsmen informally as he makes his rounds of various construction projects. He will probably confer with other business agents servicing related crafts and attend meetings of the joint bodies in his area. From this combination of meetings and interviews, the business agent will develop an idea of what to shoot for at contract time. He will then formulate his own union's demands as he participates in coordinated bargaining with the other construction unions and an association of the major contractors in the area.

In a large industrial union, major negotiation objectives are determined by the top international officers. A lengthy and complex procedure of gathering and sifting opinions usually precedes the reopening of any major contract. All local unions affected will hold special meetings to bring out matters that the rank and file feel require action. Demands emerging from these local meetings will be discussed and separated into local issues and those relating to international union policy. District or regional meetings attended by local officers follow a similar procedure. There is usually a candid interchange of views between local union officers and international representatives. If the top international officers have decided that a particular contract demand is a must in the next negotiations and no substantial grass-roots sentiment for it has emerged, an effort to build support is made through the union newspaper and by international representatives. Public media of communication may also be used. The larger unions can assign their full-time economic research units the task of developing the factual underpinnings for key demands decided upon by the policy-making officers.

In all unions, large or small, regardless of the structure and degree of internal democracy, there is considerable communication between membership and leadership. To take one illustration, the United Mine Workers (UMW) was never a shining example of internal democracy during the heyday of John L. Lewis, but few questioned Lewis's ability to remain sensitive to the economic goals and aspirations of the great majority of UMW members.

The task of union preparation for bargaining—certainly for the major industrial unions, if not for the relatively homogeneous craft unions—is complicated by the constant necessity for reconciling a variety of internal pressures before and during contract negotiation.

INTERNAL PRESSURES ON UNION LEADERSHIP IN NEGOTIATION

The life of an industrial union leader is not an easy one. Industrial unions are not homogeneous organizations. The typical industrial union has a variety of conflicting interests and pressures that need to be welded together in cohesive fashion at negotiation time, particularly when a strike appears likely.[4] In many industrial unions, there is a built-in conflict between a skilled trades minority and the preponderant majority of semiskilled production workers. The craft worker invariably holds that the current wage schedule, whatever it may be, does not reflect a suitable differential in his favor. By the same token, the typical production workers's thinking is likely to be that his job demands greater effort than the craftsman's and also calls for considerable skill and knowhow. He is likely to think that the craftsman is overpaid by comparison.

Another source of internal conflict that sometimes plagues industrial union leadership relates to the different goals of the low-seniority and high-seniority members. The former is frequently concerned about being laid off. He may thus give a high priority to contract demands for job security provisions. The high-seniority worker is less concerned becausehe knows his length of service will protect him in most layoff situations short of plant closure.

The battle of the sexes is also a matter of concern for some industrial union leaders. Problems may arise as to alleged discriminatory treatment in distinguishing between so-called male jobs and female jobs. When both men and women are employed in the same job categories, a different set of problems may arise. The traditional equal-pay-for-equal-work mandate has had greater operational significance in many plants through the impact of Title VII of the Civil Rights Act and the Equal Pay Act.

Another facet of expanded job horizons for female workers is reflected in demands for inclusion in the contract of a no-discrimination-against-spouses policy on hiring. Employers are being asked to abandon historic policies against hiring spouses of incumbent employees into bargaining unit jobs. Management, understandably enough, may have mixed feelings on this matter. So also may union leaders in a previously male-dominated union. Yet the handwriting is on the wall. There will be an increase of contract clauses adding "marital status" to the customary list of race, creed, color, religion, and so forth as still another factor that an employer may *not* consider either in hiring or in on-the-job treatment of employees.[5]

Craft unions do not ordinarily encounter internal problems because of their more uniform composition and interests. However, when several

---

4. The structural problems of maintaining an "appropriate" differential between occupational rates for the skilled trades and production workers is one that faces most industrial unions each time a contract comes up for renegotiation. To cite just one example, the 1976–79 agreement between the General Motors Corporation and the United Auto Workers provided a first-year pay increase of 3 percent plus 20 cents per hour for an average of 37 cents. Skilled workers covered under the agreement were granted *additional* increases of 15 cents per hour for the first year and 10 cents per hour for the second year (1976–79 Agreement, p. 28).

5. As of 1978, the states of Alaska, California, Michigan, Minnesota, New Hampshire, and New York had enacted laws prohibiting job discrimination on the basis of marital status.

craft unions bargain either jointly or separately with the same employer(s), they confront a variation of the industrial union leader's dilemma. A necessity arises for accommodation of conflicting pressures among the separate craft groupings, each of which is likely to regard itself still as a sovereign state.

Unions are not alone in facing the problem of reconciling internal pressures. Ryder, Rehmus, and Cohen found that the concept of a consensus within management ranks is frequently an illusion. The "management position" at any one time often reflects the dominance of one viewpoint over other conflicting views rather than a true consensus.

In any enterprise there is always a potential for conflict between production-minded "line" management and contract-oriented "staff" personnel from industrial relations. The latter at times have more in common with their union counterparts than with their management peers or superiors. In other words, it is dangerous to visualize the internal profile of management in unitary terms.

EXPERIMENTATION IN JOINT PREPARATION FOR BARGAINING

The discussion to this point may have left an impression that since preparation precedes bargaining it is not a part of the negotiation phase. This is true only in a literal chronological sense. *The main reason for thorough preparation is to facilitate the agreement-making process.*

Establishment of joint study committees on special problems of a continuing nature (for example, relating manpower adjustments over time in terms of technological changes or locational shifts) offers recent evidence of intelligent preparation for negotiation. We would be wrong in assuming that management and union negotiators are in contact only at contract negotiation time. In all relationships there is continuous interaction of some type during the life of the contract, even though not of a formalized character. Regular sessions for grievance adjustment under an existing contract, for example, may be devoted in part to a discussion of extracontractual problems that have arisen or are anticipated. Any discussion of this nature can properly be regarded as preparation for bargaining at contract renewal time.

A joint study committee has no special magic.[6] However, the use of such

6. Miracles should not be expected from such committees. Some of the pitfalls are candidly discussed by William Gomberg in "Special Study Committees," in John T. Dunlop and Neil W. Chamberlain, eds., *Frontiers of Collective Bargaining* (New York: Harper & Row, 1967), pp. 235–51.

For a more recent and somewhat more favorable view see Charlotte Gold, "Employer–employee Committees and Worker Participation," Key Issues Series, No. 20, New York State School of Industrial and Labor Relations, Cornell University, Ithaca, N.Y., 1976.

committees is encouraging evidence that some employers and unions appreciate the need for continuing rather than intermittent attention to key problem areas. The findings and conclusions of such joint study committees are not binding upon negotiators at contract time. However, the net impact in most cases has been to facilitate the agreement-making process.

Logic would suggest continued growth of joint study committees and related procedural devices. One pressure comes from the increasingly complex and technical character of many bargaining subjects. Another is the growing impatience of the public at large with "conventional" bargaining methods. Any new procedure that gives promise of enhancing the prospects for industrial peace is likely to find favor in the public's eyes. A third reason to develop continuing joint approaches to problem solving is recognition that it is *to the mutual advantage of the parties* to consider long-run problems in a calm context divorced from the immediate pressures of the bargaining table. Finally, with bargaining units increasingly refusing to ratify negotiated settlements, there is added incentive for employers to acclimate the rank and file to the costs, benefits, or provisions of new proposals. Since NLRB rulings make some direct communication with the workers risky for the employer, these joint committees have potential as effective selling tools to facilitate contract ratification.

The casualty rate has been high among these new joint approaches outside the bargaining table. One observed difficulty has been the suspicion of the rank and file as to what is going on behind closed doors between contracts. Valid findings may be rejected if the joint committee operations have been clothed with secrecy. Communication channels need to be kept open. One answer to suspicion is to broaden the base of participation, although this may reduce the operating efficiency of such committees.

CONTRACT NEGOTIATION PROCEDURES

Success in bargaining requires a combination of factors, including the following: (1) knowledgeability of one's own case and the other party's case as a result of careful preparation for bargaining; (2) contract proposals that are both attainable and workable; (3) an economically strong position from which to negotiate; (4) personal skill and experience in negotiations; and (5) a positive approach to the bargaining function based on good faith and a willingness to reach agreement.

The mutual purpose of negotiation should be achievement of a collective agreement that will work. The attitude of the parties in negotiation and the procedures they employ should be governed by a continuing joint awareness of this fundamental objective.

Workability Test of Agreement

The goal of negotiation is an instrument that can serve as the "statutory law" governing the parties' relationships over a period of usually three years. The contract will be good private law only if it permits smooth administration of its provisions for its duration. A contract that avoids or straddles fundamental conflicts of interest will produce, at best, an armed truce. A contract that attempts to conceal or gloss over actual differences of intent will be productive of continuing friction and disagreement in subsequent attempts at application. These are considerations that the able negotiator keeps constantly in mind.

Which negotiation procedures are best suited to achieve a workable collective agreement? Experienced negotiators hold that sound procedures can be of great value in facilitating agreement on substantive issues. Advance accord on negotiation procedures can be an excellent medium for establishing a constructive relationship between the parties. The bitterness on such explosive substantive issues as union security, wages, seniority, and management rights can frequently be alleviated by intelligent initial attention to desirable and efficient negotiation procedures.

The actual procedures employed will vary considerably from one case to another. Much depends on whether the bargaining is between one company and a local union, between one company and the international union, or between a multiemployer group and a local or international union.

In multiemployer bargaining, even in a first contract experience, the parties have developed a degree of sophistication through individual plant negotiations that should minimize difficulties over bargaining procedures. But when single employers are bargaining with a local union or with the union's international representatives, prior agreement on procedures to be followed in negotiation is particularly helpful.

No one procedure can be put forward as suitable to the requirements of all parties in all situations. It is nevertheless possible to list some common sense guidelines that appear to have general utility:

1. Both the union and management negotiating committees should be reasonably small. If the union or company committee is too large and everyone insists on participating, much time will be consumed, tempers will become frayed, and much irrelevant material may be introduced.

2. One person must be in charge of conducting the negotiations for each side. Division of authority in negotiation is fatal to orderly procedure and usually impedes the agreement-making process.

3. The parties should agree in advance on the time of day and desired length of bargaining sessions. Each side can then make its plans accordingly.

4. Careful preparation for negotiations should include exchange of demands or proposals for study before actual bargaining begins. A frequent source of trouble is the springing of a complicated new proposal during negotiations.

5. Advance agreement on procedures will eliminate such unnecessary arguments as whether subject X is "in order at this time."

6. Negotiators should have authority to make decisive commitments in the course of negotiations. Company negotiators generally have the power to bind their principals. In most unions the negotiated terms are subject to ratification or rejection by the membership. Membership rejection can be a serious problem.

7. Negotiations should begin with a well-planned agenda that includes a complete statement of all disputed issues, together with a listing of proposals and counterproposals on the disputed points.

8. If possible, an agreed-upon statement of relevant economic data should be employed. This can be done when the parties have made effective use of the prenegotiation conference.

9. The negotiators should first resolve the less controversial issues and reduce their agreement to writing before proceeding to the tougher issues.

10. The difficult issues can be divided into those that involve money outlays and noneconomic demands.

11. Many noneconomic issues can be negotiated individually in terms of their intrinsic merit rather than in terms of the bargaining strength of the principals. This generalization would clearly not apply, however, to union demands relating to such "noneconomic" matters as union security or seniority.

12. Finally, and of critical importance in most negotiations, a decision must be made as to whether to bargain out the demands involving money outlays one by one or to negotiate on an economic package basis.

ECONOMIC PACKAGE BARGAINING

Nearly all management negotiators and most union negotiators favor disposing of all labor cost items on a unified and related basis rather than separately. The key decision is generally over how much money may be available *in total* for allocation between wage or salary increases as such and a miscellany of money fringe proposals.

Management may be comparatively indifferent as to the "mix" between wage increases and fringe benefits. Yet no prudent employer can commit himself to an increased outlay for specific fringes without a clear idea of what the total tab is going to be. Most union negotiators arrive at the bargaining table with a mandate to achieve more than is realistically attainable. They know that at some point they will have to cut and trim their proposals involving labor cost in some fashion. Thus, it becomes important to the union to know how much total money may be extractable in any particular negotiation before deciding how much emphasis to place on wage increases as such and how much on new or expanded fringes.

Package bargaining is therefore the rule and likely to remain so. Both management and union practitioners are becoming skilled in the art of translating the cost of a particular fringe item into x cents per hour if given out in the form of an across-the-board wage or salary adjustment. The particular mix between wages and fringes is usually of greater concern to the union than to management, but not necessarily so. Management recognizes that introduction of a new fringe item into its complex of labor costs may prove burdensome in the future, even though not seemingly significant at the time of its negotiation. Fringes are readily institutionalized and not easily retractable. The problem of being saddled with an excessive fixed-cost fringe commitment is one of special concern to smaller firms.

Management is always concerned over labor cost increases, whether in the form of wage increases or new or expanded fringes. Unions at all times strive to negotiate visible gains that can be publicized as bargaining victories, whether they be wage increases as such or a much-sought-after fringe benefit. Thus, for different but equally compelling reasons, both management and union prefer to know the overall dimensions of the economic package before either is willing to forego any one economic demand or to make a particular economic concession.

Some economic package items are difficult to cost out. It is hard to know, for example, what the net increase in labor cost will be from adopting a guaranteed annual or monthly income security plan for production workers, or to estimate the cost of converting blue-collar workers from an hourly method of payment to a weekly or monthly salaried basis.

Package bargaining is more complex when the give-and-take at the bargaining table involves a tradeoff at some point between a key noneconomic demand and a money issue. Circumstances can arise when it makes sense to the union leadership to forego a substantial potential gain on a money demand in return for an important noneconomic concession such as, for example, a union shop clause or an improved understanding on subcontracting.

In summary, in any negotiation today there are likely to be several disputed issues involving increased money costs to the employer as well as a number of noneconomic issues to which the parties attach varying degrees of importance. The consensus among practitioners on both sides of the bargaining table clearly favors deferring formal commitment on *any one* economic issue until tentative agreement has been reached on *all* such issues. Such an approach is the one sure way for each party ultimately to determine the true bargaining priorities of the other party and what the probable requirements for a mutually acceptable package will be. The most common method appears to be the reaching of a preliminary understanding as to how much additional labor cost (if any) the employer is willing to accept for the coming contract period, and then to engage in the requisite bargaining for allocating this estimated overall sum among the various competing economic demands.

INTEGRATIVE BARGAINING

Concern over the quality of life at work has increased dramatically in recent years. Rising educational levels, equal rights movements, and the increasing bureaucratization of business all have contributed to the growing interest in self-fulfillment at the workplace.

This interest in human needs at the workplace has been concentrated in two major areas. One, work redesign, involves the reformulation of tasks for the purpose of making the job more meaningful to the employee. Forms of work redesign such as job enrichment and job enlargement operate on the assumption that variety, autonomy, and responsibility are highly desirable to the worker.

"Worker participation," based on the notion that "participation increases acceptance," has also received much attention. Allowing workers a voice in managing the business enterprise increases approval of managerial decisions. But does increased employee approval at the cost of decreased managerial control provide a positive tradeoff for management? Management will oftentimes protect valuable rights by allowing worker participation only on select issues.

The types of problems that lend themselves to negotiated employee consultation agreements or to joint study committees are usually distinct from conflict issues (like wages or pensions). Through cooperative labor–management relationships like these, the optimal solution to select problems such as safety, selection of insurance carriers, and technological displacement of the work force may be more easily found.

The perceived merits of quality-of-work bargaining differ, depending upon whether the subject is viewed from a worker or managerial perspective. The worker hopes that such bargaining would lead to a more pleasant and rewarding work environment. Management's primary objective, stemming from its responsibility to direct the business enterprise, is to increase productivity. But increased worker satisfaction does not always translate to increased productivity. In fact, the relation between these two goals is blurred. However, since there is potential for mutual benefit, integrative bargaining over the quality of life at work does take place.

Despite the apparent utility of integrative or cooperative bargaining practices they are oftentimes difficult to implement. It is difficult to shift gears as one moves from the negotiation of a conflict issue to that of an integrative problem. To operate from a cooperative stance while the other party anticipates a conflict process could be dangerous. Some question taking such a risk when the rewards are so uncertain. Lastly, if management approaches collective bargaining with a "you win, I lose" attitude, then it usually follows that protecting management prerogatives becomes more important than cooperation.

Joint study committees have enjoyed small success. However, they suffer the same pitfalls as other attempts at cooperative management. They are primarily utilized in an advisory capacity and have little authority. The low incidence of usage is evidence of their restricted application.

THE ATMOSPHERE OF NEGOTIATION

The atmosphere of contract negotiations will vary from one relationship to another, depending on such factors as (1) prior relations between the parties, (2) the basic attitude of the employer toward unionism, (3) the economic circumstances of the employer, and (4) the compulsions operating upon union leadership, which may or may not be related to the specific situation in which the union is negotiating. Each of these factors deserves brief attention.

If the parties have a past history of conflict, or if tensions have built up during the administration of the contract about to expire, the bargaining is likely to be tough, long drawn out, and perhaps unsuccessful. On the other hand, many employers and unions renegotiate contracts with a bare minimum of friction time after time.

When past relations have been unsatisfactory, negotiations may be conducted on a "goldfish bowl" basis, with a maximum of partisan communication designed to impress constituents. If conditions have been stable and peaceful, negotiations may involve only the principals directly concerned (the firm's industrial relations director and the union's business agent or international representative). Membership ratification of the agreement in such circumstances is often merely a formality.

The pattern of negotiations may be affected by the economic circumstances of the employer. The union must always seek "improvements" in the new contract. A company that accepts the union will not begrudge such political compulsions operating upon union leadership. In a situation where the company in question cannot grant any contract changes involving added labor cost (or may even require a decrease in labor costs), however, a realistic union will recognize the requirements of a hard-pressed firm. In one such case, when asked what he obtained from the negotiations, the union representative replied cryptically, "We couldn't get any money, but we got a lot of language." This statement acknowledged the straitened economic condition of the employer, but stressed the presumed "gains" to the membership from a firming up of contract language on various noneconomic issues.

The pattern and atmosphere of negotiations can also be affected by conditions external to the company or union. A particular employer may be under pressure from other employers to resist a particular union demand. On the union side, the policy of the international may involve pressing hard for a certain demand (such as an income security plan) that the local union(s) may not be particularly enthusiastic about. In such cases, the external pressures on one or both participants may be strong enough to convert the negotiations into an endurance contest that is desired by neither.

The lay observer is often puzzled by the apparent ferocity with which negotiators attack one another during the early stages of bargaining. He is disturbed by the extremity of the union's initial demands and the niggard-liness of the employer's original counteroffers. What is not appreciated is that collective bargaining has many attributes common to other types of bargaining in human society.

To abstain entirely from a certain amount of melodramatic buildup by approaching the matter coldly and logically would "take all the fun" out of bargaining. It would also destroy the maneuverability and flexibility that each party needs to maintain until reasonably sure in his estimates of the relative strength or weakness of the other party, and also of what the other party's true minimum demands or real offers are likely to be.

We do not mean to suggest that negotiators should not endeavor to rely more on objective facts. Nor are we suggesting that all negotiations proceed until the participants are physically and emotionally exhausted with a strike deadline staring them in the face before concluding an agreement. No harm is done, however, by judicious respect for the dramatic unities in the negotiation process. Considerable harm to union–management relationships can come from such approaches as "boulwa-rism" that intentionally circumvent bargaining conventions by stressing a "first and last offer."

Contract negotiation is the most dramatic part of the collective bargaining process. There is a constant awareness that, if agreement is not reached, a strike or a lockout can result. *The possibility of economic force is the chief sanction that keeps the parties at the table in search of an agreement.* Each party has a minimum position from which he will not retreat. In the great majority of cases, an accommodation of conflicting demands is found through negotiation. Resort to economic force is thereby avoided. The union's minimum requirements and the employer's final ability to grant improvements can generally be made to overlap or dovetail in such a way as to make agreement possible. Where this is not possible, collective bargaining is continued by harsher methods of producing agreement, such as a strike or a lockout. Bargaining behaviors and the threat of economic force are further considered in Chapter 13.

PERSONAL REQUISITES FOR NEGOTIATION

The most skilled negotiator is not likely to be successful at the bargaining table if the party he represents lacks "bargaining power," as this term is used in Chapter 13, or if the positions he is required to support lack merit or feasibility. The reverse is also true. A party bringing impressive economic strength and intrinsically meritorious proposals to the bargaining table can be poorly served by an inept negotiator or a badly designed strategy of negotiation. It is thus important to have a well-thought-out approach to bargaining and to place its execution in the hands of the most skilled personnel available. Carl Stevens has properly stressed that there is such a thing as "negotiation power," which, along with other kinds of power, determines the final result.[7] What are some of the personal requisites needed for success in negotiation?

First, there can be no substitute for personal integrity and courage. Second, a negotiator must have an intimate knowledge of the essential facts relevant to the positions of his own party and those of the other party. Third, he must have a highly developed understanding of the pressures and compulsions that condition the conduct of the other party's negotiator.

A knowledgeable management negotiator, for example, will not become disturbed when his union opposite number begins negotiations with a flaming speech about the callous, hard-hearted, stingy company whose profits are enormous but whose offers are meager. Nor will an adept union leader become incensed when the management negotiator launches into a prolonged dissertation on the inviolability of certain managerial prerogatives. In each case, other things being equal, there is an awareness of the need for a certain amount of speechmaking for the benefit of constituents.

---

7. In Stevens's frame of reference, negotiation power comes from such attributes as "facility and shrewdness in the execution of negotiation tactics such as manipulation of the communications structure of the situation to achieve commitment of a threat, use of rationalization of a position to win allies." Carl M. Stevens, *Strategy and Collective Bargaining Negotiations* (New York: McGraw-Hill, 1963), p. 3.

Such conduct in negotiations is not deliberately deceitful or harmful, provided it is not carried to extremes. No poised negotiator will be thrown off balance by such tactics.

Negotiating is a demanding, wearing kind of business. It requires a rather unusual personal chemistry, an abundance of physical and mental vigor and specialized knowhow. The model negotiator lives only on the printed page. Few, if any, mortals satisfy all criteria in the required amounts.

We shall consider next the available evidence on whether the practitioners of bargaining are facing up successfully to the various procedural challenges posed earlier in the chapter.

ARE NEGOTIATORS IMPROVING
THEIR PERFORMANCE?

Negotiation performance in general has been improving by whatever standard one chooses. Work stoppage data for recent years indicate the overall record on industrial peace to be an excellent one. Another index of improvement would be sequential analysis of contract language. Most experienced arbitrators would, we think, agree that many employers and unions have improved the clarity of their contracts, if not their brevity. Negotiators are becoming more skilled at saying what they actually intended. They are thus avoiding disputes caused by poor draftsmanship or unintentionally fuzzy language.

Another index of maturity and stability is the apparent consensus among experienced negotiators that three years is an optimal duration for a contract. The five-year contracts of the 1950s were demonstrably too long to satisfy the "living document" concept. On the other hand, most management and union negotiators join in the view that it is neither necessary nor economical to negotiate once a year or every two years (unless, of course, uncertainties of future inflationary pressures make longer term agreements prohibitive).

Additional evidence of improved negotiation performance can be found in such developments as: (1) creation of joint study committees to give systematic, continuing attention to long-range problems outside the framework of contract deadlines; (2) use of various prenegotiation procedures to facilitate the agreement-making process; (3) instances of renegotiating new contracts well in advance of expiration deadlines; (4) evidence of a disposition to consider the public stake in private bargains—for example, the willingness in some cases to consider utilizing binding arbitration for resolution of disputes over future contract terms; and (5) evidence of a declining propensity to strike in some key bargaining relationships, including a willingness to operate without a contract if necessary in marked contrast to the previously rigid "no contract, no work" stance.

Such developments illustrate the professionalization that marks negotiation in many bargaining relationships. Although there is a darker side of the picture, it is simply not accurate to say that collective bargaining as a process has remained procedurally static and unreceptive to new ideas.

CONTINUING PROBLEM AREAS
FOR NEGOTIATORS

Negotiators are concerned about their inability to cope effectively with a number of procedural problems. Perhaps the most disturbing problem is the one posed by the high rate of membership rejection of negotiated settlements. As shown in Table 5–1, cases involving membership rejection have hovered between *9 and 12 percent*. The cases covered in this table were presumably among the more difficult to settle, since they required the services of the Federal Mediation and Conciliation Service (FMCS).

What factors lie behind this contract rejection phenomenon? In some cases, rejection is clearly a consequence of overselling the membership on management's ability to pay. When union leaders prior to negotiations promise more than they can conceivably deliver the membership, in reviewing the ultimate settlement, may suspect that they have been "sold out" by their representatives. Although this is seldom the true explanation, union leaders can justly be blamed when they themselves create a gap between expectations and reality.

Table 5–1
Percent of Closed FMCS Joint Meeting Cases Involving
Rejection of Tentative Settlement, 1970–79

FISCAL YEAR	PERCENT REJECTIONS
1970	11.2
1971	9.9
1972	10.1
1973	9.6
1974	12.4
1975	11.1
1976	9.8
1977	11.5
1978	11.9
1979	11.9

Source: *Federal Mediation and Conciliation Service, Thirty-Second Annual Report, Fiscal Year 1979*, Federal Mediation and Conciliation Service, 1980, p. 19.

Some rejections are due to rank-and-file conviction that the settlement can be "sweetened" (improved) following failure to ratify. This has happened often enough to lend credence to such beliefs. A well-known case of this type concerned membership rejection of a settlement that triggered New York City's garbage strike in the winter of 1968. The initial contract terms agreed upon by union and city negotiators were voted down by the sanitation workers. The resultant strike created a potentially explosive crisis for our largest city. The ultimate settlement was in fact "sweeter" than the initial terms. It thereby created headaches for the city's negotiators in subsequent bargaining with other municipal unions.[8]

The 1978 coal miners' strike is a recent illustration of this same tactic. Miners were given an opportunity to vote on a contract proposal approved by the negotiating team. The proposal was overwhelmingly rejected, with the hopes that further negotiations would result in a more favorable settlement. To a certain extent, these hopes were realized in the subsequent industry settlement.

COPING WITH CONTRACT REJECTIONS

What is the best way of dealing with the rejection phenomenon? As long as union constitutions require membership ratification, the most direct way to improve matters is for the unions to do a far better job of educating the membership toward greater realism in their expectations from negotiations. Experienced union representatives usually know what is attainable and what is feasible in a forthcoming negotiation. They have a responsibility to themselves and to the membership, as well as to the employer with whom they are dealing, to avoid creating either false or excessive expectations.

One approach would be to eliminate the membership ratification requirement. Management negotiators have the authority to bind their principals in most cases. Should not union negotiators be armed with the same authority? Union leaders are accountable to their members and must bear the burden of showing that they did the best they could in any negotiations. In today's economy, however, it is more difficult to defend the kind of direct democracy required by the ratification process. It does not make sense to have the work of "professionals" subject to veto by "amateurs." The normal union electoral processes should suffice to replace incompetent or complacent leaders.

Moving to eliminate membership ratification would require amending many union constitutions and provoke formidable resistance. Yet, if we are to insure the continuing viability of collective bargaining as a process for

---

8. At that time, the City of New York negotiated with some seventy unions representing employees in about two hundred bargaining units. One can thus imagine the burdens imposed on the Office of Collective Bargaining (OCB), the city's official labor relations agency established in 1967. The bargaining structure has been simplified considerably since then.

resolving increasingly complex economic and noneconomic issues, we must think in terms of more representative government rather than more direct democracy.

The probability of contract rejection by the membership can be reduced in specific negotiations in two related ways. One calls for a firm, unambiguous management statement that a negotiated settlement will not subsequently be improved upon should ratification be withheld. Another is to insist on provision that the effective date of any monetary benefits, whether in the form of wage increases or new or improved fringes, will be the date on which management is officially notified of membership ratification rather than going back to the expiration date of the prior agreement. Such an approach has the merit of underlining the importance of the negotiations and the status of the negotiators. It also makes clear that no retroactivity windfalls or better terms will be gained by a settlement rejection strategy.

The Kennecott Copper Company and the coalition of unions headed by the United Steelworkers of America used such an effective date definition in their March 1968 settlement agreement following an eight-month strike. The pertinent sentence reads as follows:

> For purposes of this Agreement, date of settlement shall be the date on which the appropriate Company Director of Industrial Relations is notified by Union that the settlement has been approved as the result of Union-required approval or ratification procedures.

OTHER PROBLEMS
IN CONTRACT BARGAINING

Another challenge that negotiators have not met effectively is how to prevent contracts from becoming excessively long and detailed. The prevalence of lengthy contracts perhaps reflects the American passion for the written word. British employers and unions, in sharp contrast, follow their country's dedication to an unwritten constitution by not reducing to writing most of the shop rules and customs under which British unionized firms operate on a day-to-day basis.

Written contracts, no matter how lengthy, are not a serious problem if they include arbitration for final and binding disposition of interpretation disputes arising under the contract. About 95 percent of all agreements in the United States so provide. The salutary result has been that few work stoppages occur in this country under contracts already in effect. In Great Britain, on the other hand, such work stoppages are numerous and are directly traceable in many cases to conflict over the meaning or application of the unwritten industrial contract (constitution). To be realistic, no serious moves in the direction of contract shrinkage and/or simplification appear to be likely.

Another formidable task is that of removing from a contract a provision that no longer has any reason for being there, particularly if such a provision gives a real or fancied advantage of some sort to a few incumbent employees. Many work rules fit this category.

An effort to eliminate an obsolete contractual provision can be successful only through a convincing demonstration that the provision no longer serves a useful purpose. Realistically, there must also be assurance that no incumbent will be adversely affected. This latter point has been the rock on which many well-intentioned management efforts have foundered through suspicion or misunderstanding. If a group of employees continues to benefit from an obsolete working rule, they must usually be offered some kind of a *quid pro quo* if the rule is to be eliminated.

In this connection, use of a joint committee to develop ways and means of increasing productivity and reducing costs logically comes to mind. Properly handled and publicized, the findings of such a joint committee that certain provisions or rules are obsolete or vestigial could facilitate their elimination from the contract at negotiation time. Such surgery will not work, however, unless provision is made to insure that no present employee or group of employees will be disadvantaged thereby.

Companies and unions plagued with elephantine contracts could charge a special joint committee to recommend ways of simplifying the contract without loss of essential meaning and to identify portions of the contract suitable for deletion. Such a committee could also be given the task of preparing an informal contract synopsis in layman's language.

In recent years another difficult problem resulted from changes in employment regulation. Antidiscrimination measures, for example, mandated extensive changes in many contracts. Legislation forbidding mandatory retirement before age seventy may produce another class of problem: how to write contract language defining procedures and standards for determination of the competence of all, but especially older, workers.

CONTRACT BARGAINING
IN THE PUBLIC SECTOR

Preparation and negotiation in the public sector can be more complex than in the private sector. Management authority to decide is usually spread among several bodies, such as the executive and the legislative branches.[9] Multilateral bargaining can occur if unions appeal directly to elected

9. The most often cited study in this area is Thomas A. Kochan, "A Theory of Multilateral Collective Bargaining in City Government," *Industrial and Labor Relations Review*, 27 (July 1974), 525–42.

officials rather than to civil service negotiators, or if elected officials choose to intervene in negotiations. Other problems can occur if the employer negotiating team signs a contract but administrators refuse to implement it.[10]

Some public jurisdictions have passed laws requiring interest arbitration of unresolved contract disputes. Preparation, however, is still necessary and negotiation desirable. Generally, both sides can live better with a negotiated agreement they both understand than a contract written by a third party perhaps unfamiliar with the workplace. Unions and management are likely to prepare somewhat differently under arbitration; most important to each side is obtaining evidence that the arbitrator will view as favorable to its case.

SPECIAL PROBLEMS
IN FIRST CONTRACT NEGOTIATIONS

Most of the discussion has contemplated parties that have been bargaining collectively over a considerable period of time. We now consider briefly some difficulties encountered when a newly certified union is bargaining with an employer for the first time.

The atmosphere in negotiation of a first contract generally ranges from uncertainty to outright hostility. A strike or a lockout may be imminent or actually in progress. Negotiations are often being held following certification of the union as exclusive bargaining agent by the National Labor Relations Board.

Most first contract cases generally have the following features:

1. The union has to make a good showing. This is a political necessity in dealing with a recently unionized employer.
2. Management is generally determined to give as little as possible.
3. The negotiators probably do not know one another. They do not know each other's strengths and weaknesses. Suspicion, if not outright distrust of the other party, is usually present.
4. The parties often lack experience in negotiation.
5. The local union committee may attempt to convert the negotiations into a complaint session over an accumulation of past grievances. Such a tactic can hamper negotiation of the basic contract.
6. When the company is one of the last to be organized in its industry or area, the pressure to achieve at one stroke the gains accrued in years of bargaining with other firms may seriously complicate the agreement-making process.

---

10. Extensive multilateral involvement is a doubtful long-term bargaining strategy. Negotiations and contract administration are likely to remain unsettled, distracting, and sometimes disrupting work efforts.

Such difficulties common to first contract negotiations will not be overcome by procedures alone, but knowledge and use of effective methods can help. With the possible exception of the prenegotiation conference, the procedural suggestions outlined earlier can be utilized effectively in first contract cases. The prenegotiation conference requires stability and mutual understanding in the relationship. These qualities are not usually present in the first contract situations.

SUMMARY

In this chapter, we have examined a number of procedural and substantive problem areas challenging the parties responsible for contract negotiations. A major lesson learned in this discussion is that there is no substitute for deliberate *preparations* for contract negotiations. Early preparations, and perhaps joint preparations, for negotiations should greatly facilitate the process and allay negotiation problems that otherwise might surface. We discussed the importance of knowing well the pressures and motivations underlying each others' positions as well as the cost of proposals prior to their acceptance or rejection. Among other subjects covered, the problem of contract ratification failures was examined along with ways of coping with its reality. Consideration of problems arising when negotiation has failed, with a strike or lockout resulting, has been intentionally omitted. These topics are considered in later chapters.

We turn next to how collective bargaining contracts are administered. This subject is treated in two parts. The next chapter lays out the conceptual basis upon which our subsequent discussion of contract administration will rest. It contains a brief discussion of the nature of managerial authority in labor relations; then it structures the divergent roles assigned to labor and management during the term that the labor agreement is in force. Management has the right to put the contracts provisions into effect through its directives and decisions, and the union has the right to object to these initiatives through the grievance procedure.

Questions for Discussion, Thought, and Research

1. You have been appointed to the union negotiating team by the union president. Your first assignment is to define a strategy for preparing for negotiations. Briefly, outline some of the issues your strategy must address.

2. In what ways are the steps involved with preparing for bargaining by management similar to that of a union? In what ways are the processes different?

3. Assume that a medium-sized public employer in your state is negotiating a contract at the present time. What political, economic, legal, and social factors impact on these negotiations?

4. Why is it necessary for negotiators to disguise their true positions on issues?

5. Of what use is a bargaining book? Discuss.

6. The divergent interests of local and occupational groups present the union negotiator with some difficult structural problems. Some of the obvious divisions include craft versus semiskilled, male versus female, high versus low seniority, and racial or ethnic majority versus racial or ethnic minority. What are some of the ways that a union leader can reconcile these pressures? Does the management negotiator have an obligation to address these problems? Discuss.

7. Management does not always have a unified position. One source of potential conflict is between line management and staff personnel. What are other sources of conflict?

8. Does the skill of the negotiator make a significant difference in the outcome of bargaining? Explain.

9. What services does an international union provide for its local negotiators?

10. Democratic unions are often the most difficult unions with which to negotiate. Why?

11. How should labor and management address the increasing contract ratification problem?

12. Computing contract costs is critical. What information is required to come up with an estimate of the direct and indirect costs to the employer of a 10 percent across-the-board wage increase?

Selected Bibliography

Granof, Michael H., *How to Cost Your Labor Contract*. Washington, D.C.: Bureau of National Affairs, 1973.

Richardson, Reed C., "Positive Collective Bargaining," in Dale Yoder and H. G. Heneman, Jr., eds., *Employee and Labor Relations*. Washington, D.C.: Bureau of National Affairs, 1976, pp. 7–111–43.

Ryder, Meyer S., Charles M. Rehmus, and Sanford Cohen, *Management Preparation for Collective Bargaining*. Homewood, Ill.: Dow Jones–Irwin, 1966.

APPENDIX:
CALCULATING SETTLEMENT COSTS

During negotiations, perhaps the most critical piece of information labor and management can possess relates to the future cost implications of proposed contract changes. Costing out change in the labor agreement is a must, particularly from management's point of view. More often than not, management negotiators operate within rather precise and limiting guidelines. During prenegotiation conferences with top management, these representatives are given cost increment parameters within which the settlement must fall.

The following contains a discussion of one method by which either party may cost out demands.*

INTRODUCING THE PROBLEM

As has already been mentioned, "compensation" consists of both salaries and/or wages and fringe benefits. It encompasses all forms of wage payments (including, for example, bonuses, commissions, and incentive payments) as well as the cost to the employer of all types of fringes.[1] Obviously, the higher-paid, senior employees in the bargaining unit tend to enjoy higher compensation, while the compensation of those at the opposite end of the salary and seniority spectrums tends to be lower.

For bargaining purposes, the most relevant statistic is the unit's average compensation or, more specifically, its *weighted* average compensation. The weighted average compensation (hereafter "average compensation" or, simply, "compensation") is merely an expression of how much it costs the employer, on the average, for each person on the payroll. It is this figure which presumably will be increased through negotiations.[2]

---

*Excerpted from a U.S. Department of Labor publication entitled, *The Use of Economic Data in Collective Bargaining,* as written in 1978 by the Labor–Management Services Administration.

1. Technically, employee compensation may also include the cost of legally-required employer payments for programs such as social security, unemployment compensation, and worker's compensation. These items are disregarded in this analysis.

2. It is also referred to as the "base" compensation—that is, the compensation figure against which the cost of any settlement will be measured in order to determine the value of the settlement.

Although precision in computing these compensation costs depends very much on detailed data usually available only in the employer's payroll records, it is possible to develop some reasonably accurate approximations even without such detailed information. . . .

These computations (to repeat) are not performed simply to engage in a mathematical exercise. The reason for seeking out this type of information is its usefulness at the bargaining table.

The value of salaries and fringe benefits must be known so that the value of any bargaining offer or settlement can be judged. Logically, therefore, the base compensation costs as of the point in time of negotiations—or, more accurately, immediately prior to the receipt of any increase—must be known.

The information that is needed in most cases in order to compute compensation costs is (a) the salary scales and benefit programs, (b) the distribution of the employees in the unit according to pay steps, shifts, and length of service, and (c) for purposes of some medical care programs, the employees' coverage status. If this information is in hand, just about all but one item of compensation can be readily computed.

The sole exception is the cost of the overtime premium. Overtime is apt to vary widely from week-to-week or month-to-month. Consequently, the data for any one pay period are an inadequate gauge where overtime is concerned. Simply by chance, it may cost the employer more one week than the next. It is common practice, therefore, to cost-out the overtime premium by averaging the cost of that benefit over the prior 12 months.

So far as the other elements of compensation are concerned, however, it is not necessary to study a full year's experience. With salaries, vacations, holidays, etc., the costs can be based on a snapshot taken at a fixed point in time on the basis of the provisions in the current collective bargaining agreement and the current distribution of the employees in the bargaining unit. That snapshot of compensation costs should be made as of the time the parties are at the bargaining table.

The purpose of this Appendix is to provide guidance on how to perform those computations, as well as the computations to determine the cost—the value—of an *increase* in compensation. The development of such compensation information gives the parties a basis for weighing the value of any particular wage and fringe benefit package.

Before the value or cost impact of any increase in compensation —whether in salaries, fringes, or both—can be gauged, the first step is to develop the base, or existing, compensation figure. A pay increase of $500 per employee, for example, means something different for a bargaining unit whose existing salary and fringe benefit cost per employee amount to $20,000 per year than for a unit whose compensation is $10,000. In the latter case, it represents an increase of 5 percent, but on a base of $20,000 it amounts to only 2½ percent. Thus, the base compensation figure is essential in determining the percentage value of any increase in compensation.

In order to demonstrate the computation methods for arriving at the base compensation figure, a Sample Bargaining Unit of firefighters has been constructed and certain levels of employment, salaries, fringe benefits and hours of work have been assumed:

Sample Bargaining Unit

(a) Employment and Salaries

CLASSIFICA-TION	NUMBER OF FIRE-FIGHTERS	SALARY
Probationary		
Step 1	5	$10,100
Step 2	10	11,100
Private	65	12,100
Lieutenant	15	13,500
Captain	5	14,500
	100	

(b) Longevity Payments

LONGEVITY STEP	NUMBER OF FIRE-FIGHTERS	LONGEVITY PAY
Step 1	20 Privates	$ 500
Step 2	10 Privates	1,000
Step 2	15 Lieutenants	1,000
Step 2	5 Captains	1,000

(c) Hours of Work

The scheduled hours consist of one 24-hour shift every three days (one on; two off), or an average of 56 hours per week and a total of 2,912 hours per year.

(d) Overtime Premium

All overtime hours are paid at the rate of time-and-one-half. The sample bargaining unit is assumed to have worked a total of 5,000 overtime hours during the preceding year.

(e) Shift Differential

The shift differential is 10 per-cent for all hours between 4 p.m. and 8 a.m. However, 10 members of the unit work exclusively on the day shift, from 8 a.m. to 4 p.m.

(f) Vacations

15 employees—(probationers)
5 shifts
35 employees—(privates)
10 shifts
50 employees—(all others)
15 shifts

(g) Holidays

Each firefighter is entitled to 10 paid holidays, and receives 8 hours pay for each holiday.

(h) Clothing Allowance

$150 per employee per year.

(i) Hospitalization

TYPE OF COVERAGE	NUMBER OF FIRE-FIGHTERS	EMPLOYER'S MONTHLY PAYMENT
Single Coverage	15	$20.00
Family Coverage	85	47.00

(j) Pensions

The employer contributes an amount equal to six percent of the payroll (including basic salaries, longevity, overtime and shift differentials).

COMPUTING BASE COMPENSATION

On the basis of the foregoing information on employment, salaries and benefits, we are now in a position to compute, for the Sample Bargaining Unit, its average base compensation—in essence, the cost of compensation for the average employee.

(a) Average Straight-time Salary

(1) CLASSIFI- CATION	(2) NUMBER OF FIRE- FIGHTERS	(3) SALARY	(4) WEIGHTED SALARIES (2) x (3)
Probationary			
Step 1	5	$10,100	$ 50,500
Step 2	10	11,100	111,000
Private	65	12,100	786,500
Lieutenant	15	13,500	202,500
Captain	5	14,500	72,500
	100		$1,223,000

Average Annual Basic Salary=
$1,223,000÷100; or $12,230 per year

(b) Longevity Pay

(1) LON- GEVITY STEP	(2) NUMBER OF FIRE- FIGHTERS	(3) LON- GEVITY PAY	(4) TOTAL LON- GEVITY PAY (2) x (3)
Step 1	20	$ 500	$10,000
Step 2	30	1,000	30,000
			$40,000

Average Annual Longevity Pay=
$40,000 ÷ 100,* or $400 per year

*Since the unit is trying to determine its average base compensation — that is, all the salary and fringe benefit items its members receive collectively — the total cost of longevity pay must be averaged over the entire unit of 100.

The combined average salary cost and average longevity cost amount to $12,630 per year. On an hourly basis, this comes to $4.337 ($12,630 ÷ 2,912 hours). This hourly rate is needed to compute the cost of some fringe benefits.

(c) Average Cost of Overtime

Overtime work for the Sample Bargaining Unit is assumed to be paid for at the rate of time-and-one-half. This means that part of the total overtime costs is an amount paid for at straight-time rates and part is a premium payment.

	(1) ANNUAL COST	(2) NUMBER OF FIREFIGHTERS	(3) AVERAGE ANNUAL COST (1) ÷ (2)
Straight-time cost (4.337 x 5,000 overtime hours)	$21,685.00	100	$216.85
Half-time premium cost (½ x $21,685.00)	10,842.50	100	108.43
Total Overtime Cost	$32,527.50		$325.28

It can be seen from these overtime-cost calculations that the half-time premium is worth $108.43 per year on the average, while the straight-time portion is worth $216.85. This means, of course, that total pay at straight-time rates amounts to $12,846.85 ($12,630 plus $216.85) per firefighter.

(d) Average Cost of Shift Differential

The Sample Bargaining Unit receives a shift differential of 10 percent for all hours worked between 4 p.m. and 8 a.m. But 10 members of the unit who work in headquarters are assumed to work hours that are not subject to the differential. This leaves 90 employees who receive the differential.

Since the differential is paid for hours worked between 4 p.m. and 8 a.m., it is applicable to only two-thirds of the normal 24-hour shift. It, therefore, only costs the employer two-thirds of 10 percent for each 24 hours. That is the reason for column (5) in the following calculation. Each employee receives the differential for only two-thirds of his 24-hour tour.

(1) CLASSIFICATION	(2) NO ON SHIFT PAY	(3) SALARY	(4) 10% OF COL. (3)	(5) .667 OF COL. (4)	(6) TOTAL COST (2) x (5)
Probationary					
Step 1	5	$10,100	$1,010	$ 674	$ 3,370
Step 2	10	11,100	1,110	740	7,400
Private					
Longevity–0	35	12,100	1,210	807	28,245
Longevity–1	17	12,600*	1,260	840	14,280
Longevity–2	7	13,100*	1,320	880	6,160
Lieutenant	12	14,500*	1,450	967	11,604
Captain	4	15,500*	1,550	1,034	4,136
	90				$75,195

Average Annual Cost of Shift Differential = $75,195 ÷ 100;** or $751.95 per year

*Basic salary plus longevity pay.
**Since the unit is trying to determine its average base compensation—that is, all the salary and fringe benefit items its members receive collectively—the total cost of the shift differential must be averaged over the entire unit of 100.

(e) Average Cost of Vacations

Vacation costs for the unit are influenced by (a) the amount of vacations received by the employees with differing lengths of service, and (b) the pay scales of those employees.

(1) CLASSIFICATION	(2) NUMBER OF FIREFIGHTERS	(3) HOURLY RATE*	(4) HOURS OF VACATION**	(5) TOTAL VACATION HOURS (2) x (4)	(6) TOTAL VACATION COSTS (3) x (5)
Probationary					
Step 1	5	$3.468	120	600	$ 2,080.80
Step 2	10	3.812	120	1,200	4,574.40
Private					
Longevity–0	35	4.155	240	8,400	34,902.00
Longevity–1	20	4.327	360	7,200	31,154.40
Longevity–2	10	4.499	360	3,600	16,196.40
Lieutenant	15	4.979	360	5,400	26,886.60
Captain	5	5.323	360	1,800	9,581.40
	100				$125,376.00

Average Annual Vacation Cost = $125,376 ÷ 100; or $1,253.76 per year

*Derived from annual salaries (including longevity pay), divided by 2,912 hours (56 hours x 52 weeks). The 10 firefighters who do not receive shift differential would be on a regular 40-hour week and would, therefore, have a different hourly rate and vacation entitlement. The impact on cost, however, would be minimal. It has, therefore, been disregarded in this computation.
**Since each firefighter works a 24 hour shift, the hours of vacation are arrived at by multiplying the number of work shifts of vacation entitlement by 24 hours. For example, the figure of 120 hours is obtained by multiplying 5 shifts of vacation x 24 hours (one work shift).

(f)   Average Cost of Paid Holidays

Unlike vacations, the number of holidays received by an employee is not typically tied to length of service. Where the level of benefits is uniform, as it is with paid holidays, the calculation to determine its average cost is less complex.

In the Sample Bargaining Unit, it is assumed that each firefighter receives 8 hours of pay for each of his 10 paid holidays, or a total of 80 hours of holiday pay:

1.   Average Annual Cost of Paid Holidays = $346.96 (80 hours x $4.337 average straight-time hourly rate), or

2.   Total Annual Cost of Paid Holiday hours per year = 8,000 (80 hours x 100 employees)

   Total annual cost of paid holidays = $34,696.00 (the unit's average straight-time hourly rate of $4.337 x 8,000 hours)

   Average annual cost of paid holidays = $346.96 (34,696.00 ÷ 100 employees)

(g) Average Cost of Hospitalization

(1) TYPE OF COVER-AGE	(2) NUMBER OF FIRE-FIGHTERS	(3) YEARLY PREMIUM COST TO EM-PLOYER	(4) TOTAL COST TO EM-PLOYER (2) x (3)
Single	15	$240	$ 3,600
Family	85	564	47,940
	100		$51,540

Average Annual Cost of Hospitalization = $51,540 ÷ 100; or $515.40 per year

(h)   Other Fringe Benefits

1.   Pensions cost the employer six percent of payroll. The payroll amounts to $1,370,723 (salary cost — $1,223,000; longevity cost — $40,000; overtime cost — $32,528; and shift differential $75,195). Six percent of this total is $82,243 which, when divided by 100, yields $822.43 as the average cost of pensions per firefighter, per year.

2.   The yearly cost of the clothing allowance is $150 per firefighter.

As the recapitulation below indicates, total compensation—salary plus fringes—for each firefighter averages $16,795.78 per year.

Once having determined the base compensation costs, it is now possible to compute the value—or cost—of any increase in the items of compensation. The methods used to make these computations are essentially the same as those used to compute the base compensation data.

Average Annual Base Compensation for the Sample Bargaining Unit

(a) Straight-time		(b) Fringe benefits	$ 3,948.93
earnings	$12,846.85	Overtime premium	$ 108.43
Basic salary	$12,230.00	Shift differential	751.95
Longevity pay	400.00	Vacations	1,253.76
Overtime	216.85*	Holidays	346.96
		Hospitalization	515.40
		Clothing allowance	150.00
		Pension	822.43
		(c) Total	$16,795.78

*This is only the straight-time portion of overtime pay. The premium portion appears with the fringe benefits.

COMPUTING THE COST OF INCREASES
IN ITEMS OF COMPENSATION

In order to demonstrate how to cost-out any increases in compensation, it will be assumed that the Sample Bargaining Unit negotiates a settlement consisting of the following package:

—An increase of 5 percent in basic salaries;

—Two additional shifts of vacation for all those at the second step of longevity;

—An improvement in the benefits provided by the hospitalization program, which will cost the employer an additional $4.00 per month for family coverage and $2.50 for single coverage.

The cost of this settlement—that is, the amount of the increase in compensation that it represents—would be computed in the manner presented below, starting first with the cost-impact of the salary increase. As will be noted, the objective of the computation is to find the *average* cost of the increase—that is, the cost per firefighter, per year.

(a) Increase in Cost of Salaries. The increase in average annual basic salary (0.05 × $12,230) is $611.50. The cost of longevity pay does not increase. This is because longevity increments for the unit are fixed dollar amounts. If these payments were based on a percentage of salary—that is, if they were linked to the pay scales—then the cost of the longevity payments would also have risen by 5 percent. However, as a fixed dollar amount, these payments remain unaffected by the increase in basic salaries.

As a result, the increase in the unit's total average salary ($12,230 in basic salary plus $400 in longevity) is, in reality, not 5 percent, but only 4.8 percent ($611.50 ÷ $12,630).

This difference is important because of the way in which pay increases impact on the cost of fringe benefits. This is commonly referred to as the "roll up." As salaries increase, so does the cost to the employer of such fringes as vacations, holidays, overtime premiums, etc. This increase in cost comes about even though the benefits are not improved.

Some fringes, however, are not subject to the roll up. This is the case with respect to those fringe benefits that are not linked to pay rates. Examples of this type of fringe benefit include shift differentials that are stated in cents-per-hour (in contrast to a percentage of salary), a flat dollar amount for clothing allowance, and most group insurance programs.

(b) Cost Impact of the "Roll up." The increase in average straight-time pay (basic salary plus longevity pay) of the Sample Bargaining Unit was shown to be 4.8 percent. This means that the average cost of every benefit linked to salary will likewise increase by 4.8 percent. In our example, therefore, the average cost of compensation will go up by $611.50 per year in salaries, *plus* however much this adds to the costs of the fringe benefits as a result of the roll up.

But there is more. For our example, it is also to be assumed that the Sample Bargaining Unit will gain a vacation improvement—two additional shifts at the second step of longevity—and an improved hospitalization program.

The employer's contribution for the hospitalization program of the Sample Bargaining Unit is a fixed dollar amount and is, therefore, not subject to any roll up. Thus, we need in this instance be concerned only with the costing-out of the improvement in that benefit.

This is not the case with the vacations. Here the cost-increase is double-barreled—the cost of the improvement *and* the cost of the roll up.

None of the other fringe benefits of the Sample Bargaining Unit will be improved. Consequently, so far as they are concerned, we need only compute the increases in cost due to the roll up. The fringes which fit this

(1) FRINGE BENEFIT	(2) BASE AVERAGE ANNUAL COST	(3) ROLL UP FACTOR	(4) INCREASED COST (2) x (3)
Overtime			
Straight-time	$216.85	0.048	$ 10.41
Premium	108.43	0.048	5.20
Shift differential	751.95	0.048	36.09
Holidays	346.96	0.048	16.65
Pensions	822.43	0.048	39.48
			$107.83

category are overtime premiums, holidays, sick leave, shift differentials, and pensions.

As is indicated in the table, column (3)—the added cost due to the roll up—is obtained by multiplying the base (pre-settlement) cost by 0.048. Obviously, if shift differentials and/or pensions were based on a set dollar (or cent) amount (instead of a percentage of salary), there would be no roll up cost associated with them. The only increase in cost that would result in such a situation would be associated with an improvement in the benefit item.

Having performed this computation, we can now begin to see the impact of this roll up factor. As a result of the increase in pay, the four fringe benefit items will together cost the employer an additional $107.83 per firefighter, per year.

(c) Increase in Cost of Vacations. As noted earlier, the vacation improvement of two shifts—48 hours (2 shifts × 24 hours)—is to be limited to those whose length of service is equal to the time required to achieve the second step of longevity in the salary structure. Thus, it will be received by 30 members of the unit—10 privates, 15 lieutenants, and 5 captains.[3]

The first step in the computation is to determine the cost of the *new* benefit under the *existing* (old) salaries—that is, before the 4.8 percent pay increase:

(1) NUMBER OF FIREFIGHTERS	(2) HOURS OF INCREASED VACATION	(3) TOTAL HOURS (1) x (2)	(4) EXISTING HOURLY RATES*	(5) COST OF IMPROVEMENT (3) x (4)
10 Privates	48	480	$4.499	$2,159.52
15 Lieutenants	48	720	4.979	3,584.88
5 Captains	48	240	5.323	$1,277.52
				$7,021.92

The calculation thus far reflects only the additional cost of the vacation improvement based on the salaries existing *prior to* the 4.8 percent pay

3. In costing out an improvement in vacations, the computation should cover the cost impact in the first year *only*. There is no need to be concerned with the impact in subsequent years when, supposedly, more and more employees become eligible for the improved benefit. For computational purposes, it must be assumed that the average length of service in the unit remains constant. This constancy is caused by normal personnel flows. As the more senior staff leave because of retirement or death, the staff is replenished by new hires without any accumulated seniority. Thus, for this type of computation, it must be presumed that the proportion of the workforce which benefits from the improved vacation will be constant year after year.

It should be noted that an improvement in vacations (or any other form of paid leave) that is offset by corresponding reductions in on-duty manning does not represent any increase in cost to the employer.

raise. In other words, if there had been no pay increase, the vacation improvement would result in an added cost of $7,021.92. But there was a pay increase. As a result, the base year vacation costs—including now the added cost of the improvement—must be rolled up by the 4.8 percent factor. Every hour of vacation—the old and the new—will cost 4.8 percent more as a result of the pay increase:

(1)	(2)	(3)	(4)	(5)	(6)
	EXISTING VACATION	INCREASE	ADJUSTED BASE COSTS	ROLL UP	INCREASED COST FROM ROLL UP
CLASSIFICATION	COSTS	IN COST	(2) + (3)	FACTOR	(4) x (5)
Probationary					
Step 1	$ 2,080.80	—	$ 2,080.80	0.048	$ 99.88
Step 2	4,574.40	—	4,574.40	0.048	219.57
Private					
Longevity–0	34,902.00	—	34,902.00	0.048	1,675.30
Longevity–1	31,154.40	—	31,154.40	0.048	1,495.41
Longevity–2	16,196.40	$2,159.52	18,355.92	0.048	881.08
Lieutenant	26,886.60	3,584.88	30,471.48	0.048	1,462.63
Captain	9,581.40	1,277.52	10,858.92	0.048	521.23
	$125,376.00	$7,021.92	$132,397.92	0.048	$6,355.10

By adding the two "new" pieces of cost—$7,021.92, which is the cost of the improvement, and $6,355.10, which is the cost due to the impact of the wage increase—we obtain the total increase in the cost of vacations. It amounts to $13,377.02. In order to figure the *average* cost, this total must be divided by the number of firefighters in the Sample Bargaining Unit. The increase in the average cost of vacations, therefore, is—

$$13,377 \div 100, \text{ or } \$133.77$$

Had the vacation improvement been granted across-the-board, to everyone in the unit, the calculation would have been different—and considerably easier. If the entire unit were to receive an additional 48 hours of vacation, the total additional hours would then be 4,800 (48 hours × 100 employees). These hours would then be multiplied by the unit's old average straight-time rate ($4.337), in order to arrive at the cost of the additional vacation improvement which, in this case, would have come to $20,817.60 (4,800 hours × $4.337). And, in that case, the total cost of vacations—that is the across-the-board improvement, plus the impact of the 4.8 percent salary increase—would have been computed as follows:

(a) Roll up of old vacation costs   = $ 6,018.05
($125,376 x 0.048)
(b) Cost of vacation improvement = $20,817.60
(c) Roll up cost of improvement   = $ 999.24
($20,817.60 x 0.048)

These pieces total to $27,834.89. When spread over the entire Sample Bargaining Unit, the increase in the average cost of vacations would have been $278.35 per year ($27,834.89 ÷ 100 employees).

This latter method of calculation does not apply only to vacations. It applies to any situation where a salary-related fringe benefit is to be improved equally for every member of the unit. An additional paid holiday would be another good example.

(d) Increase in Cost of Hospitalization. In this example, it has been assumed that the Sample Bargaining Unit has negotiated as part of its new package an improvement in its hospitalization plan. As with most hospitalization programs, the one covering this unit is not linked to salaries.

This improvement, it is assumed, will cost the employer an additional $4.00 per month ($48 per year) for family coverage, and $2.50 per month ($30 per year) for single coverage. Thus, based on this and previous information about the breakdown of employees receiving each type of coverage the calculation of the increase in hospitalization costs is as follows:

(1) TYPE OF COVERAGE	(2) ANNUAL NUMBER COVERED	(3) TOTAL NEW COST OF IMPROVEMENT	(4) COST (2) x (3)
Single	15	$30	$ 450
Family	85	48	4,080
			$4,530

The unit's average hospitalization cost will be increased by $45.30 per year ($4,530 ÷ 100 employees).

THE TOTAL INCREASE IN THE AVERAGE COST OF COMPENSATION

At this point, the increase in the costs of all the items of compensation which will change because of the Sample Bargaining Unit's newly-negotiated package have been calculated. All that is left is to combine these individual pieces in order to arrive at the total increase in the unit's average cost of compensation. This is done in the tabulation which appears below.

As the recapitulation shows, the average increase in salary costs amounts to $621.91 per year, while the average increase in the cost of the fringe benefits (including *new* benefit costs, as well as *roll up* costs) comes to $276.49, for a total increase in average annual compensation of $898.40 per firefighter, per *year*. That is the total annual cost of the settlement per firefighter.

Increase in Average Annual Cost of Compensation for Sample Bargaining Unit

(a)	Straight-time earnings	**$621.91**	(b)	Fringe benefits	**$276.49**
	Basic salary	$611.50		Overtime premium	$ 5.20
	Longevity pay	—		Shift differential	36.09
	Overtime (straight-time portion)	10.41		Vacations	133.77
				Holidays	16.65
				Hospitalization	45.30
				Clothing allowance	—
				Pensions	39.48
			(c)	Total Increase in Average Annual Cost of Annual Compensation	**$898.40**

There remains one final computation that is really the most significant —the *percent* increase that all of these figures represent. The unit's average base compensation per year was $16,796. The total dollar increase amounts to $898. The percent increase, therefore, is 5.3 percent ($898 ÷ $16.796), and that is the amount by which the unit's package increased the employer's average yearly cost per firefighter.

COMPUTING THE HOURLY COST OF COMPENSATION

The increase in the cost of compensation per *hour* will be the same. The approach to the computation, however, is different than that which was used in connection with the cost per year. In the case of the hourly computation, the goal is to obtain the cost per hour of *work*. This requires that a distinction be drawn between hours worked and hours paid for. The difference between the two is leave time.

In the Sample Bargaining Unit, for example, the employee receives an annual salary which covers 2,912 regularly scheduled hours (56 hours per week, times 52). In addition, he works an average of 50 hours of overtime per year. The sum of these two—regularly scheduled hours and overtime hours, or 2,962—are the total hours paid for.

But they do not represent hours worked, because some of those hours are paid leave time. The Sample Bargaining Unit, for example, receives paid leave time in the form of vacations and holidays. The number of hours actually worked by each employee is 2,600 (2,962 hours paid for, minus 362 hours[4] of paid leave).

The paid leave hours are, in a sense, bonuses—hours paid for, above and beyond hours worked. Thus, in order to obtain the hourly cost represented by these "bonuses"—that is, the hours of paid leave—the annual dollar cost of these benefits is divided by the annual hours *worked*.

It is the same as if we were trying to compute the per-hour cost of a year-end bonus. The dollar amount of that bonus would simply be divided by the total number of hours worked during the year.

So it is with *all* fringe benefits, not only paid leave. In exchange for those benefits the employer receives hours of work (the straight-time hours and the overtime hours). Consequently, the hourly cost of any fringe benefit will be obtained by dividing the annual cost of the benefit by the annual number of hours *worked*. In some instances that cost is converted into money that ends up in the employee's pocket, as it does in the case of fringe benefits like shift differentials, overtime premiums and clothing allowances. In other instances—such as hospitalization and pensions—the employee is provided with benefits in the form of insurance programs. And in the case of paid leave time—holidays,[5] vacations, sick leave, etc.—the return to the employee is in terms of fewer hours of work.

The average annual costs of the fringe benefits of the Sample Bargaining Unit were developed earlier in connection with the computations of the unit's average annual base compensation. They appear in column (2) under average annual cost.

15 firefighters x 120 hours (five 24-hour shifts)	= 1,800 hours
35 firefighters x 240 hours (ten 24-hour shifts)	= 8,400 hours
50 firefighters x 360 hours (fifteen 24-hour shifts)	= 18,000 hours
	28,200 hours

This averages out to 282 hours of vacation per firefighter (28,200 ÷ 100) which, together with 80 holiday hours, totals 362 paid leave hours).

---

4. Each firefighter receives 80 hours in paid holidays per year. The average number of hours of vacation per year was derived as follows.

5. Typically, of course, firefighters do not receive time off, but are paid an extra day's pay for working a holiday.

In order to convert the costs of those fringe benefits into an average hourly amount, they are divided by 2,600—the average hours worked during the year by each employee in the unit. As can be seen, the hourly cost of all fringe benefits amounts to $1.518.

(1)	(2)	(3)	(4)
			AVERAGE
	AVERAGE	AVERAGE HOURS	HOURLY COST
FRINGE BENEFIT	ANNUAL COST	WORKED	(2) ÷ (3)
Overtime Premium*	$ 108.43	2,600	$0.042
Shift Differential	751.95	2,600	0.289
Vacations	1,253.76	2,600	0.482
Holidays	346.96	2,600	0.133
Hospitalization	515.40	2,600	0.198
Clothing Allowance	150.00	2,600	0.058
Pensions	822.43	2,600	0.316
	$3,948.93		$1.518

*Includes only the premium portion of the pay for overtime work.

In addition to the fringe benefit costs, compensation includes the basic pay. For our Sample Bargaining Unit this is $12,630 per year (average salary plus average cost of longevity payments). On a straight-time hourly basis, this comes to $4.337 ($12,630 ÷ 2,912 hours). Even with the straight-time portion for the year's overtime included ($216.85), the average straight-time hourly rate of pay will, of course, still remain at $4.337 ($12,846.45 ÷ 2,962 hours).

A recapitulation of these salary and fringe benefit cost data produces both the average *annual* base compensation figure for the Sample Bargaining Unit and the average *hourly* figure:

	HOURLY	YEARLY
Earnings at Straight time	$12,846.85 ÷ 2,962 =	$4.337
Fringe Benefits	3,948.93 ÷ 2,600 =	$1.519
Total Compensation	$16,795.78	$5.856

As indicated, on an annual basis, the average compensation cost comes to $16,795.78, a figure that was also presented earlier in this chapter. And on an hourly basis, the average compensation of the unit amounts to $5.856.

Essentially the same process is followed if the *increase* in compensation is to be measured on an hourly (instead of an annual) basis.

The five percent pay increase received by the Sample Bargaining Unit would be worth 21 cents ($12,230 × 0.05 = $611.50; $611.50 ÷ 2,912 =

$0.21). The annual increase in the unit's fringe benefit costs per firefighter —$276.49 for all items combined—works out to 10.6 cents per hour ($276.49 ÷ *2600* hours).

Together, these represent a gain in average compensation of 31.6 cents per hour, or 5.4 percent ($0.316 ÷ $5.856). This is one-tenth of a percentage point off from the amount of increase (5.3 percent) reflected by the annual data—a difference due simply to the rounding of decimals during the computation process.

BALANCING THE RIGHTS OF LABOR AND MANAGEMENT

6

Management's authority with respect to matters of wages, hours, and other conditions of employment is unilateral where there is no union. The unorganized employer's authority is restrained only by employment statutes and the business necessity to attract and retain a work force. This state of affairs changes once workers opt for union representation. Management's authority is now shared with the workers at the bargaining table. The negotiated labor agreement is the product of this sharing of authority. It represents a statement of the *contractual rights* of labor and management.

In this chapter, we begin with a discussion of two distinct theories of management authority held by employers with collective bargaining relationships. The theory embraced by management will influence the way it approaches negotiations and contract administration. Next, we shall underscore the often overlooked idea that management seldom, if ever, shares with the union its right to *direct* the work force. This point is perhaps too obvious. However, we will give it explicit consideration because it helps in understanding contract administration. Finally, the analysis will carry us to a discussion of how the right of management to direct the work force is counterbalanced (in most instances) by the right of workers or union to grieve management's directives. It is when the contract is being administered that disputes arise between labor's contractual rights versus management's contractual or residual rights.

ALTERNATIVE THEORIES ABOUT THE NATURE OF MANAGERIAL AUTHORITY

Of the two principal theories on the nature of managerial authority in labor relations, the one clearly preferred in management circles is the *residual rights* theory. The second theory, the *trusteeship* theory, plays down the sovereignty rationale of management rights and stresses the *multiple obligations* of modern management.[1] It emphasizes that management has responsibilities toward its employees, the community in which it functions, and the consumers of its product(s) or service(s). Many residualists do not dispute the fact that management has multiple obligations. However, they are generally more concerned to maintain functions as exclusively management's than are those in the trusteeship school.

The residualists generally seek to draw a firm line of demarcation between what *they* regard as bargainable and what they think of as being *unchallengeably* within their decision-making authority. Adherents of the trusteeship school are not usually preoccupied with sovereign prerogatives. They are more concerned with achieving a rational allocation of functions, which, in their eyes, should be pragmatically determined; that is, the division of functions should be made on the basis of "comparative advantage" rather than in terms of which party was there first. Residualists appear to be preoccupied with historical primacy. They espouse what can be termed the Book of Genesis approach (that is, *in the beginning there was management*). In such a context, the union as a "late arrival" can claim only those controls over a previously unlimited management authority that it can negotiate into the contract.

Residualists tend to view unionism and collective bargaining as a vehicle

---

1. The literature on the nature of managerial authority and the impact of the union thereon continues to be extensive. The pioneer analysis, still useful, is Neil W. Chamberlain, *The Union Challenge to Management Control* (New York: Harper & Row, Pub., 1948). An excellent treatment of more recent vintage is Margaret K. Chandler, *Management Rights and Union Interests* (New York: McGraw-Hill, 1964). Empirical evidence on the explosive subcontracting issue is of prime importance in Professor Chandler's interdisciplinary, cross-cultural treatment. A perceptive early analysis of managerial authority is that of Florence Peterson, "Management Efficiency and Collective Bargaining," *Industrial and Labor Relations Review*, 1 (October 1947), 29–49.

for progressive encroachment on a formerly exclusive management domain. The contract is viewed as an instrument that may condition or limit previously complete managerial authority. Should the contract be silent on any subject, residualists maintain with vigor (and considerable logic) that management retains 100 percent discretion. In everyday language, residualists are saying, "If we haven't given it away or agreed to limit ourselves, we've still got it completely."

The Residualist Theory of Management's Rights

In preunion days, management did have exclusive authority to determine the level of wages and type of working conditions to provide for its employees. Many employers voluntarily paid good wages and provided satisfactory working conditions. Some even established grievance procedures or fostered and supported what were usually called "employee representation plans." The latter functioned in a limited sense as a voice or channel for worker complaints. However, even under the most benevolent of managerial regimes, any rights and privileges that employees might have enjoyed were a function of *unilateral management acts rather than joint decision making.*

Whether employers were militantly antiunion or benevolently paternalistic (or both), they tended to regard union entry as an intrusion on provinces assigned by natural law to management. When employers found themselves under a legal duty to bargain in good faith with unions certified as the exclusive representatives of their employers, their attitudes were often defensive and negative in nature. Few employers welcomed the coming of unions. Instead, collective bargaining was looked upon as an instrument to limit management's essential discretionary activity. When management holds such a psychological view it is easy to adopt a "they shall not pass" approach. Few employers of such a persuasion had the vision to anticipate the positive uses of collective bargaining for improving relationships with their employees. This approach to negotiations and contract administration is negative.

Most proponents of the residual rights theory have not shirked their legal obligations to bargain, once their employees chose to be represented by labor organizations. In many cases, however, they did not go beyond satisfying the minimum legislative standards of required performance in bargaining.[2] Residualists nearly always seek to separate out exclusive management functions from those subject to negotiation.

Perhaps the most comprehensive formulation of *proposed exclusive man-*

---

2. As stated in section 8(d) of the NLRA, both parties have a mutual obligation "to meet at reasonable times and confer in good faith with respect to wages, hours and other terms and conditions of employment."

agement functions was made by the management members of a joint union–management committee at President Truman's Labor Management Conference held in November 1945. The passage of years has not diminished appreciably the basic enthusiasm in management circles for this 1945 listing. It is therefore reproduced below:

> The determination of products to be manufactured or services to be rendered to customers by the enterprise; and the location of the business, including the establishment of new units and the relocation or closing of old units. (When it becomes necessary to relocate a unit, or close an old unit, or transfer major operations between plants, management should give careful consideration to the impact of such moves on the employees involved, and discuss with them or their accredited representatives possible solutions for the resulting problems.)
>
> The determination of the lay-out and equipment to be used in the business; the processes, techniques, methods, and means of manufacture and distribution; the materials to be used (subject to proper health and safety measures where dangerous materials are utilized) and the size and character of inventories.
>
> The determination of financial policies; general accounting procedures —particularly the internal accounting necessary to make reports to the owners of the business and to government bodies requiring financial reports; prices of goods sold or services rendered to customers; and customer relations.
>
> The determination of the management organization of each producing or distributing unit; and the selection of employees for promotion to supervisory and other managerial positions.
>
> The determination of job content (this refers to establishing the duties required in the performance of any given job and not to wages); and determination of the size of the work force; the allocation and assignment of work to workers; determination of policies affecting the selection of employees; establishment of quality standards and judgment of workmanship required; and the maintenance of discipline and control and use of the plant property; the scheduling of operations and the number of shifts.[3]

Most employers prefer to include a management rights clause in union agreements. A significant minority of residualists, however, maintains that logic suggests omitting any such clause. The point is stressed that such a clause is unnecessary when management has unchallengeable authority to act on anything that is not limited or conditioned by contract. In this view, a management rights clause may in fact be dangerous because it can lead to erosion of managerial rights by interpretation in contract administration. If there is no management rights clause, there can be no limitation of authority by shortsighted grievance settlements or ambitious arbitration decisions. Its omission from the contract removes an important source of friction in cases

---

3. Division of Labor Standards, U.S. Department of Labor, Bulletin 77, *The President's National Labor–Management Conference*, November 5–30, 1945, Summary and Committee Reports (Washington, D.C.: Government Printing Office, 1946), p. 58.

where management is firm about its prerogatives and is dealing with a militant, aggressive union. A management rights clause sets up one more target for the union to shoot at, with the constant possibility of further circumscribing of managerial authority through interpretation.

To summarize, the residualist position can be stated as follows:

1. Prior to unionism, management possessed full power over all phases of employee relations.
2. Collective bargaining introduces certain specific restrictions on managerial authority and discretion.
3. Management retains all powers, rights, and privileges not specifically given away or restricted by the collective agreement. Any subject not covered by the agreement remains under exclusive, unilateral management control.
4. Management has an obligation to contain unionism and to preserve intact the essential functions of management. Supporters of the prerogative approach vary considerably in their views as to which functions are so essential as to require their remaining exclusively in management's hands.

The Trusteeship Theory of Management Rights in Summary Form

In emphasizing the multiple obligations of management, the trusteeship theory envisages the manager as a highly skilled employee hired for these specific purposes: (1) to make a profit, to satisfy stockholders; (2) to sell a quality product at a just price, to satisfy employees.[4] A rational or pragmatic allocation of functions is stressed rather than a defense of absolute rights or prerogatives. The expanding scope of collective bargaining is not regarded as a threat to effective managerial performance.

According to the trusteeship view, unilateral management control may remain as the preferred method of running an enterprise, but such a preference does not preclude a willingness to experiment with collective bargaining as a method of management. There is a recognition that

---

4. Although we continue to use the term "trusteeship theory," essentially similar views are widely referred to in the literature as the "implied obligations" concept of managerial authority. The implied obligations thesis will be found frequently in discussions within the arbitration fraternity and between management and union practitioners. See, for example, the presidential address of Charles C. Killingsworth, entitled "Management Rights Revisited," at the twenty-second annual meeting of the National Academy of Arbitrators, published in late 1969 by the Bureau of National Affairs, Washington, D.C.

collective bargaining can be the means for deciding upon the allocation of the fruits of enterprise among the various interested groups.

Once an employer has become reconciled to a long-run relationship with a union representing his employees, we can assume that he will seek to achieve maximum value from this relationship. Optimization is difficult to achieve if one is constantly saying that certain management functions are taboo for negotiation (or even for consultation). It is hard for the union leadership to take a positive line when management asserts that certain functions are exclusively and irrevocably its sole concern.

Proponents of the trusteeship theory believe management would yield greater benefits from a cooperative relationship than through establishing boundaries of negotiable and non-negotiable issues. This does not mean that adherents of the trusteeship doctrine believe in giving away their managerial right to direct the enterprise. Rather, they believe that "code-termination" is a practical method of solving certain managerial problems.

A main asset of trusteeship thinking on the nature of managerial authority is that it sees no pressing need to claim authority in terms that are absolute, unlimited, indivisible, or unchallengeable. There is instead a healthy understanding that long-run constructive relationships with unions and employees are determined through recognition of the concepts of limited government and, in the final analysis, on the consent of the governed. Viewing collective bargaining as a method of industrial government precludes regarding either managerial or union authority as inherently unlimited or unchallengeable.

The recent growth of unionism in higher education has been conducive to the development of codified trustee relations between employers and professional employees. Faculties and university administrations have traditionally worked together on a cooperative basis in securing legislative funding and have shared authority through faculty controlled governance systems. Codification of this trusteeship may be expected where formal collective bargaining is introduced into the relationship. In these situations, neither management nor faculty see their authority as inherently unlimited. Indeed, through academic institutions such as "peer review and assessment," "tenure," and "self-governance," it is not surprising that a clause like the following found its way into a labor agreement.

It is recognized that the faculty has primary responsibility for the fundamental views of curriculum, subject matter, methods of instruction, research, and those aspects of student life which relate to the educational process. The association acknowledges that, on these matters, final authority is lodged with the Board of Trustees or their delegated representatives. . . .

This authority should be exercised adversely only for good and just cause and for reasons communicated in writing to the faculty association and to the faculty senate, if requested by them.[5]

MANAGEMENT'S RIGHT
TO DIRECT THE WORK FORCE

The mere fact that a collective bargaining relationship has been established does not imply that the organized employer somehow loses the authority to manage. With or without a management rights clause in the agreement, there is no debate over the notion that the employer retains the right to make personnel decisions and orders. This concept follows from the ideas found in the residual rights theory. However, even if old-fashioned sovereignty notions are discarded, *management would continue to perform alone* most of the functions required in the running of any enterprise. Management will be managing, however, *because it is pragmatically wise to do so, and not because such functions are eternally management's by divine right.* Unions are not likely to encroach upon management's right to act because it is in the union's self-interest for management to have full responsibility for unpopular managerial decisions.

Most American union leaders have neither the interest nor the competence to direct the enterprise, even if their raw economic strength could be used to "take over." Unions serve primarily to defend the rights and interests of employees. Involvement with managerial decisions would ultimately result in a conflict of interests. Unions operate as political organizations and must devote primary attention to the expressed desires of the employees. Participation in unpopular managerial decisions would only decrease the union's popularity. Therefore, in the United States, most unions gladly relinquish rights to managerial initiative in exchange for rights to defend employees for perceived violations of the collective agreement.

Management remains in the hands of the employer unless there are special reasons for the union to perform what is customarily a management function. For example, the nature of the women's clothing industry necessitates managerial decision making by the union. In this industry, with such a large number of small firms, the International Ladies' Garment Workers Union (ILGWU) must function as a stabilizing force. This involves decisions by the union relating to introduction or discontinuance of dress lines, advertising and pricing, matters that are never performed by unions in most other industries. The ILGWU also serves as "policeman" of the industry's incentive system through its own industrial engineering department.

5. Roger Williams College, Article I—Rights and Responsibilities.

UNION'S RIGHT TO OBJECT
TO MANAGEMENT'S INITIATIVES

The management rights clause can be read as nothing more than a reminder that it is management's job to "act" and direct the work force. Management's administrative *initiative* is thereby *reasserted* by contractual language. Since management has the authority to act, it in effect interprets and applies the terms of the labor agreement in the first instance. Does this managerial potency undercut collective bargaining and assign to the union a second-class role? Certainly not. The union has the right to grieve every action management initiates which the union claims is in violation of the contract. Management's right to direct the enterprise and the union's right to protect the interests of the employees are thus distinct and counterbalancing functions. This distinction must remain clear in order for the system of industrial governance to operate effectively. It is critical to the process of contract administration.

Most labor agreements balance management's right to *act* with the union's (employee's) right to *react*. The right to react is manifest in·the negotiated grievance clause. Grievance procedures allow for objections to managerial actions without having to resort to work actions to interrupt business operations as a means of pressuring management to revise its initiative. Labor in the United States has long recognized the mutual impracticability of strikes over issues involving the interpretation and application of the negotiated agreement. Without a grievance mechanism, however, we would surely observe an increased rate of wildcat strikes in protest over managerial actions. Hence, when disputes arise over an employer directive during the life of an agreement, the union in effect has agreed via the grievance clause to *obey first and grieve later*.[6]

Diagram 6–1 is a visual summary of the major ideas presented in this chapter thus far. Management's rights originate in the residual rights theory and the management rights clause found in labor agreements is an attempt to underscore a predisposition to the residualist doctrine. The management rights clause as much as anything is an explicit note or reminder to those who read and interpret the contract that management retains the fundamental right to "act," to direct the work force, and run the enterprise. Management does not draw added authority from the management rights clause; thus, it makes explicit reference to a right that is implicitly management's, namely, *the right to "act."*

---

6. Arbitrators recognize that in some situations an overriding right or interest of the employee may require an exception to the "obey first" rule. Most arbitrators agree that under certain circumstances an employee may justifiably refuse to obey orders that would create safety or health hazards, deprive him of his right to grieve, or force him to work overtime (assuming the contract is silent on that issue). Of course, the employee may also refuse orders directing him to commit illegal or immoral acts.

The union and workers derive their right to object to a managerial initiative from the labor agreement which, in most instances, contains a grievance clause. With such a right, workers are protected against contractual violations and managerial decisions that are arbitrary, capricious, and discriminatory. Moreover, while the union and workers will obey a managerial order or decision, even though they may believe that it is in violation of their contractual or implied rights (which are discussed in the next chapter), they can *grieve* the matter and resolve it through grievance procedure negotiations or have the dispute arbitrated. The grievance clause recognizes the union's right to react to a management initiative.

DIAGRAM 6-1

Industrial Balance: Management's Right to Act; Union's Right to React

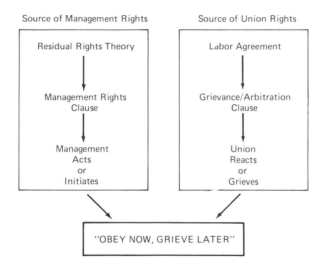

Implicit in this right is management's willingness to accept as final and binding the decision of an arbitrator if a prearbitration, negotiated settlement of the dispute is not reached; further, it is the union's willingness to obey the management directive and forego use of the strike weapon over a disputed act, knowing that the management initiative may ultimately be reversed.

Hence, a balance exists in industrial relations in the United States. This balance gives operational meaning to the success of the dictum "obey now, grieve later." Thanks to this structuring of the relationship between the parties, labor relations in the United States are relatively free of wildcat strikes which plague other industrial nations. During the term of a labor agreement the parties assume distinctive roles. Both parties understand that while they may disagree over the way their contract ought to be administered, management has the right to put its interpretations into effect and labor has the right to object.

Historically, management has not sought to process grievances against the union. The vast majority of labor agreements permit employee and union grievances, but few provide for management grievances. This observation, of course, is consistent with the thesis that management acts and the union reacts. In recent times, however, to capitalize on the advantages associated with "choosing among multiple forums for remedy," some employers have bargained provisions permitting them to grieve against union tactics. This permits management to add arbitration to the spectrum of remedial forums.

In the public sector, the doctrine of state sovereignty operates in a similar fashion to the residual rights theory. A sovereign power is supposedly immune to challenge; therefore, a union cannot lawfully threaten the state's right to manage. However, the notion of sovereignty is somewhat antiquated, as evidenced by the occurrence of strikes in the public sector. The organization of public employees is rarely viewed as a government insurrection. Rather, as in the private sector, employee organization is commonly perceived as a means of protection against managerial actions. The flow in Diagram 6–1 developed for the private sector applies to the public sector as well.

SUMMARY

We began this short chapter with an outline of the essential differences between the residual rights theory and the trusteeship theory of management authority. With these notions in mind, we presented the management rights clause as little more than an explicit codification of management's implicit right to initiate the terms of the negotiated contract; then, we viewed the grievance clause as labor's right to object to management's initiatives. In combination, these two clauses tend to balance the rights of labor and management; they motivate an explanation for the "obey now, grieve later," understanding so prevalent in U.S. labor relations.

The foundation is now set for a detailed discussion on contractual administration. This is the subject matter of Chapter 7.

Questions for Discussion, Thought, and Research

1. It is generally understood that management retains all of the rights that it has not given up in bargaining. Does this mean that a company can take any action its contract does not expressly forbid?

2. Company X has unilaterally subcontracted out work performed by

union Y's members. Union Y files a grievance. The union's sole contention is that management violated the labor agreement by subcontracting work (a subject about which the contract is silent) because the contract contained no management rights clause. Does the absence of a management rights clause restrict management's right to subcontract? Explain.

3. Why is it not customary for management to file grievances against a union? In what cases might the filing of a grievance be appropriate?

4. You have been appointed to the management negotiating committee. Your primary task is to draft a favorable management rights clause for your team. What are some of the important issues you would consider?

5. In general, unions operate in a "reactive" fashion—responding through the grievance machinery to unpopular managerial actions. Under what circumstances is the practice, "obey now, grieve later," inappropriate?

6. Contrast and compare the residual and trusteeship perspectives of management rights.

7. Obtain copies of the labor agreements of a craft union, industrial union, and public sector union. Compare the management rights clauses in each. What factors may account for the differences or similarities?

8. Is "codetermination" the inevitable and logical conclusion of the trusteeship doctrine? Discuss.

9. A union leader remarked, "I have no interest in teaching management how to run their business, as management has no right telling us how to run our union. If I were to become involved with the internal running of the company, my effectiveness as an advocate for my members declines, and so does the trust the members place in me. When I'm involved with running the company, I want to get paid for being a manager." In light of this chapter, discuss.

Selected Bibliography

Chamberlain, Neil W., *The Union Challenge to Management Control.* New York: Harper & Row, Pub., 1948.

Chandler, Margaret K., *Management Rights and Union Interests.* New York: McGraw-Hill, 1964.

Elkouri, Frank, and Edna A. Elkouri, *How Arbitration Works* (3rd ed.). Washington, D.C.: Bureau of National Affairs, 1973.

Prasow, Paul, "The Theory of Management Reserved Rights—Revisited," *IRRA Annual Proceedings*, 26th Meeting, December 1973, pp. 74–84.

Slichter, Sumner H., James J. Healy, and E. Robert Livernash, *The Impact of Collective Bargaining on Management.* Washington, D.C.: Brookings Institute, 1960.

CONTRACT ADMINISTRATION

7

GRIEVANCE PROCEDURES

Contract negotiation is the part of the collective bargaining iceberg that shows above the surface. The larger and more important part of the iceberg, seldom seen, is the administration of collective agreements. *A contract is no better than its administration.* The test of the soundness of a union–management relationship lies in how effectively the parties implement their contract in the troublesome process of living together under the agreement. In general, contract administration involves managerial decision making and union response—via the grievance process—should a management "act" conflict with the union's understanding of the agreement.

Just as contracts vary in subject matter, so also does experience vary in the matter of contract administration, making generalization hazardous. In some hostile and undisciplined relationships, the union enforces (or ignores) the contract through slowdowns, wildcats, or chronic absenteeism. In other similarly unsatisfactory relationships, management enforces (or ignores) the contract in an arbitrary and inequitable manner, knowing that the union with which it is dealing is too weak to challenge effectively such an approach to contract administration. We are not concerned here with these undesirable extremes, but with the great majority of management–union relationships where the parties have a shared desire to administer the agreement equitably in accordance with their understanding of its meaning.

The collective agreement is properly regarded as *the statutory law* of the union–management relationship for its effective length, which is increasingly a three-year period. Usually, no contract language changes can be made until the expiration date except by mutual consent. Under these circumstances, the importance of developing sound policies and procedures for smooth administration of contractual provisions can hardly be exaggerated.

POSITIVE CONTRACT ADMINISTRATION[1]

Labor agreements are the visible results of a negotiation process between two parties which have conflicting goals and points of view. Thus, in the interest of reaching agreement, each side may compromise its stance on an issue by agreeing to contract language which is vague, general, or possibly even contradictory. Written labor agreements become operational when management makes employment related decisions and when the employees and/or their labor representatives react to them on the grounds that the management decision is at variance with the negotiated agreement. Most contracts spell out a grievance procedure which provides an employee and/or a union a speedy and orderly method to raise objections to management initiatives. The grievance procedure allows for the resolution of contractual disputes with a minimum of industrial disturbance during the life of a contract and thus provides the operational flexibility needed to reach and maintain positive, cooperative management and labor relations on a day-to-day basis within an organization.[2] In effect, the grievance procedure provides the parties with a mechanism to resolve to finality any dispute involving labor relations during the life of a contract, with neither side suffering the losses associated with a strike or a lockout. Perhaps Gerald G. Somers expressed it best when he referred to the grievance procedure as being at the very heart of collective bargaining and not merely an adjunct to the process.[3]

1. For more detailed discussion of positive contract administration, see K. L. Sovereign and Mario (Mike) F. Bognanno, "Positive Contract Administration," *ASPA Handbook of Personnel and Industrial Relations,* 3 (Washington, D.C.: Bureau of National Affairs, 1976), 146–48.

2. *Ibid.,* p. 147.

3. "Grievance Settlement in Coal Mining," *Business and Economic Studies* 4, No. 4 (Morgantown: West Virginia University Bulletin, 1956), 44.

The manner in which a contract is administered is extremely important in fostering a stable and cooperative management–labor relationship. The President's National Labor–Management Conference made several suggestions as to certain employer attitudes that can aid the positive contract administration approach. Management and labor should note the following:

1. The objective of the grievance procedure is to reach fair settlements and not the winning of cases.
2. Supervisors should view the filing of a grievance as an aid in the identification and the elimination of the actual causes of discontent within their departments.
3. The tendency by either party to support previous erroneous decisions of its representatives should be discouraged.
4. Management and union representatives must both be willing to give adequate time and attention to the handling and resolution of grievances for the effective functioning of the grievance process.
5. Management and union representatives must both know the entire collective agreement for the sound handling of grievances.[4]

MANAGEMENT INITIATIVE IN CONTRACT ADMINISTRATION

Contracts do not administer themselves. As we saw in Chapter 6, the initiative for putting contract terms into effect rests with management in nearly all cases. It is management who hires, management who disciplines employees in varying degrees from verbal or written warnings to discharge in serious cases, management who initiates action on transfer and promotion of employees, management who decides on the layoff and recall of workers in response to changing production requirements, and management who introduces new jobs and abolishes existing jobs in response to technological change or other requirements. The list could be enlarged.

Few provisions are self-administering or jointly administered. The primary responsibility for giving operational meaning to the written contractual provisions governing the employment relationship is that of management as the agent for direction and control of the work force. Whenever management moves (or fails to move) on any matter covered, its

---

4. Division of Labor Standards, U.S. Department of Labor, Bulletin 77, 1946, pp. 45–46.

action must be in accord with the contract. For this reason, many employers go to considerable pains to insure that supervisors are thoroughly informed as to how their operating responsibilities are affected and conditioned by the contract.

In small firms, the production manager is usually his own labor relations man. Having negotiated the contract himself or through an attorney representing him, the small employer in theory should know the contract well enough to insure proper contract observance when he and his subordinates are performing their roles as production supervisors. In medium to large firms, the significance of the contract must be communicated to all supervisors in meaningful fashion. Many unnecessary contractual grievances can be avoided if supervisory personnel know the contract and are instructed to act in accordance with its provisions.

DEFINING THE SCOPE OF THE GRIEVANCE PROCEDURE

We have stressed the need to regard the collective agreement as the law of the relationship. This necessitates distinguishing clearly between those grievances that relate to the contract and those that relate to problems not treated by the contract or outside the employment relationship.

Intelligent positive contract administration should encompass consideration of *any* grievance relating in any fashion to the employment relationship. However, in the early steps of the grievance, the contract procedure should be clear; only grievances raising an issue of contract interpretation and application can be appealed to the arbitration step of the grievance procedure.[5]

If final and binding arbitration is available, grievances raising issues outside the statutory law of the relationship (that is, the contract) and stability and consistency in contract administration will be hard to achieve. Under such wide-open arbitration, the contract may become merely a point of departure instead of settling the rules of the game for the life of the agreement.[6] Arbitration was not invented as a process to deal with every subject under the sun.

---

5. This view is held by most practitioners and arbitrators. Under some contracts, however, virtually anything can be appealed to arbitration. Defining the limits of the arbitrator's authority and jurisdiction is a critically important policy decision that the parties themselves must make.

6. If the grievance raises a matter on which the contract is silent, under most contracts such a grievance would be held to be nonarbitrable. An important exception to this generalization relates to past practice issues, where it is contended that the practice is in fact a part of the

Most employers presumably wish to run efficient, orderly enterprises with a minimum of friction and resentment on the part of employees. Management is therefore interested (or should be) in resolving any individual or group dissatisfaction that may threaten the achievement of these objectives. Similarly, the union's principal role in contract administration is to function as an agent or a representative of employees in handling individual or group complaints that may arise. The union wishes to check independently on the way in which management is exercising administrative initiative in effectuating contract terms and conditions.

Taking this broad view of their respective functions, all employers and unions should endorse the psychological proposition that a *grievance exists whenever an employee feels aggrieved,* whether or not the source of his grievance is contractual. If an employee or some employees feel, rightly or wrongly, that they are being unjustly treated, a human relations problem exists that merits the attention of both management and the union.

The goal of intelligent and orderly administration of contracts, however, requires that a distinction be made and clearly understood by all parties between those grievances which raise a question of contract interpretation or application and those grievances that, no matter how intrinsically sincere or meritorious they may be, are outside the scope of the collective agreement. Some highly prerogative conscious managements will refuse even to discuss with union representatives any grievance that does not relate directly to the contract. Such an approach may succeed in "putting the union in its place," but it is not conducive to positive labor relations. From a realistic standpoint, a grievance procedure should be designed to carry all grievances in its early steps. Only those, however, which are rooted in the contract should be the subject of arbitration.

At some point in the grievance procedure, however, a line must be drawn. If a collective labor agreement is to mean anything, its provisions must be adhered to by both parties for its duration. It would be inviting chaos to say that all grievances must be resolved whether or not they bear any relationship to a contractual provision. At the same time, genuine grievances will arise over problems not covered or contemplated by the contract. These grievances are no less real because the contract may happen to be silent on them. Some procedural outlet should therefore be provided.

---

contract by custom and usage. To put it another way, arbitrable grievances can and do arise as to the contractual significance of contractual silence. Such grievances usually concern past practice.

COMBINING THE CLINICAL
AND CONTRACTUAL APPROACHES
TO GRIEVANCE ADJUSTMENT

Opening the early steps of the grievance procedure to *any* grievance concerning the employment relationship permits effective use of the machinery for both communication and catharsis. It permits the so-called clinical approach to grievance handling, as advocated by the late Benjamin Selekman nearly forty years ago.[7] Selekman favored seeking out the root causes of grievances rather than accepting their surface rationale. Many grievances *as filed* do not reveal the true basis for the grievant's antagonism or sense of injury. This problem has been viewed in terms of the "iceberg theory," since often only 10 percent of the problem is seen—the remainder is hidden by the iceberg.[8] Thus, the written allegation in the grievance may relate merely to a trivial surface complaint. The truth may be that the grievant is convinced in his own mind that his foreman has been systematically discriminating or otherwise administering a number of contract provisions unfairly over a considerable period of time.

The clinical approach stresses thorough investigation and treatment of the problems that may underlie the grievances rather than mechanistic handling according to whether or not they lie within the contractual frame of reference. Serious investigation of all but obviously frivolous grievances should be worth the time and effort expended. Frequently, a grievance on a noncontract matter enables management to resolve it to the satisfaction of all concerned while this potential oak of a problem is still in the acorn stage. Most employers appreciate the logic and economy of practicing preventive labor relations.

The Selekman method is in no sense inconsistent with recognizing the primacy of the contract. Grievances which do *not* raise an issue of contract interpretation and application can be received, investigated, and, where found to be meritorious, adjusted by management. At the same time, management can and should make clear that it is practicing prudent personnel administration above and beyond its contractual obligation. The contractual obligation is limited to effectuating the terms and conditions of the agreement. Only when a grievance alleges that management has failed to observe the contract should there be the opportunity to appeal the complaint for final and binding determination by an impartial outsider.

The wisdom of limiting the authority and jurisdiction of the arbitrator to grievances of this type is still questioned by some management and union practitioners who consider arbitration to be an extension of the collective

---

7. Benjamin M. Selekman, *Labor Relations and Human Relations* (New York: McGraw-Hill, 1947), pp. 75–110.
8. Sovereign and Bognanno, "Positive Contract Administration," p. 159.

bargaining process and use it for handling extracontractual disputes as well as straight contract interpretation cases. The great majority of practitioners and arbitrators, however, favor confining grievance arbitration to cases involving issues of contract interpretation and application.[9]

The needs of the clinical approach can be accommodated by a simple declaration that the grievance procedure is available to any employee or to the union desiring to present a grievance concerning any matter involving rates of pay, wages, hours of employment, or any other condition of employment. At the same time, the contract can make clear that grievances involving interpretation and application of the provisions of the contract *and only such grievances* can be appealed to arbitration.

BASIC PRINCIPLES
OF GRIEVANCE ADJUSTMENT

Certain general principles should govern the handling and adjustment of grievances. One is that grievances should be adjusted *promptly,* preferably at the first step in the grievance procedure, and that such adjustments of grievances should be *on their merits.* Few would dispute this principle, but there are cases in which the principle is ignored. In some relationships there is an inclination to bypass the departmental foreman and the union steward in grievance adjustment, although the great majority of grievances can and should be finally adjusted at the foreman–steward level. When the foreman's discretion to adjust is denied, the authority of the steward correspondingly declines. He is the foreman's opposite number. Some employers and union representatives are determined to achieve uniformity and avoid embarrassing precedents. In so doing, they destroy democratic decision making at the shop level.

The sounder approach is not to take away discretion from foremen and stewards but to do a thorough job of training both in contract administration. Training sessions for small groups of fifteen or twenty foremen and stewards at a time should be conducted shortly after a contract is negotiated. These programs are admittedly difficult to plan and administer, but the time and effort spent should be worth the trouble. Properly-trained foremen and stewards can then be encouraged and trusted to adjust grievances instead of passing them up the line.

A second principle of effective grievance adjustment is that the procedure and forms for grieving must be easy to utilize and well understood by employees and their supervisors. The functional relationship involving the employee, his union steward, and the foreman needs to be clearly

9. Frank Elkouri and Edna Asper Elkouri, *How Arbitration Works* (3rd ed.), (Washington, D.C.: Bureau of National Affairs, 1973), p. 44.

established. The employee should understand, for example, that as a matter of law he can discuss conditions and circumstances involving his work with his supervisor without his union steward being present. Also as a matter of law, of course, no adjustment of an employee complaint or grievance can be made by management that is not consistent with the provisions of the collective agreement. Whenever an employee elects to present his own grievance individually, exercising his option to do so under Taft–Hartley, the law provides that a union representative has the right to be present at such an individual adjustment session.

A third basic principle calls for a direct and timely avenue of appeal from the rulings of line supervision. The number of steps in the grievance procedure will vary in terms of the size of the bargaining unit and the needs of the parties, but in all cases the appeal ladder from one level of supervision to another must be clear and direct.

Finally, effective grievance adjustment machinery should provide for appeal to arbitration by an impartial outside party whose decision shall be final and binding upon the company, the union, and the aggrieved employee(s).

The spirit and substance of grievance handling are of the greatest importance. Sound contract administration requires that grievances be handled in an equitable, nondiscriminatory, and reasonably uniform manner in conformity with the contract provision(s) involved. At the same time, there should be a joint awareness of the need for *some* flexibility in the practical solution of problems. A good illustration of the need on occasion to depart from the letter of the contract can be found in the customary contract prohibition against supervisors doing any production work, except as instructors or in starting new jobs.[10] The historic reason for such a policy is the conservation of job opportunities for employees in the bargaining unit. Yet in daily business it may make sense occasionally for the foreman to lend a hand on a particular production job. Should the union *always* grieve in such situations, or should it occasionally look the other way? A policy of always grieving, regardless of the realities of the situation, might cause management to take an extremely strict or literal approach to contract interpretation in other types of cases where a more realistic approach might be to the employee's advantage.

In a large plant, many grievances supposedly rooted in the contract may be filed due to misunderstanding of contractual provisions. Since they lack contractual merit, such grievances must be dismissed if not withdrawn. Similarly, in any large plant, foremen will make mistakes in contract

10. A typical provision of this type is Article IV, Section 6, of the Atlantic Richfield Company and Oil, Chemical, and Atomic Workers 1975–77 agreement, which reads as follows: "No foreman or other supervisory employee shall perform duties customarily assigned employees covered by this agreement, except: A. In emergencies, B. In connection with the instruction of an employee, C. In the interest of avoiding an accident."

application, because of either ignorance or misunderstanding of the contract. Grievances can be pushed in such cases as technically sound on a strict contractual basis. Yet the interests of the parties often may be better served through a disposition to stretch a point on occasion in adjusting a grievance or to refrain from exacting literal enforcement, particularly if no one has been injured by the contractual mistake.

In each bargaining relationship, there should be a joint effort at achieving a pattern of fair-minded common sense in grievance filing and grievance handling. Such a pattern would avoid the extremes of both laxity and rigidity in applying contract language.

We dwell on this theme because, like most arbitrators, we have heard our share of cases over the years where going strictly by the contract (as the arbitrator must do) has produced a Pyrrhic victory for one party and has probably increased the friction rather than reducing mistrust or clarifying a misunderstanding. The union view in such cases is "we can't let management get away with this inch or they'll take a mile next time." Management lyrics for the same melody run as follows: "We can't grant this grievance on an equity basis when the contract does not require it. If we do, we will open a Pandora's box of similar cases lacking contractual merit."

Clearly, it is hard to generalize on when to press and when to bend in grievance handling. There must be an intuitive wisdom guiding the parties to enable them to preserve the essential meaning and force of contract provisions without ignoring the tangible values of recognizing the equities and practicalities of particular situations.

Management ordinarily takes a stricter view of the contract than the union, perhaps because of concern over the union's desire to expand the agreement's applicability. We do not say that there is not a basis for management to be cautious in this regard. However, in special circumstances where denial of the technically weak grievance would be "unjust," the employer can always win points for being fair while at the same time stressing that the settlement shall not be regarded as having any precedential value.

THE GRIEVANCE PROCEDURE

The vast majority of collective agreements enumerate a grievance procedure which is a formalized series of procedural steps that an aggrieved party must follow in the airing of a complaint. Although the grievant is typically an employee or a group of employees, the union and, in some cases, management is allowed to file a grievance when one party feels the other has acted in violation of the agreement.

The procedural steps provide the grievant with a systematic avenue of appeal through successively higher levels of the management (and union) hierarchy when the disagreement cannot be adequately resolved at a lower step. The number of steps may range from one step in very small companies up to six steps or more in large multinational corporations.[11] Although there is a great deal of variance from one multistep procedure to the next, a fairly typical five-step procedure and those listing the major participants involved at each step are as follows:

Step 1. The grieving employee, union steward, and immediate supervisor.
Step 2. The chief steward and departmental superintendent.
Step 3. The union grievance committee and/or local union president and director of personnel.
Step 4. The union grievance committee and/or local union president, union business agent and/or international union representative, and vice president of industrial relations.
Step 5. The parties involved present their cases to an arbitrator for a final and binding arbitration determination.

When a grievance is reduced to writing, it is said to have moved from the "informal" to the "formal" side of the grievance procedure.[12] Collective agreements exhibit considerable variance regarding the step at which a complaint must be put in writing. Most company and union representatives feel that it is important to formalize grievances at an early stage.[13] They argue that the process of writing out the complaint forces the grievant to set out the facts, contract provision, and contentions underlying his grievance early in the proceedings. Thus, both labor and management may better assess the merits, strengths, and weaknesses of the claim and their respective positions.[14] Grievances which are ill founded will soon fall by the wayside, while grievances which are well founded will soon be adjusted. The result is that grievances are settled more expeditiously with an accompanying savings in time, energy, and emotions for all involved.

Some organizations "formalize" the grievance procedure only in the event of impending grievance arbitration. The organizations using this approach emphasize that employees tend to accept it better since it allows for greater flexibility in the handling of grievances and attempts to adjust grievances on an equity basis rather than on a contractual basis.

---

11. Elkouri and Elkouri, *How Arbitration Works*, p. 121.
12. Sovereign and Bognanno, "Positive Contract Administration," p. 175.
13. *Ibid.*
14. Sam Kagel, *Anatomy of a Labor Arbitration* (Washington, D.C.: Bureau of National Affairs, 1961), pp. 15–19.

There is no optimal point at which a grievance "should" enter the formal grievance procedure. What is right for one relationship may not work in another. Therefore, it is important for both labor and management to assess the specific work environment and their respective organizational goals in negotiating this point.

The grievance procedure often contains specific time limitations on the filing of a grievance, on answering the complaint, and on appealing that answer to each successive step in the procedure. Time limitations are utilized because most experienced labor representatives believe that specified time limits aid in the prompt and equitable settlement of grievances, minimize the effect of stalling grievances,[15] and thus promote an atmosphere of cooperative labor relations. Of course, this proposition depends upon the extent to which the goals of the union and management relations encompass a concern for equity and promptness. In general, our experiences make it clear that time limitations do appear to be of benefit to all parties, particularly the grievant.

The contractual grievance procedure often provides for an expedited method for handling certain classes of grievances. Examples are grievances for which lower- and middle-level officals of management or labor do not have the authority to adjust, or problems requiring immediate adjudication.[16] Thus, these special grievances must be considered and adjusted by the organizational heads. Such grievances bypass the otherwise mandatory initial steps of the grievance procedure, and are first considered at the third or fourth step. Typical examples of matters treated via expedited procedures involve employee discharges, grievances filed by the unions, class action grievances, and grievances filed by management against the union.

THE POLITICS
OF GRIEVANCE ADJUSTMENT

Industrial unions in particular are not characterized by homogeneous membership with common problems and a community of interest deriving from a common background of training experience. With the exception of the longshoring and coal mining unions and perhaps a few other, conflicting pressures and interests are at work, complicating the task of union leadership in contract administration as well as in negotiation. In processing grievances relating to promotions, layoffs, and transfers, for example, the union leader is often in the unenviable position of making one employee or group of employees happy while incurring the displeas-

15. Elkouri and Elkouri, *How Arbitration Works*, pp. 145–46.
16. Bureau of National Affairs Editorial Staff, *Grievance Guide* (4th ed.), (Washington, D.C.: Bureau of National Affairs, 1972), pp. 1–2.

ure of any workers who may be adversely affected by the "winning" of the grievance. Another sensitive area in contract administration concerns allocation of available overtime work. The grievance procedure may also serve as an arena for conflicts of interest between skilled and unskilled, between hourly paid and incentive paid, or between male and female employees.

The accommodation of these conflicting interests can be a source of real difficulty for union leadership in grievance handling. This political burden is not always well understood by management. An employer who is interested in building durable relationships with a responsible union, however, usually understands the multiple pressures operating upon local union leaders. He will try to avoid actions or policies that embarrass or undercut such leadership. Much of the formalism in contract administration is due not so much to management's initiative as to the union leadership's need to insulate itself from rank-and-file pressures.

Sayles and Strauss in 1953 noted five ways in which local leaders can maintain their freedom to choose the grievances they want to push while at the same time avoiding identification with defeats: (1) requiring members to sign grievances; (2) careful screening of grievances before negotiating with management; (3) never negotiating without another officer being present; (4) relying on precedents and legalistic interpretations; and (5) "passing the buck" to the arbitrator.[17] In revising their 1953 study, Sayles and Strauss added one more technique, that of involving the international union.[18] This is nearly universal practice today prior to the arbitration step.

The current stress on individual rights has made even more difficult the unpleasant duty of screening out grievances that lack contractual merit. Every employee believes that his grievance has merit. If his leadership fails to process the grievance, the employee may conclude that he is being ignored or sold out. Although this is rarely the case, the employee may nevertheless become convinced in his own mind that he is not getting his money's worth from his dues and that he is not being fairly represented.

The current emphasis on individual rights is a healthy development, generally speaking. Such an emphasis can serve as an effective deterrent to the dubious practice of trading off legitimate grievances in the game of union or management politics. *Grievances should stand or fall on their merit.* Their political weight should not be the relevant variable.

Individual rights can be critical in bargaining units where the certified union does not have a union shop contract. When employees who do not belong to the union file grievances, the union leadership understandably may be tempted at times to give poor service or no service to these "free

17. Leonard R. Sayles and George Strauss, *The Local Union* (1st ed.), (New York: Harcourt Brace Jovanovich, Inc., 1953), p. 74.
18. Leonard R. Sayles and George Strauss, *The Local Union* (rev. ed.), ed. (New York: Harcourt, Brace Jovanovich, Inc., 1967), p. 44.

riders." Yet the only sound policy is to give good service to membership holdouts to prove to them that the union as bargaining agent for all employees takes its responsibilities seriously.

THE DUTY OF FAIR REPRESENTATION

The National Labor Relations Act (NLRA) provides in section 9(a) that a majority union shall be the "exclusive representative" of all the employees within a bargaining unit. Labor unions are required by this statute to represent not only their dues-paying members but also nonmembers who do not pay union dues. Furthermore, the union must represent all employees in an equal and fair manner.[19]

The duty of fair representation emanates from the statutory doctrine of majority rule,[20] which allows employees to "self-determine" whether they desire to be represented by a labor union and, if so, by which one. The employees' choice is determined by secret ballot with the decision of the majority ruling. If the voting majority selects a union, then that union becomes the exclusive representative of *all* the employees in the bargaining unit; that is, the minority must be afforded equal representation by that union.

The duty of fair representation requires that unions do not act arbitrarily, capriciously, or with discriminatory motivation[21] when handling an employee's grievance.[22] Usually, an employee files a grievance when he feels that the employer has acted in violation or breach of the labor contract. Now if the employee believes that his bargaining agent has not provided him with fair representation, and if the grievant has exhausted or attempted to exhaust the contractual grievance procedure or has been prevented from doing so, such as when the union has sole power to invoke the higher steps of the grievance procedure,[23] then the grievant may be on solid ground in filing suit in federal district court under section 301 of Taft–Hartley.[24] Such a suit may be filed by the employee against the union for breach of its duty to represent said employee or the employer for its breach of the labor contract.

---

19. *Steele* v. *Louisville* v. *Nashville RR*, 323 U.S. 192, 15 LRRM 708 (1944); and *Wunstall* v. *Locomotive Firemen and Enginemen, Ocean Lodge No. 76*, 323 U.S. 216 (No. 37), 9 FBP 389 (1944).

20. Robert F. Koretz and Robert J. Rabin, "Arbitration and Individual Rights," *The Future of Labor Arbitration in America* (New York: American Arbitration Association, 1976), p. 115.

21. *Vaca* v. *Sipes*, 386 U.S. 171, 190 LRRM 2369 (1967).

22. William P. Murphy, "Due Process and Fair Representation in Grievance Handling in the Public Sector," Thirtieth Annual Meeting, National Academy of Arbitration, Toronto, Canada, April 15, 1977, p. 18; and Koretz and Rabin, "Arbitration and Individual Rights," p. 121.

23. *Vaca* v. *Sipes*.

24. *Ibid.*, National Labor Relations Act, as amended.

The employee can only recover damages if he can prove that there was a "double breach," of duty by the union and of the contract by the employer. Thus, the employer's (union's) liability is dependent upon the union's (employer's) guilt or innocence.[25] In such a circumstance, the employer and union find themselves in an alliance against a common employee foe.[26]

If the employee does prove a double breach in a fair representation case, then both the employer and the union are financially liable for the consequences of each respective breach. Usually, the employer is liable for any damage caused to the employee from the time of the employer's breach of the labor contract up until the time at which the union breached its duty of fair representation. The union is usually liable for all damages accruing after the breach of duty was committed.

Although the duty of fair representation arises from *statute*, its application is left to the courts and the NLRB. Recent case law suggests a breach of the duty of fair representation has been shown when:

> The union failed to assert or only passively asserted a claim which was critical to the employee's grievance in the context of an arbitration hearing.[27]

> The union allowed the contractual time limitations to expire before the initial filing of an employee's grievance. Therefore, the grievance was barred from the grievance procedure.[28]

> The union permitted its members to vote on an employee's grievance which would affect specific employees on layoff.[29]

> The union didn't adequately investigate the facts of the case even after the employee–grievants specifically suggested and requested that the union investigate a particular accusation.[30]

> The union refused to process a nonmember grievance unless that employee reimbursed the union for processing costs. The employee was within the bargaining unit and no such demands were made of union members.[31]

> The union refused to provide an employee with representation

25. Clyde Summers, "The Individual Employee's Right Under the Collective Agreements: What Constitutes Fair Representation," National Academy of Arbitrators, 1974 *Proceedings*, 27th Annual Meeting, 1975, pp. 15, 16.

26. *Ibid.*

27. *Holodnak* v. *AVCO Corp.*, 514 F. 2d 285, 88 LRRM 2950 (2nd Cir., 1975), aff'g in part 381 F. Supp. 191, 87 (D. Mass., 1974).

28. *Ruzicka* v. *General Motors Corporation*, 523 F. 2d 306, 90 LRRM 2497 (6th Cir. 1975).

29. *NLRB* v. *Teamsters*, Local 315 (Rhodes and Jamisen, Ltd.), 545 F. 2d 1173, 93 MRB 2747 (9th Cir., 1976).

30. *Hines* v. *Anchor Motor Freight, Inc.*, 424 U.S. 554, 91 LRRM 2481 (1976).

31. *Machinists, Local 697 (H. O. Canfield Rubber Co. of Va., Inc.)*, 223 NLRB 119, 91 LRRM 1529 (1976).

during an "investigatory interview" when the employee reasonably believed discipline could result from the interview and that he must attend.[32]

FAIR REPRESENTATION IN THE PUBLIC SECTOR

The advent of collective bargaining in the public sector raises the issue of fair representation in a different context. Public employees have additional statutory protection, such as Civil Service rules, statutes, and procedures which antedate any collective agreement.[33] Few cases addressing the fair representation question in the public sector have yet been litigated. Thus, it is impossible to say whether the courts will hold public sector unions to the private sector rule;[34] not to act arbitrarily, capriciously, or with discriminatory motivation when handling an employee's grievance.[35]

Public sector employees have a statutory right to due process before the employer may take final action in a discipline case.[36] This statutory right includes a trial-like hearing.[37] Although an employer and a union may agree to settle disputes by private arbitration and thereby waive this statutory right, any subsequent arbitration of a discipline case must conform to the same due process requirement.[38] Thus, it appears that public sector employees have an absolute right to a due process hearing either by the statutory procedures or by arbitration in any discipline case, "regardless" of the grievance's merit.[39] As the doctrine of fair representation is delineated in the public sector by case decisions, it is quite possible that public sector unions will have less ability to settle cases prior to arbitration than their private sector counterparts. This is especially true in discipline cases where due process and the right to a trial-like hearing is currently a necessity.

IMPACT OF FEDERAL LEGISLATION ON THE GRIEVANCE PROCEDURE

There has been a barrage of recent legislation which regulates the employment relationship. Federal statutes such as the Occupational Safety and

32. *NLRB* v. *Weingarten, J., Inc.*, 420 U.S. 251, 88 LRRM 2689 (1975).
33. Koretz and Rabin, "Arbitration and Individual Rights," p. 152.
34. *Ibid.*
35. *Vaca* v. *Sipes.*
36. *Murphy*, "Due Process," pp. 13–14.
37. *Ibid.*
38. *Ibid.*, p. 15.
39. Koretz and Rabin, "Arbitration and Individual Rights," p. 153.

Health Act (OSHA), the Employee Retirement and Income Security Act (ERISA), and the Civil Rights Act of 1964 (Title VII), as well as local enactments, establish statutory alternatives to the grievance procedure.[40] All employees have certain statutory rights under these federal and local laws which coexist with employees' contractual rights under a collective agreement, if one is in force.

Title VII prohibits employers from discriminating against certain classes of individuals in any employment practice. These "protected classes" are sex, race, color, religion, and national origin. Any employee who feels that his Title VII rights have been violated may file a charge with the appropriate federal or state administrative agency. A federal charge would be filed with the Equal Employment Opportunity Commission (EEOC). The EEOC will then investigate the charge. If the EEOC finds that the complaint has merit, then it has the power to sue the employer. Also, the individual employee has the right to file suit against the employer under Title VII. Simultaneously, an employee may also file a Title VII–type of charge in the form of a grievance, if the alleged act also violated the collective agreement.

The U.S. Supreme Court ruled in 1974 that, even though an aggrieved employee has lost an arbitral decision, he may still file that "same charge" with the federal and/or state civil rights agency.[41] Furthermore, the same individual has an absolute right to file suit against his employer under Title VII, despite losing at arbitration and/or dismissal of the charge by either or both of the federal and state agencies.[42] However, the use of the grievance procedure by the employee does not toll the running of the Title VII statute of limitation filing requirement of ninety days from the alleged date of occurrence.[43] Therefore, under the U.S. Supreme Court's interpretation of Title VII, it is possible for an aggrieved employee to relitigate the same charge in multiple forms.

A union may not refuse to process a discrimination grievance merely because the employee has alternate recourse to remedy via the statute.[44] Accordingly, an employee may lose his case in grievance arbitration and subsequently prevail in litigation. By allowing multiple forms of relief in such cases, the U.S. Supreme Court may have weakened the finality of arbitration awards under collective bargaining relationships. However, in doing so the Court has guaranteed the rights of the "minority" over the

40. David E. Feller, "The Impact of External Law upon Labor Arbitration," in *The Future of Labor Arbitration in America*, p. 89.

41. *Alexander* v. *Gardner-Denver Co.*, 415 U.S. 36, 7 FEP 81 (1974).

42. *Ibid.*

43. *Guy* v. *Robbins and Myers, Inc.*, 529 F. 2d 801, 14 FEP 1504 (U.S., 1976).

44. Marvin Hill, Jr., "Employee Discrimination Claims," *Arbitration Journal*, September 1977, p. 188.

threatened oppression of any "majority" organization. Understandably, unions and employers have mixed opinions over this system of multiple avenues of appeal, since the path to remedy is now more complex, and for them it introduces an element of "double jeopardy."

OSHA was enacted in 1970. The statute authorizes the secretary of labor to create and enforce safety and health standards. Under OSHA, employers are required to furnish employment free from "recognized hazards that are causing or likely to cause death or serious physical harm to employees." The Department of Labor operates through the Occupational Safety and Health Review Commission (OSHRC), which investigates employee complaints and conducts spot checks on the employer's premises. At present, the full impact of OSHA upon the grievance procedure is not known.

Any employee who is injured in the course of his employment and who receives appropriate worker compensation benefits may not file suit against the employer under OSHA.[45] However, the employee may file a grievance. In and of itself, the processing of a contractual grievance does not bar the employee from filing a charge with the OSHRC. As with Title VII claims, an employee may seek remedy for an alleged health-safety violation in multiple forums.

ERISA was enacted in 1974, and it drastically reforms the area of pension plans. Under one of its many provisions, plan trustees and administrators are assigned strict fiduciary responsibility which governs their actions. Also, ERISA provides grounds for a lawsuit by the Department of Labor, plan participants, retirees, or beneficiaries against their respective fiduciaries.[46] Thus, ERISA also provides an aggrieved employee with more than one route in seeking adjudication, if the alleged fiduciary action also breaches the collective agreement.

These pieces of legislation may weaken the grievance procedure and reduce the finality of an arbitration award.[47] We are certain that over the years ahead negotiators and arbitrators alike will fashion, apply, and interpret contractual language which conforms more closely to that found in statute. In these critical areas, where public law exists, the private law of the shop must be brought into conformity if it is to be viable and if grievances are to be remedied locally.

45. John C. Unkovic, "Current Developments in OSHA," *Employee Relations Law Journal*, Summer 1976, p. 104.

46. Jeffrey D. Mamorsky, "Current Developments in Pension Programs," *Employee Relations Law Journal*, Autumn 1976, p. 225.

47. Michael E. Murphy, "ERISA and Arbitration," *Arbitration Journal*, June 1977, p. 128.

IMPROVED PROCEDURES FOR EFFECTUATING CONTRACTUAL POLICIES

In sizeable bargaining units with a considerable number of grievances filed regularly, there is a continuing need to improve the functioning of the machinery and also to control (and if possible to reduce) the volume of cases. What constitutes an "excessive" number of grievances and what is an optimal grievance procedure are questions that each union–management relationship pair must answer for itself. There is no model of universal utility. Some suggestions can be offered, however, that should contribute to improved contract administration.

We can begin by restating the conventional wisdom on the grievance procedure as such. First, the contract sections on grievance procedure should be written with special attention to clarity and directness. The task of contract administration is facilitated when the procedural guidelines in the contract are easy to follow.

Second, the contract should make clear that *any* grievance relating to the employment relationship will be processed in the early steps, but that *only grievances raising an issue of contract interpretation or application are appealable to arbitration.*

Third, the contract must treat clearly such matters as the time and manner of reducing a grievance to writing; the time limits for filing, appealing, and answering at the various steps; penalties for failure to use the grievance machinery and procedures for cases where employees elect to process their grievances independently of the union.

Many grievances can be avoided when the parties take pains to spell out in their contracts procedures for implementing substantive policies on such matters as transfers, promotions, layoffs, recalls from layoffs, discipline, merit increases, and allocation of overtime opportunities. In these and other matters, there is a need for clearly defined procedures. When this has been done in clear and even-handed fashion, much misunderstanding and confusion can be avoided.

The logic of industrial jurisprudence demands uniform, acceptable, and understandable procedures relating to on-the-job activities. If the contract is clear on the rules of the game and also on how to play the game procedurally, there will be less friction and fewer grievances. Some examples may help to underline the importance of these considerations.

Promotional Procedures

On promotions, some contracts state a policy without a procedure. The policy may be barely stated as one of filling vacancies wherever possible by promotion from within. If the contract stops here, however, many unanswered questions arise: (1) Must vacancies be posted—if so, for how long? (2) If several applicants are qualified, does the vacancy go to the senior among them or to the most qualified among them? (3) If no applicant appears to be qualified, how shall the vacancy be filled? (4) Is management obligated to give a trial on the job to any applicant who insists he is qualified to perform it? If so, how much of a trial?

Disciplinary Action Procedures

Another example of the importance of defined procedures concerns management's exercise of the discipline function. Most contracts state the policy that employees shall be disciplined only for "just cause." Such contractual protection against arbitrary or ill-founded disciplinary action is properly regarded as perhaps the most important single contribution to the meaningful democratization of industrial relations.

The just cause principle is easy to state in one sentence. However, some contracts are silent or unsatisfactory on procedures to be followed when disciplinary action is taken. A uniform procedure in all discipline cases is of great value to all parties in contract administration. Disciplinary action cases frequently result in conflicting versions of what happened and often involve serious emotional reactions. Such factors make it important to spell out in the contract the "due process of law" available to any employee charged with conduct meriting discipline.

The procedure used in administering discipline, whatever its particular form, should satisfy the following requirements:

1. The employee should be advised by management of the charges against him. He should have the right to have his union representative hear such charges and the employee's statement of *his* position.
2. Before *formal* discipline is assessed, management should conduct a hearing within a reasonable period of time after the determination that disciplinary action is required. The charged employee should be present with appropriate union representation at such a hearing. Both parties should be allowed to call witnesses in order to ascertain all the facts and circumstances of the case. Formal disciplinary action should be taken only after the completion of such a hearing.
3. Written minutes of the disciplinary action hearing should be furnished to the employee's union representative.

The objective is to assure a full review of the circumstances while they are fresh in the minds of all concerned. The testimony at the disciplinary action hearing may show that the foreman had called for discipline on the basis of erroneous or incomplete information, or the statements may make clear to the union representative that "just cause" for discipline has been proved. The disciplinary action will therefore not be grieved.

In serious discipline cases (discharge), it may be prudent to require the employee to leave the plant upon notification that disciplinary action is contemplated. In other situations, such as discipline for garnishment, tardiness, or absenteeism, such a precaution is probably unnecessary.

A NOTE ON MANAGEMENT GRIEVANCES

The grievance machinery of the contract is not necessarily a one-way street for employees and the union only. Some contracts provide for management filing of grievances, although use of such a contractual option appears to be comparatively rare.

Realistically, management does not find the grievance procedure a suitable instrument for initiating complaints against its employees or against the union as their institutional representative. One logical situation for management to use the grievance procedure would be to process a charge that employees and/or union officials had violated a union responsibility clause. Another might involve charges that the union was seeking to discredit management in the eyes of the employees.

A union responsibility clause is one stating an affirmative commitment by the union to police its membership in the interests of stable contract administration. The union agrees, for example, to condemn and discourage absenteeism, wildcat strikes, and other employee actions designed to interfere with production or to short-circuit the grievance procedure.

In any such cases, management will usually exercise its disciplinary prerogatives directly against offending employees or take formal action against the union through a civil damage suit under Section 301 of Taft–Hartley. The damage suit option has little appeal for most employers.

Even though it may rarely be used, there may be some virtue in making the grievance procedure available to management. This option supports the idea of the *joint* commitment to achieve stability, consistency, and equity in administration of contract terms. The document then becomes something more than a cataloguing of policies and procedures for the effectuation of which management assumes virtually the whole burden. The joint aspect of the undertaking can be understood by the management option to use the grievance procedure against employees or the union leadership through a "general" or "policy" grievance of its own.

This line of thinking brings us logically to the final topic on contract administration prior to discussing the uses of grievance arbitration —namely, the problem of how to prevent going outside the contract's grievance and arbitration machinery.

PENALTIES FOR FAILURE TO USE
CONTRACT GRIEVANCE PROCEDURES

BLS data for 1974 revealed that 26.6 percent of work stoppages occur under existing agreements.[48] In most contracts, walkouts of this nature are specifically prohibited by the agreement itself. Such "wildcat" stoppages are a critically serious problem whose solution is not an easy one. The grim irony is that most wildcats occur under contracts with a suitable grievance and arbitration mechanism specified as a *quid pro quo* for a sweeping no-strike clause.

Many unions have done a good job of educating the rank and file to utilize the grievance procedure instead of resorting to "direct action." In some cases, however, employers are unable to plan on uninterrupted production during the life of the contract. They are plagued intermittently (and, in some cases, with alarming frequency) by walkouts in particular departments or possibly of the entire workforce. Sometimes these wildcats may have been engineered behind the scenes by the union leadership. Usually, however, the union leadership is just as interested as management in eliminating this flouting of contract obligations.

In any valid contractual situation, there can be no excuse for a group of employees taking the law into their own hands by walking off the job, deliberately slowing down their work pace, becoming collectively "sick," or otherwise breaking their commitment to use the contract's grievance and arbitration machinery. The alleged intrinsic merit of the employee's complaint is not a valid excuse for using economic force instead of the procedures jointly agreed upon as the sole method for handling allegations of contract violation. Employees on many occasions may be restless and understandably impatient over the delays in a clogged or overloaded grievance procedure. The remedy, however, is not to go outside the contract, but to press hard for speeding up the grievance procedure through the authorized union representatives. Unfortunately, employees do not always appreciate that they themselves are the principal beneficiaries of scrupulous adherence to the prescribed contract method for adjustment of complaints.

Many wildcats are triggered by the discharge of a single employee. His fellow employees then walk off the job in protest in an effort to pressure management into reinstating him on the spot. This is perhaps the least excusable basis for direct action, if one concedes that some wildcats have a better rationale than others.

Perhaps the most plausible circumstance for unauthorized direct action would be in any case where workers are told to do a job that they believe is

48. Bureau of Labor Statistics, U.S. Department of Labor, Bulletin 1902, *Analysis of Work Stoppages*, 1974, p. 14.

dangerous to their health or safety. Even here the remedy is not to risk discharge for insubordination or a wildcat. The remedy is not a walkout or a refusal to perform, but an immediate union steward appeal to top supervision over the foreman's head.

The writers have heard discipline cases involving wildcats where the defense held that the workers were contractually correct in their position and that the foreman's order was wrong. In such cases, the discipline was sustained, even where the foreman's order was contractually in error. In labor relations, as in other phases of interpersonal relations, *two wrongs do not make a right*.

Some contracts do not provide for arbitration as the terminal step in the grievance procedure. In such, management always has the last word unless the union resorts to direct action. In a contract with a clear channel of grievance adjustment steps culminating in arbitration, however, there is no excuse for resort to economic force.

Under most contracts, the scope of the arbitrator's authority is congruent with the coverage of the contract's no-strike–no-lockout clause. If under the contract a grievance is arbitrable, the union is estopped from strike action during the life of the agreement. In some contracts, certain issues are reserved for strike action during the life of the contract by excluding them from the scope of the arbitrator's authority. However, most contracts provide that any grievance relating to contract interpretation and application may go to arbitration. In these cases, there can be no lawful strike during the life of the agreement.

A SUGGESTED SOLUTION
TO THE WILDCAT STRIKE PROBLEM

For management the problem of periodic wildcat interruptions of production is a troublesome one, particularly during periods of full employment when all employees are needed to maintain production in a race with the firm's competitors. The problem of wildcat strikes is most salient in the coal industry where 2 million man-days of production and 20 million tons of coal were lost in 1975 and 1976 due to wildcat action.[49] However, employers may have these wildcat strikes enjoined by a federal court if the strike is over an arbitrable grievance. But if the wildcat strike is an action in sympathy with another union or over any nonarbitrable issue, employees cannot be enjoined from such action even if a valid no-strike clause exists.[50]

It should be no surprise that the coal industry experiences frequent

---

49. Ed Townsend, "Coal Miners Threaten Carter's Energy Plans," *Christian Science Monitor*, May 3, 1977, p. 26.
50. *Buffalo Forge Co.* v. *United Steelworkers of America*, 428 U.S. 397, 92 LRRM 3032 (1976).

wildcat strikes. Coal mining is one of the most dangerous of all jobs. Grievable issues concerning safety are often viewed as life-and-death matters by the miners. Unlike other grievance issues, such as discharge (where back pay can be ordered), there is no adequate means to "make whole" a dead miner. Miners may pursue safety disputes with management through the grievance procedure, but many miners view this as inadequate. They perceive the grievance procedure as too slow for such a critical issue; and they perceive arbitrators as poorly informed about the unique nature of mining.

Prospects for control of wildcat strikes in the coal mining industry would appear dismal. Yet a study by Jeanne Brett and Stephen Goldberg suggests some management practices that seem to resolve most of the problems, and that could be applied to industries other than coal.[51] Brett and Goldberg compared mines that had few wildcat strikes with mines that had frequent wildcat strikes. Here are their most important findings:

1. Low-strike mines, but not high-strike mines, settled their grievances at the lowest levels of the procedure. Mine managers gave first-line supervisors the authority to settle, and made every effort to resolve grievances early.

2. At low-strike mines, but not high-strike mines, the mine committee (union) and mine management had a problem-solving relationship.

3. At high-strike mines, but not low-strike mines, miners perceived that striking was the only way to get management to discuss a problem. At high-strike mines lower level supervisors routinely forward grievances to the next step in the procedure without discussion or consideration.

Many firms without a union have grievance procedures and follow practices very much like the practices Brett and Goldberg found at low-strike mines. No union forced companies to do this; they do it because it makes good business sense. An employee, or group of employees, who get a hearing of their complaint and whose dispute is usually resolved quickly, if not always favorably, can better focus their attention and their efforts on their work.

Not all situations are as difficult as mining. Certainly, violation of the contract and the arbitration procedure by striking can serve as an invitation for future similar strikes. After a wildcat strike—once the problem has developed this far—appeasement, in the long run, may not be the most prudent management course. Solving grievances early, if possible, and maintaining a *consistent* and clearly enunciated policy of firmness toward wildcat strikes, is management's best bet for stable contract administration.

51. Jeanne M. Brett and Stephen B. Goldberg, "Wildcat Strikes in Bituminous Coal Mining," *Industrial and Labor Relations Review*, 32 (July 1979), 465–83.

SUMMARY

Most employers and union leaders agree that the heart of collective bargaining lies in the (sometimes) mundane task of contract administration. Contract negotiation is a "sometime thing." It occurs usually once every three years. *Positive contract administration requires daily initiative by management in effectuation of terms.* The contract's grievance machinery is of crucial importance in giving operational significance to the written word. It provides a peaceful way of resolving *any* dispute that may arise concerning interpretation and application.

Orderly and efficient operation of any enterprise and the logic of employee democracy require that a mechanism be available for fair disposition of any case where an employee feels aggrieved. This machinery should also be available to management for registering complaints about union or employee violation of contract.

If procedures and principles of grievance adjustment are clearly understood by both line supervision and union officials and employees, most problems in contract administration can be resolved in the early steps of the machinery. Much needless friction can thereby be completely avoided. *Perhaps most important, an effective arbitration procedure eliminates any necessity for interruption of production during the life of a contract.*

Arbitration has become such an important aspect of contract administration that we consider the process separately in the following chapter.

Questions for Discussion, Thought, and Research

1. Under what circumstances, if any, should labor and management trade grievances rather than handling each on its own merits? What are the drawbacks to trading grievances?

2. Union officials are often forced to process grievances through the arbitration step, even though the grievance lacks merit. Why? Are there ways a union leader can avoid this practice? Explain.

3. How is the duty of fair representation by the union different in the public sector than under NLRA?

4. Under present law, if an employee feels that his or her Title VII rights have been violated, he or she may pursue remedies under the labor agreement and simultaneously or subsequently commence a Title VII action with the EEOC. Explain.

5. A union business agent commented, "I don't mind having my members getting disciplined, so long as management follows the proce-

dures in administering discipline and gives the members due process. However, I'm not going to do their job. It serves neither my union nor the company to have an employer stop disciplining employees because management doesn't understand how to discipline." What problems are created for the union when discipline is warranted?

6. How does one measure the effectiveness of a grievance procedure? Propose your own measure.

7. An industrial relations professor once stated: "The union business agent is the most important member of your personnel department." Comment.

8. What is the proper role of first-line management in contract administration? How can the first-line supervisor be made more effective in handling grievances?

9. Why is it good policy to settle most grievances at the lowest level possible? Explain.

10. What is the role of the union steward in contract administration?

11. Should the grievance procedure be made available to any complaint? Why is it important for management to act on grievances even where there is no apparent contractual violation?

12. What is the importance of past practice in grievance administration?

13. Why are wildcat strikes prevalent in certain industries (e.g., mining) and unheard of in other industries?

Selected Bibliography

Aaron, Benjamin, ed., *The Future of Labor Arbitration in America*. New York: American Arbitration Association, 1976.

Bureau of National Affairs Editorial Staff, *Grievance Guide* 4th ed. Washington, D.C.: Bureau of National Affairs, 1972.

Elkouri, Frank, and Edna Asper Elkouri, *How Arbitration Works* 3rd ed. Washington, D.C.: Bureau of National Affairs, 1973.

Kuhn, James W., *Bargaining in Grievance Settlement*. New York: Columbia University Press, 1961.

Sovereign, K. L., and Mario (Mike) F. Bognanno, "Positive Contract Administration," *ASPA Handbook of Personnel and Industrial Relations*, Vol. 3 (Washington, D.C.: Bureau of National Affairs, 1976).

Trotta, Maurice S., *Handling Grievances: A Guide for Management and Labor*. Washington, D.C.: Bureau of National Affairs, 1976.

GRIEVANCE ARBITRATION

8

PRINCIPLES AND PROCEDURES

Arbitration of grievance disputes is one of the most pervasive and distinctive elements in the American practice of industrial relations. Arbitration is the final resolution of disputes of contract interpretation in 95 percent of all collective agreements.[1] Arbitration is the method that makes the collective agreement the "law of the shop."

We begin this chapter with a brief statement of the principles of grievance arbitration, followed by a review of the legal status of arbitrator decisions. Next in order is a description of some of the typical issues that go to arbitration. Finally, we discuss many of the decisions that the parties must make in setting up a grievance arbitration procedure.

---

1. *Collective Bargaining—Negotiations and Contracts,* 51 (Washington, D.C.: Bureau of National Affairs, 1979), 5.

PRINCIPLES OF GRIEVANCE ARBITRATION

A collective bargaining agreement defines a system of governance at the workplace. The collective agreement is a contract binding both parties. Inevitably, disagreements arise concerning the precise terms and conditions specified in the contract. Unlike most contracts, collective agreements are not enforced and interpreted by courts, but instead by a neutral person *voluntarily designated* by the mutual agreement of management and union representatives.

This is perhaps the most crucial principle of grievance arbitration: the arbitrator is the "officially designated reader of the contract."[2] The arbitrator's sole source of authority is from the parties. In almost all collective bargaining settings, this authority is limited to the interpretation and application of the terms and conditions of the collective agreement. The contract defines the standards of arbitration; the arbitrator cannot add to or subtract from the agreement.

In almost all contracts the arbitrator's decision is *final and binding* on both parties. Why should an employer agree to such a provision? The answer should be apparent if you consider the alternative. Suppose union and management representatives cannot agree on the meaning of particular contract language after all other grievance steps have been exhausted. Without an arbitration provision, the union must either go along with the management interpretation or use or threaten to use economic force and, in effect, begin bargaining for a new contract. In almost all collective agreements, the employer receives a no-strike agreement from the union in return for agreeing to binding arbitration; binding arbitration is the cost for a binding no-strike pledge from the union. Arbitration is a means to resolve a dispute short of economic force. Arbitrator decisions are not necessarily permanent; if either party is dissatisfied, they can attempt a negotiated change in the contract when it expires.

LEGAL STATUS OF ARBITRATOR DECISIONS

The U.S. Supreme Court, beginning with *Lincoln Mills*,[3] then forcefully in the *Steel Trilogy*,[4] has ruled that decisions by arbitrators are final and binding interpretations of the collective agreement, as long as (1) the

---

2. Theodore J. St. Antoine, "Judicial Review of Labor Arbitration Awards: A Second Look at Enterprise Wheel and ITS PROGENY," *Arbitration—1977* (Washington, D.C.: Bureau of National Affairs, 1978), p. 30.

3. *Textile Workers* v. *Lincoln Mills*, 353 U.S. 448 (1957).

4. *United Steelworkers of America* v. *American Manufacturing Co.*, 363 U.S. 564 (1960); *United Steelworkers of America* v. *Warrior and Gulf Navigation Co.*, 363 U.S. 574 (1960); and *United Steelworkers of America* v. *Enterprise Wheel and Car Corp.*, 363 U.S. 593 (1960).

arbitrator follows the contract, (2) the parties specify in the contract that arbitration is final and binding, and (3) no gross errors or procedural unfairness occur. Judges may not substitute their interpretation of the agreement for that of the arbitrator. Courts have accepted arbitrator decisions primarily because the employer and the union have voluntarily agreed to this procedure. Courts have long respected the desires of those who consent to a mutual agreement.

The most important implication of this legal standard is that under most circumstances arbitrator interpretations of the contract cannot be appealed to the courts. The only real appeal occurs the next time the contract is negotiated.

There are other reasons for appealing an arbitrator's decision to the courts; these concern conflicts between the collective agreement and public law.

DUAL JURISDICTION[5]

In Chapter 6 we mentioned that the employer-employee relationship can be set unilaterally by the employer (subject to the constraint of attracting and retaining a work force) by collective bargaining or by standards of public policy as found in public statutes. Where a collective agreement exists, two sets of standards regulate the employer–employee relationship, standards defined in the collective agreement and standards set by public policy. In the previous chapter we summarized public policies that coexist with a collective agreement, concluding that in many cases an employee with a complaint against the employer may pursue multiple avenues of appeal, through the grievance procedure and through regulatory machinery enforcing safety, discrimination, and similar public policies.

An employee losing an arbitration decision may appeal to the other jurisdiction, the jurisdiction of public law, rather than private law. Some negotiators have tried, unsuccessfully, to get around this double jurisdiction problem by including a clause in the contract stating that the parties will comply with public law. Laws banning racial discrimination, for example, can become part of the contract. In the process of interpreting the collective agreement, the arbitrator is also interpreting public law. Courts, charged with the duty to interpret *public law*, *have not* been willing to cede their jurisdiction and their duty to arbitrators (some of whom are poorly qualified to interpret public law). If the arbitrator decides a case by interpreting external law—even if a part of the collective agreement—the arbitrator's decision, if appealed, will be reviewed by the courts. Thus, an arbitrator's decision is not final if it conflicts with public law, or if the

5. This is a term used by David Feller in "The Coming End of Arbitration's Golden Age," *Arbitration—1976* (Washington, D.C.: Bureau of National Affairs, 1977), pp. 97–126.

arbitrator's decision is based on public law. As the public jurisdiction expanded throughout the past two decades, both the private jurisdiction, or the contract, and the finality of arbitration have diminished.[6]

A substantial majority of grievances filed by women and minorities allege both a violation of the agreement and discrimination. This poses a serious question about the whole procedure of grievance administration: why should employers agree to arbitration when they also may end up in court? In a sense, the dual jurisdiction regulating employment exposes the employer to jeopardy on individual rights guaranteed by public law and jeopardy on collective rights guaranteed by the union contract. The answer will probably make few employers happy.

In cases where no violations of public law are alleged, arbitration will serve its traditional function, and its traditional usefulness to both employers and unions. In cases where dual violations are alleged, arbitration may be final. Finality will occur if both the grievant and the employer find the arbitrator's ruling preferable to further litigation. Finality may occur based upon the arbitrator's understanding of the fact—that is, was there, in fact, discrimination? Finality may occur in this case if either both parties or the courts accept the arbitrator's finding of fact. Clearly, there will be a residual of cases where arbitration will be merely a prelude to litigation in the courts. Before the expansion of public regulation, the choice was arbitration versus potential strikes over contract interpretation. With the growth of public standards, the choice is to arbitrate all cases—some final and some not final—versus potential strikes over contract interpretation. If not a happy choice, most employers and unions will likely continue to choose arbitration.

REPRESENTATIVE ISSUES IN GRIEVANCE ARBITRATION

Still the most common of all cases in grievance arbitration concerns employee discipline or discharge.[7] An issue involving discharge is usually phrased in the following manner: "Did the Company have just cause under the contract to discharge Richard Roe?"

Many cases involve disciplinary penalties less severe than discharge. Most unionized employers have developed formal systems of corrective or

---

6. *Ibid.*, p. 109.

7. Taking the thousands of cases arbitrated nationally each year, the customary estimate is that more than one of every four involves a discipline issue. For further readings see Dallas L. Jones, *Arbitration and Industrial Discipline* (Ann Arbor: Bureau of Industrial Relations, University of Michigan, 1961); Orme W. Phelps, *Discipline and Discharge in the Unionized Firm* (Berkeley: University of California Press, 1959); M. C. Benewitz, "Discharge, Arbitration and the Quantum of Proof," *Arbitration Journal*, 28, No. 2 (1973), 95–104; and K. Jennings and R. Walters, "Discharge Cases Reconsidered," *Arbitration Journal*, 31, No. 3 (1976), 164–80.

progressive discipline for a variety of rule infractions by employees. Such offenses as tardiness, absenteeism, or smoking in the washroom generally call for a written warning on first offense and for a three-day disciplinary layoff for the second. A third offense may result in discharge. Such employer discipline may be challenged through arbitration when the union and the employee do not think that "just cause" existed and wish to clear the employee's personnel file.

For arbitration of discipline cases other than discharge, the issue may be phrased: "Did the Company have just cause under the contract to discipline John Doe by a three-day layoff for excessive absenteeism?"

One of the most troublesome problems in contract administration is posed by wildcat strikes—that is, unauthorized walkouts by a group of employees (or, in some cases, *all* employees in the bargaining unit) in violation of the union's contract pledge not to strike during the life of the agreement. The employer's dilemma on discipline in these cases is a real one, as we noted in the preceding chapter. Wildcat discipline cases are among the most difficult that an arbitrator can be called upon to decide. Many involve situations where the employer has discharged those he believes were responsible for triggering or leading the wildcat and meted out lesser penalties to employees who walked off or stayed off the job in response to such leadership. These cases are often "tough" for arbitrators because difficult issues as to the nature and quality of proof of cause for discipline may be involved.

Asserting a special responsibility for preventing wildcat strikes rests with union leadership, some employers would discipline union officers for their union office alone. The National Labor Relations Board has recently ruled such behavior to be an unfair labor practice. In *Precision Casting,* and again in *Gould Corporation* and *James P. Morgan,* the board has ruled that discipline based on an individual's union status, rather than conduct as an employee, is unlawful.[8]

In any discipline case the arbitrator sits as both judge and jury, deciding on both the "law" and the "facts." The arbitrator must decide in each case *on the basis of the record* whether the employer has proved "just cause" for discipline under the contract.

Many grievance arbitration cases concern disputes over the meaning and application of the contract's language as to the role of seniority in connection with layoffs, transfers, recalls to work, superseniority for union officials, promotions to higher job classifications, interplant moves, and the like. In many industrial contracts the seniority article is the longest. That is not unusual. On the other hand, some contracts are very brief on this issue. They may be limited to a general statement of policy that, in layoffs from and recalls to employment, length of service will be the controlling

8. 233 NLRB 35 (1977); 237 NLRB 124 (1978).

factor—that is, a "straight" seniority clause. In many contracts, however, ability to perform the available work is required before seniority takes on decisive importance.

A brief policy statement often reflects confidence on the part of the employer and the union in their ability to resolve disputes that may arise without spelling everything out in detail. In large bargaining units, however, the joint preference is usually for a detailed treatment. The parties must decide through experience what is the preferable approach for facilitating contract administration.

In spite of apparent clarity of contract language, seniority issues are often hard to decide. Three tough seniority arbitration issues, for example, include disputes over: (1) denial of promotion to a senior applicant in favor of a "more qualified" junior applicant; (2) transfer of supervisory employees back into the bargaining unit in connection with reductions in force; and (3) how to merge or integrate seniority rosters when company facilities are combined or shut down. Disputes are less frequent these days on straight layoffs or recalls. Contract language on these matters has been satisfactorily clarified in most relationships over the years in earlier arbitration cases or by negotiation.

Changing technology frequently requires changes in seniority policies. The impact of technology in the years ahead is likely to be substantial. One major contract innovation that required reworking of conventional seniority concepts is the guaranteed income security plan incorporated in agreements in the rubber, automobile, farm equipment, and other industries.

Management's right to subcontract work has often been a source of arbitration cases. Subcontracting issues can be explosive in nature when the exercise of one of the employer's most cherished managerial prerogagives poses an apparent (or real) threat to the job security of bargaining unit employees. We should note that arbitrators differ in their philosophies on subcontracting issues, particularly as to how to decide such cases when the contract is silent or vague.

A typical subcontracting issue might be phrased in these words: "Did Company X violate the contract by assigning the work of collecting unpaid accounts to an outside collection agency?"[9]

Other issues commonly faced by grievance arbitrators include the following:

1. Did the company violate the contract by failing to call in employee X for overtime work on Saturday?

2. Did the refusal of John Zilch to work overtime on Saturday constitute a

9. The phrasing of this arbitrable issue and those to follow are taken from actual cases heard and decided by Harold Davey. Changes in wording have been made only to avoid identification of companies, unions, and individuals.

violation of the agreement and render Zilch subject to discipline by the company?

3. Did the company violate the contract when it assigned hourly operating employees to clean and wax the ammonia production control room floor?

4. Was the company's action in assigning four bus drivers to work out of a garage other than their "home" garage on a particular Saturday a "transfer" within the meaning of the contract, or was it a "temporary assignment" that the company was privileged to make under the agreement?

5. Was the company's revision of its operating methods in department 13 and establishing of the B-20 job classification privileged or prohibited under the contract?

6. Does the company policy of refusing to hire spouses of bargaining unit employees violate the contract's no-discrimination clause?

7. Under the pertinent provision of the contract, did John Doe receive the proper amount of vacation pay?

8. Does Appendix A of the contract require automatic progression within rate ranges?

9. Is the grievance of Sam Blotto arbitrable under the contract? If so, did the company violate the contract by failing to offer the grievant overtime?

10. Did the change in method instituted on job X constitute a "substantial" change within the meaning of section 2 of Article XVI of the contract between the parties?

Issue listing could be continued for many pages. Those already noted should suffice to illustrate the range and variety of issues coming before an arbitrator. The last issue listed is representative of many issues that arise in administration of a contract's job evaluation or wage incentive system. Such "technical" cases are common today, particularly with frequent changes in "job mix" being made because of technological developments.

PROPER PHRASING
OF THE ARBITRABLE ISSUE

The reader will note that nearly all issues listed above were worded to call for a yes or no answer. The words "under the contract" can frequently be found in the statement of the issue to be decided. Most union and management representatives regard their contracts as private statutory law, binding upon the arbitrator as well as upon themselves. When they go before an arbitrator they have agreed to disagree. They do not want the arbitrator to function as a "philosopher king," resolving their dispute in terms of how *she* or *he* personally thinks it should be resolved. Nor do they want a compromise decision. They want the arbitrator to stick with the contract and decide cases in no-nonsense terms such as "under the contract, Grievance No. 99 should be and is hereby denied." If the award calls for a denial, that ends the matter. An award sustaining Grievance No. 99 would generally embrace the remedial relief sought.

If Joe Doe has been discharged, for example, his grievance usually contains a demand for reinstatement with all contractual rights restored and full back pay. Under most contracts, the arbitrator has the authority to modify penalties if his finding is that discharge was too severe under the circumstances but that the record establishes proof of cause for *some* discipline. In such cases, the award may direct reinstatement but deny some or all of the back pay that might be involved.[10]

Whatever may be the issue, arbitrators have a common concern to achieve a precise understanding at the hearing as to what they are being asked to decide. This can be done through a submission agreement drawn up by the parties in advance or through a stipulation arrived at during the hearing. The parties may prefer to leave the phrasing of the issue to the arbitrator's discretion.

THE GRIEVANCE ARBITRATOR AND HIS FUNCTION

Arbitrators owe allegiance to the contract under which they are operating. Even when the contract is clear as to the nature of the arbitrator's authority and jurisdiction, one of the parties may encourage an arbitrator to pursue a different course. If this occurs, the arbitrator must follow the contract from which authority flows. He must not permit himself to extend or to exceed his authority.

Employers and unions can make optimal use of arbitration as an instrument for improved contract administration only when they agree on the type of arbitration they want. If one party seeks a "judicial" approach to arbitration and the other wants the arbitrator to function as a mediator, the process will not work very well.

If the parties prefer an arbitrator to function as a "problem solver," they should select an arbitrator who can do so competently by mediating a solution. If they prefer the arbitrator to adhere to the judicial approach, such preference must be made clear.

Most practitioners and arbitrators hold that the arbitrator's function is

---

10. There are still contracts, however, that limit the arbitrator to a finding of whether the company has proved cause for discipline. Such contracts provide no discretion to modify penalties deemed to be excessive.

essentially judicial in nature. Most arbitrations are handled on an *ad hoc* basis, notwithstanding the rapid growth in permanent umpire machinery. In *ad hoc* arbitration, the judicial approach is clearly the more appropriate. In most permanent arbitration systems as well, the arbitrator is expected to function in a judicial manner.[11]

Only a gifted minority of arbitrators can handle the delicate dual assignment of mediator–arbitrator. Comparatively few employers and unions wish the arbitrator to depart from straight adjudication. The arbitrator is the employee of the company and the union jointly. If they wish to utilize him in a consultative capacity during negotiations or to initiate proposals for settling grievances formally submitted to him for arbitration, their wishes should be respected. The fact remains that there are few arbitrators who can function effectively in the Harry Shulman, George Taylor, Dave Cole, Saul Wallen manner.

Advisory arbitration or grievance mediation, which are two names for the same thing, should not be confused with *med–arb*. An arbitrator practicing med–arb will try to mediate a solution, while retaining the contractually stipulated final and binding authority. Advisory arbitration or grievance mediation represents a procedure which does not include a finality stipulation.[12]

Whatever their individual beliefs may be as to the arbitrator's proper function, experienced professional arbitrators will find no quarrel with the following basic propositions:

1. The arbitrator's authority is determined and governed by the contract. His duty is to the contract.

2. The parties are entitled to the type of arbitration they want, which should be clearly expressed in their contract.

3. The parties must share the same basic expectations from the arbitration process if maximum value is to be achieved.

STRICT VERSUS LIBERAL CONSTRUCTIONISTS

Notwithstanding the apparent consensus on the three propositions, professional arbitrators will differ in evaluating their interpretive functions

11. For an excellent comparative review of permanent arbitration systems, see Charles C. Killingsworth and Saul Wallen, "Constraint and Variety in Arbitration Systems," in Mark L. Kahn, ed., *Labor Arbitration: Perspectives and Problems* (Washington, D.C.: Bureau of National Affairs, 1964), pp. 56–81.

12. See James P. O'Grady, "Grievance Mediation Activities by State Agencies," *Arbitration Journal*, 31, No. 2 (1976), 125–30; and Philip Harris, "Advisory Arbitration: A Study of a Life Cycle," *Labor Law Journal*, 27 (July 1976), 420–25.

under the contract. Some regard their role as a self-limiting one. Others take an expansive view of the breadth of their discretion. This distinction in attitudes is a little difficult to pin down, but it is real. At some risk of oversimplification, it can be described as one between "strict" and "liberal" construction of contract language.

Let us take arbitrator X and arbitrator Y, each of whom is operating under typical contract language limiting arbitration to grievances concerning contract interpretation and application and prohibiting the arbitrator from adding to, subtracting from, or otherwise modifying the language of the contract. Arbitrator X is a strict constructionist with a self-limiting view of the nature of arbitral authority. Arbitrator Y is a liberal constructionist who believes that responsibilities under the contract allow for imagination and perhaps innovation in the interest of stable and progressive industrial relations.

Both arbitrator X and arbitrator Y may classify themselves as belonging to the "judicial" school of arbitration. Yet their different mental sets on the task of contract construction could lead to different decisions on identical cases. One area where such a difference might show up is in cases involving arbitrability. Arbitrator X, operating as a strict constructionist, might rule certain grievances to be not arbitrable, whereas arbitrator Y might not hesitate to assume jurisdiction.

Another category of cases where strict or liberal construction can be of critical significance might be grievances challenging managerial discretion in discipline, promotion, and job classification cases. Arbitrator X, a strict constructionist, may show greater respect for the finality of managerial discretion (unless he finds it to have been exercised in an arbitrary or discriminatory fashion). Arbitrator Y, reviewing the same factual situation, might not hesitate to modify or reverse an exercise of managerial discretion.

The distinction between strict and liberal constructionist approaches reveals itself also in the significance attributed to past practice where the contract language and the practice appear to differ. A strict constructionist inclines to the view that the contract governs when past practice and the contract are in conflict, notwithstanding the duration and uniformity of the practice in question. A liberal constructionist may hold that the parties have determined the "true meaning" of the contract language by their past practice. He may thus conform his decision to the past practice, even if this requires some "torturing" of the contract's actual wording.

Being human, arbitrators are not completely consistent or predictable. One who regards himself as a strict constructionist may be unable to resist the temptation to adopt a liberal interpretation of contract language in a particular case if he finds the equitable considerations to be compelling. On the other hand, a liberal constructionist may decide that a particular case calls for a strict or rigorous interpretation.

Differences in approaches to the task of contract construction can produce significant differences in substantive decisions. Knowledgeable employer and union representatives are therefore alert to these differences in how arbitrators look upon their duty to the contract. The selection of arbitrators on particular cases is often made with such differences in mind.

The best evidence that such games of point–counterpoint do take place can perhaps be found in selection of arbitrators for discipline cases. Experienced arbitrators acquire reputations for being "tough" or "soft" on discipline issues. In this context, tough can have two different connotations. An arbitrator can be regarded as tough because he is exacting as to the amount of proof of "just cause" he requires of management in disciplinary action cases. One who is tough on proof may be sought after by unions and shunned by management in discipline cases. However, tough can also be a fitting label for an arbitrator with strong convictions about not modifying the penalty where cause for discipline has been proved. Any union arbitrating a discipline case for the purpose of tempering justice with mercy will seek to avoid arbitrators who are reluctant to modify penalties.

Arbitrators also differ in their views as to the relative seriousness of different types of rule violations. All might agree in the abstract that insubordination, fighting on the job, reporting drunk on the job, stealing company property, and other serious offenses merit discharge the first time they occur. Arbitrators will differ, however, as to how much weight, if any, should be accorded to evidence of mitigating circumstances.

Let us suppose two employees, X and Y, are shown to have stolen equivalent amounts of company property. X has been with the company twenty years. This is his first offense of any nature. Y has been with the company only two years and already has a poor disciplinary record. Both are discharged. The proof of guilt is convincing in each case. Should the discharge be sustained in both cases, or should a requested second chance be given to X? Many arbitrators would not support a differential in penalty when theft is the basis for discharge. Others would regard the employee's entire record as proper for consideration and would review the propriety of the penalty.

Reasonable men in management and union circles can and do differ in specific situations, even though sharing similar views on the proper uses of arbitration in contract administration. So also do arbitrators differ in their views as to the proper disposition of basically similar cases and in their philosophical approaches to the task of contract construction.

Employers and unions have a right to know how the arbitrator views the task of contract construction. By the same token, the arbitrator has a right to know what the parties expect from their arbitration system. This can be made clear both in the contract language describing grievance and arbitration procedure, and also by the method of case presentation and argument.

Arbitrators are frequently urged to be "consistent" in performing their interpretive duties. The parties themselves, however, are not always models· of consistency. They sometimes depart from *their* customary positions in particular cases. Most experienced arbitrators can recall instances where company X, usually a bear for strict construction of contract language, has urged in a particular case that strict application of the contract will bring "deplorable" results unintended by the parties. Union Y, normally an apostle of equity, reasonableness, and "flexibility" in contract interpretation, may nevertheless demand its pound of flesh in strict accordance with the letter of the contract in a particular case.

Much of the difficulty in arbitration continues to be caused by inability of the parties to reach a true meeting of the minds as to the proper uses of arbitration and a consequent tendency to shift position in terms of the nature of the case being arbitrated.

JUDICIAL AND PROBLEM-SOLVING APPROACHES: A COMPARISON

In discussing strict and liberal contract construction, an effort has been made to avoid up to this point a final and binding decision as to which approach is more likely to produce better long-run results. Which approach is favored depends on how the parties and the arbitrators regard the collective bargaining contract. Do they see it as an instrument setting forth the "law of the plant," or as a set of flexible guidelines for a continuous process of mutual accommodation? In the former view, the contract becomes a binding statement of rights, obligations, and responsibilities, applicable to the company, the union, and bargaining unit employees covered by the instrument. Contract terms are assumed to stand as written for the duration of the agreement. No modification is possible save in the rare situation of mutually acknowledged necessity for change, as a result of unanticipated contingencies or the intrusion of external variables that neither party can control. If, however, the parties (and the arbitrator) regard the arbitration step as an extension (or continuation) of the process, such views will encourage a liberal approach on the arbitrator's part to his contract interpretation role. He may also be urged by the parties to *mediate solutions* of grievances appealed to the arbitration step rather than to decide such cases on a grievance-denied or grievance-sustained basis, as outlined earlier in the discussion of typical issues in grievance arbitration.

Having said this, it remains true that there *is* a difference of importance between the two conceptions of the arbitrator's task under consideration here. In judicial arbitration, *the primary responsibility for the contract always remains with the parties.* It is the employer and the union who must live with particular decisions or take on the job of changing the contract language whenever particular decisions may reveal that certain provisions are administratively impracticable or even unworkable as written, or whenever decisions enforce a significance to particular contract language that calls for a revision of such language.

On the other hand, devotees of the problem-solving type of arbitration assign a more free-wheeling role to their arbitrators. The latter are expected (in fact, encouraged) to mediate solutions in some (although not all) situations. They are not constantly reminded by their parties that they are operating under the contract as it is written. Such attitudes toward the arbitrator's task can result in excessive dependence on the outside neutral. This can result in the arbitrator actually doing what amounts to a contract-writing job through the decisional process. We do not believe that this is the way to achieve optimal results in contract administration. It permits the parties to evade their own primary responsibilities. Using arbitration for extending the negotiation aspect of collective bargaining invites both excessive arbitration and excessive dependence on the arbitrator.

SOME CONTINUING PROCEDURAL PROBLEMS IN ARBITRATION

Grievance arbitration has achieved such widespread endorsement as a procedure that it is surprising that some significant differences remain as to optimal procedures and best usage of arbitrators. We shall consider briefly the following:

1. The respective merits of *ad hoc* and permanent arbitration systems.
2. The respective merits of single arbitrators and tripartite boards.
3. The related problems of excessive use of arbitration, cost of arbitration, and "brinkmanship" as a strategy.

AD HOC OR PERMANENT ARBITRATOR MACHINERY?

Medium-sized to large employers and the unions with whom they deal can usually benefit greatly from using a permanent arbitrator to serve on all cases appealed to arbitration under the contract. Permanent arbitration systems are now firmly institutionalized in steel, automobiles, rubber, men's and women's clothing, farm equipment, and hotels and restaurants (in multiemployer urban contracts), and in many other fields. Selection of arbitrators on an *ad hoc* basis as cases arise is, however, still the most common procedure in grievance arbitration. *Ad hoc* arbitration is invariably the rule for smaller employers and small local unions. Many large firms and their unions also retain a preference for the *ad hoc* method.

Many employers and unions that operate with *ad hoc* arbitration are finding it increasingly difficult to obtain experienced, competent, and acceptable arbitrators, particularly on short notice. The delays on scheduling hearings and in getting out decisions are related matters for concern.

The permanent arbitrator system has advantages over *ad hoc* selection, both for the parties and for the arbitrator, particularly when there is a reasonably predictable arbitration caseload (such as ten or more cases per year). The parties can insure the availability of a competent professional through a suitable combination of annual retainer fee and per diem fee for cases heard and decided. An arbitrator working on such a basis can and should give priority in scheduling and deciding cases. He can also in many cases continue to handle some *ad hoc* work and perhaps even other umpireships. This would, of course, depend on the demands on his time and the need to avoid overcommitment.

The word "permanent" can be a misleading one. Contracts formerly provided that the appointee's services could be dispensed with by either party *at any time* through a "Dear John" letter to the arbitrator with a copy to the other party. This has been softened in many cases to provide tenure for the life of the agreement. The best arbitrators in the United States have been gently (or harshly) relieved of their duties in one or more permanent arbitration systems over the years. The life span of the permanent arbitrator is usually long enough to permit him to develop an informed understanding of the contract and the industry involved. His availability and understanding are important advantages to the parties. In marked contrast, under an *ad hoc* system, the arbitrator hits the hearing "cold." Even experienced arbitrators need some briefing in any case. Yet under prevailing practice the arbitrator arrives at the hearing knowing only the names of the parties and (perhaps) the bare statement of the issue(s) involved in the grievance(s) he is expected to hear and decide. He starts from ground zero.

SINGLE ARBITRATOR OR TRIPARTITE BOARD?

Grievance arbitration in the United States is usually handled by single impartial arbitrators, selected directly by the parties or from panels of five, seven, or nine names, submitted upon request by the Federal Mediation and Conciliation Service, American Arbitration Association, or a state agency. The single arbitrator concept is consistent with the judicial approach to arbitration, although there is, of course, nothing to preclude a single arbitrator using the problem-solving (mediatory) method if the parties wish him to do so.

A vigorous minority of employers and unions retain their preference for tripartite boards (usually consisting of one management-designated arbitrator, one union-appointed arbitrator, and a third impartial arbitrator who serves as chair). The use of tripartite boards is frequently (but not always) indicative of a union–management preference for the problem-solving approach. Some parties retain the tripartite mechanisms in their contracts as extra insurance for the crucial case when they wish to make certain that the impartial chairman fully understands the import of the evidence and argumentation. Customarily, however, the parties stipulate that the third man shall act in fact as though he is the sole arbitrator.

The logic of tripartite boards for grievance arbitration of the judicial type is open to question. However, the device has merit whenever final and binding arbitration is to be used for resolving disputes over future contract terms. In these cases, the decision may frequently require a "political" or "mediatory" approach. The presence of management and union-appointed arbitrators at the decision stage can thus be helpful in arriving at a solution (decision) that satisfies the needs, expectations, and capabilities of the parties.[13]

RELATED PROBLEMS OF EXCESSIVE ARBITRATION, COST OF ARBITRATION, AND "BRINKMANSHIP"

Experienced arbitrators still report that they hear much too high a percentage of cases that should probably not have been appealed to arbitration. This excessive resort to arbitration is one of the more serious ways of wasteful utilization of a critically short supply of experienced, competent, and acceptable arbitrators. It is also obviously related to the growing costs of arbitration as an instrument of contract administration. Frequently, the excess or surplus of cases appealed to arbitration is related to the strategy of "brinkmanship," a term used here to describe the contract administration equivalent of the dragsters' game known as "chicken." Some brief comments on these three interrelated phenomena follow.

13. For a full examination of the pros and cons of tripartite boards in grievance arbitration, see Harold W. Davey, "The Uses and Misuses of Tripartite Boards in Grievance Arbitration," in Charles M. Rehmus, ed., *Developments in American and Foreign Arbitration* (Washington, D.C.: Bureau of National Affairs, 1968), pp. 152–79.

The Dangers in Excessive Arbitration

Most arbitrators are (or should be) professionally concerned to make arbitration more efficient, more swift, ana less costly. There is also an obligation to encourage parties to utilize arbitration as infrequently as possible. One way to cut down on arbitration is to price it out of existence. This is not a salutary way of reducing the caseload. The logical approach is to do a far better job in earlier steps of the grievance procedure, along lines suggested in the preceding chapter. An "excessive" arbitration caseload is usually a sign of a "distressed" grievance procedure. Some excellent practical suggestions as to how to relieve such distress will be found in a paper by Arthur Ross delivered at the sixteenth annual meeting of the National Academy of Arbitrators.[14] It would be most helpful if more arbitrators would follow the Ross lead of encouraging the parties to remedy their procedures at a stage early enough to preclude the need to go to arbitration as often as many do. Arbitration is a desirable ultimate procedure. It should not become a way of life in any relationship.

One suggested cure is to make arbitration relatively expensive in order to increase pressure for screening out those grievances that are lacking in contractual merit or that are being appealed for political reasons. This view assumes that the union will go to arbitration frequently if the financial burden of doing so is not too great. Perhaps this is the case in some relationships, but there is another side to the matter. When arbitration is available only on an ability-to-pay basis, there is a constant temptation, in the face of accumulated unsolved grievances, to resort to wildcat stoppages instead of following contract procedures. In other words, to abandon arbitration and return to economic force.

It must be conceded that if arbitration is made "too easy," political or face-saving cases may be brought so that the arbitrator can absorb the heat for denial of grievances that are known to lack contractual merit. Some of these cases are doubtlessly unavoidable. The fact remains that arbitration should be reserved for the really tough cases where the parties have exhausted all possibilities of informal adjustment. Neither management nor the union should be encouraged to use arbitration as a crutch. Nor should arbitration serve as a means of escaping the consequences of sloppy or inefficient performance by either management or union representatives at earlier stages in the grievance procedure.

Clearly, there is no way to generalize as to what is an "excessive" amount of arbitration. Optimal frequency in usage will vary markedly from one situation to another. Frequency and cost will depend on such factors as

---

14. Arthur M. Ross, "Distressed Grievance Procedures and Their Rehabilitation," in Mark L. Kahn, ed., *Labor Arbitration and Industrial Change* (Washington, D.C.: Bureau of National Affairs, 1963), pp. 104–45.

the size of the company and union, tradition as to the sparing or frequent use of arbitration and the availability of acceptable arbitrators. Optimal usage is not a matter on which generalization is easy.

The Costs of Grievance Arbitration

Rising costs are a favorite allegation of those who are critical of arbitration and arbitrators. In some cases the criticism is justified. In general, however, careful review by both Federal Mediation and Conciliation Service (FMCS) and American Arbitration Association (AAA) indicates that at least the blame for increasing costs of arbitration does not properly attach to the arbitrators.[15] The villains in the picture are costs assumed by the parties themselves—needlessly, in many cases—such as using court reporters, retaining outside counsel for case presentation, and filing posthearing briefs. All these are in the category of expensive luxuries in most situations.

The arbitrator's fee is usually *not* the major cost item in grievance arbitration if the parties do a candid job of counting all the other cost factors properly attributable to appealing any case to arbitration.

It goes without saying that the surest method of reducing costs of arbitration is to resolve grievances. In a good faith relationship, it is a reasonable expectation that only rarely will it be necessary to go to arbitration. The right to arbitrate is as indispensable to good contract administration as the right to strike is to productive negotiation of future contract terms. Actual use in either case can and should be minimal. This is a particularly important consideration when one fully appreciates the fact that good arbitrators are in short supply. This is also a reason for abandoning the strategy of brinkmanship.

TOWARD A MORE EFFICIENT ARBITRATION PROCEDURE

Following are some suggestions for improving the efficiency of arbitration:

1. Switching from *ad hoc* selection on each case to regular usage of the same individual as arbitrator over a considerable period of time for any cases that may arise.
2. Formal development of prehearing statements and submission agreements.
3. More effective use of factual stipulations and consequent reduced use of witnesses.

15. See John Zalusky, "Arbitration: Updating a Vital Process," *AFL–CIO American Federationist*, 83 (November 1976).

4. Elimination of transcripts, except under special circumstances.
5. Elimination of posthearing briefs in most cases.
6. Drastic shortening of arbitration opinions.
7. Early issuance of award with brief statement of reasoning, followed later by full opinion.
8. Greater use of memorandum opinions or even the equivalent of bench rulings.
9. Use of "instant" arbitration, where feasible.

Some of these suggestions have already been discussed, some are obvious, and some will be discussed in the next three sections.

Prehearing Versus Posthearing Briefs

Prehearing statements can serve, among others, the following functions: (1) as a basis for reaching stipulations on undisputed pertinent facts that will eliminate the necessity for considerable testimony, thus saving time and preventing confusion; (2) as a basis for defining the arbitrable issue in more precise fashion; and (3) as an economical way to fill in the "cold" arbitrator.

Effective utilization of prehearing statements can greatly facilitate factual stipulations at the hearing and can make it possible in most cases to eliminate the necessity for posthearing briefs. The prehearing statement, properly prepared, will summarize the pertinent facts and indicate the line of contractual argument that each party intends to pursue. These statements can thus be used to narrow, if not eliminate, the range of disagreement on pertinent factual matters. This can often save much time (and possible confusion) by shortening or eliminating the usual parade of lay witnesses. Greater clarity and economy in presentation are the invariable result of the advance preparation that the prehearing statement requires.

Posthearing briefs seem to be more common in grievance arbitration than in former years. The busy arbitrator is not likely to protest too vigorously that he does not need briefs when he knows that their filing will put off two weeks or longer the time when he must study the record and write his decision. The fact remains that posthearing briefs are a time-consuming, expensive luxury and not a necessity in most cases. If the parties are genuinely concerned about improving the grievance arbitration process, they should devote proportionately more effort to investigation and preparation of cases. From the standpoint of reducing delays and improving performance, this is where the payoff is greatest.

The Expendability of Transcripts and Court Reporters

An arbitrator is generally pleased when walking into a hearing room and seeing a court reporter present. The arbitrator knows at once that the note-taking burden will be reduced. Yet any arbitrator worthy of hire should be willing to take notes on the average case. If the union or management representative is going too fast, the arbitrator can always ask them to slow down or repeat anything that was missed or recorded in insufficient detail.

There are *some* cases where the best interests of both parties suggest the desirability of providing for a verbatim record of the hearing. We refer to technical job evaluation or incentive-pay issues and also to future terms cases concerning wages, pension plan modifications, or other technical matters. Wherever technical terminology is crucial to the case, a transcript is certainly a justifiable expense. Transcripts may also be justified in discrimination, discipline or discharge cases that may hinge on credibility of testimony. In any such case it may be desirable to examine and, more pertinently, to cross-examine witnesses in rapid-fire fashion, too fast for most arbitrators to take competent notes. When credibility is involved, the arbitrator should be free to concentrate on the witnesses under examination.

In the great majority of cases, however, transcripts can be regarded as an expensive luxury. This is particularly true where the employer and union representatives have done a thorough job of grievance investigation and case preparation.

Expedited Arbitration and Bench Awards

Expedited arbitration has become an increasingly popular method for reducing the costs and time delays involved in arbitration. A number of national agreements—including the steel industry, Eastern Airlines, and the U.S. Postal Service—use expedited procedures of one kind or another. Expedited procedures include some of the following features: no transcript, no briefs, time limits for both argument and arbitrator posthearing study, short written opinions by the arbitrator, informal hearings, and presentation of argument by local union and management representatives.

Routine and limited application grievances are best suited for expedited arbitration. Complex issues, precedent setting issues, or issues that have expensive implications are poorly suited for expedited procedures. Most contracts provide escape clauses calling for regular arbitration at the request of either side.

Bench decisions are awarded at the conclusion of the arbitration hearing. This cuts down decision delays and the cost of arbitrator time. The tradeoff is the loss of arbitrator study time often needed to give a considered opinion. Like expedited procedures, bench awards are best suited for the simple and routine rather than the complex or unusual case. Bench award methods require some prior arbitrator familiarity with the workplace and the contract.

Instant Arbitration

In some industries, the nature of the work requires an approximation of "instant" arbitration when disputes arise over interpretation or application of the agreement. Two such widely dissimilar fields as the Broadway theater and west coast longshoring make use of the instant arbitration device. The need for a speedy disposition of cases is apparent in each industry where, for different reasons, the "show must go on," but disputes must also be resolved.

If an actress suddenly advises that she is leaving the cast of a hit play and the producer believes her action is in breach of her contract with him and his contract with Actors Equity, the union in question, he can call on one of two New York City professional arbitrators named in the Actors Equity contract to hear the matter and render a decision on virtually an overnight basis.

In longshoring, disputes may arise on the dock as to the application of the contract's manning provisions. The tightness of ship turnaround scheduling makes it mandatory that any such dispute be resolved on the spot. Such needs are covered in the contract between the Pacific Coast Shipowners Association and the International Longshoremen and Warehouseworkers' Union (ILWU) by a provision in which an "arbitrator" is designated in each port and employed by the parties on a twenty-four-hour standby basis. The port arbitrators are individuals who are knowledgeable about the contract and the problems of the industry by virtue of extensive prior experience with either the ILWU or the Shipowners Association.

Arbitrator Qualification

Arbitrators do not become arbitrators through a process of certification by a professional association or public agency. Arbitrators must meet no formal schooling requirement. The only requirement they must meet is elusive: acceptability by *both* union and management representatives. Arbitrators perceived as favoring management will not be chosen by the union; arbitrators perceived as favoring the union will not be chosen by management. Arbitrators walk the thin line of neutrality.

How persons establish themselves as neutrals, yet at the same time acquire experience in industrial relations, is the primary obstacle any aspiring arbitrator faces. After World War II, when grievance arbitration grew in acceptance by negotiators and the courts, many, perhaps most, arbitrators came from the War Labor Board. This generation of arbitrators acquired experience and a "track record" by serving, in effect, as interest (rather than grievance) arbitrators during a time of war. In recent years, there has been considerable concern expressed by senior arbitrators and professionals in the field of labor–management relations about the source of a new supply of arbitrators.

Training arbitrators in the formal setting of a classroom, such as granting master's degrees in labor arbitration, is unlikely to fulfill the "acceptable" standard. Very few arbitrators find acceptability before age 30, and arbitrators in their early thirties are unusual.[16] Union and management representatives apparently value experience. This is not surprising since many arbitration cases require million-dollar decisions. Few arbitrators win immediate acceptance; most initially arbitrate a few cases a year until they become known.

Where are the new arbitrators coming from? Considering an arbitrator needs to appear neutral, be experienced in industrial relations, and have an earnings base during the entry phase, the set of potential candidates consists, in the main, of lawyers, university professors, and government officials engaged full time in neutral work.[17] A majority of new arbitrators today are lawyers.

In order to provide some training for potential arbitrators, a number of programs have been designed with the support of such interested organizations as the AAA, FMCS, National Academy of Arbitrators (NAA), American Bar Association (ABA) and its affiliated chapters, and Centers and Institutes of Industrial Relations at major universities. These training programs are generally open only to those with a background of experience in law or industrial relations. Training usually consists of watching actual arbitration hearings, writing sample opinions, and having the opinions evaluated by experienced arbitrators.

PROFESSIONAL RESPONSIBILITIES

For the grievance arbitration method to work—that is, to avoid wildcat strikes and to settle disputes quickly, finally, and fairly—depends to a large extent on the performance and professional standards of arbitrators. Unethical or improper behavior can undermine confidence in the entire system. A joint committee of the AAA, FMCS, and NAA determined a Code of Professional Responsibility for Arbitrators of Labor–Management

---

16. Edwin R. Teple, "1976 Report of Committee on Development of Arbitrators," in *Arbitration—1976* (Washington, D.C.: Bureau of National Affairs, 1976), pp. 327–44.

17. *Ibid.*, p. 328.

Disputes. The code provides, among other things, that arbitrators should (1) conform to the wishes of the parties, except for collusion for an improper purpose, (2) disclose their work background and monetary interests, current or past, with any company or union involved in the proceedings, (3) not be influenced by personal relationships in making decisions, (4) treat the proceedings as confidential, (5) not delegate decision making to another person, and (6) complete their assignments in a timely manner.

SUMMARY

Much of this chapter is "bearish" in nature, since there has been a concentration on how to reform procedures. This should not obscure the plus side. There has been general improvement in the conduct of grievance arbitration over the years. The issues impinging on arbitration versus litigation in cases involving dual jurisdiction have quieted somewhat. The quality of those presenting cases to arbitrators has unquestionably improved.

The strong incentive to restructure procedures is not therefore to be interpreted as evidence that the process itself is working badly. At the same time the supply problem underlines the urgency of doing whatever can be done to make arbitration more efficient, less costly and less time-consuming.

Employers and unions can institute the recommended procedural changes and thereby make grievance arbitration into a more effective instrument of contract administration. The primary responsibility must rest on the users of the process. Yet arbitrators should not be passive. The jurisdiction and authority of the arbitrator are prescribed by contract, but arbitrators should do more than we have done in encouraging needed procedural changes.

We shift gears in Chapter 9. Having previously referenced the strike in numerous contexts, the next chapter is devoted to a discussion of resolving future terms disputes.

Questions for Discussion, Thought, and Research

1. Where does an arbitrator draw his or her authority?

2. Under what circumstances can an arbitrator's award be vacated? Why is there a reluctance on the part of the courts to overturn awards?

3. In general, does a contract clause which states that an employer will abide by public law benefit the union or the employer? Discuss.

4. Why is it difficult to find arbitrators who are effective at both mediation and arbitration?

5. Distinguish between grievance mediation and med–arb.

6. How would a party determine in advance of the hearing whether an arbitrator follows either the strict or liberal constructionist philosophy? In reading an arbitrator's previous awards, what items might give a clue toward his or her inclination? Does the strict versus liberal construction dichotomy make any real difference?

7. What are the advantages and disadvantages of having a permanent arbitrator?

8. Under what circumstances would the parties request a tripartite board rather than a single arbitrator?

9. Arbitrators make reasonably good money for their work. Further, there is a supply of lawyers, professors, and others with much of the necessary background to learn arbitration. Why is there a shortage of qualified and acceptable arbitrators?

10. An arbitrator's employability depends upon writing acceptable awards for the parties. An arbitrator who writes a series of poor decisions is likely to be blacklisted by the informal network of unions and management. An arbitrator becomes established by knowing or having ties with labor or management. Does the fact that an arbitrator's future employability depends upon whether he or she writes acceptable awards alter the content of awards issued?

11. In what circumstances would expedited arbitration be most appropriate? What are some of the drawbacks to this approach?

12. Why should management agree to *final and binding* arbitration awards? What is in it for them?

13. To protect individual rights of minorities and women, the courts have compromised the finality of arbitration awards. Has this development strengthened or weakened industrial relations in general?

Selected Bibliography

Coulson, Robert, *Labor Arbitration—What You Need to Know.* New York: American Arbitration Association, 1973.

Davey, Harold W., "Third Parties in Labor Relations—Negotiation, Mediation, Arbitration," in Dale Yoder and H. G. Heneman, Jr., eds., *Employee and Labor Relations.* Washington, D.C.: Bureau of National Affairs, 1976, pp. 7-183–206.

Elkouri, Frank, and Edna Asper Elkouri, *How Arbitration Works*, 3rd ed. Washington, D.C.: Bureau of National Affairs, 1973.

Feller, David E., "The Coming End of Arbitration's Golden Age," *Arbitration—1976*. Washington, D.C.: Bureau of National Affairs, 1977, pp. 97–126.

Prasow, Paul, and Edward Peters, *Arbitration and Collective Bargaining*. New York: McGraw-Hill, 1970.

St. Antoine, Theodore J., "Judicial Review of Labor Arbitration Awards: A Second Look at Enterprise Wheel and Its Progeny," *Arbitration—1977*. Washington, D.C.: Bureau of National Affairs, 1978, pp. 29–52.

RESOLUTION
OF FUTURE TERMS
DISPUTES

9

PRINCIPLES AND PROCEDURES

Use of economic force to resolve disputes over the terms of a future contract continues to be comparatively rare in U.S. labor relations. Nevertheless, whenever there is a general upturn in strike activity in any particular year or a strike occurs in an industry regarded as having critical importance, the general public's impatience is quick to surface. The contemporary bias against strike activity is especially noticeable in the public sector, where strikes by teachers, firemen, and garbage workers have produced severe adverse reactions.

How to eliminate economic force as a means of labor dispute resolution has thus come to achieve an increasingly high priority in the public mind, if not always in the minds of the collective bargaining participants. Strikes, boycotts, and lockouts are constantly under attack as anachronistic and inimical to the public interest. The origins of particular labor disputes or their merits are seldom given the attention they deserve. The emphasis is an almost overwhelming one to develop somehow a labor relations condition where production of goods or services is assured indefinitely without interruption. This is particularly notable in the public sector, where strikes are illegal for most employees and where interest arbitration is common.

THE CHALLENGE TO RESOLVE FUTURE
TERMS DISPUTES PEACEFULLY

Such a generalized preference for reason over muscle is both understandable and logical. At the same time it is important to appreciate fully why employers and unions are reluctant to forego their rights to resort to economic force, where necessary, as an ultimate means of producing agreement on the terms of a future contract. Their reluctance is based on a joint understanding that the possibility of a strike (or lockout), if agreement is not reached at the expiration of the current contract, is in itself the most powerful inducement to reach agreement. This is what keeps the parties at the bargaining table in exhausting marathon sessions. It is rarely the case that any party involved in a labor dispute seeks to resort to economic force in preference to peacefully reaching an agreement. The critical point is that it is the right to use economic force when negotiation fails that gives meaning and substance to private sector collective bargaining as we know it in the United States. It is in fact *the* distinguishing hallmark of "free" collective bargaining.

Collective bargaining, as we have seen, is an institutionalized process of joint decision making. The task of the participants in bargaining is to resolve short-run conflicts in viewpoints and desires on a wide range of economic and noneconomic issues—and to do so peacefully whenever possible. Although employers and unions have done a commendable job of institutionalizing conflict relationships in contract administration (as noted in chapters 7 and 8), the challenge to *improve the level of performance in achieving peaceful resolution of disputes over future contract terms* is a more difficult and compelling one. The stressed language in the preceding sentence was carefully chosen to avoid setting a goal of eliminating economic force entirely. In the first place, it is impossible. Furthermore, such a target would convey the false impression that labor peace is synonymous with health. In *some* circumstances, economic warfare may be a healthier and a necessary condition. The absence of conflict may be evidence of either a coercive or a "sweetheart" relationship, neither of which would be regarded as constituting a constructive or mature employer–union relationship.

We do not intend to glorify economic force at the start of a chapter whose purpose is to consider viable alternatives to the use of economic force in labor relations. It is important to appreciate, however, that many employers and unions strongly believe (perhaps correctly so) that there is no *satisfactory* substitute for economic force as an *ultimate* means of producing agreement at the bargaining table. In this same vein, it is argued that there cannot be *meaningful* collective bargaining in the public sector when the right to strike is prohibited. The key word is "meaningful." To be meaningful, each bargaining side must feel that there is at least the potential for substantial costs if they fail to reach agreement.

As we begin analysis of how to improve performance levels in avoiding use of economic force in future terms cases and to consider alternatives to its use, the first consideration is to acknowledge that if by law we choose to eliminate the right to use economic force there must be at the same time *provision for "suitable" alternative procedures* for producing agreement on future terms. "Suitable" here is defined to mean "acceptable and feasible in the eyes of the parties to the bargaining."

THE STRIKE PERFORMANCE RECORD

Use of economic force is not a problem of unusually serious magnitude. The overall record on labor peace is a reasonably good one (see Table 3–2). Approximately 1.6 million workers were involved in 4,230 work stoppages in 1978. The bare figure of 4,230 strikes in one year may sound ominously large, but we should keep in mind that only a handful of strikes are classified as major stoppages during any given year.[1] These stoppages typically account for a disproportionately large percent of all workers idled by strikes. By far the vast majority of strikes usually involve less than 250 workers.

Certain types of strikes and certain types of employer retaliatory conduct during strikes are declining, although not disappearing entirely. Strikes to enforce union recognition as bargaining representatives are comparatively infrequent. Unions customarily utilize the NLRB's representation case election machinery to establish their claim under the law to exclusive bargaining rights. Furthermore, as we noted in Chapter 3, several types of strike are prohibited by federal and/or state legislation. In this category are jurisdictional strikes, secondary or sympathetic strikes, federal employees' strikes, strikes to achieve unlawful objectives, and so on. Their legal prohibition is an important reason for the comparative infrequency of strikes in these categories. It is not the only factor. Some credit

---

1. The Bureau of Labor Statistics defines a "major" work stoppage as one involving 5,000 or more employees.

can properly be given to a maturing labor movement and growth of more constructive relationships between employers and unions.

CHARACTERISTICS OF A CONTEMPORARY STRIKE

The most common strike may be described as a *primary* strike by union X against employer Y when negotiations on future terms (the new contract) have failed to produce an agreement. Disputes over proposed general wage adjustments continue as the most important single cause of work stoppages.

As a general rule, when employer Y is struck by his employees represented by union X, the process of conflict has become institutionalized to the point where employer Y does not invite violence by initiating a back-to-work movement, by refusing to negotiate further, or by seeking to import strikebreakers.

This does not indicate that employers have gone "soft," nor can we say that labor dispute violence is entirely a thing of the past. The general absence of violence and strikebreaking activity can be regarded as evidence that today's employer recognizes the legitimacy of strike activity in such a primary dispute. Furthermore, the employer views the relationship with the union as a *continuing* one, even though the employees are on strike.

Typically, when a primary strike occurs, the parties lock horns by application of economic pressure, but there is an underlying confidence in the enduring nature of the relationship. Each strike, in other words, does not become a grim battle for survival. On the contrary, most strikes resemble the classic view of a strike as a *continuation of bargaining by other methods*. The union has no intention of breaking the employer. The latter has no intention of using the strike as a method of ridding himself of the union. Both parties assume they will resume relationships with one another after a few days, a few weeks, or, in severe cases, a few months.

This is a significant change in basic attitudes. It deserves emphasis. It reflects a maturing conception of a union–management relationship that does not rule out the possibility of industrial conflict. There is an acceptance of the proposition that conflict may at times be necessary as a means of resolving a dispute. Both the employer and the union, however, know that the institutional process of living together will be resumed after the resort to economic pressure has produced a new agreement that in the short run may be favorable to the employer or to the union, as the case may be.

A critically important characteristic of today's work stoppage concerns the disappearance of the romantic notion of the union as the underdog. On the contemporary scene, whenever employees go on strike, the burden of justifying the use of economic force falls on the union. Thus, when a strike is called, the "blame" invariably attaches to the union since it has seemingly initiated the conflict. Employer intransigence in a particular situation may have made a strike unavoidable from the union standpoint. Nevertheless, under contemporary conditions the employer rarely takes the step of locking out his employees. The lay observer is therefore prone to consider the union as responsible for the lost production, employment, and wages—not the employer. In fact, strikes begin as much from employer willingness to "take" a strike as union desire to strike.

In summary, few strikes under contemporary conditions have been popular in terms of public support. The days of union support from the underdog role are gone forever (except perhaps in agricultural labor). The psychological climate has shifted to the point where labor peace and uninterrupted production are regarded as good *per se*. A work stoppage is considered regrettable *per se*. This strong statement on public attitudes should perhaps be qualified by observing that the right to strike as part of the collective bargaining process is generally much better understood than in former years.

REALISTIC CONFLICT RESOLUTION

Outlawing the strike has been attempted often enough in the United States to conclude that it does not stop strikes. The same applies to high-pressure intervention. Extreme outside pressure on negotiations may yield a contract, but not a "livable" contract. Collective bargaining is a continuous process; a forced agreement will not last long unless both parties can tolerate the terms. Dictation of terms by third parties, who may know little about the workplace, even if tolerable, may be inefficient and detrimental to production.

The strike threat, on the other hand, forces the parties with the most knowledge and involvement to compromise, to exchange information, and to find a livable area of agreement.

Is there room for public intervention in primary labor disputes? Yes, but the public policy role is limited. The following points set the parameters for realistic conflict resolution.

1. In today's complex, interdependent society economic force as a means of resolving labor disputes must be regarded by the parties as a last-resort instrument for producing agreement. However, the right to strike and the right to lock out should be preserved. Usage in the private sector must remain a possibility. The possibility of usage should be available in the public sector as well on a limited basis (to be spelled out subsequently).

2. In any situation where use of economic force is conditioned or

prohibited by law, effective dispute settlement machinery must be available that will encourage rather than discourage bargaining to finality.

3. Public policy on labor dispute settlement should not be predicated on the proposition that peaceful solutions are always possible, or even always desirable. A primary aim of public policy should be to establish a climate that facilitates informed and rational decision making by employers and unions in future terms disputes.

4. Part of the democratic credo has always been that truth emerges from the marketplace of free ideas. Public policy can aid the labor relations process to the degree that it can reduce the tensions and pressures affecting the negotiations at the bargaining table. A principal means of doing so would be to aid the factualization of bargaining and increase the professional capabilities of neutrals assisting the parties in dispute resolution.

PRIVATE MECHANISMS FOR FUTURE TERMS DISPUTE RESOLUTION

Constructive attitudes are more powerful than any procedures. There can be no adequate substitute for the joint will to reach agreement. When such mutual willingness is present, the need for dispute settlement mechanisms, private or government, will be minimal. If the will to agree is absent, no procedure yet devised is sure to prevent ultimate use of economic force.

Positive attitudes in management–union relationships will correlate highly with joint efforts to institutionalize the bargaining process in such a way as to minimize the possible need to resort to economic force. For example, employers and unions still on a hostile basis are not likely to create joint study committees for handling continuing problems. Such committees are usually the product of mature bargaining relationships.

Assuming that improved knowledge is an aid to the agreement-making process, we can count as plus factors the increased capabilities and resources of negotiators for both employers and unions. It is logical further to assume that the higher the level of agreed-upon information at the bargaining table, the less chance there will be of negotiations breaking down. Here we can note with approval that some employers and unions engage in exploratory sessions as much as one year ahead of formal negotiation time as part of the information gathering process, and also as a way of defusing or reducing the ultimate tensions of the actual bargaining.

Comparatively few "public-be-damned" employers and unions remain on the contemporary bargaining scene. Most parties are alert to the growing public intolerance of work stoppages noted earlier. Thus another positive element can be counted in—that is, widespread and growing joint recognition of the desirability of avoiding the use of economic force wherever and whenever possible. This is not something that can be verified in statistical fashion, but we believe it to be a fact.

Related to this increasing awareness of public impatience is the hard knowledge with which some unions are faced—the technological obsolescence of the strike.[2] In telephonic communications, electric and gas utilities, petroleum refining, chemicals, and other highly automated fields, the orthodox strike has lost most of its punch. Management can use supervisory personnel to continue production for long periods of time even when all bargaining unit personnel support the strike. In such cases, the strike is more of a public information instrument than an exercise in economic strength.

Successful established unions are probably less willing to strike for another reason: past success has raised the cost—in the form of foregone earnings—of striking. To gain a marginal contract improvement, low wage earners give up less by striking than high wage earners. Each past bargaining success makes it more costly for a union to initiate a strike the next round.

When one surveys the various private procedures for future terms dispute resolution, there seems to be nothing of a genuinely new character in sight. There is nothing new about joint study committees, although they are receiving great attention as a means for avoiding crisis bargaining. Perhaps the most significant procedural development of a private nature is a less adverse disposition to consider voluntary adoption of final and binding interest arbitration as a way of resolving future terms disputes.

VOLUNTARY INTEREST ARBITRATION

Agreeing to let a neutral interest arbitrator write the new terms in a contract is unusual in the private sector. Still, it is often discussed, and it is used in some instances.[3] A necessary condition for voluntarily agreeing to interest arbitration is that both parties appreciate the high cost of delaying agreement through ponderous negotiations, especially after a strike has been called. Obviously, if the cost of delay is high enough, the immediate acceptance of an (otherwise unacceptable) arbitration determination may

2. James L. Stern was one of the first to underline technological and other factors contributing to the reduced effectiveness of the strike weapon. See his "Declining Utility of the Strike," *Industrial and Labor Relations Review*, 18 (October 1964), 60–72. See also John Dunlop, "The Functions of the Strike," in John Dunlop and Neil Chamberlain, eds., *Frontiers of Collective Bargaining* (New York: Harper, 1967), pp. 103–21.

3. West Coast Longshoremen contracts and some West Coast Teamsters contracts regularly have been written by arbitrators.

benefit the parties more than permitting costs to continue to mount if agreement is delayed any further.[4] Having agreed to submit unsettled issues to interest arbitration voluntarily does not necessarily mean that the parties will cease bargaining in an effort to reach a bilateral agreement. Without complicating the point, we merely call attention to the fact that each side knows that arbitration could leave them worse off than they would be otherwise. This realization helps to explain why there is a general aversion to interest arbitration in private sector labor relations. But, as we have already noted, there are some instances of its use.

A prime example of voluntary arbitration in the private sector is the Experimental Negotiating Agreement established by the basic steel industry in 1973. Under this agreement, either side may request interest arbitration if contract negotiations reach impasse. The ENA disallows lockouts and strikes except on local issues.

Forces creating the condition for the ENA illustrate the pressures on bargainers in an interdependent economy. For over twenty years, each time a new round of contract negotiations approached, steel customers responded by accumulating large inventories of steel. As the contract deadline approached, steel mills and steel workers went on overtime. If a strike resulted, customers would draw on their accumulated inventories; if a strike did not result, customers would again draw on their inventories, thus causing temporary plant closures or curtailment in hours worked. There was no appreciable difference to both sides whether or not a strike resulted. The threat of a strike, more than the strike itself, distorted production, employment guarantees, and vacation schedules. In addition, customers faced with a potentially unstable domestic supplier, sought to lessen their own risks of supply loss by securing foreign steel supplies. Thus, the threat of a strike reduced domestic steel sales (and employment of steel workers) in favor of foreign steel sales.[5]

The ENA was one way of meeting the challenge of finding a substitute for the strike or lockout when the costs of delayed agreement are high. The ENA also provides a practical illustration of at least one limitation faced by voluntary interest arbitration schemes. Rank-and-file union members usually have minimum information about the actual conduct of negotiations. There is always some doubt about the extent to which union officials represented their *best* interests. This doubt is sometimes voiced at contract ratification meetings. With interest arbitration, however, not only is the right to strike *forfeited*, but so is the right to contract ratification. Thus, over time arrangements like the ENA have the potential to appear as a cooperative union and management venture created at the members'

---

4. See John G. Cross, *The Economics of Bargaining* (New York: Basic Books, 1969), pp. 91–119.

5. Dunlop, ''The Functions of the Strike,'' p. 113.

expense. Such a perception is greeted with membership skepticism. In the steelworkers' case, the ENA has from its inception been a matter of intraunion controversy, and its very continuation is in constant jeopardy.

No arbitration procedure, voluntary or compulsory, will end strikes altogether. An arbitration determination that one side or the other cannot live with will inevitably lead to circumvention of procedures and occasionally to a strike.

THE IMPORTANCE OF EFFECTIVE
MEDIATION

The role of government as a conciliator or mediator of labor disputes has been historically accepted in principle, although perhaps resented in particular situations. The role of the neutral peacemaker has undeniable plus values in labor relations as in other types of conflict situations. The mediation function rests on two important basic considerations: (1) the public interest, as well as the interest of the parties immediately concerned, will normally be better served by achieving a solution to the dispute that does not require (or which minimizes) the use of economic force; and (2) in a conflict situation, third-party intervention of a voluntary kind can frequently produce a psychological climate that will lead to settlement of differences impossible to achieve when the parties are left indefinitely to confront one another. There is, however, no intrinsic magic in the conciliation or mediation function. Its effectiveness depends almost entirely on two things: (1) acceptability of the function to the parties; and (2) knowledgeability and skill of the mediators.

The mediation function has gained increasing acceptance at both the federal and state level. Most of the key industrial states have regularly established mediation agencies whose services are utilized by employers and unions as the need arises.

The Federal Mediation and Conciliation Service, an independent agency since the 1947 amendments to the National Labor Relations Act, has become a truly professional agency. The FMCS insists on previous labor relations experience as a prerequisite for becoming a staff mediator. It then puts all recruits through a rigorous academic and field regimen.[6] Both the mediation function and those performing it are highly regarded by employers and unions utilizing the service, an indispensable factor in successful dispute resolution.

---

6. A concise description of FMCS training may be found in Jerome T. Barrett, "The Training and Development of Federal Mediation and Conciliation Service Mediators," *Dispute Resolution: Public Policy and the Practitioner*, 1977 Proceedings, Society of Professionals in Dispute Resolution, pp. 68–71.

EMERGENCY DISPUTES

Now and then a lengthy strike occurs in a critical industry such as steel, transportation, or coal mining. These strikes, if allowed to continue, can, by cutting the supply of vital inputs, shut down many other industries. Extreme cost to the public by disrupted commerce provokes government intervention. A procedure for dealing with just such a strike is defined in Title II of the Taft–Hartley Act.

The president invokes Title II when a threatened or actual labor dispute "will, if permitted to occur or continue, imperil the national health or safety." Having made such a determination, the president is required to appoint a "board of inquiry" to investigate and report back to him on the issues. The board is *not* permitted to make recommendations. The president may then direct the attorney general to seek an injunction in federal district court to prevent or terminate the strike (or lockout). While the injunction is in effect, the status quo on wages and working conditions is preserved. If a strike continues or begins, the strikers would, of course, be subject to jail for contempt of the district court order. Employer and union are obligated to make efforts to resolve the dispute with FMCS aid. If after sixty days the dispute is not resolved, the board of inquiry is reconvened to make an update status report, again with no recommendations. The second report must indicate the employer's last offer for settlement, on which the NLRB must poll the employees within fifteen days and certify the result to the attorney general within five days. After this step the injunction must be dissolved. The employees are then free to resume (or begin) the strike.

This brief recital of the steps in the Title II minuet reveals its rigidity and predictability. Title II has been frequently attacked on these grounds. Yet no alternative procedures have been successfully urged since 1947. What factors, then, account for the durability of the procedure?

For one thing, the critics are of one mind only in attacking Title II. There is no consensus as to a preferred alternative. The favorite substitute would give the President a greater range of discretion and choice of procedures in handling emergency disputes. The model for most of these proposals is the law drafted for Massachusetts by the late Sumner H. Slichter. Although the choice-of-procedures concept has wide support, the critics do not agree on which procedures to include in the President's arsenal of weapons.[7]

Another reason why Title II has remained intact is that it has not been as ineffective as the volume of criticism might suggest. Studying the chronology of the twenty-six disputes in which Title II injunctions have been granted over the years shows only six cases were strikes resumed after the

---

7. Choice-of-procedures allows an elected official to choose a remedy from a list of permitted remedies such as injunctions, fines, mandatory fact finding, strike or arbitration.

eighty-day cooling-off period of the injunction. Five of these were in the stevedoring industry in Atlantic and Gulf Coast ports. However, in no case has a dispute been ended by employees voting to accept the employer's last offer.[8]

A third factor in Title II survival has been its sparing use. All White House occupants since 1947 have frequently avoided use of Title II in favor of a variety of informal procedures for inducing settlement. The most recent case since 1971 involved the 1977–78 bituminous coal strike. In this case, President Carter waited about three months after the strike began to initiate Title II procedures. In retrospect, the President probably should not have acted even when he did. After the board of inquiry issued its report to the President, a temporary injunction was issued ordering the miners back to work. This injunction was met with almost total defiance (as were two other coal mining eighty-day injunctions issued in the period from 1948 to 1950). But to complicate matters further, a few days later (on March 17, 1978), the injunction was vacated when the issuing judge concluded that the government had not shown a national emergency justified its extension. Thus, we cannot count this case as a fully executed Title II initiative. To complete this story, President Carter was spared added embarrassment when the miners voted to accept the operators' final offer on March 24.

The restrictive semantics of Title II insure sparing use. Its procedures cannot be wheeled into action unless the dispute can fairly be characterized as one which constitutes a genuine threat to the national health and safety. In any event, the President probably has a sufficient aresenal at his disposal to pressure both sides of a critical dispute toward compromise. Government influence as customer, regulator, and tax agent all restrict open defiance of critical public interests by either employers or unions.

COMPULSORY AND BINDING ARBITRATION OF FUTURE TERMS DISPUTES

Compulsory and binding interest arbitration as a terminal procedure for resolving future terms disputes has grown rapidly in the public sector. This growth is easy to explain. Interest arbitration is represented as a strike substitute process in hotly contested debate over the advisability of permitting collective bargaining in the public sector. Advocates of public sector collective bargaining have been willing to substitute interest arbitration for the right to strike in order to appease those holding that public sector collective bargaining is *wrong* if it means legalizing the strike. Chapter 15 is devoted in part to tracing the public sector collective

---

8. Donald E. Cullen, *National Emergency Strikes* (Ithaca: New York State School of Industrial and Labor Relations, 1968).

bargaining growth record. At this point, it is sufficient to note that the first state statutes requiring interest arbitration for some public sector disputes took effect in 1968.[9] By 1980, the number of states with interest arbitration laws grew to twenty.[10]

There is a great deal of variation among the states with public sector interest arbitration laws regarding the nature and requirements for using negotiation, mediation, and fact-finding steps prior to accessing arbitration; further, there are interstate differences in the *structure* of the interest arbitration process the parties must use. Mediation is a part of the settlement process in most states, although it is voluntary in many of these. Mediation has been completely eliminated for fire and police bargaining units in Wyoming, Pennsylvania, and Rhode Island. Most of the laws have provisions for fact finding and for binding arbitration awards.

Among the states with binding interest arbitration, *conventional* arbitration is the most widely used structure followed by *final-offer selection*. Under a conventional interest arbitration structure, the arbitrator is free to order any reasonable settlement consistent with decision-making criteria spelled out in the law. For example, many laws require that the arbitrator give due consideration to the public employers' (1) ability to pay, (2) ability to efficiently manage and conduct government operations, and (3) other statutory rights. Under final-offer selection arbitration, the arbitrator must select the final position of one of the parties (except in Iowa, where there is a third option: the fact finder's recommendations). In some states the arbitrator must choose between the parties' last position on each of the disputed issues (for example, issue-by-issue selection); in other states, the arbitrator must choose the entire set of final positions of one or the other party (for example, package selection).

Where compulsory and binding arbitration is law, it is usually the final step to be implemented in resolving future terms disputes. We qualified this statement with the word "usually" because, under a 1980 amendment to Minnesota's public sector law, some bargaining units and employer groups are free to select between either the strike or interest arbitration as the means to be followed in resolving bargaining impasses. Other states also permit the strike in some or all public sector jurisdictions. The point on which we wish to focus is whether interest arbitration is an effective means for resolving future terms disputes. A considerable amount of study has gone into analysis of the interest arbitration structure which *best* facilitates prearbitration, negotiated settlements. Implicit in these studies is the

9. All of the information here on state statutes is taken from Kevin J. Corcoran and Diane Kutell, "Binding Arbitration Laws for State and Municipal Workers," *Monthly Labor Review*, 101 (October 1978), 36–40.

10. Alaska, Connecticut, Hawaii, Iowa, Maine, Massachusetts, Michigan, Minnesota, Montana, Nebraska, Nevada, New Jersey, New York, Oregon, Pennsylvania, Rhode Island, Vermont, Washington, Wisconsin, and Wyoming.

criterion that the least used interest arbitration structure is the preferred structure. The threat of using interest arbitration, like the strike threat, ought to cause compromise and concessions if it is to be a genuine strike substitute. The *expected cost* of not acceding to the other party's threat of arbitration should increase, much as it would under the conventional strike threat system. With this reaction to the implicit or explicit threat to arbitrate, there will be bilateral movements toward an agreement. Thus, the actual use of interest arbitration will be minimal and, if used, the differences separating the parties will be minimal.

We know little about how arbitrators decide. It may be that arbitrators consider the same set of costs, forces, and norms that govern the bargaining relationship. Or it may be that arbitrators decide according to another set of standards.[11] For example, Sir John Hicks contended that arbitrators are prone to decide according to legalistic standards based upon considerations of justice.[12] If arbitrators substitute another set of standards, they may show consistent bias favoring one side.[13] We have already discussed how the laws restrict the arbitrator's jurisdiction with respect to the framing of decisions; left to be discussed is how this kind of structuring affects bargaining behavior.

Negotiated agreements are superior to arbitrated agreements. Negotiations involve an exchange of information more likely to result in *livable* agreements because they are the parties' creations as opposed to agreements imposed by outside arbitrators. Negotiations result in a "portfolio" of terms and conditions of employment which are (at least) minimally acceptable to and consistent with employer and union preferences. Ideally, therefore, any interest arbitration structure imposed on the public sector should encourage and spawn negotiated, rather than arbitrated, collective agreements.[14]

The best way to accomplish this objective is by enacting into law the arbitration structure that presents the parties at impasse with the highest cost associated with arbitration use, thus motivating continued negotiations. Precisely what structure that is, however, is yet to be stated.[15] At first

11. James Dworkin and Mario Bognanno have developed and tested a model of "parity" as the criterion governing interest arbitration decision. See their unpublished paper entitled "An Empirical Assessment of a Theory of Interest Arbitrator Behavior," which is available on request.

12. John Hicks, *The Theory of Wages* (Gloucester, Mass.: Peter Smith,1957), pp. 149–52.

13. Hicks thought arbitrators would favor unions.

14. For an excellent article which looks at this subject from a more general viewpoint see Carl M. Stevens, "Is Compulsory Arbitration Compatible witb Bargaining?", *Industrial Relations*, 5 (1966), 38–52.

15. Mario Bognanno, Frederic Champlin, and Ross Azevedo, "A General Theory of the Impact of Interest Arbitration on Bargaining Behavior," Working Paper 79-03, Industrial Relations Center, University of Minnesota, is a piece which begins to tackle this issue from a theoretical standpoint. Also read Vincent P. Crawford, "On Compulsory Arbitration Schemes," *Journal of Political Economy*, 87, No. 1 (1979), 131–59.

glance, we might think that conventional arbitration would be the most costly structure to use because the arbitrator can hand down any reasonable set of future terms. The uncertainty costs alone would be extremely high. However, if arbitrators deciding cases under this structure are inclined to split the difference separating the parties' last positions, then continued bargaining and concessionary behavior would be imprudent. This behavior has been hypothesized and tested. The so-called *chilling effect* associated with conventional arbitration has found some empirical support.[16]

Final-offer selection, of either the issue-by-issue or package variety, would appear to cut into the interest arbitrator's ability to split differences, thus reducing the chilling effect. While this may be so, we must still identify which of these structures is preferable. Since arbitrators are not prevented from trading issues (for example, awarding the union's final position on one issue and the employer's final position on another issue and so on) under the issue-by-issue selection structure, it seems intuitively possible that the costs of noncompromising behavior would be relatively higher under the final-offer selection by package structure. Numerous studies tend to support this conclusion. Thus, the structure most likely to motivate negotiating behavior is final-offer selection by package, followed by final-offer selection by issue, and then by conventional arbitration.[17] This whole area of research is still taking shape; empirical works abound but theory lags. For example, if arbitrators operating under a conventional arbitration structure were somehow prevented from systematically split-

16. Read, for example, Peter Feuille, "Final Offer Arbitration and the Chilling Effect," *Industrial Relations*, 14 (October 1975), 302–10; and Hoyt Wheeler, "How Compulsory Arbitration Affects Compromise Activity," *Industrial Relations*, 17 (February 1978), 80–84.

17. This conclusion was drawn from a comparative analysis of results presented in a large number of studies. In addition to the articles cited in footnotes 16 and 18, the reader should refer to the following: Ernst Benjamin, "Final-Offer Arbitration Awards in Michigan, 1973–1977," unpublished paper, Institute of Labor and Industrial Relations, University of Michigan and Wayne State University, 1979; James B. Dworkin, "The Impact of Final-Offer Interest Arbitration on Bargaining: The Case of Major League Baseball," in James L. Stern and Barbara D. Dennis, eds., *Proceedings of the Twenty-Ninth Annual Winter Meeting*, Industrial Relations Research Association, 1977, pp. 161–69; Peter Feuille, "Final Offer Arbitration and Negotiation Incentives," *Arbitration Journal*, 32, No. 3 (September 1977), 203–20; Daniel Gallagher, "Interest Arbitration Under the Iowa Public Employment Relations Act," *Arbitration Journal*, 33, No. 3 (September 1978), 30–36; Joseph R. Grodin, "Arbitration of Public Sector Labor Disputes: The Nevada Experiment," *Industrial and Labor Relations Review*, 28, No. 1 (October 1974), 89–102; David B. Lipsky and T. A. Barocci, "Final Offer Selection and Public Safety Employees: The Massachusetts Experience," in Barbara D. Dennis, ed., *Proceedings of the Thirtieth Annual Winter Meetings*, Industrial Relations Research Association, 1977, pp. 65–76; J. Joseph Lowenberg, "Compulsory Arbitration for Police and Firefighters in Pennsylvania in 1968," *Industrial and Labor Relations Review*, 23, No. 2 (April 1970), 367–79; Paul C. Somers, "An Evaluation of Final Offer Arbitration in Massachusetts," *Journal of Collective Bargaining*, 6, No. 3 (1977), 193–228; and James L. Stern, Charles Rehmus, J. Joseph Lowenberg, Hirschel Kasper, and Barbara D. Dennis, *Final-Offer Arbitration* (Lexington, Mass.: Heath, 1975).

ting differences, then the chilling effect associated with this structure might vanish.

Critics of interest arbitration have charged that it is fundamentally damaging to the negotiating process because its use can lead to a dependency (for example, a *narcotic effect*). The hypothesis is that, once used, the parties will find continued interest arbitration use preferable (in some sense) to hard bargaining in reaching settlements. Evidence on this hypothesis is mixed.[18]

The record of interest arbitration successes is open to question. Grave concerns about interest arbitrator qualifications are often raised. Likewise, the matter of using arbitration panels *versus* solo arbitrators all have a bearing on the use and abuse of interest arbitration and its record of success among various jurisdictions. We have had both positive and negative experience with interest arbitration in the public sector; we are not prepared to offer any particular structure as *the* best strike substitute, nor can we say that it is a socially more desirable alternative than the right to strike for most public service groups. The jury is yet to render its verdict.

PUBLIC SECTOR STRIKES:
A SPECIAL CASE?

Much of the literature on public sector bargaining appears morbidly preoccupied with how to resolve impasses and prevent strikes. The prevailing sentiment remains negative on granting government employees at any level the right to use economic force as an ultimate means of resolving future terms disputes. Federal employees have been denied this right since 1947 (Taft–Hartley Act). The bumper crop of state laws in recent years on public employee bargaining exhibits an astonishing variety of policies and procedures in most respects. Only eight states currently permit any public sector strikes. All eight states provide some limits to public sector strikes, such as requiring injunction or compulsory arbitration, if the "health and welfare" of the community is endangered.[19]

Yet all but the most naive realize that strikes cannot be eliminated simply by making them illegal. In fact, prohibiting strikes has little apparent effect

18. Read, for example, John Anderson and Thomas Kochan, "Impasse Procedures in the Canadian Federal Service: Effects on the Bargaining Process," *Industrial and Labor Relations Review*, 30 (April 1977), 283–301; Thomas A. Kochan and Jean Baderschneider, "Dependence on Impasse Procedures: Police and Fire Fighters in New York State," *Industrial and Labor Relations Review*, 31, No. 4 (July 1978), 431–49; and Craig Olson, "Final Offer Arbitration in Wisconsin After Five Years," *Proceedings of the Thirty-First Annual Meeting*, Industrial Relations Research Association, 1978, pp. 111–19.

19. See B. V. H. Schneider, "Public-Sector Labor Legislation—An Evolutionary Analysis," in Benjamin Aaron, Joseph R. Grodin, and James L. Stern, eds., *Public-Sector Bargaining* (Madison, Wis.: Industrial Relations Research Association, 1979), p. 203.

on public sector strikes.[20] Nor can we be sure that even the most carefully structured set of alternative mechanisms for dispute resolution will succeed in all cases in avoiding strikes by government employees.

The only true way of resolving a dispute between an employer and a union of employees requires a compromise of the underlying sources of discontent. Ignoring the discontent or prohibiting manifestations of the discontent, such as a strike, is more likely to prolong the disruption than solve the problem. The threat of a strike channels effort toward compromise and resolution. If the cost of a strike to innocent persons is too high—and a fire fighter strike, for example, is too costly—then a strike-like substitute must be found. But if the cost to innocent persons is not too high—and temporary disruption of many public operations causes little more than inconvenience—then a strike threat is the most effective means of promoting, through the process of collective bargaining, resolution of the dispute.

SUMMARY

Damage to the public from strikes over future terms can be controlled (but not eliminated) by prohibiting strikes (and substituting interest arbitration) or by making collective bargaining work better in both the private and public sectors. Collective bargaining relationships built on good faith and public policies designed to strengthen collective bargaining procedures, over the long run, have done more to achieve industrial peace than has attention to prohibition and penalties.

In the next three chapters we consider the subjects contained in labor agreements and the difficulties surrounding their negotiation. Chapter 10 focuses on negotiated wage issues.

Questions for Discussion, Thought, and Research

1. From the perspective of society, is there an argument to be made in favor of strikes? Is a strike ever in the public's best interests?

2. Without the right to strike, and the willingness to exercise this right, real collective bargaining cannot exist. Evaluate.

3. Under what circumstances is an NLRA strike legal?

---

20. John Burton and Charles E. Krider, "The Incidence of Strikes in the Public Sector," in Daniel Hamermesh, ed., *Labor in the Public and Nonprofit Sectors* (Princeton, N.J.: Princeton University Press, 1975).

4. Why is there general acceptance of arbitration for interpreting the present contract, but strong opposition for the use of arbitration in resolving issues in a new contract?

5. What is the significance of the Experimental Negotiating Agreement of 1973? Why hasn't this method of resolving interest disputes gained widespread support in other industries?

6. Has the mediation process been effective in the United States for resolving disputes? What evidence would support your conclusion?

7. Critics of Taft–Hartley contend that the emergency disputes provision is in need of reform. What type of reform would you propose? Why?

8. What are the essential characteristics of an effective procedure for interest arbitration? In other words, how does one determine whether one type of arbitration procedure is more effective than another?

9. There are many types of interest arbitration: (a) final-offer selection (issue-by-issue), (b) final-offer selection (by package), (c) conventional arbitration, (d) mediation–arbitration, and (e) types of arbitration we have yet to discover. Does the type of procedure make a significant difference in the outcome of the award?

10. How does the narcotic effect in interest arbitration differ from the chilling effect?

Selected Bibliography

Baer, Walter E., *Strikes*. New York: AMACON, 1975.

Cole, David, *The Quest for Industrial Peace*. New York: McGraw-Hill, 1963.

Cullen, Donald E., *National Emergency Strikes*. Ithaca: New York State School of Industrial and Labor Relations, 1968.

Northrup, Herbert R., *Compulsory Arbitration and Government Intervention in Labor Disputes*. Washington, D.C.: Labor Policy Association, 1966.

Simkin, William E., *Mediation and the Dynamics of Collective Bargaining*. Washington, D.C.: Bureau of National Affairs, 1971.

Stern, James L., Charles M. Rehmus, J. Joseph Lowenberg, Herschel Kasper, and Barbara D. Dennis, *Final Offer Arbitration*. Lexington, Mass.: Heath, 1975.

NEGOTIATED
WAGE ISSUES

10

Contemporary bargaining is generally concerned with economic "packages." The wage package includes a mix of direct and indirect types of pay, and a mix of hourly (or weekly or monthly) pay plus possible incentive pay. All workers may be paid at the same rate, or they may receive different rates depending upon such factors as skill, effort, or working conditions. In this chapter and the next, we consider aspects of the pay package.

In the discussion we shall sometimes simplify matters for purposes of convenience by discussing wage or salary adjustments as if they were the only economic issue at the bargaining table. As we observe in Chapter 11, nonwage compensation in most negotiations accounts for over one-third of the labor cost dollar.

Collective wage determination is a microeconomic process. This holds true whether we are considering a truly small employer negotiating with a local union or analyzing the triennial negotiations between such giants as General Motors and the UAW. In times of social concern about inflation, there is often strong sentiment for direct government control or guidelines over wages and prices. However, analysis of the relationship between macroeconomic goals and microeconomic decision making is deferred until a later chapter.

The central focus in this chapter is on wage determination by company X and union Y. In each contract negotiation the parties must confront jointly on five basic categories of wage problems. First (and usually foremost), an agreement must be reached as to whether a general (that is, across-the-board) wage increase (decrease) would be effected and, if so, how much it should be? Second, any differential wage rate among bargaining unit members must be settled. For example, what is the appropriate wage differential between the rates of top skilled craftsmen and those of semiskilled production workers?

The third category of decision making concerns methods of wage administration. Disputes over administration of incentive systems are important in this category. Another issue which can be troublesome is setting wage rates on a job which has changed during the life of the contract.

The fourth type of issue concerns the method of wage payment. This category includes problems over the level of fringe benefits such as health and welfare and pension plans. Fringe benefits are covered in the next chapter.

The fifth issue defines the distribution of wage changes over the life of the contract. This issue includes decisions of wage deferral until the second or third year of the contract or decisions about whether or not to include a cost-of-living clause in the contract. "Front-loaded" or "back-loaded" contracts were discussed in Chapter 5. Cost-of-living and wage indexing are discussed in Chapter 14.

In the remainder of this chapter the first three types of issues are covered. First, the formation and evaluation of wage policy for general pay increases is discussed. This discussion does not include labor markets and bargaining; this topic is covered in Chapter 13. Second, methods, rationales, and administrative problems for establishing different pay rates among members of the bargaining unit are discussed. Finally, incentive pay plans in the context of collective bargaining are discussed.

HOW AND BY WHOM ARE UNION WAGE POLICIES FORMULATED?

The functions of formulating economic policy and also negotiating on wages and other key issues are generally performed by top union leadership. Collective bargaining has become much too technical, complex, and specialized to be planned and conducted on a town meeting basis.

The preliminary reciprocal communication between union membership and leadership goes on months ahead of negotiation time. Firm decisions on what to press for at the bargaining table are then made by the national union leadership. There are notable exceptions, such as the building trades unions, which still leave bargaining pretty much in the hands of the locals in particular labor markets. Generally speaking, however, national union leaders call the shots for their affiliated locals. Such centralized control over wage policy formation will continue to be the way of life for most major industrial unions and many craft unions as well. In fact, as we noted in Chapter 4, structural trends do not show any likely diminution of national authority on major policy matters. Coalition or coordinated bargaining arrangements among unions with related interests are likely to continue. The AFL–CIO has computerized relevant bargaining data to be made available for the use of all affiliates in bargaining. We understand the Steelworkers Union furnishes computerized data to its representatives. In addition, the American Federation of State, County and Municipal Employees (AFSCME) and the National Education Association (NEA) have computer-based data services.

The dynamics of union wage policy are substantially different from those of management in bargaining. As political institutions, there is generally a degree of responsiveness and interaction between union leadership and the rank and file that one does not find in most management organizations. Such communication can be noted even in the most autocratically administered unions.

Unions cannot operate on a chain-of-command basis as do many business firms. There is more two-way communication in the union hierarchy, notwithstanding the usual high degree of centralization. The final formation of union wage policy, however, is the function of top leadership, in most instances.

The main factors responsible for this centralization in policy formation should be briefly restated. First, wage bargaining is a technical, complicated process. It demands a degree of expertise and a fund of information not ordinarily found among most local union leaders, let alone the rank and file. This factor alone is a powerful argument for increased centralization.

Second, union policy goals such as the standard rate and industry-wide stability in wage relationships cannot be reached through uncoordinated local union bargaining. Centralized control is essential. The consequences for big unionism in this respect are similar to those for big business. Large-scale organization precludes the luxury of pure democracy in the sense of complete rank-and-file participation.

Most union members, nevertheless, have a more effective voice on wage policy than the foregoing remarks suggest. Union constitutions, for example, generally require that agreements with employers be negotiated subject to approval by the membership.

During the 1970s ratification votes have failed on average at an annual rate of about 10 percent. The rejection phenomenon is a matter of serious concern to employers, union leaders, and federal and state mediators. A former director of the federal Mediation and Conciliation Service, William E. Simkin, notes that some aspects of the wage problem ranked foremost among causes of rejection. Simkin's study shows only 16 percent of the rejections not involving wages as a factor.[1]

Better communication is needed between union membership and union leadership if we are to achieve improved stability in labor relations. Procedures must be developed to assure that the negotiators on both sides of the bargaining table are known to have the authority to bind their constituents to an agreement. The technical character of contemporary bargaining requires the negotiation be conducted by top union leadership as well as by top management in most cases. Internal conflicting pressures within a union must be reconciled effectively before going to the bargaining table. Union leadership needs a free hand when facing management across the table. The needs of a national union negotiator are similar to those of a labor relations employer association representing large numbers of diverse small employers in a multiemployer bargaining arrangement. In each case the internal pressures must be accommodated ahead of negotiation through development of an integrated bargaining posture.

THE DYNAMICS AND DETERMINANTS OF EMPLOYER WAGE POLICY

When analyzing the decisive factors in the employer's approach to economic issues in bargaining, it is hard to generalize. As with unions, the questions must always be asked, "Which company?" and "Under what type of conditions?" Employers are pragmatic. There is thus no one standardized approach to wage determination.

The employer's task is less complex than the union leader's. The employer can concentrate on cost as the dominant consideration. A prudent employer needs the same type of data and knowhow for economic decision making, whether he is dealing with a union or operating unilaterally. In a negotiating situation, the employer's approach may appear to differ from that of a nonunion firm. This appearance is more illusory than real because it is the negotiated economic settlements that call the tune for many nonunion employers.

1. William E. Simkin, "Refusals to Ratify Contracts," *Industrial and Labor Relations Review,* 21 (July 1968), 518–40.

Most of what the employer needs to know is of an economic nature, although some factors are political for the employer as well as for the union. An employer, for example, wishes to remain in good standing with his business peers. He thus desires to stay in line with what other firms are doing, even when he is in a position to do far better (or far worse) in terms of economic demands. This consideration is the employer's version of the union comparison factor.

The employer at the bargaining table might consider the following:

1. The firm's current competitive position in the industry and in relation to possible substitute products.
2. The cost picture related to current and anticipated factor mix, that is, percentage of labor cost to total cost for whatever product(s) or service(s) may be involved.
3. Accurate comparison of his wage rates and fringe costs with those of his chief competitors in the industry and those of comparable firms in his labor market area.
4. An estimate of economic bargaining capability, involving an ability to take a strike of varying levels of duration and intensity, including an accurate estimation of firm and customer inventories and the goodwill of the principal customers and suppliers.
5. An informed appraisal of the probable cost impact of the union's economic demands, if granted, and the necessary revisions, if any, in price policy. Further price revisions in turn entail knowledge of current and prospective market conditions and the nature of demand for the firm's product(s); for example, how might consumers be expected to react to a price increase of x percent?
6. Analysis of the macroeconomic outlook as related to the probable outcome of negotiations.
7. Estimate of the tightness or looseness of the local labor supply, relating this to recruitment and retention of labor under varying conditions.

Life for the employer on economic issues is never simple any more than it is for union counterparts. A decision on a general increase is only part of the battle. The employer will need to review the internal occupational rate structure. The employer's idea of an appropriate skill differential may be at variance with what the union is pressing for in negotiations. Most employers are partial to intraplant rate adjustments suggested by their compensation administrators. These may differ from union demands for correction of alleged intraplant inequities. Also, in negotiation of such structural wage problems, the employer will usually pay more attention to local labor supply and demand factors than the union.

PATTERN-FOLLOWING ON WAGE POLICY

No part of the collective bargaining scene escapes the eyes of other employers and unions. Any change of fashion on wage policy (or on anything else, for that matter) inaugurated in a key employer–union relationship is likely to be reflected in other negotiations if the parties wish, for their own purposes, to follow suit. Employers do not like to be too far apart from their fellow employers on wage policy; they wish to remain competitive. The union leaders' constituents keep careful tabs on whether they are doing as well for them on wages and other key economic issues as other unions appear to be doing for their membership.

Occasionally, this practice of watching other bargains evolves into chronological patterns of bargaining. Typically, one negotiation sets the standard for a number of subsequent negotiations to follow. [2]

Pattern bargaining involves, as the name suggests, a practice of following the lead on wages and/or some significant nonwage bargaining development established by a union and a major employer in a particular industry, by other firms in that same industry, or even in other and seemingly unrelated industries. In meatpacking, for example, it has been customary for the pattern to be established by initial negotiations with Armour, Swift, or Wilson. The other national packers and many of the independent packers then follow suit in subsequent negotiations with the two principal unions (one since the 1968 merger) in the packinghouse field. This is what happened in negotiations culminating in the 1967–70 and 1970–73 contracts. The basic patterns on both wage increases and job security provisions set in the Armour negotiations were followed closely in negotiations with the other major packers and many of the principal independents.

Perhaps the most prominent examples of pattern bargaining are found in the auto and steel industries. In auto industry bargaining an auto company is selected as a target for negotiation by the UAW. The contract signed by the UAW and the target company serves as the standard for negotiation with the remaining auto companies, for suppliers and subcontractors to the auto companies, and often for other UAW negotiations such

2. Classical references regarding political and social forces to generate patterns include, for example, John Dunlop, "The Task of Contemporary Wage Theory," in George Taylor and Frank Pierson, eds., *New Concepts in Wage Determination* (New York: McGraw-Hill, 1957), pp. 117–39; Arthur Ross, *Trade Union Wage Policy* (Berkeley: University of California Press, 1948). Empirical works on this subject are plentiful. Relatively recent articles include D. Quinn Mills, "Explaining Pay Increases in Construction: 1953–1972," *Industrial Relations*, 12 (May 1974), 196–201; David Shulenburger, "Prior Identification of 'Key' Wage Determining Units," *Industrial Relations*, 16 (February 1977), 83–93; David Shulenburger, "A Contour Theoretic Approach to the Determination of Wages in the Building Construction Industry," *Economic Inquiry*, 16 (July 1978), 396–410; and John Lawler, "Wage Spillover: The Impact of Landrum-Griffin," *Industrial Relations* (forthcoming).

as with farm equipment manufacturers. In the steel industry the contract negotiated in industry-wide bargaining by the large steel companies and the USW is followed by the USW in negotiations with the many smaller steel fabricators.[3] Other multi-industrial unions, such as the International Brotherhood of Teamsters, Warehousemen and Helpers (IBT), or the International Union of Electrical Radio and Machine Workers of America (IUE), frequently seek to achieve a fairly homogeneous complex of bargaining demands in a variety of industrial settings. This strategy has important implications for the problem of centralized policy determination versus local union and local management autonomy.

Pattern-followers do not necessarily negotiate the precise terms in their contracts as the pattern-setter negotiates in his contract. Allowance may be made for differences among firms and union membership at the local negotiations. A small company, for example, may pay a lower wage rate than the pattern setter; however, the follower will typically increase wage rates by the same percentage as the pattern setter.

STANDARD FOR EVALUATING JOINT DECISION MAKING ON GENERAL WAGE OR SALARY INCREASES (DECREASES)

Let us assume that company X is hit with a demand by union Y for a straight across-the-board wage increase amounting to 10 percent and the company's top counterproposal reaches 5 percent. A two-month strike ensues, ending with a wage agreement for a 6½ percent general increase for each of the next three years. On what basis can the rightness or wrongness of such a settlement be evaluated?

The fact of the matter is that all evaluations of wage settlements are necessarily subjective. They are conditioned by the views and positions of those who make them. What is held to be a "responsible" bargain by a labor economist may be characterized as a "sellout" by the union membership because it does not match the increases won elsewhere in the industry (or area) or because it lacks an escalator clause in a period of rising prices for consumer goods.

Management and union practitioners must work out, in the final analysis, an agreement on economic issues that permits the parties to live together for the period of the contract (usually three years) in a compara-

---

3. Though dated, an excellent early article on the "fact," "causal forces," and "consequences" of pattern bargaining by the United Steelworkers of America was written in 1951 by George Seltzer. It is entitled "Pattern Bargaining and the United Steelworkers," *Journal of Political Economy*, 59, No. 4 (August 1951), 319–31. Contrasted with contemporary conditions in the steel industry, Seltzer's 1951 conclusion that the USW is not a form of "labor monopoly" would make an exciting debate topic.

tively harmonious pattern of accommodation. These agreements must meet the crucial pragmatic test of mutual acceptability to the parties.

Many of the criteria for evaluating general wage adjustments, such as cost-of-living changes, productivity changes, industry rates, and area rates, are in fact always coins with two sides. Their pertinence is stressed or minimized by the participants to rationalize their respective bargaining postures before, during, and after negotiations. The level of objectivity in economic negotiation has risen somewhat as more reliable data became available. It seems unlikely, however, that widely accepted standards guiding the distribution of wealth will ever be achieved in collective wage determinations.

DIFFERENTIAL WAGE PROBLEMS

Perhaps the most troublesome problem for negotiators is the proper differential in pay among bargaining unit members. In a craft union, where every member has about the same skill, wage differentials are typically not a problem; instead, a wage rate is set for journey work and another rate is set for apprentice work. In some craft and almost all industrial unions, not all members receive the same wage. Labor market forces, tradition, and internal political pressures establish different wage rates for different jobs. In some cases everyone who does the same job is paid at the same wage rate. In others, a range of pay for people working at the same job is established. Differential wage rates result from across-job differences in pay and from differences in pay among people performing the same job.

In negotiation of job rate hierarchies, significant conflicts of interest develop that must somehow be accommodated. The net result may square with one party's view of equal pay for equal work while doing violence to the other party's conception of how the goal should be achieved. How does one develop wage standards for machine-paced jobs and worker-paced jobs? Should a toolmaker (highest skill level) receive twice as much or three times as much as a yard laborer (lowest skill level)?

Within any particular occupational rate hierarchy, serious disputes between employer and union arise as to where certain jobs should be slotted on the labor grade ladder. The adjustment of alleged occupational rate inequities is an endless task in any relationship. Especially when the employer's technology is a dynamic one, there is a continuing need to revise the content of existing jobs, to create new job classifications, and, in some cases, to abolish certain classifications.

Nearly all union leaders face difficult problems at times in reconciling and accommodating the conflicting internal pressures of a heterogeneous union membership. For example, an industrial union certified as exclusive bargaining representative for an appropriate unit consisting of all production and maintenance employees periodically encounters difficulties in balancing the divergent interests and claims of highly skilled craftsmen (for example, toolmakers) with those of semiskilled production workers (for example, assemblers or machine operators). Friction, even hostility, between such groups within the same bargaining unit is often severe.

During the life of agreements, particularly those that run three years or longer, technological imperatives will produce substantial changes in the content of many existing jobs, requiring that such jobs be reclassified upward or downward. Also, new jobs will make their appearance during a contract's lifetime. Disputes are bound to arise as to whether changed or new jobs are properly placed within the hierarchy of occupational rates.

In sum, a variety of relative wage differences must be resolved in negotiations, including differences within the union, differences between the employer and the union, and differences about how to adjust wage rates for job changes during the life of the agreement. Without a union, employers make relative wage decisions. The usual employer technique involves a program of job evaluation. Many job evaluation plans have resulted from collective bargaining as well. (One of the pioneer plans in this area was designed jointly by the Steelworkers Union and steel industry management.) Although job evaluation cannot solve all the wage differential problems, it can provide a means for systematically adjusting to changing jobs once the basic job evaluation plan is established.

UNION AND MANAGEMENT GOALS FOR JOB EVALUATION

Typical management compensation goals include attraction, retention, and motivation of a work force. Besides setting wages at a level to get and keep workers, management is interested in providing incentives to workers for gaining new skills, for putting forth effort on the job, and for accepting difficult, distasteful, or dangerous jobs. If the differential between two types of jobs is not large enough, management may have an abundant supply of people willing to do one job and no one willing to do another. In a service or professional union, promotion through a succession of jobs may be a normal career path. Promotions may be part of the reward structure, so that employees who do well (work hard) are rewarded with higher pay and a promotion. If the differentials are too small between jobs, much of the reward value can be lost.

Unions are political organizations. Union views on wage differentials depend to a large extent on the political forces within the union. An ideal union approach would include reaching agreement on differentials within the union, then presenting a united front to management. The process leading to internal unity is usually called intraorganizational bargaining; this process is an important part of collective bargaining.

In general, groups important to the success of union strikes or other collective efforts will fare better in obtaining their version of the proper wage differential. These include groups with large pluralities of the membership. These large "interest groups" have another advantage: their votes are important to union officials in any reelection campaign. Smaller constituent groups with important skills for successful operation by the employer are also often influential within the union. Small groups, relatively low-skill groups, or groups whose type of work is out of the mainstream of what other workers do, are less likely to fare well in obtaining their version of the proper wage differential.

Tradition is important to union wage differential policies, since what wage differentials have been affects the way members perceive what the differentials should be. Often, the union accepts wage differentials as management set them prior to the organization of the union, then attempts to get everyone more. Problems occur, if this tactic is followed, when new jobs are created, when existing jobs change, or when new positions are created and must be classified into a job pay category. Job evaluation can be helpful here as a means of formalizing existing or agreed-upon wage differential schedules while providing a procedure for integrating new or changed jobs into this schedule.

JOB EVALUATION PROCEDURES

There are many plans for evaluating the relative pay of jobs. They range from simple ranking methods to more sophisticated schemes for weighing attributes of a job. In this section we summarize the basic steps required for a point method of job evaluation. (Those interested in this area may want to examine some of the compensation management texts for more detailed descriptions of job evaluation procedures.)[4]

Step 1. Analyze Jobs. The procedures of job analysis generate the basic data for all job evaluation plans. Job analysis must provide a reasonably complete and accurate description of the performance of the job, the working conditions in which the job is performed, and the qualifications required to handle the job. No successful job evaluation can be built on a foundation of sloppy, inaccurate job descriptions.

The procedure for collecting this data must be clear so that others may, by following the same procedure, arrive at similar results; if each person

4. David W. Belcher, *Compensation Administration* (Englewood Cliffs, N.J.: Prentice-Hall, 1974); and Richard I. Henderson, *Compensation Management* (Reston, Va.: Reston, 1979).

analyzes jobs differently, there will be no common basis for evaluation. Methods used in job analysis include observation of the work by the job analyst, interviews by the job analyst with persons doing a job, or their supervisors, or their fellow workers, descriptions by employees of their jobs, or questionnaires completed by workers or supervisors about the jobs.

Step 2. Select Compensable Factors. The object of job evaluation is to break the job down into many component parts, called attributes or factors. The idea is that more or less of each of these attributes can be found on most jobs, and that different attributes and different levels of attributes are paid at different pay rates. Thus, the process assigns so many cents per hour or per month to the many components of a job. In the intermediate stage of the process, however, we shall not refer to cents but to points for each of these degrees of a factor.

Compensable factors are those attributes of a job that make it more or less valuable relative to another. These are things about the job that make it more or less taxing or onerous, or that require more or less skill. Responsibility for others or for equipment, working conditions, job hazards, repetitive work are all examples of possible compensable factors. Experience, training, education, or certification of competency are other examples.

Step 3. Select Degrees. Compensable factors vary in their importance from job to job. Measurable differences in levels of a compensable factor are called degrees. This is easily illustrated using education as a compensable factor with, say, five degrees. The first degree might be less than a high school education *required to do the job*. (Note: a Ph.D. doing this job would receive no more points, since education is not required to perform the job.) The second degree might be high school graduation; the third degree, two years of post–high school education; the fourth degree, a college diploma; and the fifth degree, postgraduate college credits. Thus, each compensable factor comes in more than one degree. As a result of job analysis, each job can be assigned the appropriate degree of all relevant compensable factors.

It is important at this stage to develop accurate descriptions of each of the degrees. The descriptions of the degrees should fit the data developed from the job analysis. And they should be clear enough so that other people can analyze each job and assign that job the same degree of each compensable factor.

Step 4. Assign Points to Degrees. This is the crucial state where each degree of each factor is assigned a certain number of points. Using the five degrees of education from the earlier example, we might assign points in this fashion: less than high school (50 points), high school (100), some college (120), college diploma (150), and postcollege credits (170). The number of points assigned to each compensable factor is then summed across all factors in order to arrive at a composite score for the job.

Consider three jobs—assembly worker, shipping clerk, and tool and die worker—evaluated under a plan with four factors—education, experience and training, effort and working conditions, and responsibility. Finding the right degree of each factor for an assembly worker might result in this profile: education (60), experience and training (60), effort and working conditions (120), and responsibility (40), for a total point score for the job of 280. The shipping clerk might have this profile: education (100), experience and training (90), effort and working conditions (60), and responsibility (80), for a total score of 330. And the tool and die worker might have this profile: education (60), experience and training (120), effort and working conditions (90), and responsibility (100), for a total score of 370. Based on this evaluation, we would pay tool and die workers with 370 points the most, shipping clerks with 330 points less, and assembly workers with 280 points still less. How much more we pay tool and die compared to assembly work depends upon how we assign pay to points.

Who makes the decision on how many points each degree receives? Generally, this is done by a committee. Composition of the committee is discussed in the next section. What does the committee base its judgment on? Many considerations, such as the experience of evaluations at other workplaces, subjective views of managers and union members, perhaps political factors, differentials in the labor market, and, often, what fits with existing wage differentials. It is likely that this stage of the job evaluation process will reveal differences in perception about appropriate differentials; the end result will depend to some extent on the negotiations occurring within the committee.

Step 5. Assign Dollars to the Points. This decision is the final step in converting the raw job analysis data into pay levels. The simplest conversion would offer so many cents or fractions of a cent per point. Often, however, the conversion formula depends upon what criteria are chosen. Purely internal criteria depend on the negotiations within the job evaluation committee about the appropriate relation between points and wage rates. Often, purely internal criteria are used in union–management job evaluation plans. Sometimes external or labor market criteria are used either exclusively or in conjunction with internal criteria.

External pricing of job evaluation points requires additional data on the going wage for different types of jobs at places of employment. Choice of comparison places of employment may be based on employers in the same industry or similar industries or employers in the same community. It is unlikely that exactly the same type of jobs found in one bargaining unit can be found at other places. There are, however, some matches of very similar jobs between those jobs within the bargaining unit and those outside; these are called key jobs. External conversion formulas involve fitting points to the pay rates of key jobs. The fit may be accomplished by "eyeballing" the relationship, or by more elaborate statistical techniques.

Note that external pricing plays a more limited role in collective bargaining than in job evaluation without union involvement. With collective bargaining, establishment of relative wage differentials is the sole purpose of job evaluation.

Step 6. Pay Grades. For the purpose of administrative convenience, points are often reduced into several—usually less than twenty—pay grades. For example, all jobs between 320 and 339 points would be part of one pay grade, and therefore would be paid at the same wage rate.

JOB EVALUATION: DESIGN AND IMPLEMENTATION

Experience indicates that the success or failure of job evaluation depends not so much on the type of plan used as upon the manner of its introduction and administration. Many plans that seemed excellent from a technical standpoint have failed in execution because of improper or insufficient attention to the human aspects of the program. The latter must include union and employee understanding and acceptance.

Whatever the plan, it should be introduced with great care. A clear understanding is needed with the union involved on the relationship between the job evaluation plan and the wage setting. Of particular importance are the procedures for implementing a job evaluation plan in daily administration. Especially, there must be a clear understanding of the procedure for evaluating and rating new and changed jobs under the plan.

Certain intraplant rate differentials may not agree with the logic of the job evaluation plan's occupational hierarchy. If such differentials have been in existence for many years, it may not be wise to attempt to force them to conform to the plan's logic overnight. In fact, often the reverse happens; the plan's logic is forced to the existing differentials.

In order to gain wide acceptance and understanding of the job evaluation plan, the committee in charge of designing the plan should include a broad distribution of union and management members. These members should be representative of the many factions in the work setting. Members of the committee should be people who know the jobs, that is, who know how the jobs are done, and what it takes to do them. Finally, there should be lots of input from everyone with an interest in the plan.

The ultimate objective of job evaluation is to end, or at least to minimize, difficult intraunion and union–management disputes over relative pay differentials. This objective will not be accomplished if those designing the plan appear to be "putting something over" on the membership. Of course, job evaluation cannot end all wage differential disputes, since the other part of wage differentials, whether or not to pay people who do the same job at different wages, is not resolved by job evaluation. We discuss the issue of rate ranges next.

SINGLE RATES OR RATE RANGES?

The single rate concept has the appeal of simplicity in administration. It also ties in with worker and union notions of egalitarianism. Certain jobs, however, are such that individual differences in employee productivity exist. If this is the case, then management may wish to set up ranges on the grounds that differences in worker effectiveness should be rewarded. Other jobs, on the other hand, are structured in such a way that differences in worker performance do not exist, and therefore single rates are more appropriate. Even if performance differences do not exist, employees may expect seniority premiums; this too is a possible cause for rate ranges.

Management generally seeks sufficient flexibility in wage administration to permit recognition of individual differences in merit, effort, and experience. It cannot do this under a single or standard rate approach. When the rate range between minimum and maximum is a suitable one (that is, neither too narrow nor too wide) the possibility exists of starting new employees at the minimum, then advancing them to the midpoint by specified increments after specified intervals of service. Midpoint to maximum of the range can then be reserved for recognition of superior merit and effort. In some cases, however, unions have been successful in negotiating automatic progression to the maximum of the range by regular step-ups every three or six months. This may be satisfactory if performance correlates highly with the length of job tenure. If not, management may prefer performance based progression. Just what defines "performance," however, may be disputed by union and management representatives. Careful wording of this clause may save many future grievances.

SALARY ADMINISTRATION
FOR PROFESSIONAL EMPLOYEES

Should the employer's wage and salary administration program treat unionized professional employees as a breed apart? How to answer this question becomes increasingly important with intensified collective bargaining activity by teachers, nurses, and public sector employees.

Professional employees are nearly always paid on a salaried basis. We know of no evidence that they prefer another method. The prestige status of being on salary remains such that it would not make sense to remove professional employees from the category at a time when pressure is strong from blue-collar and nonsupervisory clerical employees to go on a salaried basis. In fact, the conversion of the latter to salaried status may provide the logical basis for greater homogeneity in the employer's administrative system.

Most unionized professional employees appreciate the need for a salary system that recognizes individual differences in value to the firm. There is not likely to be any objection to differential performance recognition as long as the salary classification plan clearly provides for established minima and subsequent advancement. A familiar illustration of this can be taken from union policies in the performing arts. The stress in negotiations is on improving "scale" for the various categories such as pit musician, supporting actor, extra work, and the like.

This brief discussion of individual recognition in the case of professional employees should serve as a reminder that the future will in all probability witness a similar stress on individualism on the part of all unionized workers, once the latter's drive for basic security has succeeded to the point where their economic aims can become more varied and complex. Bok and Dunlop have pointed out that the trend toward individualized choice is visible in the form of such varied negotiated accomplishments as expanded employee choice in selection of vacation periods, employer-financed training and education programs, choice of shifts, bidding opportunities, and grouping of certain fringe benefits into individualized lump-sum accounts. The last-named arrangement would permit employees and their families to adjust their contributions to their age and life style.[5]

SETTING WAGE RATES ON NEW OR CHANGED JOBS DURING THE LIFE OF A CONTRACT

No discussion of administrative decision making on wage and salary matters can end without some consideration of the perennially difficult task of setting wage rates on new or changed jobs during the life of a contract. The pace of technology and changing job design in recent years has been such as to make this phase of union–management relations more rather than less demanding. The future configuration of work patterns is certain to differ drastically from what we take for granted today. Assuming the continued prevalence of three-year agreements, we have reason to anticipate that employers and unions will need to devote considerable amounts of time and energy to this phase of contract administration.

5. Derek C. Bok and John T. Dunlop, *Labor and the American Community* (New York: Simon and Schuster, 1970), Chapter 12, "Frontiers of Substantive Bargaining," pp. 342–60.

In any one plant, the content of most jobs will not change during the life of a contract. In a dynamic industrial system, however, there always will arise a number of new jobs that cannot be fitted into existing classifications, or situations in which the duties on existing jobs may have to be changed. What procedure should be followed in setting rates or new changed jobs?

Practice varies considerably on this question. In some cases, the parties will sit down and negotiate the rate every time a new job appears or an existing job has its duties changed appreciably. In others, it is customary for management to set the rate on the new or changed job, subject to challenge by the union through the grievance procedure. Many contracts in effect prohibit management from changing the duties or rate on a job existing at the time of the contract's signing for the life of the contract.

As a general rule, the most practical and efficient approach would appear to be one which permits management to set the rate on a new job, reserving to the union the right to challenge this rate within a specified time period, such as thirty, sixty, or ninety days. This is a frequent practice on incentive jobs and has validity for new hourly jobs as well. *In plants with well-established job evaluation systems, the problem of setting rates on new or changed jobs is not likely to be as troublesome as in plants with no definite system of wage administration.*

Even under a job evaluation program, however, disputes may frequently arise, particularly in connection with changes in the content of an existing job. The normal direction of technological change is toward work simplification, with the breaking down of complex tasks into simpler, more specialized assignments. Hence, the resultant wage change is likely to be downward and therefore productive of considerable employee and union resistance. On the other hand, job enlargement as part of a "quality of work life" program may change the job profile in a way that raises the points under a job evaluation plan, though performance and efficiency may be less as a result of the enlargement program. The tradeoff of lower wages for a better (enlarged) job is a matter for negotiation.

An even more difficult issue relates to whether disputes over rates on new or changed jobs should be arbitrable or subject to strike action under the contract. An arbitrator under a contract that excludes such disputes from the arbitration step might well be grateful for the exclusion, since such disputes do not lend themselves to the "judicial" type of arbitration. The proper rate for a new job is essentially a "political" question that should be worked out by the parties. At the same time, there are real advantages, as discussed in earlier chapters, in using arbitration as an alternative to economic force for any contract dispute during the life of an agreement. Majority practice seems to favor making such disputes arbitrable.

INCENTIVE SYSTEMS: ARE THEY WORTH THE TROUBLE?

Many employers are less sanguine than in years past about the virtues of incentive methods of wage payment. Thus, it may be that the days of incentive systems are numbered in many work relationships. In many cases, a candid cost-benefit study of an incentive plan's installation and operation would reveal that this time-honored method of rewarding employee effort is not accomplishing what the employer had anticipated.

This conclusion is based on such considerations as the following:

1. An incentive system is expensive to install and costly to maintain in proper fashion.
2. If incentive dispute arbitration costs are figured into the reckoning, it is questionable in many cases whether the benefits outweigh the costs.
3. Apart from economic considerations, it may be that employee morale and rapport with management will be easier to achieve and maintain under a sound system of occupational rate differences than under an incentive payment plan.

Incentive work plans may be on the wane. However, there are still many lines of work that lend themselves to a system of payments related to worker output. Also, many instances could be cited where the employees are pleased with operating on an incentive basis.

In recent years, there has been considerable experimentation with joint administration of wage-incentive systems. Some plants have joint time study operations; others have a joint committee to review production standards and piece rates set in terms of those standards. In most cases, however, the methods analysis and time study operations remain management functions. The establishment of production standards and the setting of piece rates are also usually management functions, with the union reserving the right to challenge the fairness of the standard or the rate through the grievance process. Some international unions maintain a staff of industrial engineers to assist locals in monitoring and, if necessary, challenging standards set by management.

Union opposition to incentive methods of payment is often deep-rooted. However, when the union's institutional status is secure and job operations lend themselves to an incentive method of payment, there is less union opposition.

Most unions are not equipped for joint participation with management in administration of a wage-incentive plan. Nor do most unions wish to share responsibility for the effective operation of such plans. They prefer to insist upon the right to challenge managerial exercise of administrative initiative. If the right to challenge is secure, most unions are not interested in going further.

ELEMENTS OF A SOUND INCENTIVE SYSTEM

Variety is still the hallmark when one reviews the field of incentive systems. Some generalizations can still safely be made concerning principles to be observed for successful operation in a unionized context. These include the following:

1. To be effective, incentive systems must gain acceptance by the work force. It is therefore desirable to keep the system as simple as possible. Furthermore, if employees have input into the formulation of the system, they are more likely to accept it, and fewer grievances should arise.
2. The average normal operator should be able to earn approximately 20 to 30 percent above his guaranteed base rate.
3. The guaranteed base rate should not be set at an unrealistically low figure to create the illusion that piecework earnings are exceptionally high. It should correspond to what the job would pay on an hourly rate basis.
4. Piece rates should not be reduced unless there has been a substantial change in methods, materials, design, or equipment. Procedures should be set for changing rates.
5. The contract's grievance and arbitration machinery should be available, both for challenging rates alleged to be too tight and for reviewing those alleged to be too loose (that is, runaway standards).

SUMMARY

Collective wage negotiation sets the general wage package and especially in industrial union bargaining, divides that package in a variety of ways. It divides the package into different wage rates for different jobs, or different wage rates for different people performing the same job. It divides the package between pay for time and incentive pay for performance. And it divides the package between direct pay and many indirect or "fringe" payments. We discuss in considerable detail fringe pay issues in the next chapter; all the other issues are discussed in this chapter.

The overall size of the pay package depends upon competitive pressures on the employer side and political pressures on the union side. Given the pressures on both sides, an overall package is negotiated. We discuss some of the institutional features of wage bargaining in this chapter, and consider the same topic in a more analytical framework in Chapter 14. An agreement on wages that works—that is, settles the dispute—is probably more efficient in the long run, than the highest or lowest possible temporary settlement, since once the conflict is resolved, energy and attention can be redirected toward production.

Wage differentials pose difficult problems internally for unions and in allocation of people among jobs for employers. Negotiation problems involve settlements of the proper differential within the union, then resolution of differences between the union and the employer. Job evaluation provides an administrative framework for resolving some of the wage differential problems during the life of the agreement.

Incentive plans aid productivity and are often preferred by employees. However, incentive standards are difficult to design, and are difficult to change as new techniques are introduced. Often, incentive standards become an ongoing area of grievance and a steady source of arbitration cases. The difficulty of administration and negotiation has limited the adoption of wage incentives in collective bargaining.

Questions for Discussion, Thought, and Research

1. A union spokesperson commented, "Job evaluation is nothing more than systematic value judgments which are given the illusion of science. The problem is, the numbers the system generates are later transmitted into a person's pay. The union had no part in designing the system, and doesn't give much weight to its results." Is this assessment of job evaluation accurate? Explain.

2. The bottom line for job evaluation is its acceptability. If the logic of the system does not agree with already existing wage differentials, chances are that the system will have to be abandoned. Do you agree? Why?

3. Why does it make a difference whether an employee is paid on an hourly, weekly, or monthly salary? The outcome is the same. Evaluate.

4. In certain parts of the brewery industry, every employee receives the same pay regardless of the type of work he or she performs. In other industries, there is a formal job rate hierarchy in which more skilled jobs receive more pay. Why are differentials nonexistent in one situation while critical for feelings of internal equity in another situation? Explain.

5. What are some ways to reduce union resistance to job evaluation? Has past resistance by unions been justified? Explain.

6. In what situations are rate ranges preferable to single rates? Elaborate.

7. Company Y is opening a new plant for the manufacturing of widgets. Based on what you know about incentive systems, would you recommend installing an incentive system for factory workers? If yes, what type of plan? If no, why wouldn't an incentive system work?

8. Would you recommend a separate salary administration program for professional employees? Explain.

9. Hospital X has discovered that the starting salary for ambulance drivers is below the current market rate. The hospital is having trouble attracting new recruits. Since the hospital has a labor agreement which does not expire for two years, what steps would you suggest that it take to correct the problem?

10. Why are different occupations paid at different rates? Explain.

11. By what process are union wage policies formulated? Should union leaders or rank and file formulate wage demands?

12. What are the disadvantages to an employer in following patterned bargaining?

Selected Bibliography

Belcher, David W., *Compensation Administration.* Englewood Cliffs, N.J.: Prentice-Hall, 1974.

Bok, Derek, and John Dunlop, *Labor and the American Community.* New York: Simon and Schuster, 1970.

Edelstein, David J., and Malcolm Warner, *Comparative Union Democracy.* New York: Halsted Press, 1976.

Henderson, Richard I., *Compensation Management.* Reston, Va.: Reston, 1979.

Mills, D. Quinn, *Industrial Relations and Manpower in Construction.* Cambridge, Mass.: MIT Press, 1972.

Ross, Arthur, *Trade Union Wage Policy.* Berkeley: University of California Press, 1948.

Stieber, Jack, *The Steel Industry Wage Structure.* Cambridge, Mass.: Harvard University Press, 1959.

NEGOTIATED ECONOMIC SECURITY PACKAGES AND OTHER "FRINGES"

11

For more than three decades, employee economic security has been a major focus of union and employer negotiators. There is every reason to believe that economic security issues will continue to be of prime concern in the years ahead. Progress in the fields of health and welfare and retirement benefits has been dramatic. It must be regarded as one of the most significant developments in the recent evolution of collective bargaining as a process.

As Robert Tilove once observed, there would not have been the conversion from "progressive practices" to "standard practices" had it not been for the pressure of unions at the bargaining table.[1] Union-secured economic security benefits set the pattern followed by the nonunionized sectors of the economy. A few figures serve to highlight the change that has occurred. Table 11–1 shows trend figures on a number of health and

1. Robert Tilove, "Pensions, Health and Welfare Plans," Lloyd Ulman, ed., in *Challenges to Collective Bargaining* (Englewood Cliffs, N.J.: Prentice-Hall, 1967), p. 37.

Table 11-1

Percent of Wage and Salary Workers Under Employee-Benefit Plans[a]

TYPE OF BENEFIT	1950	1970	1975
Covered Employees as a Percent of All Wage and Salary Workers[b]			
Life Insurance	38.8	69.0	77.3
Death and Dismemberment	16.2	51.5	57.6
Hospital	48.6	70.7	72.2
Surgical	35.4	68.6	70.1
Regular Medical	16.4	63.9	69.5
Major-Medical	—	32.7	36.7
Covered Employees as a Percent of Wage and Salary Workers in Private Industry[c]			
Retirement	22.5	42.1	46.2
Sick Leave	46.2	47.9	47.5
Disability	—	11.2	17.6

[a]Excludes workmen's compensation and benefits underwritten by the government.

[b]Coverage of public and private employees in wage and salary jobs.

[c]Coverage of private employees in wage and salary jobs.

Source: Martha Ramy Yohalem, "Employee-Benefit Plans, 1975," *Social Security Bulletin* (Washington, D.C.: Government Printing Office, November 1977), p. 22.

welfare and retirement benefits. In 1975, eight out of ten workers had life insurance coverage and nearly one-half of those in the private sector had some retirement plan benefits. Twenty-five years earlier, the proportion of workers with these benefits were only four out of ten and two out of ten, respectively.

The term *package bargaining* is in itself testimony to the importance of the nonwage economic provisions of contemporary agreements. No story on a negotiated settlement is complete without a journalistic calculation of the percentage of cents-per-hour increase in so-called fringes as well as the wage increase as such. How inappropriate the term *fringes* has become can be appreciated by talking with nearly any employer engaged in collective bargaining. According to one study, an estimated 36.9 percent of payroll was spent on the nonwage package in 1978 (see Table 11–2). This ratio was up from 36.7 percent in 1977 and 35.4 percent in 1975. In dollar-and-cents terms, fringes averaged about $2.47 per payroll hour, with annual cost per employee to the employer running in the neighborhood of $5,138.[2] One usually associates the word "fringe" with a blanket, curtains, or draperies but if any of these had a fringe approximating 37 percent, it would look bizarre, to say the least.

The varied range of negotiated employee economic security programs cannot be dealt with in complete fashion in one chapter. We shall be

2. Taken from the source identified in Table 11–2.

Table 11–2

Employee Benefit Costs to the Employer as a Percent of Payroll (1978)

TYPE OF BENEFIT	ALL COMPANIES (%)
A. Legally Required Payments	9.0
FICA Taxes (Social Security)	5.6
Unemployment Compensation	1.7
Workers' Compensation	1.6
Related Railroad Law Benefits	0.1
B. Pensions, Insurance and Related Item Payments	12.2
Pensions	5.6
Life, Health, Death, Medical, Surgical, and Major Medical	5.6
Long Term Disability	0.3
Dental	0.1
Employee Discounts	0.1
Employee Meals	0.2
Separation Allowance, Moving Allowance and Misc.	0.2
C. Paid Rest Period, Lunch Period, Travel Time, etc.	3.6
D. Payment for Time Not Worked	9.7
Vacation	4.9
Holiday	3.2
Sick Leave	1.2
Funeral Leave, National Guard, etc.	0.4
E. Other Items	2.4
Profit Sharing	1.4
Thrift Plans	0.3
Bonuses	0.4
Education Allowance	0.1
Special Wage Payments (e.g., as Union Steward, etc.)	0.2
Total Employment Benefits as a Percent of Payroll	36.9

Source: *Personnel Management: BNA Policy and Practices Series* (Washington, D.C.: Bureau of National Affairs, 1980), 267:177, p. 111.

concerned primarily with tracing the evaluation, current status, and future prospects of negotiated pension plans, health and welfare programs, and, more briefly, income security and supplemental unemployment benefit (SUB) plans. In the concluding sections of the chapter we shall present a summary overview of recent developments on other standard fringes such as paid vacations, paid holidays, and the like.

Many issues that used to be troublesome for negotiators in all these categories have been resolved by a variety of means, including bad experience, grievance arbitration, legislation, and so on. To cite one example, one no longer hears debate over the once burning issue of whether a negotiated pension plan should be of a contributory or noncontributory type. The answer at the bargaining table has been overwhelmingly conclusive. Nearly all negotiated plans are noncontributory. We shall therefore forego analyzing the pros and cons on this issue.

There is no shortage of troublesome matters to test the mettle of the negotiators. In one fashion or another, most of the difficulties relate to the increasing cost problem. At each negotiation, a decision must be made as to how much of the economic package is to be allocated to wage adjustments as such, and how much to improvements and innovations in the various employee benefit programs. Notwithstanding the problem of increasing cost, the mix of benefit programs in most cases tends to become richer and more varied at each contract renegotiation.

AN OUTLINE OF A TYPICAL NONWAGE ECONOMIC PACKAGE

Referring back to Table 11–2, if we disregard the benefits associated with those federal and state programs which legally mandate employer participation, the remaining items are all negotiable and they variously appear as provisions in all negotiated agreements. Perhaps the most stable items in most negotiated packages are a retirement plan and some type of health and welfare program. The content of the health and welfare part of the package will vary markedly from one relationship to another as to both the range and level of benefits.

A fairly typical H-and-W plan will embrace the following:

1. A hospitalization care program,
2. a surgical and medical care program, and
3. a group life insurance or death benefit plan.

Important features of contemporary H-and-W bargaining not yet in the typical or customary category are provisions for hearing aids and chemical rehabilitation, whereas provisions for dental care, prescription drugs, vision care, and Medicare-related insurance appear in a growing proportion of collective agreements each year and will soon become a permanent fixture in future H-and-W plans. Today, employers with H-and-W plans are required by law to give their employees the option of joining a qualified Health Maintenance Organization (HMO) which offers prepaid medical service for one flat fee. The services which an HMO offers are very broad and include outpatient diagnostic services, X-ray and other types of laboratory services, prescription drugs, and more. The broad spectrum of HMO services cover a number of items not covered by most contracts, which were previously paid for directly out of the employee's pocket.

In health and welfare bargaining, the trend is to increase the range and coverage of benefits wherever possible. For example, some agreements call for prepaid legal services. However, this is not an easy task in the face of constantly mounting costs. Another costly development concerns extending the coverage to dependents of employees. In the pension plan phase of package bargaining, the principal current targets relate to the liberalization of early retirement provisions, to protection against layoffs, and to increased pension benefits to offset inflation. These areas will be treated in greater detail shortly.

THE FRUSTRATIONS OF PACKAGE BARGAINING

Package bargaining typically requires some agonizing choices on the part of the negotiators, especially the union representatives, who must face up to a forced choice in many cases between a substantial wage boost and improvements in the complex of employee security benefit plans. The employer's financial position is frequently such that he is unable to grant simultaneously a demand for a hefty wage increase and a considerable "sweetening" of the pension and health and welfare provisions. It is therefore a fairly common practice for the employer to advise the union representatives informally as to approximately how much of an increase in overall labor cost he is capable of absorbing over the next contract period (usually three years). In addition to negotiating over this figure, there is hard bargaining over how this lump sum shall be apportioned between wages and nonwage economic benefits. Union leaders must reveal a preference.

This is a particularly difficult decision to make during periods of double-digit inflation. Union representatives are getting strong pressure from their constituents to obtain catch-up wage increases *and* to liberalize the benefits program at the same time. If the employer's cost picture is such as to require an either-or choice, it is likely that the wage increase will get priority attention during inflationary periods. In most of the key bargaining relationships, however, it has been possible to obtain some improvements in the important fringe areas in addition to substantial wage increases.

Bargaining on economic security programs is a technical and complex business. It demands a kind of expertise that many management and union negotiators lack. Both parties have thus had to train themselves or hire specialists. No area of current bargaining is more dynamic and volatile. Costs are rising at an alarming rate. The volume of federal and state legislation mounts. At the same time, pressures for new and varied services are growing more insistent. Policies properly regarded as pioneering and imaginative in the previous three decades are relegated unceremoniously to the realm of the taken-for-granted.

THE PROSPECTS OF FEDERALIZING
BENEFIT PROGRAMS

The limits of private ability to handle economic security issues will be reached soon in many relationships. In some cases, the saturation point has already been reached. A few brief examples will help to illuminate this point.

While figures are not available, we are aware of many employers who are *demanding* that their employees begin to contribute to a share of the payments going to skyrocketing premium charges assessed by health and life insurance carriers. Throughout most of the 1970s, the "medical care" component of the Consumer Price Index increased at a faster annual rate than the "all items' " index.[3] Before health care prices began their rapid upward spiral, these same employers were inclined to pay 100 percent of premium costs for existing as well as extended and expanded health protection coverage. Now they refuse to pay for both more coverage and higher prices.

Scarcely a month has passed during the last year that we have not read a news report that a supplemental unemployment benefit (SUB) fund is in financial trouble. In auto and steel, where unemployment has been prolonged and deep, generous SUB plans have cost these industries a small fortune and, in some instances, their economic viability is threatened. Tighter control over these costs at the bargaining table is being promised by industrialists.

Lastly, soaring inflation at or near double-digit rates, plus the aging of the U.S. population (whose median age increased from 28.2 in 1970 to 30.3 by 1977) have placed many private pension plans in jeopardy, and all of them have become even more expensive to operate. As if to add insult to injury, these same factors are threatening the solvency of the nation's social security system; that is, the Old Age, Survivors, Disability and Health Insurance system (OASDHI). Why the insult? OASDHI is financed primarily through a tax on wages. Cost-conscious employers and employees (who are taxed an equal amount) are already wringing their hands about soaring private pension plan costs and now they have the added worry of increasing FICA taxes. In 1949, the employer's maximum FICA tax payment was 1 percent on maximum earnings of $3,000 or $30 per employee at the maximum wage. In 1981, the tax was 6.65 percent on maximum earnings of $29,700, or $1,975.05 per employee at the maximum wage. This figure represents a tax

3. Economic trends in health care are summarized in Glen I. Misek, ed., *Socioeconomic Issues in Health: 1979* (Chicago: American Medical Association, 1980), pp. 161–255.

increase of 6,500 percent over the 32-year period. Some employers are now questioning the basic concept of a *dual* pension system in which the social security program provides only *basic* retirement payments, while private pensions serve as a *complementary* source of retirement income. Among other strategies, these employers are advancing the concept that the two parts of the system ought to be viewed as *substitutes*. Thus, for example, an increase in social security benefits ought to be offset by a decline in private benefits.

INTERLOCKING PUBLIC AND PRIVATE FRINGE BENEFITS

Private and public benefit programs are interlocking.[4] Some privately negotiated benefits may be viewed as complementary or supplemental to public benefit programs, especially where benefit gaps or shortfalls are identified. Conversely, some private benefits may be viewed as substitutes for public benefit programs. Thus, where benefit overlaps exist, employers will press hard for rollbacks during negotiations. Whatever the case may be, employer and union negotiators usually approach the matter of fringe benefit negotiations with a strategy of coordination or integration in mind.

The following list of benefit issues are among those frequently receiving coordinated consideration in collective bargaining negotiations.

Private Benefits	*Public Benefits*
1. SUB plans.	1. Unemployment compensation insurance and federal supplemental benefit programs.
2. Sick leave and permanent or temporary disability.	2. Workers' compensation and disability aspects of OASDHI.
3. Private pension plans.	3. Retirement aspects of OASDHI.
4. Major medical insurance for retirees.	4. Medicare aspects of OASDHI.
5. Paid holidays.	5. Legal holidays.

FEDERALIZING BENEFIT PROGRAMS

Coordinating or integrating private pension plans with social security benefits is nothing new. Indeed, participants in a balanced, dual pension program fare reasonably well in retirement compared with retirees who

4. For a brief but interesting review of the interface between public benefit laws and their significance to employers, read Robert M. McCaffery, "Benefits and Services—Statutory," in Dale Yoder and Herbert G. Heneman, Jr., eds., *ASPA Handbook of Personnel and Industrial Relations* (Washington, D.C.: Bureau of National Affairs, 1979), pp. 6:157–84.

rely solely on social security benefits. This was the conclusion of the President's Commission on Pension Policy.[5] A large proportion of individual retirees who are not entitled to private pensions spend their retirement living at a substandard level.[6] The Employee Retirement Income Security Act of 1974 (ERISA) does *not* require employers to offer a pension plan. What it does is to regulate and to set minimum pension plan standards which offered plans are required to meet.

The President's commission has concluded that serious study ought to be given the idea of formally coordinating public and private pensions through law. The policy goal of this "integrative" idea is to insure an *equitable, adequate,* and *efficient* delivery of benefits for all retired workers. This conclusion has caused controversy, not the least of which has to do with who will bear the cost of any new law establishing a universal pension system.[7] We can only speculate that any new legislation in this area will significantly impact on collective bargaining relations. Note, for example, some of the effects on pension plans of the 1978 amendments to the Age Discrimination in Employment Act. This act merely raised the minimum mandatory retirement age from 65 to 70 and, in turn, questions like the following have demanded answers at the bargaining table:

1. Should the plan's "normal" retirement age be changed?
2. Should employees who work after the normal retirement age be permitted to participate in the pension plan with full credit for the additional years of service?
3. Should the employees referenced in 2 above receive partial credit for the additional years of service?
4. Should the employees referenced in 2 above have their plan participation discontinued but given actuarially increased benefits at retirement to allow for the shorter period of benefit payments resulting from shorter, postretirement, life expectation?
5. Should the employees referenced in 2 above be permitted to draw full pension payments during their years of employment beyond the plan's normal retirement age but with plan participation discontinued once this age is reached?

In the area of health care, many believe that Medicare, which became operative in 1966, was a first step toward federalizing the nation's health care system. More than 30 million people in the country who are age 65 and over are covered under this program of financing health care for the

5. *An Interim Report: The President's Commission on Pension Policy* (Washington, D.C.: U.S. Government Printing Office, 1980), pp. 1–51.
6. *Ibid.*
7. *Ibid.*

elderly, one that currently costs the federal government about $30 billion to finance.

The public and private relative health care cost burden has increased dramatically in recent years. Hence, there have been a rash of laws passed for the purpose of forcing health care providers and insurers to the more cost-conscious. Health planning, "certificate of need," hospital "cost containment," and related laws have been passed at the federal and state levels of government. A dramatic piece of similar legislation was the already mentioned 1973 Health Maintenance Organization Act. Strongly supported by organized labor, this law encouraged the formation of prepaid, comprehensive health care organizations (HMOs).[8] It requires that employers with twenty-five or more employees, who are approached by a federally qualified HMO, to offer memberships in the HMO to their employees or employees' bargaining representatives, provided the employers have a health insurance program for their employees. HMO businesses are encouraged to form. For a flat fee, which is prepaid to the HMO, it promises to provide its subscribers with comprehensive health care. The HMO is both *insuring* its subscribers against future health care costs and *delivering* necessary health care services to its members. With known revenues and unknown costs, the HMO is motivated to control costs by keeping its members healthy (e.g., by focusing on preventative health care) and by substituting outpatient care for more costly inpatient hospital care. As opposed to a traditional and bifacial health insurance, "fee for service" health care delivery system, the HMO sector should be able to operate more efficiently, introducing competitive forces into the health care markets.

The impact of proposed national health insurance (financing) programs and health care delivery programs on negotiated H-and-W plans is obviously a matter of critical importance. As with pension plan negotiations, these matters may wane as critical bargaining issues in some respects depending on the law(s) passed. Otherwise, we can expect future agreements to contain provisions which extend or augment pension and H-and-W benefits.

There is full recognition on the part of both employees and unions that even the most broadly based negotiated plans are proving to be extremely costly. Furthermore, the private plans pose a continuing psychological problem for the bargainers. Attainment of a certain level and rate of benefits invariably produces employee aspirations of "more" at the next negotiation round. Sooner or later, aspirations may not be realized.

8. Read Bert Seidman's speech on this subject, delivered on April 12, 1979, at the Annual Meeting of Group Health, in St. Paul, Minn., entitled, "The Role of Organized Labor in Development of Prepaid Group Practices." A copy of this speech can be obtained from his Washington, D.C., office. Write to Bert Seidman, Director, Social Security Department, AFL–CIO.

PENSION REFORM ACT—ERISA

After several years of congressional deliberation, ERISA was passed in 1974. In total, the law was designed to protect private sector workers and their beneficiaries from loss of deferred compensation (pension) and welfare plan rights due to theft, coercion, imprudent pension fund management, employer bankruptcy, and so forth. When the Studebaker Corporation closed its U.S. operations in the 1960s, many of its employees lost their pension benefits, despite having such rights spelled out in their collective bargaining agreement. In part, ERISA was designed to prevent a recurrence of this type of travesty.

To meet this protective goal, ERISA requires plan administrators to disclose plan provisions and financial information to employees and to file a variety of reports with the Department of Labor, Internal Revenue Service, and Pension Benefit Guarantee Corporation (PBGC). Further, it establishes standards of conduct for plan trustees or fiduciaries; it sets funding, participating, and vesting requirements for certain plans, and it makes plan termination insurance available for certain plans.

Before briefly outlining the major areas of pension reform caused by ERISA, we will pause to define a few terms already used and two phrases to be used subsequently.

> Who are *fiduciaries?* They are the people who handle pension plan funds or otherwise control the property relevant to others' retirement benefits. Under ERISA both criminal and civil suits can be brought against plan fiduciaries, including labor arbitrators who handle pension-related issues, for alleged ERISA violations.

> What is *funding?* It is a process of setting aside money specifically to pay for employees' benefit rights upon retirement.

> What is *participating?* It is a reference to employees' eligibility to take part in a pension program.

> What is *vesting?* It is a right to pension benefits that are nonforfeitable even after vested employees leave their jobs.

> How are *defined benefit* plans and *defined contribution* plans differentiated? The first states in advance the amount of money an employee will receive at retirement. This is typical of union-negotiated plans in the auto, steel, aluminum, rubber, and can industries. It states simply the flat amount per month which is multiplied by years of service. The latter category of pension plans specifies the amount of money to be contributed to an investment fund, but it does not fix the benefit amount to be received at retirement. This depends on the profitability of the fund's investment portfolio.

With the foregoing as background, we will now highlight some of ERISA's major pension plan requirements:[9]

A. Provisions Relating to Regular Employees.

    1. *Participation.* Plans must permit an employee to participate after one year of service, provided that the employee is age 25 or over. A plan with immediate vesting can require a straight three years of service. For most plans, newly hired workers age 60 and over can be excluded from participation.

    2. *Vesting.* Plans must provide that employees' contributions are fully and immediately vested. Employer contributions under most plans must vest at least as quickly as provided under one of the following three schedules: (a) 100 percent vesting upon completion of 10 years of service; (b) graded 15-year service—25 percent vested after 5 years of service, plus 5 percent for each additional year of service up to 10 years (50 percent vesting after 10 years of service), plus an additional 10 percent for each year thereafter (100 percent vesting after 15 years of service); and (c) rule of 45—when age and service (with a minimum of 5 years of service) equal 45, the employee is 50 percent vested, with an additional 10 percent for each year thereafter.

B. Provisions Relating to Other Classes of Employees.

    1. Part time and seasonal employees must be covered by the plan, provided they work 1,000 hours within twelve months.

    2. Individuals may now contribute up to a fixed dollar limit per year in one of three special retirement accounts.

C. Provisions Relating to Employers.

    1. *Funding.* Plans must be more strictly managed, with provision to accumulate funds needed over the long run to cover plan liabilities.

    2. *Termination Insurance.* Defined benefit plans must participate in a self-financing, pension benefit termination insurance program created by ERISA. The insurance program is the responsibility of PBGC.

    3. *Fiduciary Standards—Reporting and Disclosure.* The "prudent man" criterion is applied to fund managers. Standards for reporting and disclosing plan performance are set by the law.

9. See the following sources: Prentice-Hall, "Compensation," *Personnel Management* (current), pp. 50: 501–12; Coleman S. Ives, "Benefits and Services—Private," in Dale Yoder and Herbert G. Heneman, Jr., eds., *ASPA Handbook of Personnel and Industrial Relations* (Washington, D.C.: Bureau of National Affairs, 1979), pp. 6:206–16. While "welfare plans which provide medical, surgical, or hospital benefits; benefits in the event of sickness, accident, disability, death, or unemployment; vacation benefits, apprenticeship or other training programs; day care centers, scholarship funds, or prepaid legal services; etc." are covered by ERISA, they are neither insured by the PBGC nor are they subject to the participation, vesting, and funding provisions of the law.

PENSION PLANS: PAST, PRESENT, AND FUTURE

Prior to World War II there were a few private retirement plans operated by nonunion firms, but there were virtually no negotiated plans. The initial impetus for negotiated pension schemes came during and immediately following World War II. The United Mine Workers in 1946 and the Steelworkers and Autoworkers in 1949 and 1950 formed the vanguard of the drive to make some kind of negotiated retirement plan a must item thereafter on the collective bargaining agenda.

The proliferation of negotiated plans in the 1950s and 1960s was nothing short of phenomenal. Furthermore, significant improvements have been made steadily in many contracts on the level of benefits, participation requirements, vesting rights, and the like. Most contemporary negotiated pension plans bear scant resemblance to their forebears, many of which were social security "offset" plans.

Throughout this thirty-five-year period of dynamic change, both employers and unions of necessity have had to negotiate their revisions in a pragmatic fashion in order to achieve adequate benefit levels while at the same time keeping premium costs at a tolerable level. This has not been an easy task, particularly when both parties were serious about the necessity of developing a fully funded, actuarially sound plan.[10]

From a handful of workers covered by pension plans in the early 1940s, and to 9.8 million in 1950,[11] there were slightly more than 30 million individuals covered by private pension plans in 1975. This total includes multiemployee and union-administered plans, but it excludes beneficiaries and persons covered by government operated pension plans.

In 1979, nearly 35 million private wage and salary workers were not covered by a pension plan. Among the remarkable characteristics of this group was that only 9 percent were union members.[12] The obvious inference is that about 80 to 85 percent of all unionized private sector employees were covered by pension plans in 1979.

Continued growth in negotiated pension plan coverage is logical to anticipate. Workers' interests in economic security after retirement will not subside. "Growth" in this sense will persist until *all* union members have pension coverage.[13] More dramatic change over the years ahead, however,

---

10. Many, if not most, private negotiated plans did not meet rigid funding standards and other tests of actuarial soundness prior to ERISA.

11. Yohalem, "Employee-Benefit Plans, 1975," p. 24.

12. *Pensions and Profit Sharing*, p. 24.

13. We do not mean to convey the idea that existing pension plans cannot be terminated. They can be, and indeed they are. In 1975 the number of private pension plans that were terminated increased from 4,604 from a year earlier to 8,108. This may have been the result of depressed economic conditions and/or it may have been the result of increased regulatory

will relate to improved terms and provisions found in existing negotiated pension plans, which we shall discuss subsequently.

The present and future will see multiemployer pension plans changed en masse. Associations of employers can jointly offer workers in an area or industry a multiemployer pension plan. Such plans characterize the construction, entertainment, and long- and short-haul trucking industries. In these industries, workers frequently work on a project-by-project or employer-by-employer basis rather than on a single project or for a single employer on a regular basis. Hence, pension plans are organized on a multiemployer basis and they contain *portability* provisions which allow an employee to change jobs and remain covered by the plan, building up credits as long as he works for a contributing employer.

At ERISA's adoption, employers were permitted to withdraw from multiemployer pension plans without liability, unless the plan terminated within five years and with insufficient funds. Congress feared this situation would motivate employers to bail out of a plan at the first sign of difficulty, in the hope that five years would elapse before the plan collapsed, and then they would escape being stuck with having to assist in making good on benefit guarantees under PBGC requirements. To remedy this situation, Congress changed ERISA with the Multiemployer Pension Plan Amendment Act of 1980. Obviously, labor and management negotiators with multiemployer pension plans are and will be amending their plans if for no other reason than to bring them into conformity with this new law.[14]

AN ANALYSIS OF CONTEMPORARY AND PROSPECTIVE NEGOTIATED PENSION PLANS

Reviewing some features of current negotiated retirement plans will show the progress that has been made in disposing of former sources of conflict and uncertainty. As already noted, nearly all negotiated plans are *noncontributory*, which means that employees do not make plan contributions out of their own pockets. Moreover, through mandatory vesting, ERISA has helped to solve the problem of pension benefit portability. Many long-term employees in single-employer pension plans had earlier faced the prospect of forfeiting pension benefits by changing employers. One study which

---

costs associated with ERISA itself. Too, since pension startup costs are relatively higher as a result of ERISA's standards, pension plan growth may slow as a general matter. Yohalem, "Employee-Benefit Plans, 1975."

14. Plan Administrator's Compliance Manual, *A Concise Explanation of the Multiemployer Pension Plan Amendment Act of 1980* (Englewood Cliffs, N.J.: Prentice-Hall, 1980), pp. 1–62.

analyzed changes made in 131 pension funds found that among private plans without vesting provisions in 1974, all had added such provisions by 1978.[15] Furthermore, this same study disclosed that most pensions use the vesting options of either (1) full vesting after 10 years of credited service or (2) the "rule of 45." Pressure persists, however, for earlier vesting as unions continue to respond to their members' long-term economic security aspirations.

The effect of ERISA on contemporary negotiated plans is pervasive. It has led to cuts in the proportion of newly hired workers who can participate immediately upon starting work; it has led to plan changes requiring vested employees with enough service to receive accrued benefits at early retirement; as a final example, it has meant that retirement benefits under most negotiated pension plans are now guaranteed. The latter two changes stemming from ERISA have helped to remedy two areas of long-standing labor–management dispute.

The size of the normal retirement benefit is determined by a formula in most negotiated pension plans. These formulas have been and are being liberalized, a trend that is not likely to be reversed in the future.[16] As noted, most negotiated plans use some type of "dollar amount times years of service" formula. Hourly employees at General Motors Corporation in the top labor grade who retired on September 1, 1979, received $11.50 per year of credited service (per month). If these same types of employees retired on September 1, 1980, they would have received $16.93 per year of credited service and could expect periodic rate increases to $18.75 per year of credited service payable on September 1, 1982, and thereafter, or until the current pension plan benefit provision is changed through negotiations with the UAW.[17]

Voluntary early retirement provisions now appear in 97 percent of the pension plans.[18] This is part of a trend that reaches back into the 1960s. The minimum age requirement is for the most part 55, and according to one report a majority of the plans studied clustered at this age[19]—down from age 60 a decade ago. Even though pension benefits usually are proportionately reduced by the number of years an employee is under the normal retirement age, many workers are willing to pay this price in exchange for more years of life in retirement. Moreover, by and large, union members

15. Robert Frumkin and Donald Schmitt, "Changes in Major Pension Plans Since 1974," Bureau of National Affairs, *Collective Bargaining Negotiations and Controls*, 1 (1979), 14:122.

16. *Ibid.*, pp. 16:121–22.

17. *Ibid.*, pp. 21:209–10. Under the agreement, any employee in this labor grade age 65 and with 10 or more years of credited service who retired on September 1, 1981, will receive $17.90 per year of credited service. Thus, a 20-year employee meeting these criteria will receive a monthly pension of $358.

18. Bureau of National Affairs, *Collective Bargaining Negotiations and Contracts*, 2 (1979), 48:3.

19. *Ibid.*

also receive (indexed) social security benefits which, as we noted earlier, permit a reasonably comfortable retirement.

However, the unprecedented inflation of recent years has caused some to question this overall strategy. Unions have responded to retiree complaints by negotiating lump-sum benefit payments on their behalf. For example, under new contract terms, pensions for retired steelworkers were raised between 10 and 70 percent in two equal steps effective August 1, 1980, and 1981. Monthly payments will vary, but the *minimum* monthly benefit for those already on the pension rolls will be $12 per year of credited service.[20]

It is easy to conclude, as some have, that the early retirement trend may reverse itself. The arguments are complex, but any one or all of the following factors could cause a reversal: (1) normal retirement under social security is increased from age 65 to 68; (2) double-digit inflation persists; and/or (3) a slowdown in labor force growth, in combination with age 70 as the minimum compulsory retirement age.

At present, however, the *option* of early retirement characterizes the labor–management scene, and it is likely to continue to do so. We shall return to the autoworker's agreement with General Motors Corporation for illustration purposes. In that agreement, regular employees are given three early retirement options: (1) retirement at age 60 after 10 years of service; (2) retirement at age 55 but before age 60 with age plus service combined equaling 85; or (3) the "30 and out" option which permits retirement at any age with 30 or more years of credited service.[21]

From the company's point of view, the mounting pension costs implicit in the foregoing are being countered in at least three ways. First, employers are trying to negotiate benefit "caps," or maximum monthly pension plan benefits. According to reports out of the AFL–CIO, this bargaining strategy is being implemented with some success.[22] Second, some employees are succeeding in changing pension benefit formulas such that when social security benefits increase, private pension benefits decrease.[23] Lastly, employers are revealing a preference for defined contribution plans over defined benefit plans. This shift in employer policy has organized labor deeply concerned since retirement income is only guaranteed under defined benefit plans.[24]

20. Bureau of National Affairs, *Collective Bargaining Negotiations and Contracts*, 1 (1980), 29:1.

21. *Ibid.*, p. 21:209.

22. Industrial Union Department, AFL–CIO, *Labor and Investments*, 1, No. 1 (January 1981), 5.

23. Bureau of National Affairs, 1 (1979), 16:123.

24. Industrial Union Department, AFL–CIO, *Labor and Investments*.

THE ADMINISTRATION OF NEGOTIATED
PENSION PLANS

Pension funds in the private sector alone will be worth about $3 trillion by the mid-1990s. These monies constitute the largest pool of investment capital available in the United States today. Thus, control over the administration of these resources will have a major, if not determining, impact on the pace and direction of the nation's economic development. The significance of this development has recently captured organized labor's policy attention. The management of pension and welfare funds not only impacts on the immediate and long-term welfare of millions of union employees and their beneficiaries, but it also shapes the pattern of industrial growth and transnational capital flows.

Even though many of today's pension and welfare funds are the product of collective bargaining, management is in the administrative driver's seat in the overwhelming majority of negotiated plans. As required by law, multiemployer plans are jointly administered by labor and management trustees. However, in single-employer plans—which are mainly of the noncontributory variety—management almost universally controls plan trust funds, while in some cases benefit management is under joint control.

The AFL–CIO Executive Council in August 1980 adopted a policy to encourage its affiliate national and international unions to become directly involved in union-negotiated pension fund management.[25] Designed to assure that the interests of the pensioners are protected, this policy recognizes that the growth and distribution of jobs during the 1980s may be influenced by the laissez-faire economic programs promised by President Reagan. Clearly, pension fund distributions will play a key role in private sector "reindustrialization."

As an economic security instrument, pension fund management has important macro implications. Unions strongly object to the fact that their deferred wages are being used as a source of capital by antiunion corporations and by companies who are pursuing "job-exporting" policies. From a micro point of view, with a voice in pension management, unions envision investment of pension funds into worker housing, health care, day care, recreation, and retirement centers.

Pension investment management in the midst of pension cost escalation is seen as a major avenue of salvation by many employers. Obviously, improved investment performance can be translated into cost reductions, given payout obligations. Employers want control over this end of pension

25. *Ibid.*, p. 1.

fund management. In effect, employers argue that, while they may have agreed to a pension benefit plan, the resources used to fund the plan are strictly theirs. The contemporary posturing of labor and management over this issue will receive considerable attention in the 1980s, particularly when the following AFL–CIO policy recommendations are put into motion:

1. Affiliated unions ought to use the collective bargaining relationship to gain joint administration rights over funds covering its members.
2. Affiliated unions ought to secure full information about the operation of any fund covering their members.
3. Affiliated unions with a voice in fund management ought to follow the Industrial Union Department's investment guidelines.
4. The AFL–CIO may seek new federal legislation requiring that unions be given a voice in investment decision making.[26]

THE CURRENT SCENE IN "HEALTH AND WELFARE" BARGAINING

The term "health and welfare" has become a standard shorthand label for an impressive range of negotiated benefits other than pension or retirement plans. The H-and-W umbrella generally covers some, if not all, of the following: (1) sickness and accident insurance; (2) hospitalization benefits for employees and their dependents; (3) surgical benefits; (4) payments for doctors' charges in hospitals; (5) nursing and medical care in the home; (6) various outpatient services such as diagnostic X-rays, laboratory tests for allergies, and so forth; (7) prescription drugs and medicines; (8) dental care; (9) vision care; (10) treatment for alcohol and drug addiction; (11) orthodontal care; and (12) chemotherapy treatments.

Some items are doubtless missing in the above enumeration, but generally it covers the principal benefits that unions currently seek to include as integral parts of the total economic security package in contemporary bargaining. The union emphasis generally has a dual focus: (1) to extend the range of health benefits, and (2) to improve the level of benefits for each of the categories covered. The protean, diverse nature of negotiated health benefit plans is such as to defy a thorough consideration. The modest aim here will be to note trends and problems in health benefit bargaining.

26. Industrial Union Department, AFL–CIO, *Pensions: A Study of Benefit Fund Investment Policies*, 1980, pp. 3–5.

THE SPUR OF RISING MEDICAL
AND HOSPITAL COSTS

It is no secret that the costs of medical and hospital care have been rising at a rapid rate for some years with no ceilings in sight. The specter of insecurity raised by these rising costs has added to the pressure on unions to negotiate adequate coverage while trying to remain abreast of the cost picture. This is no simple task. Another troublesome concern is the search for increasing efficiency in medical plan expenditures. Some of the larger and more affluent unions and employers, profoundly disturbed at the costs of doctors, hospitals, and commercial insurance firms, have gone into the health care business on their own.

The most dramatic of health care developments lies in the field of private prepaid group health plans such as that launched in California some years ago by the Kaiser Corporation. Both the Kaiser Foundation plan and the Health Insurance Plan of Greater New York lay stress on preventive care through periodic (routine) physical examinations. The Kaiser Foundation plan provides comprehensive health care through its own clinics.

HMO health care plans are receiving more attention than ever. R. J. Reynolds, AT&T, Alcoa, IBM, U.S. Steel, and many other major organizations now offer their employees and their families an HMO option. The growth in adoption of HMO plans illustrates the extension of health and welfare benefits to dependents. HMOs protect against catastrophic illnesses and, as noted earlier, they are believed to dampen the rate of health care inflation.

PROBABLE TRENDS IN HEALTH
PLAN BARGAINING

Union pressure for additional types of health care coverage will doubtless continue in the years ahead. Cost consciousness will be a factor in seeking to obtain more efficient expenditures of health plan dollars. Union negotiated plans have clearly been in the vanguard of all private group health insurance programs for the past two decades.

Most negotiated plans provide reasonably well for basic hospital–medical–surgical coverage. However, there is a growing realization on the part of unions and their members that the so-called basics are not enough. A principal goal is to provide for major medical insurance against expenses arising from serious accident or illness. In general, organized labor is only about 30 percent away from complete fulfillment of this objective.[27] However, there remains tremendous variation in the maximum amount of

27. Bureau of National Affairs, 2 (1978), 44:6.

lifetime major medical coverage individual workers have coming. Some contracts specify a maximum coverage of $20,000; others $50,000, and so on. One source reported that in 1975 the International Brotherhood of Electrical Workers (IBEW) and RCA negotiated a $300,000 major medical benefit.[28]

Another matter of union concern is the coverage of expenses currently coming from the union members' own pockets on such items as diagnostic services, X-rays, laboratory work, and various kinds of prescribed therapy. These charges are not yet covered by most non–HMO plans. Other types of benefits currently sought by unions include the cost of out-of-hospital drugs, mental health care, alcohol and drug rehabilitation, and vision care. Last, but not least, are developments in the dental care area, a latecomer in the benefits field. The Bureau of National Affairs reported that between 1975 and 1978 the number of contracts with dental care provisions in their H-and-W plan tripled.[29] In 1978, 41 percent of the surveyed plans included dental care coverage.[30] We expect that this trend will continue.

Survivor benefits continue to be a prime negotiating target. Many unions, particularly in the highly organized manufacturing sector like aluminum, steel, or autos, are pressing to increase the percent of deceased employees' benefits allocated to spouse and family. These same industries are witnessing union pressure to require employers to continue to make H-and-W plan premium payments while employees are on layoff status.

In concluding this brief treatment of negotiated health benefits, it is appropriate to mention again the continued pressure by unions for federal health care legislation. Our system of federal social security retirement benefits has made private negotiated pension plans a feasible undertaking in many relationships. So also has the federally induced system of state unemployment compensation made viable a negotiated program of supplemental unemployment benefits (to be discussed presently). By the same token, the ultimate answer on the costly business of adequate health care for all employees may prove to be federalizing costs of the basics of medical and hospital treatment, with leeway for privately negotiated arrangements for security above and beyond the basics.

A COMMENTARY ON SUB AND OTHER FORMS OF INCOME SECURITY

For many years the goal of a guaranteed annual wage (GAW) was in the minds of union negotiators at many bargaining tables. In most cases the goal retained the status of an unrealizable dream. A scattering of successful early plans, such as that of the George A. Hormel Company, received

28. Bureau of National Affairs, *Labor Relations Yearbook* (Washington, D.C., 1976), p. 10.
29. Bureau of National Affairs, 2 (1978), 44:8.
30. *Ibid.*

envious attention periodically from trade unionists. These early plans were also studied carefully by academicians. As far back as 1945, for example, Jack Chernick and George C. Hellickson developed a plausible demonstration that a GAW plan could work in the most unlikely of all fields —buildings and construction.[31] Yet the GAW did not become a key demand at the bargaining table until the UAW's famed push in 1955.

The ultimate result of the UAW effort in 1955 was the conversion of its demand for a full-dress GAW into the first of the SUB plans. The initial SUB plan in automobiles and farm equipment (both in 1955) and in steel (1956) could be described as constituting what amounted to two-thirds of a semiannual guaranteed wage. The eligible worker upon being laid off was entitled to an amount from the SUB fund which, when combined with his payments from unemployment compensation (UC), approximated two-thirds of his normal weekly take-home pay. He could receive such payments for up to twenty-six weeks. In subsequent years, SUB plans have been liberalized in most cases to the point where the eligible laid-off employee receives from a combination of SUB and UC payments 95 percent of his customary take-home pay, less $12.50 for "work-related expenses." Furthermore, the time span for receiving such payment has been extended from an original maximum of twenty-six weeks to as long as two years presently for employees of Alcoa with more than twenty years of service.[32]

The recent massive layoffs in auto and steel have further increased worker demand for expansion of SUB benefits. The major 1976–79 auto agreements not only increased the employer contribution to SUB funds, but the Big Three (Ford, GM, and Chrysler) auto manufacturers agreed to "guarantee" SUBs regardless of account balances. Depression in the auto market has caused havoc in regard to living up to these guarantees. The point, however, is that negotiations here and the SUB developments in steel and aluminum and elsewhere reflect a continuing demand by unions for income security for their members. The current liberalization among SUB plans amounts to a near realization of the original GAW dream in substance.

ADVENT OF TIER BARGAINING[33]

Major steelworkers' contracts in the aluminum industry have moved toward "tier bargaining," which is a labor and management arrangement that allocates employment and income security benefits to workers sorted into finite seniority blocs. The 1977–80 Alcoa agreement is used to illustrate

31. Jack Chernick and George C. Hellickson, *Guaranteed Annual Wage* (Minneapolis: University of Minnesota Press, 1945).

32. The example cited here is from the Alcoa–USW 1977–80 Agreement.

33. Taken from an analysis of the Alcoa–USW 1977–80 Agreement.

the tiering of benefits. Here workers are divided into three tiers: from 2 to 10 years of employment (tier I); 10 to 20 years (tier II); and more than 20 years (tier III). Tier II and III employees are "guaranteed" SUB benefits even if the company has to liquidate some of its holdings in order to make the agreed-upon payments. Furthermore, tier II and III employees are not subject to maximum SUB benefit levels, as are tier I employees. The maximum length of time for which an eligible employee may collect SUB benefits is scaled such that tier I, II, and III employees may receive SUB benefits up to a maximum of 52, 78, and 104 weeks, respectively. Also, the income of a tier III employee is protected in the event of idleness caused by layoff, shutdown, or sickness. If such an employee opts to retire while idled, he would receive a several hundred dollar monthly supplement in addition to early retirement benefits, provided his age plus length of service is equal to or greater than 65. The monthly supplement will be paid until age 62 at which time normal retirement benefits would be paid.

Alcoa uses tiering as an income maintenance mechanism which provides special rate-of-pay protection for employees who may be assigned to lower rated jobs. Specifically, tier I, II, and III employees are guaranteed 85, 90, and 95 percent, respectively, of prior earnings despite transfers to jobs with a lower pay grade. Finally, sickness and accident benefits are also provided for by tiers.

INCOME SECURITY BENEFITS

The liberalization of SUB plans is far from being the whole story on negotiated income security. The main thrust of SUB plans, in the collective record of union negotiators, is to protect the income of laid-off employees in technologically dynamic and business-cycle-prone industries. Under these circumstances, SUB is not envisioned as *the* answer to the union goal of a guaranteed income flow to labor force participants independent of labor demand conditions.

For some relatively senior employees (for example, tier III employees in the aluminum industry), however, the union GAW goal is a reality in some measure. SUB plans are only a part of this reality. To them, we must add a host of other preferential benefits like the following: pay grade retention benefits; plant relocation opportunities; early retirement options; and the reduced risk of income loss due to disability, accident, or sickness under employee H-and-W plans.

The major nonwage economic benefit areas summarily reviewed in the preceding pages by no means completes the "fringe" narrative. It remains to note an ever expanding network of supplemental wage payment practices, a clause to cover such varied matters as paid vacations, pay for holidays not worked, reporting pay, call-in pay, premium pay practices for overtime, special rates for Saturday and Sunday work, and similar "extras."

In the next few pages we shall identify current and prospective patterns on some, but not all, of the multiplicity of fringes in the supplemental wage payment category.

VACATIONS WITH PAY

We know of no contract of recent vintage that does not provide for vacations with pay. Policies have been consistently broadened to the point where what not too many years ago was the maximum length of vacation (two weeks) has become the minimum. The maximum is often five or more weeks for long-service employees.

Recent contracts now provide for vacation pay based on a percentage of the employee's earnings during the year rather than merely multiplying his hourly rate or guaranteed occupational rate by forty hours. They also reflect an expanding of employee freedom of choice as to when to take his vacation. This greater freedom is generally subject to managerial discretion to avoid serious labor shortages that would interfere with regular production commitments.

Our subjective impression is that employers and unions have largely resolved most of their differences over such matters as eligibility requirements, vacation equities of separated employees, computation of vacation pay, and so on. Vacations with pay have been part of the compensation pattern for so long that there appear to be few if any remaining areas of ambiguity and uncertainty.

THE STEELWORKERS' "SABBATICAL" PLAN

The most unusual vacation development in recent years is the one negotiated by the Steelworkers and the basic steel industry. The contractual distinction between "regular" vacations and EVs (extended vacations) is clearly drawn. The regular vacation formula in the 1977–80 agreement is in no way startling. It provides for one week's vacation for those with service of 1 year but less than 3; two weeks for those with 3 but less than 10; three weeks for those with 10 but less than 17; four weeks for those with 17 but less than 25; and five weeks for employees with 25 or more years' service.

The EV plan, now about a decade old, was innovative. For the top half of each plant's seniority list, the contract calls for a thirteen-week paid vacation every fifth year. The employer is only required to allow ten weeks off, but must pay for thirteen weeks, in effect providing a three-week bonus. Not surprisingly, the plan was dubbed the "Steelworkers' sabbatical." During this EV year the worker does not have a regular vacation. Those in the lower half of the seniority list receive three weeks on top of their regular vacation every fifth year.

The steel vacation sabbatical rationale rested heavily on job creation rather than on concern for the worker's complete renewal of spirit and energy. Unfortunately, the EV plan has not created new jobs as the USW originally anticipated, but has eased the decline in the work force.

Other employers and unions have followed the steel industry's lead on negotiating EV plans. For example, U.S. Borax Corporation and the Longshoremen (ILWU) have developed comparable plans.

PAID HOLIDAYS

A company that schedules work on a contractually recognized holiday is either very affluent, very careless, or in dire need of production. The current tab for scheduling holiday work is frequently at triple the employee's normal rate.[34] Furthermore, the number of holidays for the employer to schedule around continues to increase from contract to contract. In the third edition of this book (1972), we projected that twelve holidays would remain the upper limit on feasible holiday observances. It is now common to find more than twelve paid holidays per year. Holidays such as Saint Patrick's Day, Bunker Hill Day, Martin Luther King's Birthday, the employee's birthday, and the first day of Buck Deer season sometimes join the more traditional holiday observances. It has also become more common to negotiate days off around such holidays as Independence Day, Thanksgiving, and Christmas.

Beginning in 1976, the UAW began negotiating off-days before and after traditional holidays. To these days off, the autoworkers initiated the concept of "personal holidays," which were allowed to fall on "prime" days (Fridays, Mondays, and days before and after regular holidays). By 1979, an autoworker's vacation time, regular paid holidays, and personal holidays could add up to 40 paid days off per year.

The chief administrative problem in holiday pay clauses has always been

---

34. Bureau of National Affairs, 2 (1978), 58:8.

insuring against excessive absenteeism before and after the paid holiday. Most contracts require the employee to work the day before and the day after the holiday in order to qualify for holiday pay. There is no difficulty in principle with such a provision. Problems still arise in attempting to determine in specific cases whether the failure to work the day before or after the holiday was due to legitimate reasons such as bona fide illness, death in the immediate family, or the like.

For a contract holiday not worked, the employee generally receives eight hours' straight-time pay. For work on a contract holiday, the employee commonly gets holiday pay plus time-and-a-half; however, as noted above, some contracts call for holiday pay plus double time.[35]

Employees on layoff during a period in which a holiday falls do not ordinarily receive pay for the holiday. This practice is in line with the theory that, since an employee already laid off is not "losing" by not working the holiday, he should not be paid. An employee on vacation is in a different category since his vacation pay is an earned equity for prior service. Many contracts provide an extra day's pay for a holiday falling within the vacation period. It is frequently labeled, however, as an extra day of vacation, to be taken on the next scheduled work day following the end of the employee's vacation period.

REPORTING PAY AND CALL-IN PAY

Our reading of agreements over the years suggests that it is customary for the contract to guarantee employees either four hours' work or four hours' pay without work, when employees report for the work at their regularly scheduled time without having been notified in advance not to report. The equity of such a provision is clear.

Similarly, we have found that many contracts guarantee at least four hours' pay to employees who are "called in" or "called back" to work after having completed their regular shift and gone home. Such clauses are usually operative if the worker is called in within sixteen hours after completing a regular shift. Some contracts provide for double time in call-back cases.

Reporting pay provisions usually give the employer an "escape clause" for failure to notify an employee not to report, if the absence of work at reporting time is for reasons beyond the employer's control such as a power failure, fire, "act of God," or strike.

---

35. *Ibid.*

PREMIUM PAY FOR OVERTIME

Premium pay for overtime hours perhaps should not be called a fringe benefit. Discussion of this practice is warranted, however, since overtime earnings constitute a principal source of additional workers' income above basic wages in many industries.

Virtually all contracts specify the length of the working day, define the work week, and make special provision for payments on hours worked beyond the normal work day or work week.

For many years, in most industries, eight hours was the prescribed normal work day and forty hours the normal work week. There has been, however, some increase in contracts specifying less than eight hours per day and forty hours per week as normal. Gradual reduction of the work day and work week is a continuing objective of union policy.[36]

Premium pay for overtime hours is universal in collective bargaining. Premium or penalty rates exhibit considerable variety. The most common is still time-and-one-half the regular hourly rate for hours in excess of the normal work day, or in excess of the work week norm. Many contracts call for going to double time after an employee has worked more than four hours of overtime in any one day. Also, double time for Saturday and Sunday work as such has become a common contract requirement.[37]

The pattern of overtime compensation is fairly complete in most unionized industries. Those unions with contracts providing for only time-and-a-half can be expected to push for double time for ordinary overtime and for triple time on holidays worked.

OVERTIME AND THE SHORTER WORK WEEK

Discussion of premium pay for overtime leads logically into the trend toward shorter work days and work weeks. It should be noted that the actual implementation of all nonconventional working schedules has fallen short of our previous expectations. It is difficult to shorten the work week and maintain productive levels. Unions are thus faced with two alternatives: (1) more leisure time per week and lower incomes, or (2) maintaining the traditional work week and bargain for higher wages.

The latter alternative continues to be their preferred choice. The length of the work day and work week are invariant in most industries. The length of the work year, however, is another matter. Clearly, the leisure-income

36. *Ibid.*, p. 57:1.
37. *Ibid.*, p. 57:2.

tradeoff is not as rigid when time off without loss of pay is negotiated in terms of annual hours.

Some unions are interested in allocating increasing amounts of the compensation package to paid leisure time off. As noted above, specific firms have made substantial concessions in the number of paid days off per year. With regard to the UAW contract cited above, former UAW President Leonard Woodcock described the 3 percent annual time-off gain as "the first step toward the shortening of the work week below forty hours."[38]

Although the four-day, forty-hour work week was widely touted during the early 1970s as a means of improving morale, reducing absenteeism, and increasing productivity, it has not gained widespread adoption. Some studies indicate that the short-run gains attributed to conversion to a compressed work week are not lasting.[39] However, as energy costs continue to spiral, the four-day, forty-hour work week becomes an increasingly attractive alternative. Both heating and commuting costs would be lowered by compressing the hours of work per week into fewer days. The energy shortage may provide the catalyst for changing the work week at a savings to both management and employees.

FRINGE BENEFITS AND MANDATORY OVERTIME

Trends toward more indirect forms of pay have created strong employer incentives to use overtime by established employees rather than to hire additional employees. This has resulted in one of the more intractable and emotional bargaining issues today—the issue of mandatory overtime. On one side of the issue are employers who prefer overtime (for reasons we will explain shortly), and on the other side are union members who prefer leisure time and discretion in the work–leisure choice, and who figure the higher marginal income tax rates reduce much of the pay premium (such as time-and-a-half) for overtime work. Mandatory overtime insures that an employer will be able to expand hours of work to meet potentially temporary increases in product demand.

Without fringe benefits, an employer would weigh the cost of hiring an extra employee (recruiting, selecting, and training costs) against the cost of overtime pay. If the demand is very short term, overtime is preferred. If the demand is longer term, new employment is preferred. Fringe benefits

38. "Slowing the Declining of the Auto Work Force," *Business Week*, October 25, 1976.

39. J. M. Ivancevich and H. L. Lyon, "The Shortened Workweek: A Field Experiment," *Journal of Applied Psychology*, 62 (1977), 34–37; and Herbert C. Morton, "Quality of Life in Work," in Dale Yoder and Herbert G. Heneman, Jr., eds., *ASPA Handbook of Personnel and Industrial Relation*, 6 (Washington, D.C.: BNA, 1977), 115.

tend to shift the weight of the employer preference toward overtime even during longer term demand increases.

Fringe benefits shift employer preference toward overtime for two general reasons. First, the cost of laying off an employee is larger. Severance pay, SUB plans, and unemployment compensation (which most employers end up paying) increase the cost of temporarily adding new employees. On the other hand, when overtime work is no longer needed, employees can return to the regular schedule without any employer layoff cost. Second, many of the fringe benefits are paid, irrespective of the number of hours worked. Thus, overtime work does not require any additional health insurance, life insurance, holiday pay, and vacation pay. Overtime may not increase the pension contribution. On the other hand, hiring an additional employee means additional health and life insurance, paid days off, and pension contributions for the employer. In some employment contracts it is nearly to the point where it is less expensive for the employer to pay time-and-a-half to established employees, rather than to pay a new employee straight time plus fringe benefits.

The issue of mandatory overtime illustrates two points that are typical in collective bargaining. First, the positions of both sides are reasonable, but not easily reconciled. It is reasonable for the employer to want the right to require overtime; this is often the least costly and most efficient way to meet production objectives. It is reasonable for employees to want leisure time, especially when the work week reaches fifty-five or sixty hours. It is reasonable for the union to want fewer overtime hours if some members are currently unemployed. The challenge to collective bargaining is to compromise two reasonable, but conflicting, objectives. Second, changes in one area of the employment contract (such as fringe payments) often result in problems in other areas of the employment contract (such as mandatory overtime). The challenge to collective bargaining is to systematically reconcile the entire employment contract.

SEVERANCE PAY PROVISIONS

No employee likes to be laid off, even for short periods of time. However, a layoff with anticipated return to work when production picks up is not particularly traumatic. In many bargaining relationships, the worker with some seniority often has the protection of SUB or the option of going to a lower-rated assignment elsewhere in the plant if bumped out of his own department or seniority unit. Unemployment compensation is another boon to temporary layoff.

Permanent displacement is another matter. Such job loss can result from technological displacement, from financial failure of the firm, or from structural or locational changes in the industry. Any of these circumstances can result in the total disappearance of work opportunities. Another common cause in recent years has been the merger of firms with net employment losses in one or both entities. The shock factor and the economic deprivation for the displaced employee are severe under the best of circumstances. Nearly all unions, therefore, seek to negotiate the best severance pay provisions they can. The problems necessitating severance pay have been treated elsewhere in this volume, notably in Chapter 10, in recognition of the primary importance of the job security problem.

In former years, some employers sought to argue against severance pay allowances, on the basis that the displaced worker had already been justly paid for all his working time and thus was not entitled to any additional payments. Such thinking is outmoded, seldom heard in unionized relationships. There is widespread agreement that a permanently displaced, satisfactory employee should have a contractual right to a lump-sum payment, with the amount geared to the worker's prior years of service. Long-service employees are often eligible for a year's (or more) pay when permanently displaced.

In 1965, according to a BLS survey, about 30 percent of major union contracts contained some sort of severance pay or layoff benefit provision.[40] A recent BNA survey found that in 1978 the number of major contracts specifying severance pay had increased to 37 percent.[41]

The increase in severance pay provisions may reflect the growing concern expressed by employees over job security. By installing severance pay provisions in labor agreements, the cost of utilizing labor-displacing technology and closing a plant increases. At the margin, an employer is less inclined to remove the variable labor costs if by so doing he then incurs the costs attributed to severance pay.

It would be surprising if the number of contracts providing for severance pay did not continue to increase. Plant closings, mergers, and multiple instances of labor-displacing technological changes will continue to mount during the 1980s as basic industries, like auto and steel, continue their reindustrialization process and as industry continues its southward migration. Any and all of these factors will lead to permanent displacements and, hence, to worker pressures for severance protection. To augment this trend, organized labor will continue to lobby for national and state laws requiring union notification prior to plant closings. In the meantime, several unions have recently succeeded in negotiating such "early warning" clauses in their labor contracts.

---

40. Bureau of Labor Statistics, U.S. Department of Labor, *Severance Pay and Layoff Benefit Plan* (Washington, D.C.: Government Printing Office, 1965), Bulletin 1425–2.
41. Bureau of National Affairs, 2 (1978), 53:1.

NEW FRONTIERS IN FRINGE BENEFITS

The relative cost of fringe compensation has been steadily increasing over the last two decades. Furthermore, the staggering pace of fringe thickening seems to be continuing. Unions generally consider that they have an important institutional stake in maintaining and improving an already impressive pattern of supplemental wage payments.

Some union leaders feel that the compensation package in the form of wages and time off from work has reached a plateau. Interest in bargaining solely for incremental increases in vacations and salaries is shifting toward an emphasis on a comprehensive income guarantee. Recent innovative benefit packages exemplify this goal of many unions to create a lifetime security program.

The Ford–UAW 1977–79 contract includes hearing aid coverage providing audiometric examinations and hearing aid evaluations every thirty-six months. The contract also contains comprehensive eye care plans providing biennial eye exams and eyeglass discounts whereby the company covers 80 percent of the expense. In addition, dental care and psychiatric coverage, plus health care during periods of layoff, were all increased.

In the 1976–78 contract between American Airlines and the Transport Workers, health care coverage was extended to provide for unique medical operations such as vasectomies, tubal ligations, and abortions. Unions recognize social illnesses, as demonstrated by the increasing prevalence of alcohol- and drug-related treatment programs in their contracts. Many contracts now provide for tuition refunds for vocational, secondary, or college education, some up to $900 per year. AT&T and the Communication Workers of America agreed for the first time in 1977 to regard pregnancy as a disability.

How far have fringes come? In 1977, the UAW and Ford provided for the so-called benefit plan representative. These full-time UAW representatives function as employee advisor and employee–management liaison by helping workers with problems that may arise in administering the agreement's complex and multifaceted benefit programs. These representatives are selected by the UAW and paid out of foregone employee wages filtered through Ford's payroll.

SUMMARY

Fringe costs have already been stressed. It would seem appropriate to conclude that the feasible limit of nonwage economic benefits of one kind or another has been reached, if not exceeded, in many bargaining relationships. This is simply not the case. A review of successive contract negotiations in a number of different industries shows no well-defined objective or pattern of optimal mix of wages and economic fringes. We must conclude that there is none, save what the employer and union agree upon, and that the ratio of wages to economic fringes will continue to shrink.

To the employer, labor cost is labor cost. He has a constant incentive to keep his unit labor costs manageable. However, he is frequently indifferent as to whether the cost is attributable to wages or to some other economic payment to his employees. An exception to this would be in the case of those fringes that give shelter from taxes.

If the employer's relative indifference as between wages and fringes is assumed and if we further assume that there is a finite limit soon to be reached on many economic fringes, the ultimate decision as to what constitutes an optimal combination must rest with the employee. There are few signs today that employees have well-defined views on the best possible blend.

Perhaps it is not too much to expect that in the 1980s there will be an increasing disposition to take stock of the complex of wages and fringes with a view to developing a more logical rationalization than simply "more." One promising avenue for such a development is to establish individual employee accounts covering amounts going into the net economic security fringes. The employee can then apportion the fringe dollar sums available for personal use and deposit them into a personalized account.

Implementing this idea of individual employee decision making on how and when to use funds accumulated in a personal security benefit account will require employee education and a great deal of contractual revision. The latter would happily be in the direction of simplification. The economic security portions of the total package currently require as many or more contract pages in most cases as the basic agreement itself. Going to a system of individual employee accounts could reduce drastically the complex, detailed verbiage now essential in most negotiated economic security programs.

Promoting employee responsibility for managing personalized economic security funds has the distinct merit of being in line with the theme of restraint and responsibility on wage negotiation that was leaned on so heavily in the preceding chapter. Our judgment is that the advantages of going to such a system far outweigh the disadvantages.

The economics and the frequency of wage and fringe benefit negotiations tends to elevate the importance of these subjects relative to other subjects which are also central to the bargaining relationship. The importance of job security, discipline, and dismissal issues to the labor and management relationship should not be dismissed. Thus, these topics are considered in the next chapter.

Questions for Discussion, Thought, and Research

1. Why is the 1973 Health Maintenance Organization Act important to the institution of collective bargaining? What forces led Congress to pass the act?

2. What is meant by the term *vesting*? Are there any vesting requirements under ERISA? Explain.

3. What are the three schedules for vesting under ERISA?

4. What is the difference between a defined benefit plan and a defined contribution plan? What are the advantages and disadvantages of each?

5. What factors led to the enactment of ERISA? Does the complexity of ERISA preclude intelligent bargaining by both sides in negotiations?

6. From a union's perspective, what are some of the most important issues concerning raising the mandatory retirement age?

7. Should an employer be compelled to make cost-of-living adjustments for pensioners, even though these people no longer work for the company?

8. What are the current trends in H-and-W negotiated benefits?

9. Why are some large firms starting their own HMOs? Is this trend likely to continue in the future?

10. Why have unions in the auto industry been successful in obtaining substantial SUB benefits, while these benefits are not found in other segments of the economy?

11. What is tier bargaining? What factors gave rise to the practice of tiering benefits?

12. What are the pros and cons of mandatory overtime?

Selected Bibliography

Ehrenberg, Ronald G., *Fringe Benefits and Overtime Behavior*. Lexington, Mass.: Heath, 1971.

Garbarino, Joseph W., *Health Plans and Collective Bargaining*. Berkeley and Los Angeles: University of California Press, 1960.

———, "Fringe Benefits and Overtime as Barriers to Expanding Employment," *Industrial and Labor Relations Review*, 18 (April 1964), 426–42.

Hetherington, R. W. et al., *Health Insurance Plans*. New York: Wiley, 1975.

Levin, N. A., *ERISA and Labor–Management Benefit Funds*. New York: Practising Law Institute, 1975.

Mamorsky, J. D., "Impact of the 1978 ADEA Amendments on Employee Benefit Plans," *Employee Relations Law Journal*, 4 (1978), 173–84.

National Commission of State Workmen's Compensation Laws, *Report of the National Commission of State Workmen's Compensation Laws*. Washington, D.C.: Government Printing Office, 1972.

President's Commission on Pension Policy, *President's Commission of Pension Policy, An Interim Report*. Washington, D.C.: Government Printing Office, 1980.

Prussin, Jeffery A., *Employee Health Benefits: HMO's and Mandatory Dual Choice*. Washington, D.C.: Aspen Systems Corporation, 1976.

Schulz, J. H., T. D. Leavitt, and L. Kelly, "Private Pensions Fall Short of Preretirement Income Levels," *Monthly Labor Review*, 102, No. 2 (1979), 28–32.

Skolnik, Jeffrey A., "Twenty-Five Years of Employee Benefit Plans," *Social Security Bulletin*, 39 (September 1976), 3–21.

Slichter, Sumner H., James J. Healy, and Robert Livernash, *The Impact of Collective Bargaining on Management*. Washington, D.C.: Brookings Institute, 1960.

Turnbull, John G., C. Arthur Williams, Jr., and Earl F. Cheit, *Economic and Social Security*, 4th ed., (New York: Ronald Press), 1973.

JOB SECURITY AND INDUSTRIAL JURISPRUDENCE

12

Job security has many faces. We shall examine such familiar aspects as seniority and protection against arbitrary discipline. We shall also consider both old and relatively new approaches to the perennial problem of adjusting to technological change.

The challenge to the bargainers is often a complex one. Employee job security requirements need to be related to a constantly changing work environment. Job content changes. Work locations and job assignments may need to be shifted frequently in response to management needs. The structure and location of the employer's operations can change in dramatic fashion. All these developments have a direct impact on the job security objectives of unions in collective bargaining. In short, job security as a policy objective is never a simple or a one-time thing. The problem concerns a complex, ever changing set of multipurpose targets. Achieving mutually satisfactory, workable contract provisions is thus a demanding task for both management and union representatives.

CONTROL OF JOB OPPORTUNITIES

In his pioneering theory of the labor movement, Selig Perlman introduced the concept of "job ownership."[1] He maintained that union policy was guided by an underlying assumption of job scarcity. "If . . . opportunity is believed to be limited, it then becomes the duty of the group to prevent the individual from appropriating more than his rightful share, while at the same time protecting him against oppressive bargains. The group then asserts its collective ownership over the whole amount of opportunity."[2] This statement implies that jobs are perceived not as *tasks*, but as a *share* in a common economic property which can be protected only through group solidarity.

Union efforts to conserve job opportunities are concentrated on controlling one side of the employment process or other. Craft unions generally seek to control the supply of labor and thus limit employer discretion in hiring. The industrial union seeks to negotiate a variety of on-the-job conditions that promote employee security and protect against layoff, arbitrary discipline, or firing.

The basic job security objective must be to reach an accommodation between the employer's interest in maintaining an efficient operation and the worker's interest in job security. Such an accommodation is often hard to achieve, especially when fairly rapid changes in structure and composition of available jobs are required. Honoring management's requirement to operate and maintain an efficient operation, plus the employee's entitlement to contractual protection of bargaining unit work, is the basis for short-run conflict.

JOB SECURITY AND INDUSTRIAL JURISPRUDENCE

A useful way to position the job security problem in its proper context is to do so in terms of "industrial jurisprudence," a term introduced in 1941 by the late Sumner H. Slichter.[3] In Slichter's usage, *industrial jurisprudence* embraced many nonwage aspects of collective bargaining, including (1) control of entrance to the trade, (2) seniority as a vehicle for regulating layoffs, promotions, and transfers, (3) negotiated controls on worker

1. Selig Perlman, *A Theory of the Labor Movement* (New York: Kelley, 1970), p. 242.
2. *Ibid.*
3. Sumner H. Slichter, *Union Policies and Industrial Management* (Washington, D.C.: Brookings Institute, 1941).

output and job assignments, and (4) negotiated provisions concerning methods of wage payment. Also embraced by Slichter's conception was the basic problem of utilizing collective bargaining as a vehicle for adjusting to the impact of technological change.

Finally, and perhaps of greatest importance, Slichter contemplated industrial jurisprudence as using collective bargaining to protect employees against arbitrary discipline or treatment on the job.

In company with most if not all students of labor relations, we consider the function of collective bargaining in establishing a system of industrial jurisprudence as of greater meaning and value to the individual employee than the more familiar function of negotiating the price of labor and various economic fringe benefits.

The individual worker is always concerned about the size of his pay envelope. However, he has a keen interest in being protected against arbitrary discipline or treatment. He wants his union to protect his job security to the fullest possible extent. Many workers may not recognize the term industrial jurisprudence, but they are insistent that their union succeed in achieving the twin objectives of such a system: job security and protection against arbitrary treatment.

ESSENTIAL ELEMENTS OF EFFECTIVE INDUSTRIAL JURISPRUDENCE

The key concepts in an effective system of industrial jurisprudence are (1) uniformity, (2) consistency, (3) fairness, and (4) predictability. The basic aim of the negotiators is to fashion policies and procedures governing on-the-job relationships so that each employee covered by the contract will know exactly where he stands in relation to his fellow employees. He will also have assurance in the knowledge that he will be treated in the same manner as all other employees in like circumstances. In short, the essence of industrial jurisprudence lies in uniform written policies and procedures, applied in a consistent, nondiscriminatory fashion.

To put it another way, under an effective system of industrial jurisprudence the contract provides intelligible, consistent rules of the game on such matters as employee discipline, layoffs, recalls, promotions, transfers, distribution of overtime opportunities, methods of wage payment, and so on. For each subject covered there is one policy only. The antithesis of industrial jurisprudence would be two (or more) standards on the same subject. Contract ambiguity and uncertainty are foreign to the spirit of industrial jurisprudence.

THE DISCIPLINE FUNCTION
AND INDUSTRIAL JURISPRUDENCE

The classic illustration of industrial jurisprudence in action concerns the exercise of the managerial right to discipline employees in accordance with principles and procedures spelled out in the contract. Guarantees of fair treatment by supervision and protection against arbitrary managerial actions are basic to the concept of democratized industrial relations.

The right to fire (or to administer lesser penalties in the form of a disciplinary layoff or written warning) is traditionally a management prerogative. Most collective agreements recognize this, although a few require union consent to disciplinary action. However, exercise of the disciplinary prerogative is manifestly one that must be subject to check and challenge if employee rights and personal dignity are to have meaning. Prior to unionization, discharged workers had no effective recourse from arbitrary action by line foremen or top supervision. The need to ensure against such wrongful exercise of the discipline function has been in many instances more compelling as a motive for unionization than purely economic factors.

Most collective agreements limit management's right to discipline. Nearly 90 percent of union contracts specify that grounds for discharge must be only for "cause" or "just cause" or discharge for specific offenses.[4] With respect to the latter, an effort is made to spell out the various offenses calling for discipline and to distinguish between the more serious ones calling for immediate discharge and lesser violations calling for disciplinary layoff or warning. Most contracts, however, state the general principle governing all discipline matters, leaving application on a case-by-case basis. This approach is preferable because it recognizes the fact that no two disciplinary cases are alike. No two sets of facts are identical any more than any two individuals are the same or likely to behave in precisely the same fashion.

The severity of a particular offense often depends on the circumstances. For example, smoking on the job calls for immediate discharge in a chemical plant or an oil refinery, but it may be only a minor offense in a plant where there is no appreciable danger from fire or explosion. Certain types of employee conduct are regarded as proper grounds for discharge in almost all situations the first time they occur. These include such breaches of conduct as fighting on the job, stealing company property, malicious destruction of company property, direct insubordination to supervision, instigating a wildcat strike, and so on. On the other hand, discharge for

4. Bureau of National Affairs, *Collective Bargaining Negotiations and Contracts,* 2 (1979), 40:1.

such offenses as chronic absenteeism, unsatisfactory work performance, or persistent inability to meet accepted production norms should be preceded by cumulative corrective discipline with clear notice that discharge will be the ultimate consequence of failure to improve performance.

Fair treatment by supervision is one factor that shows up high on any worker's listing of the requisites of a "good job." Many management disciplinary actions are protested by workers who assert that they are "not guilty" of the offense with which they are charged or who consider the penalty to be excessively harsh. No worker likes to have a disciplinary penalty on his personnel record. It may jeopardize his chances for advancement. Also, if he is discharged, it is hard to find other employment even in a fairly tight labor market. For these reasons, discipline grievances will make up a substantial part of the caseload. While reliable figures are not available, it is generally thought that about one out of four arbitration cases involves a discipline issue.

Discipline grievances are troublesome and often explosive. However, any employer and union should be able to develop policies and procedures that will safeguard management's interest in maintaining an efficient and orderly establishment and the union's interest in insuring that no worker is disciplined arbitrarily or without cause.

From time to time, complaints are heard that under union contracts employers have been deprived of their power to discipline workers. Some employers are allegedly afraid to discharge employees because they fear they might incur reprisals, such as a wildcat protest stoppage. If such an unfortunate condition exists in any enterprise, the blame can fairly be placed on management's doorstep for not exercising its contractual right to discipline, including discharge, for "good and just cause." There is no valid reason why a good faith employer should abstain from disciplining employees in a fair and nondiscriminatory manner.

Of course, the employer must be prepared to discipline. Some local union leaders will not press a grievance over discipline to arbitration if the employer's evidence and/or their investigation of the case satisfies them that the employee merited the discipline imposed. Others, however, will carry most, if not all, discharge cases to arbitration, even where they may think the employer has a good case. Their reasoning may be that a discharged employee is always entitled to full contractual due process, or that as a political entity there is a risk in not arbitrating all cases.

In any event, any employer who for any reason gives up on disciplining employees has only himself to blame for results which are bound to be unfortunate. Most employers do not share in the view that they are deprived of their power to discipline because of collective bargaining.

DIFFICULT TYPES OF DISCHARGE CASES

Possibly the most troublesome type of discharge case is one where management concludes that the employee's performance has been so unsatisfactory as to require firing. Discharge for this reason is often resisted strenuously, especially when alternative employment opportunities are scarce. The union contends typically that management had ample opportunity to gauge the employee during his probationary period. Once past this period, with seniority acquired, in the union view, the worker has developed an equity in his job akin to a property right. Discharge should never be warranted except in the most extreme circumstances after failure to heed repeated warnings.

One can agree in principle that discharge, as the ultimate disciplinary sanction, should be resorted to only when all efforts to rehabilitate the deficient employee have proved unsuccessful. At the same time, the employer needs authority to insure and maintain an efficient operation. In matters of discipline and discharge, the employer's prerogative to take action for "just cause" must be preserved.

Subject to reasonable standards sufficient to protect workers who are doing a conscientious but uninspired job, management should always be able to discharge chronically inefficient, lazy, or indifferent employees. When the reason for unsatisfactory performance is that the task is beyond the employee's abilities, he should be transferred to a less taxing assignment. This alternative is certainly preferable to discharge since discharge must be considered an admission of failure from a personnel standpoint.

The optimal approach requires searching out the root causes of poor performance and then removing these causes. When the unsatisfactory performance of the employee is shown to be a product of poor mental attitude, personal troubles outside the shop, or physical or mental deficiencies, responsible employers will make an effort through counseling to correct the condition. Discharging for poor performance has the effect of passing on the problem to another employer or to the community.

In arbitration of discipline cases two basic issues usually arise. First, did the company prove cause for the discipline? Second, did the punishment imposed fit the crime? A union will invariably challenge management discipline if it feels that the answer to either of these questions is negative.

IMPORTANCE OF SOUND PROCEDURES
IN DISCIPLINE CASES

An effective system of discipline requires the development of a uniform procedure for handling all cases where the employer believes that discipline or discharge is required. If the same procedure is used in each case, all employees know that they will be treated similarly with respect to due process and penalties. Such knowledge is important in preventing misunderstanding and reducing hostilities.

It is essential in any disciplinary investigation to discover the facts in the case at the earliest possible time before memories of the parties involved fade. One effective technique is to provide for a disciplinary action hearing within twenty-four hours after the incident that led to discipline. At such a hearing, the charged employee can state his case and call witnesses on his behalf. The supervisor calling for the discipline presents his evidence. Such an internal hearing is usually conducted by the head of the employer's labor relations department. The employee is represented by his union steward or the chairman of the local union's grievance committee. Written minutes are usually kept.

Under such a procedure, the formal decision on disciplinary action is made after this hearing. Up to this point, the employee is under suspension. He can be regarded, in a sense, as being under indictment by his supervisor. In some cases, the disciplinary action hearing record reveals that the employee was not at fault and no action against him is taken. Where management believes the evidence warrants discipline, the employee and his union representative are notified as to the reason for and content of the discipline. The employee and his union are then free to grieve the company's action as having been taken without just cause.

A procedure similar to the one described above has been in use for many years in the steel industry. This is exemplified by a paragraph in Section 8, "Suspension and Discharge Cases," from the 1980–83 U.S. Steel Corporation and Steelworkers contract.

> An employee shall not be peremptorily discharged. In all cases in which management may conclude that an employee's conduct may justify suspension or discharge, he shall be suspended initially for not more than 5 calendar days, and given written notice of such action. In all cases of discharge, or of suspension for any period of time, a copy of the discharge or suspension notice shall be promptly furnished to such employee's grievance committeeman.

DISCIPLINE CASES RAISING THE DISCRIMINATION ISSUE

The contractual difficulties associated with the employment of racial minorities, women, and older workers are real and complex. There is no question that race, sex, and age discrimination has long tainted employment relationships in this country. Statutes and agency rules and regulations have been adopted which aim at remedying this problem. Companies and unions either informally or through formal contractual language have also acted affirmatively to reverse discriminatory practices. These laws, rules, and contractual agreements, however, have neither completely clarified nor resolved the discrimination issue. While employment discrimination against protected classes is against the law, the matter of establishing practices to preferentially hire, train, or promote women and minorities is not resolved. The legal status of company–union affirmative action programs is still in question. Workers, typically white males, challenge the adoption of "reverse discrimination" policies and programs and unions are quick to challenge any idea which may place the "seniority principle" in jeopardy.[5]

There is no question that to adopt the goal of integration of the work force and of worker's opportunities is proper. Debate rages, however, as to the means society ought to follow in reaching this goal. Minorities, women, and the old have been short-changed for generations and their claim for immediate redress is valid. However, the objection raised by a traditionally favored class of white male workers that they ought not bear the cost of the discriminatory practices of earlier generations is not without merit.

The close positioning of the "public law" protecting the rights of minorities and women relative to the "private law" of the shop, which assigns rights to all employees in the unit thrusts collective bargaining in the center of the social tug-of-war over minority versus majority claims to jobs and the benefits from employment. This interface does not make it easy for management and labor to work toward the elimination of prohibited discriminatory practices at a local level. It was public enactments which triggered the impetus for local consideration and attempts at resolving the discrimination issue. Acting at the local level must continue. A "majority" union working toward an accelerated integration of the minority worker into the work force in concert with the employer can only advance the time at which industrial relations in this country are free of senseless discrimination.

Arbitrators are often faced with discharge and discipline cases in which the grievant is a minority or woman claiming that the employer's decision was motivated by discriminatory factors, and thus was a violation of the contract's nondiscrimination clause and a violation of civil rights. Cases of this type may go to arbitration because the union seeks to avoid the charge that it is failing in its duty of fair representation. If this happens and if the evidence fails to substantiate the discrimination charge (and establishes that the grievant was disciplined for just cause), the grievance will probably be denied by the arbitrator. Where this happens, however, the employer may feel vindicated but the grievant and his fellow minority or female workers may view the award as an example of "majority justice." Further, the union will get little credit for having carried the matter to

5. For a quick overview of affirmative action and reverse discrimination read the Bureau of National Affairs, *Labor Relations Yearbook—1979* (Washington, D.C., 1980), pp. 165–66.

arbitration and may be criticized for not having done a proper job of case preparation and presentation.

Turning the tables around, if the arbitrator finds discriminatory intent to have been the actuating factor, he will probably sustain the grievance. The employer that denied illicit discriminatory motivations will doubtless be outraged by the award and may charge the arbitrator with using a "double standard" to reach his decision.

The above possibilities are realistic, although hypothetical, since they are not based on actual cases. In work environments characterized by discriminating tension and suspicion, these cases will arise and there is no easy or painless end to such problems other than through eliminating the discriminatory practices and, hopefully, values.

For decades, arbitrators have dealt with discriminatory employers, and occasionally with manipulative employees. Real or fancied discrimination is not new to labor relations, however; what is new is that arbitrators are more astute and prepared to hear such cases than during earlier times. This perceived change may stem from the fact that following *Alexander* v. *Gardner-Denver Co.* it became clear that the arbitration award arising from a discrimination case is not necessarily *final*, that this subject has been well treated in contemporary labor relations journals read by arbitrators, and that it has only been within the past decade or so that civil rights have surfaced in the social consciousness to the point of changing behaviors —including that of the arbitrator.[6]

SENIORITY AS A MECHANISM FOR CONTROL OVER JOB OPPORTUNITIES

In many collective labor agreements the seniority article is the longest and most detailed, running as many as ten to twenty printed pages. In other contracts, seniority may occupy only a paragraph or so. Variety and diversity characterize seniority contract provisions. This is one subject in collective bargaining that requires custom tailoring to specific local conditions.[7] Seniority is a controlling or significant factor in determining the

6. In *Alexander* v. *Gardner-Denver Co.* (1974), the Supreme Court ruled that under Title VII of the Civil Rights Act an individual does not forfeit his private course of action against an employer through the courts if he first pursues his discrimination grievance to final and binding arbitration under the no-discrimination clause of a collective bargaining agreement. Note that discussion found in Marvin Hill, Jr., and Anthony V. Sinicropi's "Excluding Discrimination Analysis," *Arbitration Journal*, 33, No. 1 (March 1978), 16–20.

7. One of the best and most interesting ways for the reader to develop an understanding of the variety, complexity, and difficulty of seniority issues in contemporary bargaining is to read a number of recent arbitration decisions involving different industries and unions. Many seniority disputes going to arbitration have long histories as issues in labor relations but new applications arise constantly with different factual situations. Also, new contract language on an old topic may prove to be a source of controversy.

order of layoff and recall from layoff in many contracts. In every case, the governing principles and procedures must be articulated with care. Seniority also plays an important and sometimes decisive role in determining the filling of vacancies, access to overtime work, opportunities in ordering of interplant transfers, and other facets concerning the control, assignment, and direction of the work force.

Craft unions that control entrance to their trade use seniority as an internalized control within the union. Seniority is thus not an important bargaining matter for these unions. Most industrial unions, however, continue to place strong reliance on seniority provisions as a job control mechanism. They do so because the bargaining units represented by industrial unions typically contain a high proportion of semiskilled workers and a relatively small number of craft employees and unskilled. The union's "constituents" thus lack the economic power as individuals that attaches to possession of special skills. Most industrial workers are easily trained and easily replaced in a loose labor market. They frequently work at jobs whose content is defined in ways that minimize potential for differential performances based on human effort. The organization of many production operations is such that the output from the worker is machine paced or group paced. Job design affords little opportunity for recognition of individual differences in ability, attitude, or effort. In these circumstances, seniority (length of service) has a strong appeal to the individual worker as a mechanism for retaining employment during cutbacks or for securing advancement in the occupational hierarchy.

As a clear-cut, impersonal, objective yardstick, straight seniority also has considerable appeal for many employers as the basis for determining the order of layoff and recall from layoff. Within large bargaining units, in particular, seniority satisfies one of the essential requirements of an effective system of industrial jurisprudence—substitution of a uniform policy for managerial discretion, which can at times be arbitrary.

The sometimes conflicting goals of equal employment opportunity and seniority protection have received wide attention during the past decade. Government regulation of craft apprenticeship programs has represented an effort at redistributing job opportunities. But, as we have noted, the legality of affirmative action programs has not been fully established. This is certainly one aspect of job security which will continue to evolve in the 1980s.[8]

A number of other interest groups are also affected by seniority clauses and recent legislation. The Vocational Rehabilitation Act of 1973 has transformed the job rights of the physically disabled. The Vietnam Era Veterans Readjustment Act of 1972 led to a revision of veterans' job rights.

8. See Marvin J. Levine, "The Conflict Between Negotiated Seniority Provisions and Title VII of the Civil Rights Act of 1964: Recent Developments," *Labor Law Journal*, 29, No. 6 (June 1978), 352–63.

And the interests of older workers, at or near retirement age, have been substantially influenced by recent pension and age discrimination legislation. Each new act of labor legislation, and each new claim by interest groups for equal job rights, creates pressure on seniority job guarantees.[9]

EMPLOYER OPPOSITION TO STRAIGHT SENIORITY IN LAYOFF, RECALL, AND PROMOTION

Many employers continue to question the merit of length of service as the primary, if not sole, criterion governing layoffs and recalls. Employer opposition is stronger when unions seek to make seniority the governing factor in promotions. The employer thesis is that seniority places a premium on mediocrity, that it discourages initiative by making it impossible to recognize individual differences in ability and zeal, and, finally, that it hampers seriously management's need for flexibility in work assignments as dictated by the requirements of a changing job mix and a dynamic technology. In the eyes of such critics, seniority becomes a barrier to efficient operation of the enterprise.

How seniority affects employee efficiency continues to be a matter of serious debate in some bargaining relationships. Many employers consider seniority to be a prime factor in contributing to lower employee productivity and increased labor costs. On the other hand, defenders of seniority claim that it can contribute to increasing managerial efficiency by forcing employers to be more selective in their hiring and more thorough in their training programs. Seniority helps to lower costs by reducing labor turnover.[10] Some contend that improved employee morale flowing from enhanced job security has a positive effect on worker productivity. Proponents of seniority argue that any alleged losses that might flow from inability to recognize differences in individual abilities are more than offset by the elimination of grievances and resentment that invariably result from unfettered managerial discretion on layoffs, promotions, recalls, and transfers. Finally, if there is a learning curve associated with job performance, seniority will be highly correlated with performance. In this case seniority is not only an indicator of performance, but easily administered and devoid of discriminatory intent.

The argument over the vices and virtues of seniority varies in scope and intensity from one relationship to another, but the union pressure for

9. For a brief statement previewing the future for age and handicapped worker description, see *Labor Relations Yearbook—1979*, pp. 185–86.

10. For a study linking union seniority clauses to reduced turnover, see Richard N. Block, "The Impact of Seniority Provisions on Manufacturing Quit Rates," *Industrial and Labor Relations Review*, 31 (July 1978), 474–88.

retention of seniority restrictions continues. Many employers have reconciled themselves to utilizing seniority as the main governing criterion in connection with layoffs and recalls, particularly if in negotiating some flexibility and discretion for themselves to retain some key employees without regard to seniority and to avoid the phenomenon of multiple or chain bumping.

SENIORITY AND THE MANAGERIAL DRIVE FOR EFFICIENT PRODUCTION

Employers find they can live with seniority if they can negotiate certain essential qualifications on the undiluted or straight seniority application. One employer-oriented provision, for example, aims at avoiding training in connection with a layoff. An employee who wishes to exercise his seniority to bump another must always be able to do the latter's job without training.

When a layoff is necessary, any employer has an understandable desire to minimize the number of job switches and assignment changes. How successful the employer is in attaining such an objective depends in great measure on how the contract's seniority article reads. Does it provide for straight seniority with no deviations on a plant-wide basis? If so, the employer's objective cannot be achieved. The employer therefore usually tries to define seniority units in fairly narrow terms based on occupational categories or clusters of related jobs. If the working force is clearly and neatly departmentalized, it may suit the employer's objective to define seniority along departmental lines. Whatever the situation, most employers seek to assure minimal movement whenever the impact of a layoff removes X as the most junior man in his seniority unit. If X then wishes to "go plant-wide," he is often restricted by the contract to bumping the most junior (least senior) employee whose work he is qualified to perform, if he wishes to remain at work rather than taking the layoff. The sequence of chain or multiple bumping is thus successfully avoided.

How the parties handle the many difficult pragmatic questions posed by seniority is a most crucial factor in determining the overall character of the employer–union relationship. The potential is great for constructive cooperation, on the one hand, or for destructive friction and antagonism, on the other. Over the years many employers and unions have been able to work out contract provisions that reflect a workable compromise between the union's interest in protecting the job security of long-service employees and the employer's interest in maintaining an efficient work force under all conditions. Doing so necessarily involves negotiating some departures from the straight seniority application, as indicated above.

Maintaining the viability of a negotiated compromise between efficiency considerations and protected seniority is a constantly evolving responsibility whenever the technology is a dynamic one and the work force mix thus changes over fairly short spans of time. Many employers could use to advantage more flexibility than their contracts currently permit on such matters as intrafirm transfers and shifts in job assignments. How to negotiate the desired flexibility into the contract is one of the more important challenges currently facing many bargainers. To some extent, the "income security benefit plans" discussed in Chapter 11 as developed in the steel, rubber, auto, maritime, and garment wear industries is a compromise designed for the benefit of senior employees facing technological (broadly speaking) displacement.

The future impact of technology is never easy to anticipate. The employer requires some degree of freedom in manipulating the work force, retraining incumbents as necessary, and transferring those whose jobs have been drastically changed or eliminated. Seniority provisions negotiated for a former job mix frequently need to be revised if the transition is to be reasonably smooth and efficient. Further reference will be made to seniority as related to technological change in the concluding section of this chapter.

SENIORITY AND PROMOTIONAL POLICY

Most employers appear to have adjusted to seniority as the criterion governing the ordering of layoffs and recalls, particularly if they have secured contract language giving assurance that they will have qualified personnel manning the available jobs at all times. Few employers, however, are sympathetic to union contentions that length of service should be the determining factor in promotions. This is a policy area where employers generally prefer full discretion to choose among applicants for vacancies on the basis of ability. In the eyes of management, ability is more relevant than comparative length of service.[11]

Management and union thinking on promotional policy remains in conflict in a considerable number of bargaining relationships. We know of situations where a policy evolution has taken place from contractual silence (full employer discretion) to conclusive preference for the senior applicant when qualified. This latter provision has been extended to provide a trial on the job for the senior applicant held not qualified by management in the

11. Among contracts monitored by the Bureau of National Affairs, only 9 percent call for promotions on the basis of seniority alone. Thirty-three percent call for promotion of the most senior individual, provided he is qualified for the open job. Three percent of the contracts analyzed give seniority equal consideration along with other factors, and 22 percent treat seniority as determining who will be promoted if the competing employees are equal in regard to other factors. In total, seniority is assigned some role in determining promotions in 67 percent of the contracts studied. (See Bureau of National Affairs, 2 [1978], 75:2.)

initial review of applications. Management still retains authority to determine what qualifications are needed to fill any vacancy. It also exercises administrative initiative in determining which applicants are qualified and which are not qualified.

In many bargaining relationships, however, the parties still operate with provisions stating in substance that the promotion will go to the senior applicant if relative ability and fitness are equal or relatively equal. Such a policy appears to give management considerable discretion in selection, but real difficulties and conflicts can arise in particular cases over whether employees X and Y are in fact equal or relatively equal in ability and fitness.[12]

The importance of length of service as a promotional criterion is not a matter on which a scientific judgment can be made. It is an area of continuing disagreement between employer and union over what an optimal policy should be. The weight accorded to length of service in particular contracts appears to depend principally on how strongly the parties hold their contrasting viewpoints. If the contract remains silent on promotional policy, this usually indicates that the union has not seen fit to make seniority a prime negotiation demand, although such a demand is clearly within the scope of mandatory bargaining. Frequently, the contract reflects a negotiated compromise of two polarized views. In many cases, employer and union are continuing to operate with the familiar provision that calls for seniority to govern where abilities of applicants are deemed to be equal or relatively equal.

Putting to one side for the moment the issue of the contractual restriction of management discretion and speaking solely in terms of sound principles of personnel administration, one can find many organizations that rely on a promotion-from-within policy as a general rule. Furthermore, when it is recalled that only slightly more skill and responsibility is required to move up successfully in most lines of job progression, the traditional objections to seniority as a promotional yardstick lose much of their force. This is especially the case where management has assured itself the right to determine which applicants are qualified. Under those circumstances where management has ruled the senior applicants to be not qualified either before or subsequent to a trial on the job, such a discretionary determination by management should not be open to suc-

12. The reader can appreciate how troublesome disputes can arise on issues of relative or equal ability and fitness for performing higher-rated jobs. When such cases go to arbitration, the union is often undertaking a difficult and thankless task. It must show that the employer's judgment was faulty, arbitrary, or discriminatory—a difficult burden to maintain. The task is thankless because if the union "wins" the case it makes the grievant happy, but only at the cost of making unhappy the employee who received the promotion originally.

For a perceptive analysis of criteria used for measuring ability, see Thomas J. McDermott, "Types of Seniority Provisions and the Measurement of Ability," *Arbitration Journal*, 25 (Summer 1970), 101–24.

cessful challenge unless it can be shown that the decision was arbitrary, capricious, or discriminatory—a difficult burden to maintain.

SENIORITY AND INTERPLANT TRANSFERS

Seniority is properly cited as a good example of a bargaining issue that should be a "local item" in negotiation of a master contract between union X and employer Y with several plants in different locations. Differing job mixes from one plant to another frequently require that seniority arrangements be tailor made for particular locations. It is difficult in a master agreement to provide a set of principles and procedures that would fit the variety of local circumstances.

One of the more thorny seniority problems facing multiplant firms is how to provide for interplant transfers of employees displaced at their original location by a shutdown of the facility or by technological change. The job security objectives of most unions require that some consideration be given to providing transfer rights under such circumstances. Many difficult questions arise. How shall such employees be rated in seniority terms in their new locations? Must they be regarded as new employees when transferring in or shall they carry with them some, or even all, of their seniority at their former location? An optimal solution is not possible because gains to one group of employees are regarded as losses or infringements by another. Merging of seniority lists in any situation is invariably a headache for all concerned.

The transfer rights problem underlines an important attribute of seniority not mentioned up to this point. Seniority is acquired only by contract. It can be retained only by contractual agreement and not by inherent right. Thus, the very possibility of a transfer of an employee displaced at one plant to a job at another facility of the employer is contingent entirely upon what the master contract (multiplant) agreement provides. If we are talking about two different contracts, there is no way in which seniority rights acquired under one contract can be "imported" into the second and separate contract. Only when the same contract governs both plants does the possibility arise of an employee taking himself, together with some of his former seniority, to the new location.

Job security is a worrisome problem for employees working for a multiplant employer in a technologically dynamic industry. In the meatpacking industry, for example, a complete metamorphosis has taken place. Relative to earlier years, today's plants are smaller, highly automated, and specialized, and they are increasingly being located in small midwestern towns rather than in large urban centers. Seeing these changes on the horizon, the packinghouse unions began negotiating interplant transfer rights back in the early 1960s as a means of providing job security to senior workers who were displaced for either locational or technical reasons.[13] Today in the auto industry a similar phenomenon is observed. In the current agreement between General Motors and the UAW, there is an "Establishment of New Plants" provision which gives preferential hiring status to laid-off employees and to active employees, in the event a major operation is transferred, provided seniority rights have been earned.[14] This language materialized as the giant auto manufacturer has pursued a strategy of building new plants in locations south of the Mason–Dixon line. It is difficult to measure the effectiveness of interplant transfer rights as a means of calming job security worries.

SENIORITY AS A RESTRICTIVE INFLUENCE ON INTERNAL FLEXIBILITY IN JOB ASSIGNMENTS

Many employers claim to be hampered by the restrictive impact of contractual seniority provisions on internal transfer and reassignment of employees to meet changing production needs and job requirements. They emphasize their inability to stay effectively competitive under modern conditions when faced by a restrictive web of seniority entanglements that solidify employee positions within the plant and inhibit free transfers from one job to another. Such employers seek a condition characteristic of many small firms or job shops, where the work at hand gets priority without regard to particular job classifications. In this view, the new technology has served to outmode established job classification lines and underlined the need for greater freedom of worker movement from one category to another or one type of assignment to another.

We shall not treat the merits of this particular perspective. The nature and dimensions of the problem vary markedly from one industry to another. In our view, greater progress could be made in labor relations and contract administration if we shifted our focus on the seniority of the worker to his trainability or retrainability. Some years ago Neil W. Chamberlain put the emphasis where it belongs. He emphasized that the worker's only true security in a dynamic economy lies in the provision of continuing vocational education on a scale much more ambitious than we have yet attained. Chamberlain noted the essentially short-run and static

13. For a general discussion of labor relations problems in meatpacking with considerable attention to the job security problem, see Harold W. Davey, "Present and Future Labor Relations Problems in the Meat Packing Industry," *Labor Law Journal*, 18 (December 1967), 739–51.

14. Bureau of National Affairs, *Collective Bargaining Negotiations and Contracts*, 1 (1980), 21:30.

quality of seniority in underlining its shortcomings as an instrument for achieving genuine security in an age of rapidly evolving technology and changing product lines.[15] The ultimate goal must be that of provision for continual upgrading of a worker's skills over his productive lifetime. This will require a combination effort by the private sector and government agencies.

COLLECTIVE BARGAINING AND TECHNOLOGICAL CHANGE

At least a volume would be needed for proper analysis of how collective bargaining has been and can be used to respond to the impact of technological change on bargaining unit personnel. In this section we shall hit only a few high spots, recognizing that we are giving short shrift to some truly difficult policy issues on this aspect of the job security problem.

In his pioneering study, cited earlier in this chapter, Sumner H. Slichter classified union policies toward technological change as being of three kinds: (1) obstruction, (2) competition, and (3) control. Even though this classification system and the results of Slichter's study are dated, we believe that his findings contain a lesson relevant in the 1980s. Slichter's empirical research dealt with bargaining practices of the 1920s and 1930s. He identified comparatively few unions with policies of outright obstruction of technological change or of competition with such change. Most unions have recognized the legitimacy of the employer's need to improve work methods and to develop more efficient operations, even when the net effect has been to change his factor mix in such a way as to reduce permanently his requirements for bargaining unit personnel. Nevertheless, nearly all unions, with varying degrees of tenacity, have sought and will continue to seek to control the manner and rates of introduction of technological change whenever such a change contributes to reduced manpower.

In some cases, such as coal mining, the union has chosen the route of aggressive economic bargaining while ignoring adverse effects on employment. As a result, mining has become extensively mechanized. Over the years, the productivity of the individual miner has been increasing in step with an increasing capital-to-labor ratio, and the demand for coal (until recently) has been less than buoyant. The result of this combination of circumstances has been a sharp decline in employment and in the membership of the United Mine Workers. The bargaining objective of the late John L. Lewis was to make the employed coal miner the highest paid

15. These thoughts by Professor Chamberlain were expressed at a Cornell University conference dealing with seniority issues in grievance arbitration held in New York City on April 15, 1965.

semiskilled worker in the world. Lewis viewed the resultant unemployment as a macroeconomic problem with which the union was not particularly concerned.

A different union stance toward the impact of technological change is illustrated in the building and construction field. Many craft unions associated with this industry have long pursued restrictionist policies in bargaining that blocked or retarded the introduction of new technological developments. These unions did not hesitate to use their strong market power to do so. Only fairly recently have the major unions in construction moved to modernize their bargaining policies to accommodate important technological developments. This tendency may be a response to the industry's growing nonunion segment, which is proving to be a serious competitive alternative to unionized operators, through the expansion of "double breasted" operations.[16]

By way of contrast, some unions, like the sheetmetal workers, are advancing the need for technological innovation. In this case, the union is currently pressing for the introduction of new solar energy systems in new construction and developments. This development, however, instead of threatening job security, promises to add jobs and work for sheet metal workers. The Pacific Coast Longshoremen provide still another category for discussion. This union made a fundamental shift from union restrictions to receptivity toward technological innovation.

The full story of the longshoring mechanization agreement of 1961 and subsequent developments is told in a carefully researched study by Paul T. Hartman.[17] The shipping industry has moved steadily into "containerization."[18] This trend means that still further "adjustments" will be required of the bargainers, an observation substantiated by the 1978 east and gulf coast longshoring strike over a continuing job security threat presented by the advance of containerization in the industry. Although longshoring is just one industry with some individual special twists, the Hartman study contains some valuable insights for nearly any employer and union endeavoring to cope effectively and equitably with the continuing problem of accommodating the employer's need to innovate with the incumbent employees' drive for job security.

In no case is such an accommodation an easy task. However, a giant step

---

16. Double-breasting occurs when a single contractor operates two distinct companies, one union and the other nonunion. For a discussion of this phenomenon, see Jim Burstein, "The Emerging Law of the 'Double Breasted' Operation in the Construction Industry," *Labor Law Journal*, 28, No. 2 (February 1977), 77–88.

17. Paul T. Hartman, *Collective Bargaining and Productivity: The Longshore Mechanization Agreement* (Berkeley: University of California Press, 1969).

18. The containers in question are large, rigid boxes filled by the shipper or terminal operator, ranging at present from five to twenty tons when loaded. They are handled throughout the journey from origin to point of destination with special equipment such as large gantry cranes or specially designed trucks or jitneys. Ships also have to be modified to the new requirements of container loading. The productivity gains are enormous in going from the old break-bulk approach to containerization. *Ibid.*, pp. 160–61.

toward adjustment has been taken with general management recognition that meeting job security needs must be held to be a proper cost of introducing technological change.

Negotiated approaches take many and diverse forms. However, those that appear to be working the best have the common characteristic of joint acknowledgment that incumbent employees (with varying levels of minimum seniority) should not be adversely affected by technological change, either as to employment or income, whenever it lies within the private capabilities of the parties to prevent such impact. As an example, the 1978 round of newspaper talks in Washington, D.C., and New York City were bogged down in the complexities of coping with technological change. Following lengthy strike actions, the new technology formulas agreed upon will lead to the introduction of labor-saving methods which will, through attrition, eventually cut back work crew sizes. Incumbent employees, however, are protected. We believe there is general recognition that a regular cost of introducing technological change will be carrying through the retraining or relocating of workers affected by the change or, in the alternative, providing "just" compensation to those workers who cannot be absorbed and must therefore be defined as "permanently displaced."

Practically speaking, there is a good deal of variation in the degree to which this principle can be honored operationally in particular situations. On the current scene, however, most employers conceded their obligation to cope with the problem as effectively as possible. Success is easier for employers whose market demand is such that they can expand rather than contract bargaining unit personnel, even while extensive technological change is being instituted. Substantial gains in labor productivity due to mechanization can be achieved under these happy circumstances with no serious employee job security or income security problems.

In many cases, the manpower adjustment problem will not be painless and friction-free. If manpower adjustments are likely to be severe, as in meatpacking, to name one example, employer and union bargainers face a continuing challenge. In meatpacking, the parties have apparently done their best as private negotiators in several successive agreements to cope effectively with the following fundamental question: How can we introduce X amount of Y type of technology change over the next contract period without affecting adversely job and income security of incumbent employees?

NEGOTIATED POLICIES FOR COPING WITH TECHNOLOGICAL UNEMPLOYMENT

Where unemployment is contemplated as a consequence of technological change, there are a variety of ways in which collective bargaining can be utilized to deal directly with such unpleasant prospects. These include the following:

1. Adjusting by attrition to reduced manpower needs by phasing in the new or changed technology gradually to conform to the normal employee turnover rate from quits, death, retirement, and so forth, with little or no new hiring.
2. Planned retraining of incumbent employees to fit into other jobs as their old positions are eliminated or phased out.
3. Permanent transfer of employees to other plants where their abilities can be fitted to job needs elsewhere in the employer's domain.
4. Early retirement plans to encourage voluntary reduction of the work force to accommodate reduced manpower requirements caused by technological change.
5. Severance pay plans with amounts related to employee's overall length of service or to his average income in years immediately preceding separation.
6. Work sharing which involves the distribution of fewer hours of work among the work force as an alternative to mass layoff.

Which one or which combination of the foregoing will be used must depend on the conditions in the particular employer–union relationship. In a surprisingly large number of situations, planned adjustment in terms of normal employee turnover (attrition) may prove to be sufficient alone to prevent any employee displacement. In other cases, however, there will be a need for a combination approach.

Direct joint efforts of this type are becoming a familiar component of bargaining in a wide range of relationships. Such straightforward approaches do not require extensive treatment because the goal and the rationale are clear, even though operational success may not be complete.

We must take notice, however, of a considerable number of normal or conventional union bargaining demands not visibly related to technological change but which are often intimately although indirectly related. We refer to such matters as subcontracting, premium pay clauses, working rules, and the like.

SUBCONTRACTING AND JOB OPPORTUNITIES

Nothing is more certain to arouse employee fear and suspicion than the news of an employer intention to subcontract work. If over a long period of years an employer has customarily subcontracted certain types of work not directly related to that performed by bargaining unit employees, no serious problem will arise. This is especially true when the subcontracted work is of such a nature that current bargaining unit employees do not have the knowhow to handle the work in any event.

Opposition will be generated, however, when the employer seeks to subcontract work currently performed by bargaining unit personnel or which could be performed by incumbent employees. Any actual or prospective diminution of bargaining unit work activity due to subcontracting is almost certain to be challenged by the union in question. The employer will argue typically that subcontracting is a managerial prerogative. He will urge further that the business of staying competitive requires him to get the work done in the most economical and efficient manner possible. When doing so requires him to farm out (that is, to subcontract) certain duties, he will maintain that his right to do so should not be restricted by union contract. The union response will typically be that the employer has no right to subcontract bargaining unit work for any reason, particularly when a reduction in work opportunities within the bargaining unit is the likely result. This whole matter is made increasingly more complex when one looks at the analogous problem of transferring work from one plant to another within the same corporate structure or, more interestingly, when work is transferred from one nation to another within a multinational corporate structure.[19] Management's authority to act in these cases is subject to review of arbitration and is limited by the contract.

The range and limits of employer discretion to subcontract have been extensively explored in many industries via the medium of grievance among arbitrators, particularly on the matter of how to interpret contractual silence in such cases. The more conservative school of arbitrator thinking supports the conventional managerial view expressed as follows: "If we have not limited ourselves by contract, we still have discretion to subcontract as necessary according to our best judgment." The more liberal school of arbitrator thinking often applies "implied limitations" reasoning to restrict employer discretion to subcontract when the effect of such subcontracting is to diminish bargaining unit work opportunities.[20]

Negotiated contractual provisions relating to subcontracting contain a wide variety of ways of handling this potentially explosive issue. As already noted, there are still many contracts that maintain silence on the subject. One can presume that in some cases of this type the contractual

---

19. In *UFT Razor Blades* v. *District 65* (1978), a U.S. district court sustained an arbitration decision which held that a company had violated the subcontracting clause in its labor agreement by sourcing the bargaining unit work to a foreign location owned by the company. A discussion of multinational bargaining is found in Herbert R. Northrup, "Why Multinational Bargaining Neither Exists Nor Is Desirable," *Labor Law Journal*, 29, No. 6 (June 1978), 330–40.

20. According to Paul Prasow and Edward Peters, when the contract is silent on subcontracting, a "large majority of arbitrators will not sustain management if the subcontracting results in layoffs or impairment of established employee benefits." Prasow and Peters immediately qualify this generalization, however, by noting exceptions where the subcontracting has been customary in the past or where there has been "a drastic change in underlying conditions of the jobs in question." See Paul Prasow and Edward Peters, *Arbitration and Collective Bargaining: Conflict Resolution in Labor Relations* (New York: McGraw-Hill, 1970), p. 47.

silence reflects the fact that subcontracting is not a problem. In others, it might reflect a situation where management does not in fact do any subcontracting. In still others, the silence would underscore the fact that management is subcontracting certain types of work, with the union having won or lost on its challenges, depending on the arbitrator's philosophy as to how the silence should be construed.

Where the agreement is not silent in this area, there are cases wherein the employer agrees to do no subcontracting other than what he has customarily done in the past. Many employers would be wary about limiting themselves in this fashion. However, it should not be surprising to find unions seeking to enforce through collective bargaining a policy statement on subcontracting that would either prevent or limit as much as possible the contracting out of work normally done by bargaining unit personnel. Perhaps the most consistent pressure exerted by employees on any union leaders is to maintain job opportunities to the maximum degree possible.

Either contractual silence or contractual ambiguity can lead to serious disputes whenever an employer elects to subcontract in a manner that takes work opportunities away from bargaining unit personnel. The problem is one that calls for clarity and mutual understanding if the parties are going to avoid recurring instances of friction and resentment. Thus, many contracts contain provisions reflecting a joint desire to maintain a stable work force while also recognizing the employer's need for some flexibility in making arrangements to have work done.[21]

PREMIUM PAY PROVISIONS AND JOB SECURITY

Conventional union pressure to increase premium pay rates for daily or weekly overtime is another instance of a continuing type of issue that does not at first seem related to job security. Looked at more closely, however, these demands can be viewed as a strong inducement to the employer to carry more employees in his regular or normal work force than he might need to fill "normal" needs in order to avoid the financial penalties of recurringly expensive overtime.

The matter of how much to pay for overtime or for holidays when worked is frequently an issue in current bargaining. Some contracts now carry what employers must regard as truly exorbitant rates for holidays when worked (triple time is no longer unusual), or for the sixth and

---

21. Anthony V. Sinicropi's address at the 32nd annual meeting of the National Academy of Arbitrators on May 11, 1979, is an excellent statement on the court, NLRB, and arbitration award patterns developing in the area of subcontracting. The text of his address is found in the *Labor Relations Yearbook—1979* (Washington, D.C.: Bureau of National Affairs), p. 97:113.

seventh consecutive days in a work week. The contractual cost of using regular employees under these conditions is so high that it provides a most powerful incentive to the employer not to schedule work under such circumstances if he can possibly avoid doing so. Thus, the temptation might be present to carry a "regular" force of more employees than he might "normally" need in order to be sure the requisite amount of production can be obtained in straight-time schedule hours.

CONTRACTUALLY PRESCRIBED WORKING RULES AND TECHNOLOGICAL CHANGE

Any technologically dynamic situation provides the opportunity for a confrontation between the new and the old ways of getting work done. One of the stickiest areas in bargaining concerns such matters as work pace, workload, and proper crew size for a given operation. The union thrust in such cases will be to pursue a course which will preserve a fixed quantum of bargaining unit job opportunities. The typical employer will be extremely reluctant to go along with any contractual specifications that will bind him to using x number of employees on given work operations or that require him to continue doing work in a certain way. The employer desires to maintain complete freedom over "control and direction of working force." He thus comes into conflict with the union's objective of using the contract to assure maximum employment opportunities for bargaining unit employees.

The semantics are important if we are to obtain a true picture of this potential conflict area. If its demand is one that involves outright feather-bedding or make-work under current conditions, union leadership will be hard pressed to develop a plausible rationale. There are comparatively few union practitioners who will unabashedly seek to enforce such policies as a way of life. But when the manpower issue is put in less obvious and extreme terms, legitimate differences in viewpoint can develop between management and unions. To take a familiar example, problems frequently arise when a change in method or a change in machinery leads the employer to conclude that a given operation can henceforth be performed by one man instead of two. Another familiar situation arises when a sweeping technological change makes it possible for the employer to contend plausibly that producing a given amount henceforth requires a production worker component of only 100 men instead of the former 150 or 200 men.

The difficulty and seriousness of such manning controversies can be easily appreciated when one recalls such lengthy and bitter struggles of recent vintage as those concerning the diesel firemen in the railroad industry, the flight engineer position in jet aircraft, and the conversion in the municipal bus field from two men (motorman and conductor) to one man. Whenever a technological development calls for reduced manpower, there may be a serious dispute as to whether the reduction can be instituted under the current collective bargaining agreement. Whenever revision of contractual provisions on work rules or manpower components is under consideration, the union position is often that management wants to move too fast or that it is trying to cut corners by using technological change improperly to conceal an alleged increase in workload for remaining employees.

To write in meaningful fashion about such disputes would require going into the details of specific situations. Each such case has its individual variations. Sticking here to general terms, our view is that the employer must retain sufficient contractual recognition of worker equity in jobs. Where net displacement is known to be a consequence of an anticipated technological change, collective bargaining should be directed to minimizing or cushioning the adverse impact on incumbent employees.

There is no optimal solution to the work rules and manpower component problem. Furthermore, it is often hard to predict with accuracy how a given technological innovation will affect manpower requirements in a specific case. Resolution of such disputes will be a thorny problem for most bargainers, even in a full employment economy. We regard it as unfortunate, however, whenever any union chooses to use bargaining power "muscle" to force employers to maintain outmoded working rules or methods.

Achieving satisfactory accommodations between conflicting but legitimate differences in viewpoint as to proper manning on particular jobs will always be a part of the negotiators' task at the bargaining table. In most cases, detached assessment of the circumstances will reveal whether the union stance is in reality an obstructionist one designed to make the cost of instituting technological change prohibitively high. In any such case, there should no longer be any question as to proper direction. Union leadership and union membership must reconcile themselves to the need for accepting the change. They must be realistic on the matter of removal of outmoded working rules from the collective agreement. Stubborn adherence to old patterns can be sustained by muscle in the short run, but the consequent damage to the relationship between the parties will be irreparable. The damage goes far beyond the particular relationship. Society's interests are injured by the perpetuation of enforced restrictions on production that have been made obsolete by technological improvements.

SUMMARY

We have examined several critical components of the job security problem. The discussion has been structured in such a way as to illustrate the important role of collective bargaining in instituting and implementing a system of industrial jurisprudence. Whether talking about individual discipline, seniority provisions, or adaptation to technological change, the recurring theme has been the use of collective bargaining to develop jointly policies and procedures spelling out clearly the rules of the game in dealing with the problem at hand.

In each case, the acid operational test must be whether the policies and methods jointly decided upon measure up to the basic demands of industrial jurisprudence—clarity, consistency, predictability, and equality of treatment in like circumstances. The long-run health of collective bargaining as a process will be determined by how conscientiously the parties stick to the imperative of a single standard of fair and equitable treatment in their specific efforts to insure a maximum of job security to incumbent employees in a technologically dynamic and volatile labor relations scene. In the long run, there is no satisfactory alternative to the single standard for achieving and maintaining stability and equity in contract administration.

In Chapters 13 and 14 we depart from our emphasis on collective bargaining content and practice and consider the relationship of collective bargaining to labor market operations, bargaining theory, and the economic effects of collective bargaining.

Questions for Discussion, Thought, and Research

1. Local unions in construction tend to approach the issue of control of job opportunities differently from those in manufacturing. How do their approaches differ?

2. Uniformity, consistency, fairness, and predictability are the key concepts of effective jurisprudence. In what way are these elements critically linked to the concept of seniority as it relates to such decisions as layoff, recall, and promotion?

3. Does a union make it impossible for an employer to get rid of a poor employee?

4. What is required of an employer to show just cause? Why is the burden of proof in discharge and discipline cases on the employer and not on the union?

5. The seniority concept in industrial relations has affected the degree of mobility among workers. Which employees are made better or worse off? Why?

6. How do unions attempt to cushion the labor displacing impacts of technological change? Is it in a union's long-run interests to resist technological change? Why?

7. What are the benefits, if any, to an employer of seniority provisions in layoffs, recalls, and promotions?

8. Management generally views technological changes positively, while unions view such changes with great distrust. From your experience, is this statement accurate? In what ways can both labor and management reduce the tension surrounding technology?

Selected Bibliography

Dunlop, John T., ed., *Automation and Technological Change.* Englewood Cliffs, N.J.: Prentice-Hall, 1962.

Hartman, Paul T., *Collective Bargaining and Productivity: The Longshore Mechanization Agreement.* Berkeley and Los Angeles: University of California Press, 1969.

McKersie, Robert B., and L. C. Hunter, eds., *Pay, Productivity, and Collective Bargaining.* New York: St. Martin's Press, 1973.

Phelps, Orme W., *Discipline and Discharge in Unionized Firms.* Berkeley: University of California Press, 1959.

Porter, Arthur R., *Job Property Rights.* New York: King's Crown Press, 1954.

Shils, Edward B., *Automation and Industrial Relations.* New York: Holt, Rinehart and Winston, 1963.

Slichter, Sumner H., *Union Policies and Industrial Management.* Washington, D.C.: Brookings Institute, 1941.

Slichter, Sumner H., James J. Healy, and E. Robert Livernash, *The Impact of Collective Bargaining on Management.* Washington, D.C.: Brookings Institute, 1960.

Somers, Gerald, Arvid Anderson, Malcolm Denise, and Leonard Sayles, eds., *Collective Bargaining and Productivity.* Madison, Wis.: Industrial Relations Research Association, 1975.

Weinstein, Paul A., ed., *Featherbedding and Technological Change.* Lexington, Mass.: Heath, 1965.

LABOR MARKETS
AND BARGAINING—THEORY,
STRATEGY, AND EVIDENCE

13

In this chapter we briefly review two important topics: (1) how collective bargaining alters the standard wage-employment economic theory, and (2) theory and evidence about the process and outcome of bargaining.

UNIONS AND WAGE BARGAINING
IN COMPETITIVE MARKETS

Economic theory has long provided the basis for explanations of wage and price determination. We are well aware of the lesson that the market forces of supply and demand determine wages. This theory, in its pure form, does not leave room for, nor does it require, a negotiating element.

In collective bargaining situations, the terms of employment are set by negotiation and not by competitive labor market forces. This does not mean labor market forces are unimportant; the forces of demand and supply of labor set parameters which bargainers cannot ignore. At the low end, the wage package must exceed the reservation wage—that is, the lowest wage acceptable to an employee—of the work force. Below the reservation wage the employer cannot attract and retain a full work force. At the high end, incremental increases in the wage package, over the long term, often mean fewer employed union members. At an extreme, labor costs could become so high that paying them becomes less economical than simply closing down operations.

Virtually all collective agreements set a wage rate (including indirect forms of wages such as pensions and time off with pay), but leave the decision of work force size to the employer. Union influence on employment levels is still important since, over time, any change in the wage rate changes the employment incentive of the firm. For reasons we will outline in another section, wage–employment tradeoffs are not the most important factor influencing union wage negotiations. But labor markets do constrain wage negotiations and the extent of the wage–employment tradeoff determines how wage negotiations affect labor markets.

The exact effect of union on labor markets, and employment levels, is not clear from even the simplest economic models. Many economists and many employers argue from a market presumption of perfect competition. This market is depicted in Diagram 13–1, and it is discussed in this section. In later sections we discuss other presumptions about the state of the market.

Diagram 13-1

Competitive Markets with Full Unionization

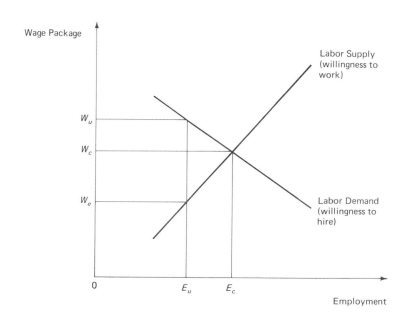

Without a union competitive markets would move to the point where supply equals demand, indicated in Diagram 13–1, at point W_c, E_c. Union entry and effective bargaining can increase the wage rate (W_u) only at the cost of less employment (E_c - E_u). We shall return to this point in the next chapter.

Two additional aspects of Diagram 13–1 characterize important elements of collective wage negotiation. First, once a work force of size E_u is set, an employer need offer a wage package no greater than W_e to retain a work force of this size. Thus, with this work force, the employer's preferred wage package is W_e, the union's preferred wage package is W_u: the difference defines a bargaining range. Second, at any wage package greater than W_e, there are some nonunion workers (indicated by the supply curve) willing to work for a lower-than-union wage. In this sense, there is always an incentive for some workers and some employers to undercut the union wage, thereby gaining a competitive advantage in the product market. Forestalling nonunion wage competition is a major union problem in otherwise competitive markets.

The employment effect of any given collective bargain depends (roughly) on the slope of the labor demand curve. If it is very steep (vertical), large wage increases have a minimal effect on employment levels. If it is almost horizontal, small wage increases may seriously diminish employment in the market.

Steep, or inelastic, labor demand is most favorable to large union wage increases, since large increases do not imply large employment losses. Labor demand is most likely to be inelastic when:

1. The demand for the product is inelastic. The demand for oil, for example, is quite inelastic. An increase in wages would increase the cost of, say, refining oil and, therefore, the price of refined oil. Because the demand for oil is inelastic, almost as much oil would be sold after the price rise as before the price rise. Almost as many employees would be required to refine this volume of oil, unless . . .

2. Equipment and other labor-saving devices cannot be technically substituted for labor in the production process; when nonunion employees cannot be substituted for union employees; or when it is very expensive to make substitutions because the supply of other inputs are inelastic. Thus, in response to higher union wages, labor will be more inelastic, and the bargaining situation will be more favorable to the union.

3. Labor costs represent a relatively small percent of total production costs. Obviously, if paying union labor is a relatively small part of total cost, union wage increases will not affect prices and sales much. Adverse employment effects will be minimized. Thus, to this extent, it is most advantageous to unions to represent a small part of total production costs.

The ideal union situation would be to organize and represent employees in firms where the product demand is inelastic, where substitution for union labor is costly or impossible, and where union labor makes up a small part of the total cost of production. The reverse situation could be the worst for a union to organize and represent: any wage increase would tend to dampen union employment severely.

A very elastic labor demand curve is most likely when a union attempts to organize one firm in an industry where other firms are nonunion. In this circumstance, higher production costs from higher wage rates cannot be reflected in higher prices by the union firm, since customers could easily shift their buying to lower priced nonunion goods. For this reason, it is extremely difficult for a union to bargain successfully for higher wage rates when no other competitors in the product market are unionized. This is the reason most unions attempt to organize a significant proportion of an industry.

WAGE BARGAINING IN NONCOMPETITIVE LABOR MARKETS

An alternative version of the market sees elements of noncompetition by employers. This may come about because an employer is very large relative to the market, or because smaller employers collude. Some economists and many union representatives and employees argue from a presumption of noncompetition by employers. An extreme version, that of one employer, is presented in Diagram 13–2.

DIAGRAM 13–2
One Employer, Many Employees

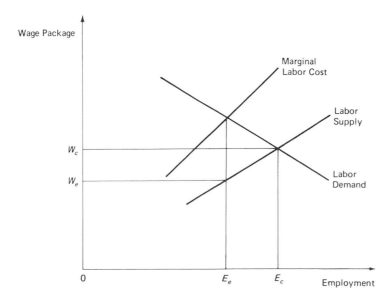

One employer acts differently toward pay and employment decisions compared to markets with many employers. Each time another employee is hired, pay rates must be raised by an employer to induce the person to come to work. As long as everyone is paid the same, the employer must pay more to hire the new employee, plus more to every other employee. The extra cost of hiring an employee (shown in Diagram 13–2 as the marginal labor cost curve) tends to restrict one employer from hiring as many people as the many employers would hire. In Diagram 13–2 one employer would hire people up to the point where the marginal cost of hiring (marginal labor cost curve) equals the marginal revenue of hiring (labor demand curve). The employer would choose to hire E_e workers.[1]

From the labor supply curve we see that the employers need only pay a wage package per employee of W_e to hire E_e employees. Both the wage rate and the number employed are less than under competitive conditions (W_c, E_c). This is an advantage with being a very large or collusive employer. It is an advantage a union can overcome, and it is one reason that motivated Congress to adopt legislation encouraging collective bargaining in the first place.

With a single employer in the market, union negotiated wage increases have the effect of increasing employment. It is, in fact, possible for the union to offset entirely the employer's advantage, and return wages and

1. Further explanation of simple labor market models may be found in Lloyd G. Reynolds, *Labor Economics and Labor Relations*, 1978, or Belton M. Fleisher and Thomas Kneiser, *Labor Economics*, 1980, both (Englewood Cliffs, N.J.: Prentice-Hall).

DIAGRAM 13–3
One Employer, One Wage

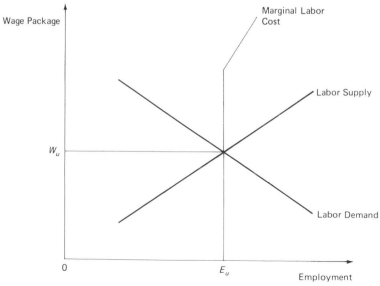

employment to competitive levels. Diagram 13–3 illustrates this point. By negotiating a wage for all employees in excess of the reservation wage, the employment incentives of the employer are significantly altered. For much of the employment range, the employer need not raise the wage rate to attract extra workers; thus, the marginal labor cost curve is not upward rising. Under exceptional circumstances, such as depicted in Diagram 13–3, the union can restore wages and employment to competitive levels, that is, where market demand equals supply.

Labor markets in the United States are probably characterized more often by competition than by employer dominance. Many of the most heavily unionized industries, however, are characterized by a few firms controlling most of the market. Precise measurement of employer's advantage of size and union impact on employment is impossible. There is enough measurement "noise" to allow advocates on both sides to give the empirical evidence the interpretation they desire. The important point is that economic laws of supply and demand leave room, under certain circumstances, for unions to increase *both* wage rates and employment levels.

UNION CONTROL OF THE LABOR SUPPLY

Craft unions have always had some voice in the selection, training, and assignment of new members. Restricted entry into the craft can be used to the unions' advantage by limiting the supply of labor. Diagram 13-4 shows

DIAGRAM 13–4
Craft Labor Market with Restricted Supply

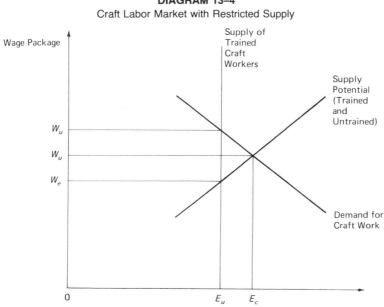

the effect of restricted entry upon wage rates. By restricting labor supply and employment to E_u, competition by employers would bid the wage rate to W_u. Union members would be better off by $(W_u - W_c)$. Craft unions could achieve this gain without the necessity of bargaining.

Achieving a restricted labor supply does not insure a union wage advantage *if the employers form a multiemployer bargaining unit*. All employers bargaining as one become a countervailing force potentially able to restrain the union advantage of limited supply. Extremely effective employer bargaining could obtain a wage rate as low as W_e in Diagram 13–4. This is the wage rate sufficient to induce all trained craft workers to supply labor. Extremely effective union bargaining could obtain a wage rate as high as W_u in Diagram 13–4. This is the maximum wage rate where all trained craft workers will be employed. The difference between W_u and W_e constitutes a bargaining range where wage changes do not imply any employment loss. Exactly where the final settlement will occur within the range depends upon bargaining.

In fact, it is extremely difficult for a craft union—or any other union—to restrict entry effectively. More and more craft skills are being taught in schools, rather than through on-the-job training. Entry to formal school-based training programs is seldom totally controlled by unions. Many people also learn the craft skill while serving in the armed forces or by trial and error. Much of the craft control has evolved from political bargaining by the union. Legal restrictions to work done only by licensed union workers is the usual method of control. Betting on the wrong candidate, however, can upset this source of supply control. Increasingly, nonunion firms are training their own employees and undercutting the competitiveness of union firms.

DO WAGE-EMPLOYMENT TRADEOFFS MATTER IN UNION BARGAINING?

The answer is yes, sometimes. The tradeoff matters a lot when a firm is failing. In 1979, for instance, the United Auto Workers union settled for a lower wage increase at Chrysler relative to Ford and General Motors in order to help prevent bankruptcy and to help preserve the 110,000 jobs Chrysler provides. Indeed, recently the union has granted Chrysler "rollbacks" and deferrals in negotiated benefits due in 1981 and 1982 in a continuing effort to permit the company to recover. The tradeoff matters a lot when higher wages at the union firm threatens employee competitiveness vis-à-vis more efficient firms and nonunion firms. As we have previously noted, this is particularly pronounced when only one firm is unionized in the product market, and during the late 1970s it was apparent in construction collective bargaining. Rising competition by nonunion firms forced building trade unions to moderate their wage demands.

Failing firms and heavy nonunion competition are extreme situations. In typical collective negotiations, failure and nonunion competition are less salient. Wage bargains may still affect employment, but this is unlikely to be an important factor in negotiations for three reasons.

First, in a dynamic economy the precise or even reasonably approximate extent of the tradeoff is not known. A labor demand curve at a point in time cannot be observed; all that is observed is one point on the curve. The curve itself certainly shifts through business cycles. Thus, even careful estimation cannot tell the extent of wage–employment tradeoff. And it is unlikely that negotiators or, especially, the rank and file carefully estimate labor demand curves.

Second, in the short run most production processes are fixed. An increase in union wages creates an incentive for labor-saving methods and equipment, but the actual substitution of labor-saving equipment for union jobs will likely not occur until the current equipment and technology are depreciated. As a result, the link between wage bargains and employment changes is not obvious, since employment adjustment may not occur until years after the precipitating bargain.

Third, union efforts may result in less employment among all potential workers, but not among union workers. As we have emphasized throughout the book, union officials are elected by the membership and must be generally responsive to the objectives of the membership. Union members probably prefer larger wage increases for themselves (especially if they are protected by seniority rules) rather than employment for future union members. Union members may prefer static employment and rapid wage increases, for example, relative to moderate employment and wage growth.

BARGAINING: THE PROCESS AND OUTCOME

In the earlier sections of this chapter, we made clear the point that labor and management do not negotiate agreements in a vacuum. These negotiations occur in a market context. The underlying market demand and supply forces operate as constraints on bargaining. These factors help us to identify the bargaining range, but they fail to tell us how bargaining proceeds and what the determined wage will be. This information is provided by bargaining theory, a subject to which we now turn.

A comprehensive discussion of bargaining behavior—process and outcome—is beyond the scope of this text. However, to understand fully the significance of the negotiation or legislative phase of collective bargaining relationships, some introductory comments are demanded. Our interest is to present in relatively easy terms an analytical framework which may serve to explain *why* the bargainers behave as they do at the bargaining table and to explain *how* bargaining proceeds and is concluded.

The novice oftentimes characterizes bargaining behavior as largely irrational (for example, without purpose), replete with meaningless ritual, and of limited value. This is a naive and dangerously misleading view of bargaining. Behavior at the negotiating table is far too systematic and predictable to be irrational. Both parties behave as if they are striving to attain specified goals and their behaviors are consistent with movement toward these objectives. The use of "threats" and the fabled "bluffing" behavior of the parties in contract negotiating are part of the bargaining ritual. However, these are critical, important behaviors essential to increasing the likelihood of a favorable bargain, and not merely ceremonial acts.

As we stated in Chapter 5, bargaining over issues for which the parties' goals or preferences are in conflict does elicit behaviors which are vastly different from those found where the parties' interests coincide. When bargaining over conflict issues, it must be remembered that each party selfishly withholds information about its own real or true preferences —particularly, that settlement or set of contractual terms which is *least* desirable although acceptable—while employing tactics to extract such information from the opposite party. Decision making is an extremely complex and risky enterprise under these circumstances. Each party *moves* in anticipation of the other's response. Each party's decision is based on sketchy (even misleading) information about its opponent's objectives and possible responses. Thus, we assert that making decisions to concede, resist, or closeout bargaining talks, where these decisions are rooted in an anticipated interaction and "poor" information, is a more "iffy" proposition than making, say, most financial investment decisions.

Collective bargaining is an extraordinarily complex exercise. Like other complex events, no one theory or explanation captures all of its nuances. By examining a small number of bargaining behaviors at a time, however, we begin characterizing bargaining processes and outcomes. By systematically piecing together the theories and the explanations of different bargaining characteristics, we can unpack some of the decision-making processes commonly called "bargaining" (or "negotiating").

REVIEW OF MORE RECENT THEORIES

We have seen that labor market theories set up the bargaining problem rather than solve it. That problem is to account for both the bargaining process and the ultimate outcome within a bargaining range. Labor market theories merely set the stage. What remains is to identify variables which affect both the process of bargaining and its final outcomes, and to show specifically how these interact to determine these outcomes.

There has been a definite historical development in which several variables have progressively been incorporated into bargaining models. We will identify and define only four of these variables. The first of these variables is risk: the idea that different potential outcomes vary in how certain one can be of their occurrence. Closely related to this is one's *attitude* toward risk. Certain people welcome or even invite risk. These people make trips to Las Vegas or Monte Carlo to enjoy increasing their risks at gaming tables where the "house" will win most of the time. Others, perhaps the majority, buy fire insurance on their homes—they are willing to pay someone a premium to assume some of their risks. The first of these are risk seekers, the second are risk averters. In between there is a group who are risk neutral; they evaluate alternatives strictly on the basis of their expected outcomes without altering their calculations to adjust for the presence or absence of risk.

Another variable to be introduced is the rate of time preference or personal discount rate. This represents a willingness on the part of an individual to defer his gratifications. A high rate of time preference indicates that the individual places a low evaluation on outcomes which may only be realized in the future and a relatively higher value on outcomes which are currently available. A low rate of time preference indicates the reverse. A person with a low rate of time preference is willing to wait.

A final variable which is introduced in a later model is referred to as a learning rate. This is the response rate which one party exhibits to the actions of the other. A high rate would indicate large changes in the party's response to an action of his opponent while a low rate would indicate a relatively small change.

OPPORTUNITY COST AND RISK

As long as an employer and union believe that they are better off agreeing with each other rather than refusing to agree, an eventual negotiated agreement is possible. Within the range of possible agreements, the opportunity cost during negotiations of each side is the offer of the other side.

For example, on wage issues the employer can agree to a union demand of $15 per hour, or hold out for his own offer of $13 per hour. The employer can be certain of a $15 per hour agreement; this is the value of his opportunity cost. However, he cannot be certain of the cost that may result from sticking with an offer of $13 per hour simply because by doing so he may run the risk of a strike.

Should our employer hold out or concede to the union's demand? If the employer is reasonably certain about the union's strike intentions, then the risk of making a faulty decision is low. Thus, if the employer is reasonably sure that the union will strike, then the cost of holding to the $13 per hour offer presumably would exceed the opportunity cost, and he should "sweeten" his offer. Conversely, if the employer is reasonably certain that the union will not strike, then the cost of holding to $13 per hour may not exceed the opportunity cost, and he should stand pat.

However, when the employer is uncertain about the union's strike intentions, the risk associated with decision making increases. Even though the employer may have some "feel" about the probability of a strike occurring, he is taking a greater chance of being wrong in whatever decision he makes. Thus, when reasonable certainty is lacking decision making becomes more hazardous. The task of evaluating and comparing the cost of one's own position *vis à vis* a known opportunity cost is obviously more difficult. In addition to a greater concern about being wrong in whatever decision is made due to the risk element, there is the added complexity of adjusting for one's attitude toward risk.

This simple illustration is sufficient to demonstrate the most frequent error made by unsophisticated observers of collective bargaining. Frequently, people remark that a labor dispute was not worth it, that the cost of the strike exceeds the extra pennies separating the parties. But this observation is made long after the bargaining parties made their decision. A risk decision can only be evaluated based on information known prior to the decision, not on information known only after the decision. In our illustration, even an employer almost certain that the union will accept the $13 an hour offer rather than strike is making a good bet. If the unlikely but possible happens and a strike results, the employer's decision is not unreasonable or irrational. It only appears unreasonable or irrational given information unknown to the employer at the time of the decision—that is, that a strike would occur.

It is true that a strike represents a succession of decisions. Perhaps seeing that the strike is inevitable, the employer could alter the $13 per hour offer. But if either a union or employer promises to call or to take a strike, then backs out, some credibility of future strike promises (i.e., threats) is lost.

VALUATION OF BARGAINING DEMANDS

In collective bargaining, small differences in dollars and cents can be big differences to union and management negotiators. Slight modifications in seniority rules, for example, might have insignificant importance in economic terms, but grave importance to the principles of management rights or union security. Or a few cents an hour in the wage rate might not seem to be a significant amount. But if the issue becomes fair or just treatment represented by the few cents, the issue can take on monumental importance. In collective bargaining, behavior is not predicated strictly on dollars and cents but on how much importance each side attaches to a given issue.

A second element in the valuation of bargaining demands includes risk, and the subjective probabilities formed by each negotiating team that their demands will be achieved. Union negotiators, indifferent between two bargaining demands on every dimension except risk, would probably prefer the least risky—that is, the demand least likely to be rejected for a strike or boycott by the employer. Since risk implies some potential cost, such as a strike, this is similar to saying that negotiators, other things being equal, prefer the least costly demand.

For convenience, we will refer to valuation of bargaining demands as the utility of the demand. Utility includes the strength of the preference the negotiating team has for the demand, risk and the subjective probability they associated with the demand.

BARGAINING THEORY WITH UNBIASED COMMUNICATION

The first model we consider will illustrate some important aspects of give-and-take and bargaining power. Our model is a simplification and synthesis of theories proposed by Frederic Zeuthen, John Harsanyi, and Sir John Hicks as treated by Robert Bishop.[2]

We designate U_ℓ and U_m as the utility gains of labor and management, respectively. Utility values as indexed by U_ℓ and U_m vary with proposals being exchanged between the parties. In wage negotiations, for example, the larger a proposed wage increase the larger U_ℓ and the smaller U_m. The reverse is also true. This relationship is implied by the negatively sloped curved line relating U_ℓ and U_m in Diagram 13–5. Defined as the parties' "utility frontier," this line traces out the combinations of maximum utility increments each party could hope for as the contract proposals under consideration vary. Thus, the union's high wage change proposal (P_ℓ) will yield a high utility increment ($U_{\ell\ell}$) for itself and only $U_{m\ell}$ for management. Conversely, management's low wage change offer (P_m) will yield a utility gain of U_{mm} for itself but only $U_{\ell m}$ for labor. The origin in Diagram 13–5 (i.e., zero utility gains going to both parties) is the point at which labor and management are fated to remain as long as they are unable to negotiate a new agreement.

2. Robert L. Bishop, "A Zeuthen–Hicks Theory of Bargaining," in Oran R. Young, ed., *Bargaining* (Urbana: University of Illinois Press, 1975), pp. 145–63, 183–90, 253–66.

Diagram 13–5

Incremental Bargaining
Utilities

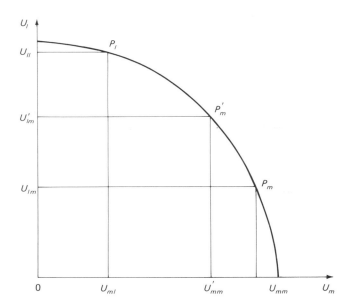

Suppose the contract under negotiation will run for t units of time, provided agreement is reached immediately. However, if a strike of s units' duration takes place, the contract will run for only $t - s$ units of time. For completeness, suppose further that both parties have zero rates of time preference.

If P_ℓ and P_m are the proposals under consideration, labor knows that they can either immediately accept management's offer and gain $tU_{\ell m}$ or hold out for its own proposal and gain $(t - s_\ell)U_{\ell\ell}$ after a strike lasting s_ℓ units of time. The union would be indifferent between these two alternative choices of action when $tU_{\ell m} = (t - s_\ell)U_{\ell\ell}$. This conclusion can be stated in another way. The union will be indifferent between striking or settling when

$$(1) \quad s_\ell = \frac{t(U_{\ell\ell} - U_{\ell m})}{U_{\ell\ell}}$$

Following a similar analytical procedure, we see that management will be indifferent between either holding out for its proposal (P_m) or accepting the union's demand when

$$(2) \quad s_m = \frac{t(U_{mm} - U_{m\ell})}{U_{mm}}$$

Expressions (1) and (2) contain critical behavioral implications. As a point of departure, note that s_ℓ and s_m indicate the *maximum* strike length labor and management, respectively, are willing to endure for a complete victory. Because we are assuming unbiased communication, the union knows s_m and management knows s_ℓ.

If $s_\ell > s_m$, then the union is willing to risk a strike longer than management is willing to endure; it's not worth it for management to hold to its offer. Management concedes. Management, however, does not have to give in entirely to the union's demand. Note what happens when management ups its offer just a little (for example, from P_m to P'_m in Diagram 13–5):

1. s_ℓ decreases; the union is less willing to strike because the value of payoff is reduced by the increased management offer. As the utility increment of management's offer ($U'_{\ell \, v}$) increases for the union, the numerator ($U_{\ell\ell}$ - $U'_{\ell v}$) declines.

2. s_m decreases; almost certainly however, this decrease is by less than s_ℓ. By raising its offer, management causes two changes in its strike risk formula. It would be less willing to strike because the difference between management's offer and union's ($U'_{mm} - U_{m\ell}$) is less. It would be more willing to strike because the proportional gain of holding out relative to its offer increases, or, in other words, the denominator U'_{mm} goes down.

In general, management only has to concede to the point where $s_m > s_\ell$.

At this level of offer, management is more willing to endure a strike than the union; it's not worth it for the union to hold onto its demand.

This theory explains why the bargaining process involves a succession of switches by management and union negotiators. The negotiating team, less willing to strike, concedes, but usually it is not necessary to make a large concession to reach the point where the other team is less willing to strike. The succession of concessions continues until $s_m = s_\ell = 0$. Concessions continue until the management offer and the union demand converge to the point of agreement.

If we define "bargaining power" as the greater willingness to strike, then bargaining power is not a constant attribute of either the union or management negotiation sides. Instead, bargaining power depends upon the relative demands and relative offers of both sides. Depending upon relative demands and offers, either union or management negotiators may have bargaining power. In the normal give-and-take of bargaining, bargaining power will switch between union and management negotiators.[3]

---

3. Observers of collective bargaining frequently and erroneously use the concept of "bargaining power" by following this reasoning: bargaining power is ascribed to one side because the other side gives in. Why give in? Because the other side has bargaining power?

THE NASH "SOLUTION"

The mathematician John Nash has advanced a theory of the bargaining process which has received considerable attention as the Nash "solution."[4] This theory is qualitatively different, however, from those already mentioned. Nash assumes there are exactly two parties who are rational in the sense that they maximize their satisfactions. He further assumes that each has a complete knowledge of his own tastes and preferences, that each has a complete knowledge of the other's tastes and preferences, and that each has equal bargaining skill. These assumptions rule out risk and bluffing as well as the need for an adjustment mechanism since each party has perfect knowledge. We are presented with a situation, then, where the parties are mirror images of one another. The result is that the parties maximize the individual product of their utility gains and reach a "split-the-difference" solution where each takes half the total utility gain available to the two.

This would seem to be a particularly sterile approach and, indeed, John Cross has argued that it leaves out the process of "disagreement–concession–agreement" and the information which leads to nonsymmetric solutions—matters which he believes are among the most interesting questions.[5] Nash's model does, however, provide a reference point from which other theoretical modes may be evaluated or compared.

THE COMMUNICATION OBSTACLE

In the bargaining models just described, there is not room for a strike. Knowledge of strike willingness is sufficient to motivate both sides to concede and settle. Sometimes strikes occur in collective bargaining because one side or the other underestimates the willingness of the other side to strike. Strikes occur because of biased communication between the bargainers as to their willingness to strike.

Generally, although not necessarily, negotiating teams on both sides know the preferences of their own constituents. They do not necessarily know these preferences, however. The union representatives, for example, may underestimate the willingness of the union membership to take a strike over a demand. Remember, as discussed in Chapter 5, the union membership rejects between 9 and 12 percent of contracts agreed to by union negotiators. Thus, union or management negotiators may signal the wrong preference to their opponent negotiators, because they have incorrectly assessed the valuation and risk perceived by their own constituents.

Because this error of logic occurs often enough, and because bargaining power is generally used imprecisely, we avoid the term whenever possible.

4. John F. Nash, "The Bargaining Problem," *Econometrica*, 18 (1950), 155–62.

5. John G. Cross, *The Economics of Bargaining* (New York: Basic Books, 1969).

Biased communication is inherent in bargaining for another, more important, reason. The incentive exists for both sides to engage in "bluffing" behaviors. Union negotiators, for example, may generally know the strike willingness of their constituents. Management negotiators, however, cannot know the union's strike willingness except through indications from the union. Yet it is to the union's advantage to indicate the strongest possible willingness to take a strike as a means to extract a concession from management. Management negotiators are well aware that the union's interests are best served by overstating its willingness to strike, and for this reason they disbelieve statements made by union negotiators. Similarly, union negotiators know management's interests lie in overstating its willingness to accept a strike, and for this reason discount statements made by management negotiators. Most union–management negotiations find the union wary of management statements of intention, and management wary of union statements of intention. Bridging this gap is the most important single element in bargaining sessions.

Negotiators certainly begin negotiation with some expectation about how the opponent will act. Bargaining may be thought of as a process that adjusts each side's expectations about how the other side will react to positions and concessions. Adjusting expectations—or communicating intent—is not simple. In the next several sections we outline some ideas about expectation adjustment and how, under certain conditions, a bargaining opponent's options may be preempted.

LEARNING AND BARGAINING

Of all the articles and books written about the bargaining process, perhaps the most realistic and revealing treatment is John Cross's learning model of bargaining.[6] Cross's bargaining model is not easy. What we report here is an overview of the structure of the model.

The central feature of Cross's approach is a system of equations which contains three sets of variables. The first set of these variables is the *concession rates*, which are simply the changes in the parties' demand per unit of time. It is assumed that a party may either concede (reduce his demand) or renege (increase his demand). It is these concession rates which the equations attempt to explain. Another set of variables deals with the party's expectations of the concession rate of the opponent. It is assumed that each party has an expectation of the concession rate of his opponent. It is further assumed that each party alters this expectation according to the discrepancy between the opponent's true and expected concession rate. The rate of change of expectations per unit of time, or learning, is related to the size of this discrepancy.

6. *Ibid.*

Finally, there is a set of three variables that represent the personal characteristics of each party. The first is the attitude toward risk. This theory implicitly assumes that all parties are risk averters, but it does not specify the degree of risk aversion. A second variable is the parties' rate of time preference. A final variable in this set is the learning or response coefficient. This measures the size of the adjustment in expectations which occurs with a given discrepancy between the opponents' actual and expected concession rate.

The Cross theory identifies two separate types of bargaining decisions. The first determines the initial bargaining positions. The second determines any concessions, or concession rates, to bargaining opponents. The first type of decision is considered first. Several forces influence negotiator decisions:

1. Costs and payoffs of bargaining occur in two forms. One cost of bargaining is the recurring cost of actual negotiation. An important aspect of this cost is the value of negotiator time. This cost may suddenly shift at critical points in the negotiations, such as at the strike deadlines. Strikes add recurring management costs, such as extra security, loss of customer goodwill, and payment of fixed costs of production. Strikes add recurring union costs, such as picketing and coordination expenses and strike benefits. Early in the negotiation, recurring costs of negotiation are usually low. But as the current contract nears the date of expiration, costs increase. Of course, the quicker negotiations are settled, the lower this cost of negotiation.

   During strikes, and for the union any time after the current contract expires, negotiations delay the payoff of settlement. This cost of negotiation usually begins low, but at some point (the strike deadline or contract expiration) rises sharply. As with recurring "out of pocket" costs of negotiation, the quicker negotiations are settled, the lower this cost of negotiation.

   On the other hand, quick settlement may require a less advantageous bargain by one side. Thus, either negotiating team could lower its demands in order to reduce negotiation cost by speeding settlement, but the usual tradeoff would be a less advantageous contract.

2. An important element in the decision is how fast a bargaining team expects its opponent to concede. An expectation of rapid concession would mean a very favorable agreement could be achieved with relatively low negotiation and delay cost. An expectation of slow concession would mean a favorable agreement could be achieved with relatively high negotiation and delay cost. Thus, the faster an opponent is expected to concede, the higher the initial bargaining demand.

3. The negotiator with a higher rate of time preference—that is, a stronger preference for a payoff today versus a payoff at some future time—will set his initial bargaining demand lower in order to speed agreement. Thus, for example, a company in the midst of introducing a new product may not want to interrupt its marketing plan with a production delay stemming from a labor dispute. Company negotiators, in this instance, may have a strong preference for a quick settlement versus some delayed, more favorable settlement.

The initial bargaining position is fixed where the present value of future benefit from the bargain equals the present value of the cost necessary to achieve the bargain. Generally, higher recurring negotiator costs, higher rates of time preference, and slower expected rates of opponent concession result in more conciliatory initial bargaining positions. Lower recurring negotiator costs, lower rates of time preference, and more rapid expected rates of opponent concession result in more extreme initial bargaining positions.

In the unlikely but fortuitous situation where the initial bargaining positions are equal, no further bargaining is required to reach agreement. In the more likely situation where the initial bargaining positions diverge, something must change to alter the initial bargaining position. Recurring negotiation cost and rates of time preferences are fixed; that leaves only change in the expected rate of opponent concession. Upward revision of expected concession rates leads to an upward adjustment in the bargaining position, and downward revision of expected concession rates lead to a downward revision in the bargaining position.

Learning enters the theory as a part of expectation adjustment. The learning premise is straightforward. If the opponent concedes at a rate slower than expected, the expected rate of opponent concession is lowered. If the opponent concedes at a faster rate than expected, the expected rate of opponent concession is raised. Thus, each party's expectations are adjusted following observation of the opponent's concession behavior.

Both bargaining teams conceding at a rate slower than expected, leads to concession by both sides and eventual convergence toward agreement. One bargaining team conceding faster than expected introduces potential instability into bargaining, since the opponent would increase its bargaining demand rather than decrease it by conceding. Under NLRB interpretations of the duty-to-bargain requirement of the NLRA, however, reneging on an offer or a demand is an unfair labor practice. Under the rules of collective bargaining, negotiators faced with concessions by an opponent more rapid than expected would cease conceding and stand on their current demand or offer. By no longer conceding, the opponent would lower its expectation of the other party's rate of concession and, therefore, concede at an even faster rate. Convergence would occur in this situation by the bargaining team initially conceding faster than expected, effectively doing all the conceding. Rapid concession, then, carries a risk that a bargaining opponent will cease conceding. Experienced negotiators are well aware of the fact that to concede too much too fast may be interpreted as a show of weakness.

Changes in bargaining demands occur in this model because of changing expectations about opponent bargaining behavior. Expectations change through learning: how quickly the bargainers learn can affect the outcome of bargaining. The slower learners end up making less of the adjustment needed to reach agreement. Fast learners end up making more of the adjustment needed to reach agreement. As an example, consider a bargaining process where both union and management begin conceding slower than the other expected, but management learns quickly and the union slowly. Management, the quick learner, immediately makes a concession, but the union, the slow learner, has not yet caught on. Because the union is not conceding much faster than before, management makes another concession. By the time the union adjusts it expectations to management's initial action, management has already made significant concessions. In this example, the slow learner may in fact be the more clever of the two negotiators.

We conclude the description of Cross's bargaining model with a report of a research result without intuitive justification. Yet this result has been logically derived from simple assumptions, and confirmed in an empirical bargaining simulation.[7] Earlier, it was noted that negotiators with high rates of time preference—that is, a strong preference for settlement today rather than at some time in the near future—tend to enter bargaining with a lower initial demand. It turns out that negotiators with high rates of time preference also concede at a slower rate. Thus, the net effect of time preference on the bargaining outcome is not clear; if negotiators start low because of high discount rates, they concede slow; if they start high because of low discount rates, they concede fast.

STRATEGIC THREATS

Within the bargaining range either union or management negotiators can, under certain circumstances, preempt all further moves by the opponent by using strategic threats. The general approach of strategic threats in

7. Mario F. Bognanno and James B. Dworkin, "Time and Learning in the Bargaining Process: A Test of Cross's Theory," *Proceedings of the Thirtieth Annual Winter Meetings,* Industrial Relations Research Association, New York, 1977, pp. 294–303.

bargaining was first developed by Thomas Schelling.[8] This section relies heavily on Schelling's work. At the outset we wish to make clear that the use of strategic threats is not riskless, and may be very difficult to apply in collective bargaining. At the close of this section we will outline some risks and some limitations.

For a threat to work it must accomplish two things: (1) it must offer a certain alternative to opponent bargainers that is acceptable—that is, within the range of possible bargainers; and (2) it must offer opponent bargainers only one other probable and undesirable alternative. Preemptive moves are essentially take-it-or-leave-it in nature. The opponent is left with a choice between an acceptable alternative and an unpleasant alternative.

The most difficult part of the threat is limiting the alternatives. To accomplish this, the bargaining team making the threat must also restrict its own options, thereby irrevocably committing itself to carrying out the threat, if necessary, however undesirable to itself. Making an irrevocable commitment to an opponent is the key element in strategic threats. We first illustrate the principle of strategic threats with an example.

Say only the issue of mandatory overtime separates union and management negotiators. Management production supervisors estimate the cost of allowing more senior workers the right of overtime refusal at $100,000 per year. Management estimates the cost of a strike at $1 million per week. No strike in the past has lasted less than five weeks. If the union can credibly commit itself to striking unless management gives in on mandatory overtime, management is forced to choose between mandatory overtime and a very costly strike. The key is management's perception of a credible commitment by the union. If management perceives a low union commitment to strike on the issue, it may prefer to risk a strike rather than give in on mandatory overtime. It does not matter that the union is in fact committed to strike on this issue. What matters is that management perceives it is committed.

Notice in this example that striking may be an unattractive alternative to the union as well. But by absolutely committing itself to a strike, it has narrowed management's choices and, in the process, gained a bargaining advantage. Management could just as easily have gained the same advantage in bargaining by committing itself first.

Once the union commits, it must convince management that the commitment is believable. Considering the cost to the union of carrying out the threat this is not an easy matter. Commitment obviates all compromises; avoiding compromise is also not an easy matter. The one thing that cannot be compromised is a principle that the other side can

8. Thomas C. Schelling, *The Strategy of Conflict* (Cambridge, Mass.: Harvard University Press, 1960).

understand. The compulsory overtime issue, for example, could be used by management as a management rights issue: the right of management to direct the work force, not a $100,000 per year nuisance. For the union a useful principle is not as clear cut. One direction would be a principle of fairness: the union has given in on many other issues; this issue is necessary for balance. Another tactic would stake the union representatives' reputations on the issue. Threats of extreme behavior are much more credible if the issue is converted into one of principle.

Simply stating a threat of principle will probably not be sufficient to establish credibility. Some form of action is usually necessary to convey a message of commitment. If the threat is a strike, unions can begin preparing to carry out the strike. Actions could include strike votes by the membership, preparation of picket signs, cleaning out desks and lockers, or bringing in international representatives as a sign of solidarity. Management strike preparations could include preparing machinery, customers, and schedules for shutdown and adding to security, as well as stocking extra inventory. Certainly, past actions add or detract from threat credibility. Negotiators caught bluffing in the past may have a very difficult time convincing opponent bargainers of their sincerity. Unions or managements with a history of fulfilling promises, on the other hand, will be more readily believed.

Countermoves to avoid threats include, foremost, blocking communication of the threat, and helping the opponent find a way out of the threat. Perhaps the simplest way out of the threat is not to react to it. Continuing negotiations as if the threat had not occurred may be enough to keep an opponent from trying again. Mediators may also serve to block threats; by communicating only through a mediator, noncompromising messages are difficult to deliver with any force.

At the outset of this section, we mentioned that strategic threats may be risky and difficult to effect. Strategic threats work best on a one-time bargain, such as purchasing a used car, and worst on a continuous relationship. Continuous relationships change the payoff structure of a threat; an opponent may project acceding to one threat as increasing the likelihood of future threats. Instead of a choice between acceptable and unpleasant alternatives, the threat may present an opponent with a choice of two unpleasant alternatives. Remember, a threat is effective only if it is not carried out. Giving an opponent two unpleasant alternatives carries a high probability that the threat will be carried out.

Threats of any sort are unpleasant to many people. The disutility of acceding to a threat may be sufficient to convert the opponent's choice into two very unpleasant alternatives. As Carl Stevens has noted, the tension of two unpleasant extremes may force negotiators to seek other options.[9] A

9. Carl Stevens, "On the Theory of Negotiations," *Quarterly Journal of Economics*, 72 (February 1958), 77–97.

scenario not uncommon in labor relations finds a threat leading to a counterthreat perhaps leading to a further threat and so on. This reciprocal cycle is associated with the most vicious and intractable of labor disputes. The calamity of negotiation decay raises costs for both sides far in excess of potential gains from the use of strategic threats.

Strategic threats offer negotiators a chance to obtain favorable outcomes in collective bargaining. It takes a deft touch, however, to make the strategy work to advantage. Poorly conceived threats can easily backfire, even leading to catastrophic results.

EMPIRICAL EVIDENCE

We here examine a series of six studies which attempt to apply theoretical models to real world data. The idea is to test these models against actual observations to see if they are consistent with real world events. These can be divided into two general categories. The first deals with the frequency and causes of industrial conflict—strikes. The second category attempts to assess the validity of models such as the ones we have discussed above, which deal essentially with the process of reaching agreement. In the first category is work done by O. Ashenfelter and G. E. Johnson and H. S. Farber. In the second category are pieces by D. S. Hamermesh, a comment on Hamermesh's work by M. F. Bognanno and J. B. Dworkin and articles by R. L. Bowlby and W. R. Schriver and a final article by Bognanno and Dworkin.

Both Ashenfelter and Johnson[10] and Farber[11] test a model of strike activity developed originally by Ashenfelter and Johnson. They argue that strikes are a mechanism by which the expectations of the union members are brought into alignment with "reality." The minimum wage increment which the membership will agree to, then, is a decreasing function of the length of the strike. In other words, the membership progressively reduces its minimum acceptable wage demand as strike length increases. There is, however, a minimum rate below which the membership will not agree, no matter how long the strike. This minimum acceptable rate schedule may be graphed as in Diagram 13–6. Here, y_0 is the minimum wage rate the membership will agree to when there is no strike and y_* is the absolute minimum wage which the membership will ever ratify.

The firm in this model is assumed to be a profit maximizer, and so must pick a wage offer which accomplishes this goal. Since any wage increase it agrees to will become a permanent part of its wage costs (that is, it lasts

10. Orley Ashenfelter and George E. Johnson, "Bargaining Theory, Trade Unions, and Industrial Strike Activity," *American Economic Review,* 59, No. 1 (March 1969), 35–49.

11. Henry Farber, "Bargaining Theory, Wage Outcomes, and the Occurrence of Strikes: An Econometric Analysis," *American Economic Review,* 66 (June 1978), 262–71.

DIAGRAM 13–6
Union Concession Curve

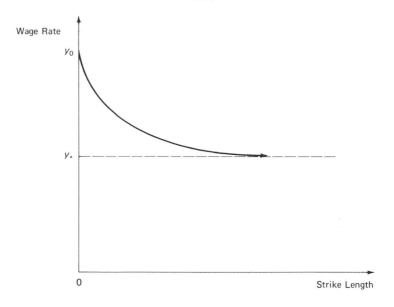

forever), the firm thinks in terms of a stream of profits lasting indefinitely into the future. The firm's goal, then, is to maximize the present value of this stream of profits. To do this, it must select a wage offer which balances the effects of a strike on this stream of future profits against the effects of a wage increase. In Diagram 13–7, we have a set of curves, each of which represent a combination of strike lengths and wage increases that result in equal present values for the firm. It can be seen that the firm's goal is to get as near to the origin as possible, since profits and present value decrease with both increases in strike length and agreed-to wages. If we combine the information in Diagrams 13–6 and 13–7, as we do in Diagram 13–8, we see that the firm will make a wage offer at the point where the lowest present value curve just touches (is tangent to) the union membership's curve of just acceptable wages. This gives us the point which maximizes the present value of the firm and is still acceptable to the union membership. The firm offers wage $\overline{w}$ after a strike of length $\overline{s}$ and achieves present value $\overline{V}_2$.

In their test of this conception, Ashenfelter and Johnson argued that the strikes were more likely, the higher the minimally acceptable rate demanded by the membership without a strike (y_o). They further argue that unemployment reduces this rate and that it is dependent on previous changes in real wages (that is, wages adjusted for changes in the price level). Their test, then, related the number of strikes in the United States in each quarter from 1952 through the second quarter of 1967 to the unemployment rate and to past changes in real wages. (Other variables were included for technical reasons which are not discussed.) Ashenfelter and Johnson found a substantial relationship between the number of

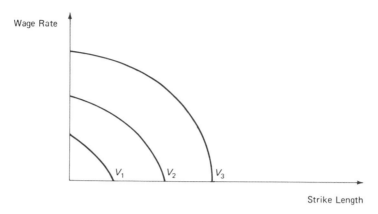

Diagram 13–7

Firm Profit Function

Wage Rate

V_1 V_2 V_3

Strike Length

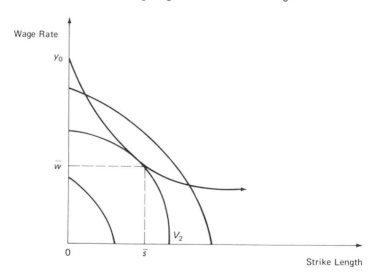

Diagram 13–8

Determining Wage Offers and Strike Length

Wage Rate

y_0

$\bar{w}$

0 $\bar{s}$

V_2

Strike Length

strikes and these variables. They concluded that their test supported the model they advanced and that the number of strikes was related to the degree of "tightness" of the market and past changes in real wages.

A similar model was tested by Farber. He used data from ten large manufacturing firms. There was a total of 80 contracts covered in the 16 years from 1954 to 1970. Farber used this data to estimate two quantities not estimated by Ashenfelter and Johnson. One was a number controlling the rate of decrease in the curve of minimum acceptable wage rates. The other was the absolute minimum acceptable wage increase (y. in Diagram 13–6). Farber then used these estimates to relate the proportional increase in wages negotiated to the variables which determine the two quantities mentioned above and to the total wage cost of the firm as a fraction of total sales. His results, while not so strong as Ashenfelter and Johnson's (possibly because Farber worked with so many more unknown quantities relative to the amount of data he had available), supported the Ashelfelter and Johnson model. Farber's work had the advantage of giving us an estimate of the rate of decrease in minimum acceptable wages and also of the absolute minimum acceptable rate (and other similar quantities as well), which we could never reach with the methods originally used by Ashenfelter and Johnson.

We now move from the question of the strike activity to the issue of where agreements occur when there is no strike. It will be recalled that Nash advanced a theory which, under the conditions specified, predicted that parties would "split the difference" in reaching their bargaining outcomes. A part of these conditions was that there be no "bluffing." Hamermesh[12] attempted to test Nash's conclusion by examining the results of forty-three negotiations concluded between September 1968 and December 1970. These were all public sector negotiations.

He constructed an index for each contract equal to the difference between the union's initial demand and the final settlement less the difference between the final settlement and management's first offer. These were all expressed as percentage changes in the rate existing when negotiations began. If the Nash theory is correct (and all other things are equal), then this index should be equal to zero since the bargainers split the difference; that is, the difference between union initial demands and the final settlement should equal the difference between management's initial offer and the final settlement. Hamermesh found that for the 43 contracts he examined, the average of the index was 7.23, which was different from zero even when the random variations due to sampling are taken into account. He concluded that either the basic assumptions of the theory are not met, especially the assumption that the union did not engage in bluffing, or that the theory is incorrect.

Bognanno and Dworkin,[13] in a comment on the Hamermesh article, pointed out that in 38 of the 43 cases the union was legally prevented from striking and was not able to resort to any other method of dispute resolution. This left the union in a position of "taking or leaving" what was offered. After reexamining Hamermesh's data, they found that this occurred in 11 of the 43 cases. When these 11 instances were removed, it was found that Hamermesh's index was equal to zero and thus supported the Nash conclusion.

If the institutional arrangements of public sector bargaining were different, it would be less likely that the union would engage in bluffing to

12. Daniel Hamermesh, "Who 'Wins' in Wage Bargaining?", *Industrial and Labor Relations Review*, July 1973, pp. 146–49.

13. Mario F. Bognanno and James B. Dworkin, "Comment," *Industrial and Labor Relations Review*, July 1975, pp. 570–72.

a greater extent than management. The Nash theory would then be applicable. One question to be answered, then, is whether this differential bluffing (where one side exaggerates its initial demand to a greater extent than the other) on the part of unions is a general feature of collective bargaining.

Bowlby and Schriver[14] examine the results of 252 distinct wage bargains made in the sixteen years from 1960 to 1975 between the Tennessee Valley Authority and various unions (apparently, mostly construction trade unions). These authors found that the index described above was positive for these bargains as well. They were then able to confirm Hamermesh's main empirical finding. They conclude that differential bluffing on the part of unions causes this phenomena.

These authors argue that unions bluff more than management because union negotiators must play to two audiences. One is the union membership, which must be placated with strident demands, and the other is the opponent's bargaining team, which must be dealt with in a business-like way. This "role conflict," they argue, causes the union negotiator to advance publicly demands which are soon dropped for more realistic aspirations.

Bowlby and Schriver tested this argument by attempting to relate the index to a number of economic variables. They found little relation here other than between the rate of inflation in the previous three years and the index. These authors theorize that the rate of inflation is related to worker militancy. From this, they conclude that union bluffing is related to the attitudes of the rank and file, which they interpret as support for their role conflict theory.

Bognanno and Dworkin[15] used experimental methods to test a variation of Cross's bargaining model described above. It will be recalled that this theory related the party's concession rate of his opponent. These authors related the difference in the party's concession rates to initial offers and initial expectations of the other party's concession rates. In this way they estimate two quantities. The first is the "learning rate" or rate of adjustment of expectations, and the second is the rate of time preference. Estimates of these quantities furnished support for Cross's theory. It was found that the model explained a reasonable part of the variation in differences in concession rates and that the estimated quantities were consistent with the hypotheses made about them prior to the work.

SUMMARY

We have covered a large number of difficult concepts in relatively few pages. Some of the important points covered include:

14. Roger L. Bowlby and William R. Schriver, "Bluffing and the 'Split-the-Difference' Theory of Wage Bargaining," *Industrial and Labor Relations Review*, January 1978, pp. 161–71.
15. Bognanno and Dworkin, "Time and Learning."

1. Standard economic models of the labor market are not adequate in explaining wage setting under collective bargaining. Forces of supply and demand limit negotiators, but there remain large areas for discretionary settlement.

2. Collective bargaining is a complex exchange that defies simple analysis, simple models, and simple solutions.

3. Bargaining settlements depend, in part, on how the opposing negotiators value alternative bargaining outcomes, how they view risk, and the subjective strike probability of the opponent that they assign to their own bargaining demands.

4. Perhaps the most difficult bargaining obstacle to overcome is biased, incomplete communication of intent. Incomplete communication occurs because sometimes the bargaining representatives do not know their constituents' position, and because there is an inherent suspicion in bargaining that the opponent is bluffing. Although sophisticated negotiators can minimize this problem, it cannot be eliminated.

5. Much of bargaining can be characterized as a learning process —learning by the negotiating parties which demands are strike issues and which are not. The one bargaining model that explicitly incorporates learning has been proposed by John Cross. Predictions made by the Cross theory hold up in bargaining simulations.

Study remains to be done in understanding the contract negotiating phase of collective bargaining. Many of the collective bargaining practices and public policies regulating collective bargaining could be improved with a better theoretical and empirical understanding of the bargaining process.

Assessing the impact of collective bargaining on wages, productivity and technological change, and aggregate price inflation are the main subjects discussed in Chapter 14.

Questions for Discussion, Thought, and Research

1. Do the classical economic theories of labor markets have any practical use for negotiators? Explain.

2. In what ways do a union's wage-setting practices differ from the practices of a monopolist employer?

3. Define the term *bargaining range*.

4. Compare wage settlements in competitive and noncompetitive labor markets. What are some of the important differences?

5. Show graphically how craft unions restrict the labor supply. What

is the effect of the employer joining other employers to form a multi-employer bargaining unit?

6. In general, wage–employment tradeoffs matter only when there is serious unemployment at stake. Why is the union not deeply concerned about the possible unemployment of a few of its members caused by wage increases for other members?

7. Many of the theories concerning bargaining and behavior fail to address the behavior of individual union members. Many strikes are of such long duration that the employee never makes up the loss in earnings through the wage increases won. If strikes cause great disruption and economic hardship on family life, why do individuals vote to strike? Do any of the theories adequately address this issue?

8. What are the significance and the limitations of the Zeuthen–Hicks–Harsanyi–Bishop bargaining model? Draw on this model to explain why we observe labor and management alternating concessions.

9. John Cross's model examines learning by the negotiating parties. Why is learning behavior important in understanding the bargaining process?

10. "Forces of supply and demand limit negotiations, but there remain large areas for discretionary settlement." Why under standard economic models of collective bargaining is the wage level indeterminate?

11. Does it make sense to have a negotiating committee that projects a high rate of time preference characteristic? Discuss.

Selected Bibliography

Carter, Allan M., *Theory of Wages and Employment*. Homewood, Ill.: Irwin, 1959.

Cross, John G., *The Economics of Bargaining*. New York: Basic Books, 1969.

Dunlop, John T., *Wage Determination Under Trade Unionism*. New York: Macmillan, 1944.

Leninson, Harold M., *Determining Forces in Collective Bargaining*. New York: John Wiley, 1966.

Ross, Arthur M., *Trade Union Wage Policy*. Berkeley: University of California Press, 1948.

Walton, Richard E., and Robert B. McKensie, *A Behavioral Theory of Labor Negotiations*. New York: McGraw–Hill, 1965.

Young, Oran R., ed., *Bargaining: Formal Theories of Negotiation*. Urbana: University of Illinois Press, 1975.

THE ECONOMIC IMPACT
OF COLLECTIVE BARGAINING

14

No understanding of contemporary collective bargaining is complete without considering the effect of unions and the collective bargaining process on important economic issues of today. Collective bargaining creates change in the operation of labor markets. It alters wages, employee mobility, productivity, and other important economic relations. The influence of collective bargaining spreads well beyond the boundary of a bargaining unit. In particular, the influence spreads to the conduct of national economic policy. This chapter is about two economic impacts of collective bargaining: (1) the impact on individuals, some of whom are and some of whom are not represented by unions, and productivity; and (2) the impact of collective bargaining on economic policy, especially efforts to control wage and price inflation.

A REMINDER OF NONECONOMIC EFFECTS

Certainly an important function, perhaps the most important function, of collective bargaining is to provide due process at the workplace to individual employees, and a collective voice by employees in defining the standards of due process. Discussion of the economic effect of bargaining, then, is only a partial perspective from which to evaluate contemporary collective bargaining.

Due process and collective voice do have important economic consequences. As a result of union representation, definition of contractual rights, and systematic enforcement and interpretation of rights, the work force stabilizes, protest is diminished, and some disincentives for employee–employer cooperation dissolve. We examine this effect more extensively under the heading "Economic Efficiency and Collective Bargaining: Two Views."

COLLECTIVE BARGAINING AND NONUNION WAGES

We observe union and nonunion wage rates. But both union and nonunion wages are likely to be changed, either by collective bargaining or by the prospect of collective bargaining. The problem is that we can only guess at what the labor market would be like without unions, and therefore measure imprecisely how union and nonunion wages are changed by collective bargaining, or the prospect of collective bargaining.

Collective bargaining creates a number of pressures, both positive and negative, on nonunion wage rates. Nonunion employers may raise wages because they are threatened by union organization; nonunion employees may be the beneficiaries of union efforts. Nonunion employers may raise wages to avoid losing valuable and experienced employees to higher wage union employers, or to keep wages high enough to retain a choice among more qualified job applicants. Nonunion employers may also increase wages as demand for their product increases when consumers substitute lower priced nonunion goods for higher priced union goods. On the other hand, as union wages rise, employers probably choose to employ fewer workers, either by producing less (but selling at a higher price) or by substituting machinery and equipment for labor. Employees who would have been hired, absent collective bargaining, end up in the nonunion market. As the supply of nonunion workers increases, nonunion wages are driven downward, thereby extending the union–nonunion wage differential.

Evidence suggests that, on balance, collective bargaining tends to depress the wage of nonunion workers.[1] In other words, some part of union wage gain comes at the expense of nonunion workers. This is not, however, uniform among nonunion employees. Where threats of union organization force nonunion employers to raise wages, nonunion employees gain the benefit of union services without financially supporting a union.

COLLECTIVE BARGAINING AND INDIVIDUAL UNION WAGES

Estimates of wage differences between union and nonunion workers are many, and the results are varied. After controlling for other factors affecting wage rates, such as education and experience, estimates vary between about zero and 25 percent for the average difference between union members versus the nonunion workers. Most estimates fall between 10 and 15 percent. Since some part of this difference may result from lower nonunion wage rates, the probable effect of unions on wage rates may be somewhat less than 10 to 15 percent. On the other hand, this may be an understatement because most estimates measure direct wages and unions tend to increase the distribution of the wage package toward indirect or fringe payments.[2]

If the average is 10 to 15 percent higher as a result of collective bargaining, not all union members gain in equal proportions. In general, collective bargaining tends to standardize wages and other aspects of the employment relation.[3] This means employees previously treated unequally, such as minorities, are less likely to be treated unequally. It also means that wages are not as responsive to local labor market conditions or to individual attributes, such as education and experience, under collective bargaining.[4] Union standardization of wages to some extent also may be an attribute of the kind of jobs covered by collective bargaining: production or operative work, especially work on assembly lines, is paced by machines and coworkers; in some instances, individual differences in skill or effort may have a negligible effect on output.

Following is a summary of how union wage effects vary among groups. Most of the studies referenced use data from the private sector.

Education. Union wage increases are larger for less educated workers and

1. Lawrence M. Kahn, "The Effect of Unions on the Earnings of Nonunion Workers," *Industrial and Labor Relations Review*, 31 (January 1978), 205–16.

2. Richard B. Freeman, "The Effect of Trade Unionism on Fringe Benefits," Working Paper 292, National Bureau of Economic Research, October 1978.

3. Richard B. Freeman, "Unionism and the Dispersion of Wages," *Industrial and Labor Relations Review*, 34 (October 1980), 3–23.

4. Farrell E. Block and Mark S. Ruskin, "Wage Determination in the Union and Nonunion Sectors," *Industrial and Labor Relations Review*, 31 (January 1978), 183–92.

smaller for more educated workers.[5] Well-educated persons certainly gain from collective bargaining, but not nearly as much as less educated persons.

Age. Negotiated seniority provisions and standardized treatment affect wage rates of older workers most, younger workers next, and workers at their prime (about age 49) least.[6]

Occupations. Unions have been most successful organizing in blue-collar settings. It is no surprise that unions are more successful raising blue-collar wages compared to white-collar wages.[7] Among blue-collar workers, the craft worker is the elite among workers represented by unions, and the unskilled fare better under collective wage bargaining than the semi-skilled.[8] There is evidence that collective bargaining by sales and managerial occupations lowers the wage rate.[9]

Sex. Groups discriminated against by society are affected by collective bargaining in two ways: wage rates on the job and entry into the job. The former way generally operates toward overcoming discrimination. Collective bargaining raises the pay of women more than men, or, put another way, women are discriminated against less when the employment contract is collectively bargained. The evidence is ambiguous, however.[10] Women tend to especially gain on men in blue-collar unions, but lose to men in white-collar unions. Women are also less likely to be in union jobs than men; this may eliminate the counterdiscrimination force of collective bargaining. It does seem safe to say that the absolute effect of male–female earnings differentials eliminated (or created) by collective bargaining is small.

Race. Black men working in unionized settings fare considerably better than white men when compared to their nonunion counterparts.[11] Equal treatment guaranteed and enforced through the collective agreement has tended to overcome the effects of discrimination. Among industrial unions,

5. George Johnson and Kenwood Youmans, "Union Relative Wage Effects by Age and Education," *Industrial and Labor Relations Review*, 24 (January 1971), 171–79; and Sherwin Rosen, "Trade Union Power, Threat Effects, and the Extent of Organization," *Review of Economic Studies*, April 1969, pp. 185–96.

6. *Ibid.* (both articles).

7. Daniel Hamermesh, "White Collar Unions, Blue-Collar Unions, and Wages in Manufacturing," *Industrial and Labor Relations Review*, 24 (January 1971), 159–70.

8. Sherwin Rosen, "Unionism and the Occupational Wage Structure in the United States," *International Economic Review*, June 1970, pp. 269–86.

9. Ronald L. Oaxaca, "Estimation of Union/Nonunion Wage Differentials Within Occupational/Regional Subgroups," *Journal of Human Resources*, Fall 1975, pp. 529–37.

10. Orley Ashenfelter, "Discrimination and Trade Unions," in *Discrimination in Labor Markets*, Orley Ashenfelter and Albert Rees, eds., (Princeton, N.J.: Princeton University Press, 1973), pp. 88–112; Hamermesh, "White Collar Unions"; Lung-Fei Lee, "Unionism and Relative Wage Rates: A Simultaneous Equations Model with Qualitative and Limited Dependent Variables," *International Economic Review*, 19 (June 1978), 415–33; Oaxaca, "Estimation."

11. Ashenfelter, "Discrimination"; Lee, "Unionism"; Oaxaca, "Estimation."

black and white men have equal access to jobs. Thus, the net impact of wage rates on the job plus entry restrictions overcome discrimination. Among craft unions, blacks have less than equal access to jobs. By restricting entry, craft unions have the net effect of adding to racial wage discrimination.[12] Because most union membership is in industrial unions, the net impact for males is counterdiscriminatory.[13]

Among black women, collective bargaining may not be as successful in overcoming discrimination. The evidence here is mixed. One estimate found that black women gained relative to white women as a result of collective bargaining.[14] Two other estimates found that white women gained relative to black women.[15]

PUBLIC SECTOR UNIONS AND PUBLIC SECTOR WAGES

During the 1950s and 1960s, when public sector union organization began to emerge as an issue, much concern was expressed about public sector unions gaining unfair bargaining advantages relative to private sector unions because of the vital character of many public supplied services. Experience with public sector collective bargaining has dispelled most of this concern. If anything, public sector unions have been somewhat less successful in raising wage rates than their private sector counterparts.

Estimates of relative union wage effects by fire fighters,[16] by municipal employees,[17] by teachers,[18] by hospitals,[19] and in large cross-sectional studies[20] have been equal to or somewhat below the results found in the

12. Distributional evidence taken from Ashenfelter.

13. See also Duane E. Leigh, "Racial Differences in Union Relative Wage Effects—a Simultaneous Equations Approach," *Journal of Labor Research*, 1 (Spring 1980), 95–114.

14. Lee, "Unionism."

15. Ashenfelter, "Discrimination"; Oaxaca, "Estimation."

16. Orley Ashenfelter, "The Effect of Unionization on Wages in the Public Sector: The Case of Fire Fighters," *Industrial and Labor Relations Review*, 24 (January 1971), 191–202; and Ronald Ehrenberg, "Municipal Government Structure, Unionization, and the Wages of Fire Fighters," *Industrial and Labor Relations Review*, 26 (October 1973), 36–48.

17. James Freund, "Market and Union Influences on Municipal Employee Wages," *Industrial and Labor Relations Review*, 28 (April 1975), 391-404; and Roger Schmenner, "The Determination of Municipal Employee Wages," *Review of Economics and Statistics*, February 1973, pp. 83–90.

18. Richard B. Freeman, "Should We Organize? Effects of Faculty Unionism on Academic Compensation," Working Paper 301, National Bureau of Economic Research, November 1978; and Schmenner, "The Determination of Municipal Employee Wages."

19. Myron Fottler, "The Union Impact on Hospital Wages," *Industrial and Labor Relations Review*, April 1977, pp. 342–55; C.R. Link and J.H. Landon, "Monopsony and Union Power in the Market for Nurses," *Southern Economic Journal*, April 1975, pp. 644–59; and Brian Becker, "The Union Impact of Compensation Levels for Nonprofessionals in Hospitals," Ph.D. dissertation, Industrial Relations Research Institute, University of Wisconsin, 1977.

20. Daniel S. Hamermesh, "The Effect of Government Ownership on Union Wages," in Daniel Hamermesh, ed., *Labor in the Public and Nonprofit Sectors* (Princeton, N.J.: Princeton

private sector. Where the relative wage effects of public and private collective bargaining are directly compared, public sector estimates are lower.[21] Most estimates are lower than 15 percent wage increases, and for some types of white-collar professional jobs are near zero and may even be negative.

Public sector unionism had not led to inordinate wage increases for public sector workers. Nor is the magnitude of estimates such as to merit undue concern about collective bargaining bankrupting cities, states, hospitals, or school districts. While many bankruptcy or near-bankruptcy cases can be cited where public sector unions are present, their causes are varied and go far beyond the "unionism" argument.

ECONOMIC EFFICIENCY AND COLLECTIVE BARGAINING: TWO VIEWS

Many classical economists and recently much of the general public have viewed unions as monopolistic, counterproductive organizations. Viewed as monopolistic organizations, unions interfere with the free operation of the marketplace which, in turn, has the effect of decreasing economic efficiency. (Whether any employer is truly "competitive" has been challenged in modern economic research.)[22] Part of every collective agreement, in addition, contains restrictive work rules which may include excessive staffing requirements, restrictions on work assignment, job bidding policies with little transfer of skill, and protection of incompetent employees. Restrictive work rules are especially prominent in craft union contracts where the market is local.[23] Seniority provisions are also seen to block the assignment of the most able worker on the job. From this perspective, unions act to lower labor productivity, distort market forces, and thereby interfere with optimal location of resources within the economy.

A counter view of unions has been argued by specialists in industrial relations, and recently has been stated in an innovative form by Richard B. Freeman and James L. Medoff.[24] The crucial question is which economic, social, and political mechanism can be used to make undesirable employer

---

University Press, 1975), pp. 227–55; and David Shapiro, "Relative Wage Effects of Unions in the Public and Private Sectors," *Industrial and Labor Relations Review*, 31 (January 1978), 193–204.

21. Hamermesh; Shapiro, "Relative Wage Effects."

22. For example, see W. Kip Viscusi, "Unions, Labor Market Structures and the Quality of Work," *Journal of Labor Research*, 1 (Spring 1980), 179–92.

23. Sumner Slichter, James Healy, and Robert E. Livernash, *The Impact of Collective Bargaining on Management* (Washington: Brookings Institute, 1960), p. 336.

24. Richard B. Freeman, "Individual Mobility and Union Voice in the Labor Market," *American Economic Review*, 66 (May 1976), 361–68; Richard B. Freeman and James L. Medoff, "The Two Faces of Unionism," *Public Interest*, pp. 69–93; and Richard B. Freeman and James L. Medoff, *What Do Unions Do?* (New York: Basic Books, to be published).

practices more desirable. The classical economic story is that inferior employers are faced with substantial employee exit (quit), and therefore must either improve their practices or face continual difficulties in retaining a work force. If there are many alternative employers, where the attributes of jobs are well known, and where the cost of leaving one job and taking another is minimal, this is an effective way of insuring socially and economically desirable employer practice. In most labor markets, however, similar alternative jobs are not many, information about alternative jobs involves significant search costs, and benefit rights losses are significant to the employee. Quits are a very costly method of correcting problems from the employee's perspective.

Employers usually have a vague idea about the true reason for an employee quit. Employers cannot correct problems they do not know about. Because quits provide inferior information to employers, and because job quitting can be very costly to the employer as well, employee exit is often a poor mechanism for resolving problems from the employer's perspective.

Another way of correcting undesired employment conditions is for employees to voice their complaints to the employer. This is precisely the function of collective bargaining. The advantage of a collective employee voice is reduction of employee exits and changes in some of the incentives for employer–employee cooperation. Of course, employees can voice their complaints without a union, but to do so may jeopardize their job. One thing unions do, as guaranteed by section 8(a)(1) of the National Labor Relations Act (see Chapter 3), is to protect employee activists when they voice complaints. Another problem with individual voice is the individual versus collective incentives to work for change and to participate in achieving collective benefits (see the discussion of right-to-work laws in Chapter 3).[25]

Collective negotiations and grievance procedures encourage employees to voice their dissatisfaction and, through joint decision making, to resolve problems. Collective bargaining, in the broad sense, is a mechanism that efficiently communicates to the employer the problems of the workplace, and the preferences of the employees. The result of this process is a better, and more suitable, employment contract than would result without a collective voice.

A key part of this perspective is the empirical question of whether employee quits are reduced with collective bargaining. This reduction could be expected because union jobs pay a higher wage, therefore nonunion jobs are less attractive. This result is more a union "monopoly"

25. An alternative reference is Mancur Olson, *The Logic of Collective Action* (Cambridge, Mass.: Harvard University Press, 1971).

effect than a beneficial social product. Another reason for a reduction in quits is the industrial jurisprudence role of collective bargaining. Standardized procedures and due process, which is enforced through contracts and grievance procedures, make a better workplace. This valuable service is produced through the process of collective bargaining. One study found that unionized workplaces do have fewer quits, partly because they pay higher wages but, equally important, because they provide industrial jurisprudence.[26]

As a result of collective bargaining, productivity may be increased in several ways. First, as mentioned, quits are reduced. Turnover of employees diminishes productivity through the loss of firm-specific skills, through the additional recruitment, selection, and training costs for a replacement, and through the disruption of the production process from the temporary absence of qualified workers. Second, protection of senior employees and job security provisions in the collective agreement (see Chapter 12) provide a climate where employee–employer and employee–employee competition lessens and, perhaps, cooperation begins. Senior employees, for instance, may be more willing to teach job skills to less experienced employees, since the contract eliminates the replacement threat to the existing work force. Employees afforded job security may also be willing to point out to management potential improvements in the production process. Without job security guarantees, improved productivity may threaten the jobs of some members of the work force. The threat of job loss may chill employee initiated productivity improving suggestions. Third, though speculative, the improved employment contract may improve employee morale, which in turn may be linked to improved performance. And, finally, as a result of higher wages, employers hire a better quality work force. This last change operates more as an offset to higher wages than as a positive social benefit of unionism.[27]

Inherent in collective bargaining, then, are two contradictory forces operating on the production process: an overly restrictive, counterefficient force and a cooperative, proefficiency force. In any given situation, it may be that one dominates the other. One study of the manufacturing sector, at least, found a proproductive union force dominating a counterproductive force. Brown and Medoff estimate that unions increase productivity by 20 to 25 percent in manufacturing.[28] Freeman and Medoff cite four additional studies, three of which find positive union effects on productivity, and one

26. Richard B. Freeman, "The Effect of Unionism on Worker Attachment to Firms," *Journal of Labor Research*, 1 (Spring 1980), 29–62.

27. Edward Kalachek and Frederic Raines, "Trade Unions and Hiring Standards," *Journal of Labor Research*, 1 (Spring 1980), 63–76.

28. Charles Brown and James Medoff, "Trade Unions in the Production Process," *Journal of Political Economy*, 86 (1978), 375; and Freeman and Medoff, "The Two Faces," p. 79.

of which finds a negative effect of unions on productivity.[29] Additional industry studies will undoubtedly continue to find mixed results.

The fact is, unions have a long-run stake in improving productivity. In the short run, however, a union may oppose more efficient production methods. We review long-run, short-run union interests in productivity in the next two sections.

PRODUCTIVITY AND COLLECTIVE BARGAINING

Productivity is the relationship of some volume of output flowing from the production process to a volume of input(s).[30] Examples of productivity measures are cars produced per man-day, insurance policies issued per salesman, and pages typed per secretary. Productivity indexes may reflect the use of labor alone, as in output per man-hour measurement, or they may incorporate the use of both labor and capital in the production of output.

An increase in productivity indicates that the efficiency of resources used has increased. An increase in labor productivity can be the result of one of many factors. Among these factors are greater employee effort, which can be the result of improved skills through training, improved supervision, tighter work rules and discipline, or higher motivation. Labor productivity can also be influenced by high rates of capital investment, the educational mix of the work force, high rates of invention resulting from large investments in research and development, the technical efficiency with which factor inputs are combined, and economic and social regulations. Obviously, productivity, while a simple concept, is extremely complicated in reality because of the wide range of factors which can affect it.

By increasing productivity, employers gain through reductions in unit labor costs and expanded markets and profits, and workers enjoy improved earnings and a better standard of living. The nation as a whole benefits from productivity increases through improvements in real output, employment, and international trade. Therefore, it is not surprising that both unions and employers should view increases in productivity as a desirable goal. When labor and management meet at the bargaining table, however, disputes with respect to productivity arise, especially about new technologies.

29. Freeman and Medoff, "The Two Faces." See the following article for a report on one of these: Kim B. Clark, "The Impact of Unionization on Productivity: A Case Study," *Industrial and Labor Relations Review*, 33 (July 1980), 451–69.

30. Leon Greenberg, *Collective Bargaining and Productivity* (Madison, WI.: Industrial Relations Research Association, 1975), p. 3.

COLLECTIVE BARGAINING
AND TECHNOLOGICAL CHANGE

An important facet of collective bargaining and productivity is the extent to which the bargaining process blocks or delays new, more efficient technologies. All unions oppose the introduction of new technologies at some time. The crucial question is, To what extent is new technology blocked or delayed and, if delayed, is this a positive or negative impact? In considering this question, it is useful to distinguish between industrial and craft unions.

Within the span of a decade, an annual 2 percent rate of productivity improvement in wages would exceed virtually all of the estimated distributive gains by unions from employers. Over time the most likely and important means to raise employee wages is through increased labor productivity. Thus, it is to the union members' advantage, as well as to the employer's advantage, to introduce new technologies improving labor productivity.

Technological bargaining in the industrial setting usually concerns an adjustment and displacement program, and the distribution of gains from increased productivity; the inevitability of change is assumed. As George Meany once stated:

> Organized labor welcomes technological change, as providing the basis for potential benefits for the nation and all Americans. . . . But organized labor insists that the burdens of rapid technological change must be cushioned, that Government and business must assume their responsibilities to minimize social dislocations and to provide adequate cushions that will protect workers, their families and communities against the hazards of rapid technological changes.[31]

Issues of work force adjustment involve reassignment and retraining of existing employees whose jobs are changed by new technology. Union adjustment concerns include seniority rights, wage and working condition comparability, job transfers, and other issues of this sort. Displacement concerns by unions include slowing the pace of technological introduction in order to minimize layoff of established workers, and, where layoff results, to share the dislocation costs between the employer and employee. Technological displacement of employees involves two costs: the cost to the employer of introducing change (including capital costs) and the cost to the employee of job loss (including loss of seniority related benefits, unemployment, and the trauma of job loss). Collective bargaining is a means to

---

31. U.S. Congress, Joint Economic Committee, *New Views on Automation*, 86th Cong., 2nd Sess. (1960), pp. 336–37; as quoted in *Collective Bargaining and Productivity* (Madison, WI.: Industrial Relations Research Association, 1975).

factor the employee interest into decisions about technological change.

Industrial unions organize many jobs in the same employment setting; technological obsolescence of one or two jobs among many seldom threatens the organizing base of the union. Craft unions, on the other hand, organize a single skill. Technological change rendering the skill obsolete, in effect, renders the union obsolete. Thus, craft unions, especially in entertainment, printing, and construction, are especially concerned about forestalling technologies threatening their existence. Often a method of slowing new technologies, and maintaining employment, is achieved by negotiating restrictive work rules. Craft unions have a more pronounced negative impact on the introduction of productivity improving technologies.

Inevitably, however, even craft unions yield to major new technologies. Examples of two craft or craft-like union concessions include the displacement by computer and other equipment of traditional typesetting jobs in the printing industry, and the displacement of many longshoring jobs by containerization in the shipping industry. In both cases collective bargaining slowed the introduction of technological change, and guaranteed job and income security to many long-time employees threatened by the change: the process of collective bargaining obtained an accommodation of diverse employer and employee interests, not an outright obstruction of more efficient methods of production.

Technological change brought about by the desire to increase productivity has presented serious problems to organized labor. Thousands of collectively bargained plans have been instituted in an effort to protect workers' job and economic security from the impact of new technology. Some of these plans, such as SUB, GAW, and "Long Range Sharing Plan" in the steel industry, have previously been mentioned. There are other examples of union responses to technological change. In the retail food industry, the Retail Clerks' union negotiated a provision in their 1974 contract designed to protect workers against displacement due to the installation of electronic checkouts. The agreement provided that advance notice be given to the union and that regular employees working on the day of the installation of the new system would be kept on the payroll, subject to transfer, or laid off in accordance with seniority, provided that the layoff was for reasons other than the installation of the new system.[32] Clearly, the union's major concern is to provide economic security for workers whose jobs are in danger as a result of technological change brought about by the quest for higher productivity.

---

32. Joseph P. Goldberg, *Collective Bargaining and Productivity* (Madison, WI: Industrial Relations Research Association, 1975), p. 35.

BRIDGE-BUILDING
BETWEEN MICROECONOMIC NEEDS
AND NATIONAL POLICY GOALS

The public expects from employers and unions *some* tangible concern beyond lip service for the macroeconomic impact of their bargains. At the same time, there is no disputing the fact that the bargainers must be expected to pursue their own calculated economic self-interest as they see it. The result of this pursuit may often be inimical to national policy objectives of price stability.

One neglected way to bridge the alleged chasm between national goals and practitioner needs is the union–management cooperation plan. This deceptively general term has a restricted meaning. It is reserved for describing *joint efforts by employers and unions to increase productivity and reduce costs.* If the efficacy of such plans had to be judged on the basis of their proved general acceptance over the years, there would be little point in continuing the discussion. Such plans have never enjoyed any vogue among employers and unions, principally because employers were worried about their managerial prerogatives and employees were fearful about working themselves out of jobs. The only time when union–management cooperation plans were plentiful was during World War II under the special stimulus of a national emergency psychology. We can also name some scattered examples of such joint efforts born in desperation to save particular firms.[33]

The union–management cooperation plan, nevertheless, remains a logical vehicle for facilitating negotiation at the individual firm level that can satisfy simultaneously the employer desire to keep labor costs stable, the employee desire for increased income, and the community interest in promoting noninflationary bargains. These plans have potential for those employers and unions who *on their own initiative* would like to adopt policies that are compatible with national economic goals. The bridge is thus available for those employers and unions that wish to use it.

JOINT LABOR–MANAGEMENT
COMMITTEES IN THE UNITED STATES[34]

One form of union–management cooperation is to establish formal committees designed to permit labor and management to work together in

33. The classic treatment of joint efforts to save individual firms remains that of Sumner H. Slichter, *Union Policies and Industrial Management* (Washington, D.C.: Brookings Institute, 1941). The best account of World War II plans is that of Dorothea de Schweinitz, *Labor and Management in a Common Enterprise* (Cambridge, Mass.: Harvard University Press, 1949).

34. This section borrows greatly from Scott Blum, "Labor Participation in the United States: Productivity Committees in the Basic Steel Industry," master's thesis, University of Minnesota, 1978.

advancing their mutual benefit. Joint committees can be classified as those which provide a financial incentive for employee cooperation and those which offer no direct incentive to the employees.[35] Incentive-type committees are typified by Scanlon plans. These plans are designed to encourage employee participation and cooperation between labor and management in order "to improve organizational efficiency and to share benefits realized from such improvement."[36] Scanlon plans have two distinct features. One feature is a system whereby employees are asked to offer cost reduction and work-saving suggestions. Committees are set up to screen, review, and evaluate employee suggestions. The second feature of Scanlon plans involves the distribution of cost savings to employees. The ratio of labor costs to sales is computed. If in a particular period labor costs are reduced in relation to sales value, this cost reduction is distributed to employees in the form of a bonus. Periodically, the ratio needs to be renegotiated in order to compensate for changes in product mix, or other exogenous factors.

Nonincentive type committees may be grouped into three different categories: information committees, advisory committees, and joint decision-making committees.[37] Information committees are established for the purpose of exchanging information between management and labor and do not necessarily involve employee input into the problem-solving process. In contrast, advisory committees serve the purpose of discussing issues in an effort to solve problems in addition to the mere exchange of information. Joint decision-making committees are relatively rare in that they involve direct employee input into the decision-making process.

In addition to labor–management cooperation at the plant level, committees may form at an industry level with participation by the national or international union. These committees are often formed for the purpose of coordinating union and management lobbying efforts and/or to increase demand for a particular product.[38] An example of this type of labor–management cooperation would be joint efforts to increase tariffs or import quotas in order to make specific products or product lines more competitive with foreign imports. This type of cooperation is not necessarily a boon to the achievement of national economic objectives.

35. Sumner Slichter, *Union Policies and Industrial Management* (Washington, D.C.: Brookings Institute, 1941).

36. Brian Moore, *A Plant Wide Productivity Plan in Action: Three Years of Experience with the Scanlon Plan* (Washington, D.C.: Government Printing Office, 1975), p. 509.

37. Charlotte Gold, "Employer–Employee Committees and Worker Participation," *Key Issues No. 20* (Ithaca, N.Y.: Cornell University Press, 1975), pp. 1–2.

38. Neil Chamberlain and James Kuhn, *Collective Bargaining*, 2nd ed. (New York: McGraw-Hill, 1965), pp. 429–33.

CONDITIONS FOR EFFECTIVE OPERATION
OF A UNION-MANAGEMENT
COOPERATION PLAN

We need to be realistic about the fears of employers and unions that have obviously discouraged support for the union–management cooperation idea in the past. We must think in terms of a plan specifically tailored to lay these fears to rest. This means that the prospects for success are brightest in technologically dynamic growth fields where labor-saving and cost-saving proposals would accompany employment increases rather than reduced job opportunities. In fields where for market or technological reasons the employment prospect is static or declining, the odds would appear heavy against introducing a plan successfully. Even in such cases, however, the idea need not be written off completely. Ways could be worked out to coordinate joint private efforts with ongoing public programs for alleviating structural unemployment and providing continuous training for upgrading work force skills.

For the moment, we will summarize essentials of a viable plan assumed to be operating in a growth environment that minimizes employee insecurity. The first requirement is purely educational. That is, top management, union leadership, and the affected employees must all have a clear understanding and acceptance of the nature and objectives of the plan. This will require some fundamental rethinking and changing of entrenched attitudes in many cases.

Assuming the necessary reeducation and initial enthusiasm for the venture, what are the essential features of a model plan? In our view, the heart of the matter lies in appointing a joint committee whose membership is related to experience and interest in productivity gains and cost reduction rather than to the individual's position in the management or union hierarchy. It is also critically important that the joint committee's jurisdiction be carefully defined. It should be made clear that the committee is advisory in nature. Its findings and recommendations should not be binding on the employer and union in their collective bargaining operations, although much of the committee's work will have great importance for the negotiators.

The range of the committee's jurisdiction will vary from one relationship to another. Committees should deal with topics such as productivity, health, and safety, and human relations issues. The National Commission on Productivity and Work Quality suggests that productivity committees deal with the following issues.[39]

---

39. National Commission for Productivity and Work Quality, *Pointers for Labor Management Committees: Discussion Paper* (Washington, D.C., 1974), pp. 8–9.

1. Conserving energy and eliminating waste of material, supplies, and equipment.
2. Reducing equipment breakdowns and delays in repairs.
3. Improving quality of workmanship and reducing need for redoing work.
4. Using production time and facilities more efficiently.
5. Focusing employee awareness on importance of productivity improvement.
6. Planning introduction of new machinery.
7. Training for new technologies.

DO UNIONS AND COLLECTIVE BARGAINING CAUSE INFLATION?

If the question is whether at some point unions and the process of collective bargaining have inflated prices, the probable answer is yes. If the question is to what extent has collective bargaining caused the inflation of the 1970s and 1980s, the probable answer is very little.

Consider the first question first: How much has collective bargaining raised prices? In order to make this calculation, we start with an estimate on the high end of the relative union wage effect, 15 percent. In 1974, 26.3 percent of wage and salary workers were represented by unions; thus unions raised 26.3 percent of wages by 15 percent, or, on average, unions raised the wage and salary level by 3.9 percent (15 percent of 26.3 percent). Since wages and salaries comprise 68.4 percent of Net National Product (1977), the potential union effect on prices further reduces to about 2.7 percent (3.9 percent of 68.4 percent). If all of the increased wage cost were reflected in prices, then over the course of many years collective bargaining would inflate prices by 2.7 percent. Note that the inflation rate for any one year would be considerably less, and once the full price increase is achieved, the annual inflation rate would be zero. The actual price effect would be less than 2.7 percent for two reasons: (1) some part of the wage increase ends up as lower profits rather than higher prices, and (2) capital may be substituted for labor, partially offsetting the effect of the wage increase on prices.[40]

Collective bargaining could also increase unit costs, and prices, not by raising wages but by lowering productivity. Judging from Brown and Medoff's estimate for the manufacturing sector, this has not been the case. If anything, union-induced productivity increases have offset the union-

40. A similar calculation is made in Albert Rees, *The Economics of Trade Unions* (Chicago: University of Chicago Press, 1977), pp. 96–97.

induced wage increases. It may even be that, on average, unions have no effect on prices because productivity increases offset wage increases.

The second question, concerning the relationship between collective bargaining and today's inflation, can be considered in light of this fact: rapid inflation has coincided with a decline in the proportion of workers unionized. Today's inflation rates are far higher than inflation rates during the late 1930s, and 1940s, and the early 1950s; inflation rates are far higher today, when union representation is declining, than during the period when union representation was rapidly growing. There is evidence, however, that union–nonunion differentials have slowly increased through time; thus, unions may have imparted a slight upward pressure on prices.[41]

As a cause of general inflation, unions and the institutions of collective bargaining are not that significant a factor. This does not mean, however, that collective bargaining practices do not create a significant problem in efforts to curb inflation. It is the nature of this problem that we consider next.

CONTRACTUAL WAGE RIGIDITIES
AND EFFORTS TO STEM INFLATION

Wage changes in the first year of a collective agreement tend to reflect expectations of economic conditions at the time of negotiations. Economic conditions in this sense include recent price changes, plus the state of the overall economy, often represented by the unemployment rate. The second and third years of the three-year agreements without cost-of-living clauses seem to reflect economic conditions anticipated at the time of negotiations.[42] Thus, if negotiators anticipate inflation to be high, and the unemployment rate to be low, large wage increases would occur in the second and third years, even if inflation in fact ends up being low and unemployment in fact ends up being high. Or, the other way, if inflation is anticipated to be low and unemployment high, smaller wage increases would occur in the second and third years, even if inflation is in fact unexpectedly high.

If demand and prices in the aggregate grow faster than expected, real wages, or purchasing power, will fall behind expectations during the second and third years of the contracts. In the short-run, wage moderation, resulting from too low expectations of inflation, will hold down the

41. Daniel J. B. Mitchell, *Unions, Wages, and Inflation* (Washington, D.C.: Brookings Institute, 1981), p. 209.

42. Daniel J. B. Mitchell, "Union Wage Determination: Policy Implications and Outlook," *Brookings Papers on Economic Activity*, No. 3 (1978), 537–92.

inflation rate. The next contract negotiation, however, will find a union attempting to catch up for the loss in real wages. Catch-up wage increases boost operating costs of employers, which end up boosting the product price. Note that collective bargaining is not the cause of inflation; bargainers are only making up for past inflation. But collective bargaining does extend the duration of the inflationary period, initially moderating inflation, then sustaining inflation for a time.

If demand and prices grow slower than expected, real wages will grow faster than expected. This has a serious adverse effect on the employer: wage increases larger than demand increases squeeze profits and, because high unit costs of production resulting from wage increases establish a floor for price adjustments, cut sales. Product cutbacks lead to layoffs, and layoffs lead to high rates of unemployment. The next contract negotiation can adjust wages to economic conditions; in this case, wage increases would be moderated, thereby moderating pressure on prices, lowering inflation and unemployment. Contractual wage rigidities create adjustment obstacles in the economy that make anti-inflation efforts more difficult.

As a general rule, nonunion labor markets are much more responsive to labor market conditions than union labor markets.[43] Unexpected monetary and fiscal economic policies to slow inflation are relatively quickly reflected in wage moderation in the nonunion market. In the union labor market, however, wage moderation occurs more slowly, extending the period of high unemployment longer and slowing the rate of inflation moderation.

The economic dilemma, and the problem facing practitioners of collective bargaining, is how to speed up the response rate of union wages to changes in economic conditions. Practitioners have done this in two ways: by shorter contracts or negotiating contracts with wage reopener clauses and through cost-of-living adjustment clauses. In the next section we review what a cost-of-living adjustment is, why it is used, and how extensive it is in practice. The section after considers the economic implications of cost-of-living adjustments.

COST-OF-LIVING ADJUSTMENTS (COLA) IN COLLECTIVE AGREEMENTS

A cost-of-living escalator clauses is a formal union–management agreement providing for an automatic linkage of employee compensation to changes in an index of consumer prices.[44] COLA clauses are inserted in

---

43. Michael L. Wachter, "Comment," *Brookings Papers on Economic Activity*, No. 3 (1978).
44. Robert H. Ferguson, *Cost of Living Adjustments in Union–Management Agreements*, Bulletin 65 (Ithaca: Cornell University Press, 1976), p. 1.

order to protect the workers' purchasing power. (As prices increase, workers' real wages decrease unless their money wages are adjusted upward. Between 1967 and 1980, the Consumer Price Index [CPI] more than doubled. Thus, a worker who was being paid $5 an hour in 1967 would need over $10 in 1980 to maintain a 1967 level of purchasing power.) In recent years, the number of workers covered by COLA has risen, as shown in Table 14–1. In 1980, 57 percent of all workers covered by major agreements[45] were also covered by escalator clauses. This ratio represents a total of 5.4 million workers. If we counted the number of workers in small units and public sector employees, available statistics suggest that over 8 million workers were covered by escalator clauses.[46]

The development of cost-of-living adjustments has contributed to the growth of multiyear agreements. By providing workers with protection against a drop in their real wages during the life of the collective agreement, escalation has made it more attractive for workers to accept long-term contracts. Without the protection offered by a COLA clause, many unions are reluctant to enter into long-term agreements in times of inflation. Employers, in turn, by accepting the costs and uncertainties presented by COLA clauses, are benefiting by the added labor relations stability derived from long-term agreements.[47]

While escalator clauses provide for an automatic adjustment of wages to changes in consumer prices, there are other contract provisions which safeguard employees against inflation during the term of a multiyear agreement. One such device is deferred wage increases. In contracts continuing deferred wage provisions, employees may be given wage increases through the life of the contract. For example, the agreement may call for an 8 percent first-year increase on wages and a 7 percent increase in each of the last two years of a three-year contract. The term "front end loaded" refers to contracts which provide for heavy increases in the first year. Other agreements contain a contract reopener clause which permits wage negotiations (and the threat of strikes) to commence at fixed time intervals during the life of a multiyear agreement while not opening other contractual provisions to renegotiation. In this way, if the prices have risen higher than expected, the union may reopen the contract and bargain for a wage increase before the expiration date of the entire agreement. Table 14–2 shows the occurrence of these provisions in labor agreements.

45. Contracts covering 1,000 workers or more.

46. Peter Kuhmeiker, "Scheduled Wage Increases and Escalator Provisions in 1976," *Monthly Labor Review*, 99, No. 1 (January 1976), 42–44.

47. For an analysis of employer risks and benefits in accepting indexing, see David Estenson, "Relative Price Variability and Indexed Labor Agreements," *Industrial Relations*, Spring 1981.

Table 14–1

The Growth of Cost-of-Living Provisions in Major Contracts,
1947–76 (as of January 1 of each year)

YEAR	ALL WORKERS UNDER MAJOR CONTRACTS[a] (MILLIONS)	WORKERS COVERED BY ESCALATION (MILLIONS)	PERCENT OF WORKERS COVERED BY ESCALATION	PERCENT INCREASE IN CPI[b]
1947	n.a.	n.a.	n.a.	8.9
1948	n.a.	0.25	n.a.	2.7
1949	n.a.	n.a.	n.a.	-1.8
1950	n.a.	0.8[c]	n.a.	5.8
1951	n.a.	3.0[c]	n.a.	5.9
1952	n.a.	3.5[c]	n.a.	0.8
1953	n.a.	n.a.	n.a.	0.6
1954	7.5[d]	n.a.	n.a.	-0.5
1955	7.5[d]	1.7	23	0.4
1956	7.75[d]	n.a.	n.a.	2.9
1957	7.8[d]	3.5	45	3.0
1958	8.0	4.0	50	1.8
1959	8.0	4.0	50	1.5
1960	8.1	4.0	49	1.5
1961	8.1	2.5–2.8	31–35	0.7
1962	8.0	2.5	31	1.2
1963	7.8	1.85	24	1.6
1964	7.8	2.0	26	1.2
1965	7.9	2.0	25	1.9
1966	10.0	2.0	20	3.4
1967	10.6	2.2	21	3.0
1968	10.6	2.45	23	4.7
1969	10.8	2.66	25	6.1
1970	10.8	2.8	26	5.5
1971	10.6	3.0	28	3.4
1972	10.4	4.3	41	3.4
1973	10.5	4.1	39	8.8
1974	10.3	4.0	39	12.2
1975	10.2	5.3	50	7.0
1976	10.2	6.0	61	4.8
1977	9.7	6.0	60	6.8
1978	9.6	5.8	58	9.0
1979	9.4	5.6	59	13.3
1980	9.3	5.4	57	10.7
1981[d]	9.2	5.3	56	n.a.

[a]Contracts covering 1,000 workers or more. Prior to 1966, the construction, service, finance, insurance, and real estate industries were excluded. Government employees are excluded for all years.

[b]December-to-December increase in U.S. City Average Consumer Price Index.

[c]September figures.

[d]Estimated. n.a. = not available.

Sources: Bureau of Labor Statistics, U.S. Department of Labor, *Current Wage Developments*, 25, No. 2 (February 1974), 45; and the January or December issue of the *Monthly Labor Review*.

Table 14–2

Wage Adjustment Provisions in Agreements Covering 1,000 or More Workers by Duration of Agreement, July 1, 1974

		DURATION OF AGREEMENT			
Type of Wage Adjustment	All Agreements	23 months or less	24–36 months	37–47 months	48 months or over
Number of agreements	1,550	87	1,359	59	45
Number of workers	7,218,000	228,900	6,461,600	334,450	193,050
		(Percentage Distribution by Agreements)			
Cost of living only	1.5	1.2	1.5	0	2.2
Deferred wage increase only	40.8	33.3	41.9	33.9	31.1
Contract reopening only	5.2	10.3	5.0	0	8.9
Cost of living and deferred wage increase	26.6	4.6	27.5	52.5	6.7
Cost of living and contract reopening	0.5	0	0.5	1.7	0
Deferred wage increase and contract reopening	11.2	2.3	10.8	8.5	42.2
Cost of living, deferred wage increase, and contract reopening	8.5	1.2	9.2	3.4	8.9
No reference to wage adjustments	5.7	47.1	3.5	0	0
Total	100.0	100.0	100.0	100.0	100.0
Cost of living alone/or with other adjustments	37.1	7.0	38.8	57.6	17.8

Source: Bureau of Labor Statistics, U.S. Department of Labor, *Characteristics of Agreements Covering 1,000 Workers or More, July 1, 1974*, Bulletin 1888 (Washington, D.C.: Government Printing Office 1975), p. 41.

The terms of COLA clauses vary from one contract to another, and our experience has shown them to be rather complex statements. COLA agreements typically require one of two different methods for transmitting increases in consumer prices to increases in wages and salaries. Both methods link wages to the federal government's Bureau of Labor Statistics indexes of price changes. The Consumer Price Index is used almost exclusively.[48] One of the methods used for transmitting increases in the CPI to wages and salary is to increase (decrease) pay by a fixed percent of the increase (decrease) in the CPI. This method is the most common in units where employees are on salaries and not paid by the hour. By using this *relative base* or percentage method, relative wage differentials among job classifications remain fixed, and therefore the unit's wage structure remains unaffected. This type of clause, for example, may call for an x percent increase (decrease) in wages for every y percent increase (decrease) in the CPI. The second, and by far most common, formula used to translate a change in the CPI to a wage change is the *absolute base* method. In this case, for example, a one-cent-per-hour adjustment in wages may be

48. Ferguson, *Cost of Living Adjustments*, p. 19.

granted for each fraction of a point change in the CPI. The fraction found in most agreements is either .4 or .3 of a point change in the CPI. Both formulas typically result in less than perfect indexing. On the average, COLAs increase wages by about one-half of the rate at which the CPI is increasing.[49] Of course, general, across-the-board wage increases usually make up for rises in the cost of living.

Table 14–3
Frequency of Cost-of-Living Adjustments in Major
Union-Management Agreements, January 1, 1975

| | PERCENTAGE DISTRIBUTION[a] | |
Frequency of Review	Contracts	Workers
Annual	38.3	47.3
Semiannual	10.9	6.8
Quarterly	45.6	43.2
Monthly	0.6	0.1
CPI triggered	1.4	0.6
Other	4.3	2.4
Total number	764	5,032,000

[a]Detail exceeds total because of rounding.

Source: Bureau of Labor Statistics, U.S. Department of Labor, special tabulation, in H. M. Douty, *Cost-of-Living Escalator Clauses and Inflation* (Washington, D.C.: Council on Wage and Price Stability, 1975), p. 20.

There are four other aspects of COLA clauses which warrant mention. First, COLAs differ on the frequency of adjustments. Table 14–3 shows the distribution of frequency of adjustments in collective bargaining agreements in 1975. Needless to say, the more frequent the adjustment, the more costly the provision to employers and the greater the benefit to employees. Second, many agreements have "caps" or "ceilings" on the adjustments. For example, assume the agreement provides for a one-cent increase in wages for every .4 point increase in the CPI, subject to a maximum of 20 cents. Thus, if the CPI increased by 8 points, wages would rise by 20 cents per hour and any further increases in the CPI would not result in a COLA credit. Some COLA agreements also contain provisions calling for "minimums" or "floors." That is, workers are granted a minimum COLA whether or not there has been enough inflation to generate the payment under the clause's formula.

Third, a major negotiable issue within COLA contract language deals with determination of the "time" or dimensions on which COLA rates are to be applied. For instance, are COLA payments to be made on a basis of "time paid for'" or "time worked"? Many agreements exempt vacation,

49. Over the period 1967–77, escalators yielded an increase of 57 percent of the CPI increase. Source: Victor J. Sheifer, "Collective Bargaining and the CPI: Escalation Versus Catch-Up," *Industrial Relations Research Association*, Thirty-First Proceedings, August 1978, pp. 257–63.

sick leave, holiday, jury leave, and other paid time-off categories from their COLA causes.

Finally, most escalator clauses contain either a "roll-up" or "add-on" provision. Under the latter, increases in pay brought about by COLA adjustments are added to the wage payment, but are kept separate from the basic wage rate. This provision can be of significant economic consequence in the computation of overtime payments, incentive earnings, subsequent COLA adjustments, pension benefits levels, and so forth. Under the roll-up clause, the COLA adjustments are merged into the wage schedule.

COLA CLAUSES AND THE ECONOMY

Practitioners bargain hard over COLA. Those agreeing to cost-of-living clauses call attention to the savings for both sides implicit in longer term contracts. With the longer term contract, there is less exposure to the risk of a strike. If you doubt this, note the relationship between frequency of cost-of-living clauses and contract length in Table 14–2.

But if indexing is good for those bargainers agreeing to such a clause, is it good for the rest of us? Is it socially responsible? Let's consider the argument.

First, longer contracts mean more stable, predictable labor relations. Suppliers and customers know that, for the duration of a contract, disruption from labor disputes is very unlikely. Since the cost of labor disputes, and in particular the costs of a strike, affect supplier and customer as well as employer and employee, longer contracts with less frequent exposure to a strike risk spread benefits beyond the bargaining unit.

Second, does cost-of-living indexing of labor contracts cause inflation? Certainly if it were a cause, it would be considered a socially undesirable practice. To answer this question, think about what would be necessary to cause a cost-of-living adjustment. The necessary condition is some price movement. Clearly some price inflation (or deflation) must already exist, otherwise the COLA clause would be inoperant. Every COLA *follows* price changes. But once inflation starts, cost-of-living clauses keep it going. However, most cost-of-living clauses make only partial adjustments to price rises (as previously mentioned, the average is 57 percent) and wages make up only part of the price of a product. Thus, a price increase leads to a partial indexed wage adjustment, and the wage adjustment leads to another partial price adjustment: a price–wage–price inflationary sequence would taper off without some further price stimulus.

Third, COLA clauses are most desirable to the general public when expectations of inflation are high during contract negotiations, but the actual inflation rate for the duration of the contract is less than expected.

Under those conditions, deferred wage increases in collective agreements without COLA clauses exceed the wage adjustments in agreements with COLA clauses.

This difference was behind the 1979 policy of the Carter administration to encourage the use of COLA clauses in collective agreements. All wage increases during the second and third contract years that result from automatic adjustments for changes in the Consumer Price Index, beyond a 6 percent CPI rise, were exempted from the wage–price guidelines. This policy was devised because economic advisors to the Carter administration anticipated that restrictive monetary and fiscal policies would slow the rate of inflation more than union and management negotiators expected. In other words, the economic advisors thought wage adjustments under COLA contracts would be less than deferred wage adjustments under non–COLA contracts.

Such was not the case, primarily because of large price increases in food, fiber, some metals, and energy. The large OPEC oil price increase, for example, was an unexpected source of inflation. The oil price increases, in particular, spotlight the fourth and most negative argument about COLA clauses. Price hikes by OPEC make virtually everyone in the U.S.—wage earner, manager, and shareholder alike—poorer, and people in the OPEC nations richer. Normally wages catch up with price increases in both union and nonunion sectors, and a COLA clause merely helps union workers catch up as fast as nonunion workers. This is not the case, however, when the source of inflation is an OPEC–type price hike. In general, even collectively bargained wages have not caught up with this sort of inflation. Yet COLA clauses automatically reflect OPEC price increases into wage increases, thereby exacerbating the inflation problem. The severest critics of COLA clauses have focused on just this point: that monopoly profits of the oil cartel automatically pass to wage increases, and add to the inflation process. Nonindexed union wages and nonunion wages, on the other hand, do not usually rise with OPEC price increases. That some union wages are indexed and automatically "profit" from rapid oil price increases is the accepted explanation for the expanded union–nonunion differential during the 1974–80 time period.

From a public perspective, while the practice of indexing may benefit some and at times perhaps most, under contemporary economic conditions one can hardly argue that society in general is left better off.

INCOMES POLICY

The wage–price guidelines of President Carter are one example of an incomes policy. An incomes policy involves some form of direct government intervention in the fixing of wages and prices. For present purposes, concern is with the effect of an incomes policy on the practice of collective bargaining, and how collective bargaining generally fits within the context of an incomes policy. The discussion begins with a brief review of the U.S. experience with several wage–price control programs.

On five separate occasions, dating from World War II, the federal government has intervened in wage and price setting by using guidelines or controls.[50] On two occasions, government policies were evoked during times of war. Wartime controls took place during World War II and during the Korean conflict. For several reasons, these wartime controls were different than the more recent incomes policies. First, wartime controls were part of an overall government strategy designed to insure that the war effort was supplied with sufficient material and manpower.[51] Second, since these policies were formulated in response to a national defense emergency, it was relatively easy to gain the support of labor and business leaders. Third, these controls, in addition to regulating wages and prices, were also designed to eliminate or reduce industrial conflict.

The more recent systems of controls were aimed primarily at controlling inflation. However, there were also secondary considerations at work. A study of European incomes policies identified three other objectives which incomes policies are designed to serve.[52] This analysis is also pertinent to U.S. experience. The objectives are as follows:

1. To improve the nation's balance-of-payments position.
2. To aid in achieving a higher rate of economic growth by diverting resources into investment in plant and equipment and away from personal consumption.
3. To raise the relative incomes of the poor and low paid.

At one time or another, our incomes policy has also targeted on one or more of the above objectives, if not in principle, at least as an end result.

The United States has experimented with peacetime policies on three occasions. As our economy grows in complexity and as we have come to acknowledge the difficulties of managing the problems of inflation and unemployment via conventional monetary and fiscal policies, the appeal of incomes policies has occasionally gained and then lost ground. The

50. Control efforts date back to the American Revolution. However, for our purposes these programs can be excluded from this discussion. See Jonathan Grossman, "Wage and Price Controls During the American Revolution," *Monthly Labor Review*, 96 (September 1973).

51. Daniel J. B. Mitchell and Ross Azevedo, *Wage–Price Controls and Labor Market Distortions* (Los Angeles: Monograph Series 16, Institute of Industrial Relations, University of California, Los Angeles), p. 2.

52. Lloyd Ulman and Robert J. Flanagan, *Wage Restraint: A Study of Incomes Policies in Western Europe* (Berkeley: University of California Press, 1971), p. 6.

remainder of this chapter deals with America's experience under the three peacetime programs of incomes policies:

1. The Kennedy wage-price guideposts (1962–66).
2. The Nixon wage–price controls (1971–73).
3. The Carter anti-inflation program (1978–80).

THE ORIGINS AND RATIONALE
OF THE KENNEDY WAGE-PRICE GUIDEPOSTS

Presidents Truman and Eisenhower periodically urged upon management and union representatives the need to be restrained and responsible in their negotiations on wages and economic fringes. President John F. Kennedy, however, advanced from admonitory rhetoric to something much more specific in his wage–price guidepost approach.

The Council of Economic Advisors' (CEA) wage–price guideposts underscored the proposition that gains in real income derive only from economic growth, that is, increases in physical output per man-hour. The CEA made clear that wage increases or price increases unaccompanied by increasing output per man-hour produced inflationary consequences, that is, reduced real national income.

To allow for productivity increases, the guideposts permitted wage increases of 3.2 percent (the average productivity growth rate). Since productivity growth, on average, would offset average wage growth, the unit cost of output would remain constant. The 3.2 percent productivity growth rate, however, was not shared equally across employers: some had rapid rates of productivity growth, and others had no productivity growth. Yet more productive work forces and less productive work forces were both constrained to the average wage increase.

Initial Mistakes in the Wage–Price
Guidepost Policy

Blessed with the customary advantages of hindsight, it is not hard to see why the wage–price guideposts had a rocky road from the start and why the house came tumbling down when the CEA unblushingly refused to follow its own formula in connection with the 1966 guideposts. Several of the more serious errors or flaws should be noted.

In the first place, the consent of the governed was apparently not solicited in advance. There was a failure on the part of both the CEA and President Kennedy to take top management and AFL–CIO leaders into their confidence to secure understanding and support of the new policy. This communication gap came back to haunt the CEA and the White

House in short order. Although contacts were frequent and intense in connection with efforts to secure adherence to the guideposts as specific negotiations took place, the requisite sympathetic rapport was not often there.

A second major flaw in the wage–price guidepost approach was the single-minded concentration on the trend rate in physical productivity per man-hour as *the* criterion for evaluating negotiated economic packages and corporate price changes. From a practical standpoint, it left much to be desired. In the real world of microeconomic decision making, many factors must be considered by management and union at the bargaining table. Corporation X and union Y could not blithely agree on a 3.2 percent increase (covering wages and economic fringes) simply because 3.2 was the magic number in the CEA's calculations. In previous chapters, we described at some length the various factors that the employer and union must consider and weigh in making their wage and fringe policy decisions. To refresh understanding of the importance of this consideration, the following statement of John Dunlop is directly to the point:

> The wage and price guideposts are not expressed in criteria that are meaningful to private decision makers. The "trend rate of overall productivity increase" and the relative rate of an industry's increase in productivity compared to the average are scarcely standards which are meaningful to decision-makers on wages and prices. These concepts are not congenial or directly applicable in their operating experience. Wage decisions are typically argued in terms of comparative wages, living costs, competitive conditions, labor shortages, ability to pay, specific productivity, job content, and bargaining power. Negotiators and their constituents understand these concepts. Pricing decisions are considered in terms of specific competitive prices, quality, advertising, market prospects, responses to changes in other prices, costs, and the like. The diffuse structure of collective bargaining and pricing makes the standards of the guideposts appear remote and unrealistic. The guideposts simply "do not come through." The macro-standards not only have no simple application to specific wage or price decisions, they do not appear relevant. You cannot effectively prescribe micro-decisions with macro-precepts. I suggest that unless guidepost standards are formulated in terms much more directly applicable and specific for decision-makers, in terms they ordinarily utilize, the guideposts will command neither respect nor application.[53]

A third defect in the implementation of the wage–price guideposts was the discriminatorily uneven burden of their impact, even though it could not be said that this was intentional. Perhaps unavoidably, the bright light of guidepost policy was focused on our major oligopolistic industries and the giant unions with which they bargain, notably steel and automobiles. It was an easy matter to wheel the guideposts into position for close

---

53. John T. Dunlop, "Guideposts, Wages and Collective Bargaining," in George P. Shultz and Robert Z. Aliber, eds., *Guidelines, Informal Controls and the Market Place* (Chicago: University of Chicago Press, 1966), p. 86.

monitoring of negotiations involving "big business" and "big labor" where the market power of the participants was clearly visible. It was not long, however, before it became evident to both professional and layman alike that some of the most severe inflationary pressures were emanating from construction, trucking, and a variety of service trades and professions (college and university teaching, for example) rather than from the market giants. At the same time that appropriate restraint was initially displayed in steel and automobile agreements, wage and salary increases far in excess of the 3.2 yardstick were being instituted in these areas seemingly beyond the reach of the administration's educational efforts. No effective way was found to carry the guidepost message to negotiators in these fields. Steel and automobile negotiators were understandably irked about being singled out for federal attention while the decentralized bargainers were able to do their bit to feed inflationary fires in enviable obscurity.

THE NIXON WAGE–PRICE CONTROLS

Unlike the earlier attempt under Kennedy and Johnson, the Nixon administration controls were mandatory. The Economic Stabilization Act of 1970 granted the President the power of imposing direct controls on wages and prices. On August 15, 1971, the President announced Phase I of his program—a ninety-day wage–price freeze. Administered by the Cost of Living Council (COLC), Phase II began on November 14, 1971, and ran through January 1973. This phase was marked by strict controls and reporting requirements. Phases III and IV ran for only a short time and featured liberalized rules. Finally, the controls expired on April 30, 1973, after Congress refused to extend the President's control authority under the terms of an expired Economic Stabilization Act.

Most of the attention during the Nixon era of incomes policy centered around the period of Phase II controls which lasted fourteen months. The other stages were too short-lived to permit meaningful analysis. During Phase II, the Cost of Living Council divided firms and bargaining units into three categories for reporting purposes. Category I included firms with sales of $100 million or more and bargaining units with 5,000 workers or more. Organizations falling into this category were required to obtain prior approval for any wage and price adjustments. Category II included firms with sales between $50 and $100 million and bargaining units with 1,000 to 5,000 workers. These organizations were required to submit reports of any adjustments. Smaller firms and bargaining units (Category III) were subject to the same standards as larger organizations, but were not required to make any reports unless they wished to exceed the standards. In addition, firms and bargaining units falling into Category III were subject to periodic audits by the federal government.

In order to administer the program, the Cost of Living Council established the Pay Board to review wage adjustments and the Price Commission to monitor prices. The Pay Board was originally comprised of fifteen members with equal representation from business, labor, and the public. The board set up a general standard based both on trends in productivity in the economy and on general cost-of-living increases.[54] By setting a 5.5 percent limit on wage and fringe benefit increases, the board sought to hold inflation to 2.5 percent, assuming a 3 percent increase in productivity.

The Price Commission was made up of seven members, most of whom had business experience. The commission devised a different set of rules and regulations for different sectors of the economy designed to hold price adjustments at 2.5 percent or lower. The Price Commission attempted to control price increases by directly limiting weighted average price adjustments and/or by applying a general rule which required firms that increased their prices to maintain a profit margin per dollar of sales that was below the average of the highest two out of three fiscal years prior to the program.[55]

Impact of the Controls

As with the Kennedy–Johnson guideposts, the Nixon controls appear to have restrained inflation for a short time. However, it is now evident that the controls did not have lasting effects on either prices or wages. The success of any incomes policy must be judged not only in terms of its impact on wages and prices, but also on the social costs imposed by the program. From this perspective, if it were possible to measure the costs and distortions attributed to the Nixon controls in terms of time spent complying with the program, and its distortions in labor and product markets, it is unlikely that this program can be judged a success.[56]

A study by Barry Bosworth concluded that the controls program reduced the rate of increase in wages by approximately 1.5 to 2.0 percentage points below the precontrol level.[57] This study reported that the average pay increase approved by the Pay Board for Category I and II firms for the first half of Phase II was 5.1 percent for union and 4.4 percent for nonunion workers. Bosworth also showed that the major impact of the controls program was to reduce the very large increases; that is, settlements above the 9 percent level. Further, it was shown that the rate of increase in

54. Barry Bosworth, "Phase II: The U.S. Experiment with an Incomes Policy," *Brookings Papers on Economic Activity*, 2 (1972), 355.

55. *Ibid.*, p. 359.

56. Robert J. Gordon, "Wage–Price Controls and the Shifting Phillips Curve," *Brookings Papers on Economic Activity*, 2 (1972), 385.

57. Bosworth, "Phase II," p. 362.

consumer prices was slowed from 3.8 percent prior to the freeze to 2.9 percent for the first eleven months of the control program.

In another study, Robert J. Gordon concluded that the Nixon wage and price controls[58] had only temporarily slowed the rate of inflation. Through econometric analysis, Gordon simulated wage and price behavior and found that wages had been deflected downward by .68 percent and prices by 1.85 percent. The same study also concluded that a major consequence of the controls program was to benefit labor at the expense of business. By squeezing profit margins, controls generated opposition from business. Further, when controls were lifted, there was a catch-up period, as business raised prices to free market levels, during which the inflation rate accelerated.

THE CARTER ANTI-INFLATION PROGRAM

The Carter administration guidelines were installed to control wage and price increases, especially deferred wage increases in collective agreements, that might be based upon anticipated high rates of future inflation. The administration planned to take substantial steps toward slowing inflation—even to the point of inducing a moderate recession—and wanted to avoid large wage and price jumps taking place before other policies took effect.

On October 24, 1978, President Carter outlined his anti-inflation program for the nation. Carter's program was designed to attack inflation on two fronts. The first part of the program was designed to curb federal spending. The second part of the Carter anti-inflation program was an incomes policy which specified voluntary guidelines for wage and price behavior. A 7 percent pay standard had been established which limited both wage and fringe benefit increases. This standard applied to average pay for groups of workers. At the time of implementation, inflation was about 7 percent annually. Employers were directed to divide their work force into three groups: management employees, groups of employees covered by a collective bargaining agreement, and all other employees. An employer was in compliance with the guidelines if the average pay increase for each of the groups did not exceed the standard. Collectively negotiated contracts were in compliance with the standard if the total compensation increases averaged 7 percent per year or less over the life of the agreement. In addition, no single year of a multiyear contract could include an increase of over 8 percent. In computing pay increases, a 6 percent rate of inflation was assumed for cost-of-living adjustment calculations.

58. Gordon, "Wage–Price Controls."

The Council on Wage and Price Stability (COWPS) established a number of exemptions to the wage standards.

1. Employees who earn \$4 an hour or less were exempt from the standard.
2. Where employers could establish a tandem pay rate relationship (or pattern bargain), they were not subject to the standard. In order to qualify the employer must show the pay rate changes for one employee unit have been regularly linked to pay rate changes in another employee unit, and the pay rate increase of the other unit must have been made effective prior to the date when the guidelines were announced.
3. When pay increases were granted in exchange for changes in contractual work rules and other practices that positively alter productivity, that portion of the pay increase was not subject to the guidelines. In order to be in compliance, the relative cost reductions generated by the productivity increases had to be equal to or greater than the excess of the relative pay rate change over the standard.
4. Exceptions to the standards were also granted in order to "avoid extreme situations of hardship or gross inequities."[59] The purpose of this exception is to allow the COWPS to make adjustments in the standards in order to reflect labor market conditions.
5. Payroll taxes and mandatory employer contributions, such as for social security and/or worker's compensation, were excluded.

President Carter's pay standards were immediately criticized by the labor community as being inequitable and unfair.[60] Among other criticisms, the AFL–CIO believed that including all fringe benefit costs in the wage control figure was impractical.[61] The increased costs of pensions and health care made it impossible for employees to enjoy the same level of benefits at a comparable cost. Thus, the AFL–CIO argued that it was unfair to include these uncontrollable costs in the 7 percent standard. As a result of pressure from the labor community, COWPS modified the general wage to exclude some fringe increases as long as there was no benefit increase.[62]

Why else were the Carter guidelines so widely criticized by labor? First, Carter's plan for enforcing the standards was criticized as unrealistic. COWPS was initially staffed by a total of 135 persons. During the Nixon

59. Council on Wage and Price Stability, "Noninflationary Wage and Price Behavior, Voluntary Standards," *Federal Register*, 43 (November 7, 1978, Part II), 51953.

60. Statement by the AFL–CIO Executive Council on Anti-Inflation Program, October 31, 1978, p. 1.

61. *Ibid.*, p. 3.

62. Council on Wage-Price Stability, *Fact Sheet*, December 13, 1978.

controls 900 people were employed by the Cost of Living Council and another 2,800 Internal Revenue Service agents were used.[63] It is unrealistic to expect that 135 people can monitor wages and prices throughout the economy. Organized labor argued that the most visible targets were collective negotiations for major bargaining units. It would be these units that would be pressured, and it would be the many small price-setting decisions that would be unaffected.

Second, the 7 percent standard was well below the current rate of inflation by the first quarter of 1979. Although only 7 percent at the time of design, by the time of implementation the U.S. experienced an annualized inflation rate of 13 percent. It is unlikely that labor would accept such a drastic cut in real wages. This leads to the third problem.

Typical collective agreements last for three years. During that time, excepting for contracts with wage reopeners, the terms and conditions of employment cannot change, given changed circumstances or new information. Thus, unions agreeing to 7 percent annual wage increases in 1979, are typically bound to this rate of wage improvement until 1982, even if, in the intervening period, inflation soars, as it did in 1979, to double-digit levels. Employers and nonunion workers can adjust prices and wages to new circumstances, since they are usually not bound by a contract. If unions and employers accede to the pressures of wage guidelines, they are taking a far greater risk than a typical price taker or nonunion wage and salary worker: once controls are lifted, prices and nonunion wages are free to move, but the union and employer are bound to the contracted wage rate. If prices are inflated faster after controls are lifted, as happened after both the Kennedy–Johnson and Nixon controls, it is the union membership that loses relative to nonunion workers and firms.

In order to minimize this source of union concern, the Carter administration guidelines did two things: (1) as already discussed, they encouraged the use of COLA clauses (so that union wage rates would adjust upward if prices rose rapidly); and (2) they proposed a real wage insurance plan that ultimately failed to be passed by Congress. Real wage insurance was intended to protect employees covered by collective agreements which stay within the guidelines from a loss of purchasing power. Failure of this innovative proposal to pass Congress created additional union concern about the risk of conforming to the wage guidelines.

During 1979 a number of major negotiations occurred. Settlements with the Teamsters, United Rubber Workers, and United Auto Workers each bent the guidelines a little farther. Under terrific inflationary pressure, the guidelines became exceedingly difficult to enforce absolutely. It does seem likely, however, that, as with the Kennedy–Johnson guideposts, the Carter incomes plan did moderate collective bargains.

63. Statement by the AFL–CIO, p. 10.

As one of his first official acts, President Reagan dissolved COWPS shortly after his inauguration in January 1981.

COLLECTIVE BARGAINING CRITERIA
FOR INCOMES POLICIES

An effective incomes policy judged solely from the labor relations perspective should be several things.

Acceptable. Participants in collective bargaining eventually learn that "acceptable" is more important than "ideal." Terms of agreement must be acceptable for the membership to ratify them. Arbitrators must be acceptable to *both* sides to be selected. Any proposal or arbitrator that is unacceptable to either side will not work. The same pertains to incomes policies: successful incomes policies must be acceptable to both labor and management.

The Kennedy–Johnson guideposts were destroyed due to their inability to gain acceptance by the labor community. The guideposts earned early credibility when President Kennedy successfully "persuaded" the steel companies to back down after they announced price increases in excess of the guideposts. However, just as quickly and abruptly, the guideposts lost their credibility and were destroyed when the International Association of Machinists (IAM) struck the airlines and successfully negotiated a contract well in excess of the guidepost figure.[64]

In 1978 the incomes policy in Great Britain tumbled with the negotiations at the Ford Motor Company subsidiary in Great Britain. Controls were installed at a time when inflation was 20 percent. The wage limit was set at 10 percent. Toward the end of the fourth year of controls, after inflation had fallen below 10 percent, the maximum wage limit was lowered to 5 percent. Angered by the continued loss of real wages, labor unions judged the new guidelines unacceptable. The strike against the Ford Motor subsidiary was in essence a strike, not against Ford, but against the incomes policy. Ford was confronted with a dilemma: conform to the guidelines and continue the strike or compromise with the union and risk the censure of the government. Ford eventually compromised with the union; this breaking of the controls limit marked the effective end of the program. A knowledgeable observer of the British industrial relations scene told one of the authors that if the maximum had been left at 10 percent, labor unions would have accepted the limit. From the standpoint of economic planning, the 5 percent wage limit may have been ideal. But because it was unacceptable, it was ineffective.

---

64. For an excellent account, see John Sheehan, *The Wage-Price Guideposts* (Washington, D.C.: Brookings Institution, 1967), Chapter 5.

In 1979 the Teamsters' strike was also more against the wage guidelines than against the employers' council. Here again, the employers were in an uncomfortable position between a union and economic planners. The ultimate resolution of this strike was a compromise not so much between the employers' council and union as between the union and the federal government. The agreement needed some creative interpretation to stay within the guidelines.

Unacceptable standards generate opposition that can rend the whole incomes program. Short of destruction, unacceptable standards can generate strikes and other forms of disputes that are harmful to efficient labor relations and economic production.

Symmetry. When government incomes policy agents enter the collective bargaining process, they do not come as neutrals, they come with the purpose of constraining wage increases. They are trying to accomplish exactly what the employer is trying to accomplish: keep wages low. It may be that at some point the employer is willing to compromise when the economic planners are not willing to compromise. Nevertheless, from the perspective of the bargaining table, the government is clearly siding with one against the other. The one-sided nature of the intervention is enough to engender considerable skepticism among labor negotiators about the fairness of the incomes policy.

In order to obtain labor cooperation, controls on management salaries and shareholder profits must be as effective, and as visible, as controls on union wages. Ineffective controls on either nonunion wages and salaries or profits will lead unions to construe that the government intervention is indeed as one-sided as it appears. Inevitably, such one-sided treatment will bring labor opposition. Pressure that squeezes profits or nonunion wages but not negotiated wages, will bring similar opposition from employers and nonunion workers. Efforts to hold back prices right after a generous labor agreement is signed will especially incur business anger.

To be acceptable to both sides, the effect of controls must be even, or symmetric, in application to both employer and employee. Reports of large profits at the same time wages are limited, or reports of large wage increases at the same time profits are falling, foster noncompliance and political efforts to end controls.

Flexibility. A not atypical problem in administering incomes policies can be illustrated by considering two bargaining situations alike in every sense, except that one contract had a COLA clause and the other did not. In situations where inflation moved at an unexpectedly fast rate, the contracted wage without a COLA clause falls behind both inflation and the wage rate indexed to prices. When both contracts are renegotiated, should both contracts be held to the same wage standard? Or should the contract without a COLA clause be permitted a large wage increase to make up for real wage loss?

An inflexible standard would not allow the nonindexed workers to make up either inflation related wage losses or wage losses relative to the indexed contract. A flexible standard may permit different rules because the circumstances of each negotiation are different. In this illustration it seems reasonable that the nonindexed contract should be permitted a larger wage increase.

As a general rule, the more flexible the incomes policy, the more likely that the negotiated agreements will be workable and acceptable. From the perspective of collective bargaining, inflexible standards can create undue hardship on some bargainers. The cost of flexibility, however, is higher administrative cost of standard setting and enforcement. It is probable that the incomes policy best for the functioning of the collective bargaining system is excessively costly to administer. It is also probable that an easily administered, inflexible incomes policy is excessively costly to the collective bargaining system.

A CAVEAT ON INCOMES POLICIES

The collective bargaining system we have described in this book is predicated upon a principle of "free collective bargaining." This means that the parties most directly involved negotiate and settle the terms and conditions of employment. The parties must conform to certain rules —rules designed especially to diminish damage to innocent third parties —but generally the parties are given considerable latitude to choose the settlement point.

This system has considerable advantages: one advantage above all others is that ultimately only persons directly involved must apply and live with an agreement on a day-to-day basis. Only these persons have sufficient information to arrive at a workable agreement. Any standard imposed from outside must be, on some dimension, less workable than the freely bargained agreement. Setting only one, inflexible standard assumes that each bargaining situation is precisely the same, and therefore should reach precisely the same terms. Even the most naive should be a bit incredulous about accepting such an assumption.

Applying and living with an agreement implies that, at least temporarily, the most severe elements of dispute, or risk of dispute, are suspended. An unworkable agreement too often means continued dispute; if the parties are constrained from reaching a workable agreement by outside intervention, the dispute may manifest itself as a strike or lockout, or as an unproductive adjustment at the workplace. Dispute in the form of a strike, in effect, against some guideline, is costly to the economy, and especially costly to the employer who is an innocent party caught in the middle between economic planners and an unhappy union.

European incomes policies are often held up as models which the United States should emulate.[65] Because the U.S. industrial relations system differs markedly from other systems, transfer of successful programs from another system to the United Stated is probably inappropriate. In many European countries, collective bargaining is highly centralized and most of the nonmanagerial work force is represented by unions; in these countries successful negotiations take place at the national level between labor representatives, business representatives, and government representatives. The entire range of issues involving the distribution of income, including not only union wages but profits, executive pay, interest income, and so on, are resolved at this level. The result of this negotiation process is a broad social contract among the economic interests in the nation.[66]

In the United States we have a very decentralized industrial relations system. There is no organization that can act at the national level as the voice for labor, or for business. The AFL–CIO is perhaps the closest thing to a national representative for labor. But it has limited authority when it comes to commiting labor to a social contract. The AFL–CIO is first a federation with limited control over the national unions and the local bargaining units. Membership in the AFL–CIO is also a small proportion of the nonagricultural work force, primarily because only a bit more than 20 percent of the U.S. work force is unionized, but also because not all unions are affiliated with the AFL–CIO.[67] Thus, there is no national representative for labor in the way that such representation exists in some other nations.

The organizational structure for first intraorganizational bargaining at a national level on both the labor and business sides, and then trilateral national negotiations among labor, business, and public officials does not exist in the United States. We lack the mechanism to achieve an acceptable social contract. We also lack an effective enforcement mechanism for any such contract. Where the number of decision-making units are few in number, monitoring and compliance efforts are minimal. In the United States, however, we have thousands of collective agreements and thousands of price-setters; problems of monitoring and compliance are too overwhelming for a sustained incomes policy.

---

65. We do not mean to imply that European incomes policy experiences have been booming successes. Sylvia Ostry and Mahmood A. Zaidi observe that the results of postwar incomes policies in Western Europe, "particularly from a long-run point of view, are not very encouraging." See their book, *Labour Economics in Canada*, 3rd ed. (Toronto: Macmillan of Canada, 1979), p. 259.

66. For a discussion of the limitation of the social contract concept to U.S. collective bargaining see Robert J. Flanagan, "The National Accord as a Special Contract," *Industrial and Labor Relations Review*, 34 (October 1980), 35–50.

67. This problem will be partially ameliorated when the UAW reaffiliates with the AFL–CIO. In June, 1981 the executive councils of both organizations voted to reaffiliate the UAW's 1.2 million members.

SUMMARY

We have reviewed the findings of numerous studies which report the measured impact of collective bargaining on individual wages and productivity. This chapter also related the aggregated impact of these negotiated wage and productivity determinations to their macroeconomic consequences and public policy implications.

In summary, there is evidence that collective bargaining increases the wages of union members relative to nonunion members, and that it even tends to depress the wages of nonunion workers except in those instances where management reacts to the threat of unionization by granting employee wage increases as a way to avoid becoming organized. Union wage gains are not distributed evenly; they depend on industry, occupation, race, sex, education, and age.

The empirical record is mixed with respect to the impact of collective bargaining on productivity. What is certain, however, is that while labor and management share a common interest with regard to the long-run benefits from productivity growth, the reverse may be true in the short run. When productivity gains in the short run can only be achieved through technological change with resulting staff reductions, a conflict develops. We advance the use of union-management cooperation plans as a way of avoiding such conflicts, and as a means for bridging the chasm between national economic goals and specific negotiation needs of the parties. Such plans could help balance the interests of labor, management, and society.

Incomes policies do not hold much promise as a way to regulate wage, price, and productivity aggregates. The industrial relations system in the United States is too decentralized and dynamic to regulate through controls. The best regulators are the union and management, and the American worker.

In the next chapter, we discuss contemporary developments highlighting collective bargaining in the public sector.

Questions for Discussion, Thought, and Research

1. In a broad sense, why must real wage increases be linked to productivity?

2. It is generally agreed that the average wage paid to union members exceeds that of unorganized employees. Is this proof that unions secure higher wages for its members than they would obtain without a union? Explain.

3. Does collective bargaining cause inflation? What evidence could you draw upon to support your argument?

4. Two employees in different industries are represented by equally aggressive and competent unions. In the last decade, wages have increased by three times for employee A, and doubled for employee B. What forces might explain the difference in increased wages between these two employees?

5. Why is it so difficult to determine the amount unionization raises or lowers wages?

6. Under what conditions is a union–management cooperation plan likely to succeed?

7. How does a cost-of-living escalator work? What are some of the key issues involved in negotiating a COLA clause?

8. What are some of the lessons we have learned from previous efforts at wage–price controls? Is it possible to design an incomes policy which doesn't seriously erode "free collective bargaining"? Explain.

9. What criteria should be used in evaluating an incomes policy? Why?

Selected Bibliography

Bok, Derek, and John Dunlop, *Labor and the American Community*. New York: Simon and Schuster, 1970.

Greenberg, Leon, *Collective Bargaining and Productivity*. Madison, Wis.: Industrial Relations Research Association, 1975.

Mitchell, Daniel, *Unions, Wages and Inflation*. Washington, D.C.: Brookings Institute, 1980.

Rees, Albert, *The Economics of Trade Unions*. Chicago: University of Chicago Press, 1977.

Ulman, Lloyd, and Robert J. Flanagan, *Wage Restraint: A Study of Incomes Policies in Western Europe*. Berkeley: University of California Press, 1971.

PUBLIC SECTOR
COLLECTIVE BARGAINING

15

Recent years have found the practice of collective bargaining extended to a number of areas where, if not unheard of, collective bargaining was minimal. Hospitals, schools, government bureaucracy, public safety agencies, and sports have all struggled to adapt bargaining processes to their different conditions. Throughout the book we have occasionally included public and nonprofit sector examples with private sector examples; we see public and private sector bargaining as variants of a fundamentally similar process. In this chapter we will briefly review public sector topics not readily suited for other chapters or covered incompletely in other chapters. In the next chapter we review three other emerging sectors of collective bargaining—health, sports, and higher education.

WHAT'S DIFFERENT ABOUT PUBLIC SECTOR COLLECTIVE BARGAINING?

The first thing that is different about public sector collective bargaining is that it has been growing rapidly at all levels of government in recent years. This contrasts with the relatively slow growth in the private sector. With rapid growth, however, have come many new problems. As we review in this chapter, public sector collective bargaining is not readily suited for all aspects of private sector practices.

For one thing, employees who have unionized in the public sector are much more diverse; they are not just craft and production workers, but also professionals, clerical and administrative workers, and public safety workers. These employee types are organized by a diversity of sometimes competing unions into many, often fragmented, bargaining units. The many new "communities of interest" create new tensions for collective bargaining.

Employers, like employees, are different in the public sector. Government as a representative system does not reflect a single voice on matters of policy, as well as matters of collective bargaining. The system of checks and balances in government decision making creates problems, as we shall discuss, for the bargaining process. Fitting the electorate—the ultimate employer—into the bargaining process is also an issue not present in the private sector.

Strikes by government workers have become more frequent events compared with the early 1960s and 1950s. To deal with this problem many states and the federal government have adopted innovative means, such as interest arbitration, as substitutes for a strike. Public sector unions have the strike weapon in common with private sector unions. They also have a weapon not found in the private sector; the public sector union can use political campaigns as methods to persuade and coerce employer representatives.

Impasse procedures such as interest arbitration are examples of regulation of the collective bargaining process in the public sector. Governments and their employees are not covered by the National Labor Relations Act (NLRA). The federal government has passed a law regulating labor relations in the federal sector. This law differs in some respects, but not all respects, from the NLRA. The states have been left to regulate government collective bargaining at the state and local level. The states have responded with a variety of statutes. The many experiments going on among the states may provide the foundation for future reform of our private sector policies. We devote much of this chapter to a summary and discussion of state regulation of public sector collective bargaining.

GROWTH

During the last two decades there has been no more important, more controversial, and more discussed collective bargaining event than the rapid growth of public sector unionism. Yet there is nothing new about unionism among government employees. Blue-collar craftsmen working for government agencies at various levels have been represented by labor organizations for many years—in some cases quite effectively.[1] Also, in particular circumstances, professionals and technicians have enjoyed an approximation of collective bargaining for long periods of time. The case of TVA employees comes readily to mind.[2] David Ziskind's painstaking research serves to remind us of many past occasions when government employees have gone on strike.[3] Public sector collective bargaining appears to be a firmly entrenched part of the U.S. system of industrial relations.

Rapid growth of public sector collective bargaining beginning about 1960 has three sources: (1) the greater willingness and ability of public sector employees to form unions, (2) the transformation of traditional public sector representative and professional associations into bargaining organizations, and (3) the growth of public sector employment.

Even in retrospect, it is not clear why public sector employees suddenly began joining unions and associations around 1960. This is especially surprising since, at the same time, private sector unions grew slowly. A variety of reasons are offered for this sudden transformation, including a changing political environment (marked especially by President Kennedy's 1962 Executive Order 10988, which permitted bargaining in the federal sector), low pay and poor personnel practices in the public sector compared to the private sector, and growing public employment which attracted unions and politicians. John Burton concludes, after an exhaustive survey, that individually or cumulatively none of the reasons adequately explains growing public sector unionism![4]

Table 15–1 presents U.S. Labor Department statistics documenting the growth in public sector employee organizations. From 1956 to 1978, public sector unions increased 500 percent, while total union membership in-

1. For the early history see Wilson R. Hart, *Collective Bargaining in the Federal Civil Service* (New York: Harper & Row, 1961).

2. See Arthur A. Thompson, "Collective Bargaining in the Public Service: The TVA Experience and Its Implications for Other Government Agencies," *Labor Law Journal*, 17 (February 1966), 89–98; Aubrey J. Wagner, "TVA Looks at Three Decades of Collective Bargaining," *Industrial and Labor Relations Review*, 22 (October 1968), 20–30.

3. David Ziskind, *One Thousand Strikes of Government Employees* (New York: Columbia University Press, 1940).

4. John F. Burton, Jr., "The Extent of Collective Bargaining in the Public Sector," in Benjamin Aaron, Joseph R. Grodin, and James L. Stern, eds., *Public Sector Bargaining* (Madison, Wis.: IRRA, 1979), pp. 1–43.

Table 15-1

Public Union Growth: 1956–78

YEAR	TOTAL PRIVATE AND PUBLIC UNION MEMBERSHIP[a,b]	PUBLIC SECTOR UNION & ASSOCIATION MEMBERSHIP[c]			NUMBER OF PUBLIC EMPLOYEES		PERCENT PUBLIC UNION AND ASSOCIATION MEMBERS OF ALL UNION MEMBERS[b]	PERCENT PUBLIC EMPLOYEES UNION OR ASSOCIATION MEMBERS[b]
		Total	Unions	Assoc.	Year	Total		
1956	17,490		915		1956	7,278	5.2	12.6
1958	17,029		1,035		1958	7,839	6.1	13.2
1960	17,049		1,070		1960	8,353	6.3	12.8
1962	16,586		1,225		1962	8,890	7.4	13.8
1964	16,841		1,453		1964	9,596	8.6	15.1
1966	17,940		1,717		1966	10,784	9.6	15.9
1968	20,721	3,857	2,155	1,702	1968	11,839	18.6	32.6
1970	21,248	4,080	2,318	1,762	1970	12,554	19.2	32.5
1972	21,657	4,520	2,460	2,060	1972	13,334	20.9	33.9
1974	22,809	5,345	2,920	2,425	1974	14,170	23.4	37.7
1976	22,660	5,582	3,012	2,840	1976	14,871	24.6	39.4
1978	22,880	6,094	3,625	2,469	1978	15,476	26.7	38.9

[a]Totals in this column exclude reported Canadian membership and members of single firm unions.

[b]Numbers in percentages represent union membership only for 1956–66; union and association membership 1968–78. Note that the percentage increase from 1966–68 in the last two columns primarily results from including association membership with union membership.

[c]Totals in these columns may include some reported members outside the United States.

Sources: Bureau of Labor Statistics, U.S. Department of Labor, *Directory of National and International Labor Unions in the United States*, for the data covering the period of 1956–66; Bureau of Labor Statistics, U.S. Department of Labor, *Directory of National Unions and Employee Associations*, for the data covering the period of 1968–78; Bureau of Labor Statistics, U.S. Department of Labor, *Monthly Labor Review*, for the number of public employers, 1956–78.

creased in the United States by only 33 percent. If union-like associations in the public sector—such as the National Education Association—are included, the percentage increase would be more. Statistics on public sector association membership, unfortunately, were not collected prior to 1968.

Part of the increase in public sector union and association membership resulted from the increase in publi: sector employment. Public sector employment more than doubled between 1956 and 1978 (Table 15–1). Part of the increase resulted from the greater percent organized for bargaining. By 1978 almost 40 percent of all public employees were represented by unions or associations. This percent is greater than the private sector peak of about 36 percent achieved shortly after World War II. Public employee membership exceeds 6 million.

The rise of public sector unionism has also altered the composition of union and association membership in the United States from a minor portion in the public sector to a rather significant 25 percent (Table 15–1). What kind of organizations are these new bargaining agents? And whom have they organized?

COMPOSITION OF PUBLIC UNION MEMBERSHIP

Initially government unions grew faster in the federal sector. President Kennedy's 1962 Executive Order 10988 was an important encouragement to federal sector unions. Executive Order 10988 supported union recognition, including exclusive bargaining units, and permitted negotiated agreements (though it did not permit strikes or arbitration of interest disputes). Since the late 1960s, federal union representation (Table 15–2) and federal employment have stagnated. Today, almost 60 percent of all civilian federal employees are represented by a union.

Table 15–2

Composition of Public Sector Unions and Associations: Federal Versus State and Local

YEAR	FEDERAL	STATE AND LOCAL	PERCENT FEDERAL
1968	1391	2466	36
1970	1412	2668	35
1972	1383	3137	31
1974	1433	3911	27
1976	1334	4518	23
1978	1420	4674	23

Source: Bureau of Labor Statistics, U.S. Department of Labor, *Directory of National and International Labor Unions in the United States,* for the date covering the period of 1956–66; Bureau of Labor Statistics, U.S. Department of Labor, *Directory of National Unions and Employee Associations,* for the data covering the period of 1968–78; Bureau of Labor Statistics, U.S. Department of Labor, *Monthly Labor Review,* for the number of public employers, 1956–78.

Since the late 1960s, the growth area for public sector unionism has been the organization of state and local government employees. Over the decade 1968–78, state and local government unions and associations grew by over 85 percent. By 1980, less than one-fourth of all public sector union members were in the federal sector (Table 15–2).

Public employees are represented by a wide variety of unions and associations which provide union-like services. Most unions and associations operate exclusively in the public sector, although some unions, such as the Service Employees International (SEIU) and Teamsters, organize both public and private workers. In the federal sector, the largest unions are the American Federation of Government Employees (AFGE), National Association of Letter Carriers (NALC) and the American Postal Workers Union (APWU). These three unions each exceed a membership of 200,000; each is an affiliate of the AFL–CIO.[5]

Among state and local unions and associations, the largest is the National Education Association with about 1.7 million members in 1978.[6] Other educational representatives are the American Federation of Teachers with 500,000 members in 1978 and the American Association of University Professors (AAUP) with 60,000 members. Both of the associations, the NEA and the AAUP, represent fewer persons in collective bargaining than they have members.

The largest union or association outside of education is the American Federation of State, County and Municipal Employees with over 1 million members. AFSCME is the largest public sector union belonging to the AFL–CIO. Other than AFSCME, state and local government employees are represented by a wide variety of specialized unions representing fire fighters, police officers, service workers, and nurses. The largest organization after AFSCME is the Assembly of Government of the State Employee Associations, a federation of independent associations representing employees of the various state governments.

Several public sector unions and associations have formed a federation, called the Coalition of Public Employees, or CAPE, to further the broad interests of public sector employees and their unions. AFSCME and the NEA are dominant members of CAPE.

Much more than in the private sector, public sector unions compete among each other for members and for representation rights. Much of the competition is between traditional public sector unions, usually affiliated with the AFL–CIO, and the associations, which have been transformed from professional advancement and lobbying organizations into collective

5. For a more extensive review of the composition of public sector unions see James L. Stern, "Unionism in the Public Sector," in Aaron et al., *Public Sector Bargaining*, pp. 44–79.

6. *Directory of National Unions and Employee Associations*, Bureau of Labor Statistics, U. S. Department of Labor, Bulletin 2079, 1980 (Appendix).

bargaining agents. Prominent competitors include the National Education Association affiliates against American Federation of Teachers affiliates, the American Federation of Government Employees (federal) versus independent federal associations such as the National Federation of Federal Employees and the National Association of Government Employees, and affiliates of the American Federation of State, County and Municipal Employees against affiliates of the Assembly of Government of the State Employee Associations. Rivals in the public sector also include exclusive public sector unions such as AFSCME versus primarily private sector unions such as the SEIU or Teamsters. The result of this rivalry is that most public sector employees may choose from more than one type of representative organization, and employer representatives must negotiate with a variety of very different unions.

Public sector unions specialize. Most specialize by level of government, either federal, state, or local. Many specialize by occupation; specialty occupations include unions of letter carriers, fire fighters, teachers, police, and nurses.

The diversity of public sector unions reflects the diversity among public sector employees and employers. But as these highly specialized unions have evolved, it has made it more difficult to avoid fragmentation of public employees into many competing bargaining units, and it is more difficult to discover the common interest among public sector employees.

EMPLOYEES AND EMPLOYEE INTERESTS IN THE PUBLIC SECTOR

Throughout most of this book, discussion of union employees has been oriented toward production and maintenance (P & M) bargaining units, with references also to craft bargaining units. In the private sector, P & M and craft workers are the primary portion of the work force represented by unions. Both types of workers are found in the public sectors, and both are represented by unions in the public sector. The public sector, however, has many types of work also unionized that have no substantial private sector counterpart.

Professionals such as engineers have organized in the private, for-profit sector, but unions have not been successful in organizing a sizeable plurality of any professional work. In the public sector we do find extensive unionization of professional workers, the most notable being teachers, but also including other types such as social workers or nurses. In some situations administrators have also been unionized in the public sector. Well-educated professional and administrative workers are concerned with pay and working conditions, just like any other unionized employee. Professional workers often take a broader view of working conditions, however, than workers in fairly routine jobs. Professionals and administrators especially want to participate in decision making about the delivery of services to their clients. Decision making about production and delivery is usually left to management in the private sector; the encroachment of unionized professional workers into this area in the public sector has been a source of continuing conflict over the demarcation between management rights and working conditions.

Police, fire fighting, and other types of public safety work also have no substantial private sector counterpart. Public safety workers have very different interests from typical production and maintenance workers. They work odd hours, in dangerous conditions, in a military-like operation, sometimes in emergency situations. They also do things to or for members of the public which may not be popular with everyone, and therefore citizen complaints affect the job security of the public safety officers. The proper role of industrial jurisprudence for this type of work will have different limits than in the typical private sector union.

When private sector unions are discussed, it is usually in the context of a factory or a special project such as in construction. The private sector bureaucracies, the banks, the insurance companies, the corporate offices, are largely not unionized. In the public sector they are unionized. A bureaucracy is characterized by an extreme division of labor divided further into many separate divisions, departments, and groups. Skills range from maintenance and operation to clerical to professional and administrative. There is unlikely to be one dominant skill group at one dominant level in the hierarchy of jobs. How to group the diversity of bureaucratic skills and job types together for bargaining purposes remains one of the ongoing problems in the public sector.

In the bureaucratic setting, and elsewhere in the public sector, the division between supervisor (or manager) and union employee has not been distinct. Back in the days when associations were low-key, fraternal, and "advancement" organizations, before they became collective bargaining agents, people from top to bottom joined. As associations acted more like unions, the appropriateness of having "management" in the union was questioned. But exactly who was management and therefore who should be kicked out of the union or association was dealt with in a variety of ways by the parties involved.

To be successful in bargaining, and in dispute resolution, a union must represent a community of interest. What we have been discussing here is a rather large number of communities of interest in the public sector. The worker performing routine clerical tasks is probably not especially sympathetic to the demand of professional workers for reform of the delivery system for their service. The professional worker is probably not aware of or especially interested in the safety and discipline problems of interest to public safety workers. Public safety workers are probably not too worried

about the hours and working conditions of production and maintenance workers, who in turn may not want to give up anything to resolve the issues of interest to clerical workers. Far more than any other industry, government has spawned a variety of unions; the many unions have formed to represent the many communities of interest. There is not a typical public sector employee or public sector union.

The many communities of interest have created the problem of fragmentation of bargaining units that we discussed in Chapter 4. At some point, the number of bargaining units reaches a point where it is very inefficient and almost unmanageable for the employer to conduct simultaneous negotiations with each union. Unions, as well, may be too small to afford a staff to handle negotiations. In these situations the different unions often end up competing as much against each other for a bigger piece of the same budget, than for a bigger budget for all workers.

Chapter 4 also discussed coordinated and coalition bargaining. In this type of bargaining several unions join together to coordinate negotiation of several separate contracts, or join in a coalition to negotiate a common agreement with a single employer. Coalition and coordinated bargaining by several unions has occurred in the public sector (the most notable example occurred during the financial crisis in New York City), but this has not become an extensive practice.[7] The diversity of public sector unions and employees, and the diversity of public sector employers (see the next section), make it unlikely that there will be a sufficient common interest in coalescing, except under the most adverse conditions.[8]

Legislatures and regulating agencies have developed rules and procedures for dividing employees into bargaining units. These rules and procedures are discussed in a subsequent section entitled "Recognition Rights and Procedures."

EMPLOYER DECISION MAKING AND COLLECTIVE BARGAINING

We have one federal government, fifty state governments, and tens of thousands of local governments, ranging from city and county governments to special districts operating such services as schools, water works, sewage disposals, transportation systems, and mosquito controls. Each unit of government is an employer and may be engaging in collective bargaining with one or frequently more unions. Government employing units differ greatly in their size, complexity, and administrative structure,

7. See David Lewin and Mary McCormick, "Coalition Bargaining in Municipal Government: The New York City Experience," *Industrial and Labor Relations Review*, January 1981, pp. 175–90.

8. *Ibid.*

and in their decision-making procedures by elected officials. Just as there is no typical public employee, there is no typical public employer.

In the private sector, management represents shareholders or a sole owner. There is a well-defined chain of command from a board of directors to top managers and then down through the managerial hierarchy. In the public sector, management represents the voting public. Sometimes the chain of command is quite clear in the public sector, very much like the private sector. (We set aside for a time the issue of involvement by the public in collective bargaining and the jurisdiction of civil service systems.) Often, however, the system of checks and balances built into government offers no clear chain of command, and therefore no clear managerial voice.

Examples of a public sector decision-making structure reasonably parallel to a corporate decision-making structure include school districts and other special districts where an elected board operates much like a corporate board of directors, and single council types of city and county government. A superintendent or manager reports to and is directed by a board, council, or commission, and oversees the administration of government, including collective bargaining.

The federal government, state governments, and many municipal governments, rather than have a single board, council, or commission, operate with a legislative branch—Congress, legislatures or assemblies, and city councils—and with an executive branch—the president, governors, and "strong" mayors. In cities where authority of elected officials is split between the branches of government, nonelected city managers sometimes gain some authority over many decisions in government. Government decisions with this type of structure are multilateral. Collective bargaining is a bilateral process. It has been troublesome to fit this bilateral process into an inherent multilateral process. Yet, for collective bargaining to work, proper identification of an employer is essential to prevent confusion and buck-passing.

Diffusion of employer authority creates several problems in collective bargaining. First, the union can play all sides until it achieves the most favorable terms. A solid employer position is the starting point toward eventual compromise. When there are many, fluid management positions, negotiation becomes an ongoing process without the strong emphasis on compromise and resolution usually associated with collective bargaining. Also, there may be no agent on the employer side taking responsibility for collective bargaining. Disputes may continue to simmer without anyone able to reach agreement.

Collective bargaining is a process that brings about compromise because of changes in attitude and decision criteria shaped by the interaction of negotiators. Agents sitting on the sideline, such as a council or legislature, do not receive the information that those directly involved in negotiation receive. As a result, their attitudes and decision criteria do not change; this can act as an obstacle to agreement. Finally, if an agreement is reached, it may be difficult to administer because of the many lines of authority. For example, an elected official may refuse to enforce a provision negotiated by another elected official, or a legislative body may refuse to allocate funds to fulfill a contract negotiated by a professional negotiator for the employer, or by an elected executive official.

Further complicating this problem of diverse employer authority is the division of duties among the levels of government. Often, local government officials depend on funding sources and guidelines established by states or by the federal government. On many of the issues most important to local employees, local officials have little control and therefore little room exists for collective bargaining.

There is one remaining area where collective bargaining confronts the problem of shared authority in the public sector. Collective bargaining infringes on the traditional jurisdiction of the civil service systems. Civil service was designed to insulate public employees from some political influences, especially by encouraging merit principles over political crony-ism. In order to do this, civil service boards and directors were given some responsibility for areas previously controlled by elected officials. In many cases unions seek to change rules established by civil service systems. In adapting collective bargaining to the public sector, civil service has been largely confined to serving the role of a personnel department. Re-sponsibility for labor relations has been removed from the civil service jurisdiction. Just where personnel ends and labor relations starts, how-ever, is never entirely clear; thus, we continue to encounter jurisdictional differences.

Of course, the ultimate voice of the employer comes from the electorate. Just where the electorate fits into the collective bargaining process is a question we address in a later section.

COLLECTIVE BARGAINING WEAPONS

What makes an employer concede to at least some union demands? In the private sector strikes are the primary vehicle for gaining concession, although boycotts have been used with occasional success. Private sector strikes impose costs directly on the employer; economic loss promotes concession. Although strikes are used by unions in the public sector, pressure on the employer is more political than economic.

In the public sector, the source of revenue (taxes) is independent from the actual delivery of the service. If a school day is lost due to a teachers' strike, taxpayers seldom receive a rebate on their taxes for service not delivered. Even with fee for service operations, such as mass transit, taxes usually cover part of the operating expense. Thus, the loss of revenue and fear of bankruptcy is not the pressure that forces employer agents to compromise in the public sector.

What other pressures are there? For a strike to be successful the clientele of the service must put pressure on elected officials to settle the dispute, and elected officials must be less able to withstand the pressure than the striking workers. With very visible, vital services, strikes succeed for unions with sufficient frequency to be a useful weapon. Police, fire, health, some transportation, sanitation, and public education fall in the visible, vital category.

Other types of public service are not in the effective strike category. In some cases the clientele is not sufficiently concerned or influential to exert pressure. Many services for the poor, services not vitally affecting citizens, such as libraries and parks, or services whose continued delivery is already politically marginal are examples. Other services are not in this category because work can cease for a time without seriously affecting the quality of service. Highways can be maintained, at least for a while, with a minimal staff, and research and planning services can be delayed. Thus the strike can be an effective weapon in the public sector, but it influences employer representatives in a different way than in the private sector, and the strike is not an effective weapon for many public sector unions.

Public sector unions, however, have another weapon that they may employ in an effort to win better conditions of employment. They may invest time and money in support of political candidates favorable to their cause. They may also invest time and money persuading the public about the merits of their cause. And they may invest time and money supplying information before executive and legislative officials that is favorable to their cause. Many unions exist primarily by using this method as their vehicle toward gaining collective bargaining status.

Through legislation, as discussed in a subsequent section, many states have established impasse procedures, such as interest arbitration, as a substitute for the strike. Fear of an unfavorable arbitration award, as discussed in Chapter 9, may force both employer and employee to bargain. Sometimes arbitration laws were passed to substitute the arbitration threat for the strike threat. At other times the arbitration threat was created for unions that presented a minimal strike threat. In this case, the arbitration threat was usually gained as a result of political activity and persuasion by unions.

STRIKES IN THE PUBLIC SECTOR

Strikes by public sector employees are nothing new. The U.S. Bureau of Labor Statistics has compiled data showing at least one strike in the public sector every year since 1942. These strikes occurred despite the almost universal illegality of public sector strikes. Beginning about the mid-1960s the number of public sector strikes increased substantially (Table 15–3). Today public sector strikes are frequent occurrences.

Table 15–3

Number of Public Sector Work Stoppages, 1960–78

YEAR	TOTAL	FEDERAL	STATE	LOCAL
1960	36	—	3	33
1961	28	—	—	28
1962	28	5	2	21
1963	29	—	2	37
1964	41	—	—	42
1966	142	—	9	133
1967	181	—	12	169
1968	254	3	16	235
1969	411	2	37	372
1970	412	3	23	386
1971	329	2	23	304
1972	375	—	40	335
1973	387	1	29	357
1974	384	2	34	348
1975	478	—	32	446
1976	378	1	25	352
1977	413	2	44	367
1978	481	1	45	435

Source: *Work Stoppages in Government, 1978*, Bureau of Labor Statistics, U.S. Department of Labor, Report 582, April 1980.

Most public strikes are found at the local level of government (Table 15–3). This is not surprising, since this is the level with the most bargaining units. Strikes are not spread evenly across the different functions of government. An inordinate number take place in education. Table 15–4 shows that in 1978 over half of all strikes were in education. Although teachers are frequent strikers (see Table 15–4), the majority of strikes in education are not by teachers. There seems to be something about education (rather than teachers), perhaps the single-board method of employer control and the effect of a strike on the public, that makes both union and management agreeable toward the use of the strike weapon. Also note in Table 15–4 that production and maintenance workers conduct a significant share of public sector strikes.

The issues in public sector strikes are little different from issues in the private sector. In 1978, 73 percent of all government strikes were over issues related to pay, compared to about 70 percent in the private sector.[9] Well less

9. The source for these and other figures in this section is *Work Stoppages in Government, 1978*, Bureau of Labor Statistics, U.S. Department of Labor, Report 582, April 1980.

Table 15-4

Number of Work Stoppages by Government Function and by Occupation, 1978

FUNCTION	NUMBER[a]	OCCUPATION	NUMBER[a]
Administrative		Professional and	
Welfare Services	16	Technical	161
Public Safety	46	Teachers	125
		Nurses	9
		Other	27
Public Utilities	55	Clerical	10
		Production and	
		Maintenance	146
Education	246	Police	21
Parks, Libraries,		Fire	15
Museums	1	Combinations	
		or Other Public Safety	9
Hospitals and Health	18	Other	119
Transportation	20		
Others and			
Combinations	57		
Total	481		481

[a]Does not equal the sum of individual entries because some strikes occur in two or more groups.

Source: *Work Stoppages in Government, 1978,* Bureau of Labor Statistics, U.S. Department of Labor, Report 582, April 1980.

than 1 percent of all strikes in both sectors involve issues of hours worked. Union organization and security are the issues in a little more than 5 percent of strikes in both sectors, and working conditions and job rights issues account for about 21 percent of all strikes in both sectors. The strike issues indicate that government unions have essentially the same concerns and goals for their members as unions in the private sector.

Public sector strikes are shorter than in the private sector, 9 days versus 23 days in 1978. Public sector unionized workers also strike less frequently than their unionized counterparts in the private sector. As a result, days of idleness as a percent of total work time due to work stoppages remain very small in government, about four one-hundredths of 1 percent in 1978.

In sum, strikes are occurring with greater frequency in the public sector than in the past, though the frequency is still less than in the private sector, and the strikes are shorter than in the private sector. Government strikes start over essentially the same set of issues as other strikes.

Most states have made strikes by government workers illegal. Reasons given for this policy include the lack of market discipline on public employers, therefore the fear that public employers will give in too easily, and that the burden of a strike falls on a small portion of the community, yet the whole voting (and taxpaying) community must, in effect, agree to end the strike.[10] Strike laws are enforced either with a court-ordered injunction or by statutory penalties. Failure by a union official to comply with a court-ordered injunction can result in the jailing of the union official. Statutory penalties include, for example, the loss of union recognition, loss of dues checkoff, job loss for striking workers, fines against strikers and unions, and imprisonment.

Strike penalties are not always successful in practice. If they were effective we would have few strikes by government workers. Jailing union leaders makes them martyrs; rather than deterring strikes, jailings tend to rally striking workers around their cause. Penalties, if viewed as "unfair" or excessive, or if the union cannot pay, are often not levied by courts or other agencies. Often, as a condition for settling the strike, unions require dismissal of any penalties. In practice, if not in law, many of the penalties against government strikes have been removed.

The trend in statutory penalties by the states has been toward less severe penalties, such as forfeiture of checkoff privileges.[11] These penalties are viewed as more likely to be enforced, and therefore more effective. Another state trend is toward the granting of a conditional right to strike to public sector employees. These experiments in legal strikes are discussed under the section headed "Impasse Procedures."

States have adopted extensive regulation of public sector collective bargaining in part to control strikes. These regulations are summarized in the next six sections.

REGULATION OF COLLECTIVE BARGAINING

In Chapter 3 we summarized national public policy toward collective bargaining. None of this policy applies to collective bargaining in government. For state and local government units, regulation is left to the states. Some states have no laws; to the extent that there is any regulation it is by common law (interpretations by judges not based on legislation). States with laws (the majority of states) typically have separate regulations for different types of public employees (teachers, police, fire fighters, etc.) and for state and local governments. The number and complexity of these regulations has been changing rapidly in recent years.

The diversity of regulations among the states serves one useful purpose:

10. Robert E. Doherty, "Public Policy and the Right to Strike," in Muriel K. Gibbons et al., eds., *Portrait of a Process—Collective Negotiations in Public Employment* (Fort Washington, Pa.: Labor Relations Press, 1979), p. 252.

11. Walter J. Gershenfeld, "Public Employee Unionization—an Overview," in Gibbons et al, *Portrait of a Process*, p. 20.

it has created a massive experiment in the regulation of collective bargaining. As different units try different methods, much is learned about which regulations work and which do not work. State control also permits state governments to tailor regulations to their own wants and circumstances. It may be that the experience gained from the states will eventually serve as the basis for reform of the National Labor Relations Act.

In the next sections we provide tables summarizing some of the statutory regulations by state. We focus on the five main areas for regulation: recognition rights and procedures, the scope of bargaining, unfair labor practices, impasse procedures, and union security. Later, we briefly summarize the law regulating collective bargaining by federal government employees.

Recognition Rights and Procedures

Recognition rights and procedures establish the union as the representative of employees and settle any questions over which employees are represented by the union. Recognition rights and procedures are an integral part of the National Labor Relations Act, and have become an integral part of the regulations established by most states. In general, the states have chosen to model this area of regulation after that set in the NLRA. It must be emphasized, however, that not all states have chosen to regulate this area of collective bargaining, and of those states that do regulate this area of collective bargaining, rights and procedures may apply to only a subset of public sector employees.

Under the National Labor Relations Act, a certified union becomes the exclusive union representative of a group of employees. The union is certified by the National Labor Relations Board after a demonstration of employee support for the Union, or, if there is any doubt about employee support, after an election supervised by the NLRB. If there is any question about which employees are in the bargaining unit, the NLRB resolves the matter by defining the unit.

Exclusive representation is an important collective bargaining practice in the United States. As is apparent in Table 15–5, states with laws have chosen to adopt this practice for public sector collective bargaining. With exclusive representation a group of workers speaks with one voice, and employers must bargain with only one union for each group of employees. In states without exclusive representation laws, it is up to the union to assert enough pressure to force the employer to recognize and bargain with it. It has been common in the public sector, where there is extensive competition among unions, for an employer to have more than one union seek recognition as the representative of a group of employees. Procedures to establish exclusive recognition can remove any ambiguities about the true representative. Exclusive representation usually carries with it a responsibility for the union; the union must represent fairly all members of the bargaining unit.

Many states have set up administrative agencies that are similar to the NLRB. These agencies, often called Public Employee Relations Boards, or PERBs, certify the exclusive union representative, conduct representation elections, and, as discussed shortly, sometimes determine the bargaining unit. PERBs have a variety of other duties: they adjudicate unfair labor practice complaints; many provide mediation, fact-finding, and interest arbitration services in addition to maintaining a list of arbitrators for grievance arbitration; they compile statistics about labor relations and matters of interest to negotiators, such as comparative wage and salary data; and they analyze the workings of these sometimes experimental laws in order to determine if they are working properly or need reforming.[12]

A PERB conducts an election for the union representative and sets rules governing the conduct of the election. Under the NLRA, a majority of employees *voting* in an election determine the outcome. This allows employees to choose whether they want union representation, and, if so, which union they want. Some states use an election criterion more rigorous than the NLRA by requiring a majority of those eligible to vote, not those who actually vote, for union representation. The rationale for this rigorous standard is avoidance of having a union forced on public employees. So far this standard has had no significant effect, since the percent of eligible voters actually voting has been very high.[13] Table 15–5 shows that most states with laws have opted for one form or another of supervised union election.

Often, which employees should be included in the bargaining unit, and therefore eligible to vote in the union election and to be represented by the union, is hotly contested. Most state regulations determine methods to resolve this dispute. Some refer the decision to an administrative agency such as a PERB (see Table 15–5). The agency may determine a set of rules for bargaining units or handle each dispute on a case-by-case basis. The problem the PERB must resolve is where the community of interest lies. Factors a PERB might consider include the job functions of employees, their rates of pay, whether pay is hourly or salary, different employee training, education and experience, types of fringe benefits, and the location and conditions of work.[14] Besides the employees' community of interest, the board must look at where the employer's administrative authority is located. If the agency controls few of the important issues, then

12. Robert D. Helsby and Jeffrey B. Tener, "Structure and Administration of Public Employment Relations Agencies," in Gibbons et al., *Portrait of a Process,* pp. 31–54.

13. Richard Pegnetter, "Majority Voting Requirements in Public Employee Bargaining Unit Elections," *Thirty-third Industrial Relations Research Association Proceedings* (1981), pp. 234–40.

14. Parker A. Denaco, "Conceptual Considerations for Unit Determination," in Gibbons et al., *Portrait of a Process,* p. 112.

Table 15–5

Public Sector Regulations Governing Recognition Rights
and Procedures by State: 1980

STATE[a]/EMPLOYEE GROUPS[b]	EXCLUSIVE UNION RECOGNITION	SUPERVISED REPRESENTATION ELECTION	BARGAINING UNIT DETERMINATION	
			BY PERB[c]	BY STATUTE
Alaska				
State and Local	x	x	x	
Public School Teachers	x	x		x
California				
State, Schools, Colleges	x	x	x	
Local Government	x	x	(d)	
Connecticut				
State and Municipal	x	x	x	
Public School Teachers	x	x		x
Delaware (All)[e]	x	x	(d)	
Florida (All)[f]	x	x	x	
Georgia (State)	x	x		
Hawaii (All)	x	x		x
Idaho				
Teachers/Fire Fighters	x	x		
Illinois (State)	x	x	x	
Indiana (Teachers)	x	x	x	
Iowa (All)	x	x	x	
Kansas				
Teachers	x	x	(d)	
All Other	x	x	x	
Kentucky (Louisville Fire Fighters)	x	x		
Maine				
State and Local	x	x	x	
Maine University	x	x		x
Maryland (Public Schools)	x	x		
Massachusetts (All)	x	x	x	
Michigan				
State Civil Service	x	x	(d)	
Local	x	x	x	
Minnesota (All)	x	x	x	
Missouri (All)	x	x	x	
Montana				
Nurses	x	x	(d)	
All Other	x	x	x	
Nebraska				
Teachers	x	(g)		x
Other	x	x	(d)	
Nevada (Local)	x	x	x	
New Hampshire (All)	x	x	x	
New Jersey (All)	x	x	x	
New Mexico (State)	x	x	(d)	
New York (All)	x	x	x	
North Dakota (Teachers & Administrators)	x	x		
Oklahoma				
Public School		x		
Police/Fire Fighters	x	x	x	
Oregon (All)	x	x	x	

Table 15-5 *(continued)*

STATE[a]/EMPLOYEE GROUPS[b]	EXCLUSIVE UNION RECOGNITION	SUPERVISED REPRESENTATION ELECTION	BARGAINING UNIT DETERMINATION	
			BY PERB[c]	BY STATUTE
Pennsylvania				
Police/Fire Fighters	x			
All Other	x	x	x	
Rhode Island				
Fire Fighters, Police				
& Teachers	x	x		x
State and Other Local	x	x		
South Dakota	x	x	(d)	
Tennessee (Teachers)	x	x		
Texas (Police/Fire				
Fighters)	x	x		
Vermont				
State/Municipal	x	x	x	
Teachers	x	x		x
Washington				
State	x	x	(d)	
Municipal/Teachers	x	x	x	
Community College	x	x		x
Wisconsin				
State	x	x		x
Local	x	x	x	
Wyoming (Fire Fighters)	x	x		

Exclusive Union Representation: The certified (usually elected) union is the only representative of employees for the purpose of collective bargaining.

Supervised Representation Election: Any questions about which union, or if any union, represents a majority of employees are resolved by an election conducted by a state authority.

Bargaining Unit Determination: Decisions about which employees are included or excluded from the bargaining unit are either specified by statute, left to a board for resolution, assigned to an administrative agency, or there is no legislative guidance on the issue.

aStates omitted from the list have no legislation dealing with union recognition rights and procedures in the public sector (13 states not listed).

bWhen more than one employee group is mentioned, they are covered by separate, somewhat different, legislation.

cPERB: a public employee relations board, or a board of a like name, usually similar in concept to the National Labor Relations Board.

dBargaining unit decisions are made by a department, e.g., departments of industrial relations, education or personnel, rather than by a board.

eIndication of "All" does not mean that every state and local employee is covered; every statute excludes some employees such as supervisors, political appointees, and those with confidential information. Rather, "All" indicates that state, local municipal, and school board employee groups, at least, are covered by this legislation.

fFlorida offers a local option on collective bargaining that is overseen by a State Public Employee Relations Commission.

gNebraska teacher union recognition is based on union enrollments over the most recent two years. This is used in lieu of an election. Note, as well, that Nebraska uses state labor courts, now called commissions of industrial relations, instead of administrative boards in overseeing application of labor–management regulation.

Sources: *Summary of Public Sector Labor Relations Policies: Statutes, Attorney Generals' Opinions and Selected Court Decisions, Labor-Management Services Administration,* U.S. Department of Labor, 1979; and Richard R. Nelson, "State Labor Legislation Enacted in 1978," and "State Labor Legislation Enacted in 1980," *Monthly Labor Review,* January 1980, January 1981.

the employer has little to bargain about. If the bargaining unit is too broad, on the other hand, many of the local concerns of administrators and employees are not reflected in bargaining.[15]

Other state regulations define bargaining units by statute rather than by referring the decision to a board (see Table 15–5). The legislature with this approach must consider the same factors as the board in its deliberation. When the bargaining unit is fixed by statute, it is relatively inflexible. When determined by a PERB or other agency, it allows for some element of voluntary agreement by a union and an employer.

Whether some or all administrators—persons who supervise—should be part of the bargaining unit is one of the difficult questions legislatures and public employee relations boards must answer. Since supervisors enforce the contract, it is argued, they should be eliminated from the bargaining unit. Perhaps they should have a separate bargaining unit, or, since someone must administer the contract, a separate contract for each hierarchical layer. This strategy, of course, adds to the problem of fragmentation of public sector bargaining units. Since administrators have much in common with the interests of all other career employees, goes the counterargument, they should be in a common bargaining unit. The latter argument is especially appropriate if bargaining issues are primarily money issues decided by a legislative body.

States have taken different approaches to supervisors and bargaining units.[16] Some have excluded supervisors completely from bargaining units covered by regulations. This approach is the same as contained in the National Labor Relations Act. Another approach is a rigorous definition of supervisor so that many persons with supervisor titles, but limited supervisory authority, are included in the bargaining unit with nonsupervisory employees. "Bona fide" supervisors are excluded from the bargaining unit. In some states, bona fide supervisors are allowed to form their own bargaining unit. More states give supervisors bargaining rights than exclude supervisors.[17]

Scope of Bargaining

·The National Labor Relations Act requires labor and management to bargain over wages, hours, and other conditions of employment. Under the *Borg–Warner* interpretation, the board has ruled that private sector bargainers may strike over issues of wages, hours, and other conditions of

15. *Ibid.*

16. Steven L. Hayford and Anthony V. Sinicropi, "Bargaining Rights Status of Public Sector Supervisors," *Industrial Relations,* February 1976, p. 59.

17. Hugh D. Jascourt, "Recent Trends and Developments," in Hugh D. Jascourt, ed., *Government Labor Relations: Trends and Information for the Future* (Oak Park, Ill.: 1979), p. 11.

employment, and may not strike, but may bargain, over all other legal issues (see Chapter 3). The question of bargainable issues has largely been settled in the private sector for over twenty years.

In the public sector, which issues are bargainable and which are restricted solely to the employer remains to be settled. The "scope of bargaining" defines the permitted bargaining issues. The problem of defining limits is more complicated in the public sector than in the private sector. No clear demarcation exists. Most people seem to agree that collective bargaining should be confined to wages, hours, and other conditions of employment, just as in the private sector.[18] Traditionally, and where management rights are spelled out by statute, elected officials have retained sole control over public policy decisions. The problem is that virtually every employment condition issue affects in some way the decision-making flexibility to determine policy by elected officials.

Legislation or administrative agencies must resolve the difficult problem of finding those issues that cut "too much" into the decision-making duties of elected officials and of finding those employment issues that only incidentally restrain elected officials. As in any area where the boundaries are imprecise, there are disagreements among interested parties on just which issues are bargainable. Guidelines that do emerge represent a compromise of many viewpoints.

An issue representative of this type of problem is the number of pupils per class in public education.[19] Class size clearly affects working conditions for public school teachers. On the other hand, class size directly translates into cost-of-education issues, including such policy decisions as tax rates, capital improvements (such as more buildings to house smaller classes), and the like that are traditionally reserved for elected representatives. Costs and therefore tax rates are vital to this debate since 70 percent of government costs are for wages and salaries.

Even before the advent of collective bargaining, attempts were made to separate the purely political decisions from employment decisions. Mostly, the separation was made by giving civil service commissions the responsibility for most employment decisions. Even then, it was not clear where the authority of civil service should end and where the authority of elected officials should begin. Collective bargaining has replaced civil service in many areas today, but the problem of separating pure politics from employment decisions remains.

Issues typically within the scope of bargaining include pay, fringe benefits, transfer rights, performance evaluation procedures, and seniority. Issues typically outside the scope of bargaining, and therefore reserved

18. Arvid Anderson and Joan Weitzman, "The Scope of Bargaining in the Public Sector," in Gibbons et al., *Portrait of a Process*, p. 173.

19. Steven C. Kahn, "The Scope of Collective Bargaining in the Public Sector: Quest for an Elusive Standard," *Employee Relations Law Journal*, 4, 1979 562–75.

exclusively for employer decision, are budgeting, employee selection, discipline, standards of performance, policies and programs, and choice of technologies.[20]

Unfair Labor Practices

Unfair labor practices set ground rules for the conduct of collective bargaining. Unfair practices as defined by statute and as interpreted by a board are collective bargaining behaviors against the rules of the game. Many states have followed the precedent set by the National Labor Relations Act and forbidden certain practices in their statutes regulating collective bargaining for government employers and employees. Most states with unfair labor practices include some of the same unfair practices as found in the NLRA.

A requirement that both unions and employers must bargain in good faith is a central part of the NLRA. In one way or another, most states with unfair labor practice statutes include a good faith bargaining provision (see Table 15–6). Some are fairly weak requirements to "meet and confer." Others are much stronger requirements creating a duty to bargain.[21] Meet and confer requires that the parties listen to arguments and proposals made by their opponents, but does not require that a sincere attempt be made toward reaching agreement. Duty to bargain requires a sincere attempt toward reaching agreement. Sometimes statutes require meet and confer on some issues—for example, education policies (for teachers), and a duty to bargain on others—for example, wages, hours, and conditions of employment.[22]

A variety of other rules to facilitate good faith efforts toward agreement are part of these statutes. Deadlines require that bargaining begin a sufficient period of time before such administrative cycles as legislative sessions or fiscal years. Deadlines for notifying mediation boards prior to either the start of negotiations or the termination of unresolved negotiations also is required. Public employers are sometimes required to furnish relevant information to the union, such as financial statements, hiring procedures, and job classifications. Information to the union is required by statute or by PERB or court rulings in order to put negotiations on as strong a factual foundation as possible.

Oregon, in an effort to maintain the integrity of the collective bargaining process by avoiding "end runs" from bargaining representatives to other agents, makes it an unfair labor practice for the public employer to communicate with employees other than bargaining representatives, and

20. Anderson and Weitzman, "The Scope of Bargaining."

21. Joel A. D'Alba, "The Nature of the Duty to Bargain in Good Faith," in Gibbons et al., *Portrait of a Process*, p. 149.

22. *Ibid.*, p. 153.

for public employee representatives to communicate with officials other than employer bargaining representatives.[23] Bad faith bargaining tactics are usually prohibited under this type of provision. Unilateral changes in wages or working conditions or breaking off negotiation without following through on all possible impasse settlement procedures are examples of what is considered a bad faith gesture.

Another type of unfair labor practice is designed to keep union representatives truly representative of employee views. This type of unfair labor practice also follows the example set in the NLRA. Unfair labor practices against employer efforts to coerce employees in their choice of a union representative, or in their expressions of union support, and unfair labor practices against union efforts to coerce employees into supporting the union, are prevalent in states with bargaining statutes (see Table 15–6). Another part of the anticoercion rules is directed toward ending any union and employee efforts to intimidate employer representatives. In the same spirit, employers are restricted from forming company unions or dominating any employee organization (see also Table 15–6).

States have enacted a number of other unfair labor practice statutes. Some examples of restricted union practices include featherbedding demands (this is also part of the NLRA), engagement in work slowdowns, solicitation of student support (in education), striking, endorsement of political candidates, making campaign contributions, and jurisdictional disputes over work assignments. Some restricted employer practices include discriminating against an employee who testifies before a PERB or other agency, and spying on a union or on employees. Some other unfair labor practices that apply to both unions and employers include refusal to agree to a written contract, discrimination, or forcing employer discrimination against employees on the basis of race, religion, sex, and so on, and on the basis of political affiliation and mechanical eavesdropping on conversations pertaining to contract negotiations.

Chapter 3 discussed interpretation and enforcement of provisions of the NLRA, including unfair labor practices. States have dealt with interpretation and enforcement in a variety of ways. In general, the approach to unfair labor practices has been remedial rather than punitive.[24] A board finding on unfair labor practice may order the guilty party to cease and desist in the unfair labor practice, to take affirmative action to end the practice, such as by eliminating certain rules, or to "make whole" any person harmed by the unfair practice, such as reinstating that person with back pay. Remedies do not require agreement to contract terms. Bad faith bargaining is usually dealt with by an order to return to bargaining and to cease certain acts.

23. *Ibid.* p. 161.
24. For a discussion see Shlomo Sperka, "Unfair Labor Practice Remedies and Judicial Review," in Gibbons et al., *Portrait of a Process*, pp. 311–25.

Table 15–6

Public Sector Unfair Labor Practices by State: 1980

STATE[a]/EMPLOYEE GROUP[b]	EMPLOYER			UNION	
	Good Faith[c]	Coercion[d]	Dominance[e]	Good Faith	Coercion
Alaska (All)	x	x	x	x	x
California					
State, Schools, & Colleges	x	x	x	x	x
Other Local		x			
Connecticut (All)	x	x	x	x	x
Florida (All)	x	x	x	x	x
Hawaii (All)	x	x	x	x	x
Illinois (State)	x	x	x	x	x
Indiana (Teachers)	x	x	x	x	x
Iowa (All)	x	x	x	x	x
Kansas (All)	x	x	x	x	x
Kentucky					
(Louisville Fire Fighters)	x	x	x	x	x
Maine (All)	x	x	x	x	x
Maryland (Public Schools)		x			
Massachusetts (All)	x	x	x	x	x
Michigan (All)	x	x	x	x	x
Minnesota (All)	x	x	x	x	x
Montana					
Nurses	x	x	x		
All Other	x	x	x	x	x
Nebraska (All)		x	x		
Nevada (Local)	x	x	x	x	x
New Hampshire (All)	x	x	x	x	x
New Jersey (All)	x	x	x	x	x
New Mexico (State)	x	x	x	x	x
New York (All)	x	x	x	x	x
North Dakota (Teachers)		x			
Oklahoma					
Public School		x			
Police/Fire Fighters	x	x	x	x	x
Oregon (All)	x	x	x	x	x
Pennsylvania	x	x	x	x	x
Rhode Island					
State		x			
Municipal	x	x	x	x	x
Teachers	x	x	x	x	
South Dakota (All)	x	x	x	x	x
Tennessee (Teachers)	x	x	x	x	x
Vermont (All)	x	x	x	x	x
Washington (All)	x	x	x	x	x
Wisconsin (All)	x	x	x	x	x

[a] States omitted from the list have no legislation dealing with unfair labor practices in the public sectors (total of 18 states not listed).

[b] Reference corresponding note to Table 15–5.

[c] Good faith: Refusal to meet and confer, to bargain in good faith, or to participate in impasse procedures in good faith (at least one of the above three items).

[d] Coercion: Interfere, coerce, threaten, discriminate, or restrain employees (because of union support or opposition) or union representatives.

[e] Dominance (of the union): To involve employer representatives in any way in the formulation or operation of employee unions.

Sources: *Summary of Public Sector Labor Relations Policies: Statutes, Attorney Generals' Opinions and Selected Court Decisions, Labor-Management Services Administration,* U.S. Department of Labor, 1979; and Richard R. Nelson, "State Labor Legislation Enacted in 1978," and "State Labor Legislation Enacted in 1980," *Monthly Labor Review,* January 1980, January 1981.

We also discussed in Chapter 3 the problem of delays to decision with the NLRB. This same problem is now being faced by the states. They can speed up the process, thereby ending the offending practice sooner, but the cost is a loss of information and deliberation in the decision-making process. One way states have speeded up the decision-making process is by taking complaints directly to the PERB rather than by relying on hearing officers as a first stage of review.

PERB decisions are ordinarily not self-enforcing; they must petition the courts for enforcement.[25] In general, the courts do not substitute their judgment for the board's in review. Legal questions, however, are reserved for the courts.

Impasse Procedures

Because strikes by government employees are either illegal or highly restricted, much attention has been directed toward providing means of labor dispute settlement short of a strike or strike threat. Of all the regulatory areas, this has been the area of greatest focus and innovation. The public sector, in general, has relied much more on the use of neutral agents to resolve contract disputes than the private sector. Neutral agents enter the bargaining process as mediators, fact finders, and arbitrators (both advisory and binding). Many states have adopted one or a combination of more than one of these forms of neutral intervention (see Table 15-7).

With mediation, a person with no direct stake in the dispute attempts to bring the parties together in agreement by listening to their proposals and suggesting alternatives. The mediation option has been popular in both the private and public sectors. There has been some debate over the role of the mediator in the public sector.[26] Some argue that the mediator should perform a public service by bringing the parties together. This is the mediator's duty in the private sector. Others argue that mediators should bring the voice of the public's interest to the bargaining table. Under the latter assignment, the mediator is less a neutral and more an advocate in the bargaining process. Most states provide mediation services to the parties.

Fact finding and advisory arbitration go a step beyond mediation by having the neutral make a public judgment about the positions of the disputants. Fact finders or arbitrators bring together relevant evidence supporting the positions of each party, make informed assessments as to the relative merits of each party's position, and recommend a settlement. Fact finding and advisory arbitration perform two functions that assist resolution. First, the neutral makes a determination about disputed facts,

---

25. *Ibid.*, p. 322.
26. Walter J. Gershenfeld, "An Overview," in Gibbons et al., *Portrait of a Process*, p. 17.

TABLE 15–7

Public Sector Bargaining Impasse Resolution by State: 1980

STATE [a] EMPLOYEE GROUP [b]	MEDIATION	FACT-FINDING OR ADVISORY ARBITRATION	INTEREST ARBITRATION	LIMITED RIGHT TO STRIKE
Alaska				
Selected State and Local	x			x
Public Safety and Hospital	x		x	
Teachers	x	x		x
California				
State–Municipal	x			
School–University	x	x		
Connecticut				
State–Teachers	x	x	x	
Municipal	x	x	x	
Delaware (Teachers)	x	x		
Florida (All)	x	x		
Georgia (State)		x		
Hawaii				
Fire Fighters			x	
All Other	x	x		x
Idaho				
Teachers	x	x		
Fire Fighters		x		
Illinois				
State	x	x		
Fire Fighters		x		
Indiana (Teachers)	x	x		
Iowa (All)	x	x	x	
Kansas (All)	x	x		
Kentucky (Louisville Fire Fighters)	x	x		
Maine (All)	x	x	x	
Maryland (Public Schools)	x	x		
Massachusetts				
Police and Fire		x	x	
All Other	x	x		
Michigan				
Public Safety	x		x	
All Other	x	x		
Minnesota				
Essential Employees	x		x	
All Other	x		x	x
Montana				
Fire Fighters	x	x	x	
Nurses				x
All Other	x	x		x
Nevada (Local)	x	x	x	
New Hampshire (All)	x	x		

394

Table 15–7 *(continued)*

STATE [a]/ EMPLOYEE GROUP [b]	MEDIATION	FACT-FINDING OR ADVISORY ARBITRATION	INTEREST ARBITRATION	LIMITED RIGHT TO STRIKE
New Jersey				
Police and Fire	x	x	x	
All Other	x	x		
New Mexico (State)	x	x		
New York (All)	x	x	x	
North Dakota				
Teachers and School Administrators	x	x		
All Other	x			
Oklahoma				
School, Police, Fire		x		
Oregon				
Public Safety	x	x	x	
All Other	x	x	x	x
Pennsylvania				
Police, Fire			x	
All Other	x	x	x	x
Rhode Island				
State		x	x	
Police, Fire			x	
Teachers	x		x	
Other Local	x	x	x	
South Dakota (All)	x			
Tennessee (All)	x	x		
Texas				
Police, Fire	x	x		
Vermont				
State	x	x	x	
Local	x	x		x
Washington				
Teachers (including Community College)	x	x		
Other Local	x	x	x	
Wisconsin				
State	x	x		
Local	x	x	x	x
Wyoming (Fire)			x	

[a] States omitted from the list have no legislation dealing with impasse procedures in the public sector (14 states not listed).

[b] Reference corresponding note to TABLE 15–5.

Sources: *Summary of Public Sector Labor Relations Policies: Statutes, Attorney Generals' Opinions and Selected Court Decisions, Labor-Management Services Administration,* U.S. Department of Labor, 1979; and Richard R. Nelson, "State Labor Legislation Enacted in 1978," and "State Labor Legislation Enacted in 1980," *Monthly Labor Review,* January 1980, January 1981.

thus removing much of this source of uncertainty from negotiations. For example, a union may believe a school district has surplus funds, despite protests by the district administrators. The veracity of the administrators is questioned since it is to their advantage to claim no surplus, even if there is a surplus. The neutral serves an auditing function in this case; in the process, the neutral enhances information exchange by resolving issues of fact.

The second function of the fact-finding or arbitration report is one of persuasion. The audience to be persuaded includes the bargaining representatives *and* their constituents. A well-publicized, reasonable recommendation can serve as the focal point of opinion about the "fair" settlement. There is some evidence that fact finding and advisory arbitration reduce public sector strikes.[27] As can be seen in Table 15–7, this has also been a popular option among the states.

Under interest arbitration, a neutral third party resolves any disputes over contract terms. This option has been used extensively in the public sector (Table 15–7). Interest arbitration has reduced, though not eliminated, strikes by public employees. The primary issue concerning interest arbitration has been the effect of arbitration on bargaining, and on the quality of judgments made by outsiders (arbitrators) compared to judgments made by negotiators intimately aware of the day-to-day operation at the workplace. A variety of interest arbitration schemes have been devised to promote exchange by the parties before the arbitration stage. We discuss these issues in Chapter 9, the dispute resolution chapter, and therefore do not repeat the discussion here.

Table 15–7 shows another alternative for resolving disputes—the strike threat. Several states have granted public employees a limited right to strike. The right to strike is a last resort, permitted *only* after all other means for resolution, mediation, fact finding, or a combination of the two, have been used. The argument for a legal strike is that the fear of a strike will create an incentive for both parties to resolve bargaining impasses, and that strike prohibitions do not work anyway. Where the right to a strike is granted, it is limited in one form or another. In some states, certain types of "essential" employees such as police or fire fighters may not strike. In some states, courts are allowed to issue injunctions against strikes that endanger the public's health, welfare, and safety.

States have adopted other, more limited, methods for resolving disputes. Nebraska turns unresolved disputes over to a court of industrial relations for a decision. Some state and local governments use the public referendum as the final word on employee contracts. Other states direct

---

27. David Estenson and Harvey Hyatt, "Teacher Strikes and Labor Relations Regulation," unpublished, 1977.

fact-finder or advisory arbitrator reports to a legislative body if the dispute remains unresolved. The latter two alternatives make the public or the legislative body the ultimate arbitrator.

This brings us to a final form of impasse procedure—grievance arbitration. In the private sector, as a result of court decisions and tradition, binding arbitration of grievance disputes is well accepted and the dominant practice. Binding grievance arbitration is the *quid pro quo* received by the union in exchange for a no-strike pledge during the contract term. This bargain is not yet completely accepted in the public sector, either in practice or by law. The problem in the public sector is that the conflicting authorities of laws and agencies leave doubts about just how far a grievance arbitrator can go in binding an agency to a contract.

Union Security

Before a union can represent employees effectively, it must itself be secure and stable. Union security is usually used as a description of a stable source of revenue to support the union. Revenue collection can be eased by dues or fee checkoff, and secured by some form of fee payment requirement as a condition of employment. A secure union is one of the first goals of a new union. It is an important enough issue for a union to strike. Over 5 percent of public sector strikes include this issue.

Checkoff regulations permit public employers to deduct union dues or "fair share" payments from employee paychecks. Before any deductions are made, the employee must authorize employer deductions. As we see in Table 15–8, checkoff permission is fairly extensive among the states. The advantage of checkoff to the union is that union representatives do not have to spend their time running around the workplace collecting dues. Since dues collection activity tends to divert employee attention from production, there is an advantage in checkoff to the employer.

A more important form of security to the union is a required payment to the union for services rendered as a condition of employment. Agency shop, maintenance of membership, and union shop all require employee payment to the union as part of the collective agreement. Many states have chosen to permit this form of contract language. Though not always true, there is a presumption that the union or agency shop in the public sector is not permitted unless authorized by legislation. Some states, as we discuss in Chapter 3, have right-to-work laws explicitly prohibiting agency or union shops in both the public and private sectors.

On required fee issues, state legislation often provides for exemptions for those with religious beliefs which do not permit union membership or contribution. In Washington state and California, for example, persons

Table 15–8
Public Sector Union Security by State: 1980

STATE[a]/EMPLOYEE GROUP[b]	CHECK-OFF	AGENCY SHOP	MAINTENANCE OF MEMBERSHIP	UNION SHOP
Alabama (Teachers)	x			
Alaska (All)	x	x		x
Arizona (State)	x			
Arkansas (State)	x			
California				
State, Teachers	x		x	
Connecticut				
State, Teachers		x		
Delaware (All)	x	x		
Florida (All)	x			
Hawaii (All)	x	x		
Indiana (Teachers)	x			
Kentucky				
Louisville Fire Fighters	x			
Louisiana (All)	x			
Maryland (Noncertified Public School)		x		
Massachusetts (All)	x	x		
Michigan (State)	x			
Minnesota (All)	x	x		
Montana (All)	x	x		
New Jersey (All)	x	x		
New Mexico (State)	x			
New York (All)	x	x		
North Dakota				
Teachers	x			
Ohio (All)	x			
Oregon (All)	x	x		
Pennsylvania			x	
Rhode Island				
Teachers		x		
All Other	x	x		
Texas				
(Most Municipal)	x			
Utah (All)	x			
Vermont (Local)		x		x
Washington				
State, Municipal	x	x		x
State Higher Education		x		x
Teachers	x	x		
Wisconsin (All)	x	x		

[a] States omitted from the list have no legislation dealing with Union Security in the public sector (20 states not listed).

[b] Reference corresponding note to Table 15–5.

Sources: *Summary of Public Sector Labor Relations Policies: Statutes, Attorney Generals' Opinions and Selected Court Decisions, Labor-Management Services Administration,* U.S. Department of Labor, 1979; and Richard R. Nelson, "State Labor Legislation Enacted in 1978," and "State Labor Legislation Enacted in 1980," *Monthly Labor Review,* January 1980, January 1981.

with such religious beliefs may contribute to a nonreligious charity an amount equal to union dues or agency fees.

Agency shop (sometimes called "fair share") permits public employers to require a union payment from nonunion employees for union services rendered. This fee is an amount less than union dues, since the value of services received exclusively by union members, and not by nonmember workers in the bargaining unit, is subtracted from established levels of union dues. As we find in Table 15–8, a number of states permit agency shop provisions in collective agreements.

Under a maintenance-of-membership contract clause, employees who are union members at the outset of a contract, or who subsequently join the union, must remain union members for the contract duration. This saves the union the trouble of constant membership drives. Maintenance-of-membership clauses are permitted for public sector employees in Pennsylvania and for selected workers in California.

Under union shop provisions, union membership becomes a required condition for continued employment. Membership is not required at the time of hire, but all new employees must join the union within a fixed number of days after hire. Union shop is not a popular option among the states (see Table 15–8).

The argument for agency shop, maintenance of membership, and union shop is familiar from Chapter 3. Unions argue that since all members of the bargaining unit benefit from union efforts, all should help defray the costs. Those who receive the benefit without paying are known as "free riders." Agency shop and other similar provisions are intended to solve the free rider problem. In an earlier section of this chapter, we noted that most states now grant exclusive representative status to unions, and that this status usually carries a requirement to represent all members of the bargaining unit. If they must represent all, unions argue, all should contribute their fair share to the union.

It must be emphasized that an agency shop law does not require an employer to agree to an agency shop clause in the contract. Why would a public employer grant such a clause? Perhaps in return for favorable treatment by the union on another issue more important to the employer. Another reason is that a secure union is more flexible and focused in collective bargaining. For instance, Nels Nelson cites several studies where unions reduce their activity in processing grievances after gaining an agency or union shop.[28] From the employer perspective, this is a favorable result that in some circumstances may outweigh the negative aspects of agency shop or similar provisions.

The Supreme Court permitted limited agency shop in government in its

28. Nels E. Nelson, "Union Security in the Public Sector," *Labor Law Journal*, 27 (June 1976), 339.

famous decision *Abood* v. *Detroit Board of Education.*[29] The Court declared agency shop fees were constitutional, but money collected must be used for collective negotiation and contract administration. This decision has been controversial.[30] By restricting funds to traditional collective bargaining activities, the Court cut off the use of funds for political activities such as lobbying legislatures, vote support, referendum opposition or support, and other activities that are fundamental components of the public sector union's "arsenal of weapons." In some situations, as discussed earlier, political activity is a public sector union's only effective alternative. Thus, under *Abood*, those employees who can strike gain, those who cannot strike lose.

FEDERALIZING PUBLIC EMPLOYEE BARGAINING

Today, state and local public employee bargaining is regulated by many states. As we have just shown, states have chosen alternative regulatory strategies. There have been efforts to end state control of regulation by establishing a federal law covering state and local government employees, or even by amending the National Labor Relations Act to include state and local government employees. This proposal for a unified bargaining law parallels what happened in the private sector, where the NLRA supplanted state jurisdiction over collective bargaining.

Foremost among the advocates of this legislation have been large public sector unions such as AFSCME and the AFT. Since many states have enacted no bargaining laws or have adopted restrictive bargaining laws, these public sector unions reason that a federal law will be, on average, more favorable to labor. Certainly this will be the case if the law approximates the NLRA.

Further complicating this issue is the question of whether a federal statute would be constitutional. The Supreme Court may rule that a federal statute usurps constitutionally protected state rights, as the Court ruled with attempts to extend the Fair Labor Standards Act to state and local government employees.[31]

Extending federal jurisdiction over state and local government bargaining will provide many more government employees the opportunities of a collective bargaining system. The cost will be a loss of state choice from among the diverse approaches to regulating collective bargaining.

29. 431 U.S. 209 (1977).

30. See, for example, Charles M. Rehmus and Benjamin A. Kerner, "The Agency Shop After *Abood*: No Free Ride, but What's the Fare?" *Industrial and Labor Relations Review,* October 1980, pp. 90–100.

31. *National League of Cities* v. *Usery,* 426 U.S. 833 (1976).

CIVIL SERVICE REFORM ACT OF 1978

Because the federal government is the largest public body bargaining collectively with employees, and because the federal sector has been a leader in developing public sector collective bargaining ever since President Kennedy's historic signing of Executive Order 10988, we briefly summarize here labor–management relations established by the Civil Service Reform Act of 1978. Provisions of this act govern labor–management relations for civilian employees of the U.S. government. Note the close parallel with the National Labor Relations Act as summarized in Chapter 3.

The Reform Act sets up a Federal Labor Relations Authority with duties similar to those of the National Labor Relations Board. The authority functions as a neutral interpreter and administrator of the act. The authority determines who is in the bargaining unit, supervises and conducts representation elections, and conducts hearings and resolves complaints of unfair labor practices.

Federal agencies and certified unions have a duty to bargain in good faith. Management, however, retains exclusive control over the budget, organization, hiring, and retention of employees and the assignment of work. These issues are designated as more "policy" than "employment" and therefore are not bargainable.

A labor organization elected as the representative by a majority in the bargaining unit becomes the exclusive union representative of the employees in the unit. In exchange for the exclusive status, the labor organization must be responsible for representing all employees in the bargaining unit. Since a grievance procedure is required to enforce the collective agreement, the elected union must represent all grievants in the unit.

The Civil Service Reform Act departs remarkably from the NLRA on strikes. Federal employees are *not* permitted to strike. Hence in 1981, federal air traffic controllers were summarily discharged by President Reagan for striking. To assist in resolving negotiation conflicts, a Federal Service Impasse Panel was established. The panel may use a variety of procedures to resolve impasses, including binding arbitration.

WHERE DOES THE PUBLIC FIT INTO COLLECTIVE BARGAINING?

The public is the ultimate government employer, and the electorate is ultimately responsible for employer decisions. Where is the public input into the employer side of collective bargaining? How does the public obtain sufficient information to make an informed evaluation and judgment?

These are important questions to resolve if collective bargaining is to be adapted successfully to the public sector.

In an important sense, the public already has input through the normal election process. The public elects executives and legislatures to office. In many state and local jurisdictions, the public votes on referenda issues affecting collective bargaining outcomes. And the public participates in hearings and other communications with elected officials.

The model that is increasing in use in the public sector illustrates where the public can fit in through the normal political process. The employer is represented by a professional negotiator in all collective negotiations with unions. The professional negotiator may report to a governor, mayor, or other elected official in the executive branch. The employer agent obtains the most favorable terms possible. These contract terms are then taken to a legislative body or board for ratification. Deliberations at this stage are open for public comment, and are generally reported. Failure by the legislative body to ratify the contract terms means negotiations must be resumed with the union by the professional negotiator.

Note the similarities in this process on the employer side to the process followed on the union side in both the public and private sector. Professional union agents negotiate contract terms, then take these terms back to the membership, or to an elected assembly representing the membership, for ratification. Sometimes the membership rejects a contract, and negotiations must again resume. The process of contract ratification allows for input by union members and, on the employer side, by the public. Debate and discussion about the contract informs the union member, and the public, about the contract.

States have dealt with this problem of public input and public information through other legislation.[32] California has attempted to provide a means for public input by modifying the bargaining procedure. Initial bargaining proposals by the employing agency must be presented at a public meeting. Any new substantive ideas proposed after the commencement of negotiations also require a public hearing. After receiving public comments, negotiations are conducted in private. Presumably, public comments will make employer representatives more responsive to public opinion. And the information brought out at the start of negotiations will provide a benchmark for judging the performance of employer negotiators. In practice, however, the public has not always availed itself of the opportunity to spend an evening listening and discussing bargaining proposals. The most interested citizens are the union members directly

32. See James J. Sherman, "The Role of the Public in the Bargaining Process," in Gibbons et al., *Portrait of a Process*, pp. 269–77.

affected by the proposal. Not surprisingly, union members are the main representatives of the public at the hearings.

Several states have adopted "sunshine" laws that require all negotiating sessions to be open to the public. This allows the public to keep up with the latest developments as bargaining unfolds. Sunshine laws have been severely criticized by labor relations professionals. They argue that negotiation sessions are opportunities to probe the opponent in order to discover areas of strength and weakness. Many of the statements during the course of negotiations are exploratory, bluffs more than committed positions. The compromise and concession of bargaining unfolds as bluffs are slowly withdrawn and committed positions exposed. Public display has the unfortunate effect of often turning bluffs into committed positions. Public observers or media reporters, lacking expertise in bargaining and perhaps in the issues, may focus attention on one aspect or another of exploratory statements. Concession from these publicized bluff positions subsequently may be made only at the cost of lost respect and prestige with the public or union membership by the negotiators. Rather than promoting compromise and resolution, sunshine laws have an opposite, chilling, effect.

DO PUBLIC UNIONS EXCESSIVELY INFLUENCE GOVERNMENT DECISIONS?

During the early stages of the surge in public sector union growth, strong reservations were expressed about excessive bargaining and political influence by government unions.[33] In retrospect, these reservations were overstated, though the arguments do point toward differences between private and public sector bargaining and to some problems with collective bargaining in the public sector. Foremost among expressed reservations were that public unions dominate local politics, that public unions would obtain an unfair advantage by controlling the labor supply for essential community services, that labor disputes in the public sector would endanger the public health and safety, and that public sector unions would not face the same employment constraints as private sector unions.

This latter argument is based on estimates of the labor demand elasticity for public services. In general, it takes a fairly large percentage increase in wages to create an appreciable percentage reduction in public employment.[34] Chapter 13 discussed the effect of possible employment loss on

33. See Harry H. Wellington and Ralph R. Winter, *The Unions and the Cities* (Washington, D.C.: Brookings Institution, 1971).

34. See Orley Ashenfelter and Ronald Ehrenberg, "The Demand for Labor in the Public Sector," in Daniel S. Hamermesh, ed., *Labor in the Public and Nonprofit Sectors* (Princeton, N.J.: Princeton University Press, 1975), pp. 55–78.

union wage demands, including why this is probably not a powerful constraint, even in the private sector. If unions have an excessive advantage in the public sector, inelastic labor demand is not the most significant source of this advantage.

The high cost to the public of work stoppages by public employees is another matter. Some fear was initially expressed that public officials would give in to almost any public union demand rather than take a strike. It was feared that the private sector cost constraint of economic competition would not force public officials to bargain diligently. With experience we have found public officials willing to take a strike, although the cost to the public is sometimes very high during these strikes. Controlling costly public union strikes, and perhaps the excessive bargaining advantage gained by some public sector unions, remains a serious concern, especially in crucial services such as police, fire, health, and transit.

In this respect, the difference between public and private sector collective bargaining is at most one of degree; strikes in the coal, steel, airline, and railroad industries, for example, also carry the potential for extreme cost to the general public.

Domination of the political process by public sector unions has three possible sources: (1) disproportionate voting by public sector union members (they, after all, have the most at stake), (2) campaign contributions (of time and money) by public sector union members to public officeholders, and (3) lobbying by public sector union officials. It is a possibility that any strong vested interest—such as public employees—could overwhelm the less interested public in controlling government by speaking with one unified voice.[35]

There remain then, some advantages that public sector unions have that private sector unions do not have, or do not have to the same extent. Recent experience, however, indicates that public sector unions have not obtained inordinate improvements in the terms and conditions of employment. In the previous chapter, for example, we noted that estimates of public sector relative union wage effects seem to be no larger, and may even be smaller, than similar estimates in the private sector.

What was not factored into the initial analysis of public union effects was the reaction of the third force in collective bargaining—*the public*. Government workers have the public as neighbors, as family, as friends; they go to the same churches, clubs, bowling alleys, and bars as the public. Government workers are not immune from, or indifferent to, what the public thinks. Elected officials have reacted to public sentiment by limiting budgets, by putting ceilings on taxes (sometimes through refer-

35. See Clyde W. Summers, "Public Employee Bargaining: A Political Perspective," *Yale Law Journal*, 83 (1973–74) 1156–1200.

enda), and by running for office by opposing the goals of public sector unions.

In short, government unions are constrained by political competition rather than by the constraint of economic competition found in the private sector.

FUTURE GROWTH

In the near future, public sector union membership and representation is unlikely to grow at as fast a rate as during the last two decades. There are several reasons for this projection.

First, beginning in 1978, public sector employment stopped growing; budget balancing efforts by federal, state, and local governments and "tax revolts" seem likely to continue to limit public sector employment growth through most of the 1980s.

Second, public sector unions organized the most easily persuaded and sympathetic bargaining units first. Those left unorganized are less able or less willing to join unions and to bargain collectively.

Third, highly publicized public reaction to government unions in San Francisco, New York, and other parts of the country reduced public tolerance of public sector collective bargaining. Collective bargaining in the public sector is unlikely to be as successful in bargaining as in the past—or as attractive to public employees.

Any forecast of the future, however, must be tempered by knowledge of our inability to explain past growth. Some sudden burst could occur again, just as it occurred beginning in 1960. Among the unknown elements is the reaction by public employees to simultaneous inflation and budget cutbacks. Greater militancy by public sector workers could create a stronger union attachment: failing to make significant gains through collective bargaining, disenchanted public employees may reject unionism.[36]

It is clear that public sector collective bargaining will continue to undergo change. Employers must adapt, often through trial and error, the multilateral decision-making process of government to a collective bargaining environment. New information will develop about the operation of the many new state collective bargaining statutes. Some regulatory provisions will prove unworkable. Others will work with minor refinements. Others, we hope, will be highly successful and give new insight into the regulatory process.

---

36. For a discussion see Benjamin Aaron, "Future of Collective Bargaining in the Public Sector," in Aaron et al., *Public Sector Bargaining,* p. 293.

Whether or not public union membership continues to grow, public sector collective bargaining will continue as one of the dynamic centers of contemporary collective bargaining.

Questions for Discussion, Thought, and Research

1. What factors have led to the expansion of public sector collective bargaining? What factors may inhibit future expansion?

2. The business agent for a police union in a large metropolitan area commented: "In the history of our relationship with the city, we have never really prepared for collective bargaining. Rather, we negotiated with the city council. Our preparation for bargaining consisted of endorsing and electing the right candidates for council. In effect, the council would make a political decision and disguise it in the collective bargaining process." Discuss. What are some of the problems for the union of this approach to bargaining?

3. Why have public sector unions been so politically active during the last few years?

4. The NLRA has been amended very infrequently (about once every twelve years). Public sector labor legislation on the state and local level is in a constant flux. Why does public sector legislation change so rapidly? If Congress passed a national law providing for public sector collective bargaining, do you think it would be subject to frequent change?

5. What evidence would you examine to determine if public unions excessively influence government decisions?

6. Are there equivalent market-like constraints on the public employer which preclude excessive wage increases?

7. To what extent should federal employees enjoy the same rights guaranteed to workers covered by the NLRA (e.g., should they have the right to strike, and to bargain on the issue of wages)? Discuss.

8. Government tends to be very labor-intensive. Is the tradeoff between higher wage increases and employment opportunities greater for the public sector than for the private sector?

9. Under what circumstances, if any, do you feel that public employees should have the right to strike?

10. Public sector employee unions want what private sector unions want—better wages, hours, and conditions of employment. Why is scope of bargaining a greater issue in the public sector?

11. Compare and contrast the NLRA approach to regulating collective bargaining with the approaches to regulation taken by the states.

Selected Bibliography

Aaron, Benjamin, James R. Grodin, and James L. Stern, ed., *Public Sector Bargaining*. Madison, Wis.: Industrial Relations Research Association, 1979.

Gershenfeld, Walter J., J. Joseph Loewenberg, and Bernard Inkster, *Scope of Public-Sector Bargaining*. Lexington, Mass.: Lexington Books, Heath, 1977.

Gibbons, Muriel K., Robert D. Helsby, Jerome Lefkowitz, and Barbara Z. Tener, eds., *Portrait of a Process—Collective Negotiations in Public Employment*. Fort Washington, Pa.: Labor Relations Press, 1979.

Gunderson, Morley, ed., *Collective Bargaining in the Essential and Public Service Sectors*. Toronto: University of Toronto Press, 1975.

Hamermesh, Daniel, ed., *Labor in the Public and Nonprofit Sectors*. Princeton, N.J.: Princeton University Press, 1975.

Jascourt, Hugh D., ed., *Government Labor Relations: Trends and Information for the Future*. Oak Park, Ill.: Moore, 1979.

Lewin, David, Peter Feuille, and Thomas A. Kochan, *Public Sector Labor Relations*. Glen Ridge, N.J.: Horton, 1977.

Weitzman, Joan P., *The Scope of Bargaining in Public Employment*. New York: Praeger, 1975.

EMERGING COLLECTIVE BARGAINING RELATIONSHIPS IN HEALTH CARE, PROFESSIONAL SPORTS,* AND HIGHER EDUCATION

16

For the past two and a half decades, the American economy has shifted in relative terms from a "goods" to a "service" producing economy. Unionization has followed these shifting relative trends. The relative (and in some instances absolute) decline in employment among traditionally strong union industries like mining and manufacturing is a cause for union membership stagnation. As we discussed in earlier chapters, public sector unionism is an exception to this overall trend in union membership. Other exceptions in both the public and private sectors also exist. Unionization among agricultural workers is an example of a goods producing private sector work force in which collective bargaining relationships are a new and growing phenomenon. Unionization developments in the service producing private sector are even more apparent. Scarcely a week goes by without reference to a threatened or actual strike among health care workers, professional athletes or professors. In this chapter we will briefly

*Some of the ideas in the section entitled "Why Won't Professional Athletes Unionize?" are taken from an article by Edwin G. Krasnow and Herman M. Levy. See footnote 39.

explore labor relations developments for each of these emerging areas.

All three of these work groups produce services. Labor relations in these areas was a development of the 1970s, and it followed the passage of enabling legislation or NLRB rulings having the effect of extending federal labor law jurisdiction to include these industries. Finally, while committed to advancing the interests of their professions, workers in these areas, like those employed in plant and maintenance occupations, have also revealed their interest in securing improved material benefits from work.

As we survey some of the contemporary trends and substantive problem areas in health care, professional sports, and faculty employee labor relations, we shall seek reasonably accurate assessments of them, their future prospects, and their impact on employment relations. It is too early to be definitive; labor relationships in the areas have not had time to stabilize; thus, we can only hope that the analytical points to be developed in this chapter will have some enduring validity.

COLLECTIVE BARGAINING
IN HEALTH CARE

Collective bargaining in the health care industry can be traced back to the predepression years in the San Francisco Bay area. However, it emerged as a significant area for unionization only in the 1970s. The Wagner Act did not specifically exclude private, nonprofit hospital, and other employees of health care facilities from its coverage. The NLRB initially asserted jurisdiction over these workers but later relented on its assertion.[1] In 1947, with Taft–Hartley, federal labor policy with respect to the labor relations rights of employees in private, nonprofit health care facilities was clarified: they were to be exempted from the federal collective bargaining laws.[2] This policy dulled collective bargaining prospects for workers in the industry until 1974 when the National Labor Relations Act was again amended and the Taft–Hartley exclusion was lifted.[3] At that time federal labor legislation was extended from mere coverage of workers in "proprietary" health care facilities to include the (then) more than 1.5 million employees in private, nonprofit hospitals, nursing homes, health maintenance organizations, health clinics, and other institutions devoted to the care of sick, infirm, or aged persons.[4]

1. Dennis D. Pointer, "The Federal Labor Relations Status of the Health Care Delivery Industry," *Labor Law Journal*, 22, No. 5 (May 1971), 278–86.

2. See Section 2(2) of the Taft–Hartley Act (pre-1974 version).

3. See P.L. No. 93–360 (July 26, 1974): 88 Stat. 395.

4. Proprietary or for-profit hospitals and health care facilities came under NLRB jurisdiction in 1969. See Emil C. Farkas, "The National Labor Relations Act: The Health Care Amendments," *Labor Law Journal*, 25, No. 5 (May 1978), 259–74.

Changing Employment Relations and Attitudes

The 1974 Health Care Amendments were not enacted without reason. Economic activity in the health care industry had increased enormously. Hospitals became large and complex organizations. As the economy grew, the health care industry grew faster. Expenditures on health care represented 4.6 percent of the gross national product in 1955. This figure more than doubled by 1977, and in 1980 it reached beyond 10 percent. In spite of technological advances, health care practices remained labor-intensive. Thus, employment growth paralleled the growth in expenditures.

The health care industry now employs more than 5 million people. The process resulting in this level of employment, however, brought with it a host of employee relations problems. Larger scales of operation and relations and greater interprofessional tensions and rivalries. Oftentimes, the pay of health care employees lagged behind the pay levels received by comparably educated groups in other industrial sectors. Hospital administrators and their trustee board members were more concerned with problems of capital financing and the introduction of new and more sophisticated medical technology. Thus, in increasing numbers, hospital employees turned to formal collective bargaining as a vehicle through which they could air their problems and advance their interests, both professional and material.

Also during this period of expansion the health care industry's basic structure changed, along with the attitudes of its workers and the public at large. Charity and philanthropic activities gave way to the expansion of third-party pay systems. Private and public (Medicare and Medicaid) insurance coverage was becoming institutionalized. Physician charges and hospital room rates skyrocketed, with the growth in demand which can partially be attributed to the spread of insurance. Patients were being hospitalized in larger and larger numbers; their period of hospitalization per admission was increasing; and they, too, were feeling a sense of alienation. The "home visit" became a thing of the past: many patients and health care critics began leveling the charge of "overdoctoring" against an industry which was once perceived as being motivated by altruism. The public health care employees and the Congress had come to view health care as just another "business."

These circumstances weakened the view that health care services were too critical to be threatened with interruptions due to strikes. Moreover, the argument that private, nonprofit health care facilities ought to be immune from collective bargaining because the burden of wage and price pressures would ultimately have to be carried by the "sick" gave way to the right of workers to be represented, negotiate, and strike. Even prior to the

1974 federal legislative initiatives, some 12 states had already passed laws permitting unionism for private, nonprofit hospital workers and other health care workers.[5]

Employees of the health care industry also began to view their jobs differently. The predominating attitude that medical–nursing standards and patient welfare ought to override a concern for material personal benefits from work gave way to a more balanced perspective.

Unionization of the Health Care Employee

As we observed earlier, union organizing activities predate enactment of the 1974 Health Care Amendments.[6] Early enthusiasm for collective bargaining, however, was limited to specific parts of the country and to but a few health occupations. It was really not until the decade of the 1970s that many professional and nonprofessional health care employee groups began to seek openly to bargain collectively and to build employee organizations designed to accomplish this end on a nationwide basis.

By the end of 1976, the nation's three largest health care employee organizations had negotiated hundreds of agreements covering thousands of employees. The Service Employees International Union had 830 contracts stipulating employment conditions for about 156,000 employees. The National Union of Hospital and Health Care Employees (popularly known as District 1199), and affiliates of the American Nurses' Association, had 413 agreements covering about 99,000 employees and 412 agreements covering about 67,000 professional nurses, respectively.[7]

The representative status of other health care professional organizations also began to advance. For instance, in 1973 there were twenty-six organizations committed to collective bargaining which claimed a membership of about 16,000 doctors and dentists.[8] While these organizations had negotiated only a handful of actual labor contracts, their motivation was to stave off encroachments into their professional domain. Doctors and dentists have consistently objected to government interventions into *how*

5. Richard L. Epstein, "Labor Relations in Hospitals and Health Care Facilities Before the National Labor Relations Act Amendments: Proprietary Versus Nonprofit Hospitals," in A. Eliot Berkeley and Ann Barnes, eds., *Labor Relations in Hospitals and Health Care Facilities* (Washington, D.C.: Bureau of National Affairs, 1976), pp. 7–12.

6. See Norman Metzger and Dennis D. Pointer, *Labor—Management Relations in the Health Services Industry* (Washington, D.C.: Science and Health Publications, 1972).

7. Lucretia Dewey Tanner, Harriet Goldberg Weinstein, and Alice Lynn Ahmuty, *Impact of the 1974 Amendments to the NLRA on Collective Bargaining in the Health Care Industry* (Washington, D.C., 1978) Federal Mediation and Conciliation Service, pp. 72–1000.

8. Mario F. Bognanno, James B. Dworkin, and Omotayo Fashoyin, "Physicians and Dentists' Bargaining Organizations: A Preliminary Look," *Monthly Labor Review*, 98 (June 1975), 33–35.

medicine is practical. Limitations and delays in cash reimbursements from private insurance companies and Medicare and Medicaid agencies were a serious problem; and finally, they resented and feared (rightly or wrongly) federal health care regulatory initiatives in the form of "controls."

Interns, residents, and fellows in hospital-based training programs have also turned to collective bargaining as a means of remedying their age-old problems of low wages, excessively long working hours, and the arbitrariness they encountered from medical supervisors.[9] On a limited basis, these employees had succeeded in forming collective bargaining relationships prior to the 1974 amendments. Tenuous though these relations were, a 1976 NLRB decision that interns and residents were primarily "students" and not "employees," as this term is used in the National Labor Relations Act, adversely affected their right to legally compel recognition and negotiations.[10] A 1979 U.S. Court of Appeals decision reversed the NLRB's holding.[11]

Between 1970 and 1976, the number of employed professional nurses covered by contracts grew at a compounded annual rate of about 14 percent. Membership in the Service Employees Union and in District 1199 grew by 12 and 8 percent, respectively, over the same period.[12] While it is dangerous to generalize from these experiences, we believe that the advent of the 1974 amendments will help to spawn continuous unionization in the health care industry. The extent of future union penetration, however, remains partly in the hands of hospital and nursing home administrators. Their personnel practices have left much to be desired. Employers having the foresight to give their professional employees an effective voice in improving standards of patient care will go far in thwarting the enthusiasm health professionals may otherwise hold for unionization. But more is required. An equitable allocation of functions between RNs and LPNs and nurses' aids must be fashioned. Supervisory methods and styles will have to be improved, and the economic welfare of hospital and nursing home employees must be given priority attention with equitable adjustments in pay being made where inequities exist.

Contract Contents and Issues

Analysis of contracts negotiated in the health care industry reveals few unique features. In general, employees in this industry seek the same set of benefits and rights as workers in traditionally unionized sectors of society.

9. Murry A. Gordon, "Hospital Housestaff Collective Bargaining," *Employee Relations Law Journal*, 1 (Winter 1976), 418–38.

10. *Cedars-Sinai Medical Center*, 223 NLRB 251 (1976).

11. "Court Overturns NLRB's Interns, Residents Ruling," Bureau of National Affairs, *Daily Labor Reports*, April 3, 1979, p. 1.

12. Mario F. Bognanno and Frederic Champlin, "Collective Bargaining in the Health Care Industry," *Socioeconomic Issues in Health*, 1979 (Chicago: American Medical Association, 1979), p. 103.

Operating engineers, maintenance, kitchen, and service employees working in health care facilities are no less interested than their counterparts in other industries in contracts which spell out their wages and hours and procedures for promotion, transfer, and layoff, and contain provisions which guarantee just cause for demotions, suspensions, or terminations with an arbitration appeal option. The Federal Mediation and Conciliation Service reports that, like other sectors, the most frequent causes of labor-management disputes in health care involve wage, pension, and insurance issues.[13]

Among professional employees, basic "bread and butter" union contract provisions dominate the pages of the negotiated agreement. However, for these employees unique professional concerns are also present in the agreements. For instance, professional nurses usually advance twin concern for both economic gains and nursing standards at the bargaining table. Thus, many of their labor agreements contain certain provisions committing management to insuring that hospitalized patients receive the highest quality of nursing care.[14] To cite another example, interns and residents in New York City have contractual provisions which call for the integration of their work schedules into models which are compatible with their educational needs, as well as the medical needs of the patients under their care.[15]

The 1974 Health Care Amendments:
Some Procedural Effects

The purpose of the 1974 Health Care Amendments was to advance both collective bargaining and the means through which labor disputes in the health care industry could be peacefully resolved. These twin objectives caused the Congress not only to extend recognition and bargaining rights to employees of the private health care industry but also to frame "special" procedural regulations which must be followed by either party wishing to change an existing contract. These special requirements are designed to minimize the prospect of work actions and to afford prospectively struck institutions the lead time required to make alternate arrangements for the care of patients and residents.[16] Each of the following statutory provisions is unique to health care collective bargaining:

13. Tanner, Weinstein, and Ahmuty, *Impact of the 1974 Amendments*, pp. 156–57; Harvey A. Juris, "Labor Agreements in the Hospital Industry: A Study of Collective Bargaining Outputs," in James L. Stern, ed., *Proceedings of the Annual 1977 Spring Meetings: Industrial Relations Research Association*, pp. 504-11.

14. Sally T. Halloway, "Health Professionals and Collective Action," *Employee Relations Law Journal*, 1 (Winter 1976), 414.

15. Peter Kihss, "Pact Ends Doctor Strike; Staff Returns to Hospital,"*New York Times*, March 21, 1975, p. 42.

16. James F. Scearce and Lucretia Dewey Tanner, "Health Care Bargaining: The FMCS Experience," *Labor Law Journal*, 27 (July 1976), 387–98; and Tanner, Weinstein, and Ahmuty, *Impact of the 1974 Amendments*.

1. The party (usually the employee organization) wishing to change the terms of an existing contract is obligated to notify the other party in writing ninety days (and not sixty days) prior to the expiration date of the agreement. Neither party may strike nor lock out until this ninety-day period has elapsed or the contract has expired, whichever is later, thus requiring considerable time during which negotiations may proceed.

2. Within thirty days after issuing the first notice, the initiating party must notify the FMCS of the existence of a dispute in the event that an agreement has not been reached.

3. FMCS mediation is mandatory (not voluntary) to further hedge against the risk of the strike or lock out that may "interrupt the delivery of the health care in the locality concerned."

4. Further, the director of the FMCS may appoint a fact finding board of inquiry thirty days prior to contract expiration or within thirty days of receiving the notice of dispute. The board must report its findings of facts and recommendations for settlement of the dispute within fifteen days and the parties must maintain the status quo for an additional fifteen days after the report is issued.

5. Finally, if neither the board's recommendations nor continued mediation and negotiations resolve the differences between the parties, then the employee organization is obligated to notify management in writing of any intention to strike ten days before the work action is to commence. The strike notice itself may be preferred during the fifteen-day hiatus following the submission of the board's report.

Analyzing strike statistics in order to assess the impact of these procedures on work actions in the health care industry is a difficult exercise. Our assertion rests on two points. First, the 1974 amendments and collective bargaining experiences under them are still a new and immature phenomenon; and, second, the time trend line of strikes in the health care industry—measured in terms of number of strikes, number of employees involved, and number of working days idled by work actions —has been positively inclined at least since 1967.

Militant unions like District 1199 demonstrated their willingness to strike against New York City hospitals back in 1959 and again in 1962. In defiance of the 1950 policy adopted by the American Nurses' Association, the California Nurses' Association struck San Francisco Bay area hospitals in 1966 and again in 1974. In 1967 alone some 27 work stoppages in medical and other health services were reported. This number increased to 71 by 1976 with interannual fluctuations occurring during the intervening years. During 1976, approximately 49,500 workers participated in these strikes, and slightly less than 610,000 days of work were lost as a result.[17] It may

17. Bognanno and Champlin, "Collective Bargaining in the Health Care Industry," p. 112.

take several years before the underlying causes of this upward trend begin to show signs of subsiding as a result of the impasse procedures listed above. Work actions attributed to recognition disputes will no doubt abate. However, as employee organizations continued to penetrate the health care industry, the statistical strike series may continue along its present trend simply because "first contracts" are more subject to strike actions than "contract renewals."[18]

According to one study, 2,585 private health care industry negotiations occurred between August 25, 1974, and December 31, 1976. Since mediation is mandatory, "active" FMCS mediation meeting occurred in about half of these cases. This represents a much greater incidence of mediation than normally occurs in the voluntary sector where mediators serve at the pleasure of the host parties. During this time period strikes occurred in 129 of the cases, representing 5 percent of the total number of contracts negotiated.[19] While comparable data are not available for industry in general, we do not believe that it would be erroneous to conclude that this figure is at least roughly comparable to that which characterized nationwide negotiating experiences. There is some evidence to suggest that the FMCS mediators worked harder to avoid strikes in the health care industry vis-a-vis industry in general in those instances where their services were used and where strikes actually occurred. During the reference period, approximately 7.1 "joint meetings" were held on average prior to a strike in health care versus 5.2 meetings on the average for all FMCS cases ending in strike during 1976.[20]

These findings support the conclusion that the FMCS is filling its statutory mandate. What is perhaps most encouraging is that more strikes have not occurred in health care. The lack of bargaining savvy because of inexperience and the fact that strike incidence is greater in new contract negotiations as opposed to renewal negotiations might cause one to predict a more precipitous increase in work actions. Boards of inquiry were not appointed for all of the cases which subsequently ended in strike. For example, a disproportionately large number of strikes occurred among nursing homes, and in some of these cases it was apparently determined that the impasse would not substantially interrupt the delivery of health care. Between August 25, 1974, and December 31, 1976, 120 boards were appointed. Settlements were reached without work action in approximately 7 percent of cases.[21] Assuming that strikes would have occurred in, say, at least half of these "emergency" cases in the absence of the fact-finding procedure, this early record of impasse resolution in the health care industry is respectable.

18. *Ibid.*, p. 113.
19. Tanner, Weinstein, and Ahmuty, *Impact of the 1974 Amendments*, pp. 110, 381.
20. *Ibid.*, p. 110.
21. *Ibid.*, pp. 234–35.

The Bargaining Unit Question

The NLRB was under union and employee association pressure to mini-mize the prospect of interoccupational disputes among different groups of employees placed in common hospital bargaining units. Moreover, there was fear that such groupings would adversely disrupt existing bargaining relationships and might seriously damage new unionization efforts. On the other side of this situation were industry arguments that the proliferation of bargaining units would result in continuous employee caused disrup-tions in the delivery of care, and that it would expose employers to intraorganizational "whipsawing" tactics.

In an effort to resolve these competing views, the NLRB held prelimi-nary hearings in the early part of 1975. After weighing the various considerations raised by the parties and drawing on its traditional unit determination criteria, late in 1975 the NLRB decided upon units struc-tured along occupational lines. The various unit decisions were as follows:

1. Registered nurses were to comprise a separate bargaining unit.[22]
2. Technical employees, including licensed practical nurses. X-ray techni-cians and laboratory technicians were to be grouped into a distinct unit.[23]
3. Maintenance and service employees constituted an appropriate unit.[24]
4. Office and clerical employees were to be assigned to a separate unit.[25]
5. Other professional employees were to be grouped together.[26]
6. In 1977, the board placed employee physicians (MDs) in a separate professional unit.[27]

Bargaining structure considerations do not stop here. For instance, in 1978 the NLRB ruled that a single hospital bargaining unit (and election district) was inappropriate for residual technicians in Saint Luke's Hospi-tal, San Francisco, since it had a long history of bargaining with other technicians on a multiemployer basis.[28] This case suggests to us that the board will be applying its traditional rules (like "established history and practices") in determining the appropriateness of "scope" issues.

Interestingly, there is a history of multiemployer bargaining in the hospital industry in some metropolitan areas in the country which consid-

22. *Mercy Hospital of Sacramento*, 217 NLRB 765 (1975).
23. *Barnert Memorial Hospital Assn.*, 217 NLRB 775 (1975); and *St. Catherine's Hospital*, 217 NLRB 793 (1975).
24. *Newington Children's Hospital*, 217 NLRB 793 (1975).
25. *Sisters of St. Joseph of Peace*, 217 NLRB 797 (1975).
26. *Mercy Hospital of Sacramento*, 217 NLRB 775 (1975).
27. *Ohio Valley Hospital's Asso.*, 230 NLRB 84 (1977).
28. *St. Luke's Hospital*, 234 NLRB 16 (1978).

erably predate the 1974 amendments. Largely a function of state law and voluntary acceptance on the part of the parties involved, multiemployer structural arrangements are found in Minneapolis–St. Paul, New York City, San Francisco–Oakland, and Seattle. The employee organization partner to these structures include the service employees, operating engineers, District 1199, affiliates of the ANA, and other associations or unions like the Society of Radiologic Technologists, New York City's Committee of Interns and Residents, and the Licensed Practical Nurses Association. One study suggests that based on its limited survey, multiemployer bargaining can be appropriate for most hospital occupational designations such as those defined through NLRB determinations. There is cause to believe that, where an employee organization succeeds in organizing numerous similar hospitals in a geographically concentrated area and when it is perceived as being able to force employer concessions through hard bargaining, then health care employers and unions alike may find it to their mutual advantage to adopt a multiemployer bargaining structure.[29]

Economic Impact of Health Care Collective Bargaining

Numerous studies have attempted to measure the effects of health care unionism on relative wages and employment, and ultimately on health care costs, which have been increasing at socially unacceptable rates for more than a decade. Critics of the 1974 Health Care Amendments pointed to the positive correlation between this inflation and the expansion of collective bargaining in the health care industry in voicing their objection to the pending legislation. Unions and associations countered this argument with the view that unionization would reduce labor turnover in the industry, and thus may serve to generate cost savings.

We will briefly report the findings of some of the studies in this area. To begin with unions have succeeded in increasing the relative wages and total compensation (for example, wages plus fringe benefits) flowing to their units. One study found that the annual salary of RNs is from 4 to 7 percent higher for those nurses working in unionized hospitals.[30] Another study determined that, where nurse unions are present, the metropolitan-wide average wage of RNs in private hospitals is increased by slightly more than 7 percent.[31] Nonprofessional unionized employees have been receiving even higher relative wage gains than those received by professional

29. Peter Feuille, Charles Maxey, Hervey Juris, and Margaret Levi, "Determinants of Multiemployer Bargaining in Metropolitan Hospitals," *Employee Relations Law Journal*, 4 (1978) 98–115.

30. C. R. Link and J. H. Landon, "Monopsony and Union Power in the Market for Nurses," *Southern Economic Journal*, 41, No. 4 (April 1975), 644–59.

31. David L. Estenson, *Hospital Union Wage Effects*, unpublished Ph.D. dissertation, Industrial Relations Center, University of Minnesota, 1978.

nurses.[32] In terms of total compensation, there is some evidence that—aggregating across unionized hospital occupations—the union–nonunion differential is about 8 percent.[33]

Given the relative wage gains brought about by hospital unionization, it would not be surprising to discover that unionism has also resulted in a reduction in the relative employment of workers under contract. There is some evidence supporting this deduction; however, the adverse employment effect of unionism is quite modest. The demand elasticity for hospital labor is relatively low.[34] Nevertheless, hospitals do substitute among occupational work groups in response to relative wage changes among them.[35] Thus, for example, one study reported that if unionized LPNs and nurses' aides were to increase their wages 10 percent faster than unionized RNs, then the demand for RN services would increase by about 2.5 percent (at the expense of lost LPN and nurses' aide jobs).

When it comes to the problem of assessing the impact of unionization on hospital costs the required analytical job is more complex. We know of one serious study which tackled this problem.[36] After considering the increased cost effects hospital unions have on both relative total compensation and administrative outlays, plus the reduced cost effects unions have on relative labor turnover, from this study it can be predicted that unionization may increase relative average cost per patient day in a short-term general hospital by about 3.8 percent.[37] This particular relative average cost estimate is subject to numerous limiting assumptions. Thus, we offer it as merely a "ballpark" estimate. All things considered, the impact of unionism on hospital inflation is hardly overwhelming. The fundamental causes of increasing costs per patient day are largely those which lie in other spheres of the hospital and health care delivery sector.

COLLECTIVE BARGAINING IN PROFESSIONAL SPORTS

Unionization in professional sports was a phenomenon of the 1970s. This is not to imply that earlier attempts at unionization had not been tried.[38] In

32. See Myron D. Fottler, "The Union Impact on Hospital Wages," *Industrial and Labor Relations Review*, 30, No. 3 (April 1977), 342–55; Estenson, *Hospital Union Wage Effects*; Brian E. Becker, *The Union Impact on Compensation Levels for Nonprofessionals in Hospitals*, unpublished paper, Industrial Relations Research Institute, University of Wisconsin, 1977.

33. *The Union Impact on Compensation Levels*.

34. Frank A. Sloan and Richard A. Elinicki, "Professional Nurses Staffing in Hospitals," in Frank A. Sloan, ed., *Equalizing Access to Nursing Services: The Geographic Dimension* (Washington, D.C.: U.S. Department of Health, Education and Welfare, Publication No. HRA 75–51, 1978).

35. *Ibid.*

36. Brian E. Becker, *The Impact of Unions on Hospital Costs*, (unpublished paper, Industrial Relations Research Institute, University of Wisconsin, 1977).

37. Bognanno and Champlin, "Collective Bargaining in the Health Care Industry," pp. 116–21.

38. Lee Allen, *100 Years of Baseball* (New York: Bartholomew House, 1950).

the case of baseball, representation and collective efforts date back nearly a century. Today, wages, hours, and working conditions in professional sports are determined through collective bargaining. Professional baseball, basketball, football, hockey, and soccer are represented by professional associations which negotiate opposite their respective club owners' groups on a multiemployer basis.

Bargaining by professional athletes was decades in coming; indeed, many knowledgeable individuals predicted that it would never occur. The reasons for this prediction are wide-ranging. We will review briefly some of these reasons before turning to a discussion of the development of collective bargaining in professional sports.

Why Won't Professional Athletes Unionize?[39]

From a modern-day perspective this is a moot question. However, from a historical perspective, the very reasons listed for the pre-1970s lack of unionism in professional sports highlight the barriers to unionism which were subsequently removed through the long process by which player unions would ultimately come on the scene. Club owners' resistance to changing fundamental employment practices which deprived athletes of their perceived rights to job mobility was the historical catalyst which led to the repeated attempts by players to use both legal avenues and collective bargaining means to change these employment relations. We can only speculate whether collective bargaining would have ever materialized in professional sports had the owners been more flexible and had they seen the "handwriting on the wall."

Later in this chapter, we will develop the basis on which club owners totally controlled the professional athlete's playing career. With such power it was relatively easy for club owners to discourage dissident athletes from objecting too loudly to unfavorable employment practices. The threat of being "benched," "shipped back to the minor leagues," "blacklisted," and so forth is a strong deterrent to collective representation attempts. It must be noted that for years professional athletes were not protected by the coercion and discrimination prohibitions in the NLRA. Several other reasons for the predicted failure of professional athletes to organize for collective bargaining can also be listed.

The strike threat, in many ways the key to collective bargaining success, was thought to be lacking. Athletes are young and their professional careers are short. Thus, it was questioned whether they would engage in short-run sacrifices in order that benefits might accrue to others over the long run. This was particularly true among superstars who had relatively

---

39. The difficulties in unionizing professional athletes are discussed in Edwin G. Krasnow and Herman M. Levy's article entitled "Unionization and Professional Sports," *Georgetown Law Journal*, 51 (Winter 1963).

more to lose from a strike than do the average players. For players making the minimum basic salary the 1972 baseball strike cost only $675, but for a superstar like Hank Aaron it cost nearly $10,000.[40] In the 1981 baseball strike, superstars assumed a leadership role. This will cost. For example, Pete Rose could not hope to break Stan Musial's National League hit record until the strike ended, but he is a solid *union man*.

Open to relatively better employment opportunities outside of professional sports, and with wide fan support, the superstars have been able to do a relatively better job of representing their individual interests vis-a-vis management. Why should they join in collective action with other journeymen athletes who would obviously be far better off as a part of a collective bargaining unit? Moreover, without the support of superstars, successful organizing would be a near impossibility. It was the lack of star support that weakened and led to the collapse of the American Baseball League in 1946. The star players' reputation, media appeal, and leadership positions on the team made them a critical element to unionism in professional sports. Lastly, it was argued that the array of interplayer differences in ability, positions, interest, and number of playing years remaining were so great that it would be difficult to successfully forge a broad enough community of interest to effectively compel managerial recognition and bargaining.

Professionalism and the Oppressive Reserve and Draft Systems

Though unique in many respects, professional athletes have been as concerned with their employment conditions as any other set of workers. The "sporting" aspect of professional athletics can hardly be said to be less important than the "employment" aspect of such endeavors. Field conditions, the pressure of field competition, arduous playing and traveling schedules, the threat of economic loss due to injuries, and so on have long been a part of the general employment conditions over which players have demanded a larger voice.[41] Nevertheless, like so many other professional employee groups demonstrating enthusiasm for organized dealings with management, professional athletes have chosen to be independent of blue collar unions.

Like professional health care employees, the vast majority of schoolteachers and professors, airline pilots, and other professional groups, professional athletes turned to unionization through such contemporary associations as the Major League Baseball Players Association (MLBPA), National Basketball Players Association (NBPA), National Football League

---

40. Joseph Durso, "Baseball Strike Is Settled; Season to Open Tomorrow," *New York Times,* April 14, 1972, p. 1.

41. "The Balance of Power in Professional Sports," *Maine Law Review,* 22 (1970), 474.

Players Association (NFLPA) and National Hockey League Players Association (NHLPA).

Some years ago the Teamsters made a bid to organize pro football players. This effort received a great deal of publicity but little support from the players themselves. The players gave support to their own association while showing little sentiment for dealing with the owners through an AFL–CIO union or through the independent but muscular Teamsters. (In late 1979, the NFLPA did finally affiliate with the AFL–CIO.) Football and baseball players, in large numbers, have always been somewhat ambivalent toward unionization. Even Bob Feller, an early MLBPA official, was reported to have denied that the organization was a "union."[42] The general aversion on the part of professional athletes to join labor organizations raises questions central to an analysis of whether professional athletes are truly of a special category. Experience would suggest that professional athletes and other professional occupations are. The reasons for being so, however, are puzzling. In recent years the professional associations representing football and baseball players were lacking considerably in the quality of their representative function. Yet they were the preferred instruments for unionization. It was not until baseball and football hired nonplayer executive directors having considerable blue-collar union experience during their previous years as union representatives that the MLBPA and NFLPA became viable representative organizations. Football's Ed Garvey was a labor lawyer representing union and association clients of the Minneapolis based law firm of Lindquist and Vennum and baseball's Marvin Miller was a Steelworkers representative prior to joining the Baseball Players Association.

The "professionalism" hangup may have been another factor retarding the onslaught of unions in professional sports. But as we stated earlier, the persistent use of specific employment practices by the leagues which the players found objectionable served as a catalyst to keep collective bargaining activities alive. The two practices imposed on professional athletes, from the very inception of league sports, were the reserve and draft systems. While intersport variations in these systems existed, they were found in all of the sports in one form or another.

The reserve system (for example, "reserve" or "option" clause found in individual player contracts) ties the professional playing life of an athlete to the discretion of his hiring club.[43] Once acquired, the club owner has the sole and exclusive rights to a player's contract. The owner decides whether to play, trade, or release a player. Under the reserve system, the athlete was

42. "Players Ask Joint Meeting," *New York Times,* December 11, 1956, p. 52.

43. An interesting statement of the history and recent changes in the reservation systems in baseball, basketball, football, and hockey is found in James B. Dworkin and Thomas J. Bergmann, "Collective Bargaining and the Player Reservation/Compensation System in Professional Sports," *Employee Relations Law Journal,* (August 1978), 241–56.

prohibited from soliciting bids from other teams and, conversely, other teams were prohibited from dealing directly with a player. The adverse effects of the reserve system from the player's point of view are obvious. First, it is unsettling, to say the least, to have one's professional career dictated exclusively by the predispositions of the "boss." In most cases, the player's employer was in a "make or break" position which gave him tremendous control over the player, a level of control unmatched by that of employers in any other industry. Second, a player could not decide for whom he would play and/or where he would work. Finally, since clubs in the league were barred from bidding for a player's services, it is quite possible that the player would receive compensation which was less than that which the "market would bear." In respect to this last point, several economists have estimated the extent to which professional athletes were in fact being economically exploited.[44] Obviously, the reserve system offered ample motivation for attacking the legitimacy of league employment practices, attacks which would ultimately be waged in the courts and at the bargaining table.

To regulate operation of the reserve system, the leagues created "rules" to which all member clubs were bound. These rules were enforced by a league commissioner who, in every instance, was granted exceptional powers. For instance, the commissioner could fine, suspend and/or invalidate player contracts determined to be in violation of league rules. Thus, even though individual teams were hungry for star talent, if a team were to place a player under contract who was already the "property" of another club in the league, then the commissioner would void the contract, order the acquiring team to cease making salary payments on the contract, and order the player to return to his former team or bar him from league play. This kind of authority assured the orderly operation of the sports cartel.[45]

The player draft system was equally oppressive from the players' standpoint.[46] Under this sytem, amateur players were variously brought into the professional ranks through a common draft which in effect permits the last-place team in the league to make the first amateur selection, then the team with the second worst record would make its selection, and so on up to the first-place team in the league. In each case, the amateur athlete

44. See, for example, Gerald W. Scully, "Pay and Performance in Major League Baseball," *American Economic Review*, 54 (December 1974), 915–30; Marshall H. Medoff, "On Monopolistic Exploitation in Baseball," *Quarterly Review of Economics and Business*, 16 (Summer 1976), 113–21; and James G. Scoville, "Wage Determination and the Development of Collective Bargaining in Baseball," in James Stern and Barbara Dennis, eds., *Proceedings of the Twenty-ninth Annual Winter Meetings, Industrial Relations Research Association*, 1976, pp. 317–23.

45. Lance E. Davis, "Self Regulation in Baseball," in Roger G. Noll, ed., *Government and the Sports Business* (Washington, D.C.: Brookings Institution, 1974), pp. 349–86.

46. The player draft system is defined in operational terms in Daniel I. Shapiro, "The Professional Athlete: Liberty or Peonage," *Alberta Law Review*, 13, No. 2 (1975), 212–41.

selected must negotiate with the selecting team and was prohibited from negotiating with any other organization. Again, competition was restricted and the recruited player, once signed to a contract, was bound thereafter to the interests of the club with which he signed.

Early Bargaining Attempts

In 1885 the National Brotherhood of Professional Baseball Players was formed. Among its many goals was the desire to free players from the mobility limitations of the reserve clause. The Brotherhood was so intent in its resolve to change employment conditions that it went so far as to establish its own Players' League which rivaled the existing leagues. The financial stress, however, was too great. The new player owned league failed and by 1889 the Brotherhood had dissolved. Since then numerous other collective efforts were made, and in one way or another the reserve clause and/or draft system provided the rallying call.

In 1913 the Ball Players' Fraternity was formed. It extracted a few concessions from the owners, but due to player apathy it soon vanished. The reserve system survived this assault only to be tested in the courts in 1922 when (for the first time) the U.S. Supreme Court held that baseball was not subject to the antitrust laws of the land.[47] It seems that the Supreme Court found that, unlike a normal business, baseball teams compete on the playing field and not on the field of business *per se*. From this time forward baseball remained as the only professional sport exempted from federal antitrust laws. Baseball players (though they were to seek legal recourse against the reserve system again in future years) would ultimately be forced to find relief through collective action inasmuch as the 1922 Supreme Court decision provided the judicial immunity the team owners required to perpetuate use of the reserve clause.

In 1946, Robert Murphy, a Harvard educated labor lawyer, founded the American Baseball Guild. The guild advanced specific demands, including the freedom of players to contract at will. The team owners refused to concede to these demands; further, the National Labor Relations Board refused the guild's petition for representative status on the grounds that baseball was not a genuinely commercial pursuit. Thus, this organization also met an early demise. Player apathy and the compromising reactions of baseball commissioner A. B. Chandler to the threat posed by the guild by involving player representatives in discussions regarding employment conditions were elements of the guild's decline.[48]

In 1954 the Major League Baseball Players Association was established. It floundered as a purposeful labor organization for more than ten years. In

47. *Federal Baseball* v. *National League*, 259 U.S. 200, 208 (1922).
48. Krasnow and Levy, "Unionization and Professional Sports," pp. 762–64.

1966 Marvin Miller was hired as the Baseball Players Association's executive director and the organization's history as a bona fide employee advocate was established. By the late 1960s, the club owners granted voluntary recognition to the Baseball Players Association. In 1969, the National Labor Relations Board asserted jurisdiction over baseball in a case involving the American League and an association representing the league's umpires (who also organized).[49] Inroads into the owners' long-cherished reserve system were to materialize in baseball through the grievance arbitration provision embedded in the baseball players' master agreement.

In the late 1950s professional players' associations were also formed in basketball, football, and hockey. Each progressed toward representative status at slow and uneven rates. However, unlike baseball, the professional athletes in these sports were all victorious in various legal actions brought against the reserve and draft systems.[50]

Why the ultimate success at unionization?[51] Many reasons can be given. Each probably has merit for inclusion. First, baseball's legal battles against the reserve clause were going nowhere. In 1969 Curt Flood was traded by the St. Louis Cardinals to the Philadelphia Phillies. Flood refused to be traded on the grounds that he had not been consulted in advance of the trade and that he sought employment with other teams in the league. Baseball commissioner Bowie Kuhn enforced the reserve clause in Flood's player contract. Other teams in the league boycotted Flood. Thus, he brought charges against the league all the way to the Supreme Court, contending that the trade and the reserve clause constituted a violation of the Sherman Anti-Trust Act. Citing *Federal Baseball* (1922) and *Toolson* v. *New York Yankees* (1953), the court ruled against Flood in 1972.[52] Thus, baseball remained exempt from federal antitrust laws. The players had little recourse but to turn to collective bargaining. This time, however, their efforts paid huge dividends. The hiring of Marvin Miller in 1966 was critical to the players' subsequent unionization successes. Moreover, the diversity of philosophies, financial resources, and owner personalities left the league open to attack. Some owners were "hard-liners" in regard to their labor relations philosophy, while others viewed the reserve clause as indefensible. Some American League owners harbored suspicions that their National League counterparts were selfishly resisting needed changes in the game. Lastly, clubs having a solid financial base were suspected by the

49. 5 CCH Lab.L. Rep, 21, 448, at 27,431 (NLRB, 1969).

50. A brief review of the legal challenges facing professional sports can be found in Thomas P. Gilroy and Patrick J. Madden, "Labor Relations in Professional Sports," *Labor Law Journal*, 28 (December 1977), 768–76.

51. Arthur A. Sloane, "Collective Bargaining in Major League Baseball: A New Ball Game and Its Genesis," *Labor Law Journal*, 28 (April 1977), 200–209, contains an excellent discussion of the factors behind baseball's ultimate success at unionization. Many of our answers to this question first appeared in this article.

52. *Flood* v. *Kuhn*, 404 U.S. 880 (1972).

have nots like the Baltimore Orioles, Minnesota Twins, Chicago White Sox, Houston Astros, and Cleveland Indians. Another reason for the success lies in the fact that the industry was experiencing an unparalleled financial boom, despite pockets of poverty, which permitted concessions to many of the Baseball Players Association's demands. Too, the times were ripe for professional unionization. White-collar and public sector unionism were on the upswing, and the concept of negotiating a master contract with "minimum" salaries and group benefits in conjunction with the player option to interest arbitrate individual player salary disputes was the combination that linked the diverse interests of the rookie and star athletes. With the potential benefits to all arising out of the prospects for collective bargaining, and having removed some of the earlier barriers to collectivity through the promise of unique contract language, unionism finally caught on.

The owners' arguments that the reserve clause and the common draft system were necessary to maximize league balance to insure fair competition on the field of play lost its impact. The players and the public turned a deaf ear to the contention that without the reserve and draft systems the "rich" clubs would initiate bidding wars "destined to corner the market" for superstars, resulting in league imbalances, jeopardizing club finances, and threatening club investments in player training and physical care.

Baseball's first basic agreement negotiated in 1968 established grievance arbitration as the means for resolving player–management disputes not having to do with matters which may endanger the "integrity of the game." The latter issues remained in the exclusive jurisdiction of the commissioner of baseball. Under the terms of the negotiated grievance arbitration provision, the Baseball Players Association filed a grievance on behalf of Angels' pitcher Andy Messersmith in 1975. Messersmith claimed that under the terms of the Uniform Players Contract he could become a "free agent" at the end of the 1975 season and thus would be free to negotiate a contract with other teams in the league. Subsequently, his claim was joined with that of Expos pitcher Dave McNally. Both pitchers played the 1975 season without a contract. They interpreted the reserve clause to mean that their respective teams could renew their old contract for only one year, after which time the reserve clause was no longer binding and they would become "free agents." The owners argued that the grievance was not arbitrable and that the reserve clause was also part of the renewed contract, implying that the owners could renew individual player contracts forever. On November 21, 1975, the two grievances came to arbitration. Arbitrator Peter Seitz ruled that the matter before him was arbitrable and in deciding on the merits of the case, he determined that the reserve clause did not grant "perpetual renewal" of a players' contract. Having played a full season without a signed contract, the players were freed from any further obligations to their respective clubs. Seitz further observed that the parties were free to negotiate a more rigid reserve clause.[53] The club owners were shocked by the awards. Seitz was immediately fired as the neutral party to the arbitration panel and the owners sought to have the awards vacated by the courts on two separate occasions but to no avail. Thus, baseball's 1976 labor agreement contained a mutually acceptable, negotiated reserve clause. For the first time in baseball history, though limited in a number of respects, professional baseball players were granted free agent rights.

In basketball, football, and hockey, unionization succeeded for some of the same reasons it flourished in baseball. The player "stars" provided a boon to the organizing and representation thrusts. Kyle Rote and Norm Van Brocklin in football, Ted Lindsay in hockey, and Bob Cousy in basketball were among the category of star association representatives.[54] Further, the courts and favorable NLRB rulings were important to successes among these sports. In a series of cases, the federal courts found various applications of baseball-type reserve clauses and draft systems to be in violation of the Sherman Act. These decisions provided invaluable moral and legal aid to the player associations. In these cases, the courts also designated arm's length bargaining as a proper way by which these matters of employment may be fashioned; provided, of course, that the resulting language was not intended to accomplish an anticompetition conspiracy.

In basketball, a district court indicated in 1976 that the National Basketball Association's draft and reserve practices might be in violation of antitrust laws.[55] In hockey, two court rulings were handed down in 1972 against the National Hockey League. The most far reaching decision held that the reserve clause and NHL's farm team relationship which restricted the flow of amateur players outside the league (and in this case, to the rival World Hockey Association) constituted a violation of the Sherman Act and represented an illegal restraint to the freedom of individual mobility. In football,[56] the Supreme Court made clear in 1957 that the reserve clause was a trade violation and that football was not exempt from the Sherman Act. In its place, therefore, the owners substituted the "option clause" buttressed by the "Rozelle Rule" (named after football commissioner Pete Rozelle). The former clause gave the club owner exclusive bargaining rights to a player during the term of his contract, plus one additional contract period (the option year); therafter, having played out his option, a player would become a free agent. The Rozelle Rule authorizes the commissioner of football to require an acquiring team to compensate the free agent's

53. *Professional Baseball Clubs*, 66 LA 110 (p. Seitz, 1975); also, Peter Seitz, "The Gotterdammerung of Grievance Arbitration," *Employee Relations Law Journal*, (Spring 1977), pp. 386–95.

54. Krasnow and Levy, "Unionization and Professional Sports," pp. 764–65.

55. Gilroy and Madden, "Labor Relations in Professional Sports," pp. 770–71.

56. *Ibid.*, p. 771.

previous team for the new hire. This rule stripped the free-standing option clause of its original intent. Owners were being penalized in effect for hiring free agents, and free agents were discouraged in effect from playing out their option. This matter was soon set right. In *Kapp* v. *National Football League* (1974) and *Mackey* v. *National Football League* (1976), two federal courts held that the Rozelle Rule was illegal.[57]

About the only employment condition which players negotiate as individuals is salary. Even here there are minimums and other cash compensation benefits which are a part of the master agreement. Collective representation has replaced individual representation. Court actions, NLRB decisions to extend the NLRA's jurisdiction to include professional sports, and critical board decisions enjoining managerial unfair labor practices, gifted union leadership, improvement in the leagues' financial posture, a social climate conducive to professional unionism, ingenious contractual ways of combining diverse player interests, the strike threat, and sheer tenacity explain the rise of modern-day unions in professional sports.

The Current State of Collective Bargaining Relations in Professional Sports[58]

Labor relations problems are frequently aired on radio and television sports shows. Sports magazines and the sporting press do not permit us to escape the daily reminder that collective bargaining has emerged in professional sports. Even though work actions have been few in number, the sports industry has not been immune from strikes. In 1968 and early 1969, many professional baseball players refused to sign their individual player's contracts until the club owners agreed to a substantial improvement in the players' group pension plan. The athletes' refusal to sign their player agreement created a media stir; however, the worst was yet to come. In 1972, again over the pension issue, the MLBPA and the owners reached an impasse. In the spring of that year, the association led a players' strike, the first general players' strike in baseball history. Buttressed with nearly unanimous player support, the 1972 season was delayed until the second week in April as a result of the strike. The owners were furious over the strike; many owners supported the possibility of opening the season with minor league players, and others would have accepted the consequences of a prolonged strike rather than to compromise their position. Obviously, the moderate view of compromise prevailed. Labor relations had arrived in

---

57. *Ibid.*, pp. 771–72.

58. Many of the factual statements contained in this section first appeared in Gilroy and Madden, ''Labor Relations in Professional Sports,'' pp. 773–75.

baseball; the owners and the players responded to the 1972 strike in a sobering way. The 1973 and 1976 negotiations resulted in hard bargaining aimed at avoiding the need for subsequent work actions. The same was true in 1980, even though there was a partial walkout during spring training. Baseball players engaged in their first mid-season strike in June of 1981. The strike was precipitated by the failure to reach agreement over the issue of compensation for teams losing free agents.

Two other strikes are on record in professional sports. In 1970 and again in 1974 the National Football League Players Association called general strikes. In an attempt to cut losses, the club owners substituted rookies for veterans in exhibition games. The results were disastrous. The quality of football played was poor. Attendance fell off dramatically and eventually the strike fizzled. The players returned to the field and it was not until 1977 that a players' agreement was again reached. During the interim, the NLRB ruled against various management actions which discriminated against the union activists among the players; moreover the federal courts found football's reserve system and the Rozelle Rule to be in violation of federal antitrust laws. These legal blows to football management and the association's improved cohesiveness caused the club owners to recognize that a collective bargaining agreement would be a less costly option than pursuing the antiunion policy that had been followed for years.

The historical divisions between players and club owners created by the reserve and draft systems has narrowed considerably. Baseball remains as the only professional sport that is exempt from federal antitrust laws. However, pressures on Congress to remedy this legal problem through legislative actions have subsided as a result of the Seitz arbitration. Subsequent negotiations have led to revisions in the reserve clause. Baseball's 1976–79 basic agreement permitted all players who desire to become free agents to do so after acquiring six years of major league service. Limits were placed on both the number of free agents a team can acquire during a season and on the number of teams with whom a free agent may negotiate.

In 1976, the NBA's labor agreement contained provisions on a new college draft, option clause, interteam compensation and the "right of first refusal." The latter provision essentially gives a player's current team an opportunity to retain the player's services by matching the bids received by the athlete from competitive teams in the league. The right of first refusal went into effect with the end of the NBA playoffs in 1981 and is to be in effect for a period of six years. Given that no compensation is required for teams losing free agents under this new system, it can safely be predicted that both player mobility and salaries in basketball will increase as a result. The NHLPA and league management agreed to a one-year option clause in place of the old perpetual reserve clause. In professional football, the parties agreed in 1977 on a new draft system; player contracts were issues devoid of option clause for players who have at least four years of participation in the league pension plan and the contract included a right of first refusal clause. However, in football, teams losing free agents are guaranteed compensation for their player losses, in some cases as much as two first round draft choices, Thus, free agency is weak in football. The issue of free agency will surface again in the early 1980's.

While all of the above referenced contracts contain grievance machinery provisions and other standard provisions found in the typical union contract, the mobility and draft provisions are unique to professional sports. From the players' point of view, the emergence of collective bargaining has indeed played a major role in improving their economic and labor market situation. Minimum salaries have increased by leaps and bounds since the installation of unions. In baseball, the minimum salary increased from $10,000 in 1968 to $21,000 in 1978, and to $32,500 in 1981. By 1977, football players averaged $55,288; baseball players, $76,349; and hockey players, $90,000. Basketball players averaged about twice as much as football players. These are averages, of course. A superstar like Pete Rose may earn eight times the average player's salary.[59] Unionization can be associated with fatter expense allowances, greater compensation levels for postseason games, and considerably improved pension, health, life, and disability insurance benefits. And, in baseball's case, interest arbitration is the agreed-upon basis for resolving individual player salary disputes.[60]

COLLECTIVE BARGAINING IN HIGHER EDUCATION[61]

Teacher unions date back to the late nineteenth century, but, as discussed in Chapter 15, it was not until the general growth of public sector unions in the 1960s that literally thousands of elementary and secondary school-teachers turned to collective bargaining as the instrument for resolving a

59. *Sporting News,* May 17, 1980, p. 38, and December 29, 1979, p. 30.

60. A brief statement on the use and impact of final-offer arbitration in baseball is found in James B. Dworkin, "The Impact of Final-Offer Interest Arbitration on Bargaining: The Case of Major League Baseball," in James Stern and Barbara Dennis, eds., *Proceedings of the Twenty-ninth Annual Winter Meetings: Industrial Relations Research Association,* 1976, pp. 161–69. From a practical standpoint, final-offer procedures in baseball are discussed in the following articles: Peter Seitz, "Footnotes to Baseball Salary Arbitration," *Arbitration Journal,* 29 (June 1974), 98–103; and Peter Seitz, "Are Professional Sports or Business? or How Much Would You Pay for Catfish Hunter?" in James Stern and Barbara Dennis, eds., *Proceedings of the Twenty-ninth Annual Winter Meetings, Industrial Relations Research Association,* 1976, pp. 324–28.

61. This section relies heavily on two articles by Joseph W. Garbarino, namely: "Faculty Unionism: The First Ten Years," *Annals of the American Academy of Political and Social Science,* 448 (March 1980), 74–76; and "Faculty Unionization: The pre-Yeshiva Years, 1966–1979," *Industrial Relations,* Spring 1980, pp. 221–31.

large number of industrial relations issued facing education. Led by the schoolteacher experiences, during the 1970s collective bargaining among professors emerged. This section of the chapter will trace some of the unique aspects of faculty collective bargaining. Huge collective bargaining inroads have already been made at the community college level; thus, this section will deal exclusively with collective bargaining in four-year colleges and universities—a newly emerging sector.

Patterns and Trends in Faculty Unionism

Professional collective bargaining, like that among health care employees and professional athletes, is truly a phenomenon of the 1970s. In 1969 only twenty-four institutions of higher education had unionized faculties; the first four-year college to be organized was the U.S. Merchant Marine Academy in 1966. By 1979, the faculty unionism picture had changed dramatically. Excluding law and medical school unions on campuses where other faculty members had not organized, a total of 227 institutions were unionized, representing about 86,000 professors. The vast majority of these unionized institutions were publicly owned and operated, 161 out of 227. As one might expect, slightly less than nine out of every ten unionized professors worked in a public sector college or university.[62] In relative terms, nearly 30 percent of all public and 5 percent of all private institutions had faculty unions in 1979.

A geographic analysis of ths state-by-state location of institutions with faculty unions and the amount of faculty unionism existing in each state reveals that public sector unions were almost exclusively located in states with laws permitting faculty organizing. In 1979, twenty-two states and the District of Columbia had faculty bargaining laws. Every unionized public institution of higher learning was located in these jurisdictions with the exception of nine organized colleges or universities which were located variously in the states of Illinois, Ohio, and Maryland. Every public sector college or university located in Connecticut, Delaware, Florida, Hawaii, Maine, Massachusetts, New Jersey, New York, Rhode Island, South Dakota and Washington, D.C., has faculty unions. In the remaining eleven states with faculty bargaining laws (excluding California, whose law took effect only on July 1, 1979) there were 76 institutions of higher learning, and all but 27 of these had faculty unions (with 20 being large, "Big Ten" types of universities).[63]

The importance of the association between the level of union organizing activity and the existence of enabling labor laws has been discussed many times throughout the book. The significance of this relationship, however, is most vividly illustrated in the case of public sector faculty bargaining. It is

62. Garbarino, "Faculty Unionization: The pre-Yeshiva Years, 1966–79," p. 223.
63. Garbarino, "Faculty Unionism: The First Ten Years," p. 76.

dangerously tempting to overstate this point; we have to be careful because counterillustrations are easy to find. In fact, counterevidence can be also found in the higher education industry itself. After decades of refusing to assert jurisdiction over private sector colleges and universities, the NLRB reversed itself in 1970.[64] Again, in the following year, in its 1971 *C. W. Post* decision, the board held that the policy making role of full-time and part-time faculty did not exempt them as "employees" under the NLRA.[65] In spite of having enjoyed federal representation rights for ten years, however, only about 5 percent of all of the nation's private colleges and universities are unionized.

It seems safe to conclude that enabling labor legislation does spawn a flurry of early organization activity but, thereafter, the rate of union penetration (for a host of reasons) begins to slow. This was the case in higher education's private sector, where the number of unionized institutions began to increase at a considerably reduced rate after 1975.

Future collective bargaining initiatives in private sector higher education are less promising even than this trend analysis would suggest. In a 1980 case involving Yeshiva University in New York City, the Supreme Court ruled 5 to 4 that faculty members at private colleges and universities are generally not employees under the NLRA.[66] The Court's majority held that faculty members have absolute authority over academic matters and, in effect, make key employment and service decisions which cause them to be classified as managerial personnel who are outside the coverage of federal labor law. While this decision does not apply to public sector college and university professors, and while it may leave the "technical door" to collective bargaining open to faculty members not engaged in managerial decision making, there is little question that, short of a court reversal and/or amending the NLRA, collective bargaining growth in private higher education institutions may come to a halt. In fact, management in private institutions that are currently unionized are within their legal rights to refuse continued union recognition.

The prospects for continued public sector union penetration in higher education are only marginally brighter. Without passage of higher education bargaining laws in states without them, there is little reason to expect the 1970s trend to continue. The Yeshiva decision, moreover, will most certainly have an adverse impact on any new (and perhaps existing) public sector labor laws that will be enacted at the state level in the future. The number of additional public college and university faculties turning to union representation has already begun to slow. Most of the institutions *without* faculty bargaining from among the twenty-two states with faculty

---

64. *Cornell University*, 193 NLRB 41 (1970).
65. *C. W. Post Center of Long Island University*, 189 NLRB 109 (1971).
66. *NLRB* v. *Yeshiva University*, 48 U.S.L.W. 4175 (U.S., February 20, 1980).

bargaining laws may be classified, like we did earlier, as "Big Ten" types of universities (for example, the University of California, Iowa, Michigan, or Minnesota).[67] From among these large institutions, Colorado, Michigan State, Minnesota, Nebraska, Oregon, Penn State, and Pittsburgh have already rejected unionism through representation elections.[68] Most assuredly, more elections will be held from among these candidates. For example, a second election at the University of Minnesota, Twin Cities campus, should be held in the fall of 1981. The University of Minnesota's Duluth and Waseca campuses, have recently unionized, but whether the Twin Cities faculties at Minnesota or at any other institution will soon unionize is an open question.

Having observed the faculty electioneering process at the University of Minnesota, a large segment of that faculty unquestionably believe that unionism would negatively affect the prestige of the university, the quality of research and education, and thus the acceptability of the university as a place of work. Faculty members at the larger research universities are quick to point out that none of the fifty institutional members of the prestigious Association of American Universities (AAU) are unionized, and that all nine of the representation elections held at AAU universities resulted in rejections.[69]

Professional employees in general have been demonstrating an increased enthusiasm for organized dealings with management. However, as we noted earlier in this chapter, they generally favor working through professional associations rather than unions (and, as will be shown momentarily, the same is true for higher education). This avoidance of "unions" is partially a consequence of elitist feelings, but perhaps more importantly, it arises from a genuine conviction that there is merit in blending bargaining with professionalism. Among the research universities the "blending" argument has not been selling. The very legitimacy and necessity of bargaining itself is attacked by many professors. Indeed, prior to the 1978 election at Minnesota, and in deference to this antibargaining sentiment on campus, the local chapter of the American Association of University Professors (AAUP) seemed to go out of its way to avoid the use of blue-collar or "hard-hat" labor relations terms and moreover objected to the thought of being viewed as a union. It was sometimes questioned whether the AAUP chapter was campaigning for or against representation. The rival local of the American Federation of Teachers (AFT), which was also vying for representation rights at Minnesota, was quick to point out this ambivalence with the charge of "company unionism." When the second election is held at Minnesota's Twin Cities campus, the likelihood is

---

67. Garbarino, "Faculty Unionism: The First Ten Years," p. 67.
68. *Ibid.*, p. 80.
69. *Ibid.*

that this time around the AAUP and a relatively newly formed affiliate of the National Education Association (NEA) will be pitted against each other. The second round will involve an interassociation rivalry.

The propensity to organize the Big Ten types of universities is blunted by other factors as well. Relative to other intrastate higher educational institutions, it is fair to say that, on average, the faculties at the research universities are better paid, have lighter teaching loads, enjoy a more effective role in university governance matters, and have a greater day-to-day involvement in faculty hiring, promotion, and retention decisions. Leading institutions of higher education are not likely to turn away from the traditional form of faculty representation (i.e., governance through a faculty senate) and toward the industrial form or representation (i.e., collective bargaining) unless they are neglected or alienated by university administrations and/or treated inquitably by state government authorities who are often faced with budgetary decisions which may favor unionized over nonunionized public colleges and universities.

Professor Bargaining Agents

The philosophical differences among the AAUP, AFT, and NEA are widely touted and researched. With membership limited to exclusively higher education faculty, the AAUP is a relative newcomer to collective bargaining dealings. From its inception, the AAUP has championed the concept of "tenure" as the principal employment rule needed to effectively protect the constitutional right of professors to "academic freedom." It has protected these twin measures on behalf of faculty members through the decades via faculty–administration dialogue, lobbying, and legal actions; it has set academic standards; and in the area of faculty compensation it has consistently advanced the idea of "pay for merit." The transition of the AAUP from a strictly professional association to a bargaining organization as well was difficult. Following considerable intraorganizational trauma, however, in the early 1970s the AAUP, like the NEA had done a half decade earlier, threw its hat into the bargaining agency ring.

The NEA is the nation's oldest, best financed, and largest teachers' organization. Drawing members from all rungs of the academic ladder, the NEA was converted from a professional association (which featured educational programs and enunciated policies ranging from school finances to class size to teaching methods to academic standards) to a labor relations association in the late 1960s. Here again the conversion was arduous. Inititially, NEA affiliates rivaled the AFT as a public school teacher representative and then as a community college representative. It shied away from strike talk; instead, it favored "sanctions." It stressed the use of "professional negotiations" and eschewed "collective bargaining." Over this period, of course, the NEA was sneered at by the AFT, a "real" union and an AFL–CIO affiliate. Time has blunted the antistrike, nonunion label sought by the NEA as it has repeatedly struck in various jurisdictions as a means of effectuating its economic and noneconomic demands. The NEA's full conversion to unionism, however, has not meant that the association has discarded many of its initial goals and professional interests. It has merely meant that wages, hours, and employment conditions, bargained collectively, have assumed a new and perhaps greater importance than ever before.

The AFT's roots date back to the late nineteenth century, but it was not until 1961 that the first major teacher bargaining breakthrough occurred. Following a strike and protracted negotiations, New York City's board of education accepted collective bargaining and the representative status of an affiliate of the AFT, which in one full sweep became the representative of about 30,000 teachers. Using standard bargaining tactics, the AFT has come to represent nearly 500,000 schoolteachers and professors during the years which have elapsed. Included among the professors represented by AFT locals are two huge bargaining units in New York's higher education system—namely, the City University of New York (CUNY) and the State University of New York (SUNY) complexes.

While cast as a bread-and-butter union, it would be inaccurate to conclude that AFT affiliates as opposed to the NEA or AAUP chapters show little or no interest in academic issues like tenure, academic freedom, or faculty governance. One analysis of labor contracts negotiated in colleges and universities concludes that with few exceptions the similarities in contract provisions negotiated by these three organizations are more pronounced than the differences.[70] This may explain why, contrary to expectations, affiliates of the AFT, NEA, and AAUP have not in any impressive sense been victorious in winning representative rights in large public, small public, and private colleges and universities, respectively. The AAUP has succeeded in organizing more institutions (41) than the other organization; whereas the AFT represents the most professors (nearly 43,000).[71]

A Comment on Faculty Bargaining Issues and the Impact of Faculty Bargaining

The evidence on the impact of faculty unions on relative wages is mixed. Specific institutions can be identified as having realized significant gains in compensation as a result of unionizations. However, it is difficult to know what faculty salaries would have been at these institutions in the absence of the union. A leading scholar and observer on the higher education bargaining scene, Professor Joseph Garbarino, concludes that after ten

70. Mario F. Bognanno, David L. Estenson, and Edward L. Suntrup, "Union-Management Contracts in Higher Education," *Industrial Relations*, May 1978, pp. 189–203.

71. Garbarino, "Faculty Unionism: The First Ten Years," p. 81.

years of higher education collective bargaining there is no conclusive evidence on the effects of faculty unions on salaries. He observed that whatever the effects have been thus far they are neither significant nor substantial.[72] While the promise of economic benefit is one of the reasons faculty members turned to unions during the 1970s, as the academic marketplace began to show signs of increasing slack, it would appear that this promise has not materialized in any measureable sense.

This, however, is not true in other important areas of academic employment relations. No single topic has received more attention in relation to faculty collective bargaining than that of faculty governance. Because of their professional experience and knowledge, faculty members hold the attitude that they ought to have input into critical college and university decisions having to do with faculty hiring and retention, academic programs, student admissions, graduation criteria, and budget allocation decisions which, in the final analysis, go far to determine a given institution's academic strength, faculty, staff, and student body size and the extent of teaching and research program support. Typically, faculty involvement in these decision-making processes occurs at the all-college/ university level through a faculty senate or at the specific college/ department level through a faculty committee structure.

Many of the institutions which have been organized to date are those that lack a strong tradition of faculty governance. At other institutions where organizing attempts have been made but failed—for example, at the University of Minnesota—an important union campaign issue was the lack of an effective faculty governance system. Among the charges leveled against the Minnesota administration was the assertion that the university senate was so fragmented in its committee structure that it did not have an effective general policy voice. To this charge was added the claim that the senate was no more than a "rubber stamp" body to which already agreed-upon administrative decisions were being submitted. The list of charges goes on. In some instances, faculty groups claimed that the veto power of the college dean or university president in effect reduces faculty input to a meaningless state. It is difficult to accurately assess the validity of these charges. Do, for example, departmental faculty deny a given professor his promotion because of the belief that the dean or a higher administrative figure has already "let it be known" that he opposes the promotion? On occasions, arguments against promotions are made on the grounds that an affirmative decision would be unpopular with the administration; unfortunately, the matter of merit is sometimes lost in such discussions.

Collective bargaining in higher education has most definitely affected the processes by which a faculty member's performance is reviewed in

72. Garbarino, "Faculty Unionism: The First Ten Years," p. 84.

regard to retention or promotion decisions. Unions have forced personnel reviews into a more systematic framework, complete with decision-making criteria, and open to broad general scrutiny. Further, many academic contracts have provisions which permit individual faculty members to appeal adverse decisions and even to take the decision "outside" to be tried before an impartial arbitrator or panel of arbitrators. Where review systems had been procedurally flawed, collective bargaining has led to improvements. Perhaps even the quality of the final decisions made has improved. This, however, is a purely speculative and questionable judgment. It may be that the subjective judgments of colleagues or administrators about the quality of one's teaching, research, and service is not being given the weight it would have received in the absence of collective bargaining vis-a-vis pieces of objective evidence, like the numbers of classes taught or articles published. The latter kind of evidence is easier to measure and evaluate against standards of consistency and past practices. Whether unions have helped or hurt the academic sense of "collegiality" and "peer review" remains open for debate.

As for the matter of governance, collective bargaining has shifted the locus of participation in the wages and hours decisions from the faculty senate floor to the bargaining table. However, the evidence is mixed in regard to the other matters of faculty governance which had before been within the exclusive jurisdiction of the senate. For example, issues involving educational and research programs, faculty reductions, intercollege or departmental budget allocations, athletic programs, faculty consulting policy, and so forth are sometimes discussed within the context of collective conferences and negotiation settings, and sometimes these issues are distinctly earmarked for discussion within the traditional governance framework.

Questions for Discussion, Thought, and Research

1. Should health care employees have the right to strike? Explain.

2. One force which impeded the development of nursing unions is the notion of Nightingalism—nurses were in the profession for altruistic reasons and not for money. Is this attitude changing?

3. "The height of professionalism is to be able to assert control over your own economic destiny. Unions allow professionals to assert such control." Evaluate this contention.

4. How does the NLRB treat interns and residents?

5. Is a promotion system based on seniority incompatible with professionalism?

6. What are the special procedural requirements health care employees must follow before they have the right to strike? Have these procedures been effective?

7. What labor organizations are the fastest growing in the health care industry?

8. Is multiemployer bargaining going to become more prevalent in the health care industry in the near future?

9. Has the impact of unionization on hospitals been favorable or unfavorable? Explain.

10. In the absence of issues such as the reserve clause and draft system, would collective bargaining have evolved in professional baseball?

11. What factors impeded unionization by professional employees?

12. Why is unionism among college faculty not likely to spread?

Selected Bibliography

Allison, D. J., "Professional Sports and the Antitrust Laws: Status of the Reserve System," *Baylor Law Review*, 25 (1973), 1–25.

Begin, James et al., *Academic Bargaining: Origins and Growth.* New Brunswick, N.J.: Institute of Management and Labor Relations, 1977.

Carr, R. K., and D. K. Van Eyck, *Collective Bargaining Comes to the Campus.* Washington, D.C.: American Council on Education, 1973.

Dworkin, J. B., *Owners versus Players: Baseball and Collective Bargaining,* Boston: Auburn House, 1981.

Dworkin, J. B., "The Impact of Final Offer Arbitration on Bargaining: The Case of Major League Baseball," *IRRA Annual Proceedings,* 29th Meeting, (December 1976), pp. 161–69.

Fottler, Myron D., "The Union Impact on Hospital Wages," *Industrial and Labor Relations Review*, 30, No. 3 (April 1977) 342–55.

Garbarino, J. W., *Faculty Bargaining, Change and Conflict.* New York: McGraw-Hill, 1975.

Gilroy, T. P., and P. J. Madden, "Labor Relations in Professional Sports," *Labor Law Journal*, 28 (December 1977), 768–76.

Juris, Hervey A., "Labor Agreements in the Hospital Industry: A Study of Collective Bargaining Outputs," James L. Stern, ed., Proceedings of the Annual 1977 Spring Meetings: IRRA (Madison, Wis.: IRRA, 1977), pp. 504–11.

Kemerer, F. R., and J. V. Baldridge, *Unions on Campus.* San Francisco: Jossey-Bass, 1975.

Krasnow, E. G., and H. M. Levy, "Unionization and Professional Sports," *Georgetown Law Journal*, 51 (Winter 1963), 749–82.

Ladd, E. C., and S. M. Lipsett, eds., *Professors, Unions and American Higher Education*. Berkeley: Carnegie Commission on Higher Education, 1973.

Metzger, N., and Dennis D. Pointer, *Labor–Management Relations in the Health Services Industry*. Washington, D.C.: Science and Health Publications, 1972.

Miller, Richard U., Brian B. Becker, and Edward B. Krinsky, "Union Effects on Hospital Administration: Preliminary Results from a Three-State Study," in James L. Stern, ed., *Proceedings of the Annual 1977 Spring Meetings: IRRA*. Madison, Wis.: IRRA, 1977, pp. 512–19.

Mortimer, Keeneth, ed., *Faculty Bargaining, State Government and Campus Autonomy*. Denver: Edcuation Commission of the States, 1976.

Noll, R. G., ed., *Government in the Sports Business*. Washington, D.C.: Brookings Institution, 1974.

Scearce, James F., and Lucretia Dewey Tanner, "Health Care Bargaining: The FMCS Experience," *Labor Law Journal*, 27 (July 1976), 387–98.

Scully, G. W., "Pay and Performance in Major League Baseball," *American Economic Review*, 54 (December 1974), 915–30.

Shapiro, D. I., "The Professional Athlete: Liberty or Peonage?", *Alberta Law Review*, 13, No. 2 (1975), 212–41.

Sloane, A. A., "Collective Bargaining in Major League Baseball: A New Game and Its Genesis," *Labor Law Journal*, 28 (April 1977), 200–10.

COLLECTIVE BARGAINING: THE CHALLENGES AHEAD

17

Many challenges to the collective bargaining process and the nature of the response to them have been discussed and evaluated in earlier chapters. In these concluding pages we must be mindful once again of the heterogeneous character of collective bargaining relationships in these United States. No summary overview can reflect faithfully the entire collective bargaining spectrum. A summary listing of the challenges—current and prospective —to collective bargaining is realistically within our grasp. Thus, these are listed in this chapter. We then identify the qualities and tasks of the model collective bargaining practitioner who must deal with these challenges as a part of his or her daily responsibilities. Lastly, the text would be incomplete without presentation of a brief inventory of collective bargaining accomplishments and short-comings, and without our thoughts about the future state of collective bargaining as an institution.

PERENNIAL CHALLENGES
TO PUBLIC POLICY

The evolution of collective bargaining in the United States has gone a long way toward realizing the potential of three major public policy goals which have been a matter of record for nearly half a century. More can be done, however. The goals or objectives we have in mind are as follows:

1. To achieve full employment without inflation while maintaining "free" collective bargaining (that is, without direct control over wages and prices.)
2. To achieve effective democratization of industrial relations, although faced with an increased amount of centralization in bargaining structures and in decision making in both union and management organizations.
3. To achieve a stable, equitable condition of industrial peace while avoiding undue government control.

These three challenges remain significant ones for now and the predictable future. Each challenge embraces a mixing of public interest goals with private needs and requirements. Viable responses require achieving in accommodation of public policy objectives with those of the private decision makers. How to dovetail private and public policy in ways that will maximize the discretion remaining to the practitioners while insuring the attainment of economy-wide goals continues to be *the* fundamental challenge.

Throughout the book we discussed specific problem areas involving public–private jurisdiction. Tension between the private jurisdiction and public jurisdiction in the employer–employee relationship has always existed. In recent years this tension has increased and created new problems in collective bargaining. One only has to recount contemporary developments in the areas of discrimination, OSHA, pensions, "finality of arbitration awards," and wage–price controls, to mention a few.

Students of collective bargaining must look beyond the specific requirements of particular union–management relationships. We must be concerned with the macroeconomic impact of thousands of microeconomic bargains arrived at separately. However, the practitioners of bargaining focus naturally on the short run and on their particular needs as they see them. The analysis must begin by acknowledging that *collective bargaining must remain a microeconomic process if we are to continue stressing the values of private decision making.* Our inventory of challenges, however, *appropriately includes macroeconomic problems whose solution can be affected by the practitioners of bargaining.*

SOME MACRO-ORIENTED
PROBLEM AREAS

Without elaboration, we list some major challenges posed in macro-oriented terms and then turn to problems faced by and within the control of those who actually engaged in collective bargaining.

Our inventory of macro challenges is as follows:

1. How to inject macroeconomic awareness into the consciousness of collective bargaining practitioners in a manner that will *effectively condition* their joint action on economic issues in bargaining.
2. How to minimize the possible use of economic force to resolve disputes over future contract terms in critical bargaining relationships while avoiding such extreme measures as compulsory arbitration or government seizure.
3. How to reformulate our national labor relations policy in ways that will strengthen the institutional processes of private collective bargaining and eliminate abuses.
4. How to coordinate national policy measures aimed at preventing inflation with related private approaches through collective bargaining.
5. How (or whether) to encourage those engaged in conventional collective bargaining to develop joint solutions to problems beyond or outside of the employment relationship.
6. How to improve knowledge and understanding of the economic effects of collective bargaining on the economy as a whole as well as on particular industries and particular labor markets.
7. How to improve the general public's knowledge and understanding of what collective bargaining involves, what it can do, and what it should not be expected to do.

JOB SECURITY PROBLEMS: THE MAIN
CHALLENGE TO COLLECTIVE BARGAINING
PRACTITIONERS

At a micro level, the principal challenge to bargainers concerns how to insure job security without infringing upon management's right to innovate, to change factor and job mixes, and to relocate and restructure plants. This statement should not be interpreted as minimizing the importance of wages as a central issue. In inflationary times, wage increases receive top billing. Nevertheless, with the advent of business cycles in the 1970s and early 1980s, the complex of problems relating to job security has been and will remain of crucial significance to both management and union.

The conflict potential inherent in the job .security problem can be illustrated by stating two propositions. The first conditions management thinking. The second is mandatory for union leadership to consider. These two propositions are as follows:

1. Management must retain freedom to innovate in terms of technology, structure of industrial operations and location of plants, involving the shutting down of obsolete installations, and the construction of optimal size units. In a period of stagnating productivity, innovation and technological change must be accorded top priority.

2. Employees are entitled to contractual protection of bargaining unit work opportunities to the maximum extent consistent with point 1 above and to negotiated provisions for *cushioning the impact* of either technological displacement or loss of work occasioned by plant closures and/or removal to a different location.

Specific illustrations of job security issues were given in Chapter 12. Since job security poses perhaps the most difficult problem area in contemporary bargaining, it has been accorded special mention in beginning this inventory. Other challenges are listed summarily, with editorial comment excluded at this stage. The ordering of these challenges has no particular significance.

CHALLENGES TO THE PRACTITIONERS OF BARGAINING

1. How to negotitate master contracts and local supplemental agreements in such a fashion as to minimize the likelihood of strikes over the latter after the former have been peacefully negotiated.

2. How to achieve meaningful collective bargaining in the public sector, without full recourse to the traditional private sector instrument of economic force as a means of producing agreement.

3. How to achieve efficient collective bargaining in the public sector that reconciles but still respects the highly fragmented authorities and specialties of government.

4. How to achieve greater individual employee interest and participation in collective bargaining policies and procedures, including making the process more "relevant" in terms of the aspirations of minority, females, and younger workers.

5. How to develop effective procedures for joint consideration of such long-range continuing problems as the impact of technological change and industrial relocation, outside the crisis atmosphere of regular contract negotiation periods.

6. How to achieve a sensible balance between wages, on the one hand, and monetary fringe benefits, on the other.

7. How to negotiate mutually satisfactory provisions on the explosive issue of subcontracting work.

8. How to negotiate the elimination of outmoded policies and procedures that are still regarded as sacrosanct (for example, outmoded working rules negotiated originally to cover a condition that no longer exists but whose continuance may benefit some incumbent employees).

9. How to conform to government employment requirements such as EEO, HMO, and ERISA.

10. How to prevent collective bargaining contracts from expanding into "Roman codes" that are too detailed and too technical for the average working mortal to comprehend.

11. How to adjust wages and fringes for the duration of a contract to allow for inflation.

12. How (and when) to make use of "informed neutrals" to facilitate negotiation and administration of collective agreements.

13. How to cope rationally with the enduring problem posed by the confrontation between management's cherished reserved rights and the union's penchant for enlarging the scope of collective bargaining.

14. How to encourage the use of joint union–management committees in dealing with such matters as increasing productivity as well as with the more conventional areas of joint safety committees, joint job evaluation committees, and so forth.

15. How to encourage creativity and innovation in collective bargaining, both procedurally and on substantive policy problems.

16. How to safeguard the procedural right of the individual worker to fair representation without sacrificing the institutional objectives of management and union aimed at stability in contract administration.

The foregoing challenges are microriented in the sense that the parties themselves have the capacity and the power to respond. The nature and adequacy of responses were reviewed throughout the book. It is apparent that how the parties solve (or fail to solve) these problems can have ramifications far beyond the purview of company X and union Y. It is also clear that some of these challenges cannot be met effectively by microeconmic decisions alone but require complementary and supportive public policy. The job security problem, for example, calls for a high degree of cooperation between private and public policy.

In brief, these are some of the principal challenges faced by the practitioners seated at the bargaining table. In foregoing chapters, we have seen the astonishing variety of responses to these challenges. We very much doubt that the pattern of variety will narrow in the years ahead.

However, we are hopeful that the nation's labor, management, and government leadership will focus more of their energies on working out a better coordination on private and public policy toward collective bargaining. Contemporary political and economic conditions, both national and international, beg for studied and reasonable solutions to the micro and macro challenges inventoried.

THE QUALITIES OF A MODEL PRACTITIONER OF COLLECTIVE BARGAINING

Today's practitioner of collective bargaining, whether union or management, needs more than a robust physical constitution, basic honesty, and native intelligence. To be effective in today's collective bargaining, the union or management representative must be intelligent, resourceful, and hard-working. He or she can be dedicated to the shorter work week only as a bargaining target for others, not as a personal goal.

Today's bargainer must be emotionally balanced and knowledgeable on the economics of the firm or industry in question, as well as on current practices in other fields. A true professional must have the talent to be flexible in one context and firm in another. The bargaining function requires a sense of humor and a sense of proportion. One must have the ability to "keep one's cool" in crisis stages of bargaining.

Perhaps most important of all, a competent union or management representative must be able *to see a problem whole.* An understanding of the compulsions and pressures operating on practitioners on the other side of the bargaining table is an indispensable requisite to intelligent bargaining.

Effective negotiators and contract administrators are mature realists who appreciate when it is desirable to compromise and when it would be fatal to concede. They must be capable of handling rather than hating difficult or unpleasant situations.

The picture of today's model professional now emerges as a combination of diplomat, tactician, technical expert, and psychologist. Such a "package" is obviously hard to come by. However, the professional nature of the task is generally appreciated in today's labor relations.

COLLECTIVE BARGAINING AS A PROFESSIONAL TASK

The labor relations function demands trained professionals. Excluding a few "neanderthal" situations, collective bargaining is rarely performed any more by management representatives as a part-time chore or by union leaders without some training. The president of a very small firm may still handle collective bargaining along with numerous other responsibilities, but he needs specialized knowledge to cope effectively with his union counterpart.

Collective bargaining is a relatively new venture for both parties in fields like basketball, nursing and higher education. Where this is the case, it has not taken the participants long to realize that intimate knowledge of their line of work is not enough. Both management and union organizations understand their need to develop specialized talent. The labor relations function is increasingly regarded by management as of primary importance. Unions are experiencing an acute need for more trained negotiators and backup staff specialists to remain on a par with their management "rivals."

Developing professional expertise is easier for management. When management experiences a need, it can proceed to hire or develop the requisite professional talent. Unions are somewhat handicapped by their political nature. The tradition still holds that collective bargaining should remain in the hands of elected leaders at both the local and national union level. Honoring this particular past practice has sometimes been done at the cost of inadequate representation of union interests.

Long-standing union distrust of "intellectuals" dates back to the time of Samuel Gompers. This had been overcome somewhat in recent years, perhaps in part by the example of such public sector unions and associations as the American Federation of Teachers, National Education Association, and the American Federation of State, County and Municipal Employees. Also, it has been overcome because of the growing use and force of now permanent fixtures on the nation's educational landscape, like university-based short-course training programs for union leaders, two-year and four-year labor studies degree programs, institutions like the AFL–CIO's George Meany Center for Labor Studies and even graduate degree programs in industrial relations. Change in the occupational composition and location of industry, changes in the labor force, and changes in labor and employment laws have spurred contemporary interests in union and association membership growth and organizational maintenance concerns. A collateral development is the surging interest in professionalism and study on the part of unions and associations.

THE COLLECTIVE BARGAINING BALANCE SHEET

We are now prepared to detail the successes and failures of collective bargaining. This discussion should take on sharper relief after having inventoried the challenges to collective bargaining and the qualities of the model collective bargaining practitioner. What we have portrayed as a contemporary challenge could easily have resulted from past successes as well as from failures. For example, we have cited job security as the main challenge to collective bargaining practitioners. Likewise, effective approaches to the solution of this challenge through joint study committees and other negotiated approaches to job security matters must be counted among the plus factors for contemporary collective bargaining.

Much criticism of collective bargaining comes from frustrated idealists or crusaders who expect too much from the process. Criticism also comes from those who think collective bargaining has worked too well, that is, that unions are too powerful. Such critics yearn for the days when unions were weak or nonexistent. In this analysis, we have not been concerned particularly about criticisms from these two camps. The focus has remained on how collective bargaining is working for those who utilize it conscientiously as a method of determining the price of labor and other conditions of employment.

Collective bargaining is not championed as an ideal system by anyone close to the scene. *At best, it is an imperfect institutional process that works reasonably well in an imperfect society.* It is the best we have. No one up to now has come forth with any alternative procedure that will work any better.

Collective bargaining is necessarily a pragmatic process. The standards for its evaluation should also be pragmatic. We are concerned mainly with two questions: (1) *How well has collective bargaining worked?* (2) *Where it has not worked well, what is needed for its improvement?* These questions are central to the analysis and this summary statement.

Although perfection is not a realistic goal, striving for improvement is an imperative for a constructive employer–union relationship. Experienced good faith bargainers understand intuitively that change is a pragmatic necessity if collective bargaining is to continue to perform effectively. The distinctive characteristic of a progressive and mature collective bargaining relationship is the capacity to adapt and to stay attuned to changing requirements at the microeconomic level. There must also be an awareness of the need to follow policies and procedures that will be complementary with national goals and aspirations.

Collective bargaining performance regarded as effective for current requirements can become outmoded rather quickly if the parties should fail to adjust to changed conditions and circumstances. Collective bargaining can become a failure if the joint willingness and ability to adapt should somehow be lost along the way. For example, bargaining in the steel industry can be justifiably criticized on a number of points. Blithe disregard for the inflationary and competitive impact of outsized wage and benefit settlements and failure on labor's part to cooperate with attempts at innovations are two often heard negative points. For its part, steel management has not been creative in its bargaining approaches to the nation's steel crisis. For these reasons and others, collective bargaining in this field could be labeled a failure. Similar assertions are heard in regard to automobile manufacturing.

Our listing of pluses and minuses for collective bargaining will now be set forth in outline fashion.

PLUS FACTORS FOR CONTEMPORARY COLLECTIVE BARGAINING

1. Effective approaches to solution of such continuing problems as adjustment to technological change through *joint study committees* and other negotiated approaches to *job security matters.*
2. Improved caliber of both management and union negotiators and contract administrators; acknowledgment of the professional and technical character of the labor relations task; increasing availability and use of reliable data in negotiating economic issues.
3. Joint awareness that collective bargaining can no longer be a matter of solely bilateral concern, but that it is a process that requires recognition of the public stake in responsible contract negotiations and administration.

Specific developments illustrating the foregoing factors include the following:

    a. widespread use of long-term (usually three-year) contracts;

    b. nearly universal utilization of binding arbitration for final disposition of grievances raising issues of contract interpretation or application, with no-strike clauses congruent with the arbitrator's authority under the contract; and

    c. a clear inclination to utilize binding arbitration on future terms issues in the public sector in those jurisdictions which bar the economic strike.

4. Improved contract administration on such formerly troublesome issues as arbitrability, subcontracting, intrafirm wage structure problems, equitable distribution of overtime and the role of seniority in relation to layoffs, recalls, and promotions. (Note: Cases still arise on these issues but at a more sophisticated level. Many formerly tough issues have been resolved by better contract language.)
5. In the private sector, many employers and unions are no longer at odds over *union security and scope of bargaining.* The union shop

prevails. A satisfactory modus vivendi has been reached on what is bargainable. The parties have stopped looking over their shoulders to see what is the newest NLRB ruling in the *Borg–Warner line.*

6. The parties are becoming more adept in the demanding task of contract administration.

7. Today's contracts are generally marked by substantial improvement in clarity and force of language. The evidence is convincing that contracts do change over time in response to changing conditions.

These favorable developments suggest that the performance record of collective bargaining is better than the torrent of critical comment might indicate. Granted that bargainers have performed poorly in some instances, the process has nevertheless worked rather well on the whole. The quietly successful employer–union relationships do not receive much attention or praise. There is a minus side of collective bargaining, however, that must be reviewed.

MINUS FACTORS IN CONTEMPORARY BARGAINING

1. Neither management nor union is yet prepared in some cases to develop a basis for stable mutual accommodation for the long pull. One party is often labeled as the "villain." Usually, however, neither party is entirely blameless. The NLRB's unfair practice caseload continues to grow. It is obvious that we have many employers and labor organizations that are still unwilling to observe the law of labor relations.

2. A low level of professionalism exists in some important employer–union relationships. This is a real problem in some public sector jurisdictions, and in the hospital industry. Whenever inept negotiation or irresponsible brinkmanship results in an unnecessary strike or interest arbitration, the image of collective bargaining as a whole suffers.

3. Excessive arbitration continues to be the rule in some relationships. This generally reflects either hostility or poor understanding of how to use arbitration as an instrument of contract administration. Such a condition is doubly unfortunate when there is a serious shortage of competent, experienced, and acceptable arbitrators.

4. Employers and unions in some cases have failed to modernize their contracts by eliminating outmoded provisions. To stay competitive most employers need to stay loose in terms of freedom to change methods, introduce new equipment, and restructure plant layout. Union concern over the job rights of incumbent employees is one

thing, but stubborn refusal to scrap outmoded working rules endangers collective bargaining as a process.

5. Employee rejection of negotiated contract settlements is creating serious difficulties in a number of industries. In some cases such rejection may be a healthy reaction to excessive power centralization and an encouraging example of participatory democracy at work. Too often, however, such rejection of negotiated settlements reflects unrealistic rank-and-file aspirations.

6. Wildcat strikes are presenting a serious problem in some relationships where it was formerly the custom to utilize the grievance and arbitration machinery. Employers are not getting the uninterrupted production span of the contract's lifetime for which many of them have paid a stiff price in economic benefits.

7. In some cases there is evidence of rigid adherence to patterns set in other bargaining relationships instead of attempting to negotiate "custom-made" contracts better suited to the particular needs and requirements of the employer and union in question. Using language or policies from other contracts frequently does not work well when application is attempted in a management–union situation for which they were not originally devised. The uniformed public services are a case in point.

8. Bargaining in some cases remains on a strictly short-run horizon. Little attention has been paid to long-range problems that need study on a continuing basis.

9. The potential of joint efforts to increase productivity and lower unit labor costs has been largely ignored. Related to such disinterest is a continuing lack of concern over the macroeconomic impact of microeconomic decision making. The focus of most bargainers remains bilateral. The public interest in responsible and constructive bargaining has not become a significant factor in the parties' assessments of their bargaining posture and demands.

10. An insufficiency of "creative" bargaining can be noted in many cases where innovation is urgently required. In the public sector, we continue to hope that the necessities may prove to be the mothers of invention where private sector experience is not readily or happily transferable.

THE FUTURE OF COLLECTIVE BARGAINING

These pluses and minuses reveal that there is much unfinished business for many employers and unions. In fact, collective bargaining is never finished. Working out a durably satisfactory pattern of accommodation requires change as our social and economic imperatives continue to evolve and shift. The real question remaining is whether collective bargaining change will occur rapidly enough to insure future success. If it does not, then the *guarantee of continued privacy* of collective bargaining may be placed in real jeopardy. Public collectivization always stands on the sideline as a ready substitute for "free" collective bargaining.

The future of collective bargaining as an institutional mechanism for private decision making on wages, hours, and other conditions of employment depends on how well the bargainers face up to the challenges inventoried in the preceding pages and analyzed in earlier chapters. What is needed is a realistic recognition of the community of interest on many vital points between *private needs and public policy*. Determined action by negotiators to meet the challenges we have outlined can produce a more effective mix of private discretion and public policy than we have witnessed so far. The ability to act courageously and imaginatively is present. Today's negotiators and contract administrators are far better informed and more professional than their predecessors. They have succeeded already in overcoming some previously troublesome problems of conventional bargaining. There is no reason to suppose that they cannot move beyond conventional policies and toward the kind of joint forward progress required by positive collective bargaining and the needs of the community at large—where positive collective bargaining is a calling for a high order of rationality, intelligence, and social vision on the part of all concerned with the bargaining process, including the employees themselves.

Collective bargaining remains the most valid institutional approach for strengthening the essential components of our private enterprise system, while at the same time enhancing the dignity and freedom of the individual worker in our society. Assuming that we wish to strengthen the role of the individual through a democratized system of labor relations in both the private and government sectors, the energy and imagination of all concerned will be needed to effectuate the conversion from conventional to positive bargaining. The alternatives to such an effort are not pleasant to contemplate.

Questions for Discussion, Thought, and Research

1. Do you think that the apparent conflict between labor and management is inherent and inevitable, or can it be eliminated by an intelligent rational approach to the matter?

2. What criteria or measures would you suggest for evaluating the collective bargaining processes in a particular organization?

3. Should the government's role in labor relations be enhanced? Have labor and management failed in their social responsibility? Discuss.

4. How would you change the collective bargaining institution to make it more responsive to contemporary social and economic conditions?

5. What qualities would you look for in someone hired to represent your interests at the bargaining table?

6. List as best you can the various ways collective bargaining contributes to society. List the adverse social effects of collective bargaining. How does your list of pros and cons net out?

7. Write a short essay developing your thoughts regarding the future of collective bargaining in the United States.

Selected Bibliography

Somers, Gerald G., ed., *The Next 25 Years of Industrial Relations.* Madison, Wis.: Industrial Relations Research Association, 1973.

Shaffer, Bertram, "Some Alternatives to Existing Labor Policies," *Labor Law Journal*, 27 (June 1976), 370 78.

AUTHOR INDEX

Page numbers in italics denote references within tables in both the Author and Subject Indexes. **455**

Gordon, Murry A., 412n
Gordon, Robert J., 359n-60
Granof, Michael H., 113n, 133
Greenberg, Leon, 340n
Grodin, Joseph R., 222n, 223n, 371n
Gross, James A., 42n, 49n, 52
Grossman, Jonathan, 355n

Halloway, Sally T., 413n
Hamermesh, D. S., 325, 328, 335n, 336n, 403n
Hanslowe, Kurt L., 46n, 49n, 52, 57n, 61n, 99n
Harris, Philip, 193n
Harsanyi, John, 315, 331
Hart, Wilson R., 371n
Hartman, Paul T., 295
Hayford, Steven L., 388n
Healy, James, 337n
Hellickson, George C., 265
Helsby, Robert D., 102, 385n
Henderson, Richard I., 235n
Herman, Jeanne B., 69, 77
Hicks, Sir John, 221, 315, 331
Hill, Marvin, Jr., 175n
Hyatt, Harvey, 396n

Ivancevitch, J. M., 271n
Ives, Coleman S., 256n

James, Estelle, 95n
James, Ralph, 95n
Jascourt, Hugh D., 388n
Jensen, Vernon H., 3n
Johnson, George E., 325-28, 335n
Jones, Dallas L., 188n
Juris, Harvey A., 413n, 417n

Kagel, Sam, 169n
Kahn, Lawrence M., 334n
Kahn, Mark L., 87n, 193n, 200n
Kahn, Steven C., 389n
Kalachek, Edward, 339n
Kasper, Hirschel, 222n
Kerner, Benjamin A., 400n
Kihss, Peter, 413n
Killingsworth, Charles C., 153n, 193n
Klauser, Jack E., 81n, 103n
Kneiser, Thomas, 308n
Kochan, Thomas A., 130n, 223n
Koretz, Robert F., 172n, 174n
Krasnow, Edwin G., 408n, 419n, 423n, 426n
Krider, Charles E., 224
Krislov, Joseph, 86n
Krock, Arthur, 42n
Kuhmeiker, Peter, 349n
Kutell, Diane, 220n,

Lasser, David, 96n
Lawler, John, 231n
Leigh, Duane E., 336n
Levi, Margaret, 417n

Levine, Marvin J., 287n
Levy, Herman M., 408n, 419n, 423n, 426n
Lewin, David, 377n
Link, C. R., 336n, 417n
Lipsky, David B., 222n
Livernash, Robert E., 337n
Lowenberg, J. Joseph, 222n
Lumsden, Keith, 54n
Lung-Fei Lee, 335n
Lyon, H. L., 271n

McCaffery, Robert M., 252n
McCormick, Mary, 377n
McDermott, Thomas J., 291n
McNally, Dave, 425
Madden, Patrick J., 424n, 426n, 427n
Mamorsky, Jeffrey D., 176n
Marshall, Ray, 58n
Maxey, Charles, 417n
Medoff, James L., 337n, 339, 340n, 346
Medoff, Marshall H., 422n
Messersmith, Andy, 425
Metzger, Norman, 411n
Mills, D. Quinn, 231n
Misek, Glen I., 251n
Mitchell, Daniel J. B., 347n, 355n
Moore, Brian, 344n
Moore, William, 54
Morton, Herbert C., 271n
Murphy, Michael E., 176n
Murphy, Robert, 423
Murphy, William P., 172n

Nash, John F., 318, 328-29
Nelson, Nels E., 398n, 399
Nelson, Richard R., 387, 392n, 395, 398
Nesbit, Murray B., 103n, 104n, 107
Newman, Robert, 54n
Northrup, Herbert P., 298n

Oaxaca, Ronald L., 335n, 336n
O'Grady, James P., 193
Olson, Craig, 233n
Olson, Mancur, 338n
Ostry, Sylvia, 366n

Pegnetter, Richard, 385n
Perlman, Selig, 279
Peters, Edward, 298n
Peterson, Craig, 54
Peterson, Florence, 150n
Pointer, Dennis D., 409n, 411n
Prasow, Paul, 298n

Rabin, Robert J., 172n, 174n
Raines, Frederic, 339n
Rees, Albert, 335n, 346n
Rehmus, Charles M., 113, 117, 133, 222n, 400n
Reynolds, Lloyd G., 308n
Rosen, Sherwin, 335n